Family Therapy Case Conceptualization

This textbook provides a comprehensive and in-depth exploration of the primary models of family therapy and helps readers conceptualize various theories around a single case. Designed as a core text for marriage and family therapy courses, this edited volume presents the conceptualization of problem formation, problem resolution, and diversity considerations from 15 of the most influential family therapy models. By applying traditional and contemporary models to a single case, the reader is able to compare and contrast the models. Each theory chapter is divided into five parts: 1) the therapeutic story of problem formation; 2) diversity considerations; 3) the therapeutic story of problem resolution; 4) a hypothetical case transcript of a first session with explanations of how and why the therapist is creating a specific therapeutic story; and 5) the developed therapeutic story. This textbook serves graduate and doctoral students in marriage and family therapy, mental health counseling, clinical psychology, and social work. The book is also a useful resource for practicing professionals who want to explore how to apply a specific model of counseling to family systems.

Michael D. Reiter, Ph.D., LMFT, is an American Association for Marriage and Family Therapy (AAMFT) Approved Supervisor, a therapist with over 30 years of experience, and a full-time faculty member for over 25 years. He currently teaches and supervises at Capella University.

Family Therapy Case Conceptualization

Creating Therapeutic Stories Across Models

Edited by Michael D. Reiter

Routledge
Taylor & Francis Group
NEW YORK AND LONDON

Designed cover image: Getty Image

First published 2027
by Routledge
4 Park Square, Milton Park, Abingdon, Oxon OX14 4RN

and by Routledge
605 Third Avenue, New York, NY 10158

Routledge is an imprint of the Taylor & Francis Group, an informa business

Cover art is from Michael Reign

British Library Cataloguing-in-Publication Data
A catalogue record for this book is available from the British Library

ISBN: 978-1-041-13186-1 (hbk)
ISBN: 978-1-041-13184-7 (pbk)
ISBN: 978-1-003-66851-0 (ebk)

DOI: 10.4324/9781003668510

Typeset in Times New Roman
by SPi Technologies India Pvt Ltd (Straive)

This book is dedicated to all our teachers and mentors, who taught us what it means to be a family therapist. Special recognition to a few who are no longer with us: Insoo Kim Berg, Norman Epstein, and Salvador Minuchin.

Contents

Figures

About the Editor

Michael D. Reiter, Ph.D., LMFT, is an AAMFT Approved Supervisor and family therapist for over 30 years. Throughout his career, he has worked in private practice, community mental health centers, home-based programs, and university counseling centers. Michael has been a full-time faculty member for over 25 years. He was a Professor of Family Therapy at Nova Southeastern University in the Marriage and Family Therapy program and also taught in the Psychology, Clinical Psychology, School Guidance and Counseling, and Mental Health Counseling programs at NSU. Currently, Michael is a core faculty member at Capella University in the Marriage and Family Therapy program. He has written 14 books and co-edited three books. These books include *Substance Abuse and the Family* (3rd ed. Routledge, 2026), *Family Therapy: An Introduction to Process, Practice, & Theory* (2nd ed) (Routledge, 2025), *A Therapist's Guide to Writing in Psychotherapy* (Routledge, 2023), *Family Therapy: The Basics* (Routledge, 2022), *Therapeutic Interviewing* (2nd ed. Routledge, 2022), *It's Not You, It's Them…And You* (2020), *Systems Theories for Psychotherapists* (Routledge, 2019), *The Craft of Family Therapy* (2nd ed. Routledge, 2021)—written with Dr. Salvador Minuchin, one of the most important figures in the field of family therapy, edited *Case Conceptualization in Couple Therapy* (Routledge, 2025), and co-edited books with Dr. Ron Chenail, *Behavioral, Humanistic-Experiential and Psychodynamic Approaches to Couples Counseling* and *Constructivist, Critical, and Integrative Approaches to Couples Counseling* (Routledge, 2017). Michael has written over 20 journal articles and has been a Special Edition editor for the *Journal of Systemic Therapies* and the *American Journal of Family Therapy*. Michael has presented at many state, national, and international conferences on various issues in psychotherapy and family therapy. He currently lives in South Florida with his wife, Yukari, and their children Maya and Koji.

Contributors

Roxanne Bamond, Ph.D., LMFT, is an AAMFT Approved Supervisor and a Professor at Capella University. As a Marriage and Family Therapist Professor for 20 years, her academic interests include mentoring AAMFT Approved Supervisors, pre- and postgraduate clinical supervision, ethics, and teaching clinical skills. She has a private practice in Colorado and specializes in couples therapy.

Marina Bluvshtein is a Professor and Director of the Center for Adlerian Practice and Scholarship at Adler University, and President of the International Association of Individual Psychology.

Weston Crafton, Ph.D., LMFT, is a Licensed Marital and Family Therapist in Tennessee and Texas, an AASECT Certified Sex Therapist, and an AAMFT Clinical Fellow and Approved Supervisor. He is an Assistant Professor of Marriage and Family Therapy at Capella University, where he teaches residency and internship courses. He is also a Clinical Therapist at Family Care Center in Nashville, TN, where he works with individuals, couples, and families.

Keran Flynn-Kroska, Ph.D., LMFT, is a licensed marriage and family therapist and AAMFT Approved Supervisor in Minnesota, and has worked in rural, community, and tribal mental health since 2008. Dr. Flynn-Kroska is a specialist in early childhood mental health and trauma and is trained and certified in a number of evidence-based models, such as Parent-Child Interaction Therapy, Attachment Bio-behavioral Catchup, Internal Family Systems (IFS), and EMDR. Dr. Flynn-Kroska is a full-time Associate Professor at Capella University.

Arlene Brett Gordon, Ph.D., LMFT, collaborated with Insoo Kim Berg to integrate solution-focused work into social service systems in South Florida and ran two university family therapy clinics. Since 1993, Arlene has provided solution-focused trainings and sessions to keep this work close to its original models of delivery. She currently provides training and other services to local and international audiences.

Anastasia B. Hanson, M.S., MFTC, works in private and group practice settings with clients whose sexual, relational, and gender expressions have been marginalized. They employ an integrated approach in their therapeutic work, which prioritizes parts-work, feminist theory, and anti-carceral approaches. They are a member of AASECT and are working to become a Certified Sex Therapist.

Coreen Haym, Ph.D., LMFT, is a full-time faculty member at Capella University, teaching Social Justice and Gender and Sexuality, among other related marriage and family therapy topics. She enjoys private practice, provides feminist-informed clinical supervision, and holds licenses as a Marriage and Family Therapist and Clinical Professional Counselor. She is a digital nomad and finds home wherever she lands.

Kelly Heenan, Ph.D., LMFT, is the Program Director for the Marriage and Family Therapy program at Capella University. She is a seasoned clinician with over 15 years of experience across private practice, K–12 school settings, community mental health, and higher education. Kelly is passionate about fostering academic excellence and supporting innovative teaching practices.

Tequilla Lynn Hill, Ph.D., LMFT, is a somatic psychotherapist and Assistant Faculty Director at Capella University. With over 17 years of clinical, supervisory, and teaching experience, she specializes in systemic therapy, Bowen family systems theory, and mindfulness-based approaches to therapist wellness. She is also the founder of *Refill with Dr. Hill*, a wellness brand supporting therapists in cultivating balance, confidence, and vitality.

Todd C. Workman Jesness, Ph.D., LMFT, is an Associate Professor of Marriage and Family Therapy at Capella University and an AAMFT Approved Supervisor. Over the course of more than two decades, Todd has been a clinician, educator, supervisor, and assistant clinical training coordinator. His writing interests include the analysis and clinical application of theories and methods as well as ethics.

Kyle D. Killian, Ph.D., LMFT, is a Professor of Marriage and Family Therapy at Capella University and an AAMFT Approved Supervisor. His research foci include intercultural and interracial couples, trauma and loss, vicarious resilience, and assessment. Frequently cited works include “Helping till It Hurts? A Multimethod Study of Compassion Fatigue, Burnout, and Self-Care in Clinicians Working with Trauma Survivors” (2008) and “Advancing Science and Practice for Vicarious Traumatization/Secondary Traumatic Stress” (2017), and his book *Interracial Couples, Intimacy and Therapy: Crossing Racial Borders* (2013). Dr. Killian is also the developer of easy-to-use measures of emotional intelligence, vicarious resilience, and cultural assumptions and beliefs, and a subtle screening for suicidal ideation.

Rosemary A. Leone, M.A., LMFT, is the Past Chair of the Rocky Mountain Family Therapy Network, a geographical interest branch of AAMFT. She is the proud founder of the Center for Strategic Change, a private practice focusing on the effective use of Strategic Family Therapy. She owns and operates the Lionheart Forum, where clinician members train using collaboration and reflecting teams, modeling the group after the Mental Research Institute of Palo Alto. Her publication themes include Ambiguous Loss and Gender Wage Gap in Higher Academia. She uses a multicultural orientation in the clinical supervision she provides.

Pei-Fen Li, Ph.D., LMFT, is an Associate Professor in the Couple and Family Therapy Department at the Dr. Kiran C. Patel College of Osteopathic Medicine, Nova Southeastern University. She is an AAMFT Approved Supervisor, with clinical experience both in Taiwan and the U.S. She is guided by systemic thinking and brief therapy principles. Her therapeutic and supervisory approach emphasizes observing interactional patterns within people's relational contexts and using their strengths to facilitate purposeful change.

Claire Loucka, Ph.D., LMFT, is an Assistant Professor at Capella University in the marriage and family therapy program. Her research interests include substance abuse and SFBT. Claire sees clients in private practice and supervises for licensure.

Ashley McErlean, Ph.D., LMFT-S, is a marriage and family therapist supervisor in Texas and an adjunct faculty member in the marriage and family therapy program at Capella University. She is the founder of The Opal Center, a nonprofit LGBTQIA+ resource center offering pro bono mental health and support services to members of the LGBTQIA+ communities in her area. Her research interests are in the areas of systemic model application, gender and sexuality, ethical non-monogamy, culturally competent practice and education, and the therapeutic applications of role-playing games.

Cindy McIntire, Ph.D., LMFT, is an AAMFT Approved Supervisor and Assistant Professor at Capella University. With extensive experience in clinical practice, supervision, and higher education, she serves as the Clinical Training Coordinator for Capella's Marriage and Family Therapy program. Dr. McIntire specializes in supporting neurodiverse families through inclusive, strengths-based therapy that promotes growth and well-being across the lifespan. A dedicated advocate for the profession, she also serves on the board of the Florida Family Therapy Alliance, advancing the visibility and impact of family therapy throughout the state.

Carol Messmore, Ph.D., LMFT, is a Professor in the Capella University MFT program and a licensed marriage and family therapist. Dr. Messmore has worked extensively with social service organizations supporting families with young children in South Florida. She trained with Insoo Kim Berg and Steve de Shazer and has been presenting and teaching for more than 30 years, and is committed to sharing her knowledge of Solution-Focused Brief Therapy.

Matthew Pace, Ph.D., LMFT, is an Associate Professor of Marriage and Family Therapy at Capella University and an AAMFT Approved Supervisor. With over 20 years of experience, his work has included roles as a clinician, educator, supervisor, and clinical training director. His teaching focuses on social justice and cultural competence in clinical practice, as well as systemic approaches to grief, loss, and trauma. His research and publications in the field center on the role of emotion in family therapy, clinician burnout, and ethics in systemic practice.

Woochul Park, Ph.D., received his doctorate in Family Science from the University of Maryland and is currently a Professor of Child and Family Studies at Duksung Women's University in Seoul, South Korea. He developed the Korean Couple and Marriage Checkup (KCMC), a program officially adopted by the Seoul and Busan Metropolitan Governments and implemented in more than 30 local Family Centers nationwide. He also leads a government-funded project that develops and provides after-school programs for children's emotional and social development in elementary schools across Seoul.

George A. Pate, Ph.D., is an AAMFT Approved Supervisor, LMFT-S, LPC-S in Texas, and an Internationally Certified Alcohol and Drug Counselor. He is an Associate Professor with Capella University in the Department of Marriage and Family Therapy and is the former Clinical Director of an adolescent treatment center, which focuses on adolescent substance abuse and chronic, complex trauma. Both individually and in association with other presenters, he has presented at numerous local and regional conferences and workshops on issues of chemical dependency, family therapy, and integrative approaches, including the Texas Behavioral Health Institute, the Constructivist Psychology Network, TNOYS, Texas Psychological Association, Texas Association of Addiction Professionals, Mental Health America (Dallas), National Association for Alcoholism and Drug Abuse Counselors (NAADAC), AAMFT, and Texas Association of Marriage and Family Therapy (TAMFT).

Anne M. Prouty, Ph.D., LMFT, provides clinical supervision and teaches feminist-informed marriage and family therapy as a full-time faculty at

Seattle Pacific University, and as an occasional lecturer and consulting supervisor for Daybreak University. She is a licensed marriage and family therapist who specializes in medical family therapy. She enjoys the beautiful Pacific Northwest with family and friends.

Carlos A. Ramos, Ph.D., is a licensed marriage and family therapist, an Associate Professor in the psychology department, and the Certificate Director of Psychological Services for Spanish Speaking Populations at Our Lady of the Lake University in San Antonio. His interests include relational hypnotherapy, bilingual supervision and therapy, and qualitative research.

Natalie Richardson, Ph.D., LMFT, is the Assistant Program Director for the Marriage and Family Therapy program at Capella University. With a background in medical family therapy, Natalie has extensive experience in clinical practice, research, and education. Her work has primarily focused on moral injury, grief, traumatic stress, and biopsychosocial-spiritual health, with numerous publications and national presentations. Currently, she is passionate about curriculum development and fostering supportive learning environments for the next generation of helping professionals.

Kayleigh N. Sabo, Ph.D., LMFT, is an AAMFT Approved Supervisor. She is Adjunct Faculty at Nova Southeastern University and works in various clinical settings, including private practice and nonprofit.

Jon Sperry is a Professor of Clinical Mental Health Counseling at Lynn University. He holds a diplomate in Adlerian Psychology and is currently the co-editor of the *Journal of Individual Psychology*.

Len Sperry is Professor Emeritus at Florida Atlantic University and the Medical College of Wisconsin. He currently co-edits the *Journal of Individual Psychology* and co-authored *Learning and Practicing Adlerian Therapy*.

The views expressed in this work are those of the authors and contributors and do not reflect the views of Capella University.

Preface

I want to tell you a story. A story about how this book came into being. It was born over 30 years ago, when I was first becoming a family therapist. However, that is not quite true. It was born over 100 years ago, when people first began working therapeutically with families. Actually, that's not quite true either. It was born when people began trying to conceptualize why people have "problems" and how those problems can be ameliorated. So, what I am saying here and what will be presented in this book is partial. That is all we ever see is partiality, but we make do with what we have.

Over my career, I've written and edited several books that have a similar format to this book: a sample case; presentation of the theory of problem formation; presentation of the theory of problem resolution; and a sample transcript (see Reiter, 2014, 2019, 2025; Reiter & Chenail, 2017a, 2017b). I've found that this method of theory presentation, where it is embedded within the application of the theory to a case, is extremely useful for students to help them learn the concepts as well as know how they would be used in a session.

What makes this book unique is the slant of creating therapeutic stories. Through my own clinical practice and my years of supervising Master's and Doctoral family therapy students, particularly doing live supervision, I've realized that therapy is all about storytelling. Clients come to therapy telling us their current story—one that they don't want continued. Their problem story usually involves them experiencing a limited identity (Reiter et al., 2020). In therapy, the therapist attempts to change this story so that the client experiences themselves as having more personal agency.

The question becomes: What is the therapeutic story that gets developed? That is the crux of this book. Each model of therapy has its own slant to what is included in the therapeutic story. Some will focus on the client's parents and grandparents. Others will include the client's childhood and relationship with parents. Others will highlight what is happening in the therapy room. Others will include the future in the therapeutic story. While not all therapists operating from the same model will construct the same therapeutic story with the same family, there will likely be consistent themes. What is presented in this book is just one construction of a therapeutic story from the model. I encourage you to explore how, based on your understanding of each model, you might have constructed a different story.

This is a book about family therapy but also about family. For over 20 years, I was a faculty member at Nova Southeastern University. That was my family, as I received my doctorate in family therapy from there as well as met my wife there—as we both were hired the same week in 1999. Recently, I have been a faculty member at Capella University. They have taken me in so that I could become part of that family as well. Most of the authors in this book are either my Nova or Capella "family members." A few other authors I have gotten to know are from outside of the family. I want to thank all of the contributors to this book: Roxanne Bamond, Marina Bluvshtein, Weston Crafton, Keran Flynn-Kroska, Arlene Brett Gordon, Anastasia B. Hanson, Coreen Haym, Kelly Heenan, Tequilla Hill, Todd Workman Jesness, Kyle Killian, Rosemary Leone, Claire Loucka, Pei-Fen Li, Ashley McErlean, Cindy McIntire, Carol Messmore, Matt Pace, Woochul Park, George A. Pate, Anne Prouty, Carlos Ramos, Natalie Richardson, Kayleigh Sabo, Jon Sperry, and Len Sperry. Thanks also to my wife, Yukari Tomozawa, for creation of the genogram of the Daniels family. Special thanks to my good friend, Michael Reign, for allowing the use of one of his paintings as the cover artwork.

References

Reiter, M. D. (2014). *Case conceptualization in family therapy*. Pearson.

Reiter, M. D. (2019). *Systems theories for psychotherapists*. Routledge.

Reiter, M. D. (Ed.). (2025). *Case conceptualization in couple therapy*. Routledge.

Reiter, M. D. & Chenail, R. J. (Eds.). (2017a). *Behavioral, humanistic-experiential, and psychodynamic approaches to couples counseling*. Routledge.

Reiter, M. D., & Chenail, R. J. (Eds.). (2017b). *Constructivist, critical, and integrative approaches to couples counseling*. Routledge.

Reiter, M. D., Jung, W. F., Popham, J., Fitzgerald, C., Garcia, E., de Perez, M. G., Lockhart, T., & Villanueva, N. (2020). Training through naming: A process of psychotherapist skill development utilizing recursive frame analysis. *The Qualitative Report*, *25*(8), 2085–2099.

1 Creating Therapeutic Stories

Michael D. Reiter

What occurs in the process of psychotherapy? How does psychological and interpersonal change take place? What mechanisms enable clients to leave therapeutic sessions with a transformed experience of themselves and their lives? These fundamental questions have occupied the field of psychotherapy since the emergence of talk therapy approximately 150 years ago. The answers to these questions vary depending on the theoretical orientation of the practitioner. This book examines how 15 distinct models of family therapy conceptualize and address these core issues. Through an exploration of case conceptualization and the construction of therapeutic stories, the book investigates the diverse ways in which these models facilitate therapeutic change.

Case Conceptualizations

Case conceptualization is widely regarded as a foundational competency for mental health professionals (Sperry & Sperry, 2020, 2023; Stanton & Welsh, 2011). It serves as a critical mechanism through which therapists organize clinical information, formulate treatment goals, and develop effective intervention strategies. As Gilboa-Schechtman (2024) articulates, a robust case conceptualization comprises three core elements: (1) an accurate depiction of the client's current psychological functioning, (2) the identification of appropriate and achievable therapeutic goals, and (3) the development of a coherent plan—or roadmap—for facilitating change. Through the integration of these components, clinicians are better able to understand the client's presenting concerns, envision meaningful outcomes, and delineate a pathway toward therapeutic progress.

Stanton and Welsh (2011) propose a similar tripartite framework for case conceptualization, emphasizing the sequential progression through three stages: *Problem Identification*, *Case Understanding*, and *Treatment Planning*. In the first stage, Problem Identification, clinicians define the presenting issues, typically during the initial phase of treatment. The second stage, Case Understanding, involves the construction of an interpretive framework that

DOI: 10.4324/9781003668510-1

explains the development and maintenance of the identified problems. Finally, Treatment Planning focuses on selecting interventions that are both theoretically grounded and practically suited to resolving the client's difficulties.

Sperry and Sperry (2023) expand upon these models by delineating four interrelated domains of case conceptualization: *diagnostic*, *clinical*, *cultural*, and *treatment* formulations. The **diagnostic formulation** addresses the question, "What is happening?," and aims to assess the nature, scope, and severity of the client's presenting issues. The **clinical formulation** focuses on the underlying question, "Why is this happening?," seeking to explain the etiology and maintenance of the problem through a specific theoretical lens. Depending on the therapist's orientation—whether cognitive-behavioral, solution-focused, psychodynamic, or systemic—the explanation for a given concern will vary, integrating intrapsychic dynamics, relational patterns, and broader contextual influences.

The **cultural formulation** further explores the "what," but does so through a sociocultural lens. It examines how aspects of the client's cultural background, identity, and lived experiences shape the emergence and expression of psychological distress. Finally, the **treatment formulation** addresses the question, "How can change occur?" This component outlines the goals of therapy, specifies the interventions to be employed, and details a strategy aligned with the client's values, context, and therapeutic needs.

At its essence, case conceptualization operates as a working hypothesis or clinical theory that explains the client's experience and behavior. It synthesizes empirical data, contextual knowledge, and theoretical insight to guide the course of therapy (Eels, 2022). As such, it functions as a dynamic and evolving roadmap, informing therapeutic decision-making throughout the treatment process.

A point of ongoing debate in the literature concerns whether case conceptualization and treatment planning should be conceptualized as discrete processes. Zubernis (2016), for instance, argues for treating them as distinct, while others—such as Reiter (2014, 2025)—advocate for a more integrated view, in which case conceptualization inherently includes both an understanding of problem formation and an articulation of how change is expected to occur.

In this book, case conceptualization is framed as encompassing two interdependent narratives: the *therapeutic story of problem formation*, which accounts for how the client has arrived at their current state of functioning; and the *therapeutic story of problem resolution*, which outlines a prospective pathway toward improved functioning and well-being. This dual-focus approach positions case conceptualization not merely as a diagnostic tool, but as a narrative and strategic framework that underpins the entire therapeutic process.

Therapy and Storytelling

"Stories can powerfully communicate what it is like to be in the world and can provide opportunities to change our view of reality" (Crawford et al., 2004, p. 1). Mental health professionals frequently incorporate metaphors and storytelling into their sessions to help individuals see their experiences through a different lens. Often, these narratives parallel a client's own life circumstances. What is often overlooked, however, is that therapy itself unfolds as a narrative. The therapist co-constructs a therapeutic storyline that guides the client toward transformation.

Stories are deeply embedded in how humans understand themselves and their environments. They function as the medium through which individuals define their identities and roles in the world. According to White and Epston (1990), this "storying" of experience allows people to feel continuity and coherence in their lives, offering a framework to structure daily life and interpret new situations. Dwivedi and Gardner (1997) further emphasize that individuals assign meaning to their lives through the act of storytelling, creating narratives that help them make sense of their experiences. These stories are usually personal since stories that are pertinent to the client tend to be remembered (Bergner, 2007).

Narratives not only help us process our own lives—they also enable us to connect with others. As Crawford et al. (2004) observe, stories have the unique ability to convey lived experiences and reshape our understanding of reality. When individuals internalize a story, it begins to regulate their self-perception, reinforcing or filtering experiences based on its message. For example, someone who identifies as socially anxious may consistently recall moments when they avoided interaction, while ignoring instances where they engaged confidently. However, if they were to view themselves differently—not as a socially anxious person but as a socially comfortable person—they would likely pay more attention to those times that they were more easily able to connect to others socially rather than those times they avoided interactions.

One widely recognized framework for understanding narrative structure is **Freytag's Pyramid**, introduced in 1863 by Gustav Freytag. Originally designed to map out the structure of fiction, this model has been widely applied across fields such as digital storytelling (Ciğerci & Yildrim, 2024), marketing (Quesenberry & Coolsen, 2019), and music (Simon, 2019). The pyramid outlines five components of plot development: exposition, rising action, climax, falling action, and dénouement.

The **exposition** introduces the characters, setting, and foundational context. In family therapy, this phase would involve understanding the relationship history of the parents, when children were born, demographics, and social identities of the individuals. For instance, Sheldon and Sondra Parsons have been together for 15 years. Sheldon is a 48-year-old African American from the Southern U.S. working in pharmaceutical middle management, while Sondra, 46, is an Asian American science teacher who immigrated from China to New York during childhood. They have two children, Yumi and Zaden, who are 12 and 10, respectively.

Rising action introduces the central issues—why the family has sought therapy. These might include trust issues, frequent conflict, or communication struggles. Unlike single-protagonist stories, family therapy typically involves two or more main characters with differing views. For example, Sheldon feels Sondra is too lenient with the children, while Sondra believes Sheldon is too strict. Though their interpretations differ, both agree that the relationship is strained and needs repair. Yumi and Zaden are intimidated by their father and tend to seek out their mother.

The **climax** is the critical turning point, often marked by breakthroughs in therapy. Here, therapeutic intervention helps transform conflict into understanding and distance into emotional closeness. This shift often brings forward the main theme of the family's narrative—moving from disconnection to reconnection. Kühn and Boschoff (2023) note that this central message is usually crystallized during the climax phase. For the Parsons, the therapist presented a reframe of rather than viewing their parenting differences as a conflict, Sheldon and Sondra's contrasting approaches can be understood as a blending of cultural strengths—discipline and warmth—that, when integrated, could offer their children a more balanced and adaptive developmental environment.

At this stage, various therapeutic models can be applied. Research shows that while no single method dominates in effectiveness (Miller et al., 1997), using a defined model accounts for about 15% of therapeutic improvement (Lambert, 1992). Other factors include clients' lives outside therapy (40%), the quality of the therapeutic relationship (30%), and client expectations and hope (15%) (Lambert, 1992; Lambert & Bergin, 1994). Regardless of the model used, this part of the journey involves helping clients reshape their existing story into one that aligns more closely with their goals and values.

The **falling action** reflects how the family starts adapting to this new narrative. This is when entrenched patterns are replaced with healthier dynamics. In the Parsons family case, Sheldon and Sondra begin to see their relationship as a partnership built on mutual support rather than disconnection. Their focus shifts from past grievances to present connection and future possibilities. They shift from a story of being at odds with one another to a story of being a team, working together to parent their children. Further, the foursome shifts their story from "Dad is too strict" to "We are a family that gets along."

Finally, the **dénouement** marks the resolution and closure. This typically aligns with the conclusion of therapy, where the family transitions from therapeutic support to independent functioning, ideally with a renewed sense of connection and hope. This stage happens for many families since family therapy tends to produce positive change, as the efficacy of family therapy is well-documented (Carr, 2020; Wittenborn & Holtrop, 2021).

Recursive Frame Analysis

Within the broader landscape of psychotherapy, Brad Keeney's *Recursive Frame Analysis* (RFA) offers a distinctive framework for understanding the dynamic, evolving structure of therapeutic dialogue (Keeney, 2009; Keeney et al.,

2012, 2015). RFA conceptualizes therapy as a performative and recursive process, organized into a narrative arc composed of three acts. These acts reflect the trajectory of therapeutic transformation: from an impoverished experience, through a transition, and culminating in a resourceful experience.

The first act captures the initial state of client distress, characterized by rigid self-concepts and problem-saturated stories that constrain behavior and perception. Drawing on Watzlawick et al.'s (1974) notion of problem maintenance through attempted solutions, Act I represents a condition of being "stuck"—a state in which clients operate from habitual interpretations of self and others that reinforce dysfunction and erode hope. For the Parsons family, this act is illustrated by ongoing conflict regarding parenting styles and a mutual expectation that their difficulties are enduring and intractable. Within this narrative frame, the family perceives itself as locked into a pattern of interpersonal frustration and diminishing connection.

The second act introduces a critical turning point. Here, the therapist facilitates the emergence of alternative perspectives through reframing,[1] thereby creating narrative space for change. This phase is marked by a movement away from the impoverished storyline toward a therapeutic re-storying process. Regardless of theoretical orientation, therapists shift the initial problem-saturated narrative to one that promotes greater client personal agency. In the case of the Parsons family, Act II is initiated when the therapist frames their parenting conflict—not as a dysfunction, but as a reflection of diverse strengths that, if integrated, could enhance family functioning. This reframing signals the beginning of a new therapeutic story, imbued with hope and possibility.

The third act signifies the consolidation of change. Clients begin to internalize and enact a revised, more empowered narrative identity—what Reiter et al. (2020) describe as the transition from a limited identity to a resourceful one. This stage involves not only insight but behavioral embodiment of the new story in everyday life. For the Parsons family, this might involve a shift from viewing themselves as a "family in conflict" to a "collaborative team," capable of adaptive and responsive parenting. The new narrative promotes agency, resilience, and redefined relational patterns.

RFA is a versatile heuristic that can be integrated across therapeutic models to both track and facilitate change. For example:

- **Bowenian Family Therapists** may map the progression as:

  Act I—Emotional fusion and reactivity
  Act II—Exploration of multigenerational patterns and differentiation
  Act III—Thoughtful, differentiated decision-making

- **Narrative Therapists** might frame the journey as:

  Act I—Dominant, internalized cultural discourses
  Act II—Deconstruction and externalization
  Act III—Re-authoring preferred stories grounded in agency

- **Emotionally Focused Family Therapists** could represent the transformation as:

  Act I—Entrenched negative interaction cycles
  Act II—Exploration of attachment needs and vulnerabilities
  Act III—Development of secure, emotionally responsive engagement

While the thematic contours of each act may vary based on the family's cultural context and the clinician's theoretical orientation, the underlying structure remains consistent: clients begin with limited identities, move through transformation, and end with a sense of a more expansive and resourceful identity.

Structuring Change Through Conceptual Frameworks

In family therapy, therapists rely on their case conceptualization to understand relationship dynamics and guide therapeutic change. For this framework to be meaningful, it must shape the structure and delivery of therapy. Clients place high value on their therapist's ability to organize the therapeutic process effectively (Madden & Timulak, 2024). A core element of this structure involves crafting a **therapeutic story**—a storyline that engages clients and moves them toward their goals. For this narrative to be effective, it must resonate with the clients, capturing their interest and encouraging their participation. As Crawford et al. (2004) note, the stories constructed in therapy reflect the intentions of the storyteller and the cultural and professional context in which they arise.

Conceptual frameworks, while rooted in theory, only become impactful when they are enacted and embraced by clients. Corrie and Lane (2010) pose a critical question: "Who owns the case formulation—and who has the authority to approve, reject, or revise it: the therapist, the client, or someone else?" (p. 51). While clinicians develop and present these stories, clients are ultimately the ones who determine whether the story fits and whether change is possible. Therapists create the conditions for transformation, but it is the clients who must engage with and act on those possibilities. Thus, therapeutic stories are only beneficial when therapists and clients utilize them.

Therapy is inherently a collaborative endeavor. A therapist's conceptualization cannot singlehandedly lead to change. Unless clients accept and engage with the therapist's framing of the problem, they are likely to remain embedded in their own initial perspective. Framing, therefore, is a central element of persuasive and effective therapy (Cheng, 2016). Each individual in the room brings a unique worldview or position regarding the issue at hand. Fisch et al. (1982) referred to this as the "patient's position," asserting that the therapist must understand and work with this viewpoint to foster therapeutic engagement.

In family therapy, each family member often arrives believing that the source of the problem lies in another person. Clients may cite communication breakdowns but typically believe the breakdown stems from the other's behavior. One of the family therapist's primary responsibilities is to shift these individual frames into an interpersonal context. While clients tend to interpret problems as individual flaws, the therapist redirects focus to relational dynamics (Reiter & Chenail, 2016). Over time, this shift encourages clients to reframe their experiences as part of a shared interaction, rather than a one-sided issue (Moran et al., 2005).

For reframes to be effective, they must align—at least partially—with the client's worldview. As Fisch et al. (1982) explain, it's not just the content of a suggestion that matters, but the manner in which it is presented. What works for one client might be unconvincing to another. Understanding a client's position—including factors like culture, race, gender, age, and sexual orientation—helps therapists shape feedback in a way that feels authentic and acceptable. The therapist's systemic insight becomes truly impactful when this feedback is both relevant and agreed upon by the client (Stanton & Welsh, 2011).

Frames function as vehicles for progress. According to Sussman (1999), framing provides structure, justification, and meaning. For the therapist's narrative to take hold, it must make logical and emotional sense to the clients. The frame's perspective gives context; its rationale links the evidence (such as client behaviors or exceptions) to that context; and its structure shapes how clients interpret past, present, and even future events. In this way, framing helps construct a cohesive therapeutic story.

In family therapy, **reframing** is a vital tool. It does not alter the facts but reinterprets their significance (Watzlawick et al., 1974). As Weeks and D'Aniello (2017) describe, reframing invites clients to see the same circumstances through a new lens—one they co-create and are willing to accept. Effective reframes in family therapy are often interactional, reducing blame and increasing hope (O'Brien & Young, 2014). They help shift emotional tone and foster more constructive attitudes (Robbins et al., 1996). A systemic reframe offers a fresh angle that helps families make better sense of their shared experience (Weeks & D'Aniello, 2017).

Clients frequently arrive in therapy with a narrow, zoomed-in view of what's wrong—usually placing blame on the identified patient. Family therapists, however, work from a broader vantage point, offering alternate interpretations that open new possibilities (Minuchin et al., 2021). A well-placed reframe expands the clients' sense of identity and agency, revealing that they are more resourceful than they previously believed.

Constructing the Therapeutic Story

When a reframe becomes part of a case conceptualization, it often evolves into a **therapeutic story**. These narratives are usually constructed in story form, which helps clients integrate new perspectives into memory and identity

(Bruner, 1990). Though reframes are often brief, those rooted in case conceptualization provide a lasting foundation for change.

Therapists tend to develop affirming and optimistic frames in their conceptualizations—developing a therapeutic story that emphasizes growth, connection, and possibility. While these positive frames are typically helpful, there is a risk that clients may perceive them as overly persuasive or disconnected from their lived experience, triggering resistance or disbelief (Koch & Peter, 2017). This highlights the importance of grounding reframes in observable client strengths and experiences, such as exceptions or unique outcomes.

However, negative or undermining frames—such as viewing the relationship as beyond repair or suggesting separation as the only option—are associated with poorer outcomes and shorter therapy duration (Doherty et al., 2024). Fortunately, such approaches are rare. Most therapists frame the therapeutic story in a way that aligns with the family's aspirations, reinforcing the belief that improvement is achievable. Hoyt (2000) explained that "therapy can be understood as the purposeful development of a more functional story; 'better' stories are those that bring more of what is desired and less of what is not desired" (pp. 21–22).

While the use of storytelling has been frequently utilized in psychotherapy (see Bergner, 2007; Crawford et al., 2004; Perrow, 2012), these stories may be separate yet adjacent to the client's actual experience. They tend to be metaphors in hopes that the client takes some meaning from. The therapist may have stock stories that they can use for a multitude of clients who fall within a certain category (e.g., for individuals experiencing depression; for couples dealing with an infidelity; or for families who had a member recently die). In this book, we will talk about therapeutic stories—how the therapist conceptualizes and explains the client's situation. Andolfi et al. (1989) explained the purpose of constructing a therapeutic story, "Within this temporary and 'artificial' story, it is possible for the family to learn how to find different meanings for the events and interactions of family life and eventually to try out new alternatives in real life" (p. 16).

Each model of therapy has various techniques associated with them. Yet, techniques and interventions on their own are just techniques. They are not cure-alls. However, how techniques are put together and interwoven leads to the construction of a therapeutic story that can be useful.

Continuing the Story of Case Conceptualizations

Developing effective case conceptualizations in family therapy extends beyond the identification or diagnosis of problems. It involves the construction of therapeutic stories that facilitate meaningful change and resonate with clients' lived experiences. Through the processes of framing and reframing, clinicians introduce alternative perspectives on interpersonal difficulties—shifting the focus from blame to relational understanding, and from limitation to potential.

These therapeutic stories not only clarify the direction of treatment but also invite clients to envision themselves and their relationships in more hopeful and empowering ways.

Chapter 2 examines the utility and impact of case conceptualizations within the context of family therapy. Importantly, no single theoretical model holds a monopoly on effective case formulation. Rather, each model offers a valid and potentially transformative pathway toward the family's goals. This reflects the systems theory principle of **equifinality**, which posits that there are multiple routes to achieving the same outcome.

Chapter 3 introduces the Daniels family—a fictional composite drawn from clinical experience—who will serve as a case study throughout the remainder of the volume. The subsequent chapters present 15 distinct models of family therapy, each illustrating how the Daniels family might be conceptualized and how a unique therapeutic story might emerge from that model's perspective.

It is important to note that while 15 distinct case conceptualizations are offered, these represent only a subset of the possible stories that could be generated—even within a single theoretical model. Therapeutic stories are inherently co-constructed within the specific therapeutic system that includes the practitioner, the family, and the broader context in which therapy occurs. They are shaped not only by theoretical orientation but also by timing, relational dynamics, and the particular needs and resources of those involved.

The aim of this book is to encourage readers to reflect on their own clinical work through the lens of case conceptualization. Specifically, it invites emerging and experienced clinicians alike to consider: How do I construct case conceptualizations that lead to the creation of therapeutic stories which are both useful and transformative for my clients?

Note

1 Reframing is being used here to explain how a therapist takes the client's initial problem-focused frame and reframes it into a therapeutic story that highlights the client's strengths and resources.

References

Andolfi, M., Angelo, C., & de Nichilo, M. (1989). *The myth of Atlas: Families and the therapeutic story*. Brunner-Routledge.

Bergner, R. M. (2007). Therapeutic storytelling revisited. *American Journal of Psychotherapy*, *61*(2), 149–162.

Bruner, J. (1990). *Acts of meaning*. Harvard University Press.

Carr, A. (2020). Evidence for the efficacy and effectiveness of systemic family therapy. In K. S. Wampler, R. B. Miller, & R. B. Seedall (Eds.). *The handbook of systemic family therapy: Volume 1: The profession of systemic family therapy* (pp. 187–220). Wiley.

Cheng, M. (2016). The power of persuasion: Modality and issue framing in the 2012 Taiwan presidential debates. *Discourse & Society*, *27*(2), 172–194.

Ciğerci, F. M., & Yildrim, M. (2024). From Freytag pyramid story structure to digital storytelling: Adventures of preservice teachers as story writers and digital story tellers. *Education and Information Technologies*, *29*, 5697–5720.
Corrie, S., & Lane, D. A. (2010). *Constructing stories, telling tales: A guide to formulation in applied psychology*. Karnac.
Crawford, R., Brown, B., & Crawford, P. (2004). *Storytelling in therapy*. Nelson Thomes Ltd.
Doherty, W. J., Harris, S. M., & Mussa, K. (2024). Relationship undermining in couple therapy. *Contemporary Family Therapy: An International Journal*, *46*, 243–248.
Dwivedi, K. N., & Gardner, D. (1997). Theoretical perspectives and clinical approaches. In K. N. Dwivedi (Ed.). *The therapeutic use of stories* (pp. 19–41). Routledge.
Eels, T. D. (2022). History and current status of psychotherapy case formulation. In T. D. Eells (Ed.). *Handbook of psychotherapy case formulation* (4th ed., pp. 1–35). Guilford Publications.
Fisch, R., Weakland, J. H., & Segal, L. (1982). *The tactics of change: Doing therapy briefly*. Jossey-Bass.
Gilboa-Schechtman, E. (2024). Case conceptualization in clinical practice and training. *Clinical Psychology in Europe*, *6*, e12103.
Hoyt. M. F. (2000). *Some stories are better than others: Doing what works in brief therapy and managed care*. Brunner/Mazel.
Keeney, B. (2009). *The creative therapist: The art of awakening a session*. Routledge.
Keeney, H., Keeney, B., & Chenail, R. (2012). Recursive frame analysis: A practitioner's tool for mapping therapeutic conversation. *The Qualitative Report*, *17*(38), 1–15.
Keeney, H., Keeney, B., & Chenail, R. (2015). *Recursive frame analysis: A qualitative research method for mapping change-oriented discourse*. The Qualitative Report Books.
Koch, T., & Peter, C. (2017). Effects of equivalence framing on the perceived truth of political messages and the trustworthiness of politicians. *Public Opinion Quarterly*, *81*(4), 847–865.
Kühn, S., & Boschoff, C. (2023). The role of plot in brand story construction: A neurophysiological perspective. *Journal of Strategic Marketing*, *31*(2), 471–497.
Lambert, M. J. (1992). Psychotherapy outcome research: Implications for integrative and eclectic therapists. In J. C. Norcross, & M. R. Goldfried (Eds.), *Handbook of psychotherapy integration* (pp. 94–129). Basic Books.
Lambert, M. J., & Bergin, A. E. (1994). The effectiveness of psychotherapy. In A. E. Bergin, & S. L. Garfield (Eds.), *Handbook of psychotherapy and behavior change* (4th ed., pp. 143–189). Wiley.
Madden, L., & Timulak, L. (2024). It takes three to tango: Clients' experiences of couple therapy-A meta-analysis of qualitative research studies. *Counselling Psychology Quarterly*, *37*(1), 1–24.
Miller, S. D., Duncan, B. L., & Hubble, M. A. (1997). *Escape from Babel: Toward a unifying language for psychotherapy practice*. Norton.
Minuchin, S., Reiter, M. D., & Borda, C. (2021). *The craft of family therapy: Challenging certainties*. Routledge.
Moran, G., Diamond, G. M., & Diamond, G. S. (2005). The relational reframe and parents' problem constructions in attachment-based family therapy. *Psychotherapy Research*, *15*(3), 226–235.
O'Brien, E. R., & Young, M. E. (2014). The big reframe: Helping couples develop an interactive definition. *The Family Journal: Counseling and Therapy for Couples and Families*, *22*(3), 347–349.

Perrow, S. (2012). *Therapeutic storytelling: 101 healing stories for children*. Hawthorn Press.

Quesenberry, K. A., & Coolsen, M. K. (2019). Drama goes viral: Effects of story development on shares and views of online advertising videos. *Journal of Interactive Marketing*, *48*, 1–16.

Reiter, M. D. (2014). *Case conceptualization in family therapy*. Pearson.

Reiter, M. D. (2025). An introduction to couple therapy. In M. D. Reiter (Ed.). *Case conceptualization in couple therapy: Comparing and contrasting theories*. Routledge.

Reiter, M. D., & Chenail, R. J. (2016). Defining the focus in solution-focused brief therapy. *International Journal of Solution-Focused Practices*, *4*(1), 1–9.

Reiter, M. D., Jung, W. F., Popham, J., Fitzgerald, C., Garcia, E., de Perez, M. G., Lockhart, T., & Villanueva, N. (2020). Training through naming: A process of psychotherapist skill development utilizing recursive frame analysis. *The Qualitative Report*, *25*(8), 2085–2099.

Robbins, M. S., Alexander, J. F., Newell, R. M., & Turner, C. W. (1996). The immediate effect of reframing on client attitude in family therapy. *Journal of Family Psychology*, *10*(1), 28–34.

Simon, G. (2019). Tell me a story: Teaching music composition through narrative design. *College Music Symposium*, *59*(2), 1–24.

Sperry, L., & Sperry, J. J. (2020). *Case conceptualization: Mastering this competency with ease and confidence* (2nd ed.). Routledge.

Sperry, L., & Sperry, J. (2023). *Core clinical competencies in counseling and psychotherapy: Becoming a highly competent and effective therapist* (2nd ed.). Routledge.

Stanton, M., & Welsh, R. (2011). *Specialty competencies in couple and family psychology*. Oxford Academic Press.

Sussman, L. (1999). How to frame a message: The art of persuasion and negotiation. *Business Horizons*, *42*(4), 2–6.

Watzlawick, P., Weakland, J., & Fisch, R. (1974). *Change: Principles of problem formation and problem resolution*. W. W. Norton & Company.

Weeks, G. R., & D'Aniello, C. (2017). Teaching reframes in a Master's level marriage and family therapist program. *Journal of Family Psychotherapy*, *28*(4), 303–316.

White, M., & Epston, D. (1990). *Narrative means to therapeutic ends*. Norton.

Wittenborn, A. K., & Holtrop, K. (2021). Introduction to the special issue on the efficacy and effectiveness of couple and family interventions: Evidence base update 2010–2019. *Journal of Marital and Family Therapy*, *48*, 5–22.

Zubernis, L. (2016). *Case conceptualization and effective interventions: Assessing and treating mental, emotional, and behavioral disorders*. Sage Publications.

2 The Effectiveness of Case Conceptualization

A Brief Primer

Kyle D. Killian

A central premise of this edited volume is that case conceptualization is crucial to successful therapeutic processes and outcomes. Effective case conceptualization is a core clinical competency for all trainees and therapists. This chapter focuses specifically on the use of case conceptualization by family therapists, given this book's focus on family therapy case conceptualization. A successful case conceptualization provides a systemic, context-sensitive, parsimonious model of client functioning; outlines relevant, overarching treatment goals and their associated assessment procedures; and presents a treatment plan with intervention phases. This chapter presents evidence for case conceptualization's contributions to positive processes and outcomes, making the case for why it is a critical component of our work as clinicians.

Importance of Case Conceptualizations

Through case conceptualization, we seek to write a concise and coherent story (Reiter & Sperry, 2025) that offers a credible framework for understanding the client's difficulties and informs treatment planning (Eells, 2022; Persons, 2022; Sperry & Sperry, 2026). A theory-informed, comprehensive conceptualization can lead to the development of a flexible, effective treatment plan (Gilboa-Schechtman, 2024). Ideally, case conceptualization: (1) strives to provide a comprehensive understanding of clients' presenting concerns, strains and symptoms, and systemic, relational patterns, and (2) is an *ongoing* process wherein the therapist works to revise, update, and refine it "via new information, insights, and responsivity to specific triggers and interventions" (Gilboa-Schechtman, 2024, p. 2). In best practice, therapists would remain open and attuned to signals from clients (e.g., communications about misalignments in treatment tasks or goals) (Zilcha-Mano et al., 2020), indicating directions for possible modifications or fine-tuning of the case conceptualization (Kealy & Curtis, 2025). Thus, therapists' openness to feedback and responsiveness via reevaluation of a case formulation over the course of treatment is crucial to fostering positive outcomes.

DOI: 10.4324/9781003668510-2

It can be argued that since case conceptualization is a metacognitive competency of couple and family therapists, training and practice are necessary (Seif et al., 2014; Wall, 2021). Trainers and supervisors can seek to develop trainees' ability to assess the completeness of their case conceptualizations by aiming to fulfill the following seven characteristics:

> (a) *comprehensive* in addressing multiple aspects of a client's functioning; (b) *understandable* to the client and thus use language that is precise and non-technical; (c) *parsimonious* yet not simplistic; (d) *coherent*, providing an internally consistent model of the individual's problems, explaining the presenting complaints by reference to predisposing vulnerabilities and strengths, precipitating events, etiological and maintaining factors; (e) *science-informed*, offering explanatory hypotheses linked to knowledge about personality and psychopathology; (f) *generative*, highlighting the ways in which the treatment plan logically flows from the explanatory hypotheses and predicts measurable outcomes; and finally, (g) *cohesive*, offering a treatment plan that links the hypotheses with a therapeutic course of action.
>
> (Gilboa-Schechtman, 2024, p. 6, emphasis in the original)

As we seek to aid therapists to form ever more comprehensive case conceptualizations, specific teaching activities include Chalkboard Case Conceptualization (Eells, 2013), Concept Mapping (Novak & Cañas, 2010), Creative Role Play Activity (Hinkle & Dean, 2017), and Scenarios with Fictional Characters (Cook, 2018).

Case conceptualization skills have been studied using different methods, with researchers attempting to parse different skill sets and/or levels. Lee and Tracey (2008) cited examples of the conceptual level (Holloway & Wampold, 1986), convergent or divergent conceptual strategies (Hirsch & Stone, 1983), cognitive processing (Hillerbrand & Claiborn, 1990), concept mapping (Martin et al., 1989), and cognitive complexity (Ladany et al., 2001). Perhaps unsurprisingly to systemically oriented practitioners, the major takeaway from this research is that conceptualization is best when it reflects high levels of complexity, convergence, abstraction, and integration (Lee & Tracey, 2008). The general conclusion of the research is that clinicians with more training or experience tend to create conceptualizations that demonstrate higher-order cognitive skills outshine their peers on expert ratings.

CFTs engaging in a comprehensive case conceptualization apply multiple metacognitive skills, including monitoring of client and therapist responses, analysis, synthesis, and evaluation of diverse "information streams to develop a cohesive narrative or structure that fosters an understanding of clients' presenting concerns and strengths (e.g., development, course and maintenance) within the clients' varying sociocultural context" (Wall, 2021, p. 5). Case conceptualization also steers CFTs through the steps of diagnosis, recommendations, goals, and interventions (Haynes et al., 2021; Wall, 2021).

A subarea of interest is *multicultural* case conceptualization. There has been a dearth of process-oriented guidance for increasing the cultural responsiveness of evidence-based practice in family therapy. Nevertheless, studies have highlighted how cultural context can deeply affect the way in which individuals and families view therapy and therapy services (Georgiadis et al., 2020; Graham-LoPresti et al., 2017; Kirmayer & Jarvis, 2019; Lewis-Fernandez et al., 2020; Zigarelli et al., 2016). Ideally, therapists seek to develop a picture of clients' functioning across multiple systems and domains, including work, school, social network, and culture (Ridley et al., 2017; Wall, 2021). Sanchez et al. (2022) pointed out that "most evidence-based treatments have been developed mostly within the majority White culture and largely by White clinical innovators and researchers, leading to a lack of systematic consideration of cultural factors relevant to mental health care" (p. 751). Sanchez et al. (2022) stressed the need for more culturally responsive approaches, underlining "how leading case conceptualization models fail to systematically incorporate cultural formulation into assessment and treatment planning" (p. 751), and offered practice guidance for systematically incorporating relevant cultural factors into case conceptualization in the context of family therapy. They defined cultural responsiveness in terms of "the intentional use of strategies that incorporate their [the clients'] cultural backgrounds, beliefs, and values into treatment" (p. 751).

Eschewing a "one size fits all" treatment approach that tends to ignore important individual differences, as well as the significance of intersectionality, a culturally informed case conceptualization allows therapists to ensure that treatment interventions and strategies are relevant to clients' specific needs and contexts (Easden & Kazantzis, 2018; Sanchez et al., 2022). Leveraging cultural assessment permits incorporation of cultural factors into the five stages of Christon et al.'s (2015) science-based case conceptualization model. Conducting a cultural assessment as part of Stage 1—integrating evidence-based assessment—can improve the therapists' understanding of the family's presenting problems. Asking families about their cultural values and strengths shows that therapists value their perspectives. Therapists can identify presenting problems in a culturally responsive way by asking questions such as what is the client's/caregiver's description of their problem, and what troubles the client/caregiver most about their problem? The second stage, generating and assigning diagnoses, can be made culturally responsive by including a review of the cultural definition of the problem and reviewing DSM-5 cultural contexts of distress. Stage 3, development of hypotheses, can include the following questions from the Cultural Formulation Interview: What does the client/caregiver think is causing their problem? Are there stressors that make the client's problem *worse*? Are there aspects of the client's/caregiver's background that make a difference to their problem or are causing them more difficulties (Sanchez et al., 2022)? For Stage 4, treatment plan and selection, Sanchez et al. (2022) suggested inclusion of the following Cultural Formulation Interview questions: Are there any kinds of supports that make the problem better? What types of help have been most and least useful to the client/caregiver? Has anything prevented the client/caregiver from getting the help they needed? For Stage 5, ongoing treatment monitoring and evaluation, Sanchez et al. (2022) suggested that therapists discuss cultural strengths, acknowledging values consistent with treatment goals.

Evidence of Effectiveness of Case Conceptualization and Case Conceptualization Training

Case conceptualization is the core of evidence-based practice (Hass et al., 2022). However, studies (e.g., Lau et al., 2017) demonstrate that there continues to be a shortage of clinicians who have received training in the use of case conceptualization to guide decisions regarding treatment, and who have developed the capacity to consistently utilize evidence-based treatments (Austin et al., 2025). Studies on case conceptualization skills in training are of vital importance because these skills are associated with therapy outcomes (Kendjelic & Eells, 2007; Kuyken & Dunn, 2022; Lee & Tracey, 2008). For instance, in the field of psychotherapy, case conceptualization skills are correlated with the degree of therapeutic skill (Morran, 1986) as well as client and observer ratings of therapeutic effectiveness (Morran et al., 1994). Accuracy of therapist conceptualizations has also been found to correlate with client progress (Silberschatz et al., 1986) and positive treatment outcomes (Crits-Cristoph et al., 1988). Despite the importance of understanding how psychotherapy trainees develop in case conceptualization skills, a dearth of research has been conducted in this area (Kendjelic & Eells, 2007; Ladany, 2007; Neufeldt et al., 2006). What follows is a brief review of studies conducted on case conceptualization and the effectiveness of therapy.

Research indicates that "effective case conceptualization is associated with improved client outcomes and shorter lengths of treatment" (Austin et al., 2025, p. 2). For instance, using a sample of 72 early- to mid-career clinicians, Austin et al. (2025) provided a series of trainings using an iterative process where feedback was incorporated throughout and participants' knowledge, self-efficacy, and clinical practice (i.e., evidence-based treatments or EBTs) were assessed pre- and post-completion of the series. The training included dissemination of information on evidence-based interventions and case conceptualization. Austin et al. (2025) concluded that the training was "feasible, effective for improving master's prepared clinicians' self-efficacy surrounding the utilization of EBTs and case conceptualization in clinical practice, and cost-efficient for participants" (p. 1).

Difficulties in applying case conceptualization theory and knowledge in everyday clinical practice persist (Austin et al., 2025; Dudley et al., 2015). When case conceptualization is ineffective, therapists can wind up mismatching symptoms and interventions (Austin et al., 2025; Calloway & Creed, 2022). Research has shown that beginning therapists tend to be "less methodical, more confident in their case conceptualizations, and more likely to consider less robust treatment options" (Austin et al., 2025, p. 2) when compared to their more experienced counterparts (Dudley et al., 2015). Interestingly, experienced therapists "endorse *low* confidence in their case conceptualization skills, again, indicating that experience and training in case conceptualization are needed to leverage the skills of the existing workforce (Zivor et al., 2013)" (Austin et al., 2025, p. 2). This seems to be a case of less experienced therapists not knowing what they don't know or what they aren't doing as effectively, and more seasoned therapists having an awareness that their case conceptualization skills and use of EBTs could be better.

Eells et al. (2005) conducted a study of a group of 65 clinicians, classified as novice, experienced, and expert, who constructed comprehensive conceptualizations based on six standardized vignettes with a range of presenting problems and disorders. A total of 390 case conceptualizations were created. After reading the case vignettes, therapists took five minutes to verbalize aloud a case conceptualization in an unstructured manner with instructions to "address whatever you think is important." The transcribed case conceptualizations were coded using the Case Formulation Content Coding method (Eells et al., 1998). Then, multiple 5-point Likert scales were rated by pairs of raters to judge the relative presence versus absence of specific skill sets. "Precision of language" (ICC = 0.77), "complexity" (ICC = 0.83), "coherence" (ICC = 0.75), "treatment plan elaboration" (ICC = 0.86), "goodness-of-fit" (ICC = 0.73), and "systematic process" (ICC = 0.77) reflected good to excellent levels of reliability. The study's findings indicated expert conceptualizations were rated as more comprehensive, elaborated, complex, systematic, and better quality overall when comparing experienced with beginning therapists.

Investigating therapist training in conceptualization, Kendjelic and Eells (2007) provided a 2-h conceptualization training session for 20 novice therapists; a control group of 23 therapists did not receive the training. Using data from 99 conceptualizations of anxious and depressed clients, the researchers found a large mean effect size of 1.12, with the average therapist in the training group producing a better case conceptualization than 86% of the therapists who had not received the training. In a subsequent analysis of data from this study, Eells et al. (2011) found that experts had a greater focus on treatment (d = 0.34) and psychological mechanisms of change (d = 0.25) than nonexperts, and experts generated more descriptive (d = 0.33), diagnostic (d = 0.24), inferential (d = 0.35), and treatment planning information (d = 0.32) in their case conceptualizations than nonexperts.

In a study of seven therapists delivering Cognitive Behavioral Therapy (CBT) to 28 adults presenting with depression, Easden and Fletcher (2020) used the Conceptualization Rating Scale (CRS) to comprehensively assess therapist competence in case conceptualization by rating recordings of 225 therapy sessions over the course of the first ten treatment sessions. Using multilevel modeling (MLM) analysis and controlling for time, Easden and Fletcher

(2020) found therapist competence in case conceptualization explained 40% of within-client variance, and 19% of between-client variance, measured as positive change on the Beck Depression Inventory II. Easden and Fletcher (2020) concluded that increased therapist competence in using case conceptualization is associated with greater reductions in depressive symptoms.

Regarding multicultural case conceptualization research, in a series of studies, Constantine (2001a, 2001b) provided psychotherapy trainees with a vignette about a client of color presenting with multiple culturally laden concerns and asked trainees to write a conceptualization including etiology and treatment planning (Lee & Tracey, 2008). Multicultural case conceptualization skills correlated positively with empathy (Constantine, 2001b), ethnic tolerance attitudes (Constantine & Gushue, 2003), and, importantly, multicultural training (Constantine, 2001a, 2001b; Constantine & Gushue, 2003). Further, trainees of color were found to demonstrate higher multicultural case conceptualization abilities than White trainees (Constantine, 2001a). In a qualitative study exploring the general and multicultural case conceptualization skills of psychotherapy trainees, Neutfeldt et al. (2006) exposed 17 trainees to two video vignettes of clients (one upper-middle-class, retired, European American male, and one young, Chinese American, female college student). A semi-structured interview followed each video. Interestingly, Neutfeldt et al. (2006) found psychotherapy trainees incorporated more diversity factors in their conceptualization of the White client versus the Asian client. Finally, studying doctoral-level trainees' case conceptualizations, Wright et al. (2023) investigated whether the integration of culture into the conceptualizations/formulations was influenced using the Wright-Constantine Structured Cultural Interview (WCSCI) compared to the use of the DSM-5 Cultural Formulation Interview and the Patient Cultural Identity Assessment. Clients with minoritized identities and supervisors with minoritized identities were associated with case conceptualizations that integrated culture at higher rates. However, minoritized identities in *trainees* were not a factor leading to cultural integration. Conceptualizations that utilized the WCSCI were between 3.5 and 4.5 times more likely to integrate culture than those that used one of the other two cultural interviews. The tools that therapists utilize to gather information from clients can have a significant impact on the cultural responsiveness of case conceptualization. What we ask, and how we ask it, can have a profound effect on the case formulation process.

Conclusion

To enhance therapist competence, there is a "need for robust training of therapists to become proficient in skills pertinent to…case conceptualization" (Easden & Kazantzis, 2018, p. 381). Indeed, developing case conceptualization skills is an ongoing, lifelong endeavor. This effort can be aided by supervision, training, and mentoring that help supervisees and trainees hone and expand their skill sets. Provision of additional training opportunities carries the potential of improving "the quality and effectiveness of services delivered by master's prepared clinicians who may not have had the opportunity to obtain rigorous training" in these skill sets (Austin et al., 2025, p. 13). Striking a balance, supervisors "who model intellectual humility and healthy skepticism as parts of their professional improvement process are likely to foster up to date… methods among their supervisees" (Gilboa-Schechtman, 2024, p. 6). Further, developing model-based case conceptualization skills will be useful to couple and family therapists, as a more comprehensive case conceptualization process is the launch pad for more effective treatment outcomes and increased quality of therapeutic practice.

References

Austin, J. E., Whitehead, M. R., Young, M. A., Ryan, P. M., Kramer, K. M., & McClure, J. M. (2025). A quality improvement approach to elevate clinicians' use of evidenced-based practice. *Evidence-Based Practice in Child and Adolescent Mental Health*, *10*(3), 541–555.

Calloway, A., & Creed, T. A. (2022). Enhancing CBT consultation with multicultural counseling principles. *Cognitive and Behavioral Practice*, *29*(4), 787–795.

Christon, L. M., McLeod, B. D., & Jensen-Doss, A. (2015). Evidence-based assessment meets evidence-based treatment: An approach to science-informed case conceptualization. *Cognitive and Behavioral Practice*, *22*(1), 36–48.

Constantine, M. (2001a). Independent and interdependent self-construals as predictors of multicultural case conceptualization in counselor trainees. *Counseling Psychology Quarterly*, *14*, 33–42.

Constantine, M. (2001b). Multicultural training, theoretical orientation, empathy and multicultural case conceptualization ability in counselors. *Journal of Mental Health Counseling*, *23*, 357–372.

Constantine, M., & Gushue, G. (2003). School counselors' ethnic tolerance attitudes and racism attitudes as predictors of their multicultural case conceptualization of an immigrant student. *Journal of Counseling and Development*, *81*, 185–190.

Cook, K. (2018). Brief counseling scenarios from fictional characters for counselors in training. *Journal of Educational Psychology*, *11*(3), 43–49.

Crits-Christoph, P., Cooper, A., & Luborsky, L. (1988). The accuracy of therapists' interpretations and the outcome of dynamic psychotherapy. *Journal of Consulting and Clinical Psychology*, *56*(4), 490–495.

Dudley, R., Ingham, B., Sowerby, K., & Freeston, M. (2015). The utility of case formulation in treatment decision making: The effect of experience and expertise. *Journal of Behavior Therapy and Experimental Psychiatry*, *48*, 66–74.

Easden, M. H., & Fletcher, R. B. (2020). Therapist competence in case conceptualization and outcome in CBT for depression. *Psychotherapy Research*, *30*(2), 151–169.

Easden, M. H., & Kazantzis, N. (2018). Case conceptualization research in cognitive behavior therapy: A state of the science review. *Journal of Clinical Psychology*, *74*(3), 356–384.

Eells, T. D. (2013). The case formulation approach to psychotherapy research revisited. *Pragmatic Case Studies in Psychotherapy*, *9*(4), 426–447.

Eells, T. D. (Ed.). (2022). *Handbook of psychotherapy case formulation* (3rd ed.). Guilford.

Eells, T. D., Kendjelic, E. M., & Lucas, C. P. (1998). What's in a case formulation? Development and use of a content coding manual. *The Journal of Psychotherapy Practice and Research*, *7*(2), 144–153.

Eells, T. D., Lombart, K. G., Kendjelic, E. M., Turner, L. C., & Lucas, C. P. (2005). The quality of psychotherapy case formulations: A comparison of expert, experienced, and novice cognitive-behavioral and psychodynamic therapists. *Journal of Consulting and Clinical Psychology*, *73*(4), 579–589.

Eells, T. D., Lombart, K. G., Salsman, N., Kendjelic, E. M., Schneiderman, C. T., & Lucas, C. P. (2011). Expert reasoning in psychotherapy case formulation. *Psychotherapy Research*, *21*(4), 385–399.

Georgiadis, C., Peris, T. S., & Comer, J. S. (2020). Implementing strategic flexibility in the delivery of youth mental health care: A tailoring framework for thoughtful clinical practice. *Evidence-Based Practice in Child and Adolescent Mental Health*, *5*, 215–232.

Gilboa-Schechtman, E. (2024). Case conceptualization in clinical practice and training. *Clinical Psychology in Europe*, *6*(Spec Issue), e12103.

Graham-LoPresti, J. R., Gautier, S. W., Sorenson, S., & Hayes-Skelton, S. A. (2017). Culturally sensitive adaptations to evidence-based cognitive behavioral treatment for social anxiety disorder: A case paper. *Cognitive and Behavioral Practice*, *24*(4), 459–471.

Hass, M. R., Maupin, Z., & Doria, M. (2022). Case conceptualization as an alternative to educationally related mental health assessments. *Contemporary School Psychology*, *26*(3), 290–298.

Haynes, S. N., Godoy, A., & Frias, A. (2021). Selecting treatment foci in clinical case formulations: Estimating the clinical benefits of modifying causal variables. *Psychological Assessment*, *33*(5), 452–458.

Hillerbrand, E. T., & Claiborn, C. D. (1990). Examining reasoning skill differences between expert and novice counselors. *Journal of Counseling & Development*, *68*(6), 684–691.

Hinkle, M. S., & Dean, L. S. M. (2017). Creativity in teaching case conceptualization skills: Role-play to show the interconnectedness of domains. *Journal of Creativity in Mental Health*, *12*(3), 388–401.

Hirsch, P. A., & Stone, G. L. (1983). Cognitive strategies and the client conceptualization process. *Journal of Counseling Psychology*, *30*(4), 566–572.

Holloway, E. L., & Wampold, B. E. (1986). Relation between conceptual level and counseling-related tasks: A meta-analysis. *Journal of Counseling Psychology*, *33*(3), 310–319.

Kealy, D., & Curtis, J. T. (2025). Failure to evaluate and modify a case formulation across the course of therapy: A risk factor for poor psychotherapy outcome. *Journal of Psychotherapy Integration*, *35*(2), 150–160.

Kendjelic, E. M., & Eells, T. D. (2007). Generic psychotherapy case formulation training improves formulation quality. *Psychotherapy*, *44*(1), 66–77.

Kirmayer, L. J., & Jarvis, G. E. (2019). Culturally responsive services as a path to equity in mental healthcare. *Healthcare Papers*, *18*(2), 11–23.

Kuyken, W., & Dunn, B. D. (2022). Case conceptualization in mindfulness-based cognitive therapy. In T. D. Eells (Ed.), *Handbook of psychotherapy case formulation* (3rd ed., pp. 353–379). The Guilford Press.

Ladany, N. (2007). Does psychotherapy training matter? Maybe not. *Psychotherapy: Theory, Research, Practice, Training*, *44*(4), 392–396.

Ladany, N., Marotta, S., & Muse-Burke, J. L. (2001). Counselor experience related to complexity of case conceptualization and supervision preference. *Counselor Education and Supervision*, *40*(3), 203–219.

Lau, A., Barnett, M., Stadnick, N., Saifan, D., Regan, J., Wiltsey Stirman, S., Roesch, S., & Brookman-Frazee, L. (2017). Therapist report of adaptations to delivery of evidence-based practices within a system-driven reform of publicly funded children's mental health services. *Journal of Consulting and Clinical Psychology*, *85*(7), 664–675.

Lee, D. L., & Tracey, T. J. G. (2008). General and multicultural case conceptualization skills: A cross-sectional analysis of psychotherapy trainees. *Psychotherapy: Theory, Research, Practice, Training*, *45*(4), 507–522.

Lewis-Fernández, R., Aggarwal, N. K., & Kirmayer, L. J. (2020). The Cultural Formulation Interview: Progress to date and future directions. *Transcultural Psychiatry*, *57*(4), 487–496.

Martin, J., Slemon, A. G., Hiebert, B., Hallberg, E. T., & Cummings, A. L. (1989). Conceptualizations of novice and experienced counselors. *Journal of Counseling Psychology*, *36*(4), 395–400.

Morran, D. K. (1986). Relationship of counselor self-talk and hypothesis formulation to performance level. *Journal of Counseling Psychology*, *33*(4), 395–400.

Morran, D. K., Kurpius, D. J., Brack, G., & Rozecki, T. G. (1994). Relationship between counselors' clinical hypotheses and client ratings of counselor effectiveness. *Journal of Counseling & Development*, *72*(6), 655–660.

Neufeldt, S. A., Pinterits, E. J., Moleiro, C. M., Lee, T. E., Yang, P. H., Brodie, R. E., & Orliss, M. J. (2006). How do graduate student therapists incorporate diversity factors in case conceptualization? *Psychotherapy: Theory, Research, Practice, Training*, *43*(4), 464–479.

Novak, J. D., & Cañas, A. J. (2010). The theory underlying concept maps and how to construct and use them. *Práxis Educativa*, *5*(1), 9–29.

Persons, J. B. (2022). Case formulation. *Cognitive and Behavioral Practice*, *29*(3), 537–540.

Reiter, M., & Sperry, J. (2025). Creating therapeutic stories through case conceptualizations in couple therapy. *The American Journal of Family Therapy*, 53(38), 1–12.

Ridley, C. R., Jeffrey, C. E., & Roberson, R. B. (2017). Case miss-conceptualization in psychological treatment: An enduring clinical problem. *Journal of Clinical Psychology*, *73*(4), 359–375. https://doi.org/10.1002/jclp.22354

Sanchez, A. L., Comer, J. S., & LaRoche, M. (2022). Enhancing the responsiveness of family-based CBT through culturally informed case conceptualization and treatment planning. *Cognitive and Behavioral Practice*, *29*(4), 750–770.

Seif, G., Coker-Bolt, P., Kraft, S., Gonsalves, W., Simpson, K., & Johnson, E. (2014). The development of clinical reasoning and interprofessional behaviors: Service-learning at a student-run free clinic. *Journal of Interprofessional Care*, *28*(6), 559–564.

Silberschatz, G., Fretter, P. B., & Curtis, J. T. (1986). How do interpretations influence the process of psychotherapy? *Journal of Consulting and Clinical Psychology*, *54*(5), 646–652.

Sperry, L., & Sperry, J. J. (2026). *Case conceptualization: Mastering this competency with ease and confidence* (3rd ed.). Routledge.

Wall, L. M. (2021). *Closing the case conceptualization gap: An integrative case conceptualization model and introductory workshop for helping masters-level clinicians-in-training learn and engage in case conceptualization*. Dissertation, Pepperdine University.

Wright, A. J., Vardanian, M. M., & Constantine, K. (2023). The Wright-Constantine structured cultural interview and integration of culture into case conceptualization. *The Counseling Psychologist*, *51*(1), 36–61.

Zigarelli, J. C., Jones, J. M., Palomino, C. I., & Kawamura, R. (2016). Culturally responsive cognitive behavioral therapy: Making the case for integrating cultural factors in evidence-based treatment. *Clinical Case Studies*, *15*(6), 427–442.
Zilcha-Mano, S., Eubanks, C. F., Bloch-Elkouby, S., & Muran, J. C. (2020). Can we agree we just had a rupture? Patient-therapist congruence on ruptures and its effects on outcome in brief relational therapy versus cognitive-behavioral therapy. *Journal of Counseling Psychology*, *67*(3), 315–325.
Zivor, M., Salkovskis, P. M., & Oldfield, V. B. (2013). If formulation is the heart of cognitive behavioural therapy, does this heart rule the head of CBT therapists? *The Cognitive Behaviour Therapist*, *6*, e6.

3 The Daniels Family

Michael D. Reiter

The Presenting Complaint

The Daniels family is coming to therapy because Murray (39) and Fran (38) are concerned about their daughter, Pam, who is 17 years old. Two years ago, she was diagnosed with Anorexia Nervosa. However, within the past six months, her weight has severely declined. She is five feet three inches and weighs 88 pounds. Pam is the oldest of three children, Oliver, 15, and George, 13.

Pam had been hiding her eating habits for the year preceding her diagnosis. At times, Fran would comment at the dinner table that Pam was not eating enough. Pam would counter by saying that she was not that hungry. After six months of these types of exchanges, Murray and Fran realized that things were more serious than they had realized. They sent Pam to a therapist who diagnosed her as being anorexic and worked with her, but with no positive changes. Pam continued to lose weight. The therapist recommended that Pam be placed in an inpatient facility for people with eating disorders. Murray and Fran think that it is an extreme situation to put her in an inpatient facility. They are hoping family therapy will help. If not, they are going to place her in the facility.

The Formation of the Family

Murray and Fran have been married for 20 years. They view themselves as a normal couple and family, and are very confused why Pam has this disorder. They are not sure what is wrong with her, as they believe they have provided a solid foundation for each of their children to grow and succeed. The family is a middle-class family where Murray is the primary breadwinner and Fran, who had been studying to become a teacher, became a stay-at-home mother once Pam was born. She has always had a close relationship with Pam, and the current medical issues for Pam are extremely scary for her.

Murray and Fran met on a blind date arranged by their mothers who knew each other through a book club. They hit it off and started dating. Murray was 19 at the time and Fran was 18. Murray was in his second year of college,

DOI: 10.4324/9781003668510-3

Fran her first. They attended the local community college and lived at their respective parents' houses. Murray received his Associate of Arts degree in business and began working for his father, who owned an appliance store. Fran completed her Associate's in education but did not enter the workforce because she became pregnant with Pam at the age of 20.

The transition from couplehood to parenthood seemed to be fairly smooth. Murray and Fran both had traditional U.S. beliefs, where Murray was the family's financial provider and Fran had primary responsibilities with the children and the home. After Pam was born, they had children every two years for the next four years. Fran found comfort in being a mother. She had always loved children and had planned on being an elementary school teacher before getting pregnant.

The childhood for each of the children seemed to be a normal U.S. upbringing. Each of the children was on time with their developmental milestones. Fran always seemed to be closest to Pam. Murray would joke that since they were the only two females, they had an extra-close relationship. Murray found that he gravitated more toward his sons, being able to play sports with them. Currently, he is an assistant coach on each of his sons' city baseball teams. Oliver and George are athletic, each being able to play multiple sports. They both seem to enjoy baseball more than any other sport. They are doing well academically, with low A to high B averages.

Pam is in her senior year of high school and has a low B average. She did better in middle school, with an A average in her classes. After her transition to high school, Murray and Fran became concerned as to why she had decreased her scores. They were also concerned that Pam did not seem that concerned. Fran tried harder to push Pam to do better, which led to arguments between the two of them. Murray, although concerned about the situation, let Fran attempt to deal with it.

Murray's Family-of-Origin

Murray was born into a Protestant family in the Virginia area. He is an only child. His parents, Milton and Dorothy, have been married for 65 years. They still live in Virginia and see their grandchildren quite often. Murray is close with his father, Milton, based on his working in the appliance shop his father owned, and that he eventually took over.

Milton is the oldest child of Frank and Kitty. He has two younger siblings, Christine, two years younger, and Jeffrey, five years younger. Frank originally worked on an assembly line and quickly learned how to fix and work with a variety of mechanical equipment. Eventually, he opened up an appliance store where he also fixed various machines such as sewing machines, refrigerators, and other such equipment. Milton spent much of his time after school working in his father's store. When he was 16, Milton stopped going to school and worked full-time in the appliance store.

Milton's siblings never seemed to take a liking to the appliance store. Christine went to a university and became a nurse. Jeffrey went to college and then law school and is currently practicing law in Pennsylvania. Milton was never that close with either sibling, although there were no severe disagreements and fights.

As Murray was growing up, Milton would bring him into the store. Murray seemed adept at working in the store, providing good customer service, stocking shelves, and eventually learning how to fix various pieces of machinery. Milton suggested that Murray go to business school so that he could one day take over the store. Once he received his AA degree in business, Murray worked full-time in the store. Eventually, Milton made him a partner. Two years ago, Milton informed Murray that he was going to retire and that he was giving over ownership of the business to him.

Fran's Family-of-Origin

Fran comes from a Catholic family. She is the oldest of four siblings: her brother Paul, two years younger; her brother Michael, three years younger; and her sister, Tamara, six years younger. Tamara was sickly as a child, and Fran seemed to be the person in the family who most looked after her. There were many days after school, when Tamara was between four and six years old, that Fran would go straight from school and spend several hours taking care of her.

Fran was always good with children and decided she wanted to be a teacher. She was close to her mother, Nancy, who was also a stay-at-home mother. Her father, Horace, worked in a book-binding factory. Fran was not especially close with him, but not too distant. Horace was a serious man who worked hard at his job and came home to relax. He allowed Nancy to do almost all of the parenting with the children.

Horace and Nancy both worked in the book-binding factory when they first met. They began dating, broke up, and then one year later began dating again. After several months, Nancy became pregnant, and they decided to get married. They did not have a tumultuous marriage, but it was also not very loving. Horace was not a very affectionate person. Fran does not recall ever seeing her parents kiss or hold hands.

Ten years ago, Horace had a heart attack and passed away. Nancy did not seem to be too impacted by the death. However, she decided to move to South Florida. She only sees Fran and her grandchildren about two times per year. This is distressing for Fran as she would like to have a closer relationship with her mother, not only for herself but for her children as well.

Current Status of the Family

The Daniels believe they are a close family, yet they see that there are areas where they are not as close as they think. There has evolved a division in the family between the males and the females. Murray, Oliver, and George tend to unite with one another, especially around sports. Oliver and George get into competitive battles with one another, especially around who can shoot a basketball better, hit a baseball farther, or other such athletic endeavors. Murray enjoys challenging his sons to become better at sports. He has at times talked to Fran that he will be more of an influence in his sons' lives, so that Fran can be more of an influence in Pam's life.

Pam feels isolated from her brothers, Oliver and George. She sees that they have a bond she does not have with them. Pam was never that athletic, engaging in activities such as arts and crafts and music (she had taken piano lessons for seven years). She does not fight with Oliver and George, but she does not engage them too frequently in activities, except when the family goes together as a group to some event, like their recent trip to some of the theme parks in Orlando, Florida. Ever since the diagnosis of anorexia, Pam's relationship with her brothers has become more distant. Pam also feels isolated from her father. She sees that Murray spends a lot of time with her brothers, but not really with her. She has not brought this hurt up to him. She had been close with Fran, but in the last year, the relationship has become very strained because her mother's interactions with her now usually center around her weight and what she is eating.

4 Bowen Family Systems Therapy

Tequilla Lynn Hill and Cindy McIntire

Bowen Family Systems Therapy (BFST), also known as **Multigenerational Family Therapy**, was developed by psychiatrist Murray Bowen. Originally trained in psychoanalysis, Bowen shifted his clinical focus after years of work with schizophrenic patients and their families. Through these experiences, he recognized that symptoms could not be fully understood when viewed in isolation from the family system (Kerr & Bowen, 1988). He was among the first to conceptualize human behavior as embedded in an emotional system, emphasizing how patterns are transmitted across generations rather than focusing solely on the individual's pathology (Bowen, 1985). Bowen theory, as a natural systems theory of human emotional processes, offers a framework for understanding how people emotionally engage with their environments. Rather than centering solely on individual behavior, it expands the lens to examine how relationship systems function as interconnected units, with members mutually influencing and responding to one another and to external forces in dynamic and ongoing ways (Bregman & White, 2011).

Bowen theory explains emotional process as an inherent part of human relationship systems, unfolding automatically through the reciprocal interactions of individuals with one another and with life conditions to which they must adapt for survival and well-being (Bregman & White, 2011). The Bowen approach provides individuals with tools to manage emotional processes both within themselves and in relation to their family system, especially when faced with anxiety-provoking life situations in the present and future (Titelman, 1998a).

Bowen argued that the human family must be understood through the lens of evolution, asserting that any scientific family theory needed to be grounded in biology and evolutionary processes. Unlike other early family researchers, he uniquely conceptualized the family as an "emotional system," aligning his use of the term with Darwin's evolutionary framework (Noone, 2017).

Bowen theory offers a framework for examining human behavior and functioning across multiple levels within individuals, between members of a system, and in the broader dynamics of the system. Effective application of the theory is closely linked to one's ability to observe and reflect on their own

DOI: 10.4324/9781003668510-4

emotional functioning within the relationship systems to which they are connected (Wiseman, 2011).

Family functioning is highly sensitive to anxiety and stress levels. When a family is calm, its psychological and behavioral patterns differ significantly from when it is anxious. These predictable shifts point to both the family's level of tension and the relationship processes likely to occur. The dynamics are further shaped by circumstances such as the people involved, the quality of relationships, the resources available, and how leadership is exercised within the family (Papero, 2017).

At its foundation, Bowen Family Systems Theory asserts that symptoms emerge from relational patterns rather than existing independently. By learning to observe and regulate emotional reactivity, individuals strengthen their differentiation of self, which is the ability to balance individuality with connectedness. This growth enables people to engage more effectively with their family and broader social systems, reducing chronic anxiety and interrupting dysfunctional multigenerational patterns. From a Bowenian perspective, *anxiety* is not the same as the DSM-defined disorder of anxiety; instead, it refers to the emotional intensity or reactivity that flows through relationships and systems when individuals or families feel threatened or under stress (Kerr & Bowen, 1988). Importantly, this approach does not aim to eliminate anxiety. Instead, it seeks to help individuals respond thoughtfully rather than reactively when stress inevitably arises (Meyer, 1998).

Human efforts are profoundly shaped by how we think, making it essential to examine how we approach relationships (Gilbert, 1992). Developing awareness of the emotional systems at work in our lives and in the lives of clients allows us to adopt a systemic lens and focus on processes rather than isolated events. This perspective helps both therapists and clients recognize their position within a relationship, the position of others, and how the two fit together. Such awareness strengthens one's ability to function in relationships with greater balance, clarity, and responsibility (Bowen, 1985). Bowen theory views the family as an **emotional unit**, a natural system that has evolved much like other living systems. Its central concept, differentiation of self, offers a framework for understanding how individuals function in relation to others across emotional systems of family, work, community, and society (Titelman, 2014).

Anyone living within a household becomes part of its emotional unit, or "family," regardless of blood ties. At the same time, those working within a Bowen framework observe relational patterns and systemic functioning. According to Meyer (1998), Bowen theory stands in contrast to models that frame the human condition primarily through the lens of health versus pathology or by applying discrete, differential diagnoses. From Bowen's perspective, diagnosis is better understood as perceiving emotional problems along a continuum, with qualitative differences evident across individuals and families. The emphasis is not on the surface phenomenology of symptoms, but rather on the deeper challenge all families face—the ongoing effort to balance the instinctual emotional forces of individuality and togetherness. Bowen asserted that meaningful change is not possible without knowledge of human functioning, an understanding of individual patterns of behavior, and respect for the influence of environmental factors (Meyer, 1998).

This reframing helps therapists and clients understand symptoms as products of systemic functioning rather than as the responsibility of one individual. Even highly differentiated individuals may experience symptoms when anxiety escalates, but these occurrences tend to be less severe and shorter-lived. The long-term task for people involves maintaining awareness of the broader systemic picture (Bowen, 1985).

The more differentiated the self, the greater a person's ability to preserve individuality while staying emotionally connected to the group (Kerr & Bowen, 1988). Differentiation fosters the capacity to think and reflect, rather than automatically react to internal or external emotional stimuli, allowing individuals to regulate reactive impulses even during periods of heightened anxiety (Kerr, 2019). Effectively learning and applying Bowen theory depends on one's ability to observe their own emotional functioning within the relationship systems they are part of (Bregman & White, 2011).

The Therapeutic Story of Problem Formation

Bowen family systems theory conceptualizes the family as an emotional unit, emphasizing the profound and enduring emotional connections between its members (Kerr & Bowen, 1988). Even when individuals perceive themselves as distant from their families, their thoughts, behaviors, and emotional responses remain deeply influenced by these relationships. Family members naturally respond to one another's needs, moods, and expectations, creating a complex pattern of emotional interdependence. When one person experiences change, whether positive or negative, other members often adjust in response, frequently without conscious awareness. This emotional closeness ensures that family members affect each other in consistent and powerful ways over extended periods of time (Bowen, 1985).

Building on this foundation, Bowen therapists explore how emotional patterns and behaviors are transmitted across generations. Rather than attributing problems to isolated individuals, Bowen theory frames such difficulties as manifestations of broader family processes that develop and persist over time (Bowen, 1985). For example, a family may carry forward the belief that expressing emotions is a sign of weakness. A grandfather who was taught to keep things to himself might raise a son who avoids emotional conversations, who in turn raises a daughter struggling to express her feelings in relationships. These recurring patterns become ingrained in the family's functioning, often without explicit recognition (Bowen, 1985).

Applying this framework to the Daniels family, Bowen therapists would understand Pam's anorexia not as an isolated personal issue but as a symptom rooted in multigenerational family dynamics. Fran's early experiences caring for her younger siblings established a caregiving role she now assumes with Pam. While well-intentioned, this overinvolvement may contribute to Pam's feelings of being emotionally overwhelmed or a sense of being controlled. Simultaneously, Murray replicates patterns from his own upbringing by bonding with his sons through shared activities, while leaving Fran to manage the family's emotional needs. Oliver and George, in turn, reinforce this split by aligning more closely with their father, which further deepens Pam's sense of isolation within the family system.

These roles reflect behaviors and emotional responses that have been passed down through generations. Fran's identity as the family caretaker and Murray's role as provider and mentor to the boys shape the family's emotional climate. Pam's isolation, particularly as the only daughter, may be influenced by these dynamics. From a Bowenian perspective, Pam's anorexia can be viewed as a manifestation of emotional reactivity within the family system rather than merely an individual disorder. This challenges the Daniels' perception that Pam's struggles are separate from the family context.

Symptoms

Bowen theory suggests that several key factors contribute to the development of symptoms, including one's level of self-differentiation, the amount of stress or chronic anxiety present, and the extent of isolation experienced by an individual or family. The theory also highlights how the nuclear family emotional system (NFES) and the multigenerational transmission process shape relational dynamics that influence susceptibility to physical, psychological, or behavioral difficulties (Papero, 2020).

Families often come to therapy focused on one member who seems to be causing the most trouble. They believe that if this person gets better, the rest of the family will fall back into place. BFST takes a wider view. It sees the problem as part of the entire family's emotional life, shaped not only by how the family is currently functioning but also by patterns and emotional processes passed down across generations. These multigenerational dynamics influence relationships, communication, and coping strategies within the family, contributing to the way symptoms appear and persist. The difficulties experienced by one family member often reflect these longstanding patterns within the broader family system (Bowen, 1985).

In the Daniels family, Pam is the one everyone is worried about. She is 17, refusing to eat, skipping school, and withdrawing from her parents. She is the **identified patient (IP)**, the family member who shows the symptoms (Kerr & Bowen, 1988). But those symptoms are not just hers. They reflect the stress and emotional tension that have built up in the family system over time. Pam is carrying anxiety that belongs to everyone.

Anxiety travels through the **emotional system**, the automatic ways people respond to each other based on closeness, fear, or pressure (Kerr, 2019). This shows up in how Fran reacts strongly to Pam's schoolwork and eating, while

Pam shuts down. These patterns are not planned; they are just the emotional system doing what it does. Over time, the family becomes stuck in a loop where one person's reaction sets off the next.

The **triune brain** model describes three interconnected layers of brain function: the **reptilian brain**, responsible for survival instincts; the **limbic brain**, which governs emotions and relationships; and the **neocortex**, associated with reasoning and self-regulation (Kerr & Bowen, 1988). This system allows individuals to step back from automatic or emotional reactions, observe patterns, and choose how to respond. Engaging the intellectual system supports differentiation of self by helping individuals manage anxiety, regulate emotional reactivity, and respond thoughtfully rather than being swept into the family's emotional processes. When anxiety increases, the last part of the brain to develop, the thinking system, is often the first to shut down. In these moments, individuals are more likely to function from the reptilian brain, reacting with fight, flight, or freeze responses. Currently, neither Fran, Murray, nor Pam is fully accessing their thinking systems. Fran is locked into worry and control, Murray is withdrawing and focusing on the boys, and Pam is overwhelmed by emotional responses. All three are reacting from the lower brain systems rather than reflecting with their intellectual system, limiting their ability to interrupt the family's automatic patterns.

Bowen also talked about the need to balance individuality and togetherness (Kerr & Bowen, 1988). These two forces create a core tension in every relationship system. **Individuality** is the drive to be a distinct self, independent in thoughts, feelings, and actions. However, **togetherness** is the desire to belong, connect, and maintain emotional closeness with others (Kerr, 2019). In healthy families, there is a balance between individuality and togetherness. When that balance shifts too far in either direction, where too much closeness or too much distance occurs, anxiety often increases, and symptoms may develop (Bowen, 1985). This balance is off in the Daniels family. Pam's interests and personality differ from her siblings, but instead of being supported in her uniqueness, she feels pressure to conform. Her refusal to eat as well as the conflicts with her mother may be ways of holding onto herself in a system that does not fully allow for her individuality.

Understanding Pam's symptoms in this context shifts the focus from trying to fix her alone to examining the family system. Her struggles reflect the emotional patterns and anxiety that flow through the Daniels family and across generations, showing how each member contributes to and is affected by these dynamics. By exploring how Fran, Murray, and Pam respond to one another, therapy can help them recognize their automatic reactions and begin to engage their intellectual systems. This creates opportunities for differentiation of self, allowing each family member to manage anxiety, respond thoughtfully rather than reactively, and gradually interrupt entrenched patterns. From a Bowenian perspective, lasting change comes not from changing the IP alone but from addressing the broader family system and its multigenerational influences.

Anxiety

Bowen theory recognizes anxiety as an inherent aspect of all living systems, not just human functioning (Papero, 2020). Stress is defined as a threat to the organism resulting from changes in its internal or external environment, while anxiety is understood as the variable response to those perceived threats, whether real or imagined (Kerr & Bowen, 1988). Relationships serve as both sources of stability and triggers of anxiety. The ability to balance individuality with thoughtful responses to others is a resource for managing anxiety, which may be acute or chronic (Papero, 2020).

At the family level, anxiety tends to circulate among members, though it is rarely shared evenly. While life events can influence how anxiety is distributed, it is primarily determined by established family interactional patterns. Anxiety may manifest physiologically, behaviorally, or relationally, and its intensity is influenced by both stress levels and the individual's degree of differentiation of self (Papero, 2020).

Differentiation plays a key role in how individuals adapt: those who are more highly differentiated are generally less anxious and more adaptive in the face of stress, whereas less differentiated individuals tend to be more anxious and less flexible in their responses. While most people can adapt successfully to situational anxiety, chronic anxiety more easily overwhelms one's adaptive capacity. Although both situational and chronic anxiety contain innate and learned elements, patterns of learning within family relationships play a particularly significant role in the development and maintenance of chronic anxiety (Meyer, 1998).

Bowen connected theory development with its therapeutic applications and the needs of mental health professionals, using the concept of anxiety to explain emotional responses to threat. He distinguished between **real threats**, those that are immediate and highly probable, and **imaginary threats**, those that may never occur yet persist in shaping emotional experience (Bregman & White, 2011). Bregman and White (2011) note that Bowen theory distinguishes between **acute anxiety**, triggered by immediate threats, and **chronic anxiety**, which arises from imagined or anticipated dangers. Anxiety operates within families and can move across relationships and generations. Chronic anxiety and differentiation go hand in hand: people with higher differentiation usually have lower chronic anxiety, while those with lower differentiation tend to carry higher chronic anxiety (Titelman, 1998a). Relationships serve as both sources of stability and triggers of anxiety.

Situational anxiety is evident when the family faces situational stressors. For Pam, this might include a difficult test or a challenging school assignment, triggering temporary emotional responses like irritability or withdrawal. For her brothers, situational anxiety could appear before or during a playoff game, affecting how they interact with each other and the family. Even the Daniels family can experience situational anxiety, such as the tension that arises before going on a trip or navigating other changes in routine. Chronic anxiety underlies much of the family's dynamic. The Daniels family has a longstanding pattern of unresolved emotional tension, passed through generations, that revolves around concerns about approval, identity, and connection. This chronic anxiety manifests in Pam's symptoms of anorexia, which serve as an expression of the family's deep-seated fears and unspoken emotional distress. This dynamic makes it difficult for Pam to distinguish her own needs from the family's, keeping anxiety high and leading to more reactive interactions.

Over time, the Daniels family has developed **anxiety binders**, relational strategies, or patterns that help contain anxiety within the system, often without conscious awareness (Kerr & Bowen, 1988). These include behaviors such as avoiding direct conflict, shifting focus to another family member, or forming temporary alliances to sidestep deeper emotional discomfort. While these strategies may offer short-term relief, they ultimately reinforce chronic anxiety by maintaining emotional intensity and preventing open communication. Examples of anxiety binders include Fran's overinvolvement with Pam, Murray's withdrawal into his relationship with the sons, Oliver and George's alignment with their father through sports and competition, and Pam's retreat into restrictive eating behaviors. These patterns allow the family to manage discomfort without directly addressing its root causes, keeping the system stuck and preventing meaningful change.

Eight Interlocking Concepts

Bowen developed eight theoretical interlocking concepts that emerged through his clinical work with families at the National Institute of Mental Health, where he observed emotional patterns among patients diagnosed with schizophrenia and their relatives. His research revealed that individual symptoms often reflected the larger emotional processes within the family system, particularly under stress (Bowen, 1985). These findings shaped his belief that families operate as interdependent emotional units, influenced by patterns passed down through generations. From this foundation, Bowen developed eight core concepts to describe how families manage anxiety, maintain connection, and adapt to change over time: differentiation of self, emotional triangles, NFES, family projection process (FPP), multigenerational transmission process, sibling position, emotional cutoff, and societal emotional process (Kerr & Bowen, 1988). Each concept offers a lens for understanding the emotional processes that shape individual functioning within the broader family context.

Triangles are foundational to BFST and represent the most basic unit of emotional interaction within a family system (Kerr & Bowen, 1988). A triangle forms when tension or anxiety builds between two people, prompting one or both to involve a third to manage the discomfort. This process is not typically conscious or deliberate, but rather a natural response to emotional strain. The inclusion of a third person helps stabilize the relationship by dispersing the anxiety, much like redistributing weight to keep a structure from collapsing under pressure. However, while triangulation may provide temporary relief, it does not resolve the source of tension. Instead, it spreads the anxiety throughout the system, often creating patterns of avoidance, miscommunication, or alliance that further complicate relationships over time (Kerr & Bowen, 1988).

A persistent triangle can be observed between Fran, Pam, and Murray. The relationship between Fran and Pam is emotionally intense, characterized by a push-pull dynamic of care, control, and reactivity. For example, when Pam struggles with her eating habits, tension escalates as Fran becomes critical and attempts to monitor or correct her behavior. Pam may respond with withdrawal or irritability, which heightens Fran's anxiety and frustration. Rather than addressing the conflict directly, Fran often turns to Murray to complain about Pam's behavior. In response, Murray distances himself by investing attention in his sons, subtly stepping out of the emotional fray. This shift creates a second triangle involving Murray, Fran, and the boys, where Murray's closeness with Oliver and George contrasts with Fran's sense of being left to manage Pam's struggles on her own. Rather than easing the tension between Fran and Pam, his withdrawal into the father-son alliance solidifies both triangles, reinforcing emotional distance and preventing direct engagement with the core issues. These triangular patterns allow each family member to manage their discomfort in the short term but ultimately keep the system stuck, with unresolved anxiety continuing to circulate among them.

Differentiation of Self refers to the ability to separate one's thoughts from one's emotions and to maintain a clear sense of identity while staying meaningfully connected to others. This means being able to think through decisions calmly, even in emotionally charged situations, without being overwhelmed by one's own feelings or automatically absorbing the emotions of others (Bowen, 1985). Someone with a higher level of differentiation can hold on to their own values, beliefs, and goals without becoming overly influenced by pressure from others. At the same time, they can stay connected in relationships without needing to withdraw or emotionally shut down when tension arises. Differentiation supports both individual strength and relationship stability by helping people manage themselves rather than trying to manage others (Kerr & Bowen, 1988).

Bowen (1985) described differentiation along a hypothetical **Scale of Differentiation**, ranging from 0 to 100, which he developed as a conceptual framework rather than a formal assessment tool. At the lower end of the scale (0 to 25), individuals are highly emotionally fused with others, experience intense reactivity, and have difficulty maintaining a clear sense of self apart from their relationships. In the midrange (25 to 75), where most people function, individuals demonstrate varying balances of autonomy and connectedness, capable of independent thinking in some situations but still prone to emotional cutoff or overinvolvement under stress. At the higher end of the scale (75 to 100), individuals can sustain both intimacy and individuality, think clearly under pressure, and remain connected without losing their sense of self. In this way, the scale highlights how differentiation reflects the ability to balance emotional closeness with autonomy across different levels of functioning (Bowen, 1985).

Differentiation levels in the Daniels family appear generally similar, with Pam, Murray, and Fran all functioning at a somewhat lower, semi-lower level of differentiation. They each manage and express their anxiety differently. Fran tends to overengage, becoming intensely involved with Pam and closely tying her sense of self to her daughter's well-being. Murray exhibits emotional cutoff, distancing himself from Pam and the family's tensions by focusing on the boys, which limits his capacity to help reduce the family's overall anxiety. Pam expresses her anxiety through rebelliousness, challenging parental authority, and asserting her individuality, though her responses are strongly influenced by the family's chronic anxiety and the FPP, which focuses the family's tension onto her. In contrast, Oliver and George appear to have a somewhat higher level of differentiation. Because the family's projection process targets Pam, the boys are less enmeshed in the family's anxiety and can function more independently, though they still align closely with Murray through shared activities like sports and competition. Their relative autonomy provides stability but does not fully challenge the family's polarization between the male and female subsystems.

The **NFES** is a Bowenian concept that describes how chronic anxiety is experienced, transmitted, and managed within a family. Anxiety is a natural part of family life, but when it becomes persistent or intense, it can create patterns of interaction that stabilize the tension but also contribute to problems. The NFES explains how this ongoing anxiety often leads to four common relationship patterns that shape where difficulties arise (Bowen, 1985). **Marital conflict** occurs when ongoing tension or disagreement between spouses generates stress that affects the entire family, even if the conflict is not openly expressed. **Dysfunction in one spouse** happens when a partner absorbs more of the family's anxiety, struggling emotionally or behaviorally, which limits their ability to respond effectively to the family system. **Impairment in one or more children** develops when a child expresses the family's anxiety through symptoms or behavioral issues, often becoming the IP who carries the burden of the system's tension. **Emotional distance** is another common pattern in which family members reduce closeness or connection to avoid conflict, leading to unresolved feelings, detachment, and continued anxiety within the family. Together, these patterns illustrate how chronic anxiety is not simply an individual problem but a systemic process that binds family members together in predictable ways, shaping behavior and relationships over time.

These patterns are clearly visible as Pam's anorexia represents impairment in a child, as her symptoms reflect the emotional strain she experiences within the family. This focus on Pam's struggles diverts attention from deeper family conflicts and makes her the identified source of the family's difficulties. The couple's marital conflict is subtle but present, with Fran and Murray often out of sync in their emotional responses and parenting styles. Rather than addressing these tensions directly, Murray demonstrates emotional distance by withdrawing from the conflict and focusing his attention on his sons. Meanwhile, Fran's intense involvement with Pam suggests lower differentiation in one spouse, as she carries much of the family's anxiety and struggles to remain balanced. Together, these interconnected patterns demonstrate how the Daniels family's ways of managing chronic anxiety contribute to ongoing emotional challenges and maintain Pam's role as the family's symptomatic member.

The **FPP** describes how parents unconsciously transfer their own emotional concerns, anxieties, and sensitivities onto their children (Kerr & Bowen, 1988). This often causes one child to become the primary focus of worry, overprotection, or criticism. As a result, the child's identity and behavior may be shaped by this intense parental attention, sometimes leading to increased emotional distress or the development of symptoms (Kerr & Bowen, 1988). There is usually one child who becomes the focus and develops a lower level of differentiation of self, while the other children, who are not the primary focus, tend to develop a slightly higher level of differentiation than their parents. Over time, this pattern can become deeply embedded in the family system and contribute to ongoing relational difficulties.

Fran's heightened concern and caretaking toward Pam illustrate the FPP in action. Fran's own anxieties are projected onto Pam, intensifying her daughter's emotional distress and symptoms of anorexia. Murray also directs emotional focus toward Pam, for example, by worrying about her health or offering guidance in response to Fran's complaints, which can unintentionally reinforce her dependence and maintain the emotional intensity. Because Pam is the focus of this projection, she tends to develop a lower level of differentiation than her parents, while the other children, who are not the target of this anxiety, have more opportunity to develop greater differentiation. Meanwhile, Murray diverts attention from the sons, subtly stepping out of the emotional fray and contributing to the family triangle. Furthermore, Fran may have experienced a similar projection in her own childhood. As a secondary caregiver for her siblings, she likely absorbed significant emotional responsibility early on, a role that shaped her sense of self and may have reinforced anxious caretaking patterns passed down from her mother. This continuation of projection across generations maintains the family's chronic anxiety by keeping attention on individual family members, first Pam, and then Fran, rather than addressing broader systemic issues.

The **multigenerational transmission process** explains how patterns of emotional functioning, including levels of differentiation, relationship styles, and methods of managing anxiety, are passed down across multiple generations within families (Bowen, 1985). These patterns are often subtle and operate below conscious awareness, shaping how family members relate to one another and respond to stress. Small differences in how individuals manage their emotions and relationships can accumulate over time, influencing the overall emotional climate of the family system. When family members maintain a higher level of differentiation, they are better able to manage anxiety and balance intimacy with autonomy, which can promote healthier functioning and growth across generations (Kerr & Bowen, 1988). Conversely, when differentiation is low, emotional reactivity and fusion tend to increase, leading to amplified dysfunction.

The ongoing transmission process can perpetuate maladaptive relational patterns and chronic anxiety, making it challenging for families to break free from cycles of emotional distress. Understanding the multigenerational transmission process helps clinicians see how patterns of differentiation and anxiety are passed down through families. Individuals tend to choose partners with similar levels of differentiation (Kerr & Bowen 1988). Through the FPP, parents focus their emotional energy on one child, who typically develops a lower level of differentiation. That child is then likely to select a partner at a similar level, and the FPP repeats, causing one branch of the family tree to gradually move down the differentiation scale over generations. Meanwhile, siblings who are not the focus of the FPP have more space to develop independence and self-regulation, allowing their branch of the family to slowly move up the differentiation scale. Recognizing this pattern allows clinicians to target interventions that support greater differentiation and emotional resilience across generations (Bowen, 1985).

Fran's role as the primary caregiver mirrors the traditional caregiving role of her mother, Nancy, highlighting the transmission of emotional roles through generations. Similarly, Murray's emotional distancing and his relationship with his sons follow the pattern he experienced with his own father. This modeling reflects traditional beliefs about men's and women's roles in emotional expression and regulation. Fran models for Pam a pattern of heightened emotional involvement and caretaking, which is often socially associated with feminine roles of nurturing and emotional responsibility. Murray, in contrast, models emotional restraint and avoidance, reflecting societal expectations for men to suppress vulnerability and maintain control by limiting emotional expression. Through their behaviors, Fran and Murray teach their children how men and women are expected to relate to emotions within the family system. Murray's sons may learn to handle stress by distancing themselves and avoiding emotional openness, while Pam is influenced to manage anxiety through caretaking and internalizing distress. These gendered patterns reinforce chronic anxiety in the family and limit the development of healthier, more flexible ways of relating emotionally across generations.

Emotional cutoff refers to the process by which individuals attempt to manage unresolved emotional issues with family members by reducing or completely severing emotional contact. This distancing can be physical, such as moving away or limiting visits, or emotional, such as avoiding sensitive topics or disengaging from family interactions. While cutoff may offer temporary relief from relational tension or anxiety, it often leaves the underlying emotional processes unresolved. As a result, emotional reactivity remains just beneath the surface and may resurface in other relationships or during times of stress (Kerr & Bowen 1988).

Pam's growing emotional distance from her father and brothers, as well as the heightened strain in her relationship with Fran, can be understood as a form of emotional cutoff. As Pam struggles with anorexia and becomes the focal point of the family's anxiety, her withdrawal may be a way to manage overwhelming emotional pressures. Rather than helping resolve the deeper family tensions, this distancing reinforces disconnection and isolation, limiting the family's ability to support Pam or address the systemic issues contributing to her distress. This pattern also suggests that in future relationships, Pam may be able to function well until anxiety increases, at which point she is more likely to react with emotional cutoff rather than thoughtful engagement. Similarly, Murray's limited interactions with Pam can be viewed as a form of emotional cutoff. By distancing himself and focusing on the boys, he avoids engaging with the family's heightened anxiety, which may reduce immediate tension but ultimately contributes to the family's ongoing disconnection.

Sibling position refers to the idea that birth order influences personality development, relational tendencies, and family roles. Bowen expanded on Toman and Gray's (1961) concepts when incorporating them into family systems therapy in the early 1960s (Kerr & Bowen, 1988). Toman emphasized the importance of functional position, or the role a person assumes within the family, which may or may not align with their actual birth order. The original family configuration in which a child grows up plays a critical role in shaping interaction patterns and relational dynamics. Bowen adopted this premise and integrated it into his systemic framework, showing how sibling position interacts with anxiety, differentiation of self, and multigenerational transmission of family patterns to influence how individuals function within both their nuclear and extended family systems.

Pam is the oldest child and the only daughter, which positions her as the natural recipient of Fran's intense caregiving and oversight. As the eldest, she is expected, implicitly or explicitly, to model appropriate behavior, manage responsibilities, and often carry the emotional weight of the family's anxieties. Meanwhile, Murray directs his attention more toward their sons, who are less the focus of the FPP and therefore experience greater freedom to develop independence and self-regulation. This uneven distribution of emotional involvement reinforces traditional gender roles and places significant pressure on Pam, increasing her sense of emotional isolation and intensifying her internalization of stress. Her experience demonstrates how sibling position interacts with parental expectations to shape emotional functioning, differentiation, and the broader dynamics of the family system, particularly in the context of chronic anxiety and the FPP.

Societal emotional process expands Bowen's family systems theory beyond the family unit to include the influence of broader cultural and societal forces. Just as families respond to chronic anxiety with regressive behaviors such as blame, avoidance, or rigidity, entire societies can react similarly. When under chronic stress, societies may exhibit polarization, reduced tolerance for difference, and a breakdown in effective leadership. These dynamics often trickle down into families, shaping how individuals relate to one another and manage emotional tension. Recognizing this systemic interplay helps therapists understand family functioning within a broader context of cultural pressure and social change (Kerr & Bowen, 1988).

In the Daniels family, these influences are visible in the traditional gender roles embedded in their emotional system. Fran takes on the role of the primary caregiver and emotional caretaker, while Murray assumes the position of breadwinner and emotional distancer. These patterns reflect common societal expectations about how men and women should function within the family, reinforcing gendered ways of handling emotion. As a result, emotional support in the family is unevenly distributed, with Pam receiving heightened attention and pressure from her mother and limited engagement from her father. These dynamics, shaped by the larger societal emotional process, contribute to Pam's emotional distress and may perpetuate similar patterns in future generations.

Diversity Conceptualization

According to Erdem and Safi (2018), BFST has expanded significantly in its concepts and clinical use over the past three decades. This growth has been shaped by scholars who emphasized the importance of culture, including attention to ethnicity and culture (Boyd-Franklin, 1989) as key contexts influencing family processes (Carter & McGoldrick, 1988).

Individualism and collectivism can be understood as both categorical and continuous dimensions of culture. Categorially, cultures may be described as primarily individualistic or collectivistic, depending on the dominant orientation of their social values. At the same time, these orientations exist on a continuum, with cultures and individuals varying in the degree to which they emphasize autonomy versus interdependence (Triandis, 2001). This continuum parallels the concept of differentiation of self, the balance between maintaining individuality and staying meaningfully connected within relationships. As Kerr and Bowen (1988) noted, differentiation involves the ability to "be in emotional contact with others yet still autonomous in one's emotional functioning" (p. 145). In this way, Bowen theory provides a framework for understanding how cultural values of individualism and collectivism shape family functioning and personal growth.

Carter and McGoldrick's (1988) family life cycle framework emphasizes that developmental tasks and transitions are shaped not only by individual and relational processes but also by cultural expectations and values. Their model highlights the significance of examining how cultural norms shape family roles, transitions, and patterns of intergenerational connectedness. When integrated with Bowen's concept of differentiation of self, this perspective offers a richer understanding of how families navigate the balance between separateness and connectedness within diverse sociocultural contexts.

A culturally responsive Bowenian therapist recognizes that fostering differentiation must be sensitive to the client's cultural context. While BFST has been critiqued for centering Western ideals (Brown & Errington, 2024; Chan, 2024), this limitation can be addressed by inviting clients to define what differentiation looks like within their cultural framework. Rather than imposing individualistic standards, the therapist supports a client's growth in managing their emotional boundaries in ways that honor values such as loyalty, interdependence, and family roles. Bowen's multigenerational and systemic framework is particularly well-suited to exploring the impact of culture, race, migration, and sociopolitical context on family processes. A culturally responsive therapist considers how historical trauma, systemic oppression, and cultural resilience shape functioning, and recognizes immigration and acculturation stress as significant emotional drivers. Tools such as the genogram can help map cultural histories, language shifts, migration patterns, and structural barriers. By integrating differentiation with a client's values and beliefs, the therapist helps them develop self-regulation and resilience within the family system, promoting both personal development and family cohesion while creating a path toward healing that aligns with their lived experience.

By attending to cultural expectations around gender, responsibility, and emotional expression, the therapist can help clients balance connection and individuality in a way that aligns with their values. In Pam's case, the therapist might validate her parents' intergenerational experience and cultural scripts around caregiving, reframing Fran's overfunctioning not as pathology but as a culturally shaped survival strategy. This creates space for Pam to explore how she can remain connected and loyal while also developing her own emotional clarity and identity. Situating Pam's experience within a broader context also underscores how Bowen therapy has been applied successfully across diverse cultural settings. For example, in collectivist cultures, therapists have utilized Bowen's concepts to help individuals balance loyalty to their family with personal autonomy (Chan, 2024). In immigrant families, Bowen's emphasis on multigenerational processes has helped clients explore how migration stress and cultural adaptation shape family functioning (Fishbane, 2023). The model has also been applied in faith-based communities, where cultural and spiritual traditions influence expectations around caregiving, hierarchy, and emotional expression (Bulut, 2020). These examples highlight Bowen therapy's flexibility in supporting families from varied cultural backgrounds while maintaining sensitivity to context.

The Therapeutic Story of Problem Resolution

From a Bowen perspective, therapy is not focused on symptom relief alone but on helping clients understand the emotional systems they are part of and how symptoms reflect patterns of chronic anxiety passed down through generations (Kerr & Bowen, 1988). Clients are encouraged to observe these patterns, increase their emotional awareness, and move toward greater differentiation. Pam's anorexia will not be treated as an individual problem to be fixed. Instead, her symptoms are understood as a signal of unresolved anxiety within the broader family system. By exploring how Pam's role has developed in response to her parents' functioning and family history, the family can begin to address the underlying dynamics that sustain the symptom (Kerr & Bowen, 1988).

The first task in therapy is to help the family lower anxiety to a level that allows for clearer thinking (Kerr & Bowen, 1988). Achieving this often requires patience, as the intensity of emotional reactivity may take time to subside. To support this kind of systemic change, Bowen therapy uses specific concepts and interventions that guide both the therapist's stance and the client's work in session. These tools help families gain awareness of how their patterns were formed and maintained, offering pathways toward more differentiated, less reactive functioning. The following sections describe how each concept would be applied in therapy with the Daniels family.

Therapist Stance

The therapeutic stance refers to the therapist's calm, non-anxious, and emotionally neutral presence, often described as a coach or consultant rather than a fixer or expert. This stance is crucial because the therapist's emotional tone can either increase the family's reactivity or help create space for thoughtful, regulated reflection. By modeling differentiation of self, the therapist maintains a clear sense of identity without becoming emotionally entangled in the client's process. Even when intense emotions arise, the therapist remains grounded and reflective, which helps contain anxiety and encourages clients to do the same. This stance is not cold or distant but intentionally collaborative and culturally sensitive.

The most important variable in doing therapy depends on the therapist's own emotional functioning. The therapist must avoid being drawn into the family members' emotional fusion (Titelman, 1998a). Rather than solving problems or assigning blame, the therapist helps clients take responsibility for their own behavior within the family system while modeling emotional regulation. This non-anxious, reflective presence is essential to reduce reactivity and support thoughtful family interaction. In working with the Daniels family, the therapist maintains this coaching stance by resisting the urge to side with Fran when she feels overwhelmed or with Murray when he withdraws, or with Oliver and George when they align with their father. Instead, the therapist encourages everyone to reflect on how their reactions are influenced by their own family histories and alliances. Through this approach, Fran may begin to recognize how her overinvolvement with Pam mirrors patterns from her upbringing, while Murray explores how emotional distancing was modeled in his family, and the boys gain awareness of how their identification with Murray through sports shields them from but also reinforces family anxiety. This stance is not distant or detached but intentionally collaborative and culturally sensitive. The therapist supports differentiation in ways that respect the family's cultural values around loyalty, interdependence, and family roles.

A key focus of this coaching is **differentiation work**, where the therapist models thoughtful reflection and supports clients in observing their own functioning within the family system. Instead of offering solutions or aligning with a client's emotional position, the therapist helps clients make intentional, self-directed changes in how they respond to relational stress. For example, Pam might be coached to respond to her mother's anxious phone calls not with avoidance or emotional reactivity but with calm, non-defensive communication. Through this process, she learns to maintain emotional connection without overfunctioning or absorbing anxiety, gradually shifting from a reactive stance toward greater differentiation. Similarly, Oliver and George might be encouraged to recognize when they are automatically siding with Murray during family stress and to practice expressing their own perspectives calmly, without dismissing Fran or Pam. This combined coaching stance and differentiation work creates a supportive environment that fosters insight, reduces anxiety, and encourages meaningful, lasting change (Bowen, 1985). Applying Bowen theory within a systems framework requires consistent self-reflection and disciplined observation over time. As individuals expand their ability to recognize their own emotional patterns within relational contexts, they simultaneously strengthen their capacity to apply the theory in meaningful ways. In this regard, systems thinking and self-observation develop together, reinforcing one another (Wiseman, 2011).

Acting as one of the vehicles to enable an individual to increase their own functional level of differentiation, the **"I" position** is a core communication tool in Bowen therapy that encourages individuals to express their own thoughts and feelings clearly and calmly, without blaming or controlling others (Titelman, 1998b). For instance, Pam might practice saying, "I feel overwhelmed when I am called multiple times a day, and I need to set aside time for my own studies while still staying connected," rather than reacting defensively or withdrawing.

Coaching clients to utilize I statements reduces emotional intensity and promotes personal responsibility. In therapy, Fran might practice saying, "I feel helpless when I see Pam withdrawing and don't know how to respond," rather than accusing Murray of not caring. This shift allows Fran to own her experience and creates space for Murray to respond without becoming defensive. Oliver and George can also benefit from practicing "I" statements, such as expressing, "I feel pressured to always take Dad's side," or "I feel left out when conversations only focus on Pam," which helps them develop differentiation and healthier ways of engaging. Over time, "I" statements promote more respectful and direct communication (Bowen, 1985).

Genogram Construction and Interpretation

In BFST, the genogram is a foundational tool that goes beyond a traditional family tree. It serves as a visual and narrative map of emotional patterns and relational processes across three or more generations. All members of a household are included in the genogram, which represents not only biological lineage but also the broader emotional system that shapes family functioning across generations (McGoldrick et al., 2020). The therapist works collaboratively with the family to identify patterns such as emotional cutoffs, triangulation, caregiving roles, and varying levels of emotional functioning within the family system. As an assessment tool, the genogram helps uncover long-standing dynamics like chronic anxiety, role expectations, and conflict that influence present-day family relationships (Kerr & Bowen, 1988). Importantly, the genogram also functions as a therapeutic intervention. Through its construction, family members externalize their experiences, gaining cognitive and emotional insight into how prior generations have shaped their behaviors and emotional responses. This exploration often includes culturally rooted beliefs, gender roles, socioeconomic influences, and migration histories, all of which impact family functioning and identity (Figure 4.1).

The Daniels' genogram work reveals key transgenerational patterns that contribute to current challenges. Fran's intense caregiving role toward Pam mirrors the way her mother, Nancy, acted as a primary caregiver during times

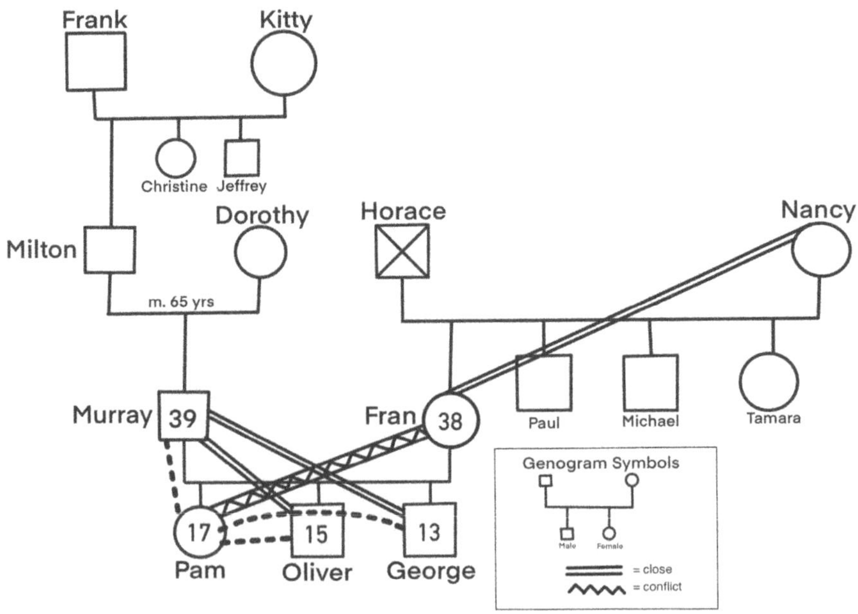

Figure 4.1 A genogram of the Daniels family.

of family stress when Fran herself cared for her younger siblings. This repeated expectation for eldest daughters to assume caregiving responsibilities reflects both family tradition and cultural norms. Meanwhile, Murray's emotional withdrawal and close bond with his sons echo patterns modeled by his father, Milton, who was emotionally reserved and focused on work and providing financially. This distancing from emotional expression aligns with traditional gender roles passed down through the generations. Oliver and George's strong alignment with Murray also reflects these gendered patterns, as they are encouraged to bond with their father through competition and achievement rather than through emotional expression, perpetuating the split between male and female subsystems. The genogram highlights these intergenerational influences, helping the Daniels family move away from blaming Pam for her anorexia and instead recognizing how broader family patterns and cultural expectations have shaped their emotional environment. This expanded awareness lays the groundwork for systemic change and more compassionate understanding within the family.

According to Kerr and Bowen (1988), a related intervention often integrated with genogram work is **multigenerational exploration**, which encourages clients to engage intentionally with their family of origin, including parents and elders. This process is not about assigning blame or revisiting past conflicts, but about fostering a more objective and compassionate understanding of how emotional patterns and family roles have been inherited. In therapy, the Daniels family members may be guided to have structured conversations or reflective exercises, such as letter writing to older relatives. Through these interactions, they can uncover stories of migration, gendered expectations, caregiving burdens, and unresolved grief or trauma that have shaped their current family dynamics. This deeper awareness helps individuals like Fran and Murray see their behaviors as part of a larger system, while also helping Oliver and George recognize how their closeness with Murray both protects them from but also ties them into the family's anxiety. This awareness allows the boys to begin developing more differentiated identities, rather than simply repeating gendered patterns from previous generations.

Detriangulation is the process of helping family members step out of emotional triangles that are three-person systems in which two people manage anxiety by involving a third. Although triangles may provide short-term relief from tension, they often maintain or worsen dysfunctional patterns over time. A key intervention in BFST is assisting clients in recognizing when they are caught in these reactive roles and supporting them to disrupt the pattern by stepping out of the triangle (Kerr & Bowen, 1988).

Pam is caught in a triangle between her parents. Fran's worry and frustration are directed toward Pam, while Murray often disengages, avoiding direct conflict. In Bowenian therapy, the focus is on helping Fran and Murray communicate openly with each other rather than expressing their anxieties through Pam. Between sessions, the therapist guides Pam in helping her notice when she is being pulled into her parents' conflict and choose not to absorb or carry their distress. With this support, Pam learns to tolerate discomfort, remain emotionally present, and set clear boundaries, such as declining to relay messages or "rescue" one parent from the other. At the same time, Oliver and George are encouraged to notice how they are drawn into a parallel triangle with Murray, aligning with him in ways that distance them from Fran and Pam. By becoming aware of this dynamic, the boys can begin practicing differentiation by expressing their own thoughts and feelings without automatically siding with their father. These intentional, skillful shifts gradually reduce anxiety within the family system, allowing Fran and Murray to address their concerns directly with one another. As the triangle dissolves, Pam is relieved of the family's emotional burden, and Oliver and George gain freedom to engage more authentically with both parents, which diminishes the chronic stress contributing to her eating disorder and creates opportunities for healthier family interactions and improved symptom management.

The process of detriangulating depends on recognizing both the subtle and the more obvious ways in which one is drawn into triangles by others. Detriangulation is considered one of the most important techniques in BFST (Kerr & Bowen, 1988). In fact, all methods and techniques in Bowen theory represent intentional efforts by the therapist and differentiating family members to define a self in the family system. Therefore, they are ultimately in the service of detriangling. According to Bowen (1985), detriangulation involves emotional nonparticipation; it means staying out of the family's emotional process and gaining some control over the pressure to take sides with any family faction. Detriangulation involves fostering direct person-to-person conversations, which help replace triangular communication with honest, clear, and calm dialogue.

Pam may be encouraged to speak directly with her father about her need for emotional support, rather than expressing these needs indirectly through her mother or through symptomatic behavior, with the therapist providing coaching to support the interaction. The therapist's best operating emotional distance is the position from which one can observe the emotional processes flowing back and forth among family members (Titelman, 1998a). When a therapist remains emotionally free while staying in contact with each member of the family, the family system itself becomes freer. In this position, the therapist can draw on knowledge of family systems to guide their work with the family (Bowen, 1985). These conversations are often practiced during therapy sessions, where the therapist helps each family member to maintain emotional regulation, neutrality, and use of the "I-position," a clear, calm way of stating personal feelings and perspectives without blame.

Bowen often encouraged the more mature side of a family member by requesting, "Give me a few minutes of your most objective thinking." In this way, the therapist seeks to bypass conflict or anxiety (Titelman, 1998b). Bowen broadly described detriangling in the following statement:

> When there is finally one who can control their emotional responsiveness and not take sides with either of the two, and stay constantly in contact with the other two, the emotional intensity within the system will decrease and both will move to a higher level of differentiation.
>
> (Bowen, 1985, p. 192)

Over time, engaging in person-to-person dialogue will help the Daniels family members to build greater differentiation, allowing them to think more thoughtfully and effectively. This shift can lead to lasting changes in family dynamics by breaking cycles of reactivity and fostering healthier patterns of connection.

Emotional reactivity is the tendency to respond automatically and intensely under stress, which Bowen (1985) identified as a major barrier to healthy functioning. Emotional reactivity manifests through physiological responses, behaviors, and relational patterns, which are regulated within emotional triangles rather than dyads. Interactions between two individuals are always influenced by a third, with dynamics such as distance, conflict, dependence, symptom development, or focus on another emerging in these triangular patterns. These relational processes are tied to neural and physiological activity, and one's ability to notice and manage their reactions reflects their level of differentiation of self (Papero, 2020).

Emotional reactions can trigger feeling responses, and those feelings, in turn, can shape thoughts that are colored by the emotional state (Kerr & Bowen, 1988). The goal is to help clients observe their reactivity, understand its origins, and respond more thoughtfully. For example, if Murray shuts down when Fran expresses fear about Pam's health, the therapist, instead of pushing for a quick fix, might pause and invite Murray to reflect on what feelings arise and whether this response relates to how emotions were handled in his family of origin. This moment of reflection also provides an opportunity for Oliver and George to observe and reflect on their own automatic responses when tensions rise, helping them practice differentiation alongside their father. Increasing the family's awareness of emotional reactivity promotes more constructive interactions (Kerr & Bowen, 1988).

Problem resolution arises not from simply eliminating symptoms, but from transforming the underlying emotional processes within the family system. Central to this transformation is increasing an individual's differentiation of self by increasing the client's capacity to think and act in alignment with one's own values while maintaining emotional connection to others. Lasting change begins when one family member responds with calm clarity and thoughtful presence instead of reactivity or blame. This subtle shift can alter the family's emotional climate, opening space for healthier patterns to emerge and sustain.

Kerr and Bowen (1988) emphasized that BFST does not require the entire family's participation; meaningful change can begin even when only one motivated family member engages in the process. The aim is not to change others directly, but to support the individual in becoming a more differentiated presence within the family system. In Pam's case, therapy helps her recognize how her anxiety is intensified by her parents' emotional reactivity, while Oliver and George gain awareness of how their alignment with Murray contributes to family tension. With this insight, Pam can interact with her family from a position of clarity rather than emotional fusion, gradually reducing the intensity of the system's overall anxiety.

Self-of-the-Therapist

When a clinician is thinking systemically, practices such as neutrality, detriangling, and monitoring one's own emotional reactivity become second nature. This orientation allows the therapeutic process to move in a more thoughtful, less reactive direction (Titelman, 1998b). The therapist's ability to apply theory is inseparable from their own level of differentiation. Many Bowen therapists engage in their own family-of-origin work to begin the process of increasing their differentiation (Bowen, 1985). A therapist who is reactive, fused, or emotionally cut off inevitably brings that functioning into the therapy room. By contrast, a therapist who has cultivated clarity, steadiness, and self-awareness through ongoing personal work creates space for the family system to breathe differently, respond more thoughtfully, and shift longstanding patterns of anxiety and triangulation.

The therapeutic relationship is never a one-way intervention but a reciprocal interaction between two systems, the family's and the therapist's. The therapist's presence and reactivity influence the process as much as the family's patterns do. For this reason, Bowen emphasized that therapists cannot expect clients to attempt work that they themselves are unwilling to pursue. Attending to one's family of origin, recognizing loyalties and emotional triggers, and identifying patterns of fusion or cutoff are core elements of self-of-the-therapist work. Grounded in systems thinking, the therapist strives to stay close to the problem without becoming absorbed by it (Bowen, 1985). This orientation grants the therapist a distinctive stance: calm, connected, and clear. It is not detachment but thoughtful presence; not fusion but engaged steadiness. By embodying this stance, the therapist models differentiation for the family, showing in real time what it means to remain a self while remaining in a relationship. Importantly, this posture also enables the therapist to function as a non-reactive third person when family members attempt to triangulate them in session, maintaining neutrality without withdrawal. This modeling is often more powerful than any single technique, as clients begin to mirror the therapist's posture and experiment with their own clarity and intentionality.

Kerr and Bowen (1988) stress that human beings can influence the functioning of their emotional systems by learning to manage their emotionality. For therapists, this underscores the lifelong task of self-regulation and self-awareness as a professional discipline. The self of the therapist becomes both the primary tool and the primary responsibility. Hill (2012) describes this as resource management: therapists must use themselves wisely in the therapy room while also investing in their continued growth and differentiation outside it. By tending to their own development through reflection, supervision, and engagement with their family of origin, the therapist expands their capacity to guide others.

Ultimately, Bowen theory positions the therapist's self not only as the medium of change but also as evidence of the theory in action. When therapists embody calmness, connection, and clarity amid intensity, they invite families to shift from reactivity toward responsibility and intentional connection. In this sense, Bowen theory is a clinical framework and a personal discipline; an ongoing practice of self-of-the-therapist work that fosters greater freedom, balance, and integrity for clinicians and the families they serve.

The Therapeutic Process

The therapeutic process in BFST reflects the theory's emphasis on multigenerational functioning. It is not designed as a brief, symptom-focused model. Instead, it unfolds gradually, emphasizing long-term growth through the development of differentiation of self. Clients are encouraged to experiment with small, thoughtful changes in how they relate to family members, while the therapist supports them in observing the ripple effects within the system. Progress is measured less by immediate symptom relief and more by the individual's growing ability to function with clarity, responsibility, and balance amid relational tension (Bowen, 1985). In practice, therapy is a process of learning to respond rather than react, of remaining emotionally connected while maintaining a solid sense of self.

Two guiding principles shape the Bowenian process: reducing anxiety relieves symptoms, and increasing differentiation enhances adaptability (Kerr & Bowen, 1988). Therapy aims to help clients lower their anxiety and emotional reactivity while strengthening their differentiation of self within close relationships. Clients are also guided to reduce patterns such as triangling, overfunctioning, or underfunctioning, and emotional cutoff in response to anxiety. To support this process, coaches must regulate their own anxiety, maintain neutrality, avoid becoming triangulated, and uphold clear boundaries without disclosing personal life details (Klever, 2014).

Early sessions often focus on lowering anxiety to allow for clearer thinking and calmer functioning which the therapist facilitates by maintaining a calm presence, modeling non-reactivity, slowing the pace of interactions, guiding clients in genogram exploration, encouraging the use of "I" position statements, and coaching self-observation rather than emotional reactivity. To effectively support clients, a Bowen-informed therapist must regulate their own anxiety, remain neutral, avoid becoming triangulated, and maintain firm interpersonal boundaries, all without disclosing personal life details (Klever, 2014). As therapy progresses, the emphasis shifts toward strengthening the client's differentiation or the ability to express convictions without defensiveness, maintain autonomy without cutoff, and stay connected without overdependence. Symptom reduction is viewed not as the ultimate goal but as a byproduct of systemic change. The focus is on supporting clients in sustaining autonomy while remaining connected. Rather than offering solutions or assigning blame, the therapist invites curiosity about how anxiety moves through the family system. This stance of neutrality and steady inquiry helps clients tolerate the discomfort of change and fosters conditions in which new patterns of interaction can emerge (Kerr & Bowen, 1988).

Assessment and evaluation in BFST focus on the functioning of the entire relationship system rather than on the individual who presents with symptoms. Key areas of inquiry include the degree of emotional reactivity within the family, the levels of differentiation of self, how anxiety is managed, and the patterns of triangulation that stabilize or destabilize the system. A Bowen therapist also considers the role of extended family and the degree of emotional cutoff across generations, recognizing that nuclear family functioning is deeply influenced by broader systemic ties (Kerr & Bowen, 1988). Intervention strategies are consistent with these systemic aims. Genogram construction provides a visual framework for reflection. **Process-oriented questions**, which are open-ended inquiries into patterns of interaction and emotional responses, guide clients to shift from blaming others to observing their own roles within the system. Clients are encouraged to use "I" statements to clarify responsibility and reduce reactivity, and to thoughtfully re-engage with extended family members when cutoff exists. Through these practices, clients gain perspective on multigenerational processes and experiment with more intentional, less reactive ways of relating (Papero, 2014).

One of the most powerful interventions in Bowen therapy is the therapist's own presence. By remaining calm, grounded, and emotionally neutral, the therapist lowers anxiety in the room and models the differentiation that clients are working to cultivate. This neutrality is not passive but active: it reflects the ability to remain in contact with a problem without becoming part of it. Each time the therapist perceives the system as it is, rather than through the lens of fear, wish, or projection, they expand their own differentiation and invite clients to do the same (Kerr & Bowen, 1988).

The goal of Bowen therapy is to increase differentiation of self, supported by intermediate goals such as detriangulation, anxiety reduction, and the cultivation of deeper intimacy in significant relationships. Differentiation involves distinguishing between thoughts and feelings, maintaining self-definition amid relational intensity, and engaging authentically without fusion or cutoff (Bowen, 1985). As individuals develop these capacities, families experience a reduction in reactivity, clearer communication, and greater flexibility. Change in one member contributes to gradual change in the larger system, often leading to symptom relief in others without direct intervention (Kerr & Bowen, 1988). In practice, Bowen therapists often prefer to work with the most differentiated family member, as that person is typically most capable of initiating change that reverberates through the system. Bowen himself emphasized working with the parents rather than the children, believing that increasing parental differentiation was the most effective way to alter patterns transmitted across generations (Kerr & Bowen, 1988). For this reason, the present case conceptualization focuses more on the dynamic between Fran and Murray than on their sons, who are not seen as "the problem." Attending to the parents' anxiety and interactional patterns is more likely to shift the overall family process than concentrating solely on the children's behavior.

Ultimately, therapy in the Bowen tradition extends beyond the consulting room. Each family interaction becomes an opportunity for clients to observe anxiety, regulate reactivity, and practice differentiation. Over time, these incremental shifts alter the emotional tone of the family system. Symptoms lessen, not because they have been directly treated, but because individuals relate to one another with greater clarity, integrity, and responsibility. In this sense, BFST is not about quick solutions but about fostering systemic change that endures across generations.

Case Transcript

Therapist: Pam, let's begin with you. How would you describe the problem that brings your family here today?

Intervention: Joining—The therapist begins by entering the family system, recognizing that parents often want to speak on behalf of their children. This approach allows the therapist to build rapport with Pam while still acknowledging her role as the "identified patient."

Pam: (*shrugs*) They think it's me. Because I don't eat. But it's not just about food.

Conceptualization: Family Projection Process—Pam reflects the family's anxiety being projected onto her, showing how symptoms often manifest in one member while originating in family patterns.

Fran: It *is* about food. She's skin and bones, and it terrifies me. Every night I watch her at the table, pushing peas around. I can't sleep, I'm so worried.

Conceptualization: Emotional Reactivity/Nuclear Family Emotional Process—Fran demonstrates chronic anxiety and the pursuer role in the family system, showing how her worry escalates tension.

Murray: I just want peace. Meals are unbearable.

Conceptualization: Emotional Reactivity/Withdrawal Role—Murray distances himself, attempting to reduce tension through avoidance, reflecting his typical pattern learned in his family-of-origin.

Oliver: I don't really know… I just see everyone stressed, and I don't want to mess things up.

Conceptualization: Emotional Cutoff/Sibling Position—The middle child attempts to emotionally distance to avoid conflict, consistent with his birth order.

George: Yeah, it's tense at dinner. I just try to stay out of it.

Conceptualization: Emotional Cutoff/Sibling Position—The youngest child mirrors avoidance, consistent with sibling position norms.

Therapist: What I hear is that Pam's eating—or not eating—creates waves for everyone. Pam, you withdraw. Fran, you pursue. Murray, you retreat. Oliver and George, you try to stay out. That cycle matters just as much as the food itself.

Intervention: Emotional System/Coach—Therapist identifies patterns, highlights the emotional system, and models neutral observation, creating a framework for understanding behavior as relational.

Fran: But if Pam would just eat, the fighting would stop!

Conceptualization: Family Projection Process—Fran externalizes the problem onto Pam, showing how the nuclear family emotional process can intensify anxiety.

Therapist: Families often locate distress in one member, but symptoms live inside relationship patterns, not individuals. Pam's body is showing the strain of the family's anxiety.

Intervention: Intellectual System/Deconstructing the Symptom—Therapist explains that the symptom is relational, not solely located in Pam, helping the family shift perspective.

Pam: (*quietly*) That feels better than being blamed all the time.

Conceptualization: I-Position/Individuality-Togetherness—Pam expresses her own perspective while remaining part of the family, beginning to increase differentiation of self.

Therapist: Would it be okay to zoom out and look at how the family manages stress collectively? Notice the patterns without blaming anyone. Who tends to step in, who steps back, and how that affects everyone else?

Intervention: Detriangling/Coach—Therapist encourages observing systemic patterns rather than focusing blame on one member.

All Members: (*anxious reluctance*) Okay.

Conceptualization: Situational Anxiety—The family reacts to the challenge of shifting focus, revealing anxiety responses.

Therapist: I'd like each of you to share what you want for yourself. Fran, let's start with you. As you speak, try to focus on your own perspective and feelings rather than what you think anyone else should do.

Intervention: Joining/Individuality-Togetherness—Therapist elicits differentiated perspectives while maintaining connection.

Fran: I want my Pammy to be happy and talk to me more.

Conceptualization: Pursuer Role/Emotional Reactivity—Fran demonstrates chronic anxiety and her tendency to push for closeness.

Murray: I want my family to be happy; I want my child to live a full life, but I can't take the constant bickering between Fran and Pam. I want it to stop, or at least to leave me out of it.

Conceptualization: Withdrawal Role/Emotional Reactivity—Murray demonstrates his distancing pattern to manage tension.

Oliver: I just want things to feel normal at dinner again, where no one is arguing or stressed

Conceptualization: Sibling Position—Middle child expresses desire for stability, showing the impact of nuclear family emotional process on siblings.

George: I just want to stay out of fights and keep things calm, so I don't get caught in the middle

Conceptualization: Sibling Position/Emotional Cutoff—Youngest child seeks peace through avoidance, consistent with sibling norms.

Therapist: Thank you. Pam, what do you want for yourself regarding food and family interactions?

Intervention: I-Position/Differentiation—Therapist invites the identified patient to voice personal needs without blaming others, promoting self-definition.

Pam: I want to feel like I can eat without everyone staring or nagging. I want to enjoy meals again.

Conceptualization: Emotional Cutoff/Intellectual System—Pam articulates her boundary and emotional need, balancing individuality and togetherness.

Therapist: That's important to notice. So, you all have different desires and ways of coping. Let's look at what happens when tension rises. Fran, what do you notice you do when Pam doesn't eat?

Intervention: Differentiation/Emotional Reactivity—Therapist elicits awareness of automatic family patterns.

Fran: I panic. I hover, I nag, I try to control.

Conceptualization: Pursuer Role/Chronic Anxiety—Fran's behavior demonstrates chronic anxiety and automatic reactivity.

Therapist: And Murray?
Murray: I step back. I don't want to make it worse.

Conceptualization: Withdrawer Role/Emotional Reactivity—Murray uses learned withdrawal strategies to manage tension, consistent with his multigenerational pattern.

Therapist: Oliver, George?
Oliver: I tune out. I don't want to fight.
George: Me too.

Conceptualization: Sibling Position/Emotional Cutoff—Sons mirror avoidance to maintain homeostasis.

Therapist: [*Therapist takes out a large blank piece of paper and markers*] Let's map this on the genogram. Pam is at the center, with lines between people that show each of your patterns.

Intervention: Family Diagram/Triangles—Visual mapping helps the family see patterns, including triangling.

Fran: I lean toward Pam; Murray steps back.

Conceptualization: Triangles/Pursuer-Withdrawer—Fran describes her automatic pattern.

Pam: You hover. Makes me want to disappear.

Conceptualization: Emotional Cutoff—Pam expresses the impact of being pulled into the triangle.

Murray: I step back to keep things from blowing up.

Conceptualization: Withdrawal Role/Emotional Reactivity—Murray demonstrates a learned strategy from his family-of-origin.

Oliver: I stay quiet to avoid trouble.
George: Me too.

Conceptualization: Sibling Position/Emotional Cutoff—Sons mirror each other's avoidance to maintain homeostasis.

Therapist: These patterns are common across families. What tools help you calm down?
Pam: Music.
Fran: Journaling.
Murray: Walking outside.
Oliver: Basketball practice.
George: Video games for a little while.

Conceptualization: Individuality-Togetherness/Emotional Reactivity—Each member identifies coping strategies, supporting differentiation and regulating anxiety.

Therapist: Great. Now, let's discuss family-of-origin patterns. Fran, how were mealtimes in your family?
Fran: Chaotic. My mother hovered; my dad stormed off.

Conceptualization: Multigenerational Transmission Process—Fran recognizes repeating family patterns.

Therapist: Murray?
Murray: Silent. My dad never spoke.

Conceptualization: Emotional Cutoff/Multigenerational Transmission Process—Murray notices learned withdrawal.

Pam: That's exactly how it feels here.

Conceptualization: Emotional Reactivity—Pam observes parallels to intergenerational patterns.

Therapist: Notice the pattern, not blame. Awareness is the first step to freedom. What might happen if Fran shared more worry with Murray instead of focusing it on Pam?

Intervention: Emotional Reactivity—The therapist encourages family members to notice relational patterns without assigning blame, fostering awareness of intergenerational dynamics and supporting differentiation within the system.

Fran: Maybe Pam would feel less suffocated.
Murray: I'd rather carry more worry myself.

Conceptualization: Detriangling/I-Position—Redistribution of anxiety shifts the family system toward balance.

Therapist: Let's talk about individuality and togetherness. When do you feel close yet maintain yourself?

Conceptualization: Differentiation—The therapist guides clients to explore balancing closeness and individuality, promoting self-awareness and the ability to maintain personal identity within family relationships.

Fran: I feel close when Pam talks to me, but I lose myself when I panic.
Pam: I feel connected when they listen instead of nagging.
Murray: When we have fun as a family, but I can also step back.
Oliver: Playing basketball with Dad feels good.
George: Baseball with Dad or video games with friends.

Intervention: Individuality-Togetherness/Scale of Differentiation—Family identifies moments of balance between connection and self.

Therapist: Today, we explored how each of you experiences and responds to tension in the family. We saw patterns of pursuing, withdrawing, and avoiding, and how these cycles affect all of you. You began noticing these patterns without blame, identified moments when you can stay connected while maintaining your own perspective, and practiced thinking about how anxiety moves through the system. Small steps toward awareness and calmer responses can gradually shift the family's emotional balance. Keep practicing your coping strategies and supporting each other as you try new ways of relating. For homework, notice triangles and practice using I statements like we went over in session. We'll reflect next time.

Intervention: Coach/Emotional System/Differentiation—Therapist closes session with concrete steps to enhance differentiation and reduce chronic anxiety.

The Therapeutic Story

At the end of the session, there has been a noticeable shift from the Daniels' initial problem story, which positioned Pam's anorexia as the sole source of family distress. Through systemic reframing and careful therapist guidance, several new perspectives have emerged in the family's narrative:

1. From individual blame to systemic patterns: Pam's eating behaviors are understood as reflecting the family's interaction cycles rather than originating solely within her.
2. Patterned emotional reactivity: Fran's pursuit, Murray's withdrawal, Oliver and George's alignment with their father, and Pam's shutdown are recognized as patterned responses to stress, not personal flaws.
3. Differentiation and self-regulation: Each member identifies strategies to manage reactivity by fostering thoughtful, intentional responses instead of automatic reactions.
4. Multigenerational patterns: Present struggles echo Fran's and Murray's family-of-origin dynamics, highlighting inherited patterns of anxiety, worry, and silence.
5. Shifted roles and collaboration: Responsibility for Pam's care is shared between Fran and Murray, while Pam is acknowledged as a competent participant capable of expressing her needs and contributing to family decision-making. Oliver and George are included in family discussions in age-appropriate ways, recognizing their perspectives and supporting more balanced family engagement.
6. Lens shift from symptom to relationship: The focus moves from "within Pam" to the relational system, emphasizing reflection, shared responsibility, and opportunities for growth and connection.

References

Bowen, M. (1985). *Family therapy in clinical practice*. Jason Aronson.

Boyd-Franklin, N. (1989). *Black families in therapy: A multisystems approach*. Guilford Press.

Bregman, O. C., & White, C. M. (2011). Introduction to bringing systems thinking to life. In O. C. Bregman & C. M. White (Eds.), *Bringing systems thinking to life: Expanding the horizons for Bowen family systems theory* (pp. 1–10). Routledge.

Brown, J., & Errington, L. (2024). Bowen family systems theory and practice: Illustration and critique revisited. *Australian and New Zealand Journal of Family Therapy*, *45*(2), 135–155.

Bulut, Ö. A. (2020). The religious and spiritual dimensions of Bowen family therapy. *Spiritual Psychology and Counseling*, *5*(1), 65–85.
Carter, E., & McGoldrick, M. (1988). *The changing family life cycle* (2nd ed.). Gardner Press.
Chan, P. (2024). Bowen theory, culture and therapeutic applications to Asian families. *Australian and New Zealand Journal of Family Therapy*, *45*(2), 244–256.
Erdem, G., & Safi, O. A. (2018). The cultural lens approach to Bowen family systems theory: Contributions of family change theory. *Journal of Family Theory & Review*, *10*(2), 390–405.
Fishbane, M. D. (2023). Intergenerational factors in couple therapy. *Clinical handbook of couple therapy*, 199–224.
Gilbert, R. M. (1992). *Extraordinary relationships: A new way of thinking about human interactions*. John Wiley & Sons.
Hill, T. L. (2012). *Exploring self-care among marriage and family therapists: A qualitative study* (Unpublished doctoral dissertation). Nova Southeastern University.
Kerr, M. E. (2019). *Bowen theory's secrets: Revealing the hidden life of families*. W. W. Norton & Company.
Kerr, M. E., & Bowen, M. (1988). *Family evaluation*. W. W. Norton & Company.
Klever, P. (2014). Applying differentiation of self in one's family. In P. Titelman (Ed.), *Differentiation of self: Bowen family systems theory perspectives* (pp. 131–148). Routledge.
McGoldrick, M., Gerson, R., & Petry, S. (2020). *Genograms: Assessment and treatment*. W. W. Norton & Company.
Meyer, P. H. (1998). Bowen theory as a basis for therapy. In P. Titelman (Ed.), *Clinical applications of Bowen family systems theory* (pp. 69–116). Haworth Press.
Noone, R. J. (2017). Multigenerational family emotional process as a source of individual differences in adaptiveness. In R. J. Noone & D. V. Papero (Eds.), *The family emotional system: An integrative concept for theory, science, and practice* (pp. 45–66). Lexington Books.
Papero, D. V. (2014). Assisting the two-person system: An approach based on the Bowen theory. *Australian and New Zealand Journal of Family Therapy*, *35*(4), 386–397.
Papero, D. V. (2017). The family emotional system. In R. J. Noone & D. V. Papero (Eds.), *The family emotional system: An integrative concept for theory, science, and practice* (pp. 23–43). Lexington Books.
Papero, D. V. (2020). Bowen theory and clinical practice. In M. N. Keller & R. J. Noone (Eds.), *Handbook of Bowen family systems theory and research methods: A systems model for family research* (pp. 145–163). Routledge.
Titelman, P. (1998a). Family systems assessment based on Bowen theory. In P. Titelman (Ed.), *Clinical applications of Bowen family systems theory* (pp. 51–66). Haworth Press.
Titelman, P. (1998b). Overview of the Bowen theoretical–therapeutic system. In P. Titelman (Ed.), *Clinical applications of Bowen family systems theory* (pp. 7–48). Haworth Press.
Titelman, P. (2014). The concept of differentiation of self in Bowen theory. In P. Titelman (Ed.), *Differentiation of self: Bowen family systems theory perspectives* (pp. 1–62). Routledge.
Toman, W., & Gray, B. (1961). Family constellations of "normal" and "disturbed" marriages: An empirical study. *Journal of Individual Psychology*, *17*(1), 93–95.
Triandis, H. C. (2001). Individualism collectivism and personality. *Journal of Personality*, *69*, 907–924.
Wiseman, K. (2011). Emotional process in organizations. In O. C. Bregman & C. M. White (Eds.), *Bringing systems thinking to life: Expanding the horizons for Bowen family systems theory* (pp. 25–44). Routledge.

5 Contextual Family Therapy

Kelly Heenan and Natalie Richardson

Contextual family therapy was originally founded by Ivan Boszormenyi-Nagy, a Hungarian-born psychiatrist who became one of the early pioneers of family therapy in the United States. Born in 1920 in Hungary, Nagy was trained in medicine and psychiatry before emigrating to the United States after World War II. In 1957, he joined the Eastern Pennsylvania Psychiatric Institute (EPPI) in Philadelphia, a central site for the emerging field of family therapy. While many early models focused on interactional patterns or structural organization, Nagy's model introduced a unique emphasis on *ethical dimensions* as its primary guidance, which make up the context and dynamics of family functioning (Boszormenyi-Nagy & Krasner, 1986). Dr. Nagy defined ethics not as abstract morality or professional codes, but as the relational ethics that govern fairness, trust, and loyalty within families. He distinguished relational ethics from morality or law, noting that they are embedded in the lived fabric of close relationships rather than imposed externally (Boszormenyi-Nagy & Krasner, 1986; Böszörményi-Nagy & Spark, 1973).

The *context* of therapy refers to the ethical dimension of relationships, where trust, fairness, and accountability are negotiated across generations. This use of the term highlights the conviction that genuine healing requires attention to relational ethics in addition to psychological or systemic factors (Böszörményi-Nagy & Spark, 1973; Boszormenyi-Nagy & Krasner, 1986). From the contextual approach, Nagy argued that family relationships are sustained not only through emotional bonds or organizational structures, but also through an implicit ethical ledger in which members balance loyalty, trustworthiness, and entitlement. He described these dynamics as "invisible loyalties," the often-unspoken obligations and expectations that tie family members together, sometimes in ways that foster resilience and sometimes in ways that perpetuate conflict (Böszörményi-Nagy & Spark, 1973). Contextual therapy, thus, situates itself not only in psychological or systemic theory, but also in a moral framework that acknowledges how justice and responsibility shape intergenerational relationships.

From a contextual lens, therapy is inherently multigenerational, recognizing that past hurts and patterns of unfairness are often carried forward

DOI: 10.4324/9781003668510-5

across generations. By addressing these inherited loyalties and injustices, therapy seeks to repair trust and promote healthier patterns for the present and future (Böszörményi-Nagy & Spark, 1973; Boszormenyi-Nagy & Krasner, 1986). While contextual therapy draws on elements of both individual and conjoint family therapy traditions, its distinctive contribution lies in the recognition of merited trust as the central dynamic that sustains relationships. Therapeutic change emerges through the active restoration of trust, both within the family system and in the relationship between the family and the therapist (Boszormenyi-Nagy & Krasner, 1980).

Although Boszormenyi-Nagy's work was foundational, contextual therapy did not maintain consistent visibility across the family therapy field. Wilburn-McCoy (1993) noted that much of Nagy's corpus was neglected or underutilized in training and discourse during the 1980s–1990s, leading to a temporary decline in its application. Some critiques suggested the model was "too intellectual" and not easily accessible to lower socioeconomic or less-educated populations (Kaslow, 1987). Nagy countered this by asserting that relational ethics, trust, fairness, and loyalty are universal and not bound by class, race, or education. Feminist critiques also questioned whether contextual therapy sufficiently addressed women's unique experiences in family systems (Grunebaum, 1987). Yet, others have argued that the model's emphasis on fairness and accountability makes it particularly suitable for work with survivors of abuse, as it offers a framework that validates and gives voice to their claims and experiences (Wilburn-McCoy, 1993).

Despite the period of declining visibility, more recent scholarship points to a renewed appreciation of contextual principles, especially relational ethics and fairness in close relationships (van der Meiden et al., 2018, 2020). This "rediscovery" underscores both the durability of Nagy's insights and their ongoing relevance to contemporary clinical practice. Later interpreters have worked to make contextual therapy more accessible for modern clinicians. Ducommun-Nagy (2025) emphasizes that contextual therapy should be considered among the postmodern, collaborative approaches to family therapy rather than being limited to earlier modernist traditions, thereby reframing its relevance for modern-day clinicians. She further argues that contextual therapy is uniquely equipped to address the relational consequences of injustices, including those tied to sociohistorical and systemic factors, positioning the model as a vital therapeutic resource for the future. Hargrave and Pfitzer's (2003) *The New Contextual Therapy* reframes Nagy's central ideas, particularly relational ethics and the ledger, into a practical guide for therapeutic settings, helping extend Nagy's legacy into today's practice. These contemporary updates provide clearer frameworks for operationalizing the ethical ledger and demonstrate how contextual concepts can be integrated into evidence-based approaches, thus bridging the gap between Nagy's pioneering vision and the needs of present-day clinicians (Ducommun-Nagy, 2025; Hargrave & Pfitzer, 2003).

The Therapeutic Story of Problem Formation

Contextual therapists view problem formation as rooted in violations of *relational ethics*, where unresolved invisible loyalties and imbalances of giving and receiving undermine fairness and merited trust. When patterns of entitlement and indebtedness become distorted—such as one member consistently sacrificing while another takes without reciprocity—symptoms and relational distress emerge. Healthy family functioning is restored when members engage in *ethical accountability*, acknowledging both their **entitlements** ("what is due") and **indebtedness** ("what one owes"), thereby reestablishing fairness and trust across relationships (Böszörményi-Nagy & Spark, 1973; Boszormenyi-Nagy & Krasner, 1986).

Four Dimensions of Relational Reality

A contextual approach holds that fully understanding a family requires examining multiple, interconnected layers of experience, which Böszörményi-Nagy and Krasner (1973, 1986) refer to as the **four dimensions of relational reality**: (a) facts, (b) individual psychology, (c) interpersonal transactions, and (d) relational ethics. Each dimension offers a lens through which therapists can assess family functioning and identify sources of stress or imbalance.

The **facts** dimension includes objective realities that influence the family system, such as age, gender, health, and developmental milestones. These facts shape the expectations, entitlements, and obligations of each family member, setting the stage for relational dynamics and stressors (Boszormenyi-Nagy & Krasner, 1986).

For the Daniels family, key facts worth noting from a contextual lens include that Pam, age 17, has recently received a severe diagnosis of Anorexia Nervosa. She is the oldest of three children, with two younger brothers, which shapes the expectations and responsibilities placed on her within the family. The family also functions within established gender roles, with Murray (Dad) serving as the primary breadwinner and Fran (Mom) as the primary caregiver.

The second dimension of **individual psychology** examines intrapsychic processes, coping strategies, and emotional functioning. Böszörményi-Nagy and colleagues (1973, 1986) viewed individual psychology not as pathology in isolation, but as a reflection of relational and ethical dynamics within the family. Psychological symptoms—such as anxiety, depression, or anorexia nervosa—are often understood as responses to perceived injustices, unbalanced obligations, or unresolved invisible loyalties, rather than solely intrapsychic conflicts. Thus, understanding individual psychology helps the therapist see how each member perceives obligations, fairness, and trust, and how their internal experience interacts with family patterns (Böszörményi-Nagy & Spark, 1973). It provides clues to where the ledger is out of balance, and which loyalties or ethical debts may be influencing behavior (Boszormenyi-Nagy & Krasner, 1986).

Pam experiences significant stress and isolation, particularly in relation to her parents and brothers. She reports distress in her familial relationships, which intensifies alongside her struggles with eating. Fran carries intense anxiety about Pam's health and eating behaviors, an intrapsychic burden that reflects her caregiving role and sense of responsibility. Murray expresses concern for Pam but tends to defer caregiving responses to Fran, reflecting coping strategies consistent with his position as financial provider and less engaged nurturer.

The third dimension, **interpersonal transactions**, examines the observable patterns of interaction, communication, and relational behavior within the family system (Boszormenyi-Nagy & Krasner, 1986). Unlike individual psychology, which focuses on intrapsychic experience, this dimension highlights how family members relate to one another in concrete, often repeated ways, revealing both functional and dysfunctional relational patterns.

Boszormenyi-Nagy and colleagues emphasized that these transactions are inseparable from ethical considerations: alliances, conflicts, and communication patterns often reflect imbalances in fairness, loyalty, and obligations (Böszörményi-Nagy & Spark, 1973). For example, a parent's overinvolvement in one child's life, or a sibling coalition, may indicate over-indebtedness, over-entitlement, or hidden loyalties, which in turn contribute to stress, resentment, or symptomatic behavior in other family members.

Some of the primary intrapersonal processes to note for the Daniels family include Pam's experience of significant stress and isolation, particularly in relation to her parents and brothers. She reports distress in her familial relationships, which intensifies alongside her struggles with eating. Fran carries intense anxiety about Pam's health and eating behaviors, an intrapsychic burden that reflects her caregiving role and sense of responsibility. Murray expresses concern for Pam but tends to defer caregiving responses to Fran, reflecting coping strategies consistent with his position as financial provider and less engaged nurturer.

Interpersonal transactions further highlight these dynamics. It appears that the family is experiencing clear gender-based alignments. Murray and the two boys, Oliver and George, share close, activity-focused bonds, particularly around sports, reinforcing a father–son alliance. In contrast, Pam experiences increasing isolation from her father and brothers, which restricts meaningful engagement and contributes to relational tension. At the same time, Fran's interactions with Pam are heavily focused on monitoring eating and health, which, while well-intentioned, often result in conflict and a strained emotional connection.

The fourth dimension of relational reality, **relational ethics**, is the defining feature of contextual family therapy (Böszörményi-Nagy & Spark, 1973; Boszormenyi-Nagy & Krasner, 1986). Unlike traditional models that focus primarily on intrapsychic functioning or observable interactions, contextual therapy situates ethical considerations—fairness, trust, and accountability—at the heart of family assessment and intervention. Relational ethics encompasses both conscious and unconscious obligations, expectations, and loyalties that guide how family members give and receive care across generations.

At its core, relational ethics concerns **merited trust**: the degree to which family members can rely on one another to act fairly and honor obligations. Violations of this trust—such as one member consistently over-giving without acknowledgment, or another over-receiving without reciprocation—can create symptoms, conflict, or emotional distress (Boszormenyi-Nagy & Krasner, 1986).

From a relational ethics perspective, Pam's perception of inequity in receiving less attention from her father and experiencing a strained relationship with Fran signals a disruption in merited trust within the family. Fran's over-involvement in monitoring Pam's eating can be understood as an expression of over-indebtedness and unconscious loyalty to protect her daughter. However, this dynamic paradoxically undermines reliability in their relationship rather than fostering a sense of fairness and trust. The gendered alliances within the family, with Murray closely aligned with the sons and Fran positioned with Pam, further highlight intergenerational legacies of role expectations and obligations that constrain relational balance in the family.

Ledger

A central concept in relational ethics is the **invisible ledger**, a metaphor introduced by Boszormenyi-Nagy and Krasner (1986) to describe the implicit record of give-and-take within family relationships. The ledger tracks entitlements ("what is due") and indebtedness ("what one owes") across interactions and generations, including obligations and loyalties that may operate unconsciously (Böszörményi-Nagy & Spark, 1973). Each family member carries an internal ledger, and problems arise when it becomes imbalanced—for instance, when one person consistently gives without receiving, or another benefits at someone else's expense. Such breakdowns of fairness can generate resentment, symptoms, or destructive relational patterns, highlighting the importance of ethical accountability in family functioning. Restoring relational ethics involves acknowledging these imbalances, addressing destructive loyalties, and facilitating equitable recognition and accountability across the family (Böszörményi-Nagy & Spark, 1973; Boszormenyi-Nagy & Krasner, 1986).

Entitlement

Within contextual family therapy, **entitlement** refers to the fundamental right of each family member to receive care, fairness, and acknowledgment within relationships. These "ethical guarantees" may only become evident during a crisis or stressful situations. When individuals preserve their capacity to care about others, to be considerate of others, and to be considerate and sensitive to others regardless of past hurts or unfairness, a sense of **constructive entitlement** develops (Reiter, 2024). In contrast, when individuals experience deprivation, neglect, or injustice, they may feel deserving of specific actions or lack of judgment from others, developing a sense of **destructive entitlement**. Individuals with destructive entitlement often seek repayment in ways that perpetuate harm or imbalance, such as withholding care, acting out in resentment, or placing undue burdens on others (Boszormenyi-Nagy & Krasner, 1986; Reiter, 2024). Such individuals may feel they have the right to be preoccupied with their personal troubles, leaving little space for sensitivity to ways in which their actions affect others.

From this perspective, entitlement is not simply an individual feeling but a relational and ethical dynamic that shapes the family ledger. Constructive entitlement allows for fairness to be transmitted across generations, while destructive entitlement often fuels cycles of mistrust, resentment, and symptom development (Gehart, 2018). In the Daniels family, both constructive and destructive entitlements are evident. Constructive entitlement emerges through intergenerational patterns of loyalty and caregiving. Fran's early life established a caregiving identity, particularly through her role in raising her younger sister Tamara, which reinforced both her reliability and her sense of worth. This carried forward into her parenting of Pam, where she invested deeply from infancy through adolescence, initially creating mutual loyalty and emotional reciprocity. Murray also demonstrates constructive entitlement through his relationship with his father, Milton. Having been entrusted with responsibility in the family business, Murray responded with loyalty and hard work, maintaining balance by eventually taking over the store. Similarly, Oliver and George reciprocate Murray's investment in sports and mentorship, sustaining fairness in the father–son bond, though this alignment leaves Pam feeling excluded.

Destructive entitlement also seems to be present, particularly in Pam's experience. Pam's anorexia can be understood as a potential protest against relational imbalances, reflecting a claim that she is owed attention and care after experiencing emotional neglect from her father and excessive monitoring from her mother. Fran's overinvolvement with Pam similarly reflects destructive entitlement. Carrying unresolved longings for closeness with her own distant parents, Fran unconsciously demands that Pam meet her unmet needs, which paradoxically undermines their bond. Murray contributes to this imbalance by investing primarily in his sons while remaining disengaged from Pam, leaving her with a sense of exclusion from his loyalty. The boys' closeness with Murray, while generally positive, also contributes to this imbalance by reinforcing the division between the male and female children. His tendency to delegate responsibility for Pam to Fran further perpetuates an unfair distribution of parenting duties. Together, these destructive entitlements highlight unmet relational debts and fairness issues that drive the family's current struggles. These patterns of constructive and destructive entitlement not only shape the family's sense of fairness but also directly influence the development of trustworthiness and merited trust within their relationships.

Fairness

Fairness is a core principle of relational ethics (Boszormenyi-Nagy & Krasner, 1986; Böszörményi-Nagy & Spark, 1973), reflecting the balance of entitlements and indebtedness across relationships. It involves recognizing each person's contributions, needs, and vulnerabilities, ensuring that give-and-take is balanced and obligations are acknowledged. When fairness is disrupted, trustworthiness and loyalty are undermined, potentially leading to relational conflict, resentment, or symptoms (Boszormenyi-Nagy & Krasner, 1986). Fairness is a central dynamic in the Daniels family. Pam likely experiences unfairness in multiple ways, as her needs for attention and emotional support are overshadowed by her brothers' activities, particularly Murray's consistent investment in sports and shared bonds. At the same time, her relationship with Fran often feels defined by pressure and monitoring around eating, which leaves Pam feeling criticized rather than cared for. These experiences likely create a sense of imbalance in that while her brothers receive recognition and reliability from their father, and Fran pours her energy into caregiving, Pam feels both excluded from closeness with her parents and burdened by maternal overinvolvement. Fran herself likely feels overextended, perceiving an inequitable distribution of responsibility for Pam's struggles. Murray, though perhaps unaware, reinforces these imbalances by focusing his engagement more on the boys and leaving Fran to manage Pam's care. In therapy, naming and addressing these inequities can open dialogue about fairness, allowing family members to acknowledge contributions and unmet needs. By restoring fairness, trust can be rebuilt, enabling Pam to experience a greater sense of belonging and opening the door to repairing strained relationships.

Trustworthiness/Merited Trust

In contextual family therapy, trustworthiness—or more precisely, merited trust—is central to healthy family functioning. Boszormenyi-Nagy distinguished between **trustworthiness** (the ethical quality of being reliable and fair) and **merited trust** (the relational outcome that develops when others experience someone's fairness consistently; Boszormenyi-Nagy & Krasner, 1986). Böszörményi-Nagy and Spark (1973) argued that trust is not blind faith but is grounded in earned reliability within relationships. In other words, trust cannot be demanded—it must be earned. Nagy emphasized that family members build merited trust through patterns of acknowledgment, fairness, and responsiveness to each other's needs and contributions (Böszörményi-Nagy & Spark, 1973; Boszormenyi-Nagy & Krasner, 1986).

Within the Daniels family, we see patterns of trust and merited trust are significantly disrupted. Fran's efforts to monitor Pam's eating are likely experienced by Pam as controlling rather than supportive, undermining her sense that her autonomy will be respected. At the same time, Murray demonstrates consistent trustworthiness with the boys but has not engaged meaningfully with Pam, contributing to her perception that he is less reliable. His delegation of responsibility for Pam's care to Fran may communicate trust and confidence in her caregiving yet demonstrates a level of avoidance of shared engagement, leaving Pam without a sense that both parents can be trusted to meet her emotional needs. These dynamics illustrate how merited trust is not solely a matter of intent but of the relational impact of actions and responsiveness within the family system.

Loyalty

As trust and fairness are negotiated within families, questions of loyalty naturally emerge. **Loyalty** refers to the emotional bonds that bind family members across generations, often operating unconsciously. Loyalties often arise from family history and relational transactions across generations. They reflect implicit expectations, responsibilities, and connections that children inherit from parents and ancestors, forming what Nagy and colleagues described as *vertical loyalties* (to parents and ancestors) and *horizontal loyalties* (to siblings, partners, and peers; Boszormenyi-Nagy & Krasner, 1986; Böszörményi-Nagy & Spark, 1973). In contextual terms, these unconscious bonds are often referred to as **invisible loyalties**, reflecting the ethical and emotional obligations that family members inherit across generations (Böszörményi-Nagy & Spark, 1973; Boszormenyi-Nagy & Krasner, 1986). Loyalties often develop as a response to past hurts, fairness imbalances, or perceived injustices, creating obligations to care for, protect, or compensate for others in the family system.

In the Daniels family, these dynamics of trust and fairness intersect closely with issues of loyalty. Fran's loyalty to Pam echoes her early caregiving role with her sister, yet this deep investment sometimes creates tension in the marital relationship, as responsibilities with Pam overshadow her partnership with Murray. For Pam, this intense focus can feel both protective and constraining. She may experience unspoken pressure to meet her mother's expectations and to reciprocate Fran's devotion, while simultaneously negotiating her own desires for autonomy and connection with her father. Murray's prioritization of his sons reflects loyalty patterns carried from his family of origin, where male bonds and shared work or activities defined connection. These competing loyalties shape both closeness and distance within the family system, highlighting the need to explore how unbalanced allegiances may perpetuate relational strain and undermine trust.

Split loyalties occur when a family member feels torn between competing obligations or allegiances, often when meeting the needs of one person seems to conflict with the needs or expectations of another (Böszörményi-Nagy & Spark, 1973). When loyalties are split, for example, between competing parental expectations, they can produce tension, secrecy, and symptoms, as individuals attempt to honor competing loyalties without violating relational ethics. Contextual therapists emphasize acknowledging these loyalties rather than assigning blame, as symptoms often emerge as attempts to manage or negotiate conflicted loyalties. In the present case, split loyalties are evident not only for Pam and Fran but also for Pam's brothers, Oliver and George, and for Murray himself. Pam experiences divided attention between her parents, feeling torn between seeking closeness with Fran and navigating unmet recognition from Murray. She also experiences subtle tension in relation to her brothers, as she observes the bond they share with their father through sports. Her sense of exclusion and invisibility contributes to her feelings of responsibility, guilt, and isolation, which are heightened by her anorexia. At the same time, Fran experiences tension between advocating for Pam's needs and supporting Murray as a partner, reflecting competing relational obligations. These hidden loyalties place subtle but persistent pressure on family members, creating stress and relational strain. For Pam, the push and pull between honoring her mother's devotion and respecting her father's bond with her brothers can heighten feelings of responsibility, guilt, and isolation. Oliver and George may also experience split loyalties between their father and their sister. They are clearly aligned with Murray through sports and shared activities, and they derive validation and encouragement from his attention. At the same time, they may feel implicit expectations to recognize and support Pam, particularly as she struggles with health and relational difficulties. If unacknowledged, this tension could create feelings of obligation or resentment, producing covert stress within the sibling subsystem. For Fran and Murray, unacknowledged expectations and loyalties further complicate cooperation and mutual support. While Murray recognizes that Fran is more attuned to Pam's needs, his allocation of attention may inadvertently reinforce the gendered division in the family, creating additional pressure on Pam and Fran to negotiate relational obligations independently. By surfacing these split loyalties in therapy, family members can begin to recognize how invisible obligations shape interactions, paving the way for more balanced engagement and restored trust.

Parentification

Loyalties and split loyalties often set the stage for children to assume responsibilities beyond their developmental capacity. From a contextual perspective, when children feel compelled to meet parental needs—emotionally, practically, or relationally, they may experience **parentification**, taking on parental roles typically expected of adults to maintain relational balance or fairness (Boszormenyi-Nagy & Krasner, 1986).

From a contextual perspective, the Daniels family illustrates how patterns of parentification can be transmitted across generations, shaping current relational roles and obligations in ways that affect loyalty, trust, and fairness. Fran's early parentification, shaped by her role as the primary caregiver for her sister Tamara and her emotionally reserved family environment, carries forward into the Daniels family. Patterns of responsibility, loyalty, and unmet emotional needs are evident in her parenting of Pam, where Fran invests heavily in monitoring her daughter's eating, school performance, and emotional well-being. This overinvestment places adult-like expectations on Pam, who may feel pressured to take on responsibilities beyond her developmental capacity, including managing her mother's worries and maintaining family harmony. These dynamics illustrate how intergenerational patterns of caregiving and loyalty are enacted across generations. Fran's early experiences of responsibility and relational obligation inform her current behaviors, which in turn contribute to loyalty conflicts, relational tension, and the subtle parentification of Pam. Recognizing these patterns allows therapists to trace how historical obligations and family-of-origin experiences shape current relational ethics, entitlements, and trust within the Daniels family.

Legacy

Parentification and multigenerational loyalties are often expressions of a family's **legacy**, the enduring patterns, values, messages, and obligations, both positive and negative, transmitted across generations. In contextual therapy, legacy helps explain how past relational dynamics, unfinished business, and invisible entitlements shape current family interactions and influence both individual behavior and systemic functioning (Boszormenyi-Nagy & Krasner, 1986). The Daniels family illustrates how intergenerational legacies shape current relational dynamics. Patterns of loyalty, entitlements, parentification, trust, and fairness—both constructive and destructive—have been transmitted across generations, carrying forward unfinished business and invisible obligations. Fran's early caregiving for her younger sister established a strong sense of responsibility and nurturance that she now extends to Pam, while Murray's alignment with his father and focus on male bonding reflect inherited patterns of loyalty and selective investment.

These legacies influence the family's current difficulties. Constructive entitlements, such as Murray's and Fran's early reliability and reciprocity, coexist with destructive entitlements, including Pam's illness as a protest against perceived neglect, Fran's overinvolvement, and Murray's selective attention to his sons. Parentification is also evident across generations. Fran assumed adult-like caregiving for her sister, and Pam now bears emotional and relational responsibilities beyond her developmental capacity. Divided loyalties place additional pressure on Pam, caught between maternal expectations and paternal alliances with her brothers, creating relational strain.

In summary, contextual therapy views the Daniels' difficulties as rooted in ethical imbalances, invisible loyalties, and disrupted fairness, which shape entitlement, trust, and family interactions. Pam's anorexia nervosa can be seen as a relational response to these multigenerational patterns. This perspective highlights how personal, relational, and ethical dimensions interact, setting the stage for examining how these processes also unfold within broader cultural and social contexts.

Diversity Conceptualization

Understanding the Daniels family through contextual therapy requires a nuanced appreciation of how cultural, gender, religious, and generational norms shape relational dynamics and ethical expectations. Murray and Fran's adherence to traditional U.S. middle-class values, with Murray as the provider and Fran as the caregiver, reflects a gendered distribution of emotional labor and authority that influences loyalties, obligations, and the balance of fairness within the family ledger. Within this context, Pam's experience cannot be separated from these broader relational patterns; her needs and responses are shaped by the implicit expectations placed on her as a daughter and sister. Pam's anorexia may be interpreted not as pathology but as a silent protest of these norms, particularly the pressures of femininity, achievement, and emotional caretaking. This aligns with Gangamma et al. (2012), who found that women often report lower fairness and higher distress, suggesting that gender roles deeply influence relational ethics.

From a diversity-informed contextual perspective, Fran's early parentification and caregiving for her sister Tamara may be culturally reinforced, especially within Catholic traditions that emphasize sacrifice and duty. These legacies of care, while noble, can lead to destructive entitlement when past sacrifices are not acknowledged or reciprocated. Therapy must help Fran and Murray engage in **exoneration**, understanding each other's behaviors considering their histories, and foster **genuine dialogue** where each family member's voice is heard and validated. This process helps reset the revolving slate, allowing family members to re-engage without carrying unresolved emotional debts.

Boszormenyi-Nagy (1987) emphasized that relational ethics, fairness, loyalty, and accountability transcend culture and must be expressed uniquely within each cultural context. The therapist must consider how religious backgrounds (Protestant and Catholic), socioeconomic status, and historical trauma shape the Daniels' relational expectations. For example, Fran's intense involvement with Pam may reflect culturally embedded values of maternal sacrifice, while Murray's emotional distance may stem from Protestant stoicism around suffering and duty. These dynamics must be explored without pathologizing culturally normative behaviors.

Moreover, invisible loyalties and split loyalties, central to contextual therapy, are especially relevant in diverse families. Pam may feel torn between loyalty to her parents and her own emerging identity, while Fran may unconsciously prioritize loyalty to her family of origin over her marital relationship. These tensions are often intensified in families shaped by intergenerational trauma, religious duty, or systemic marginalization. As noted by Boszormenyi-Nagy & Krasner (1986) and van der Meiden et al. (2020), relational ethics are universal, but their expression varies across cultures. Therapists must adapt language and methods to ensure inclusivity, such as using nonverbal tools or culturally resonant metaphors.

Finally, while Nagy's framework is grounded in Western individualist notions of reciprocity, recent critiques and expansions (e.g., Comas-Díaz et al., 2019; Yeh et al., 2004) emphasize the need to account for collectivist values, systemic oppression, and historical injustices. In collectivist cultures, fairness may be defined more by fulfilling family roles than by mutual negotiation. As Boszormenyi-Nagy (1987) poignantly asked, "Who will defend the interests of those religious, cultural or national loyalty groups that have no voice?," a question that remains vital in applying contextual therapy to diverse populations.

Boszormenyi-Nagy's collected works further underscore his early recognition of cultural legacies, historical injustices, and the impact of transgenerational trauma as central to understanding diverse family systems (Boszormenyi-Nagy, 1987). Moreover, in the foreword to *Foundations of Contextual Therapy*, his own Hungarian background is cited alongside his concern for "disadvantaged minorities," reflecting a sensitivity to sociopolitical and cultural marginalization that anticipated later multicultural critiques and adaptations (Boszormenyi-Nagy, 1987).

Building on Boszormenyi-Nagy's early recognition of cultural and historical influences, contemporary research demonstrates the applicability of contextual therapy across diverse cultural and social contexts. For example, Natrajan-Tyagi and Poulsen (2025) illustrated the use of intergenerational contextual work with Asian Indian families, highlighting how attention to family ledger, loyalty patterns, and relational ethics can be adapted to culturally specific expectations around hierarchy, parent–child obligations, and gender roles. Similarly, Glebova et al. (2025) examined relational ethics in immigrant families, emphasizing how intergenerational and cross-cultural dynamics shape perceptions of fairness, trust, and obligation. Collectively, these studies highlight how contextual principles can be meaningfully applied across diverse family structures, sociocultural backgrounds, and historical experiences, reinforcing the model's flexibility and relevance in multicultural practice.

The Therapeutic Story of Problem Resolution

From the lens of contextual therapy, healing is not merely the alleviation of symptoms but the restoration of relational ethics, a process rooted in fairness, reciprocity, and accountability. Problems within families are understood not just as dysfunctional interactions but as ethical violations that disrupt trust and justice across generations (Boszormenyi-Nagy, 1987). Symptoms, therefore, are reframed as calls for justice, signaling unresolved relational debts and imbalances rather than pathology. Nagy and Krasner (1980) argued that the therapeutic task is not to persuade family members to "just trust" one another, but to create conditions in which trustworthiness can be demonstrated and merited trust gradually restored. This involves surfacing hidden injustices, acknowledging legitimate pain, and fostering new experiences of fairness within family relationships.

For families such as the Daniels, this perspective highlights the ways trust must be actively rebuilt rather than assumed. Restoring trustworthiness requires that Pam's voice be taken seriously, her experiences validated, and responsibility for her care shared more equitably. Trust is merited through small but consistent acts of fairness, such as Murray showing investment in Pam's interests or Fran cultivating moments of connection that do not center solely around food. These shifts work against the uneven distribution of relational trust—where Murray invests primarily in the sons and Fran shoulders responsibility for Pam—by rebalancing fairness across family members. In this sense, the process of therapy is less about symptom reduction and more about restructuring the ethical patterns of giving and receiving that sustain family life.

Each individual carries an intergenerational ledger of entitlements and obligations, shaped by past relationships and family legacies. When one party gives disproportionately without reciprocity, or when destructive entitlement overshadows constructive giving, relational distress emerges. Healing occurs when family members engage in mutual acknowledgment, forgiveness, and rebalancing of this ledger, restoring trustworthiness and promoting earned entitlement through care and responsibility (Boszormenyi-Nagy & Krasner, 1980). The therapist's role is not to impose goals but to facilitate dialogue among family members, allowing them to co-create treatment goals that reflect their unique relational realities (Ducommun-Nagy, 2018).

Ultimately, health is restored when individuals become ethically accountable, balancing what is owed with what is due. This process prevents the transgenerational transmission of trauma and injustice, strengthens connectedness, and promotes autonomy through relatedness rather than isolation (van der Meiden et al., 2020). Adams and Maynard (2004) emphasize, "clinical improvement will come from the restoration of fair and responsible relating… and from direct and non-sacrificial expressions of family loyalty" (p. 2).

Role of the Therapist

The therapist is not a neutral observer, but an ethical agent, and a facilitator of fairness, accountability, and trustworthiness. Their role is to guide the family in uncovering and addressing relational injustices, helping each member articulate their pain, unmet needs, and hopes for fairness (Boszormenyi-Nagy & Krasner, 1986; Ducommun-Nagy, 2018). The therapist listens for the state of the family ledger and helps clients explore how past loyalties, debts, and entitlements shape current roles and expectations. This includes recognizing invisible loyalties and destructive entitlements that may be passed down across generations (Boszormenyi-Nagy & Krasner, 1986).

From a Buberian lens, the therapist embodies "healing through meeting," emphasizing genuine human connection and mutual recognition (Friedman,

1989). The therapist's ethical engagement is not about restoring justice directly but about creating conditions where family members can reclaim agency and make responsible choices. As Ducommun-Nagy (2018) analogizes, the contextual therapist functions like a strategic player in a complex game, such as chess. The therapist must thoughtfully anticipate the emotional and relational needs of each family member. Through the practice of multidirected partiality, the therapist ensures that every voice is acknowledged and that each person has the opportunity to be treated fairly. The approach highlights the therapist's ethical responsibility to navigate and balance the diverse loyalties and perspectives within the family system, fostering a space where constructive healing and relational justice can emerge. While the responsibility for change lies with the family, by modeling fairness and facilitating dialogue, the therapist becomes a catalyst for relational healing and transformation.

Joining

In contextual therapy, joining is a relational and ethical act. It involves entering the family system with empathy, neutrality, and a deep awareness of each member's relational ledger. This ledger reflects the balance of give-and-take, loyalty, and entitlement that shapes their interactions (Boszormenyi-Nagy, 1987). The therapist must validate each person's experience without taking sides, creating a safe space for genuine dialogue. Through this process, the therapist facilitates communication that restores balance and trust. This process is grounded in the recognition of relational ethics: who has given, who has received, and who feels unseen or overburdened. As Boszormenyi-Nagy (1987) emphasized, the therapist's extended perspective becomes a source of deeper understanding.

In the Daniels family, joining requires the therapist to attune to Fran's emotional exhaustion and her deep loyalty to Pam, Murray's quiet withdrawal and his alignment with his sons, and Pam's sense of isolation and invisible burden. These positions reflect complex intergenerational legacies and unmet needs. By acknowledging each member's pain and contributions, the therapist fosters trust and opens the door to healing. This joining is not passive; it is an ethically engaged stance that honors each person's merit and suffering while gently challenging relational imbalances (Boszormenyi-Nagy & Krasner, 1986; Ducommun-Nagy, 2018).

Joining also involves listening for the family's historical truths, including patterns of loyalty, sacrifice, and injustice. The therapist must be sensitive to how these legacies shape current dynamics and avoid pathologizing culturally embedded behaviors. As Boszormenyi-Nagy (1987) emphasized, the therapist encourages clients to articulate their justified relational positions and reflect on the fairness of their actions. This process sets the stage for deeper therapeutic work, including rejunction, exoneration, and the restoration of trust.

Rejunction

Rejunction refers to the restoration of broken relational ties, particularly between parents and children, through fairness, trust, and mutual recognition. It is not merely reconciliation; it is an ethical process that involves acknowledging past injuries, rebalancing emotional give-and-take, and fostering renewed commitment to relational integrity (Boszormenyi-Nagy, 1987; Wilburn-McCoy, 1993). Rejunction is seen as a healing moment, where family members re-engage in mutual care and accountability, often across generational divides (Boszormenyi-Nagy & Krasner, 1986).

In the Daniels family, rejunction is especially needed between Pam and her father, Murray, whose emotional distance has contributed to Pam's sense of invisibility and distress. Facilitating opportunities for Murray to engage with Pam's interests, such as her music, can help rebuild trustworthiness and allow Pam to feel seen and valued. This aligns with the therapeutic goal of restoring the family's capacity for relatedness, as symptoms often emerge when trust and caring break down (Adams & Maynard, 2004). Similarly, rejunction between Fran and Pam requires shifting from monitoring Pam's eating behaviors to emotionally attuned, non-intrusive interactions that affirm Pam's autonomy and worth.

Rejunction also involves exoneration, helping Fran and Murray understand each other's behaviors in the context of their own legacies. For instance, Fran's overinvolvement is rooted in early caregiving and sacrifice. Through genuine dialogue, the therapist fosters a space where past hurts can be ethically acknowledged, and relational fairness can be reestablished. As van der Meiden et al. (2020) emphasizes, rejunction is not only a restorative act but also a preventive one, helping to break cycles of relational injustice and promote healing for future generations.

Exoneration

The process of lifting the burden of blame by helping individuals understand the contextual roots of harmful behaviors is referred to as **exoneration**. It does not excuse the harm but reframes it within the ethical, historical, and relational backdrop of the person's life (Boszormenyi-Nagy, 1987; Boszormenyi-Nagy & Krasner, 1980). This process allows family members to move from judgment to compassion, fostering forgiveness and relational healing. Ducommun-Nagy (2018) stated, "clients can see that their parents too were seeking redress for past injustice," which opens the door to empathy and emotional freedom (p. 6).

Exoneration is a critical intervention for both Fran and Pam. For Fran, understanding that her intense focus on Pam stems from her own childhood experiences of emotional neglect and parentification helps reframe her behavior as an expression of unresolved loyalty and care, rather than control.

For Pam, recognizing that Murray's emotional distance may be a learned behavior rooted in his own upbringing versus a personal rejection can soften her resentment and open space for reconnection. This therapeutic reframing emphasizes adult reassessment of past injustices and the restoration of fairness through understanding, as described by van der Meiden et al. (2020).

The therapist guides the family through this process, encouraging genuine dialogue and helping each member see the intentions behind the impacts. For example, an intervention like "Murray, Pam feels a distance from you that hurts. Would you be open to hearing what she needs from you, not as blame, but as a way to rebuild that bond?" invites Murray into a space of accountability without shame. Through exoneration, the Daniels family can begin to release destructive entitlement, reset the emotional ledger, and move toward a more ethically balanced and emotionally connected future.

Revolving Slate

The **revolving slate** refers to the intergenerational transmission of unresolved relational debts and entitlements. It describes how children may unconsciously carry the burdens of their parents' unmet needs, injustices, or emotional wounds, often reenacting these legacies in their own relationships (Adams & Maynard, 2004; Boszormenyi-Nagy, 1987). This cycle of destructive entitlement, where individuals feel justified in harmful behaviors due to past injustices, can perpetuate emotional imbalance and relational dysfunction across generations (Gangamma et al., 2012).

In the Daniels family, this concept is vividly illustrated. Fran's unresolved longing for maternal closeness, shaped by her early parentification and emotional neglect, appears to be playing out in her intense focus on Pam. Her caregiving may be an unconscious attempt to resolve her own unmet needs through her daughter. Similarly, Murray's emotional stoicism, likely inherited from his father, contributes to his limited engagement with Pam, perpetuating a legacy of emotional distance. These patterns reflect how legacy obligations, unspoken expectations to repay or reenact past roles, can shape current family dynamics (Boszormenyi-Nagy & Krasner, 1986).

Therapeutic work with the Daniels family involves helping each member recognize and interrupt these cycles. Through interventions like "What would it take for this family to feel fairer and for everyone to feel seen, supported, and acknowledged?," the therapist invites reflection on relational fairness and emotional accountability. Exoneration helps family members understand the origins of their behaviors and consciously choose to break the cycle (van der Meiden et al., 2020). The ultimate goal is to clear the emotional ledger, allowing each person to move forward freely and prevent the transmission of unresolved trauma to future generations.

Multidirected Partiality

Multidirected partiality is a foundational clinical strategy in contextual family therapy, emphasizing the therapist's active and empathic engagement with each family member's perspective (Boszormenyi-Nagy & Krasner, 1986). Unlike neutrality, which may risk emotional detachment, multidirected partiality involves sequentially siding with all parties, validating their experiences, grievances, and truths (Boszormenyi-Nagy & Krasner, 1986). This approach fosters trust, fairness, and mutual accountability, helping families move from cycles of blame and silence to ethical dialogue and connection (Boszormenyi-Nagy & Krasner, 1980).

In the Daniels family, multidirected partiality is essential for navigating the complex emotional terrain between Pam, Fran, and Murray. The therapist listens deeply to Pam's feelings of isolation and emotional neglect, Fran's guilt and fear rooted in her own history of parentification, and Murray's quiet sense of inadequacy and emotional distance. By validating each person's subjective truth, the therapist models fairness and ethical engagement, creating a space where each member feels seen, heard, and respected. This opens the door to genuine dialogue, where Pam can express her need for emotional connection, Fran can acknowledge her fears without projecting them, and Murray can begin to step into a more emotionally present role.

Importantly, multidirected partiality also aligns with multicultural competencies, as it requires honoring diverse voices and experiences. However, as noted by Hardy & Laszloffy (1995) and McDowell (2012), therapists must be cautious not to fall into "both-sides-ism" that ignores structural power imbalances such as sexism, racism, or generational hierarchies. In the Daniels case, this means being sensitive to how gender roles and cultural expectations may have shaped Fran's caregiving identity and Murray's emotional stoicism. The therapist must integrate cultural humility and explicitly address these dynamics to ensure that multidirected partiality does not inadvertently reinforce oppression.

Ultimately, multidirected partiality is not just a humanistic stance—it is a clinical strategy to break cycles of negative reciprocity and promote relational fairness (Boszormenyi-Nagy, 1987). By advocating for each family member's voice and guiding them toward mutual recognition, the therapist helps the Daniels family move toward healing, accountability, and deeper connection. This approach also takes into consideration the broader relational web, including the potential impact on future generations, such as the children of the current children, aiming to prevent the continuation of burdens and imbalances that have historically affected the nuclear family. By attending to both present and future relational obligations, multidirected partiality supports the creation of patterns of fairness and trust that can endure across generations.

The Therapeutic Process

Using contextual family therapy, we can approach the Daniels family by focusing on relational ethics, fairness, loyalty, and multigenerational influence within the family system. The primary focus is on the web of obligations, legacies, and relational balances that span generations. The therapist's role is not to impose solutions but to illuminate patterns of giving and receiving, to identify relational debts and entitlements, and to facilitate opportunities for repair and mutual recognition (Böszörményi-Nagy & Spark, 1973; Noone & Papero, 2015). In essence, the therapist is both a witness and an active participant—helping the family see imbalances, explore their origins, and consider ways to restore fairness without assigning blame.

In approaching the Daniels family, the therapist has focused on uncovering patterns of loyalty, transgenerational caregiving, and parentification that shape current dynamics. This approach helps us understand Pam's anorexia not just as a psychological issue, but as a relational and ethical message about invisible injustices in the family system. Her restriction of food can be seen as a protest against feeling excluded from her father's attention, reduced to a "problem child" in her mother's anxious caregiving, and burdened by loyalties that leave her siblings' needs overshadowed. In contextual terms, Pam's symptoms point to an imbalance in the family ledger; she has been giving loyalty, patience, and silence while receiving little in return. Likewise, Fran's overinvolvement reflects her own history of parentification, repeating a generational pattern where caregiving becomes a primary expression of love but also a source of hidden cost. Seen in this manner, anorexia is not simply a disorder to be resolved, but a signal of deeper inequities in giving and receiving that need acknowledgment and repair.

The interventions, therefore, center on highlighting relational costs, building trust, and opening space for each family member's perspective, particularly those, like Pam, whose experiences of exclusion or burden may have gone unrecognized. The following transcript illustrates how these principles and interventions were applied in a first family session. The dialogue captures both the emotional experience of the family and the deliberate, ethically guided approaches the therapist uses to facilitate awareness, acknowledgment, and relational repair. It provides a window into the complexity of family dynamics from a contextual perspective, showing how understanding obligations, trust, and loyalty across generations can guide the therapeutic process.

Case Transcript

Therapist: Thank you all for being here. I know this isn't easy. I want to start by saying that each of you will have space in this room to share your perspective. My role is to listen to everyone's story fairly and to understand how each of you has been giving and receiving in this family. I'd like to begin by understanding what brings you to therapy?

Intervention: Joining through Multidirected Partiality—Similar to other family therapy models, a Contextual therapist needs to establish a strong therapeutic foundation of empathy, understanding, and trust with each member of the family system. From the beginning of the therapeutic process, the contextual therapist wants each member of the system to understand that their voices are important, signaling fairness and balanced allegiance to each member.

Fran: We're really worried about Pam. Her weight has dropped again, and we're scared. We don't want to send her to inpatient care unless we have to.

Murray: We thought maybe family therapy could help. We've always tried to be a good family, and now it feels like we're failing somehow.

Therapist: I hear that you both care deeply about your family. Mom, you want to protect Pam, but you also don't want to lose her trust by pushing her too hard, and Murray, you're worried that something may have been missed despite your best efforts. Pam, how are you feeling about being here?

Intervention: Multidirected Partiality—A contextual therapist is intentional about validating each family member's perspective to restore a sense of fairness (Boszormenyi-Nagy & Krasner, 1986). The therapist guides the session so each member of the family feels heard and ethically recognized.

Pam (quietly): I don't know. I guess I'm tired of being talked about like I'm broken.

Therapist: That makes sense. It sounds like you feel more like a problem than a person right now.

Intervention—Multidirected Partiality—The therapist ensures to validate Pam's feelings about her role in the family without judgment, avoiding invalidating other members of the system.

Pam: Yeah. Everyone's always watching what I eat. It's exhausting. I don't think they understand me. It's not just about food.

Fran: I'm just trying to help. I don't want to lose you, Pam!

Therapist: Mom, it sounds like you're carrying a lot of fear. And Pam, it sounds like that fear feels like pressure at times. Is that fair?

Intervention—Multidirected Partiality—The therapist is intentional about validating both sides without taking one over the other.

Pam: Yeah. I miss when we used to just talk about normal stuff.

Therapist: Can you tell me more about what it's been like for you these past two years?

Pam: I just… I feel like I don't belong. Dad spends so much time with Oliver and George. It's like they have their own little club, and I'm not part of it. They're always talking about baseball, practicing in the yard, going to games. I don't even bother trying to join in because I know I'll just be on the outside. And Mom… I love her, but lately, it feels like all she cares about is what I eat, or if I've eaten enough, or if I'm lying about eating. Every conversation turns into food. It's exhausting.

Therapist: So, what I'm hearing is that you've been missing the sense of belonging you once had—missing conversations that were just about you and your life, not your weight, while also feeling a bit disconnected from both your dad and brothers. That sounds both tiring and lonely.

Pam: Yeah, I mean, I used to feel close with Mom at least, like she was the one person I could talk to about school or friends or whatever. But now I feel like I can't go to her either because it always turns into questions like, "Have you eaten today?" So, I just feel like I don't have her anymore either. And when I'm around everyone else, I just feel… extra. Like the (*signals air quotes with hands*) "problem child." I pretty much feel like the fifth wheel in my own family.

Therapist: Wow. Thank you for sharing so openly, Pam. It sounds like you've been feeling this intense pressure to hold in your feelings, trying not to burden anyone—but at the same time, the balance of what you're receiving back feels unfair. It sounds like your personal "ledger" of give and take within the family feels a bit unbalanced. For example, feeling like your brothers have Dad's attention, and Mom's primary concerns are about your eating due to fear. Which leaves you carrying these feelings of being alone all on your own.

Pam: Yeah, it just doesn't seem fair.

Therapist: Sure, that makes sense. Having to bear that pressure and those feelings of isolation and loneliness feel unfair to you. Mom, I couldn't help but notice your tearfulness while Pam was describing her feelings. What's it like to hear that your concern for her health and well-being can often feel like a lot of pressure, creating a bit of a wedge between the two of you where she doesn't feel connected?

Intervention—Multidirected Partiality—It's important for the therapist to approach the family from an impartial perspective to authentically validate all parties' perspectives while still naming the imbalances and unfairness felt among members of the family.

Ledger Balancing—In the above example, the therapist also works to build trust and connection with Pam (something she feels is lacking within her family) and draws attention to imbalances in giving/receiving (e.g., Pam gives loyalty but receives isolation). The goal is to make unfairness visible and create opportunities for repair.

Fran: I'm just terrified. Every time she skips a meal, I panic. I feel like if I don't watch her or don't check in, I could lose her.

Therapist: That sounds incredibly scary and heavy. I imagine you've been carrying that fear alone. Does it feel like you have to be strong for everyone?

Intervention—Multidirected Partiality & Trust-Building—Here, the therapist practices multidirected partiality by centering the mother's fear and validating its weight. Rather than framing her worry as overbearing, the therapist highlights her strength and the isolation of carrying this burden. This builds trust and opens space for Fran to reflect on how caregiving has shaped her role in the family.

Fran: Yes… kind of. It's just like when I was younger and had to care for my sister. I guess I've always taken on that role.

Therapist: I wonder if part of your love for Pam is wrapped in that same caregiving thread. Do you sometimes feel she's pulling away from that connection?

Intervention—Revolving Slate—The therapist works to connect Fran's current over-vigilance with Pam to her earlier experiences of parentification—being required to care for her younger sister. This frames her behavior as part of a transgenerational pattern, helping her see that her intentions are rooted in love and learned responsibility.

Fran: Yes. And it terrifies me.

Therapist: Thank you for sharing that, Mom. Pam, what's it like hearing your mom say this?

Intervention—Multidirected Partiality—Turning to Pam, the therapist attempts to ensure fairness in hearing her perspective too. This balances attention in the session and begins to make the family ledger visible, showing that both giving and receiving matter in relationships.

Pam(quietly): I didn't know she saw it that way. I just… feel smothered sometimes. I get it, but I just want space. I want to be seen for more than my eating.

Therapist: So, Pam, for you, the closeness that comes from Mom's caregiving feels like too much—it tips the balance. And Fran, for you, stepping back feels terrifying, because caregiving has always been how you've shown love and kept people safe. What we're naming here is an imbalance in the family ledger: both of you are giving, but not both of you are receiving in ways that feel fair.

Intervention—Ledger Rebalancing & Relational Ethics—From a contextual lens, the therapist's job is to hold multiple truths simultaneously (multidirected partiality). Here, the therapist is linking Fran's caregiving pattern to her past (revolving slate) and framing Pam's push for space as a fair bid for balance in the ledger. The interactions above capture how Fran's fear, rooted in her own history, collides with Pam's need for space and fairness.

Pam: It's just a lot sometimes. I get that she loves me, I just want to be trusted and seen for more than my eating. I mean, I'm into music, but no one really asks me about that. I want them to know me for the things I like, not just the things they worry about.

Therapist: That makes sense. You're at a stage where independence matters. And at the same time, it sounds like part of you wants to be closer to your parents and for them to really *see* you. Earlier, you talked about the unfairness of being outside of the "Boys Club." Can you tell me a little more about what it's been like with your dad in those moments?

Intervention—Ledger Awareness and Relational Ethics—The therapist is highlighting ledger awareness and relational ethics, connecting Pam's feelings of exclusion to a broader pattern of relational fairness. By inviting her to describe her experience with Murray, the therapist validates her perspective and opens space for Murray to hear the impact of his actions without assigning blame.

Pam: I mean, he loves me, I know that. But sometimes it feels like he doesn't really *see* me. Like when I won a competition at school last year, he didn't even ask to look at my writing submission. Or when I try to talk about music, it just goes unnoticed. It's like if it's not sports, it doesn't matter.

Therapist: Dad, Pam is describing a longing to feel seen by you—not only as your daughter, but as someone with her own interests and gifts. What is it like to hear that?

Intervention—Multidirected Partiality—Here, the therapist maintains multidirected partiality by shifting focus to Murray while maintaining Pam's perspective. This invites Dad to recognize the cost of his inattention, fostering awareness of imbalance in giving and receiving within the parent–child relationship.

Murray (pauses, visibly moved): It hurts. Because I never wanted her to feel that way. I thought since Fran and Pam were close, it made sense for me to be the one more involved with the boys. And honestly, sports were the way I knew how to connect with them. That's how my dad and I bonded. I didn't think she would want to hang out with the boys and me.

Therapist: So, for you, Dad, being on the field with your sons was a way of passing on what your father gave you—a sense of connection through activity.

Intervention—Exoneration and Rejunction—Exoneration includes reframing past harm in context to reduce blame and guilt while fostering ethical accountability (Boszormenyi-Nagy & Krasner, 1986; Friedman, 1989). Here, the therapist reframes Murray's behavior as rooted in loyalty to family legacy rather than intentional neglect. This reframing can also be understood through Nagy's concept of "seed planting" (Boszormenyi-Nagy & Krasner, 1986), in which the resources, values, and relational capacities Murray models and invests in with his sons act as seeds for future ethical and relational growth. By consciously planting these seeds, Murray contributes not only to their current development but also to the intergenerational transmission of trust, fairness, and constructive entitlement. At the same time, the therapist emphasizes that even well-intentioned actions can create relational costs, setting the stage for repair and eventual rejunction in order improves family cohesion while enhancing mutual accountability.

Pam (looking at Murray): I get that. But it still felt like I'm always left out. You never ask me about anything that matters to me or offer to do things with me. You never even offer to have me join you and Oliver and George.

Murray: I didn't think you wanted me to.

Therapist: That's a powerful moment. Pam, it takes courage to say that. Dad, would you be open to hearing more from her?

Intervention—Multidirected Partiality—The therapist acknowledges Pam's courage while inviting Murray to listen without defensiveness, fostering relational fairness.

Murray: Yeah. I guess I haven't been fair. I got caught up in the boys' lives with all the different practices, games, and activities.

Therapist: And that's important, too. Yet, Pam has experienced the cost, even though the intention came from love and loyalty.

Intervention—Ledger Rebalancing—Rebalancing makes visible the invisible obligations, entitlements, and trust in relationships (Böszörményi-Nagy & Spark, 1973). In this example, the therapist names the imbalance in giving and receiving without blame, helping Murray understand the relational cost of his prior focus.

Murray: I see that now. I didn't realize she was paying the price for me not making that space with her.

Therapist: That awareness is a step toward fairness, acknowledging both the gift you tried to give, and the debt Pam has carried. Pam, you've given so much—your honesty, your effort, even carrying worries that weren't really yours. And this all builds up in the family ledger. Children who give so much also deserve something back.

Intervention—Ledger Awareness/Rebalancing—The therapist frames the family ledger practically, prompting Pam to articulate what she needs to restore balance, linking feelings to concrete actions.

Murray: That makes sense. I can do more to balance that ledger. For me that means not just assuming Pam is fine because she is quiet but taking the initiative to ask about her day or joining her in something she enjoys. Even small things like checking in with her the way I do with the boys.

Pam (smiles a little): That would help. More than anything, I want help feeling like I don't have to carry everything by myself. If Dad could share that with me and show me versus just telling me, it would make it easier to trust him again.

Therapist: You're entitled to that kind of support and recognition.

Pam: I want to trust him. But I need him to try. When he spends all his time with Oliver and George, it's like I don't exist sometimes.

Murray: I didn't mean to make you feel that way. I just thought you weren't interested in the same things. I don't always know how to talk about girl stuff.

Therapist: That's an important point, Dad. Sometimes fairness isn't about equal time; it's about feeling seen. Pam, what would it look like for you to feel seen by your dad?

Intervention—Ledger Rebalancing/Rejunction—The therapist highlights the entitlements and imbalances currently being experienced, while also softly holding Dad accountable for this role. At the same time, the therapist draws on the family's existing relational resources (i.e., the love, loyalty, and capacities for connection already present among family members) to facilitate repair and strengthen bonds. By asking Pam about what it would be like to feel seen by her dad, this encourages the family to begin working toward restoring broken relational bonds (rejunction).

Pam: I don't know... maybe if he asked me about my music or just sat with me without talking about food or school.

Murray(nods): I can do that. I didn't realize how much that mattered.

Therapist: Oliver, George, I'd like to check in with you, too. Sometimes when one child is struggling, the others feel they shouldn't ask for anything.

Intervention—Multidirected Partiality—To this point, Pam's brothers have not been included in the conversation. The therapist uses multidirected partiality and joining by inviting Oliver and George into the conversation. After initially amplifying Pam's voice to address her isolation, the therapist now ensures the siblings' perspectives are heard, promoting fairness and helping the family recognize relational costs and needs.

Oliver: Yeah... I didn't want to make things harder for Mom. Like when I need help with a school project, I just figure it out on my own.

George: Same. I kind of stayed out of the way. I didn't want to add to the stress.

Therapist: That shows loyalty to your sister and your parents. But it can also mean your needs got overlooked. In a family, each person is entitled to their share of care and attention. How do you both feel hearing that?

Intervention—Ledger Rebalancing—The therapist acknowledges Oliver and George's loyalty in stepping back to reduce family stress, while also naming the cost: their own needs being overlooked. By framing this dynamic in terms of fairness and entitlement within the family ledger, the therapist validates their sacrifices while also legitimizing their right to care and attention. This intervention helps rebalance relational accounts and fosters trust by ensuring the siblings' voices and needs are recognized alongside Pam's.

Oliver: Relieved, actually. It makes me feel like it's okay to need Mom too.

George: Yeah. It'd be nice to get time with Mom too, not just always Dad.

Fran (tearfully, nodding): I want that as well. I see how much I've been wrapped up in watching Pam, and I've missed those moments with you two. I don't want to feel like you have to stay quiet to protect me. I want to be there for you, too.

Therapist: Mom, how do you feel hearing all of this?

Fran(tearful): I feel guilty. I've been so focused on Pam's health that I forgot to just be her mom, to laugh with her, ask about her day, or simply sit with her without an agenda. And I see I now that I've overlooked Oliver and George too. They needed time and recognition apart from all this, and I didn't give it.

Therapist: That's a powerful insight. You've been trying to protect her, but it may have felt more like control. Pam, do you feel like you can trust your mom to just be with you?

Intervention—Multidirected Partiality & Ledger Awareness—The therapist validates Fran's experience while also bringing Pam's perspective into the dialogue. This highlights the relational costs of overprotectiveness and opens space for both mother and daughter to express needs without blame. Fran articulating that she now sees fairness as not just "protecting," but "being with." This highlights the principle of mutual responsiveness.

Pam: Sometimes. But lately it's been hard. I feel like I'm always disappointing her.

Fran: You're not. I'm just worried, that's all. I don't want to lose you.

Therapist: Mom, what would it mean to acknowledge Pam's pain without trying to fix it?

Intervention—Trust-Building—The therapist encourages Fran to recognize Pam's experience without immediately problem-solving. This supports fairness in the ledger and nurtures emotional connection by validating Pam's feelings.

Fran: It would be hard. I won't lie. Helping is what I do, and if I can fix something so she or her brothers don't have to feel pain, I will. But I think I need to try. Maybe I can start by asking how she feels instead of what she's eating.

Therapist: That's a great start. Dad, I'd like to invite you to think about how you could also spend 30 min this week with Pam doing something she chooses. No agenda—just presence.

Intervention: Rejunction/Ledger Rebalancing—Here, Dad is invited to show up for Pam in a way that emphasizes giving without expectation or control. This practical action begins to repair relational imbalances and rebuild trust.

Murray: Absolutely. Pam, would you want to go for a walk or listen to music together?

Pam (smiles slightly): Maybe. I'll think about it.

Therapist: That's all you need for now—a little hope and a little effort. We'll keep building from here. Today, we began to make visible some of the imbalances in the family. Fran, you were able to share your caregiving fears and recognize how they sometimes feel controlling to Pam. Pam, you were brave in naming your need to be seen beyond your illness. Murray, you reflected on how your way of connecting with the boys may have unintentionally left Pam feeling left out. That's big! Oliver and George, you shared how stepping back to protect your parents also meant your own needs sometimes went unnoticed. Naming that opens the door for fairness to flow in both directions, where care and attention can be more evenly shared. We'll continue to build on this in our next sessions. The goal isn't perfection, but awareness, repair, and creating opportunities for each of you to feel seen, heard, and valued in this family system.

The Therapeutic Story

In the Daniels case, ethical imbalances that had previously remained invisible were illuminated. Specifically, Pam's experience of parentification, her loyalty conflict between parents, and the inequities of the family ledger. Through multidirected partiality, the therapist validated each member's perspective while highlighting patterns of over-giving and unmet entitlements. This strategy builds trust and models relational fairness, encouraging mutual care and accountability (van der Meiden et al., 2020). In doing so, the therapist also drew on the family's existing relational resources, planting "seeds" for future ethical and relational growth (Boszormenyi-Nagy & Krasner, 1986). Thus, the therapist helped create a different story in the family—one that centered around demonstrating due concern for each member. Boszormenyi-Nagy (1987) wrote, "The therapist's extended perspective became the source of a broadened and deeper understanding" (p. 17). Interventions such as ledger balancing and explicit acknowledgment of Pam's care reframed her anorexia as a relational signal rather than individual pathology. Specifically, these interventions highlighted the ways Pam has given more than she has received, reframing her symptom as a plea for fairness and prompting Murray and Fran to consider new ways of giving.

The session also modeled exoneration, helping Fran and Murray to reinterpret their behaviors based on intergenerational legacies, and began to dismantle the revolving slate by inviting new transactions with more fairness in mind. For example, Murray could reframe his focus on the boys as an act of loyalty to his father's legacy, softening his guilt while inviting accountability. Including Oliver and George reinforced fairness and broadened the family's sense of mutual responsibility. Practical tasks, such as Murray spending intentional time with Pam and Fran shifting from food-focused monitoring to emotional attunement, allowed the constructs of fairness and trustworthiness to be put into actional behaviors. This also activated the family's relational resources, allowing fairness and trustworthiness to take root in everyday interactions.

Finally, revolutions of the slate encourage Fran to differentiate between her past role as a parentified child and her current role as mother, opening possibilities for new, more equitable patterns of connection. Together, these interventions offer the Daniels family pathways toward repair, mutual recognition, and the restoration of relational trust.

The session exemplifies Nagy's (1986) principle that trust cannot be demanded but must be merited through consistent, ethical engagement. From a Buberian lens, the therapist embodies "healing through meeting," emphasizing genuine human connection and mutual recognition (Friedman, 1989, p. 402). Additionally, by uncovering hidden injustices, acknowledging legitimate pain, and fostering new experiences of fairness, the therapist set the stage for relational repair and sustainable change.

Next Steps, Treatment Goals, and Prognosis

As the session closed, the therapist emphasized that the Daniels family's path forward would not rest on quick solutions but on deliberate efforts to restore fairness and merited trust. In practical terms, this meant small but meaningful commitments. Murray was invited to spend intentional one-on-one time with Pam each week, engaging in activities of her choosing, while Fran was encouraged to shift from food-focused monitoring toward emotional attunement. The siblings, Oliver and George, were included in this restorative process by being reminded that their needs for attention and care also matter, reinforcing a sense of fairness across the family ledger.

For this case, treatment moving forward could focus on acknowledging Fran's history of parentification and helping her renegotiate her role as a responsive, rather than rescuing, parent. Murray will be invited to work on becoming more emotionally present and trustworthy, particularly with Pam and outside the realm of sports, while Pam will be supported in moving from destructive entitlement, expressing distress through unhealthy symptoms, to constructive entitlement, where her needs for attention and validation can be voiced directly. Through structured dialogue, the family will be encouraged to practice mutual recognition, ensuring that each member's contributions and vulnerabilities are acknowledged without blame.

The prognosis for the Daniels family is cautiously optimistic. With commitment to the therapeutic process, they have strong potential to rebalance fairness, repair fractured bonds, and develop a relational ethic that honors loyalty, accountability, and care. Importantly, while Pam's physical health remains an ongoing reality that shapes the family's dynamics, the contextual therapist looks beyond pathology, attending instead to the ethical dimensions of fairness, trust, and relational accountability. Contextual therapy frames this as a generational investment: by addressing hidden injustices and practicing earned trust, the Daniels family not only works toward healing Pam's immediate struggles but also lays the groundwork for healthier patterns of relating to be carried forward.

References

Adams, J. F., & Maynard, P. E. (2004). Contextual therapy: Applying the family ledger to couple therapy. *Journal of Couple & Relationship Therapy*, *3*(1), 1–22.

Boszormenyi-Nagy, I. (1987). *Foundations of contextual therapy: Collected papers of Ivan Boszormenyi-Nagy*. Brunner/Mazel.

Boszormenyi-Nagy, I., & Krasner, B. R. (1980). Trust-based therapy: A contextual approach. *The American Journal of Psychiatry*, *137*(7), 767–775.

Boszormenyi-Nagy, I., & Krasner, B. R. (1986). *Between give and take: A clinical guide to contextual therapy*. Brunner/Mazel.

Böszörményi-Nagy, I., & Spark, G. M. (1973). *Invisible loyalties: Reciprocity in intergenerational family therapy*. Harper & Row.

Comas-Díaz, L., Hall, G. N., & Neville, H. A. (2019). Racial trauma: Theory, research, and healing: Introduction to the special issue. *American Psychologist*, *74*(1), 1–5.

Ducommun-Nagy, C. (2018). Contextual family therapy. In J. L. Lebow et al. (Eds.), *Encyclopedia of couple and Family therapy* (pp. 1–8). Springer.

Ducommun-Nagy, C. (2025). The essence of contextual therapy, its place in the field of family therapy, and its role in the future. *Family Process*, *64*(1), e13070.

Friedman, M. (1989). Martin Buber and Ivan Boszormenyi-Nagy: The role of dialogue in contextual therapy. *Psychotherapy*, *26*(3), 401–409.

Gangamma, R., Bartle-Haring, S., & Glebova, T. (2012). A study of contextual therapy theory's relational ethics in couples in therapy. *Family Relations*, *61*(5), 825–835.

Gehart, D. R. (2018). *Mastering competencies in family therapy: A practical approach to theories and clinical case documentation* (3rd ed.). Cengage Learning.

Glebova, T., Lal, A., & Gangamma, R. (2025). Relational ethics in immigrant families: The contextual therapy five-dimensional framework. *Family Process*, *64*(1), e13071.

Grunebaum, J. (1987). Multidirected partiality and the "parental imperative". *Psychotherapy*, *24*(4), 581–589.

Hardy, K. V., & Laszloffy, T. A. (1995). The cultural genogram: Key to training culturally competent family therapists. *Journal of Marital and Family Therapy*, *21*(3), 227–237.

Hargrave, T. D., & Pfitzer, F. (2003). *The new contextual therapy: Guiding the power of give and take*. Brunner-Routledge.

Kaslow, F. W. (1987). Marital and family therapy. In M. B. Sussman & S. K. Steinmetz (Eds.), *Handbook of marriage and the family* (pp. 835–859). Plenum Press.

McDowell, T. (2012). Social class in family therapy education: Experiences of low SES students. *Journal of Marital and Family Therapy*, *39*(1), 72–86.

van der Meiden, J., Noordegraaf, M., & van Ewijk, H. (2018). How is contextual therapy applied today? An analysis of the practice of current contextual therapists. *Contemporary Family Therapy*, *41*(1), 12–23.

van der Meiden, J., Verduijn, K., Noordegraaf, M., & van Ewijk, H. (2020). Strengthening connectedness in close relationships: A model for applying contextual therapy. *Family Process*, *59*(2), 346–360.

Natrajan-Tyagi, R., & Poulsen, S. S. (2025). Contextual family therapy and intergenerational work with Asian Indian families. *Family Process*, *64*(1), e70011.

Noone, R. J., & Papero, D. V. (Eds.) (2015). *The family emotional system: An integrative concept for theory, science, and practice*. Lexington Books.

Reiter, M. D. (2024). *Family therapy: An introduction to process, practice, and theory* (2nd ed.). Routledge.

Wilburn-McCoy, C. (1993). Rediscovering Nagy: What happened to contextual therapy? *Contemporary Family Therapy*, *15*(5), 395–409.

Yeh, C. J., Carter, R. T., & Pieterse, A. L. (2004). Cultural values and racial identity attitudes among Asian American students: An exploratory investigation. *Journal of Counseling Psychology*, *51*(2), 139–150.

6 Object Relations Family Therapy

George A. Pate and Michael D. Reiter

Object relations theory addresses the question of how we develop the lens or filter through which we establish our sense of self and view the presentations and meanings of family members and others around us. Although based on psychoanalysis, it represents an alternative psychodynamic approach to Freud's psychosexual drive theory. Consistent with psychoanalysis, object relations theory focuses more on how the internalization of external objects (major caregivers) creates the sense of self and influences the development of subsequent relationships than with a proscribed therapeutic practice (Scharff & Scharff, 1987). The model was initially proposed in 1917 by Sandor Ferenczi (Ferenczi, 1949; Soreanu, 2018) and later addressed by Harry Stack Sullivan in his discussions of how familial and social processes influence the development of self (Cortina, 2020; Gaarder, 2006; Sullivan, 1953). It was more formally developed as object relations theory in the 1940s, primarily by Melanie Klein (1946).

While object relations theory deviated from Freud's focus on psychosexual development, it continued to focus on drive theory related to the internalization of external objects (representations of primary caregivers). It became closely associated with the British Psychoanalytic Association. While Klein addressed the internalization or **introjection** of the primary caregivers, Fairbairn (1954, 1958, 1986) focused more on the process of seeking out the desired relationship suggested by the infant's experiences with primary caregivers. Other contributors to object relations theory, such as Kohut, Kernberg, and Winnicott, have tended to fall into either Klein's drive theory or Fairbairn's relationship seeking theory. In both approaches, the significance of early experiences with primary caregivers provides the foundation for the infant's development of self and their sense of emotional and physical safety in their relationship with others, social structures, and the world at large. In essence, the introjection of externalized objects creates a lens that filters all relationships and interactions (Scharff & Scharff, 1992; Sussal, 1992).

DOI: 10.4324/9781003668510-6

The Therapeutic Story of Problem Formation

Klein's initial concepts relate strongly to Bowlby's **attachment theory**, in that the type of attachment style is dependent on the quality of the interactions with primary caregivers (Bowlby, 1958, 1960). Similar to Bowlby's concepts, internalized objects that represent a sense of nurturing and emotional and physical safety might correlate with the development of secure attachment. Conversely, those that represent unpredictable, capricious, temperamental, or rejecting/abusive objects might correlate with insecure, anxious, or reactive attachment processes. In both Klein's and Fairbairn's approaches, the internalized objects are the foundation of the **ego**, or sense of self, and shape subsequent adolescent and adult interactions and relationships.

In the Daniels family, the parents have experienced difficulties establishing secure attachments in their respective families of origin and appear to have maintained a family environment conducive to similar restrictions on their daughter. The Daniels have experienced multigenerational processes of anxious or insecure attachments, which seem to represent internalized black/white, good/bad concrete "part-objects" as evidenced by both parents and their children. Murray, as an only child, and Fran, as the firstborn, experienced periods of distance from their mutual parents, suggesting that they are being arrested in the black/white or good/bad developmental stage, which Klein (1946) described as the "paranoid-schizoid" position. Fairbairn (1954, 1986) and Winnicott (1969) would describe this as the maturational failure to internalize the quality of the parental relationship as "good enough" as opposed to dichotomous distinctions between "good" vs. "bad." Pam, as the oldest child in this 3rd generation family pattern, maintains increasing anxiety and secretiveness, which have progressed into anorexia that has not been amenable to conventional individual psychotherapy. The anxiety that she experiences appears to be exacerbated by her distance from her father and brothers, her unmet expectations of support and affection from them, and the change in the quality of her relationship with her mother. The development of anorexia has resulted in her mother now functioning to some extent as an external superego, or what Berne (1964) would describe as the "critical or controlling parent," mostly concerned with Pam's eating habits rather than with her emotional experiences.

Pam's difficulties in accomplishing the transition from early to late adolescence are further demonstrated by her growing emotional distress, anorexia, and decreasing grades, and suggest that, like her parents, she internalized part-objects of her parents and is arrested at the "paranoid-schizoid" position. Or, as Fairbairn (1954, 1986) and Winnicott (1969) might have described, she has failed to internalize or introject the object identification of the "good enough" parent, thereby projecting her own sense of being either "good" or "bad" onto the perceptions of others' beliefs about her. In the absence of what Winnicott (1969) would have been described as a **holding environment**, she remains pinned in all-or-nothing self-perceptions, experiencing a continuous positive feedback loop, gradually spiraling downward into further distress and symptomatology.

Theory

Object relations theorists recognize how the perception of external objects follows a process of normal development. Klein (1946) described instinctive drives and actions, such as rooting for the mother's nipple, as **unconscious phantasy** [her spelling], stating that the integration of neural perceptual and behavioral templates (unconscious phantasies) combines with actual experience to form the foundation of the child's development. Considering that infants are theorized to lack a sense of differentiation between self and major caregivers, the actions of major caregivers represent either nurturing or threat to the existence of the self. To protect from the threat of negative interactions, infants are believed to **split** the external object into separate entities of good and bad, or "**part-objects**" in what Klein termed the "paranoid-schizoid position" (Klein, 1946). The process of splitting between the good parent and bad parent (sometimes referred to as the "good breast" as opposed to the "bad breast") is typically resolved subsequently during the second quarter of infant development into the "**depressive position**" of the "good enough" parent, representing an acceptance of certain areas of ambivalence in relationships. If this acceptance is not accomplished, the child continues to see the world and relationships in terms of black/white, good/bad, all/nothing extremes, possibly leading to the development of arrested **positions** (Klein's term for developmental milestones) including borderline personality disorder (Klein, 1946). Klein described the introjection of the good breast as a significant defense against the anxiety associated with unpredictable interactions and events. Essentially, phantasizing about the existence and stability of the good breast during the paranoid-schizoid position is important for normal development and allows the child to project the good breast (a part-object) onto external objects to hide in a secure concept of safety and nurturing emotionally. Klein (1946) described this defense, which fails to establish a boundary between self and the other, as **projective identification**. In essence, the person projects onto another aspects of themselves, whether good or bad. The other person then introjects these parts, which the initial person identified with (Sussal, 1992). While in one way this connects the two people, it also leads to each losing parts of their personality.

Fairbairn offered a different focus from Klein, stating that the child seeks the internalization of the quality of the relationship with the external object as opposed to concrete internalization of the object itself (Fairbairn, 1986). In essence, he described the child as "relationship seeking" rather than "object seeking" or "drive seeking" (Cassullo, 2014; Fairbairn, 1986). He also advocated the **moral defense** as an extension of projective identification. In situations in which children are abused or neglected, they might claim responsibility for the other's behavior and introject the negative traits of the other upon themselves. By accepting a part-object of the other as good, and a self-description as negative, they preserve their ability to maintain a sense of safety with the other as in trauma-bonding (Celani, 2010). In the Daniels family, the concern is that Pam might split off her frustration and anger at her parents, accepting Fran's failed attempts to fix Pam's eating behaviors and weight loss with the justification that there's something inherently wrong with her (Pam). In doing so, she split her mother and herself into part-objects of good vs. bad as a means of saving some aspect of an attachment relationship (Celani, 2010).

Winnicott (1969) recognized the significance of parents providing emotionally safe and nurturing interactions and settings, essentially a holding environment for their child, thereby allowing the child to emotionally and physically explore their world in a safe setting. Winnicott described this process as "primary maternal preoccupation" in which the baby is offered the "illusion" that they and the mother are fused in emotions and experiences, absent of boundaries. The mother's task is to eventually wean the child from that illusion, possibly offering an alternate external object that will bring the child comfort and security for times when the mother is not present—a **transitional object** (Winnicott, 1969). Winnicott recognized that transitional objects are also objects of projection of part-objects, either good/comforting or bad/distressing (such as teddy bears vs. clowns), and cannot sustain the child's development. Consequently, the mother's task is to assist the child to recognize the ambivalence between the "good" and "bad" of external objects and to come to terms with the more mature understanding of the "good enough" mother or parent who represents the continuum of traits. As this happens, the child borrows or absorbs the good enough parent's ego strength and gradually develops a more stable sense of self, allowing them the opportunity to test personal limits and explorations.

Winnicott (1965) further maintained that if the parent cannot present themselves in a "good enough" light, the child internalizes this continued splitting and develops a "false self" as an external representation, often in conflict with the underlying "true self." While some degree of development of the false self is important to meet the demands of society, an overly constructed false self leaves little room for the development or expression of the true self.

In addition to theory-based concerns, Framo (1976) pursued object relations therapy within the framework of family of origin theory. Through several case examples, he described and demonstrated how vertical, multigenerational processes of part-object introjection influence the introjections of split objects in successive generations, resulting in misunderstandings and heightened reactions between marital partners and between parents and children and within sibling relationships. He wrote that "… intergenerational interventions [provide] a direct route to etiological factors—the parental introjects that had so heavily influenced [couples] lives" (Framo, 1992, p. 170).

Summary of Theories

The fundamental point of all approaches through object relations is that early childhood experiences with major caregivers influence attachment style, which in turn creates a lens through which all subsequent relationships are experienced (Bowlby, 1958, 1960; Fairbairn, 1954, 1986; Klein, 1946).

- Elements of early relational experiences, whether identified parts or the overall quality of the relationship, are internalized in the construction of self.
- In the absence of a safe or holding environment, the restricted or limited aspects of self become fixed, so that the individual tends to overrespond to indications of ideal or negative perceptions of the other and does not perceive or appreciate the full presentation of the other.
- The restrictions of internalized objects are multigenerational, in that the limitations of parents also function to inhibit their ability to provide a holding environment for their children, resulting in limited psychological development on the part of the children.
- Children who are impacted by their parents' projective identification (expression of part-objects) choose partners who complement or reflect their own internalized objects, thus continuing in many ways the conflict that their parents experienced with each other and with their children.
- The request for therapy might be in the form of couples therapy or due to difficulties of one or more children. In either case, therapy involves the creation of a therapeutic holding environment in which parents, and eventually adolescent and younger children, gain an understanding of internalized part-objects, how part-objects have impacted communication patterns, and how they can communicate more authentically and openly.

Shapiro (1998) stated, "during the course of his development, and depending upon his particular emotional meaning to his parents, the adolescent who is disturbed has not been supported by his parents in his efforts to accomplish phase-appropriate life tasks" (p. 231).

Assessment and Plan

Based on the present and multigenerational information that the therapist gathered during the initial phone contact, assessment documents, and session, the therapist constructed an assessment of the family based on the assumptions of object relations. To assist in the assessment, the therapist administered the **Object Relations Technique** (ORT) developed by Phillipson (1955) and as reviewed by Knafo (2010). The ORT consists of ambiguous figures similar to the Rorschach Technique, but suggestive of personal elements as in the Thematic Apperception Test (TAT). However, the elements of the ORT are not as direct or restrictive as the TAT, but similar to the TAT in that the technique allowed for a full and personal projective and narrative account of the individual's relational perceptions. The ORT provides information concerning developmental sophistication from infancy to adolescence and adulthood and corresponds with Piaget's cognitive developmental stages. Particularly significant for the

Daniels is the extent to which they perceive and make use of the "gray areas" of interpersonal perceptions and interactions.

The results of the ORT, coupled with the therapist's assessment procedures and observations, confirm the earlier description of Pam and her family. Both parents evidence difficulties in relating to "gray areas" of their concepts of self and of their relationships with others. They have split off their developmental emotional losses from their relationships with their parents. Consequently, they have internalized part-objects of black/white perceptions of self/others, focusing primarily on prescribed concrete functions as a defense against the possible emotional pain involved in confronting ambiguous interactions. They remain in Klein's (1946) definition of the paranoid/schizoid position and, per Winnicott (1969), have not developed or communicated the role of the "good enough" parent. Consequently, through projective identification, they view others through the same lens of black/white, nurturing/rejecting, or good/bad, and have created an environment in which their children have done the same.

The therapist's concern for Pam is that she has sustained and introjected the paranoid/schizoid position so that she views herself in the same black/white manner. With the challenges of adolescence, she has found less in herself and in her environment to feel positive about and has drifted further into finding rejection of self in terms of her beliefs and perceptions of the reactions of others. Per Fairbairn's model (1986), compounded by her mother's attentiveness to her anorexia rather than to her emotions, she is less able to seek out or conceptualize supportive or nurturing relationships. She also appears to be at risk of maintaining Fairbairn's moral defense in which she castigates herself as a means of preserving what limited attachment she currently maintains with her mother and other family members (Celani, 2010).

Diversity Conceptualization

Considering that object relations theorists were primarily from the United Kingdom, diversity considerations might initially appear questionable. However, Klein, Fairbairn, and Winnicott did not suggest that infant development and the processes of internalization of external objects and subsequent maturity could be distinguished across ethnic divisions of the human species. Klein (1946), in particular, addressed these processes as neurologically and instinctively driven. Although one might speculate that economic, educational, and geographic diversity might significantly impact object relations theory, this was not a primary concern for the theory. Rather, each family was viewed as an individual culture dependent on the quality of "good enough" parenting established by the primary caregivers within the parameters of their own culture. The extent to which the primary caregivers fail to accomplish effective parenting approaches produces predictable degrees of part-object introjection and subsequent projection by their children. The consequential projective identification by their children results in predictable patterns of restricted maturity, partner selection, and projection of part-object conflict with partners and children (Fairbairn, 1986; Framo, 1992; Klein, 1946; Winnicott, 1969).

Gender is a more modern diversity consideration. The early object relations theorists addressed the major caregiver as the mother, resulting in accentuation of maternal guilt during therapy (Bitter, 2014). However, modern object relations therapists are becoming more focused on the generic term "caregiver" rather than specifically addressing the mother. Although much of the emphasis on the child-caregiver relationship has been placed on the mother, this change in emphasis will likely soften the guilt related to attachment concerns when the mother returns to work while the child is an infant or toddler.

Financial resources constitute another diversity concern that affects longer-term therapies. Since object relations therapy is not brief, payment through personal resources or through third-party agencies (e.g., managed care) will likely be limited. Therefore, many working-class or poor families will not be able to sustain object relations therapy past the problem formation stage (Bitter, 2014).

The Therapeutic Story of Problem Resolution

Object relations therapists are typically more concerned with the assumptions of the model, addressing the family's understanding and gradual resolution of internalized objects and part-objects rather than following a set of proscribed techniques or interventions. In the journey of self, the compass is significantly more important than the map (Klein, 1985; Lenormand, 2018; Scharff & Scharff, 1991). Since addressing these processes, which are often unconscious or semi-conscious, produces a considerable degree of anxiety, problem resolution begins with the emotional safety of the therapy setting. The ability of the therapist to foster and maintain an emotional holding environment for the family determines the extent to which family members feel a sense of safety in being able to express their feelings and concerns (Scharff & Scharff, 1991). This is partly accomplished through the therapist openly asking the family, "How can we talk about difficult things in a respectful manner?" (Pate, 2025, p. 36).

In object relations, therapy centers around open conversation, and change happens as family members disclose their relational (attachment) experiences and how those experiences influence their relationships with each other. Considering that some of these experiences involved the splitting of relational percepts (the introjection of negative part-objects), the disclosure of these experiences and interpretations raises the concern that they will be harshly criticized by their projective identifications of others in the family. Therefore, the risk to self and desire for secrecy is exacerbated by their fear of criticism and rejection. Consequently, gaining the ability to effectively talk about difficult things in a respectful manner approaches a direct challenge to the part-object introjects and projections of family members. In the face of such direct challenges, the family is likely to withdraw emotionally or physically, demonstrating either superficial compliance per "false selves" (Winnicott, 1969) or perhaps withdrawing from therapy altogether.

Scharff and Scharff (1991) explained, "The object relations approach to families provides emotional space for a rediscovery of each other and of the lost parts of the self that have been put into each other" (p. 169). This occurs within the therapeutic frame, where the therapist provides the holding space for family members—the therapist sets the format of therapy, whether it be weekly, biweekly, inclusive of all family members, subsystems, or individuals. The therapist's stance is similar to a parent's holding relationship for their child (Diekmann-Tapon, 1999). Thus, the therapist becomes a "good enough" parent.

Given this, one of the first tasks of the therapist is to develop the working alliance. To do so, the therapist must develop a capacity to tolerate anxiety (Scharff & Scharff, 2008). When the family tries to "bend the frame," the therapist understands this as information about the family's defenses.

The holding environment is benefited by the therapist holding a neutral position (Scharff & Scharff, 2008). Benefiting the therapeutic alliance, this neutral position prevents the therapist from being colluded into the family's interpersonal dynamics, such as siding with parents against child, child against parent, or spouse against spouse (Slipp, 1993). The therapist moves back and forth between each individual's intrapsychic world, the family's interpersonal process, as well as the process occurring between the family and the therapist. Further, the therapist's neutral position shows that they do not have skin in the game—they are not tied to the family having a specific outcome.

A key role of the object relations family therapist is to analyze the client's resistance (Scharff & Scharff, 1991). When clients feel anxiety in the therapy room, they tend to sabotage the progress being made. Sussal (1992) described this process,

> Creating a storm prevents making contact with the inner emptiness which has come about as a result of infantile trauma. Therefore before this can happen as a result of someone else's doing, people make it happen themselves. It then at least is perceived as being in their control.
>
> (p. 318)

Object relations family therapists will need to decide, many times over the course of therapy, about the core affective exchange; whether they will work in the here-and-now or the there-and-then (Scharff & Scharff, 1991). They will also move back and forth between the intrapersonal and the interpersonal levels (Jordan & Shaw, 2008). The intrapersonal level focuses on the person's early parent/child attachment experience that has led them to have a current ego position in relation to others. The interpersonal level explores how the individual seeks adult attachments, usually in ways that replicate their early attachment relationships.

There are four main areas of intervention: organizing the session; giving support and advice; facilitating communication; and interpretation (Scharff & Scharff, 1991). Therapists organize the session by setting the therapeutic frame. Like parents in a family, the therapist is responsible for the structure and running of the session.

Object relations family therapists give support by encouragement or validation. Scharff and Scharff (1991) explained, "For most families, the most supportive thing we can do is the be interpretive so that the holding capacity improves" (p. 185). While advice may sometimes be given, the intent behind the advice is usually explored in an exploratory way first. One way of doing this is modeling ways of working together by suggesting possibilities for how the family might function better (Jordan & Shaw, 2008).

Facilitating communication is one of the intermediate goals of family therapy (Scharff & Scharff, 1991). The therapist works in the here-and-now, exploring the emotional exchanges between family members and assessing possible transference that may be occurring.

Interpretation is a central process of ORFT. Scharff and Scharff (1991) proclaimed, "Interpretation is the workhorse of the object relations approach" (p. 189). It is a process of sharing information that happens over the course of therapy rather than at one specific time. Usually, the therapist's interpretative focus is on the family member's holding environments with one another. Interpretation is important since "insight is essential to change" (Scharff, 1989, p. 11).

Individual family members, as well as the full family, will likely have times when they display defensiveness and resistance as they try to maintain their status quo. When this happens, the therapist engages in **working through**, continuing to peel away the client's resistance (Scharff & Scharff, 2008). This is an expected process as change usually happens over time rather than in one fell swoop. Diekmann-Tapon (1999) explained, "Working through does not occur just through understanding one's inner motivations but needs long-term work on the issues explored. This is achieved by repeatedly talking about the topic and slowly gaining better self-awareness" (p. 239).

Interpretation rests upon a solid therapeutic alliance, since clients may experience the therapist's statement as being critical. Three techniques that are useful when interpreting the client's projective identification are reframing, linking, and clarifying (Slipp, 1988). Through **reframing**, the therapist shifts the aim of the projective identification from a negative attribution to a positive attribution. An example of this might be a statement to Fran and Murray,

> When your daughter restricts food, it can awaken parts of your own history that never felt fully held or understood. Sometimes a child's symptoms can carry unspoken family feelings, and you may feel compelled to over-manage because it's painful to see those emotions outside yourself. Exploring how to reclaim those feelings can help you stay connected with her in a steadier, less pressured way.

The second technique to ease the interpretation is linking. **Linking** occurs when the therapist connects the current with the past. Instead of just making a statement of someone's behavior, the therapist links it to past relationships. For instance, the therapist might say,

> It sounds like an internal drama from your childhood may still be playing out: a vulnerable child-part of you and a very controlling, anxious caregiver-part. At times, your daughter may carry the vulnerable role for you, while you step into the controlling one. We can look at how these old internal relationships might be shaping the way you respond to her now.

By connecting the person's behavior to their past, they may not feel as blamed but rather appreciate the insight into their behavior.

The third technique to provide interpretations that will be accepted by the client is **clarifying**. "Clarifying the reason for the patient's past conflict about owning the problem is helpful, since it may have originated in the desire to protect others, to preserve self-esteem, or to respond to family rules" (Slipp, 1988, p. 197). The therapist might say to Fran,

> In your childhood, you often felt responsible for keeping things together emotionally. When your daughter becomes fragile with food, it seems to reactivate that old internal conflict between feeling overwhelmed and needing to appear capable. Taking a highly controlling stance now may be your psyche's way of preserving your sense of competence and value—maintaining a familiar self-esteem structure that once kept you safe.

Transference and Countertransference

At the heart of ORFT are transference and countertransference:

> They offer the living bridge between therapist and family through which the family's shared unconscious assumptions, mutual projective identifications, pained relationships, and deficits in providing holding to one another can be experienced, understood, and fed back to the family in modified form.
>
> (Scharff, 1989)

Transference and countertransference are concepts developed by Sigmund Freud and expanded on over the years by therapists of a range of orientations. **Transference** refers to a client's projection of their past relationships onto their therapist. This might occur in therapy with the Daniels if Pam begins to resist the therapist's inquiries, experiencing them similarly to the inquiries and demands that Fran has made upon her over these last few years. Throughout the session, the therapist pays attention to each individual's transferences as well as their shared transferences. Exploring people's transference is enhanced when the therapist maintains a neutral position, where the therapist uses themselves as a projection screen for the client's identifications. In essence, the client engages with the therapist in ways that signify and demonstrate early attachment difficulties. The therapist will then be able to feed this process back to the family through interpretation so that the family members can work through their chronic interaction patterns.

Transference could also be seen when a client acts toward another family member in ways that signal something about themselves. Those aspects of another that they don't like may actually be the things they don't like about themselves (Sussal, 1992). Murray may be frustrated by Fran's overbearing nature, which is a demonstration of his own concern about his parts that are overbearing, which tend to come out concerning his son's sporting life.

Countertransference occurs when the therapist has reactions to the family members. This may be related to the therapist's early relational experiences with their own parents or can be viewed simply as the therapist's response to the family's demands. Usually, in psychoanalytically oriented therapies, transference is encouraged while countertransference is attempted to be minimized. This is why ORFT supports therapists going for their own analysis or therapy (Diekmann-Tapon, 1999). Further, therapists who have gone through their own analysis may be better able to be empathetic to the family (Jordan & Shaw, 2008).

There are two types of countertransference (Scharff, 1989; Scharff & Scharff, 2008). The first is **focused countertransference**, the therapist's reactions to a single family member. "'Focused countertransference' occurs in response to the focused transference, namely, feelings the patient transfers to the therapist as an object for intimate relating" (Scharff & Scharff, 2008, p. 178). For instance, the therapist may be triggered in their interactions with Fran, experiencing her as too overbearing, similar to their own mother, who was quite overbearing during their childhood.

The second type is **contextual countertransference**, which arises based on the therapist's internal issues of whether they can hold a space for this family and their expectations and needs of the therapist. Scharff and Scharff (2008) described this process:

> "Contextual countertransference" refers to the therapist's reaction to the patient's contextual transference, namely, the patient's response to the therapeutic environment, shown in attitudes about the frame of treatment, unconscious resistance in general, specific conscious feelings, and behavior toward the therapist as an object for providing a holding situation. (p. 178)

The Daniels family will likely come to therapy quite desperate, as Fran and Murray are viewing family therapy as the last-ditch effort before they put Pam into an inpatient eating disorders facility. The family's anxiety for the therapist to "do something" will need to be contained; otherwise, the therapist may be reactive rather than thoughtful. This is to prevent **parallel process**. Jordan and

Shaw (2008) noted, "Parallel process suggests that what is happening in key family member relationships is also happening between therapist and client (s) and needs to be addressed as part of the ongoing therapy" (pp. 219–220).

By remaining neutral, the therapist can attempt to avoid any countertransference that arises. Slipp (1988) compared the object relations family therapist's role to that of a boxing referee. They are not there to help one side win over the other. Rather, they try to allow the parties to engage one another while preventing them from throwing low blows or an all-out melee.

Goals of Object Relations Family Therapy

The goals of ORFT have many overlaps with other models of family therapy. Here, we cover those specific to object relations. Slipp (1988) stated, "Object relations family therapy attempts to deepen the self-awareness of each of the family members by analyzing their unconscious internalized object relations and verbally interpreting the genesis of their behavior" (p. 193). As explained here, ORFT holds to the notion of the unconscious and that people utilize defenses as a means of avoiding anxiety and protect their ego. Further, the unconscious represses past relational encounters (usually from primary caretakers from early childhood), yet they are played out in the current, with people who are usually different from those early caregivers. This is the process of transference. Based on this understanding of how intrapsychic and interpersonal dynamics overlap, the object relations therapist shares this information with the family through interpretations.

The goals of ORFT can be delineated even further, as Scharff and Scharff (1991) explained:

The general goals of object relations family therapy include the following:

1 The recognition and reworking of the defensive projective identifications that have previously been required in the family.
2 The treatment of the family's capacity to provide contextual holding for its members so that their attachment needs and conditions for growth can be met.
3 The overall reinstatement or construction of the series of centered holding relationships between each of its members to support their needs for attachment, individuation, and growth sufficient to allow each individual to "take it from there."
4 The return of the family to the overall developmental level appropriate to its tasks as set by its own preferences and by the needs of the family members.
5 The clarification of remaining individual needs in family members so that they can get them met with as much support as they need from the family. By this, we specifically include individual needs for psychotherapy, as well as more general needs for other growth endeavors. (p. 448)

During initial sessions, assessing the family's ability or willingness to tolerate emotional stress sets the pace at which therapy can progress. The therapist identifies that member and attends to their demonstration of anxiety, working to either stay beneath their emotional tolerance level or be prepared to "bring them back" if that level is exceeded. In addition to how this process provides the therapist with helpful information, it also provides a sense of agency and control for each family member, assures that they have some voice in the early minutes of the process, and assures each member of the therapist's attentiveness to their emotional safety. In this manner, it initiates sequential gentle changes and creates a positive holding environment for the family.

This is particularly important when working with families with an adolescent. Scharff and Scharff (1991) explained that:

> One of the jobs of the adolescent therapist is to help the adolescent get a "shell" around the penchant for externalizing the turmoil and inner struggle. This shell normally derives from the family's capacity to form a container for the child, and its deficiency in doing so during growth is what is reflected in sum in the adolescent's own, now internalized, difficulty in providing self-holding. (p. 337)

This can be seen in the Daniels family as Pam does not feel secure in her relationship with her parents, with one parent (Fran) being too overbearing and overwhelming, while the other parent (Murray) is extremely distant. The object relations family therapist will work with the family to help the parents provide a safer holding environment for Pam, one in which she feels secure and connected yet still independent. It would be interesting to know to what extent Pam sees her situation as related in some way to her relationships with parents and siblings, or if she adopts Fairbairn's moral defense, demeaning herself and blaming herself for her parents' anxiety over her situation (Celani, 2010). ORFT therapists tend to find that, when the IP is a child or adolescent, family therapy is indicated, since one of the best ways for an individual to heal is by healing the family system (Nilsson & Belfort, 2025).

Object relations therapists are more concerned with the assumptions of the model (the compass) than with specific or proscribed techniques (the actual map). As such, object relations therapists utilize elements of traditional and Jungian psychoanalysis, including free association, dream analysis, role playing, imagery and visualization, and artistic representations in the service of promoting awareness and resolution of projective identification. The selection of procedures depends on the general preference of the therapist and on their assumption as to what might best meet the client or family's communication style and needs (Klein, 1985; Lenormand, 2018).

As a psychoanalytic approach, object relations is not a brief model and requires time for assessment and therapy. To promote an overall family approach, the therapist can consider an initial timeline of the client's concerns

(Schauer, 1986). Of particular interest in the Daniels family, in addition to the overall understanding of Pam's attachment history, is her progression through the developmental milestones of adolescence. Per object relations, current problems seldom occur spontaneously but evolve out of developmental history (Fairbairn, 1954; Framo, 1976; Klein, 1946; Winnicott, 1969). Historical accounts are likely to vary, so therapists should be prepared to honor the intent of each account while attempting to arrive at as clear an understanding as possible of the actual timeline.

During therapy, the therapist sets the stage for the clients to have a corrective emotional experience with various family members (Jordan & Shaw, 2008). By focusing on past family of origin issues, family members are able to decrease the intensity of their internalized objects. This provides them with the opportunity to engage one another differently in the present. During family therapy or when it ends, it may be advantageous for one or more members to also engage in individual therapy (Slipp, 1993).

ORFT therapists might also establish a therapeutic contract with the family that determines the goals and rules of therapy. For example, Slipp (1993) described:

> Members should be encouraged to try to avoid premature closure and to listen to others' opinions, rather than judging, condemning, or blaming, especially if they disagree; to try to communicate as openly and honestly as they can; to try to be helpful to one another; not to interrupt or speak for one another; and, whenever possible, to speak directly to the individual they are talking about. One can propose a rule that issues brought up during the session not be used as ammunition against one another after the session. (pp. 203–204)

Thus, when working with the Daniels family, the therapist will first attempt to develop a strong therapeutic alliance so that there is a strong holding environment for the difficult work of exploring how the past is showing up in the current.

Case Transcript

All five members of the Daniels family were asked to come to the first session, since having the adults as well as children of all ages there provides a fuller understanding of the family (Scharff, 2004).

Therapist: Thank you all for coming together today. First sessions are about getting to know not just what's been happening outwardly but also the emotional world of this family. Each of you has a perspective that matters here.

Intervention: The therapist begins the session by establishing a holding environment. By explicitly acknowledging that every family member's perspective is important, the therapist is creating a sense of safety and containment. This introduction serves to communicate that the session is a space where feelings can be expressed without judgment, which is crucial for families in which emotional expression has historically been constrained or unsafe.

Fran: We're overwhelmed. We're desperate for help.

Therapist: It sounds like this fear has been living with all of you for some time.

Intervention: Here, the therapist is containing Fran's emotional intensity by reflecting it back in a calm and validating way. This intervention communicates understanding and empathy, while also externalizing the fear as something the family shares rather than something that resides solely in Fran or in one child. This helps reduce shame and validates the emotional experience of the family as a whole.

Murray: I wouldn't say desperate. Let's not exaggerate.

Therapist: I notice, Murray, you're working to keep the emotional intensity manageable for yourself and everyone else. It's as if worry feels too big, so you try to shrink it.

Intervention: The therapist noted the internalization of part-objects by the parents and the multigenerational transmission of the same with their children. That there is a possible arrestation of both parents in the "paranoid/schizoid" position. In other words, each parent experiences projective identification of their children, interpreting questions, emotions, or reactions (which children are likely to demonstrate) as criticism or rejection and splitting their children's responses and characteristics into categories of "good" or "bad." To protect from "bad" responses, they carefully structure and limit their emotional interactions as a means of avoidance. The therapist is gently interpreting Murray's defensive minimization. By naming the function of his behavior as a protective response to overwhelming emotions, the therapist reduces the likelihood that Murray feels criticized or blamed. This helps the family recognize patterns of defense, and it also begins to make unconscious relational dynamics explicit.

(Murray shifts slightly, showing subtle acknowledgment of the therapist's observation.)

Therapist: Pam, when you hear your mother say she's overwhelmed and your father say it's not that bad, what stirs inside?

Intervention: The therapist invites Pam to access her internal experience in relation to each parent. This brings attention to her internal object world and to the splitting she may perceive between her parents' responses. By encouraging Pam to articulate her feelings, the therapist also creates a safe space for emotional expression and helps her recognize the relational dynamics in real time.

Pam: I feel like I'm stuck between them… and that everything is somehow my fault.

Fran: You're not at fault! That's not fair.

Therapist: Fran, I hear your protectiveness. And Pam, I also hear a part of you that feels you're carrying the family's distress. That part of you deserves our attention.

Intervention: The therapist validates both Fran's protective impulse and Pam's sense of over-responsibility. By acknowledging both perspectives, the therapist reduces potential defensiveness while also highlighting Pam's role as the identified patient and emotional container of the family. This helps the family members become conscious of the unspoken roles they have adopted and sets the stage for later interpretations of internal object dynamics.

Therapist: George, when Pam says she feels like the cause of everyone's stress, what's that like for you to hear?

Intervention: Inviting George into the conversation expands the emotional field to include siblings and prevents Pam from remaining the sole focus of family tension. This encourages him to reflect on his internal experience, which may help him recognize his own defensive patterns and increase his emotional awareness.

George: I just… wish things could go back to normal. Before all this.

Therapist: There's a longing for an earlier family—an idealized version that felt safer.

Intervention: The therapist interprets George's statement as a reflection of his attachment to an idealized past internal object. This helps the family understand that longing for a different time is a normal emotional reaction and also begins to make explicit the internalized relational templates that influence current interactions.

George: I don't want to talk about it too much. It just makes things worse.

Therapist: I hear that you're trying not to stir anything up. Sometimes resistance comes from fear—fear that speaking might destabilize things.

Intervention: The therapist identifies George's withdrawal as a defensive maneuver. By naming the underlying fear rather than criticizing his behavior, the therapist reduces potential shame and opens a pathway for discussing the function of his resistance. This helps the family observe the protective patterns each member employs when emotions become intense.

(George looks down, showing acknowledgment of the observation.)

Therapist: Oliver, what do you notice when the family gets tense?
Oliver: It feels like… everyone's holding their breath.
Murray: That seems a little dramatic.
Therapist: Murray, I hear you pulling away from intensity again. And Oliver, I hear your sense that the whole family becomes tight and still.

Intervention: The therapist names both Murray's avoidance and Oliver's perception simultaneously. By reflecting these experiences without judgment, the therapist creates a containing environment that validates multiple viewpoints and also highlights patterns of splitting and avoidance in the family. It makes the unconscious enactments visible for later exploration.

Fran: We're not frozen. We're just tired of worrying.
Therapist: Worry can be exhausting. Sometimes, when worry gets too heavy, families move into a kind of emotional holding pattern without meaning to.

Intervention: Here, the therapist normalizes the family's defensive pattern and frames it as an adaptive response to overwhelming emotions rather than as a failure. This reduces defensiveness and encourages curiosity about the functional role of worry in the family system.

Fran: It feels like you're saying we're doing something wrong.
Therapist: Not wrong—human. Defenses are survival strategies.

Intervention: The therapist explicitly reduces shame by reframing the family's defensive behaviors as understandable and human. This helps the family feel safer to explore their internal experiences without fear of blame.

Therapist: Murray, earlier, when emotions rose, you leaned back. What happens inside for you in those moments?
Murray: I just don't think getting emotional helps anything.
Therapist: For you, rationality seems safer than emotion. That's a defense that probably protected you in difficult earlier experiences.

Intervention: The therapist interprets Murray's distancing as a protective measure that developed in response to past relational dynamics. By linking current behavior to past adaptive strategies, the therapist helps Murray understand his reactions without judgment and encourages him to observe the underlying emotions that the defense is shielding.

Murray: I'm not defending. I'm being practical.
Therapist: Practicality is your way of managing something inside that feels otherwise too much.

Intervention: This interpretation frames resistance as an adaptive strategy rather than defiance. It allows Murray to recognize his coping mechanism as functional and understandable, which reduces the likelihood of reactive defensiveness and helps integrate awareness of internal object dynamics.

(Pam begins to cry quietly. Fran leans in, Murray stiffens, George looks away, and Oliver hunches inward.)

Therapist: Let's slow this down. Pam is becoming emotional, and everyone else's bodies are tightening. What's happening inside each of you right now?

Intervention: The therapist highlights the live enactment of internal objects in the family system. By naming bodily and emotional reactions as they occur, the therapist creates awareness of projective identifications and unconscious defensive patterns.

Fran: Pam, honey, don't cry—please don't cry.
Therapist: Fran, those tears feel dangerous to you. What threatens you about Pam's sadness?

Intervention: The therapist explores Fran's immediate reaction as a window into her internalized persecutory object. This encourages reflection on unconscious fears that shape defensive behavior and reduces the likelihood that Fran's reaction will be interpreted as criticism.

Fran: It reminds me of when things were really bad. I'm afraid we're going back there.
Therapist: So Pam's sadness activates an old internal fear—a persecutory feeling of danger.

Intervention: This interpretation links Fran's defensive urgency to earlier relational experiences, highlighting the ways in which internal objects influence current behaviors.

Therapist: I'm noticing a pattern: Fran, you hold the emotional panic; Murray, you hold the calm. Together it's as if the fear is split between you, and Pam is caught between these two internal poles.

Intervention: The therapist interprets parental splitting to make explicit the unconscious distribution of affective roles in the family. This helps the family understand relational dynamics that contribute to Pam's symptom expression. To this point, the therapist has been concerned that Pam has accepted Fairbairn's "moral defense" (Celani, 2010), believing that her difficulties are completely her fault, and her parent's inability to help her were because she is a "lost cause" thereby freeing her parents from her judgment of them and preserving what limited attachment she has with both of them. To help all members gain some insight about the larger picture of attachment, introjection of part-objects and emotional maturity past Klein's description of the paranoid/schizoid position (1946), the therapist has begun more direct inquiry about intergenerational processes per Framo (1976, 1992). Intergenerational inquiry will assist the parents in recognizing what was needed in their own development and applying that understanding to what might be needed now in their relationships with their children. The therapist is providing an open discussion in which they will spread out the family map to provide an emotional holding environment, especially for Pam. The goal is for the parents to come to terms with understanding and accepting "good enough" parenting and demonstrating that understanding with their children and in their relationships with each other. In accepting her understanding of her parents' good enough interactions, Pam might then be better able to reconcile her part-object internalization of a good/bad dichotomy of self and come to terms with how to more graciously address her sense of limitations and shortcomings.

Therapist: George, what's happening for you right now?
George: Nothing. I'm just annoyed. Crying doesn't help.
Therapist: Annoyance can be a shield for feelings that feel too vulnerable—like fear.

Intervention: The therapist reframes George's apparent irritation as a defensive mechanism, allowing him to observe underlying emotions without shame and reducing resistance to emotional exploration.

George: I'm not afraid.
Therapist: Part of you isn't. Another part may be.

Intervention: The therapist introduces the concept of multiple self-states and normalizes internal conflict. It helps George recognize that defensive behaviors may mask more vulnerable feelings.

Therapist: Oliver?
Oliver: It feels like she's going away when she cries.
Therapist: That distance feels scary.

Intervention: The therapist names Oliver's attachment-based fear and validates his emotional perception. By doing so, the therapist acknowledges Oliver's internal object experience and promotes reflective capacity.

Therapist: Pam, it seems you've come to carry the family's pain for them—like the emotion-keeper. That's a heavy internal role.
Pam: It does feel that way…
Fran: She's always been strong.
Therapist: Strength doesn't mean carrying everything alone. Sometimes being 'strong' is a defense against showing need.

Intervention: The therapist interprets Pam's false-self adaptation and the internalized caretaker object, helping the family recognize how roles maintain the status quo while limiting emotional expression. The therapist is introducing the concept that Pam might be unconsciously taking care of her mother (the "good-self" part-object) by continuing to need assistance for her "bad self" part-object. Ironically, demonstrating sufficient recovery to leave home might threaten her attachment to her mother.

Therapist: There's another thing I notice. When Pam shows vulnerability, Fran rushes in, and Murray pulls back. Both responses make true closeness hard. This is a kind of resistance—born from fear, not lack of love.

Intervention: This interpretation identifies resistance to intimacy and helps the family see that defensive behaviors serve a protective function rather than expressing rejection or indifference.

Therapist: George and Oliver, when you go quiet or shrink back, it seems like you've learned there's no room for your feelings. Like an internal message says, 'Stay small to keep the peace.'

Intervention: The therapist addresses the internalized invisibility of siblings and interprets defensive withdrawal as an adaptive response to relational constraints.

Therapist: Pam, you've carried the family's fear for a long time. That fear doesn't belong to you alone. Little by little, we'll help each person carry what's theirs.

Intervention: The therapist restores boundaries and returns projected emotions to their rightful owners, facilitating the redistribution of emotional responsibility within the family.

Therapist: Today, we saw how each of you protects yourselves: Pam carries the distress, Fran rushes to prevent collapse, Murray minimizes to avoid overwhelm, George withdraws to avoid conflict, and Oliver shrinks to stay safe. These defenses make sense—they come from old internal patterns.

Intervention: The therapist integrates observations into a coherent narrative, which normalizes defensive behaviors, reduces shame, and provides a framework for understanding internal object relations within the family.

Therapist: Next time, we'll explore how these patterns began and how we can shift them so everyone has room for their own feelings.

Intervention: The therapist consolidates the session, providing a holding function, and establishing a clear direction for ongoing therapy.

A note about countertransference: During the session, the therapist noticed strong emotional responses arising within themselves that mirrored the dynamics in the family. They experienced a mix of protectiveness toward Pam, frustration at the defensiveness of Murray and George, and sadness at the intensity of Fran's worry. At times, the therapist felt pulled to intervene more actively to manage the anxiety in the room, reflecting their own discomfort with emotional chaos. They also became aware of a desire to rescue or soothe Pam, which mirrors the family's pattern of over-relying on her emotional strength, highlighting the therapist's need to remain attentive to professional boundaries. Recognizing these feelings allowed the therapist to monitor their responses carefully and use them as a tool for understanding the internal object projections and defenses occurring in the family, rather than acting on them. By observing their countertransference, the therapist was able to maintain a holding environment, contain the emotional intensity, and provide interpretations in a manner that remained empathic but neutral, ensuring that their reactions supported the therapeutic process rather than introducing bias or over-identification.

Given that ORFT is typically not a brief therapy, and usually not one done in a single session, here are some ideas about how therapy with the Daniels family might play out. In subsequent sessions, the therapist invited each family member to freely discuss their experiences individually and with each other over the past several years. As the sessions progressed, therapy consisted of relevant symbolic work, accumulation of family stories, history, and genograms, including those of Fran and Murray.

After several sessions addressing the family's experiences in open discussion, a multigenerational approach was implemented. Per Framo (1976, 1992), the therapist provided information about the structure of three generational genograms and questions that assisted in their construction. The therapist explained the purpose of the procedure in terms of awareness and improving the family members' relationships with each other. Pam conducted a genogram interview with both of her parents during a two-hour session while the therapist diagramed the information from the interviews.

In addition to how the genogram interviews provide important multigenerational information, they repositioned Pam in the family—giving her the voice that she needed to communicate effectively and more emotionally with her parents. As her brothers looked on and participated during this session, they obtained new information and experienced a more direct emotional connection with Pam. This connection involved a combination of anger/irritation with Pam for breaking the rules of the family, but also involved some empathy for her experience and the experiences of both of their parents in their respective families of origin. The next several sessions addressed further development and family interpretations of the genograms.

In therapy, Pam expressed that she needed to be heard and recognized by her family. Finding her voice and expressing her hurt over her parents' relationships with her suggested steps toward resolving the introjection of part-objects, moving past the limitations of her false self (Winnicott, 1969) and viewing herself and her parents in a more balanced manner. Her mother's acceptance of the content and emotion of Pam's expression and her acknowledgment that she was not present emotionally for Pam at critical times, but stating obvious concern now for Pam's feelings, suggested a movement toward Winnicott's descriptions of the "good enough" mother (1969). As suggested by Winnicott (1969), a good enough mother will always do a better job than a perfect mother, meaning that a "perfect mother" is more concerned about activities, duties, and functions than emotional processes. As Pam experienced her mother's limitations balanced with her caring abilities, she began to internalize or introject that perception into her own sense of self, gradually ameliorating the need for her use of the moral defense (Celani, 2010) or reliance on a false self (Winnicott, 1969).

The Therapeutic Story

The family came to therapy with a story of a daughter who is out of control; not with acting out behaviors (e.g., drugs, sex, or fighting) but rather internalizing behaviors in the form of isolation and anorexia. The parents viewed themselves as being good parents with little role in the symptoms of their child. At the end of therapy, many changes to this story occurred.

1 The therapist shifts the focus from Pam as the identified patient to the family's shared emotional experience, emphasizing that the distress lives in the system rather than in one person.
2 The therapist identifies and normalizes defensive patterns in parents and siblings (minimizing, withdrawing, rushing in) as protective strategies shaped by past experiences, rather than signs of blameworthy behavior.
3 The therapist invites each family member to explore their internal reactions, distributing emotional meaning across the system and reducing Pam's burden of responsibility.
4 By naming live emotional enactments in the room, the therapist highlights relational patterns in real time, showing how anxiety, avoidance, and fear circulate among family members.
5 The therapist reframes Pam's symptoms and emotional expressions as responses to family dynamics—such as carrying others' fear or adopting a false self—rather than as purely individual pathology.
6 The therapist helps the family recognize how splitting, projective identification, and internal object relations shape their interactions, shifting the narrative from symptom management to emotional understanding.
7 The therapist integrates these observations into a coherent story about how each member copes with fear and overwhelm, setting the stage for future work on how these patterns developed and how they can change.

References

Berne, E. (1964). *Games people play: The psychology of human relationships*. Balantine Books.

Bitter, J. R. (2014). *Theory and practice of family therapy and counseling* (2nd ed). Brooks/Cole.

Bowlby, J. (1958). The nature of the child's tie to his mother. *International Journal of Psycho-Analysis, 39*, 350–373.

Bowlby, J. (1960). Separation anxiety. *International Journal of Psycho-Analysis, 41*, 89–113.

Cassullo, G. (2014). Splitting in the history of psychoanalysis: From Janet and Freud to Fairbairn, passing through Ferenczi and Suttie. In G. S. Clarke & D. E. Scharff (Eds.), *Fairbairn and the object relations tradition*, (pp. 49–58). Taylor & Francis Group.

Celani, D. (2010). *Fairbairn's object relations theory in the clinical setting*. Columbia University Press.

Cortina, M. (2020). Harry Stack Sullivan and interpersonal theory: A flawed genius. *Psychiatry, 83*, 103–109.

Diekmann-Tapon, D. (1999). Case report: Object relations family therapy as a model for genetic counseling. *Journal of Genetic Counseling, 8*(4), 235–246.

Fairbairn, W. R. D. (1954). *An object-relations theory of the personality*. Basic Books.

Fairbairn, W. R. D. (1958). On the nature and aims of psycho-analytical treatment. *International Journal of Psychoanalysis, 39*(5): 374–385. In: D. E. Scharff & E. F. Birtles (Eds.), (1994), *From instinct to self: Selected papers of W. R. D. Fairbairn, Volume I: Clinical and theoretical papers* (pp. 74–92). Jason Aronson.

Fairbairn, W. R. D. (1986). *Psychoanalytic studies of the personality*. Routledge & Kegan Paul.
Ferenczi, Sándor (1949) [1932]. Confusion of the tongues between the adults and the child (The language of tenderness and of passion). *International Journal of Psycho-Analysis*, *30*(4), 225–230.
Framo, J. L. (1976). Family of origin as a therapeutic resource for adults in marital and family therapy: You can and should go home again. *Family Process 15*, 193–210.
Framo, J. L. (1992). *Family-of-origin therapy: An intergenerational approach*. Taylor & Francis Group.
Gaarder, K. R. (2006). Commentary on "Transcription of fragments of lectures in 1948 by Harry Stack Sullivan": The life and legacy of Harry Stack Sullivan. *Psychiatry*, *69*(2), 107–109.
Jordan, K., & Shaw, R. (2008). Object relations theory in family therapy. In K. Jordan (Ed.). *The quick theory reference guide: A resource for expert and novice mental health professionals: A resource of expert and novice mental health professionals* (pp. 209–225). Nova Sciences Publishers, Inc.
Klein M. (1946). Notes on some schizoid mechanisms. *International Journal of Psycho-Analysis 27*(Pt 3–4), 99–110.
Klein, M. (1985). The psycho-analytic play technique: Its history and significance, In P. Heimann, M. Klein, & R. Money-Kyrle (Eds.), *New directions in psychoanalysis* (pp. 14–32). Karnac Books.
Knafo, D. S. (2010). The O.R.T. (the Object Relations Technique): A Reintroduction. *Psychoanalytic psychology*, *27*(2), 182–189.
Lenormand, M. (2018). Winnicott's theory of playing: A reconsideration. *International Journal of Psychoanalysis*, *99*(1), 82–102.
Nilsson, M., & Belfort, E. (2025). Psychodynamic influences on contemporary family therapy. *Child and Adolescent Psychiatric Clinics of North America*, *34*(3), 435–443.
Pate, G. A. (2025). *Counselor training manual*. Sundown Ranch, Inc.
Phillipson, H. (1955). *The object relations technique (plates and manual)*. Tavistock.
Scharff, J. S. (1989). Object relations theory and its application to family therapy. In J. S. Scharff (Ed.). *The foundations of object relations family therapy* (pp. 11–22). Jason Aronson Inc.
Scharff, J. S. (2004). Play and very young children in object relations family therapy. *International Journal of Applied Psychoanalytic Studies*, *1*(3), 259–268.
Scharff, D. E., & Scharff, J. S. (1987). *Object relations family therapy*. Jason Aronson Inc.
Scharff, D. E., & Scharff, J. S. (1991). *Object relations family therapy*. Jason Aronson Inc.
Scharff, J. S., & Scharff, D. E. (1992). *The primer of object relations therapy*. Jason Aronson.
Scharff, J. S., & D. E. Scharff (2008). Object relations couple therapy. In A. S. Gurman (Ed.). *Clinical handbook of couple therapy* (4th ed.) (pp. 167–195). The Guilford Press.
Schauer, A. H. (1986). Object relations theory: A dialogue with Donald B. Rinsley. *Journal of Counseling and Development*, *65*, 35–39.
Shapiro, R. L. (1998). Family dynamics and object relations theory: An analytic, group-interpretive approach to family therapy. In J. S. Scharff (Ed.). *The foundations of object relations family therapy* (pp. 225–245). Jason Aronson Inc.
Slipp, S. (1988). *The technique and practice of object relations family therapy*. Jason Aronson Inc.
Slipp, S. (1993). *Object relations: A dynamic bridge between individual and family therapy*. Jason Aronson Inc.

Soreanu, R. (2018). The psychic life of fragments: splitting from Ferenczi to Klein. *The American Journal of Psychoanalysis*, *78*, (421–444).
Sullivan, H. S. (1953). *The interpersonal theory of psychiatry*. Norton.
Sussal, C. M. (1992). Object relations family therapy as a model for practice. *Clinical Social Work Journal*, *20*(3), 313–321.
Winnicott, D. W. (1965). Ego distortion in terms of true and false self. In M. Khan (Ed.), *The maturational processes and the facilitating environment* (pp. 140–152). Hogarth Press and the Institute of Psycho-Analysis.
Winnicott D. W. (1969). The use of an object. *International Journal of Psycho-Analysis*, *50*, 711–716.

7 Adlerian Family Therapy

Len Sperry, Marina Bluvshtein, and Jon Sperry

In 1921, Alfred Adler introduced a systemic perspective that shifted the focus of psychotherapy from an individual's internal drives to their social environment and relationships. Adler's work laid the groundwork for the modern, systemic view of family dynamics and is credited with influencing family therapy pioneers in the mid-20th century like Minuchin, Bowen, Satir, and Dreikurs (Bitter & Carlson, 2017). While several excellent publications describe the overall practice of Adlerian Family Therapy (Devlin et al., 2024; Dreikurs, 1946, 1948; Dreikurs et al., 1959; Grunwald & McAbee, 1999), this chapter focuses primarily on one component of this practice: case conceptualization. It begins by defining case conceptualization and Adlerian case conceptualization. Then it analyzes the Daniels family from the Adlerian case conceptualization perspective in terms of the therapeutic story they bring to family therapy. Finally, it illustrates the Adlerian case conceptualization perspective in a transcription of how the first session with the Daniels might unfold from an Adlerian perspective.

Basically, a case conceptualization is a method for understanding and explaining a client's presenting issues and for planning and guiding the therapy process to increase the likelihood of achieving treatment goals (Sperry & Sperry, 2020). "Family case conceptualizations are case conceptualizations that incorporate family or systemic dynamics. They are essential in achieving positive changes in couple and family dynamics" (Sperry & Sperry, 2022, p. 128). Clinically useful case conceptualizations "focus on the unique contexts, needs, and resources of the individual members of couples or families and the system as a whole" (Bitter, 2025, p. 485). From the Adlerian perspective, these dynamics include family constellation, birth order, early recollections (ERs), lifestyle, and tasks of life.

Terms

Lifestyle refers to one's beliefs and convictions about belonging and finding a place in the world.

DOI: 10.4324/9781003668510-7

Family constellation refers to the early developmental influences on an individual, including parents, siblings, peers, neighbors, and other key individuals like teachers.

Birth order refers to the unique psychological position a child occupies in a family, which shapes their personality and lifestyle.

ERs are *specific memories associated with childhood but remembered as vividly as though they* were happening in the present. They are understood to be projections of the present-day self onto the past.

Life tasks are the main challenges—love, work, and friendship—that life presents to all individuals.

The Therapeutic Story of Problem Formation

Lifestyle

The core of Adlerian understanding of problem formation and its dynamic maintenance is lifestyle. Lifestyle is a pattern of how an individual views themselves, others, and the world, how all of that systemically operates, and how an individual finds their place in that world (Adler, 1931; Ansbacher & Ansbacher, 1956). The lifestyle is formed very early in one's life as a result of observations and trial and error in achieving what the person wants most—a sense of belonging, having a place, a feeling of being the one with life, and mastery in life (Adler, 1930). Once developed, the lifestyle and its constituent strategies carry an individual through both ordinary life events, normative stressful transitions (such as starting a school or becoming an empty nester), and the non-normative stresses (such as losing a child to suicide or living in a war zone). Lifestyle is a pattern of life as it is lived by an individual in their social field and throughout the lifespan, and it helps an individual to carry out life tasks (love/intimacy, occupation, fellowship/friendship) (Ansbacher & Ansbacher, 1956; Dreikurs, 1950). It is only through a significant personal crisis or effective therapy that lifestyle can change. Adlerian therapists distinguish several major windows into lifestyle, including family constellation, ERs, and dreams, among the most significant ones.

The following sections will focus on the constituent parts of lifestyle, their formation, interrelationships, impact on individual emotional health, and the health of a family, as well as how lifestyle works in therapeutic relationships. The Daniels family will serve as an example in these discussions.

Current distress in the Daniels family exemplifies this discussion. In the family, a system disruption takes place on levels greater than those visible to the naked eye. We see traditional continuity and the crisis of discontinuity across democratic demarcation lines. We observe autocratic parenting, disguised as a normal and traditional division of roles. Both Pam and, likely, her mother are not valued by Murray, a breadwinner and apparently the decision-maker (including the decision not to be involved in Pam's parenting). The Daniels family is built hierarchically. The benevolent autocracy in the Daniels family is likely reinforced by multigenerational, never-challenged, rigid gender and generational roles.

Family Constellation

As previously noted, family constellation refers to the early developmental influences on an individual interacting with parents, siblings, peers, neighbors, and other key individuals like teachers (Ansbacher & Ansbacher, 1956; Sicher, 1991). Adlerian family therapists tend to focus on childhood situations, viewing the in-depth exploration of these dynamics as a key to understanding a developing personality, its strengths and challenges, and the strategies a person employs to achieve success and overcome challenges (Adler, 1964b; Ansbacher & Ansbacher, 1956; Shifron, 2020). By observing immediate family members as they deal with life, trying the same or different strategies, and making mistakes, a child learns to navigate life. That is how the lifestyle is formed within the first four to five years of life. Parents' and other adults' attitudes toward a child and the resulting treatment of each child play a key role here. Among different types of attitudes, Adler wrote about unloved children and favorite children, "the danger of favoritism can hardly be overdramatized. Almost every discouragement in childhood springs from the feeling that someone else is preferred" (Ansbacher & Ansbacher, 1956, p. 376).

In the Daniels family, we see Pam, especially in her relationship with her father, as an unloved child. Although Pam and her family are somewhat connected, this connection seems unstable and fractured, as she does not have active and cooperative relationships with her father or brothers. Pam's early childhood training for cooperation was likely deficient, and the deficiency was not visible until recently. Now Pam is 17 and facing a life transition (high school), when even the healthiest lifestyle strategies would be tested. Pam's lifestyle strengths are clearly inadequate to what is needed for successful overcoming of even known developmental challenges (high school, adolescence). Adlerian therapists would question not only the purposefulness of Pam's symptoms, but the purposefulness of Fran's parenting helplessness and concerns and confusion.

The central question related to Fran would be: what might Fran have to deal with, and possibly face imperfection or failure, if Pam were healthy? Fran would likely have to, developmentally, go back to when she was 18–19, finish her education, and pursue the career she dreamed of. Does she feel ready and courageous for that? If discouraged, would she, subconsciously, benefit from Pam's sickness, keeping her (Fran) from having to revisit her earlier occupational dreams and changing the status quo in her family arrangement?

An Adlerian family therapist would likely see in the Daniels a very discouraged family system, with two discouraged parents and a discouraged oldest child. The parents dealt with discouragement by adhering to century-old, rigid roles. The rigidity of multigenerational roles and the contagious discouragement likely reached their saturation point in Pam, who, due to her natural sensitivity and attunement to the arts and music, threw a wrench into the machinery of a "normal family." An Adlerian family therapist will engage the family in educating it (calling on Fran's longtime dreams of becoming a teacher) and repairing it (appealing to Murray's expertise).

Birth Order

Adlerians see family constellation as not a cause of lifestyle development, but a social field in which the lifestyle is developed (Sicher, 1991). From it, and from the earlier exercises with it and interactions within it, "a child first draws conclusions about life, about his/her own worth as compared to others, and his/her feelings about belonging or not belonging" (Grunwald & McAbee, 1999, p. 61).

Within the constellation, we see the child's siblings (whether alive or not), parents, and other adults. It is also important to inquire about miscarriages, stillbirths, and children who died in infancy. In many traditional families, grandparents are not only mentioned as extended family or historical figures, but also as active participants in the unique social sphere of the family.

Adlerian therapists consider the firstborns as potentially having a unique psychological situation (Grunwald & McAbee, 1999; Sicher, 1991; Seidler, 1930). For some time, they are the only children, and then later they are dethroned by the next child. The greater the distance between siblings, the greater the chance that the oldest child meets the next sibling with a similar established lifestyle. The firstborn child meets the next one more painfully because they have never had the experience of cooperating with somebody else. The therapy may focus on the strengths of firstborns, which include their inclination to protect others, help the helpless, be responsible, and organize. There are other considerations that an Adlerian family therapist will take into account, such as family values related to education, religion, child raising, right and wrong (Bitter, 2025).

Psychologically, Pam can be considered both the oldest child (with her two brothers following her) and the only child (as the only girl born into the family, adhering to traditional values). She is likely seen as less worthy by her father's side of the family. Her becoming interested in arts and music—fluid, unstructured, not "useful" interests, and foreign to the family—could have reinforced that attitude. As a psychologically only child (only girl), she may occupy one of the two positions related to her family values—to embrace these values or to fight them (Bitter, 2025). She might have tried to seek connection through emotional openness, but when this effort went unrecognized—particularly given Murray's disregard for her artistic sensibilities—she instead chose to assert herself through conflict. Paradoxically, she achieves a form of success in this struggle by drawing her family together in therapy, prompting them to focus their concern and care on her. In that "sport," she is her father's daughter.

Once at school, assuming she started at the age of 5, Pam was unlikely to have an opportunity for exclusive attention, and, in the absence of good parenting, Pam may have experienced being dethroned in three waves—once by Oliver, then by having two closely related boys taking the family attention, and then by having to blend in the entire class of peers.

The birth order of the parents is quite revealing in the Daniels family. Like her daughter, Fran was also the firstborn, with the same age difference between her and the next sibling, and they were both raised by traditional parents. Fran's life story is marked by what we may call empathy deficiency. She and her mother, Nancy, seem to have a difficult time recognizing, naming, and experiencing complicated feelings. Not being good at dealing with feelings and with Pam being only two at the time Oliver dethroned her, Fran would have, using Dreikurs's language, "no way to explain this to the child; the only way to compensate for loss is to give the child extra attention" (Dreikurs & Grey, 1970, p. 11). With no chance of winning her father's attention, Pam needed to find ways to make her presence known and win her mother's attention. We may see Pam being quite powerful in fighting and winning her mother's exclusive love—and if healthy love is unattainable, then making her mother worry would be the second-best choice.

Murray is the only child. As the only child, he may be more traditionally oriented and more ambitious, with goal posts set against adults rather than peers. Murray is the only child, as well as a male, in a traditional family. Being competitive and prideful, Murray nevertheless cannot win Pam.

The lonelier Pam feels, the more extreme her strike against her "normal family" might be. Contrary to the expectations of the girls in "good" traditional families, she does not do well at school anymore. Having lost significant weight, she is no longer a "neat" girl, and she "misbehaves" in the only way she knows how—by starving herself. She is not supposed to be heard, and she is not heard. She is seen, and paradoxically, the less of her body that is seen, the more she is seen. So, we may understand her as a perfect example of a child who is (unseeingly) seen but not heard. Her "abnormal" scream in this normal family can hardly be louder.

Early Recollections (ERs)

ERs are a projective technique used to determine a client's self-view, view of others, worldview, and their overall strategy in dealing with others and life's challenges (Ansbacher & Ansbacher, 1956; Shifron, 2020). ERs also reflect the client's level of social interest, and their lifestyle convictions. This method can be utilized in family therapy as it can assist family members to better understand each other and their collective family stories, which often include other family members in such recollections.

ERs also suggest the individual's basic movement in relation to others. There are four such types of movement. They are movement toward, movement against, movement away from, and ambivalent movement, which can be toward-against or toward-away from (Sperry & Sperry, 2022). These basic types of movement are suggestive of basic personality styles or personality disorders. For example, movement toward suggests the Histrionic Personality or Dependent Personality, while movement toward and against is suggestive of the Obsessive-Compulsive Personality or the Passive Aggressive Personality (Sperry & Sperry, 2022). In working with the Daniels, Adlerian family therapists would see personality-styled movement of family members as underlying individual strengths and challenges, patterned interpersonal dynamics, expressions of lifestyle strategies in times of crises, as well as marking the risks of therapeutic impasses.

Tasks of Life

Adlerians identify three life tasks (or life challenges) that each person faces and interrelates holistically: the task of intimacy, the task of occupation, and the task of friendship/fellowship (Ansbacher & Ansbacher, 1956). These three are the only unavoidable ones among all the rest of the possible life tasks one can imagine. Holistically, success on each task cannot be without success on the other two. The tasks carry two distinctive features: all three are necessary for the continuity of humanity, and all three require at least one other human being to join and collaborate (Ansbacher, 2011; Ansbacher & Ansbacher, 1956). Lifestyle strategies are formed and are traceable in each of these tasks.

Strauch and Erez (2009) linked anorexia to "restrictive personality," pointing to a common feature of "feeling inferior and berating oneself" (p. 204). "Restriction" describes and explains the way people with Anorexia Nervosa react to life challenges. Control and restrictions allow the child to feel safe. Other restrictions would follow, such as in the "work, social, and love tasks" (Strauch & Erez, 2009, p. 205), with avoidance and obsessive thoughts as prominent features. Additional features are perfectionism, criticism, self-doubt, and doubts about others, maintaining a restricted engagement with all three life tasks.

Pam and her parents have challenges with life tasks. Pam, Fran, and Murray struggle to form intimate bonds within their family. Murray appears to be successful at work, likely has friends, and is mentoring and coaching his sons in sports. However, none of his undeniable tangible assets would explain his decision not to partner with Fran in supporting Pam. Pam's illness may be too challenging for Murray to understand, and her body weight numbers may not seem like a winnable fix for him. So, he resorts to winnable sports. Fran, on the other hand, with having had some teaching training, may likely feel a failure with her only "student," Pam, who is failing at school and at home. Pam cannot succeed occupationally (as a student). We do not know much about her friends, but we can suspect that friendship and intimacy tasks often evolving in friends' circles are both a challenge for her now, given that teens' social life often involves food. Not feeling useful, friendly, and intimately connected in her family, she must feel very discouraged.

Inferiority Feeling and Compensation: Anorexia as Organ Jargon

Adlerian therapists view **inferiority feelings** as a starting point for overcoming and promoting healthy development, with cooperative compensatory activities as an integral part of everyday life. Adler wrote, "To be human means to feel inferior" (Ansbacher & Ansbacher, 1956, p. 116). Occasionally, some people overdose on compensation and begin to overcompensate, usually at a heavy neurotic price. Both normal compensation and neurotic overcompensation always occur in a relational context. Whether to compensate or to overcompensate, we really need others. Feelings of being not good enough, less than, worse than, not as good as—all breed insecurities and relational problems, in couples, in parenting teams, in dyadic and other relational groupings.

Adlerians see symptoms as strategies developing to solve the overdose on feelings of inferiority and providing a paradoxically safe excuse from healthy, albeit risky, compensation and courageous movement in the direction of self-betterment. Symptoms are seen as an "attempt at compensation" (Ansbacher & Ansbacher, 1956, p. 282). The stronger the insecurities a child experiences about their "future and success in life," the stronger this compensation is, and the more we will see how a child would detour around the problems of life (Ansbacher & Ansbacher, 1956). Other lifestyle characteristics observable in individuals with eating disorders are self-criticalness, preoccupation with self-image, low stress tolerance threshold, and high anxiety.

It is likely that Pam's lifestyle, steeped in discouragement, rigid gender and age roles, prepared her to see normative transitions in life (such as starting high school and now preparing to enter adulthood) as threatening and to see herself as incapable of dealing with changes. Through interviews and observations, an Adlerian therapist will develop hunches about the goals of Pam's misbehavior (attention, power, revenge, or display of inadequacy) and what maintains that behavior. We will likely see how, back in her earlier childhood, she was able to find a place in a socially useful way until her strategy stopped working and she lost confidence in her ability to find a different, more adaptive way. At that time, as a discouraged teen, she tried the only method she could imagine at her disposal—the disordered eating.

It could be that Pam has a tall order of conditions for feeling belonging, safe, and significant, for viewing self as the whole with the world. She would need not just love, but continuous assurances of love by both parents. Pam may sabotage her previous therapy's attempt because getting better may seem more dangerous to her than staying sick. Suppose she abandons her symptoms and starts gaining weight. In that case, she will have to face emerging adult responsibilities, including doing better at school, deciding on her future occupation, possibly starting to date, and more. However, she likely feels inferior to the prospect of becoming an adult. Her mother, whose lifestyle dances right along Pam's, too, has an incentive—if Pam is symptom-free, Fran would have to face the reality of Pam leaving home in just two years. With the boys being taken care of by her husband, Fran would need to find something to occupy her life, such as entering the workforce or possibly returning to school, if she still aspires to become a teacher. Fran's possible subconsciously held invested interest in Pam's symptoms should not be ignored.

Hypothesizing Pam's, Murray's, and Fran's lifestyles would allow us to see the psychodynamics of the family challenges, the purpose of their behaviors (including Pam's symptoms), the strategic patterns the family uses to address these challenges, whether actively changing them or reinforcing them, and pinpointing the family strengths at the core of possible interventions. Adlerians operate with therapeutic hypotheses and bring those to clients for confirmation or rejection. That process, often employing Socratic questioning, is therapeutic in its own right. The initial story of a problem would never be a chapter book. The story will continue in each of the four stages of Adlerian therapy: building an alliance, assessment, developing insight, and reeducation/reorientation (Dreikurs et al., 1959). In each stage, the story of the problem will become richer. It will be complemented by the story of strengths, as well as the mistaken strategies that the system and each family member use—for the system's betterment or its detriment. Built on the therapist's hunches, the overall story will ultimately be authored by a client, with all the rights and responsibilities attached to the authorship.

Diversity Conceptualization

Adlerian family therapy employs a holistic approach to addressing family life challenges, strengths, and successes, emphasizing the importance of meaning-making and meaning-carrying throughout all stages of treatment. The meaning and the way it is explored in Adlerian therapy are always culturally expressed—within the family system, between the family and larger systems, and between the family and the therapist.

In Adlerian therapy, culture is a complex, multilayered, and dynamic phenomenon. It exists at the intersection of many demographics. It is placed in and possibly changes over one's lifespan. It is also not a passive backdrop, but an active participant, perhaps the major player in the meaning-making process. That reminds us of Adler's famous assertion that "every human being is an artist on his life's road" (Ansbacher & Ansbacher, 1956, p. 281) and brings us to the concept of creativity, which, in its many definitions, is also a deeply cultural phenomenon.

Another uniquely Adlerian cultural consideration in working with families is democracy, which has been reflected in significant cultural changes in the U.S. in the second half of the 20th century. Dreikurs (1957) wrote:

> We are living between two major cultural epochs, and the changes which we witness are the birth pains of a completely new era of human existence. We can distinguish three phases of human society: a primitive, an autocratic, and a democratic culture. The autocratic phase of society began with our civilization about eight thousand years ago. The democratic era is about to be established.
>
> (p. 18)

That discussion is fundamental to understanding and treatment considerations with couples, families, and especially parenting challenges in families with teenagers.

Although both fairly traditional, Murray and Fran came from different cultural backgrounds, Catholic for Fran and Protestant for Murray. That could help a family therapist understand some of the value systems that may be ingrained in the values carried out by both parents and the relative difficulties of negotiating between these values within the family during times of family distress. A therapist would guess the strong presence of Protestant work ethics—and Murray was likely steeped in it, as were at least two generations of the men in his family before him. However, Fran, being raised Catholic, may likely carry strong values related to the roles and responsibilities of women in a family, as well as the central role of guilt in processing perceived failures.

In working with the Daniels family, the call for a definition of "normal" (and they characterize themselves as being a *normal* family) will likely yield divergent responses. Murray will emphasize the idea that normal is proper and that one should obey the rules. Fran may underscore the importance of comfort and her responsibility to maintain it as essential features of normalcy. As different as these two definitions seem to be, there is a common cultural theme of traditionalism visible here and expressed by parents who are hesitant to and trying not to get Pam into inpatient treatment. Should that happen, the centuries-old, molded, and inscribed definitions of normalcy could be shattered, because *normal families* (especially those with a coach father and an educator mother) do not have abnormal children.

The Therapeutic Story of Problem Resolution

One of the unique foci in Adlerian therapy is viewing symptoms not as a problem but as a solution to a problem (Adler, 1964a; Ansbacher & Ansbacher, 1956; Shifron, 2020). Thus, the meaning of the word "solution" is two-layered: a solution in the form of symptoms and a solution as an informed and educated cooperative resolution to an actual systemic problem. Adlerian therapists look for patterns connecting the two points on the line, which in turn reinforce the patterns and explain what might seem unexplainable. For example, how can good or normal parenting produce a pathology, as we see in the Daniels family?

This is done in a therapeutic environment that is egalitarian, friendly, encouraging, and empowering, aimed at achieving the goal of mastery and belonging more effectively (Ansbacher & Ansbacher, 1956; Grunwald & McAbee, 1999). The goal is not for a therapist to understand, but for a client to understand, whether through new insight or by experiencing a new behavior. Therefore, in the context of family therapy, Adlerian education is always collaborative (Dreikurs et al., 1959). The development of insight is not always a primary goal or a main vehicle of change; instead, Adlerian family therapists may focus on changing motivation and immediate prosocial behavior, building respect, confidence, cooperation, and communication—all delivered with a good dose of encouragement (Dinkmeyer & Dreikurs, 1963; Dinkmeyer & Losoncy, 1980).

In working with the Daniels family, a therapist might say to Fran and Murray,

> You said you are confused about why Pam has anorexia. I am too. This makes no sense for Pam to become so unwell, given how much parenting you do with all three children. I know you have gone through all sorts of possible explanations and ways to deal with the problem. *What were your explanations of Pam's symptoms that would include you as a family? Would you rank them from most possible to least possible? Let us talk about the least possible one.*

The purpose of the first question is to encourage parents and permit them to consider explanations other than default ones. Another line of questioning might include "*What is it like to believe this thought?*" (after Murray mentions the family to be a normal family), or, following a few positive changes, a question might be introduced: "*What needs to happen for the change to keep happening?*" These are examples of **Socratic questioning**. The parents are encouraged to be less rigid and to see a range of explanations, of which there are no wrong explanations. Socratic questions are actively used by Adlerian therapists (Millar, 1999; Overholser, 2018; Stein, 1991). The questions are motivating, sufficiently interesting, map the consequences, and invite alternative responses. The questions draw a participant and do not just keep a listener busy listening. Murray and Fran, both fairly rigid and likely very discouraged, need permission to think outside the straight lines of useless logic. Once less logical (more analogical/more psychological) explanations are explored, a therapist will ask, "*How did it feel for the two of you to explain Pam's illness in a way you typically don't explain*?" That would open the door to a teaching moment, bringing flexibility and collaboration they have never experienced and can now practice consciously within this parenting team. That might lead to a second educational opportunity, and a therapist might ask, "*What was your very first thought about yourself as a parent when Pam was diagnosed with Anorexia?*" Exploring their own feelings as parents could become a key to changing parenting dynamics, both within the parenting dyad and between the generations.

In Adlerian family therapy, next to each difficult child, we tend to see a discouraged parent—a parent who does not believe they *can* (Bettner, 2020, 2023). This is an example of mistaken beliefs held by the parents that need to be confronted and reeducated. Finally, the third question—"*Have you tried to do things differently with your children, opposite to what you are doing now, like switching the roles of who is in charge of what children?*"—could become a homework assignment to experiment with different arrangements, such as Fran spending a weekend with the boys, while Murray takes Pam to an art show. The Adlerian basis for such intervention is our firm belief and Adler's stated, "golden rule of Individual Psychology: Everything can be different" (Ansbacher & Ansbacher, 1956, p. 363).

Another aspect of social equality and mutual respect in Adlerian therapy is aligning the goals and transparency (Dreikurs et al., 1984). In dysfunctional families, this is immensely therapeutic as a role model of cooperation. Training and education will take time because they aim to challenge and change established family patterns and individual lifestyles. When using specific recommendations, a therapist will ask the clients to articulate their understanding.

For the Daniels, we should note that the patterns are more deeply rooted due to stable multigenerational patterns, resulting in possibly much greater resistance to change. Not only Pam, but Murray, Fran, and the boys may have a difficult time accepting the necessary family changes. A professional repairman, Murray may find it challenging to accept changes that may affect his role and require him to do things differently from the traditional parenting/family manual he follows. His modus operandi is to fix what is broken, not to replace it. He will need to learn to differentiate firmness and domination, and to experience the power of firmness without domination. However, Fran may also need to learn firmness—a respectful firmness without indulgence for Pam's or Murray's wishes (Dreikurs, 1957).

Insight-Building Exploration of Family Patterns

Adlerian family therapists work with the family system that is holistic, dynamic, and consistent (Ansbacher & Ansbacher, 1956; Sherman & Dinkmeyer, 2015). Consistency is established and maintained by the family members' unique and stable lifestyles, as well as the predictable pattern of their family interactions when facing life challenges. Therapists may even talk about the family's lifestyle and interactional patterns. Therapeutically examining a typical family day is perhaps one of the best approaches (Bitter, 2025; Grunwald & McAbee, 1999). It serves as both an assessment and a great psychoeducation, tapping into clients' insights and encouraging them to see the family life and themselves in it with much greater insight, and to engage in a conversation with each other.

With the Daniels, we will ask them (the whole family at once or in its various groups—gender—or generation-based) to describe *a typical day* and who does what at any given time, from when the first family member wakes up until the last family member goes to bed at night. If needed, the therapist would use the prompt, "What happens next?" Although mealtimes seem to be crucial moments due to Pam's diagnosis, we really want to see a whole day-long snapshot of the family's and each member's activities and interactions, especially what happens right after the "problem" (Pam refuses to eat). Knowing what happens next (what Fran says and does, what Murray says and does, what each of the boys says and does) will help us understand the systemic purpose of Pam's symptoms and the *mistaken goal* of her behavior (Dreikurs & Soltz, 1968). Adlerians hold the view that all behavior is purposeful and that we are always in pursuit of the ultimate fictive goal, whether we use healthy or unhealthy strategies to achieve our goals (Dreikurs, 1950; Sicher, 1991). The therapy with the Daniels will focus on *misguided strategies* that a child adopts in pursuit of the goal of belonging, having a place, safety, and significance. That part of the family therapy will be expressively strengths-based. "Most dangerous is yielding to the child's conviction that he is bad or can't be liked" (Dreikurs, 1957, p. 25). Pam excels at building such conviction and maintaining it daily at mealtimes. She "requests" the love to be served daily, and we can easily imagine Fran doing just that by expressing concerns and trying to persuade Pam to eat or eat more. Not knowing how to be loved, Pam accepts worries. Not knowing how to love, Fran offers worries. Each of them gets something valuable from the pattern and will maintain it until a new incentive is brought up. An important step would be to engage Oliver and George in the family work. Although they do not have any reported problems, and seem to be good kids overall, an Adlerian therapist will see that pattern as being a model child next to a problem one. Quite often, the excellence of a model child is achieved at the expense of a problem child. The consequences are that once Pam starts improving, one of her brothers may lose their model child dynamics and become symptomatic in some way. So, while the work with Pam is an intervention, working with Oliver and George will be a preventive measure. Revealing this pattern will be key to successful therapy, and it can occur linearly or non-linearly. The linear approach will take shape in education. A nonlinear approach can also be used, such as spitting into a client's soup, employing a pushbutton technique, or acting as if.

Spitting into the client's soup is a technique of making the secondary gain (the mistaken socially useless payoff) less desirable, less appealing (Mosak & Maniacci, 1998). A therapist would essentially suggest the hidden goal of the client's symptoms, revealing it to the client, in the form of a "could it be" hunch. Once the mistaken goal is revealed, the symptoms are no longer palatable. Mosak developed the **pushbutton technique** as a way to interrupt the depression (Mosak & Maniacci, 1998). In the three-step process, a client is asked to recall a happy moment, then switch to an unpleasant memory, and then return to the pleasant one. A follow-up discussion focuses on the client's ability to push the buttons, to have control over their emotional experiences, and to master their feelings about themselves and their lives. Thoroughly explained by Watts, the **Reflecting As if** and **Acting As If** approaches involve asking a client to identify a problem, take a "reflective" step back from it, and then step forward to act as if the client were the person they would like to be (Watts & Garza, 2008). The client is then asked what some of the initial indicators might be that would demonstrate they are moving in the right direction. Following this initial step, the therapy focuses on the plan's viability and steps, ranking the items, and planning the enactment of the selected steps as homework. The best of Adlerian family therapy is holistic on many levels, engaging the entire family and weaving various, seemingly disparate interventions into the powerful texture of therapeutic change. Bitter defined Adler's clinical work as "a gift for intuitive guessing, teleological interpretation, storytelling, and even physical metaphor" (Bitter, 2025, p. 138).

Encouragement, Optimism, and Building on Strengths

Adlerian family therapy uses encouragement not as a technique or a time-specific approach, but as a main therapeutic fabric, both the content and the context of therapy (Ansbacher & Ansbacher, 1956; Dreikurs, 1967). This is based on the proposition that discouragement is at the root of every psychopathology. Here, we might add systematic discouragement as being at the root of family dysfunction and calling on systemic interventions as the only lasting solution to family problems.

With the Daniels family, especially with Murray, Fran, and Pam, encouragement will be crucial. That encouragement will be two-layered. The first will be the therapist's encouragement in the form of engaging the entire family, planning the sessions together, using the *"as if"* tasks, motivating Murray and Fran to overcome their feelings of not being good enough, empowering the parental team, and finding and planting more strengths and a sense of worth. The second, concurrent layer will be to encourage Murray and Fran to become encouragers for all three of their children. The family members will be prompted to do things together in various groups: first, Fran and Murray, then Fran and the boys, then Murray and Pam, and finally, the three kids by themselves. There will be only two non-negotiables in these times together: regularity and goodwill. The location or the activity can be negotiated at the family meeting and can rotate to value and exercise different family members' ideas.

Social Interest

Social interest in family therapy is not only a general philosophical concept; it can and should be clinically operationalized, based on the Adlerian assertion that "[in the family], social interest—the concerns for others—must be nurtured"

(Ansbacher, 1977, p.92). Evii (as cited in Ansbacher, 1977) noted interpersonal problems and impaired empathy as core features of eating disorders and suggested that "The individual suffering with Anorexia Nervosa may exhibit more social interest toward others and develop a greater sense of self-love by practicing social interest through helpfulness, warmth, and concern for the well-being of others" (Ansbacher, 1977, p. 277).

The goal of clinical work with Pam, within the family system, is to encourage her to become less self-focused, self-absorbed, and more focused on people around her. That, however, may not happen fast enough given the severity of her symptoms and the rigidity of the family system. Pam's interest in art may create an intermediate goal of connecting with nature and focusing on the environment, thereby turning her attention away from herself. Pam's homework may involve photography, starting with nature and moving toward photos of people. During the family therapy sessions, Pam will be asked to show selections of the images and describe them. Another approach in working with Pam might be to have special weekends working with rescue animals in the animal shelters. The important point is to bring the family together and use the power of that togetherness to nourish and validate social interest in Pam and the rest of the family. The rationale is that while Pam lacks a good measure of social interest openly, other family members do not demonstrate a healthy sense of community, too, despite not being symptomatic. Because they (Murray, Fran, and the boys) seem to be busy with life and are not physically symptomatic, their social interest deficiency may go unnoticed.

Reconstructed ERs

Reconstructed ERs are a unique and powerful immediate Adlerian intervention that can be used with family members (Shifron, 2020). In using that approach, the Adlerian therapist would first gather a traditional ER, ask for the most vivid moment, and the feelings that accompany it. The memory is the most vivid representation, a metaphor of one's lifestyle—the pattern of life, the strategies used to maintain that pattern, and the strengths expressed in those strategies. The ER will serve as a window into one's view of themselves, of others, of the world, and of all that *should* and *should not* be carried by the person in that world. Most importantly, the ER will have a metaphorical representation of the current life struggle that a person experiences and seeks to solve (Shifron, 2020). In the reconstruction stage, we will ask a person to change the most vivid moment in any way to *make it right by them*. Once the most vivid moment is reconstructed, we should be able to map the path of their striving, the image of their sense of ultimate oneness, and the strengths they have to achieve it. That investigation will be open, collaborative, and therapeutic, with the client as an expert. An Adlerian family therapist may decide to use ERs with all the Daniels family members, working with them individually and strengthening their insight.

Therapist's Lifestyle

Adlerian therapists' and supervisors' lifestyles (psychological birth order and other aspects of family constellation; self-others-life convictions hidden and revealed through dreams and early memories) would play an active role in both understanding the client's dynamics and influencing those dynamics, and ultimately impacting the therapeutic and supervisory relationships. In this chapter, the authors' lifestyle also influenced their interpretation of the family dynamic. Therefore, in therapy, we would present insights as hunches only, approaching the case phenomenologically, and recognizing the family and its members as the true experts in their unique lives and equally valuable experts in life in general.

Case Transcript

Therapist(facing each family member): Are you Murray? You must be Fran? And you are Pam? And how about you two? Oliver and George, right? Good morning to you all! Grab a chair, wherever you feel would be the right place for you to sit.

Interventions: Respect; seeing and treating family members as equally valuable, important, and having a place in the upcoming therapeutic process.

Murray: Hi, Doc!

Fran: Good morning, Mr. T! Pam, honey, is it OK for me to sit next to you?

Pam: Good morning! Yeah, sure. I don't care, actually.

Oliver: Hi.

George: Hi.

Therapist: Do you know why you are here?

Oliver: Some family stuff. Dad says we have to come and talk to someone; and then we can go to a game.

George: I don't want to practice today. Dad, you told us we can play Fortnite after we are back home.

Murray: I told the boys it is important to fix their sister's issues… whatever they are. And that the family comes first… and no video games today. You've heard me, boys.

George: Oh no.

Oliver [to George]: I told you.

Fran: [*no response*]

Pam: I am not sure I really wanted to come.

Therapist: I want to meet with you all as a family to talk about the family life, to get to know how your family works, to learn about each of you—and from each of you, too—and to figure out together how your family can work better. We will meet today, and we will then talk if you all want to come back to see me again. Does this make sense? (*Everyone nods*.)

Interventions: Education (by modeling) about equal values and respect for the free will of all participants. Validating "not sure" and other verbal and non-verbal signs of discouragement and treating people not as they seem to be, but as they can become, or "as they might be", (Sicher, 1991, p. 515), encouragement and epistemological optimism. Pam especially needs encouragement. When a person says that they are not sure whether they want to do anything, that must be read as "I am discouraged."

Murray: Yes, we talked about that with the kids. I guess we are all on board with that.

Therapist: So, you all came here as a family, even though each of you could have had some other plans. What did you all have to give up to come here?

Pam: I have something to finish reading… [*a long pause*]. A book… "Tender is the Flesh" …. and some other school things…

Fran [gently and worryingly]: Honey, we're all here for you, and you can always finish reading later. I'll help you with other things.

Oliver: It's always this way. [*slightly mocking*] Honey, I'll help you… I'll do things for you… We're all here for you…. We don't get that from you, Mom.

Murray: Oliver, apologize to your mother for your rude language immediately! I'm not going to say that twice.

Oliver: Ok, I'm sorry. I didn't mean to be rude. It's just irritating how she gets a pass on all the stuff, and we don't.

Fran [to Oliver]: I love you, baby. You know that.

George: What about me? And what is this whole thing anyway? What are we doing here?

Fran [to George]: And I love you too, Georgie. The doctor will tell us what to do and how to help your sister.

Murray: I had to leave a shop for an associate, and we have a shipment of parts coming. So, let's get started and get things done, whatever should happen here [*adding under his breath*], which I don't believe can do a thing.

Fran [quietly to Murray]: You promised me, Moe … please…

Therapist: It looks like all of you are pretty busy with many important things in life. Pam and Murray, you seem to be very serious about your responsibilities in life. Oliver, you have an excellent eye for how relationships work and how to make them fair. George, your curiosity is contagious. Fran, you seem to be busy with keeping everyone happy—that feels like a full-time job, and I don't know how you manage that. But we don't need to talk about that now, of course.

Interventions: Strengths-based reframing; validation of the promising efforts regardless of the motivation; optimistic forecast of teams and alliances where there are frictions. At the same time, the therapist challenges both Murray and Fran: encouraging Murray to see Pam as a serious, capable, and responsible team member and briefly confronting/probing Fran on some of her mistaken beliefs. A little later, Fran will be challenged on the topic of love. The question should never be whether a parent loves the child. The answer here is always affirmative. The question is how a parent loves their child. But right here, we might have pampering leading to the deprivation of the experience of one's own psychological strengths. This may likely contribute to Pam's symptoms and may present risks for the boys' health as well.

Therapist: This is how we will work today. I will have some time with Murray and Fran. Then some time with the three of you. Then, a little time with Pam, and then we will all come back together for a bit of talk. I want to learn as much as I can about your family from all of you. Will that work? You guys have cell phones, right? Would one of you be a timer and send a text in like 10–15 minutes?

Interventions: The therapist shares plans and rules (ensuring predictability, safety, and structure) and allows the clients to see their unique place in therapy. The latter might serve as a role model for parents. The therapist integrates Murray's focus on rules, Fran's focus on care, yet still gives power to the boys, and special, yet structured, clear, and thus safe, time to Pam. With that, the therapist also treats the parents as a team. Although not using the open forum counseling approach here, having initial agreed-upon meetings with subgroups is consistent with the common Adlerian practice of open forum counseling, as practiced by Adler in the 1920s and later adopted by Adlerian family therapists (Dreikurs et al., 1959; Garrison & Eckstein, 2013). Having a special time, as described above, provides a safe environment for each family member to share their experience and a tailored educational opportunity for the therapist, both during each interview segment and when the family comes back together.

[Pam, Oliver, and George leave the room.]

With parents

Therapist: What do you hope happens or does not happen here?

Murray: Well, Pam doesn't want to eat, and that's not OK. I don't know anything about why and how to fix that. I am busy with work and with the boys. My wife is dealing with Pam. This is [*softly joking*] the sort of girls' thing. But I don't think Fran knows how to fix that either. It's frustrating because we raise the kids well and they are healthy and well taken care of, and we pay for their sports, music, and whatnot. How did Pam get this illness? Is this a new thing, Doc? In our families, nobody ever had that. Sorry, this is not what you asked. I'm so busy at work and with the boys—I don't get to talk about much. So, if you can help us fix that for Pam, that is my only hope. Fran, the boys, and I—we're all Ok. Are you going to talk to Pam so that she respects the food on the table that her mother cooks?

Fran: I agree with my husband. I just want to help Pamela. We don't want her to go to the hospital. What's going to happen there? And she is not sick like other people are. She just does not eat well.

Therapist: I see that you are deeply committed to the health of Pam and also want to do the right things for your children. That you both are very sincere in seeking help and explanation of what might be confusing and strange.

Intervention: Socratic approach in the introductory question, giving power of choice to the couple. Validation of parents' concerns. The therapist avoids a premature confrontation by not immediately responding to "she is not sick," as that trivializes and minimizes the problems and would also shift the responsibility to Pam. For now, the task is to build relationships, validate, and strengthen the team by believing in them, seeing them as experts, and seeing their shared strengths.

Therapist: Tell me about your family. What would you like me to know about you? How do you find a place in your family and life in general, especially now during the crisis? How do your kids find their place and get their way? How is it to be a parent, an adult in your family?

Murray: We're just a normal family. I'm busy at work. When I'm not in the shop, I coach the boys' baseball team. My wife takes care of Pam and all the home stuff. We're a family. Everyone belongs alright, if that is what you are asking about. We all pitch in when we have to.

Fran: I agree with my husband. There's nothing special about us. We're like everyone else. Kids are healthy, well, except for Pam. They go to school, and the boys play sports. But see—they came here today. We told them it was important, and they came with us. They're very good kids. I'm just very confused about the eating illness in Pam. What is that illness? I just can't stop worrying.

Therapist: How is that like to be a parent in your family now?

Murray: I do my job the best I can and as my father did… and see I turned out OK… It is all good with the boys, but Pam's not eating right. You talk to Fran about this.

Fran: It's stressful, and I don't know what to do. Murray takes care of the boys, and it's all good there. But I don't know what to do with Pam, and it is all on me, but I don't know what to do about her not eating.

Therapist: People always seek to find a place in life. We need to feel we have a place so we feel safe and significant, that life makes sense, that we are a part of something, and that we can contribute in our roles, whether as a parent or a child in a family, a friend, or a colleague. In looking for a way to belong, each person is unique, and each family is unique. Your family is unique in more ways than I know. When someone feels they don't have a place in a useful and healthy way, that person will do all they can to find a place, often in a useless side of life. This is when we usually see some symptoms. We can talk about that later if you want.

Intervention: The therapist displays a genuine concern about the parents as a team and each of them as a unique contributing individual adult. While asking a series of open-ended questions, and opening a space for a variety of possible responses, the therapist keeps focus on the central point—what is it like to be a parent + in your family + now? This is an appropriate place to bring a good dose of family education related to mistaken beliefs and corresponding unhealthy family dynamics to very discouraged parents. The purposefulness of behavior has already been suggested.

Therapist: What have each of you done about the situation? I hear that you, Fran, worry a lot. I am sure you tried more than that, right? How did it work? Who is best suited to handle the situation?

Intervention: Optimism and helping a client to see how things can be different/what more they can do, faith in the client's desire to do well; search for strengths.

Fran: I talk to poor Pam. I mean, I try to speak to her, but she's avoiding me. Some days, I cook special meals just for her, but she's never hungry. I talk to her about how in the world she will become an adult if her grades are sliding down and she's so skinny. She behaves like a 2-year-old. She is sort of a bookworm now. I mean, this isn't bad—I used to read books too, and Murray and I met because our mothers were in the book club together. But we did it right back then. So, really, nothing works. I wish I could ask my mom, but my mom isn't in touch with me much. I guess I'm just a bad parent.

Therapist: So, you cater to Pam and serve her as if she were 2, but want her to act as an adult? Hmm… Must be so tiring for you to have a 2-year-old for that long, mustn't it? And, you are ready to get help, right? By the way, if you feel sorry for the child, she will feel sorry for herself, and nobody is as miserable as the one who feels sorry for themselves. Feeling sorry for the child comes from a lack of belief that the person can handle things. Do you believe in Pam?

Intervention: The therapist provides education about the dangers of pity; focuses on mistaken beliefs; and engages in paradoxical questioning to reveal the nature of mistaken beliefs.

Fran [seemingly surprised]: I guess yes. I never thought about that… And yes, I need help. Well, Pam needs more help, but I can use some help too.

Therapist: What about you, Murray? You must have tried something too—you are good at figuring this out.

Intervention: Finding strengths and building on strengths.

Murray: Yes, I am. It's just so much easier with broken fridges than with girls. Boys are easier too—they're simple to understand, and I can see my two boys through. I always know how to fix things with the boys. Pam is really Fran's job—we decided on that a while ago. I oversee the boys, and she deals with Pam. As I said, all these talks are the girls' things.

Therapist: Thank you for being so open about that, Murray. Later, let's talk about your way of disciplining children and how it might hurt your boys in the long run.

Intervention: Education. Punishment leads to an increase in antagonism, shaking a child's faith in oneself.

Murray: Yeah, you get what you see with me. I have nothing to hide—a little tap didn't hurt anyone yet.

Therapist: Just curious, with your many years in the repair business and just in running a business, have you ever had something not working to the point that no user manual can help you? If you did, what would be a secret of handling something like that?

Intervention: Using metaphors based on occupation and occupational strengths. That should also empower Murray (he only seems powerful and is, in fact, very discouraged) and help him to see his relationship with Pam differently.

Murray: Well, I like you, Doc. Nobody ever cared to ask me about my trade tricks and secrets. I can see the real repairman by how he would handle exactly what you just asked, Doc! My secret is that I spend some time with the broken piece of appliance or whatnot. Just spend time with it, get a feel of it, think about it, and be careful not to break more of it. Some pieces are really beautiful, once you figure out how to fix them right.

Therapist: So, you're a true artist in your trade.

Intervention: Uncovering and validating Murray's unique talent to later use in improving his relationships with Pam.

Murray [pleased]: You can say that, yes.

Therapist: Now we know how Pam became so good with art and music, and so sensitive to beauty. We can guess from whom she got those talents, right?

Intervention: Suggesting the stronger bonds between Murray and Pam than Murray would acknowledge, and seeing a client, how he might become with a good dose of encouragement (vs. how he is now).

Murray: Not exactly, but something of that nature.

Therapist: Of course. Now, a question to the two of you—If you were to work on rearranging the family routines in any way to improve the situation for all of you, what would that be?

Murray and Fran [spontaneously, in one voice]: Not that much right away!! We need to think.

Therapist [laughing]: Wow, you actually are a good team! How about you take it as homework? Just one change, please—no more. Like you said, "not that much right away!" Start with small portions.

Intervention: Using humor and encouragement. Use of a metaphor of portions. Paradoxical suggestions. The therapist "prescribes" a specific small dose of changes as homework for the parents. Whether the parents follow the prescription and make only small changes or violate the prescription and introduce greater changes, the therapist will witness parents winning control of the changes and doing so as a team of responsible adults. The therapist also, paradoxically, finds the strengths ("You actually are a good team") where others would default to seeing as a collective resistance to change.

(With the Boys)

Therapist: Thank you for being patient, boys, and for sticking around too. Can you tell me about your family? What would you like me to know about you? What kinds of things do people usually do? How is it to be a child in your family?

Intervention: Genuine interest and insight-building.

Oliver: Ha! That's easy. Dad fixes. Mom cries. We play ball. Pam fusses. We are OK. My brother and I are OK, not in trouble. Right, Georgie?

George: Yes, Pam fusses and fusses and fusses. That should be triple fussing. Kind of irritating.

Therapist: So, you see how unhappy your sister is about something in her life, right?

Intervention: Reframe as modeling for the siblings to encourage them to see things differently. And at the same time, the therapist points to their strengths in being able to see how unhappy their sister is.

Oliver: Yeah, you can say that. But what is wrong with her? And how come we have to talk about that?

Therapist: Did you notice who is good at dealing with this and how well?

Intervention: Insight building; encouragement to see strategies and strengths.

George: Nobody. It all always ends with mom and dad arguing, and dad goes to his shop, and mom goes to her bedroom to cry, and Pam just gets her way. Mom and Dad think we never see them arguing, and they whisper—and the more they whisper, the more we hear them.

Therapist: What do you mean by "Pam gets her way"?

Oliver: It's like she's never asked to do any chores because she's sick, and we do that for her, and she gets special treatment.

George: And Dad never teaches her any rules or about consequences like he does with us. That's unfair!

Therapist: I see. How do you get your way?

Intervention: Insight building. Probing the purpose of the symptoms.

Oliver: We play ball. And do well at school. So, how they deal with Pam is unfair—like the way she's sick, and mom tells us to take care of her when we grow up.

George: Yes, it's unfair. We play, and we earn privileges. Pam gets things by playing sick.

Therapist: So, you all get your way in some way, but it looks like some of your ways don't play well with some other ways, right?

Intervention: Insight building.

Oliver and George: Yes!!

Oliver: It's actually cool, I mean, this family therapy thing. Can we come here again?

Therapist: We'll have to check with your parents, but I say yes. Your observations have been very helpful to me in learning about your family.

Intervention: Validation.

(With Pam)

Therapist: You waited the longest of all, Pam. How did you handle that?

Pam: It's OK. I'm used to being alone. I like it.

Therapist: You seem to be quite self-sufficient in that. Good skill, and many find it hard to be on their own for a long period of time.

Intervention: Reframe Pam's tendency to self-isolate. Later, that strategy can be considered on a continuum from self-isolation and loneliness to solitude, and the purpose of the chosen strategy.

Pamela [smiling]: Not me.

Therapist: Can you tell me about your family? What would you like me to know about you? What kinds of things do people usually do? How is that to be the oldest child/daughter in your family? If you were to think about your family as an object, as a thing, what would it be?

Intervention: Genuine interest, curiosity. The use of a metaphor (building on Pam's strengths with her artistic abilities), while also maintaining therapeutic safety at the initial stages of therapy.

Pam [after a long pause]: I don't know. I guess it's like a big lump of clay, with twigs and small pieces of gravel mixed in it and sticking out. I don't know why I see it—it's kind of ugly, and wet, and doesn't hold a form.

Therapist: Tell me more about it, and where are you in relation to it?

Pam: It's big and heavy and smells like wet grass. The twigs and gravel—I don't know how they get there and why, but I can't get them out, and they don't let me hold and shape the clump of clay. I don't like ugly when it's senseless. When it makes sense, I'm Ok. But not like this.

Therapist: That lump of clay—how did it get to be that way? What was there before?

Intervention: Insight building in the process of metaphoric exploration.

Pam: Funny you asked… [*half-smiling*] I actually made it that ugly. I had a piece of clay and wanted to make a person, a dancer, and twigs and marbles, and pieces of straw would be hands, eyes, and feet. But I struggled with the clay, and it started drying, and crumbs started falling off it.

Therapist: So, you just stuck the twigs in?

Pam: Yes, I know this sounds stupid to you, but I thought to keep it together in some way, and now I can't even hold it, with all the things sticking out. I guess you can't make a dancer out of a piece of clay. A stupid idea anyway.

Therapist: If that clay sculpture were a family, then where are you in that?

Intervention: Insight building, stressing the relational aspects of Pam's life and the social field; at the same time, building on the creative nature of personality and the power of an individual in carving out their place in a community.

Pam: I am the twigs.

Therapist: The twigs?

Pam: Yes, is that OK? I know I'm sticking out.

Therapist: Absolutely, you can be anything you want in your family… for as long as it holds together. We become truly free when we stop being concerned with successes and failures.

Intervention: Education about freedom and the creative power of the self.

Pam: Yes, it does. I mean, I do it the wrong way, but I still do.

Therapist: And if you were to change it to make it right by you, what would that be?

Pam: I'm not sure I can. It's pretty hard and dry—I think we need to wrap it in a warm and moist fabric first to make it malleable. Then, maybe I won't have to be a twig anymore. I can be one of the marbles. I actually just thought of signing up for a ceramics class in my senior year. You think that would be good for me?

Therapist: This is a change already, pretty brave too. Thank you for sharing the process with me. And that ceramic class idea—it sounds like you already have your answer to a question, right?

Intervention: Transformation of therapeutic metaphor and bridge-building as a part of the transformation.

Pam: (*Nodding and smiling*).

The Family Together for the Closure of the Session

Therapist: I want to share something with you all, something that I observed in each of you that gives me lots of hope. Would that be Ok with each of you?

Intervention: Reaffirming respect, valuing each family member's opinion, and transparency with needed safety measures when it comes to sharing.

All: Sure.

Therapist: I saw lots of unique strengths that make your family unique and also keep it together. I shared these strengths with each of you, and I wonder what everyone can do, just one thing, from what they are good at doing, to make things right by all as a family and right by each of you as an equally valuable family member. What can each of you contribute to the team? You don't need to say it right now, but do what you believe is right, and also watch what others do. Next time, I would love to hear from you what you will notice in others and how other family members contribute. Would that be OK?

All: Yes! Yes!

Intervention: Strengths building, encouragement, specific optimistic planning, and strengths-based recommendations (homework and next session). Stressing the responsibility for finding solutions and bettering the family life shared between the children and the adults. The rationale here is that we only do what we decide, so the decision is a key to actions.

George: Dad, can we now go home and play?

The Therapeutic Story

At the end of this session, several important changes seem to have taken place:

1 The family system and each family member have heard at least one of their former self-perceived weaknesses being reframed as a strength, allowing for the next step, next chapter in the family story.
2 All five family members become more encouraged, and they now have a specific homework assignment building on their strengths.
3 The family constellation was critically revisited, prompting the family members to constellate healthier.
4 The so-called problem was shifted from Pam to a discouraged family system with rigid gender and generational guiding lines and a lack of education
5 Pam seems the most encouraged and ready to make changes in her life strategies from useless, psychologically costly, symptomatic to more joyful, socially useful, and likely to provide enough confidence to her for abandoning her symptoms.
6 The family (Pam especially) seems to be willing to benefit from focused interventions, suggesting improved insight.
7 Mistaken assumptions about self, others, and how the world operates were identified and gently challenged for Murray, Fran, and Pam.
8 The possible purposes of symptoms were suggested for Pam, Fran, and Murray.
9 The solid therapeutic alliance seems to be forming, promising a new chapter in this therapeutic story.

References

Adler, A. (1930). *Guiding the child on the principles of individual psychology*. George Allen & Unwin Ltd.
Adler, A. (1931). *The pattern of life*. Kegan Paul, Trench, Trubner & Co., Ltd.
Adler, A. (1964a). *Problems of neurosis. A book of case histories*. Harper Torchbooks.
Adler, A. (1964b). *Superiority and Social Interest: A Collection of Later Writings*. (H.L. Ansbacher & R. R. Ansbacher, Eds.). Northwestern University Press.
Ansbacher, R. R. (1977). The happy family, Adlerian style. In C. L. Morse (Ed.), *Proceedings of the symposium: The Individual Psychology of Alfred Adler* (pp. 79–94). University of Oregon Press.
Ansbacher, R. R. (2011). The life tasks: Opening convocation, Meredith College, August 27, 1979. *Journal of Individual Psychology*, *67*(1), 9–12.
Ansbacher, H. L. & Ansbacher, R. R. (1956). *Individual psychology of Alfred Adler. A systematic presentation in selections from his writings*. Harper Torchbooks.
Bettner, B. L. (2020). Are Alfred Adler and Rudolf Dreikurs relevant for parents today? *Journal of Individual Psychology*, *76*(1), 70–78.
Bettner, B. L. (2023). *Encouraging parents courageous children: The crucial cs handbook*. Family Leadership Center.
Bitter, R. J. (2025). *Theory and practice of couples and family counseling* (4th ed.). American Counseling Association.
Bitter, J. R., & Carlson, J. (2017). Adlerian thought and process in systems of family therapy. *Journal of Individual Psychology*, *73*(3), 307–327.

Devlin, J. M., Birkey, J., & Smith, J. (2024). Contemporary Adlerian family counseling. *The Family Journal: Counseling and Therapy for Couples and Families*, *32*(2), 263–268.
Dinkmeyer, D. & Dreikurs, R. (1963). *Encouraging children to learn*. Hawthorn Books, Inc.
Dinkmeyer, D. & Losoncy, L.E. (1980). *The encouragement book. Becoming a positive person*. Prentice-Hall, Inc.
Dreikurs, R. (1946). *The challenge of marriage*. Duell, Sloan & Pearce.
Dreikurs, R. (1948). *The challenge of parenthood*. Duell, Sloan & Pearce.
Dreikurs, R. (1950). *Fundamentals of Adlerian Psychology*. Greenberg, Publisher
Dreikurs, R. (1957). *Child guidance and education*. Alfred Adler Institute of Chicago.
Dreikurs, R. (1967). *Psychodynamics, psychotherapy, and counseling*. Alfred Adler Institute of Chicago.
Dreikurs, R., Corsini, R., Lowe, R., & Sonstegard, M. (1959). *Adlerian family counseling. A manual for counseling centers*. The University Press.
Dreikurs, R. & Grey, L. (1970). *Parents' guide to child discipline*. Hawthorn Books, Inc.
Dreikurs, R., Shulman, B.H. & Mosak, H.H. (1984). *Multiple psychotherapy: The use of two therapists with one patient*. Alfred Adler Institute of Chicago.
Dreikurs, R., & Soltz, V. (1968). *Children: The challenge*. Meredith Press.
Garrison, R., & Eckstein, D. (2013). Ethical considerations involving informed consent in Adlerian open forum counseling. *Journal of Individual Psychology*, *69*(4), 344–356.
Grunwald, B.B. & McAbee, H.V. (1999). *Guiding the family: Practical counseling techniques* (2nd ed.). Taylor & Francis.
Millar, A. (1999). The use of Socratic questioning in Classical Adlerian Therapy. In P. Prina, C. Shelley, & C. Thompson (eds.), *Adlerian society of the United Kingdom and the institute of individual psychology year book* (pp. 55–65). Adlerian Society of the United Kingdom and Institute of Individual Psychology.
Mosak, H. H. & Maniacci, M. P. (1998). *Tactics in counseling and psychotherapy*. Peacock.
Overholser, J. (2018). *The Socratic method of psychotherapy*. Columbia University Press.
Seidler, R. (1930). Rivalry among children of the same family. In A. Adler (Ed.). *Guiding the Child on the Principles of Individual Psychology* (pp. 183–192). George Allen & Unwin Ltd.
Sherman, R. & Dinkmeyer, D. (2015). *Systems of family therapy: An Adlerian integration*. Routledge.
Shifron, R. (2020). The miracle of early recollections in Adlerian psychotherapy and supervision. *The Journal of Individual Psychology*, *76*(1), 110–127.
Sicher, L. (1991). *The collected works of Lydia Sicher: An Adlerian perspective*. (A.K. Davidson, ed.). QED Press.
Sperry, L., & Sperry, J. (2020). *Case conceptualization: Mastering this competency with ease and confidence*. Routledge.
Sperry, L. & Sperry, J. (2022). *The 15-minute case conceptualization: Mastering the pattern-focused approach*. Oxford University Press.
Stein, H. T. (1991). Adler and Socrates: Similarities and differences. *Individual Psychology*, *47*(2), 241–246.
Strauch, M., & Erez, M. (2009). The restrictive personality: Anorexia nervosa and Adlerian life tasks. *Journal of Individual Psychology*, *65*(3), 203–211.
Watts, R. E., & Garza, Y. (2008). Using children's drawings to facilitate the acting "as if" technique. *Journal of Individual Psychology*, *64*(1), 113–118.

8 Satir's Experiential Growth Model

Kayleigh N. Sabo

Virginia Satir—developer of the experiential growth model (sometimes called the human validation process movement)—is one of the original family therapists and the mother of family therapy (Hagen & Sabey, 2019). Her beginnings at the Mental Research Institute led to her work being influenced by Gregory Bateson's cybernetic theory (Reiter, 2025). Additionally, Satir drew inspiration from Eastern philosophy and practices as well as humanistic psychology, as her approach was not just about the presenting problem but about overall human well-being (Satir et al., 1991). She particularly emphasized the notion that everyone is capable of change (Satir & Baldwin, 1983), showing the influence of strength-based ideas on her work.

Satir's focus on general wellness and human potential is evident in the core principles and interventions of the growth model. Some of the core principles include the focus on one's self-esteem (with the idea of "self" being conceptualized through a self-mandala) and the importance of congruence of self (i.e., the person is whole and authentic in their experience of self, interactions with others, and experience of their context; Satir et al., 1991, 1994). In her therapy, Satir created a story of connection to self, others, and context through common interventions like sculpting, meditations, and family reconstruction. These and other core principles and interventions are expanded upon further in this chapter, starting with how Satir viewed the formation of problems that brought people into therapy.

The Therapeutic Story of Problem Formation

First, a bit of history: Virginia Satir is considered a pioneer of the family therapy field because she was one of the first in the mental health profession to see the value in working with more than one person. Satir (1964/1967) initially discussed this shift from individual work to relational work as **conjoint family therapy**. This relational work involves meeting with multiple people in the relevant system (e.g., a family, a work team) to watch the communication processes happening between people rather than hearing about these processes and other content from one person. Specific benefits of seeing the whole family

DOI: 10.4324/9781003668510-8

rather than just an individual include observing more accurate dynamics between important people in the client's life and engaging these individuals in the therapeutic process. Therefore, growth therapists (operating from a family therapy model) prefer to see multiple people compared to one person in the therapy room.

Satir did not just view clients in terms of their perceived presenting problems or even her view of the problem. Rather, she expanded her understanding of a client to include their full experience of life—not just on their current pathology but on how they were doing as a whole in terms of health and wellness (Satir, 1987). Still, the growth model has a foundational notion of how people are prevented from experiencing the fullness of their life (i.e., how problems make their way into people's lives).

Primarily, Satir believed that people start struggling in one way, shape, or form when their selves are not wholly integrated—they cease to have a flow of energies within them and between those around them (Satir, 1988b). Things within their lives are restricting their uniqueness and preventing them from being congruent and authentic. It is the person's job, however, to take responsibility for their responses rather than blame external sources (Satir et al., 1991). Satir thought that the source of the restriction of one's full self came from their family of origin, and the most basic element of one's family of origin starts with the primary triad.

The Primary Triad

Satir conceptualized conception and birth as the beginning of the growth—and also, therefore, potentially the problem formation—process (Satir et al., 1991). There are three individuals in this original life process that are of the utmost importance: mom, dad, and child (when speaking of a traditional heterosexual household). This trio is known as the **primary triad**. The primary triad, however, exists in all family types. For example, some children grow up with their grandparents as their guardians. The primary triad in this case would be the grandparents and the child. The same goes for same-sex relationships: The primary triad would be (a) mom, mom, and child or (b) dad, dad, and child. In the Daniels family, the first primary triad is Fran, Murray, and Pam (as Pam is the first child in the family). There are two other primary triads consisting of Fran, Murray, and (a) Oliver and (b) George as well.

The primary triad is important because it is one's parents who provide one's learnings of what to expect from others and the world, how to interact with others and the world, and so on (Satir et al., 1991). Therefore, parents are the ones who teach their children how to cope with life. Children then take what they have learned from their parents and either use it with others (a) in a helpful way (if the learnings promote congruence) or (b) in an unhelpful way until they figure out how to cope in a more congruent manner.

Low self-esteem emerges when one questions whether they are loved (Satir et al., 1991). This questioning would usually start with one's parents, as the parent–child relationship is the first relationship that people usually come across in life. The survival responses (which are addressed in the next section) that result from low self-esteem center around self, others, and context. In one way or another, low self-esteem—which leads to incongruent communication (Satir, 1964/1967)—essentially results in one or more of these three elements being imbalanced or outright neglected altogether.

Survival Communication Stances

There are four **survival communication stances** through which individuals cope when they are incongruent and have low self-esteem: placating, super-reasonable (computer), blaming, and irrelevant (Satir, 1972). The three elements of communication that the communication stances operate within include self, others, and context.

Someone operating from the **placating stance** does not honor the element of self and gives more power to others (e.g., through accepting blame) and to the context (Satir et al., 1991). The **blaming stance** blames others for their wrongdoing and therefore does not honor others. The **super-reasonable stance** disregards self and others and focuses on context, often by ignoring emotions and favoring logic. The **irrelevant stance** does not honor any of the three elements of communication (i.e., self, others, context) because individuals in this stance often have difficulty dealing with tough situations head-on and distract from the problem altogether as a result.

Let's look at each stance in more detail. Visually, a placating stance is often represented by someone kneeling down while reaching a hand out to be in service of another person (Satir et al., 1991). Although placating may seem similar to pleasing, it is different in that one's sense of worth suffers when they placate, as they are sacrificing their true feelings to make someone else's experience better. Fran's dynamics with her husband, Murray, demonstrate a placating stance: Fran cedes to Murray's directions for Fran to primarily deal with Pam while he handles the boys.

A blaming stance could be thought of as the other end of the spectrum compared to placating, as one who blames puts themselves and the context first at the expense of others (Satir et al., 1991). The classic pose of pointing one's finger at another person displays the essence of this stance. In terms of the Daniels family, it would make sense to perhaps see Fran as acting through the blaming stance with Pam. Fran, understandably out of concern for her daughter, gets on Pam about not eating enough and has intentions to put Pam into an inpatient facility if family therapy does not make a difference. This places the blame on Pam for her actions surrounding eating and health.

Because the super-reasonable stance ignores two components of self (i.e., others and self) in favor of the context, it is often referred to as the computer stance (Satir et al., 1991). Someone physically representing this stance may stand ordinarily straight and still with little facial expression. Those coming from this stance are often experienced as unemotional and boring. Murray might be coming from a super-reasonable stance in his thought process that he (as dad) should focus on the male children while Fran (as mom) focuses on the female child.

Last, there is the irrelevant stance that disregards all three elements of self (Satir et al., 1991). Someone in a physical pose that demonstrates this stance would look out of whack—the person is moving some body parts in one direction and other body parts in another direction (e.g., their head may be facing one way while their arms are pulling the opposite way). This pose would continuously change, however, as someone operating from this stance has a hard time staying still or keeping focused since they tend to be the distractor. Oliver and George could be seen as coming from an irrelevant stance, as it seems like they are letting mom and dad handle things with Pam and are disconnected from the process and their relationships (especially with mom and Pam). Pam may also come from the irrelevant stance when engaging with mom and dad, as she is not acknowledging others (e.g., her parents' pleas), context (e.g., the fact that she is medically underweight), or self (e.g., her own wellness and needs).

It is important to note that people utilize different stances in different contexts (Satir et al., 1991). One might placate in one scenario and blame in another (e.g., Fran toward Murray and Fran toward Pam, respectively). Although one can switch between all the survival communication stances, it is common for someone to have a primary coping stance (the default stance that the person mainly uses) and a secondary coping stance (another stance that the person usually falls back on).

Despite these stances being problematic overall, Satir believed that they "contain seeds of wholeness" (Satir et al., 1991, p. 53). As Satir et al. (1991) detailed, one placates to care about someone else; blames to stand up for oneself; is super-reasonable to demonstrate intelligence; and is irrelevant through creativity. This reinforces the model's underlying strength-based nature and the focus on health and human potential rather than pathology.

More specifically, these communication stances result "when our basic yearning to love and be loved is threatened" (Satir et al., 1991, p. 53). As noted when talking about the primary triad, the first relationship with which this idea becomes relevant is the parental relationship (Satir, 1964/1967; Satir et al., 1991). Essentially, people develop survival responses as a result of their relationship with and what they learned from their parents (and grandparents, as Satir believed in the importance of looking at three generations of communication). These learnings are carried into adulthood, where people attempt to change their own partners and/or children based on perceived faults.

A growth therapist, though understanding of why people fall into these communication patterns, sees these stances as problematic because they are based on one's expectations of someone else (Satir et al., 1991). Humans are not perfect, but people attempt to make them so and then wind up coping through these incongruent communication stances. As a whole, this basing of one's own well-being on other people's actions leads to reduced self-esteem.

Self-Esteem

Satir (1972) stated, "I am convinced that the crucial factor in what happens both *inside* and *between* people is the picture of individual worth that each person carries around with him" (p. 21). Satir (1975b) considered **self-esteem** to be an intrapersonal (self), interpersonal (others), and situational (context) concept. The essence of self-esteem is therefore the wholeness of one's experience as a human. It is an experience of being authentic with oneself and having inherent worth as a person (Satir, 1988a). Each of the four incongruent communication stances disregards one or more of these elements of communication (i.e., self, others, context). The incongruent communication stances are therefore connected to low self-esteem (Satir, 1972).

Within Satir's overall concepts of self-esteem and congruence is a more specific concept of the **self-mandala** (Satir et al., 1991). Mandala—Sanskrit for circle—is an Eastern idea that Satir applied to her conceptualization of wholeness. In the growth model, the self-mandala is divided into eight elements: (a) physical, (b) spiritual, (c) sensory, (d) interactional, (e) emotional, (f) intellectual, (g) nutritional, and (h) contextual (see Figure 8.1). The culmination of these pieces of the self creates wholeness and higher self-esteem. Each of these areas of self leads to higher self-esteem. When one or more of these pieces of the self-mandala are neglected in some way, the person tends to have lower self-esteem. This also usually results in more dysfunctional coping responses (i.e., the survival communication stances).

As part of a family therapy model, the self-mandala is systemic/relational at its core because it includes contextual and interactional elements. Contextual elements may include factors such as culture, family history, age, and gender. This piece of the mandala highlights the importance of a person's background and how their context is a part of their overall experience of self. Interactional elements include the person's relationships and dynamics with others, and this piece emphasizes the implicit relational component of self. Additionally, the coming together of all these elements does not just lead to wholeness within one person but also translates into more productive and positive interactions with others.

Again, it is the discord between these elements of communication and the imbalance of the pieces of the self-mandala that lead to low self-esteem and problem formation. If we look at the idea of the self-mandala in relation to the Daniels family, we could see how they are at odds with some elements of their self-mandalas. Take Pam, for example: It would be fair to say that she is certainly in disharmony with the nutritional and physical components of her self-mandala due to her eating habits and weight. Fran's emotional element

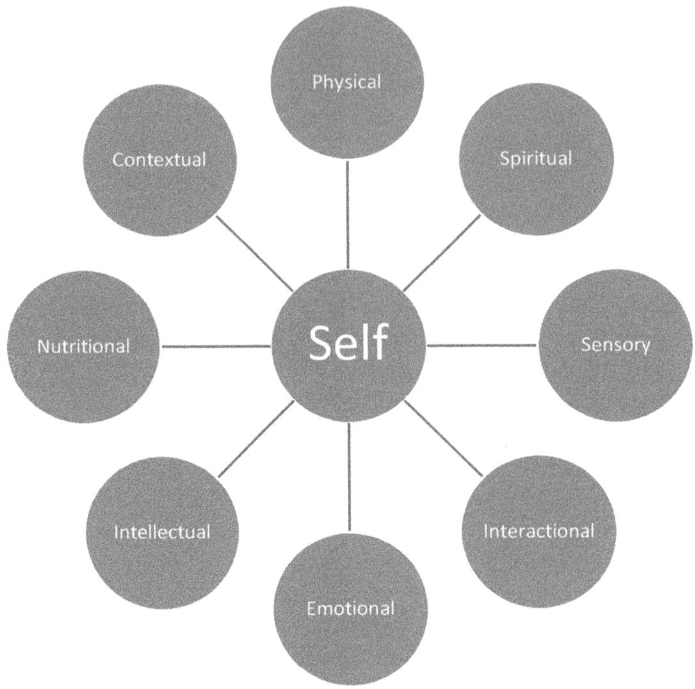

Figure 8.1 The eight components of the self-mandala.

could be strained related to her dynamics with Murray. Murray might also be neglecting the emotional component and relying too heavily on the intellectual piece. Regarding the whole family, it is likely that the interactional piece of all their mandalas is affected.

Diversity Conceptualization

The beauty of Satir's growth model is that there is an explicit emphasis on self, others, and context. These mirrored philosophies do not solely focus on the individual experience, or the experience of others, or the situation/environment. Instead, Satir's approach highlights the importance of the uniqueness of and connectedness between people, families, societies, and cultures. Also foundational to the growth model is the belief that all humans deserve basic respect and openness. This is overt in Satir's work: "Regardless of age, skin color, gender, or health, all humans are of equal value" (Satir et al., 1991, p. 8).

Satir used her growth model in many different countries—as she traveled the world providing workshops—and with a variety of client types. Satir also tailored the metaphors that she used with clients based on their culture and experiences and emphasized the ability for metaphors to bridge people of different languages (Satir et al., 1991). For example, she described using metaphors related to the Buffalo Woman (a figure in Native American culture) when working with Native American clients.

Since Satir's passing, other clinicians have also utilized her approach in various contexts. Cheung and Chan (2009) described the application of the Satir model in Hong Kong. They differentiated traditional Chinese culture (which historically promotes more hierarchy and respect for authority) and the growth model (which promotes equality and direct, honest communication). These differences led to some challenges in therapy, such as some clients having trouble integrating therapeutic changes within their traditional home environment. However, Cheung and Chan emphasized the benefit of the model in improving family dynamics for other clients and the ability for the model to be compatible with Chinese culture through focus on the shared idea of honoring not just oneself but the context and others. Similarly, Der Pan (2000) and Epstein et al. (2012) cited benefits of and promise in incorporating the growth model within Taiwanese and Chinese contexts, respectively.

In applying these considerations to Satir's concept of self, there is a necessity to acknowledge that there is an inherent individualistic, Western quality to the use of the word "self." Although Satir's use of the self-mandala is based on Eastern philosophy and incorporates individual, relational, and contextual elements, the word "self" in the Western world has an attached individualistic connotation and is often appropriated toward favoring the individual. Sedikides et al. (2011) highlighted this trend, as they acknowledged that although there are different definitions of self (i.e., individual self, relational self, and collective self) that comprise one's overall self-concept, the individual self is treated as primary and is often put above the other types of self.

The same lens can also be used to more systemically conceptualize Satir's communication stances, which also have an individualistic foundation. On the one hand, Satir's communication stances are relational in the sense that one's communication stance would affect another's stance and subsequent responses and dynamics between people (Satir et al., 1991). On the other hand, the stances themselves are about an *individual's* way of communicating by primarily tapping into intrapersonal experiences, whereas other cultures may conceptualize communication as primarily occurring at an interpersonal level with multiple people.

It is also important to acknowledge that postmodern theorists posit that Satir did not directly provide instruction on incorporating social location factors into the growth model itself (Maxey, 2021). Satir commented on the unhelpfulness of stereotyping people based on various factors such as gender and race throughout her work (Freeman, 1999). However, her primary belief was that all humans are connected at an energetic level; everyone is simply trying to get through life, and everyone deserves the same basic respect (Satir et al., 1991). Critics of her model assert that Satir left her approach at this baseline belief and did not overtly take it to the next step of considering how culture, biases, power differentials, and gender roles come into play with how people are each trying to (and are able to) get through life (Maxey, 2021). This makes sense given the context, as Satir created this model during the modernism era of the family therapy field, which has been critiqued as not including relevant factors such as culture, gender, and sex (Rasheed et al., 2011).

More recent adaptations of Satir's work blend her model with more current diversity and inclusion contexts. For example, Maxey (2021) incorporated the growth model with intersectional feminism and noted that the growth model has inherent similarities to intersectional feminist theory (e.g., Satir's emphasis on challenging societal gender expectations and promotion of egalitarian relationships). As a whole, the growth model seems to be considered an approach that—although one of the original family therapy models—is primed to be integrated with evolving diversity conceptualizations in the field.

The Therapeutic Story of Problem Resolution

Increasing one's self-esteem is a primary goal in Satir's growth model (Satir et al., 1991). Satir (1972) described self-esteem as involving components such as love, compassion, and honesty; it is an experience of self in which one has faith in oneself and believes one matters. As mentioned, Satir also believed that people inherently have the resources and strengths within them to change and grow (Satir & Baldwin, 1983; Satir et al., 1991).

Since low self-esteem would result from a restriction of uniqueness and therefore an increase in symptoms, high self-esteem would result from the opposite (Satir, 1988a; Satir et al., 1991). High self-esteem comes from the culmination of honoring self, others, and context and when the person experiences flow (Satir, 1988b). This is also known as **congruence**—the desired communication stance (Satir et al., 1994). Essentially, the person operates from their uniqueness rather than being confined by conformity and restriction (Satir et al., 1991). This, in turn, allows others to live from their own uniqueness as well.

Satir (1964/1967) noted the importance of congruent communication between family members: "People must communicate clearly if they are going to get the information which they need from others. Without communication, we, as humans, would not be able to survive" (p. 63). Communication includes both verbal and nonverbal communication (e.g., tone, expression, body language). A growth therapist's job as an outside agent of change in the family system is to help clients let go of dysfunctional coping and communication from childhood and to instead develop functional coping and communication. This promotes self-esteem and the congruence that a growth therapist is helping to bring out of each family member.

There are several ways that a growth therapist would help a client increase their self-esteem; balance their self-mandala; and allow for context, self, and others to be honored—thus promoting the client's congruence. The number of experiential techniques may be thought of as infinite, as experiential interventions are based on the creativity and flow of the therapist, client(s), and context (Reiter & McLendon, 2014). Some of Satir's traditional interventions, however, include the parts party, sculpting, metaphors, meditation, family reconstruction, temperature reading, reframing, and therapeutic touch. The use of the self-mandala is also foundational to the interventions used. Additionally, there are overarching conceptualizations of how people change regardless of intervention, which are addressed first.

Stages of Change

Irrespective of the various interventions that a growth therapist would use to increase self-esteem and congruence with a client, Satir conceptualized six stages through which people change (Satir et al., 1991). The first is the **status quo**, where the person's existing life no longer works and change is needed. At this stage, the person recognizes that there is a problematic story going on in their life. Next, there is the **introduction to a foreign element**, where the person brings up this desire for change to someone else (e.g., a therapist). Here, the person not only makes the problematic story known to others but specifically indicates a desire to shift this story. The aptly named **chaos stage** involves the shift from the status quo to the beginnings of change that causes instability. The transition from the problematic story to a more preferred story begins in this stage. The fourth stage—the **integration stage**—is where the person starts to integrate what they have learned thus far, which starts the course for a new state of being. The preferred story takes more shape at this point as the person makes efforts to breathe life into this story. The **practice stage** continues this integration of learning with further practice, and the preferred story becomes more consistent and present in the person's life. The final stage—the **new status quo**—is a more congruent state as a result of the person's efforts to make change. Unlike the old status quo (which was characterized by the problematic story), the new status quo is the manifestation of the preferred story.

People cycle through these stages of change throughout their life as people encounter different reasons for starting change (Satir et al., 1991). Some renditions of these stages may be easier, whereas some may be more challenging. The hope, however, is that the process of going through the stages becomes more fluid and even enjoyable as people move toward growth. The Daniels family is past the status quo stage (as they recognize change is needed) and is shifting from the introduction to a foreign element stage to the chaos stage (as they are starting the process of family therapy).

Self-Mandala

The self-mandala is used both as a diagnostic tool and as a framework from which interventions can be based upon. It is also sometimes an intervention in and of itself. Satir considered each of the eight pieces of the mandala—and the center element of self/"I am"—to be the universal human resources that are connected to one another (Satir et al., 1991). Although the specifics of these resources may change for each person, the basic category of each element of self is foundational to everyone.

Regarding the self-mandala's use as a diagnostic tool, a growth therapist would want to get a holistic story of a person that involves the consideration of all eight pieces (Satir et al., 1991). For example, the therapist would ask questions about the person's living situation (e.g., who they live with and where) to better understand their contextual and interactional components. The therapist would ask questions to gain information on the status of the other elements of the self-mandala as well. The therapist could either be explicit about this process or covert, asking questions for the purpose of filling in the self-mandala in the therapist's mind to better understand the client's current life story.

The intervention of the self-mandala comes into play through the process of therapy being centered around clients tapping into their inherent resources and manifesting those resources in their lives to create a therapeutic story of wholeness. Sometimes, the self-mandala informs other interventions: Satir's meditation intervention would certainly expand one's spiritual component of their self-mandala, for instance. Other times, activities directly related to the self-mandala are the intervention. For instance, Satir et al. (1991) described an acceptance-based demonstration of the self-mandala that can be used for interventive purposes. Essentially, Satir would have someone (who could be a family member in therapy or a volunteer at a workshop) identify components of the self-mandala that they are proud of and some that the person is ashamed of, does not use, etc. (e.g., the nutritional element being constrained due to ideas of thinness). Other individuals in the group would play the role of these elements. Satir would then engage the person in activities that allowed them to process their feelings with the components they struggle with and eventually invite them into a more harmonious existence with these components. Again, this leads to increased self-esteem, congruence, and overall wholeness of health.

The Parts Party

Satir believed that we inaccurately view people as their full self when we encounter them at any particular instance (Satir et al., 1991). This is not the case because if you are a night owl rather than a morning person, for example, it is likely that you are not the same person (i.e., you have different characteristics/elements of self that come forth) at night compared to the morning. The idea is that we have multiple facets of self that shift from being in the foreground to the background and vice versa.

People often get caught up in trying to ignore the less desirable parts of self (Satir et al., 1991). A common facet that people tend to disregard is their inner judge, who critiques their actions and thoughts. Satir considered this to be problematic because it denies one's full experience of themselves and, therefore, their resources. To mitigate this tendency, the **parts party** is a growth therapist's process of integrating one's inner human resources.

Satir's traditional approach to a parts party involves getting a group of people and having each person individually represent one person's (the Host) facets of self (Satir et al., 1991). The Guide (e.g., the therapist or workshop presenter) then acts as a facilitator to engage the group and the Host in various activities and steps to help the Host acknowledge their parts, engage them in conflict (i.e., get one part to try and take over the party and be in control), and then resolve the conflict to promote harmony between the parts.

In relation to the judge facet, for instance, a parts party would allow one to shift their judge from being a critic to being a support. If the Host initially thinks of the judge as a negative part, the Guide would ask the Host about situations in which the judge could be a positive part. This initial acknowledgment of the various qualities of each part challenges the black-and-white thinking that parts can be only bad or good. This would set up the Host to be able to connect the negative judge part with a more positive part—perhaps a supportive part who cares for the Host's well-being—during the resolution stage.

A growth therapist can adapt the process of the parts party based on the context, such as by guiding an individual client through an imagery-based version of the parts party. In a family session, several parts parties could be held with each family member rotating as the Host. While one family member is the Host, the other members would take the roles of the Host's parts. The parts party could be utilized in this way with the Daniels family.

Sculpting

One of the growth model's most famous interventions is **sculpting** (Satir & Baldwin, 1983). Satir originally developed the sculpt to be a movement-based technique in which the therapist moves clients around the room to demonstrate the current family dynamics and functioning. This would be considered a therapist-initiated sculpt. The therapist may also ask their clients to put themselves in the position that physically represents their experience: for example, "Mom, move yourself and your family members into the physical representation of what it feels like when you all are, as you mentioned, fighting like you're in a war zone." Though the therapist asked the client to create the sculpture, this would be considered a client-initiated sculpt because one of the clients is posing themselves and their family members based on their own experience of the family rather than the therapist choosing where each member goes. From here, the therapist would have each family member take turns posing the others to see everyone's perspective of the family dynamics.

Sculpting demonstrates the growth model's roots in cybernetics because the focus of a sculpt is on communication patterns (Satir & Baldwin, 1983). Getting a family to arrange themselves in the physical representation of their dynamics allows them to become visually aware of one another's roles. Once the family members put themselves in their corresponding sculptures, Satir would often keep them there and ask them to reflect on their emotional experience in those poses. She would additionally ask each family member to reflect on how the other members affected their own positions (e.g., "How does it feel when mom points her finger at you like that?").

Sculpting connects back to the communication stances, as Satir would use these communication stances to help make sense of the family members' roles and coping strategies (Satir et al., 1991). For example, "father could be super-reasonable and stand on a chair (expressing his power). Mother could be kneeling on the floor (expressing her coping through placating)" (Satir et al., 1991, p. 284). In most cases, families typically come into therapy with the pattern of telling each other what (or who) they consider to be the problem. This is the problematic story that the family is currently living—one in which family members likely do not listen to one another anymore since the dominant way of communicating is about what is causing the problem.

Sculpting is a way to help people move past these unhelpful communication stances and communicate in ways that are more congruent (Satir et al., 1991). Therefore, a growth therapist would not stop at the sculpts that represent the dysfunctional communication patterns. Once the family has awareness of these unhelpful patterns, the therapist may ask each family member to sculpt their desired dynamics to create a story of understanding and connection. A growth therapist focuses on the shift from what does not work to what does work for the family using their existing resources. The sculpt is a way to do this in a more active, comprehensive manner rather than simply relying on words (hence the growth model's designation as an experiential therapy).

Meditation

Satir used **meditations** both in her sessions with clients and in the workshops she gave (Haber, 2002; Satir et al., 1991), and Banmen and Gerber (1985) even published a book that compiled the collection of Satir's meditations. Satir specifically used meditations to tap into the right hemisphere of the brain, which she talked about containing our intuitive side (Satir et al., 1991). Meditation consequently allows for increased self-awareness, understanding, presence, acceptance, positivity, and more. Satir used meditations to increase wholeness of the self at both the intrapersonal and interpersonal levels to provide a connective experience within us as well as with those around us.

The purpose of Satir's use of meditations shifted over time (Satir et al., 1991). Initially, her meditations centered on one's feelings and ability to concentrate on the present moment. These meditations often included breathwork. Later in her career, Satir incorporated more thematic purposes to her meditations. For example, these intentions included focusing on positive ways of thinking, affirmations, and new choices/possibilities.

The Daniels family might benefit from various meditations. A growth therapist could initiate a possibilities-based meditation, for example, to expand the Daniels' problem-saturated story to a goal-oriented story that paints a picture of what the family wants to be different. Another beneficial meditation might include breathwork and focusing on one's feelings before engaging in a sculpt to help promote each family member's connection to their own experience to more honestly share and demonstrate this experience with the rest of the family.

Metaphors

Metaphors are both a linguistic and imaginative/visual tool for change in the growth model, specifically to add further depth and meaning to the discussion (Satir et al., 1991). Not only do metaphors create a visual bridge to words, but they also allow for increased understanding when the therapist and client do not share the same primary language. Satir described using nature-based metaphors (which she thought to be more universally understood) to help convey meaning when she was somewhere in which the language spoken was not English (Satir et al., 1991).

Like meditations, metaphors help shift the therapeutic process from being solely an intellectual endeavor, which Satir thought was limiting (Satir et al., 1991). Instead, metaphors provide an intuitive side to one's experience of self, which allows for a fuller experience of self and involvement of the brain altogether. These whole-person experiences included emotions, senses, imagery, and more.

The growth model itself is full of metaphors. Satir used an **iceberg metaphor** in which she conceptualized the intrapsychic essence of a person (Banmen, 2002; Satir et al., 1991). The tip of the iceberg (i.e., what is seen from the outside) is what people often inaccurately think comprises the entire human experience. In reality, beneath the water, there is a much deeper and more comprehensive internal human experience—one made up of feelings, perceptions, expectations, and more. This metaphor is used to remind growth therapists that it is vital to go below the surface and understand the client's full experience of self.

A metaphor that might apply to the Daniels family would represent the dynamic between Fran and Pam. Satir promoted the intuition and creativity of the therapist when applying interventions such as metaphors (Satir et al., 1991). If I (KS) were to work with the Daniels family, a metaphor I might use would involve a short story inspired by my mom and my cat: My mom loves my oldest cat and intensely seeks my cat out whenever she visits my house, prompting my cat to hide from her because she feels overwhelmed with the often overflowing attention. In contrast, my cat freely socializes with my friends who are not vying to pet her. My intention in using this metaphor with the Daniels is to paint a mirrored experience to Fran getting on Pam for not eating and Pam retreating. Perhaps this would allow them to recognize that sometimes taking a step back allows the other person to take a step forward.

Family Reconstruction

As evident in the concept of the primary triad, Satir incorporated family-of-origin work in the growth model. The **family reconstruction** is an intervention that involves bringing people back to their own family-of-origin experiences

(Satir et al., 1991). Specifically, it "provides a way of seeing ourselves and our parents with new eyes, and thus seeing the present and the future in a new perspective" (Satir et al., 1991, p. 205). Before the reconstruction happens during a family therapy session, one person (i.e., the Star) is selected to have their family of origin reconstructed (Satir et al., 1991). The Star and the therapist (i.e., the Guide) then meet beforehand to complete three specific tasks—a family map, a family chronology, and a wheel of influence—in preparation for the actual reconstruction. The following information on these three tasks is based on a traditional family (i.e., one mom, one dad, and one child). However, this process can be used with any family setup (e.g., stepfamilies, single-parent families).

A **family map** is essentially a family tree of three generations of the Star's family of origin (Satir et al., 1991). There are several stages of the development of the family map between the Guide and the Star. First, they gather the details of the Star's parents, including information on their birthdays, birthplaces, jobs, education, hobbies, cultural backgrounds, and so on. Second, three specific components are added to each parent's side of the map: (a) three adjectives to describe the parent, (b) the parent's primary coping stance, and (c) the parent's secondary coping stance. Third, the Star and Guide add information about siblings. Fourth, the Star and Guide then incorporate grandparents and additional information on the family dynamics, patterns of coping stances between family members, values and beliefs, and so on.

After completing a family map, the Star and Guide work on the **family life chronology**, a chart of important family life events in chronological order (Satir et al., 1991). These chronological events would include birthdays of all family members, significant family-specific events (e.g., marriages, divorces, deaths), and significant life-specific events (e.g., natural disasters, political events).

The pre-reconstruction planning ends with the **wheel of influence**, which is another chart of the important people/things that have influenced the Star's life (Satir et al., 1991). Specifically, these are emotional, physical, and intellectual impacts on the Star before adulthood. Obvious candidates for the wheel are members of the Star's family of origin. Other important people might include friends, teachers, and bosses, for example.

Once the family map, family life chronology, and wheel of influence are obtained and understood, the family reconstruction can begin (Satir et al., 1991). There are three main parts to the reconstruction. First, the Guide needs to understand the Star's specific goals for the reconstruction (Satir et al., 1991). In the context of the Daniels, for instance, Pam's initial goal—if she were the Star—might be to feel less pressured by her mom and less isolated from the family. The second step would involve the Guide telling the Star's family life story using the information gathered from the family map, family life chronology, and wheel of influence—especially focusing on information related to past and current family coping and resources. After the telling of the Star's family story, the Guide would then conduct a series of sculpts surrounding the Star's family of origin to help promote (a) current acceptance and understanding of what has happened in the past and (b) different ways of being and communicating in the present.

Temperature Reading

Temperature reading is a growth therapy technique that promotes congruent and honest communication between people (Satir et al., 1991), allowing for individuals in a group to express how they feel and what they think (and, inversely, receive what others feel and think) in a healthy way. Essentially, it is a process where people get on the same page and develop closer relationships as a result.

There are five major areas of content in a typical temperature reading discussion: (a) appreciations and excitements; (b) worries, concerns, and puzzles; (c) complaints and possible solutions; (d) new information; and (e) hopes and wishes (Satir et al., 1991). A temperature reading starts with appreciations and excitements about others in the group to start off on a positive note. This allows for the worries and concerns to be considered in a more receptive manner (while still promoting the use of "I" language rather than blaming language). The third topic allows individuals to take ownership of negative feelings related to complaints, but then follow them up with solutions. Talking about new information prevents assumptions and keeps everyone up to date with relevant information about one another and the group. Finally, the temperature reading ends on verbalizing hopes and wishes, which allows others in the group to support each other in these endeavors.

Satir et al. (1991) noted that in a family context, this intervention is most helpful when the family does this consistently, potentially both in therapy and in their day-to-day lives. Usually, this process can take between 30 and 60 minutes, depending on how well-versed the family is in directing a temperature reading.

Temperature reading might be useful with the Daniels family because it is evident that they are disconnected from one another and are not clearly communicating their experiences and needs. In contrast, this intervention fosters honesty and communication. For instance, Murray and Fran may use the temperature reading process to share their deeper concerns and worries regarding Pam's health. Pam might reveal some solutions that either she has not spoken about yet or that have not been truly heard by the family. Oliver and George could convey their hope to have a closer relationship with their sister. These are all things that have likely been unsaid, and a temperature reading would create a therapeutic story of direct discussions on these beneficial topics.

Reframing

Reframing "refers to interventions in which the therapist helps clients see themselves as capable and open to change" (Satir et al., 1991, p. 106). Instead of being trapped in unhelpful dynamics of defensiveness, resistance, etc., reframing allows for a more expansive (and helpful) story to be created in the client's life (Satir et al., 1991). Oftentimes, reframing can be done in a single sentence. If a client comes in and states that her husband doesn't care about her because he's at work all day, the therapist might say: "I'm hearing that you feel unseen by your husband; at the same time, I also wonder if he's so dedicated to work so that he can provide for you." The therapist would then ask the husband if this is true to verify and then engage the wife and husband in a further conversation based on this reframe.

Right now, the Daniels—especially Murray and Fran—see Pam's lack of eating and loss of weight as something negative. This is, of course, understandable. However, a growth therapist might use a reframe to help the family see that these behaviors from Pam might be a way to let them know that she needs support. This may allow Murray and Fran to recognize their role in how they can be helpful to Pam rather than this situation being a "Pam problem." Oliver and George's distance from Pam—though in one way could be seen as a lack of interest—could be reframed as a lack of understanding of what is going on or how to help Pam.

Therapeutic Touch and Connection

Satir had a distinct style of therapy in which she utilized therapeutic touch as an intervention on its own (Haber, 2002; Satir & Baldwin, 1983). In a transcript of one of her therapy videos, she discussed the importance and use of touch in a therapeutic setting:

> [Touch] says things that no words can say… . Now, for me, my touch is not going to send much to you unless I am integrated myself. Unless I really feel whole myself, then energy moves out. If I feel I have to touch, or I have to be careful about touching, that won't work. Because it's not a gimmick. And it's not a strategy.
>
> (Shoai, 2013, p. 41)

Connecting back to Satir's Eastern and humanistic approach, she viewed touch as a genuine way to move energies between people and communicate at a deeper level of humanhood.

Satir would often use touch to (a) move people around the room (such as during sculpts) to increase intimacy between family members and (b) to promote touch between the family members themselves (Satir & Baldwin, 1983). For example, she might have a couple hold each other's hands while talking to one another. In addition to touch, Satir would also look each person directly in the eyes and guide the clients to do the same with each other. For Satir, the use of touch helps promote a story of intimacy and connection.

There are several ways in which touch and connection could be utilized with the Daniels family. Having the three children—Pam, Oliver, and George—hold hands, for example, would create a story of coming together as siblings rather than feeling isolated. The therapist might also encourage each family member to look directly into one another's eyes when speaking rather than talking directly to the therapist.

Therapeutic Presence

Satir was most known for her connective, personal, and touch-based approach (Satir & Baldwin, 1983)—all of which highlighted the experiential nature of the model and her emphasis on human connection. Despite the case transcript for this chapter being readable rather than watchable, information on *how* a growth therapist would interact with the Daniels (e.g., tone, touch, movement) is included to demonstrate the full picture of a growth therapist's warm therapeutic presence and process. The foundation of this approach with clients is trust (Satir, 1975a)—for example, shaking hands with each family member, using the clients' first names, asking permission for touch, and asking each family member for their perspective.

Another important element of the therapeutic presence is the therapist's own experience of congruence (Satir, 1964/1967; Satir & Baldwin, 1983). If the therapist is not congruent, then it would be hard to facilitate a session to promote a family's congruence. Satir (1983) described the therapist's congruence in therapy through the **I-Thou relationship** between therapist and client. Just as the therapist takes responsibility for their own actions, they allow the client to take responsibility for their actions rather than telling the client how they should. This congruent approach on the therapist's end highlights the individuality of both themselves and each family member and is a model for family members' behaviors (Satir & Baldwin, 1983).

The therapeutic process is one of acceptance and understanding of one's experiences (even if they are negative experiences) because, for a growth therapist, everything is useful for the client's present-day change (Satir et al., 1991). Therefore, the use of the growth model would be based on that therapist's intuition with the family and the dynamics of the session. Although Satir would usually do a family map with clients—especially at the beginning of therapy—the case transcript focuses on other interventions for brevity's sake. The following case transcript with the Daniels family, therefore, shows one iteration of how a therapy session with a growth therapist might unfold.

Case Transcript

Therapist: Hi everyone, it's great to meet you. My name is Minnie. [*Gets up to shake each family member's hand and gets their names.*]

Intervention: The therapist makes sure to acknowledge and establish a personal relationship with each family member by individually shaking their hands, demonstrating each person's importance to the therapeutic process. She also highlights the importance of human connection through appropriate therapeutic touch.

Therapist: Okay, so we have Fran and Murray as mom and dad, Pam as sister, and Oliver and George as brothers. Do I have that right?

Intervention: The therapist continues to build trust by remembering and citing each family member's name.

Murray: You got it. [*All family members nod their heads in agreement.*]

Therapist: Great, so it would be really helpful if each of you could tell me what you are hoping to get out of our time together today. [*Leaning forward in chair and making eye contact.*]

Intervention: The therapist is asking each family member for their perspective. She is also demonstrating genuine interest in their answers through her body language.

Fran: Well, Pam's health is extremely concerning to us. I think you were told this before we came in, but Pam was diagnosed with anorexia, so she is really underweight and doesn't eat nearly enough.

Conceptualization: The fact that the Daniels family is in therapy indicates that they are in the introduction to a foreign element stage. They—particularly Fran at this moment—have already acknowledged that there is problem that they would like to resolve (i.e., the status quo stage). Now, they are introducing this problem to the therapist in an effort to make change.

Therapist: Okay, so Fran, you're saying that you see Pam's health as a concern, and you're here to find a way to help her be healthier?

Intervention: The therapist does several things using specific language and communication. First, she reflects Fran's perspective as her own rather than the "us" perspective that Fran had given. Second, she continues to build trust through validating Fran's perspective by repeating back what Fran said. Third, she addresses the problem Fran brought up but does so in a way that involves a positive goal (i.e., increasing Pam's health) based on Fran's actions (i.e., Fran helping Pam). This takes the language away from Pam being the problem and plants the seeds of the whole family's involvement in both what isn't working and how they can make it work. Essentially, the therapist is beginning to shift what in this case could be considered as a blaming stance from Fran to a more congruent stance.

Fran: Of course, I am her mother, and I just don't know what to do for her anymore.

Therapist: Fran, it sounds like this is partially coming from feeling like you can't do your job as a caring mother when you see Pam not physically at her best. Do I have that right?

Fran: Absolutely.

Therapist: That must be really tough. Pam, what is it like for you to hear that your mom doesn't feel like she does a good job as a mom all the time? Could you look at her in the eyes and tell her your answer?

Intervention: The therapist is encouraging mother and daughter to have open, congruent communication to create a better understanding of each other's experiences. The therapist also has mother and daughter look at each other in the eyes while doing so to create connection through the process. This intervention starts to initiate the chaos stage, as the therapist is getting the family members to be different with one another to promote the preferred story.

Pam: [*Turns to and looks directly at mom.*] I mean, I guess it's obvious that this whole situation has been hard for you, but this is the first time I'm hearing that you don't feel like a good mom because of it.

Therapist: Pam, keep looking at your mom, and tell her what difference it makes for you to hear this from her.

Intervention: A problematic communication pattern between Pam and Fran is that Pam feels like her mom is frequently on her back about her eating habits and weight, which has contributed to their strained relationship. The therapist is asking Pam to reflect on her mom's comment about feeling incapable as a mother to see how this shifts how Pam sees (what she finds to be) the unhelpful communication from mom.

Pam: [*Still looking at mom.*] I guess it makes me feel bad that you feel that way. I honestly thought that you were just nagging me all the time just to do it. Even if she's not doing it to nag me, it still doesn't help, though.

Therapist: Okay, and what were you hoping to get out of today's session, Pam?

Pam: Well, that is what it was. To get my parents, mainly mom, to understand that their harping on me all the time is not helping.

Therapist: Okay, so you want to be able to tell your parents that their attempts to help you—which you now know a bit more about from mom's perspective—aren't what you need.

Intervention: The therapist once again reframes what the client shares as her goal surrounding her identification of the problem (i.e., her parents' harping) to something that the client can take ownership of as well (i.e., telling her parents that this is not working for her). The previous comment from Pam shows that she is also in the introduction to a foreign element stage because she sees and speaks about a problem in the current family functioning (even if her idea of the problem is different from Fran's).

Pam: Yes.

Therapist: Okay, and do you know your dad's idea of what he wants from this session? [*Pam shakes her head "no."*] Could you turn to him and ask?

Intervention: The therapist is still getting each family member's perspective but is doing so through the engagement of the family. Specifically, the therapist is trying to promote more open communication between the family members since it seems that they are not necessarily on the same page about things (e.g., Pam's not knowing Fran's true feelings about the situation). The therapist is also demonstrating the I-Thou relationship by asking Pam to take responsibility for her actions and be able to ask dad for his perspective. Additionally, Pam has felt isolated from dad, so the therapist is trying to engage dad and Pam into a more direct interaction. The chaos stage continues to unfold.

Pam: [*Turns to dad.*] What do you want from coming here today?

Therapist: Murray, could you come sit next to Pam and look at her as you tell her your answer? Fran, could you scootch over a seat to allow Murray to fit?

Intervention: Pam was sitting next to Fran on one side of the therapist while Murray was sitting next to Oliver and George on the other side of the therapist. The therapist asks Murray to look at his daughter but also to get up and get closer to her. This should decrease the isolation between Pam and Murray and promote a closer relationship between them instead. The disruption of current family dynamics in the chaos stage is now involving the movement of family members.

Murray: [*Moves to the chair next to Pam.*] I want to figure out what is going on that is leading you not to want to eat and lose this much weight. It is scary, honey, for both me and your mom.

Therapist: Murray, similar to Fran, you both are here to figure out how you can better help Pam out of concern for her well-being as parents.

Murray: Yes.

Therapist: Okay, and what about the boys? Oliver and George, what are you hoping happens today?

Oliver: I agree with mom and dad about Pam. Ever since she stopped eating, she doesn't really talk to us anymore. I get that me and George do more boy stuff anyway, but still. The only time I see her is when she's at dinner, but that ends after mom tells Pam to eat more and then Pam usually gets up and leaves.

Therapist: So, you share the same concern for your sister as mom and dad do. It also sounds like you don't like that you and your brother don't do as much with Pam as perhaps you'd like. [*Oliver nods his head "yes."*] So, George, what are your thoughts? What do you hope for today's session?

George: The same as Oliver. We do more stuff by ourselves and with dad than with Pam. She's older than me, but we used to still have fun at the house and watch movies and stuff.

Conceptualization: Oliver and George also have their own version of the problematic story and are therefore in the introduction to a foreign element stage as they tell the therapist their concerns and wants.

Therapist: Okay, so it sounds like you both—you and Oliver—want to have a closer relationship with Pam. [*George nods his head "yes."*] Alright, so I am going to ask you all to stand up and do something a little different with me today. [*Therapist stands up, and the family follows.*] I'm a visual person, so it would help me to get a more concrete picture of what usually happens in this family. Pam, I would like you to create a sort of sculpture using your family members and yourself by putting everyone in the positions that represent what it feels like for you being in this family now.

Intervention: So far in the session, the therapist has started to engage the family members in different ways (e.g., having them ask for each other's perspectives, look at one another, and move closer to one another). These have been examples of therapist-initiated sculpts to initiate more helpful communication patterns compared to what currently seems to be happening in the family. Now, the therapist is initiating a sculpt that the family, specifically Pam, will arrange based on the current dynamics. The therapist chose Pam since she is the one feeling isolated from most of the family, and the therapist wants Pam to have a more active role. However, the sculpt now engages the entire family in the chaos stage.

Pam: Alright, well I guess I would be by myself.

Therapist: How far away by yourself? Could you move your family around and then put yourself somewhere in relation to them to show me?

[Pam puts her brothers and dad in one corner of the room.]

Therapist: And how should dad and your brothers be standing in relation to one another?

[Pam puts her dad standing behind her brothers with one hand on each of their shoulders.]

Therapist: Okay, and where is mom?

[Pam puts her mom more in the middle of the room—but closer to the other corner. Pam then puts herself in that other corner of the room facing away from everyone.]

Therapist: So, is mom standing facing you or is she facing your dad and brothers? What exactly is she doing?

Pam: She's sort of in between everyone, but she is more focused on me. [*Pam faces mom toward her with one arm reaching out to Pam and the other one waving her finger at Pam. Pam goes back to her corner facing away from everyone.*]

Therapist: Alright, everyone stay right there for a second. [*Lets a few moments go by.*] Fran, how does it feel to be placed in this position?

Fran: It's tough. I feel alone and like I'm doing something wrong. Especially with where Pam is in comparison to me. It hurts that she's over there by herself and isn't even able to look at me.

Therapist: Fran, it sounds like as a mom, it hurts you to see your child so far away from you, and I'm assuming then that you'd like to be closer to her. Is that right?

Fran: Yes.

Therapist: Is this how this dynamic feels for you?

Fran: The part where I am reaching out to her, yes. But I suppose I don't feel like I wave my finger at her. I feel more like I am fully trying to reach out to her out of concern.

Therapist: Can you move around and show us what it feels like for you when you are fully reaching out to Pam?

Intervention: Pam seems to experience Fran as communicating to her via a blaming stance (as evidenced by Pam having Fran point her finger at Pam). When Fran described a more positive dynamic of wanting to provide support because she cares, the therapist focuses on that and asks Fran how she can show what that more congruent communication would look like.

[*Fran moves closer to Pam and reaches both arms out toward her.*]

Therapist: And is Pam still facing away from you even when you feel like you are reaching out to her?

Fran: Yes, I don't think she wants my help most of the time.

Therapist: Pam, is mom right?

Pam: Recently, for sure.

Therapist: Okay, is it alright, Pam, if I place my hand on your back and ask you to turn around? [*Pam nods her head "yes" and turns around.*] Based on what you all have told me and shown me so far, it seems like there is some disconnection from one another. I want to ask you, Pam, to do something.

Intervention: The therapist has allowed the family to start to move themselves into how they see and experience their dynamics right now. The therapist sees the separation between family members and the unhelpful way that they are currently communicating. The therapist is now initiating a part of the sculpt that will allow the family members to explore more congruent communication and coping. She also utilizes touch to promote connection.

Therapist: Pam, what difference does it make for you to be facing mom and seeing her reach out to you?

Pam: I guess I am actually seeing her try. But, like I said, it's not the kind of try that I need all the time.

Therapist: Could you let mom know how she could reach out to you in a helpful way?

Pam: Mom, sometimes I just need you to ask me if I'm okay instead of saying that I need to eat. Telling me to eat makes me want to eat less, and you sent me straight to that other therapist when you realized what was going on instead of talking to me about it.

Therapist: Could you show mom what reaching out would feel like? Move her into the spot where you feel like she is reaching out and it is helpful, where you feel supported.

[Pam has Fran step closer to her and puts Fran's hands on Pam's shoulders.]

Therapist: Okay, hold it here, you two. Pam, go ahead and tell mom how you feel differently here.

Pam: I feel like you are actually coming to me and trying to listen to me. You are asking me what is wrong directly.

Therapist: [*Puts a hand on both Pam's back and Fran's back.*] Fran, would you be able to ask Pam that question?

Fran: Honey, what is wrong? [*Begins to tear up.*] I really do want to know.

Therapist: Alright, stay right there for a second. Pam, how does it feel to have mom ask you that?

Pam: It's the first time she has really asked me that question, so it feels nice. It feels like she cares about me rather than just being worried about the food thing.

Therapist: Okay, and where is dad in all this? You originally put him over in the other corner with the boys. Murray, how does it feel for you to be over there with Oliver and George?

Murray: I feel like I'm not involved in something important. Obviously, the boys are important, as are all the kids, always. But there's something really important right now going on between mom and Pam over a big issue.

Pam: I know he means I am the issue. That is why he doesn't want to deal with me. That's why I put him over there with Oliver and George.

Therapist: I hear where you're coming from with that, Pam. I also heard something else in there where it sounds like dad sees something important going on with his daughter, and as a parent, that concerns him. I'm also hearing that there might be some regret in not being involved in this as a parent. Is that right, Murray? [*Murray nods head "yes."*] Pam, do you want dad to be involved?

Intervention: The therapist validates where Pam is coming from and also gives a reframe of what Murray said. This reframe allows for a greater understanding of Murray's intentions and a deeper understanding about how Murray feels.

Pam: I do, I just feel like he doesn't want to be involved all the time.

Therapist: Could you ask him to come join you and your mom?

Intervention: The therapist continues to help the family develop more open and honest communication with one another.

Pam: Dad, will you come here please?

[*Dad walks over to Fran and Pam.*]

Therapist: Murray, now that you're over here, can you show Pam how you'd like to be here for her? Not just physically be over here but the picture of what it represents for you to be here for her when she needs you for support.

[*Murray wraps his arm around Pam.*]

Therapist: Pam, is this more so what you are hoping from dad?

Pam: Yes.

Therapist: Murray, what about for you? What's going on for you here?

Murray: I feel more involved. I hope Pam knows that I love her very much. I guess I just don't know how to help her all the time, and I wind up spending more time with the boys.

Therapist: And what about your wife? You're here with your arm around Pam, so what are you doing in relation to Fran since she is a part of this picture as well?

Murray: [*Puts his arm around Fran.*] These are both my girls. I love'em both.

Therapist: Fran, do you often feel this love from Murray?

Fran: Well, honestly, this feels newer for me because I feel like I've been on my own with the whole situation with Pam. Murray and I have talked about it logistically, but I'm the one who practically has been trying to deal with it. I know he loves me, but I don't always feel supported in this.

Therapist: This relationship between you two is really important both as parents and as partners. Pam, do you mind if mom and dad face each other for a moment? [*Gently has Pam step out to the side and away from mom and dad. Steps in between Pam and her parents and puts a hand on Murray's shoulder and Fran's shoulder to face them toward each other.*] Fran, can you tell Murray what you need from him?

Intervention: The therapist brings the focus to the parental and partner relationship between Murray and Fran, as this relationship is where the communication in the whole family stems from. This shift also takes away the focus on just Pam (who has been brought to therapy as the problematic person in the family) and puts the focus on how others in the family contribute to communication patterns as well.

Fran: [*Looking back at therapist.*] I need more support from him.

Therapist: Look at him and tell him what support you need.

Fran: I need you to support me more with this. I know that you feel more comfortable helping the boys with things, but we need to be a team on this. Pam needs both of us, and I don't feel like I know what to do all the time either.

Therapist: [*Takes Murray's hands and places them on Fran's.*] Respond to Fran from here. Look at her solely in the eyes as you speak with her.

Murray: Okay, I do get it. I just need you to tell me exactly what you need because I also don't always know all the time.

Therapist: Fran, how does this feel for you to have Murray hold you like this and look at you as he tells you this?

Fran: [*Tears up.*] Much better. Like we're actually talking about this together. And I do know I need to tell him this more. I just let it go usually.

Therapist: Okay, stay right here for a moment. Oliver and George, I know you've been a bit of a ways away while all this has been going on. What are you seeing from over there?

Intervention: The therapist makes sure to include all members of the family during the sculpt.

Oliver: I haven't seen mom and dad stand that close in a while.

George: Yeah, they're always stressed.

Therapist: Okay, and do you two want to be over there? Does that feel right for you?

[Oliver and George both shake their heads "no."]

Therapist: Where do you want to be instead? Let's start first with how you would like to be in relation to Pam. Can you both move yourself to make the picture that you want to see happening with her?

[*Oliver walks over next to Pam. George stands next to him.*] Alright, so you both came closer to Pam. Pam, your brothers chose to come closer to you. Do you prefer this experience?

Pam: Yeah, I do.

Therapist: Would you all be willing to get a bit closer for a moment? Take each other's hands in a circle together. [*Moves Pam, Oliver, and George closer together and clasps their hands together.*] What about now? George, do you prefer being here instead of way in the corner?

George: Yeah. This is how it sort of felt when we would do movie nights together. Although I'm a boy and do need my space sometimes, so I don't want to be this close always. Pam used to joke that I have the smelliest feet in the world.

[Family laughs.]

Pam: That's true.

Therapist: [*Laughs.*] Well, that makes sense. Just like it's too much to never be close to someone, it's also sometimes too much to always be close to someone. It sounds like, though, that when you all want to feel close as siblings, this is what it would be like. Pam, Oliver, George, is this the case?

[*Pam, Oliver, and George nod their heads "yes."*]

Therapist: Great, so I am going to ask you all to do something now. Could you all—Murray and Fran as well—get in a circle and put your arms around each other's shoulders? [*Each family member stands in a circle and puts their arms around each other's shoulders.*] How does it feel to be here?

Intervention: It is clear to the therapist that the interactional piece of each family member's self-mandala was strained at the beginning of the session. Through the use of various interventions, especially the last two therapist-initiated sculpts between the siblings and the whole family unit, the therapist helps the family enrich this component of their self-mandala.

George: It feels like we are about to get ready for a sports game.

[*Family laughs.*]

Therapist: Does that mean it feels like you all are a team?

Intervention: The therapist takes George's joke about a sports game and makes it a meaningful metaphor about the family being a team—further promoting their connection.

[*Oliver and George nod their heads "yes."*]

Fran: Yes.

Therapist: Murray, Pam, what about for you?

Murray: It does. [*Rubs Pam's arm.*]
Pam: Yeah, I can't remember the last time we did something like this.
Therapist: That's a great note to leave you all on. Before our next session, I'd like you to pay special attention to when you all feel like you are in this pose together during the week. Perhaps not literally, but notice the moments in which you feel like you are representing this family sculpture of being a team. Does that work for everyone?

Intervention: Growth therapists may give clients experiential activities to do outside of the therapy room to continue experiencing the desired communication skills learned in the therapy room. In this case, the therapist asks the Daniels family to take this ending family "team" sculpture and notice when this desired, more congruent communication stance is happening between the family. This is shifting the Daniels into the integration stage as they begin to incorporate what they learned in therapy into their day-to-day lives. Future sessions and experiential tasks in between sessions will move the Daniels to the practice stage (where they continue to implement what they learn in therapy), and the Daniels will hopefully eventually find themselves in the new status quo stage (i.e., where the congruent story has taken hold).

[*Family agrees.*]
Therapist: Great. It was really a pleasure meeting you all today, and I look forward to seeing you next week.

The Therapeutic Story

The Daniels came into the session with their eyes on Pam. From Fran and Murray's perspective, the primary concern included Pam's health and eating habits. Oliver and George commented on their lack of a close relationship with their sister. As the therapist started getting each family member's perspective through both conversation and the various sculpts, it was clear that this family was feeling disconnected in various ways and did not openly talk about their experiences or perspectives with one another.

The strategies the therapist implemented challenged the idea that one specific problem within a family (in this case, the Daniels' initial perspective that Pam was not eating) is the source of the current discord. Instead, the therapist took the viewpoint of looking at the family's overall well-being and saw how various members' incongruent communication stances contributed to the issues they were experiencing.

The therapeutic story that was created is one of connection and honest communication. First, the therapist promoted connection between the family members through multiple techniques. These included utilizing physical touch, asking family members to directly speak to one another, and moving family members into more desired ways of being via sculpting. Second, the therapist invited a broader viewpoint of the problem within the family and engaged the family in a way that revealed other important dynamics that were contributing to their lack of flow. For example, Pam's sculpt of her experience showed Murray that his daughter felt distant from him. Third, the therapist demonstrated and invited clearer and congruent communication from the family. The therapist exhibited this communication herself by checking in to see if she understood someone's perspective (e.g., "Do I have that right?") and by providing reframes of the family's statements. She also asked the family to communicate differently themselves (e.g., "Look at him and tell him what support you need."). Overall, the authentic approach from the therapist and the experiential nature of the model allowed the Daniels family to transform their problematic story of disconnection and strained communication into a preferred story in which they openly communicated and came together as a team.

References

Banmen, J. (2002). The Satir model: Yesterday and today. *Contemporary Family Therapy*, *24*(1), 7–22.

Banmen, J., & Gerber, J. (Eds.). (1985). *Virginia Satir: Meditations and inspirations*. Celestial Arts.

Cheung, G., & Chan, C. (2009). The Satir model and cultural diversity: A Hong Kong reflection. In J. Banmen (Ed.), *Satir transformational systemic therapy* (pp. 205–221). Science and Behavior Books.

Der Pan, P. J. (2000). The effectiveness of structured and semistructured Satir model groups on family relationships with college students in Taiwan. *The Journal for Specialists in Group Work*, *25*(3), 305–318.

Epstein, N. B., Berger, A. T., Fang, J. J., Messina, L. A., Smith, J. R., Lloyd, T. D., Fang, X., & Liu, Q. X. (2012). Applying Western-developed family therapy models in China. *Journal of Family Psychotherapy*, *23*(3), 217–237.

Freeman, M. L. (1999). Gender matters in the Satir growth model. *The American Journal of Family Therapy*, *27*(4), 345–363.

Haber, R. (2002). Virginia Satir: An integrated, humanistic approach. *Contemporary Family Therapy*, *24*(1), 23–34.

Hagen, L., & Sabey, A. (2019). Satir model of transformational systemic therapy. In J. L. Lebow, A. L. Chambers, & D.C. Breunlin (Eds.), *Encyclopedia of couple and family therapy* (pp. 2549–2557). Springer.

Maxey, V. A. (2021). The intersectional growth model: The Satir growth model informed by intersectional feminism. *Contemporary Family Therapy*, *43*, 54–68.

Rasheed, J. M., Rasheed, M. N., & Marley, J. A. (2011). *Family therapy: Models and techniques*. SAGE Publications.

Reiter, M. D. (2025). *Family therapy: An introduction to process, practice, and theory* (2nd ed.). Routledge.

Reiter, M. D., & McLendon, J. (2014). Satir growth model. In M. D. Reiter (Ed.), *Case conceptualization in family therapy* (pp. 82–104). Pearson.

Satir, V. (1967). *Conjoint family therapy* (Rev. ed.). Science and Behavior Books. (Original work published 1964).

Satir, V. (1972). *Peoplemaking*. Science and Behavior Books.

Satir, V. (1975a). Problems and pitfalls in working with families. In V. Satir, J. Stachowiak, & H. A. Taschman (Eds.), *Helping families to change* (pp. 133–160). Jason Aronson.

Satir, V. (1975b). *Self esteem*. Celestial Arts.
Satir, V. (1983). *Conjoint family therapy* (3rd ed.). Science and Behavior Books.
Satir, V. (1987). Going behind the obvious: The psychotherapeutic journey. In J. K. Zeig (Ed.), *The evolution of psychotherapy* (pp. 58–74). Brunner/Mazel.
Satir, V. (1988a). *The new peoplemaking*. Science and Behavior Books.
Satir, V. (1988b). The tools of the therapist. In J. K. Zeig & S. R. Lankton (Eds.), *Developing Ericksonian therapy* (pp. 513–523). Brunner/Mazel.
Satir, V., & Baldwin, M. (1983). *Satir step by step*. Science and Behavior Books.
Satir. V., Banmen, J., Gerber, J., & Gomori, M. (1991). *The Satir model: Family therapy and beyond*. Science and Behavior Books.
Satir, V., Stachowiak, J., & Taschman, H. A. (1994). *Helping families to change*. Jason Aronson.
Sedikides, C., Gaertner, G., & O'Mara, E. M. (2011). Individual self, relational self, collective self: Hierarchical ordering of the tripartite self. *Psychological Studies*, *56*(1), 98–107.
Shoai, S. (2013). *Instructor's manual for Of Rocks and Flowers: Dealing with the abuse of children*. Psychotherapy.net. https://www.psychotherapy.net/data/uploads/525722432f413.pdf

9 Brief Therapy: Mental Research Institute

Pei-Fen Li

Mental Research Institute (MRI) was one of the earliest clinical centers devoted to family therapy during the 1950s and 1960s. It was founded by Don D. Jackson in 1959 in Palo Alto, California (Mental Research Institute, n.d.). MRI founders (e.g., Don D Jackson, John Weakland, Jay Haley, Paul Watzlawick) collaborated with and were highly influenced by Gregory Bateson's National Institute of Mental Health (NIH)-funded research project on communication in families with one member having schizophrenia (Ray & Schlanger, 2009). They developed the **double-bind theory** (Bateson et al., 1956), in which individuals receive contradictory messages at different communication levels (e.g., verbal and non-verbal). No matter how people respond, they cannot win the situation. They feel trapped and punished (e.g., if you don't do it, you will be punished; if you do it, you will be punished as well).

With the collaboration and the influences of Gregory Bateson's work, MRI therapists perceive that symptoms are communication and are maintained and embedded in interaction patterns (Watzlawick & Weakland, 1977). The shift from viewing symptoms from individual and psychoanalytic perspectives to understanding the problem in an interactional context was a significant paradigm shift in the field of psychotherapy.

The Therapeutic Story of Problem Formation

Problem

MRI therapists view the problem as undesired behaviors in the present (Weakland & Fisch, 1992). It is unwanted behavior that occurs repeatedly and constitutes an ongoing difficulty, reinforced and maintained within reciprocal interactions among family members (Fisch et al., 1982). MRI therapists observed that one person's behavior elicited and structured another's behavior and vice versa (Watzlawick & Weakland, 1977). If two people are in contact over time, repetitive patterns of their interactions will arise. When a problem happens, people attempt to resolve or alter it. When a problem is not successfully resolved, people tend to use similar or the same attempted solutions to fix

DOI: 10.4324/9781003668510-9

the original issue, assuming that if they try harder, they will fix it. Unfortunately, the attempted solutions, rather than alleviating the original problem, often become repetitive patterns that inadvertently maintain or exacerbate the problem.

Cybernetics and Communication

From a cybernetic perspective, a human system constantly maintains its homeostasis to ensure its functionality. This self-regulatory mechanism influences how individuals in the system respond and adjust their behaviors in relation to each other. Bateson (1972) once stated, "all changes can be understood as the effort to maintain some constancy and all constancy is maintained through changes" (p. 381). As individuals and families seek change in therapy, they also seek stability, which is a cybernetic system (Keeney & Ross, 1985). Human systems adapt to change for survival, and these adaptations stabilize the system's overall functioning. Stability isn't no change; it requires the system to self-regulate and restore equilibrium while adjusting to internal and external demands and differences. Throughout the feedback process, the system responds either by reinforcing stability or by supporting change, creating a circular causality that organizes human communication.

Feedback Loops

Feedback loops are the circular processes where the output of the system flows back as input (information) that further informs and allows the system to adjust based on this information (Watzlawick et al., 1974). If the system receives **negative feedback**, it reduces and corrects deviations to maintain homeostasis. For example, when the weather is too hot, people sweat, which removes heat from the skin's surface to lower body temperature and cool down. When the weather is too cold, the human body shivers to generate heat and warm up. When shivering is not enough to warm the body, people need to put on a coat. Human bodies respond to the temperature around them to return to equilibrium, a state in which they feel comfortable and can function.

Unlike negative feedback, which corrects deviations from the original status quo, **positive feedback** reinforces or amplifies changes, leading to growth within the system or to further deviation from the initial state (Watzlawick et al., 1974). For example, a person shares a video online, a few friends or followers see it, find it interesting, and share it on their social media. Once they share it, their friends or followers see it, continuing to build a bigger audience. This cycle repeats, attracting more viewers and increasing its popularity, which might be unexpected given the first person's intention.

In Daniels family, when Pam started eating less and lost weight, Fran commented that she was not eating enough and wanted to bring her back to a "normal" weight. However, Pam minimized the mother's concern and responded that

"I am not that hungry." The family temporarily dropped the topic and kept the peace without resolving Pam's control of her restrained eating habits. In addition, Fran has taken the primary caretaking role in the household and monitored Pam's eating habits, while Murray has taken a withdrawal role and let Fran handle it. Negative feedback loops show how each family member has tried but continues to maintain the family's homeostasis, preventing relational tensions and protecting the belief that "we are a normal family."

Positive feedback loops escalate Pam's eating habits to receive a clinical diagnosis of Anorexia, and she continues losing weight. Fran worried and continued pressuring Pam to eat more. Pam felt threatened with losing her autonomy and resisted Fran's comments and restricted her eating, as this is one way for her to preserve her sense of control. Pam's resistance and withdrawal made Fran feel more anxious and controlling, which intensified her interaction with Pam, who became even more withdrawn not only from her parents but also from her siblings. As Murray spent more time with the boys to avoid potential relational conflicts with Pam and assumed it was Fran's role and responsibility, Pam felt even more emotionally excluded by her father, and Fran felt unsupported by her husband. The mutual disengagement among family members reinforced emotional distance and Pam's symptoms.

Circular Causality

Circular causality refers to the cause-and-effect relationship within feedback loops, in which each element in the system repeatedly influences and is influenced by the others (Watzlawick et al., 1967). Circular causality emphasizes reciprocal and mutually reinforcing interactions that sustain the system over time. In circular causality, no single person is the cause, as each person's behavior is both a response and a trigger for another's behavior. Through multiple circular interactions among family members, the system self-regulates to sustain equilibrium or pursue a desired change.

Applying the concepts of feedback loops and circular causality, MRI therapists perceive human communication through the patterns of symmetrical escalation and complementary communication.

Symmetrical Escalation

Symmetrical escalation means that each person responds to the other's behavior similarly, leading to an escalation point (positive feedback) for change (Watzlawick et al., 1967; Watzlawick & Weakland, 1977). This can result in healthy growth when both behaviors are constructive, such as both partners mirroring and competing for mutual career accomplishments, or destructive conflicts when both behaviors are harmful, such as partners' or family members' repetitive arguments or intensified conflicts. For example, Fran worries about Pam's health and school performance, so she reminds Pam of her eating behavior at the dinner table. Pam perceives Fran's reminders as pushing and pressuring her, so she restricts her eating and arguing back, which further worries Fran, who then pushes Pam to eat even more. The more Fran pushes, the more Pam pushes back by eating less and arguing further to preserve her autonomy and control overeating.

Complementary Communication

Complementary communication refers to each person responding to the other's behavior in a complementary way, thereby stabilizing and balancing the system (negative feedback) (Watzlawick et al., 1967; Watzlawick & Weakland, 1977). In this complementary communication, one takes a more dominant or directive role, while the other takes a more subordinating or supportive role. Although complementary communication maintains the system's homeostasis, the rigidity of this pattern can make family members feel stuck when their needs change and they no longer want to play the submissive role. Murray and Fran take complementary roles in responding to Pam's eating behavior. Fran is undoubtedly more involved, monitoring Pam's eating habits, even pressuring her to eat when Pam resists. Murray takes a withdrawal role in relation to Pam, lets Fran take charge of the issue, and often focuses on interacting with his sons, Oliver and George. When Fran takes charge, Murray steps back. This complementary communication pattern between Fran and Murray stabilizes the marriage, as Fran's over-functioning matches Murray's under-functioning. However, this rigid complementary communication between Fran and Murray maintains Pam's eating behaviors as Fran's over-functioning and controlling role, and Murray's disengagement makes Pam feel pressured and avoidant, which finally perpetuates family distress.

Report and Command Levels of Communication

When people communicate, they convey two levels of messages: report and command aspects (Watzlawick et al., 1967). **Report-level communication** refers to the literal content or factual information people share with others. In interaction, it is a statement of fact. **Command-level communication** means the relational or meta-communicative aspect of the message. It defines the nature of the relationship between two communicators (e.g., power, expectations, and roles) and provides a context for interpreting the report message. The command message can be conveyed nonverbally, through body language or facial expressions. Problems arise when there is an inconsistency between report and command communications, leading to mixed messages and confusion among family members.

As Fran comments at the dinner table that Pam is not eating enough, Pam would counter by saying that she was not that hungry. The mother and daughter's argument of "not eating enough" is not just about food consumption (the report level of communication). A metacommunication (the command levels of communication) about the mother's control and authority of deciding what is best for the daughter, the daughter's attempts to seek independence and autonomy through her eating behavior, and their rigid relational roles to each other, such as the mother's dominance and the daughter's submissiveness, do not fit with the daughter's developmental needs any more.

First-Order and Second-Order Change

Informed by cybernetics and systems theory, MRI therapists perceive family systems as a self-regulating unit based on the feedback loops it receives, which create circular causal interactions that either maintain or change the system's homeostasis. When a problem arises, individuals or family members modify their behavior to address the issue (the new information). When individuals and family members attempt to resolve the problem based on the same or existing governing rules and structure of the system, that is considered **first-order change** (Watzlawick et al., 1974). Attempted solutions may seem varied, but the principles and rules underlying those solutions remain the same. It is like doing more of the same. For example, first-order changes occur in the Daniels family when Fran monitors Pam's eating more frequently, and Murray steps back to avoid further relational conflicts and maintain family peace (homeostasis). Each parent adjusts their behaviors to handle Pam's worsening eating, but the principles of Fran's taking charge and Murray's avoidance remain unchanged. Even though they seek therapy, they continue to see the problem as Pam's issue. They are not aware that their rigid interaction patterns make Pam feel stuck and resistant to giving up her autonomy and independence by controlling her eating.

However, when individuals and family members alter their strategies to handle the problem by changing the rules and structures of the system, this constitutes a **second-order change** (Watzlawick et al., 1974). The initiated changes bring about a fundamental shift that interrupts old interactional patterns and reorganizes the system's structure and family roles. In the Daniels family, the second-order changes occur when the parents start taking co-parenting seriously. Fran is not the only parent involved in Pam's eating behavior, as Murray will share parental responsibility with Fran as a co-parent. The family will not blame Pam for being the "trouble kid" but acknowledge that it is their rigid interactional patterns that contribute to Pam's anxiety, emotional disconnection, and eating behavior. The family will adopt different communication rules so that Fran can express her concerns without trying to control, Murray can spend quality time with Pam and listen to her needs, and Pam can voice her wants without sacrificing her healthy eating to nurture herself.

Attempted Solutions

Attempted solutions are the actions or strategies that individuals and family members create to resolve the identified problem but often fail to achieve a resolution (Fisch et al., 1982). MRI therapists want to gather information about the presented problem and the attempted solution. They assume that people often attempt solutions before coming to see a therapist. MRI therapists want to know why those solutions do not work, either to avoid them or to assess the underlying principles for further interventions (second-order changes). Attempted solutions often represent first-order changes, as they are based on the same rules and principles without altering the system's underlying rules and structure. To address Pam's anorexia, attempted solutions include Fran's consistent monitoring and increased control of Pam's eating, Murray's withdrawal to avoid further conflicts, and the parents' sending Pam to individual therapy and potentially to an inpatient facility.

Problem-Maintaining Solutions

Problem-maintaining solutions are those repetitive attempts that perpetuate or worsen the problem (Fisch et al., 1982). As individuals and family members attempt to resolve the problem (e.g., who does what to whom to handle the situation), their repetitive attempts at solutions are embedded in behavioral and interactional sequences among family members. Rather than resolving the problem, the interactional sequences often leave people feeling stuck and lead to unintended or unexpected consequences of the attempted solutions, which further exacerbate the problem. In the Daniels family, the problem-maintaining solutions include Fran's increasing overcontrolling and monitoring Pam's eating, Murray's withdrawal and passivity, the parents' decision to try to ameliorate Pam's anorexia through her individual therapy, and the family's dismissal of Pam's symptoms and claiming themselves to be "a normal family." All repetitive attempts, such as Fran's control pattern, Pam's resistance, and family members' avoidance, preserve the family system's homeostasis but worsen Pam's health (e.g., by causing weight loss). Pam's anorexia is an emotional outlet not only for Pam but also for the whole family.

Problem Cycle

MRI therapists perceive the identified problem embedded in an interactional cycle as having the following components: (1) The problem definition: The problem cycle starts with individuals and family members noticing a problem, which is the current undesired behaviors from the clients' perspectives. (2) Attempted solution: Individuals and family members tend to apply strategies to handle the problem based on their experiences and knowledge. If they successfully resolve the issue, the system returns to its homeostasis and does not require further attention. If the solution does not work, people tend to repeat the same solutions with increased intensity or frequency (similarly to first-order changes). (3). The interactional sequences to maintain the problem: As people do something to resolve the issue, their actions influence the other, and vice versa. The interactional sequences consist of self-reinforcing feedback loops, in which individuals repeatedly engage in the same behaviors and fail to address the problem, creating a positive feedback loop that continues and exacerbates the issue.

Non-Pathologizing View

MRI therapy is one of the earliest systemic therapy models that deviated from traditional psychoanalytic therapy, which emphasized individuals' intrapsychic issues or defects. MRI therapy is grounded in cybernetics and systemic theories, allowing MRI therapists to hold a non-pathologizing view of clients' presented issues as problem-maintained attempted solutions embedded in family members' interactions, rather than within individuals themselves (Weakland & Fisch, 1992). The cybernetic perspective enables MRI therapists to conceptualize family members' problem-maintained or perpetuated attempted solutions as part of feedback loops that lead them to resolve the issues (negative feedback loops) to maintain homeostasis. Alternatively, positive feedback loops amplify the issues, prompting the need for help and requesting a second-order change for the system. In the feedback loops among family members, all circular information provided is considered valuable data, not a diagnosis of any individual's internal mental health conditions. MRI therapists use this information to guide further assessment and intervention aimed at breaking interactional patterns and promoting second-order change.

Interactional View

According to Watzlawick and Weakland (1977), human behavior is interactional and situated within broader contexts, such as the family, social, and cultural environments. The issues clients present are part of interactional sequential behaviors within their family, social, and cultural systems (Weakland, 2009a). An individual's behavior is not only a stimulus to another person who follows it, but also both a response and a reinforcement to the one who acts before it. For an MRI therapist, instead of thinking "What is wrong with Pam's eating (the presented problem)?" they would ask, "What is going on in the Daniels' family interactions that makes Pam's eating behaviors?" "What behaviors in the Daniels family members' interaction are functioning, and how, to maintain Pam's eating seen as the problem?" As discussed earlier, Pam's anorexia and eating behavior are part of the rigid interaction behaviors of Fran's overcontrolling, Murray's and the other family members' withdrawing and denying, and the family's dismissal and minimizing of the problem (e.g., "we are a normal couple and family"). Pam's anorexia is not just her own problem but reflects the rigid interactional patterns among family members that sustain her eating behavior and emotional distance.

Diversity Conceptualization

MRI therapy focuses on resolving clients' current problems and on interrupting the problem-maintaining interactional patterns; these fundamental cybernetic and systemic tenets make it quite adaptable to clients from diverse cultural contexts. To better assist clients, MRI therapists need to be aware of how clients' cultural contexts and worldviews shape their problem definition, attempted solutions, interactional patterns, and preferred therapeutic outcomes (i.e., desired behavioral outcomes).

MRI frames or reframes problems and interventions tailored to clients' contexts, making sense of them from their perspectives and enabling practical implementation (Fisch et al., 1982; Weakland et al., 1974). If a client is from an individualistic culture, an MRI therapist frames an intervention focused on self-needs or self-care; if a client is from a collectivistic culture, the therapist frames an intervention tailored to collectivistic values, such as self-sacrifice for group or family well-being (Reiter & Ray, 2014). While assessing interactional patterns, they not only collect information about who does what to whom and vice versa (report) but also acknowledge how clients' micro and macro contexts influence and interpret the interactional patterns that make clients feel stuck (command). MRI holds a non-pathologizing view and neutral position to understand how family members' interactional patterns maintain the problem, rather than judging what is normal and abnormal.

MRI has been applied to diverse clinical populations across settings. At the Latino Brief Therapy and Training Center in San Francisco, California, Anger-Díaz et al. (2004) emphasize universal principles of MRI, such as taking a curious stance, adopting a non-normative and non-pathological perspective, learning from clients, and treating clients as experts in their lives while working with people across cultures, including the Latino clinical population served in their clinic. In working with Chinese Americans, Soo-Hoo (1999) recommends using the client's cultural frame of reference to understand their problem definitions and tailor culturally appropriate interventions. For example, in Chinese culture, which values parental hierarchy, rather than correcting the parents' strict and critical parenting behaviors to handle a child's misbehavior, the MRI therapist would focus on "helping the parents find the proper teaching principle that will correct their child's problems" (Soo-Hoo, 1999, p. 171). By reframing the parenting issue in this way, the parents do not feel blamed for engaging in culturally expected parenting practices; instead, they feel respected and are more willing to explore alternative strategies for teaching their children.

Schlanger et al. (2020) adopt a one-down position and learn about clients' cultures and values when assisting immigrant and refugee families facing uncertainty about threatened deportation. The therapist focuses on the family's current problem, reframes the boy's fear about his parents' deportation as an adaptive emotion to uncertain situations, and calls it "our friend" to alert human beings to potential dangers. The therapist also encourages the parents to acknowledge and normalize the boy's fear rather than keep telling him nothing bad would happen with the intention of protecting him. By interrupting the parents' attempted solutions that intensified the boy's anxiety, the family gradually accepts the fear rather than avoiding it. These three highlighted studies show that MRI's fundamental principles support culturally responsive practice with diverse clinical populations. MRI therapists promote change by using reframes and interventions that align with clients' cultural values to interrupt ineffective attempted solutions.

The Therapeutic Story of Problem Resolution

According to Fisch et al. (1982), "All contacts with clients may affect treatment; therefore, if one intends to do therapy efficiently, planning is necessary at all stages of treatment actions" (p. 53). MRI therapists emphasize the importance of planning throughout different phases of therapy sessions to target the identified problem efficiently, allowing clients to experience relief from their symptoms within a reasonable timeframe. Before the first session, MRI therapists will consider who will be invited to therapy. "As a safe rule of thumb, whoever in a system is most discomforted by a problem is the one most committed to seeking change. Correspondingly, the complainant is also the one best worked with in treatment" (Fisch et al., 1982, p. 54). Those who feel distressed about the problem in the system are often more motivated to act and are more likely to cooperate with the therapist. People come to therapy with their complaints, so it makes sense for MRI therapists to work with the complainers, as they can serve as the strongest ally in implementing intervention.

The First Session

In the first session, MRI therapists focus on several key tasks, including understanding the nature of clients' complaints, the clients' attempted solutions, and their desired goals, as well as assessing clients' positions for change (Fisch et al., 1982). MRI therapists start by asking, "What brings you to therapy today?" Based on clients' statements, therapists gather information about their complaints and identify their current undesired behaviors. When the complaint is vague, MRI therapists clarify it before suggesting any intervention. The therapists listen to the problem itself (the content information) and to what underlies the presented issues (the interactional pattern and process information).

Understand clients' presented problems and attempted solutions. Based on MRI's premise that the problem is maintained by every effort clients make to resolve it, therapists also gather information about how clients have attempted to resolve the issues identified (attempted solutions). The therapists pay attention to who is involved in handling the identified problem, what they do, and how the others respond next, and vice versa. The attempted solutions provide MRI therapists with contextual information about the individual's and family members' interactional patterns, in which attempted solutions are embedded to maintain the problem. Attempted solutions often become a circular feedback loop that perpetuates the original problem and maintains the system's homeostasis. MRI therapists further identify the "basic thrust" (Fisch et al., 1982) of the attempted solutions, which serves as the driving force and organizing principle behind them. This process-level information informs MRI therapists of targeted areas for intervention. This also ensures that MRI therapists do not merely repeat the first-order changes that have previously been ineffective for the family but instead provoke the second-order changes that interrupt the problematic maintenance cycles.

Fran's anxiety leads to her control of Pam's eating, which triggers Pam's resistance and fighting back. It heightens Fran's anxiety and prompts Murray's withdrawal, which increases Fran's over-functioning and pushes Pam further away. The basic thrust (organizing principle) is family members' fear of the family falling apart and loss of control. The fears drive each family member to use different strategies to protect the family. Fran wants to protect Pam's health by controlling her eating; Murray wants to protect the marriage by not disagreeing with Fran and staying out of conflicts; and Pam wants to protect her independence and autonomy by restricting her eating and disengaging from her family. They are not comfortable sharing their vulnerabilities but use various, similar first-order solutions to avoid confrontation, create emotional withdrawal, and hide the relational issues. Unfortunately, these problem-maintaining solutions further worsen Pam's health and exacerbate family members' emotional distance from each other. The couple cannot work as a team together and continue rigid complementary parental roles in addressing Pam's eating issues. Pam does not feel close to her siblings, and they dismiss her, too.

Develop treatment goals. To make therapy work more efficiently and align with MRI's brief approach, MRI therapists ask clients about their goals. As MRI therapy is brief and strategic, the therapists often design behavioral interventions to interrupt problem-maintained interactional patterns. Goals are specific and behaviorally oriented. To change the interactional patterns that make individuals and family members feel stuck while attempting to resolve the problem, therapeutic goals are tailored to change specific behaviors in interactions (Fisch et al., 1982), rather than focusing on feelings or abstract thinking. Behavioral goals also facilitate clients' and therapists' easier evaluation of whether the desired change has occurred and if problematic interactional patterns have been altered. Behavioral goals are focused on the concrete behavioral sequences that maintain the problem. This aligns with the MRI's perspectives of "do something different" to change the system. As Fisch et al. (1982) stated, "If at first you don't succeed, you might perhaps try a second time- but if you don't succeed then, try something different" (p. 18).

Fran and Murray's desired intuitive treatment goals for the family will be to reduce Pam's anorexia, as they are not aware that the presented problem is part of their family's rigid interactions. However, from an MRI therapist's interactional views of the problems, Pam's eating behavior is part of the rigid interactional patterns of Fran's overcontrolling, Murray's withdrawal, Pam's resistance, and the family members' emotional distance. To challenge the basic thrust of the family's fear of falling apart and loss of control, MRI therapists may suggest the following behaviorally oriented treatment goals: enabling the family to reorganize their behavioral interactions toward one another, resulting in emotional closeness and connections. The first treatment goal is to reduce Fran's overcontrol and Pam's resistance in the mother-daughter dyad interaction. Fran will focus on neutral conversations on topics unrelated to food and reduce verbal commentary on Pam's eating at meals to once a day, and eventually once a week. Pam will respond verbally by simply stating, "Thanks, Mom, I will take care of it," to replace her silence or arguing back. This alternative interaction interrupts Fran's overcontrol and Pam's resistance loops, creating a less reactive pattern. The second treatment goal is to strengthen the marital dyad and increase Fran and Murray's teamwork as parents in addressing Pam's anorexia. At meals, Murray will join and facilitate neutral conversation unrelated to food to interrupt Fran's overcontrol and comment on Pam's eating. In addition, the couple can spend 15 minutes each day checking in and discussing any family concerns that require their attention. Third, Murray will increase engagement with Pam. Murray will spend 30 minutes walking with Pam at least once a week and checking in with her. This will make Pam realize that Murray is also available to listen to her needs and provide connection, reducing her feelings of isolation and Fran's over-supervision. Finally, Pam and her brothers will engage in one family activity together, such as a game or movie night, which rebuilds sibling connection and reinforces inclusion in the family.

Assess the clients' position in relation to change. MRI therapists assess the clients' positions in relation to change (Fisch et al., 1982). The clients' **position** regarding change refers to how they perceive and describe the problem, their role in it, their readiness and willingness to change, who is most willing to change among family members, and what they believe is possible for changes. Some clients can seek therapy and want the therapist to fix the problem or change others without making the effort to change themselves. This happened to the Daniels family as the parents took Pam to individual therapy and expected a therapist to assist Pam in resolving her eating issue. Some clients want to control the therapy process and use the therapist as a passive listener. Some clients work collaboratively with a therapist to create change. "Knowing what the client's position (is) allows one to formulate guidelines on how to couch/frame a suggestion in a way that the client is most likely to accept" (Fisch et al., 1982, p. 90).

MRI therapists constantly assess clients' positions regarding change and carefully listen to clients' complaints, values, and emotions. Once MRI therapists are aware of the clients' positions, they maximize "the clients' compliance with the suggestion" (Fisch et al., 1982, p. 99). MRI therapists design and deliver interventions that are consistent with the clients' change positions, meaning they frame the intervention in a way that is close to clients' beliefs, values, language, and desired goals. This makes the proposed intervention more understandable to clients, thereby decreasing their resistance to change. This also increases therapists' maneuverability, so the intervention is not prematurely rejected by clients.

Fran and Murray are both concerned about Pam's eating issues and severe weight loss, as shown by both parents requesting therapy and accompanying Pam in sessions. Fran is the one who feels more motivated to get the problem resolved. This is possibly because Fran interacts with Pam more around the eating issue and has taken a lead in attempted solutions. She experiences the problem more intensely than other family members. Murray also sees Pam's eating as an issue, but is less involved in those attempted solutions to change Pam. However, Fran and Murray's perception of change focuses more on fixing Pam's eating individually than realizing that they both also contribute to Pam's presented issues. Pam, as the identified patient (IP), does not perceive her eating behavior as a big issue, as she uses eating to reserve her autonomy in responding to Fran's intense monitoring. However, she feels bothered by Fran's severe supervision. Therefore, she does not object to coming to therapy and may perceive that Fran should have left her alone and could have felt better. For Oliver and George, as they are quite emotionally and behaviorally disengaged from Pam and are absent from therapy, they perceive themselves as not relevant to Pam's eating issues.

Formulating a Strategic Intervention

Once MRI therapists have a better understanding of the client's presented problem, attempted solutions, desired therapeutic goals, and positions to change, they start formulating a strategic intervention. The key purpose of the intervention is to alter the "basic thrust" that organizes the problem-maintaining interactional pattern. Effective intervention strategies typically disrupt clients' repetitive attempted solutions and create alternative interactions. It requires MRI therapists to identify the organizing principles underlying clients' attempted solutions that maintain the problematic cycles. For example, to interrupt the rigid interactional pattern of Fran's repeated monitoring of Pam's eating and arguing, an MRI therapist might suggest that Fran stop commenting on Pam's eating or temporarily back off and allow Pam to decide when and how much to eat. By doing the opposite of their familiar attempted solution, it interrupts the existing rigid interactional pattern and creates a space to explore alternative and more functional interactions. In other words, MRI therapists target process changes, rather than content changes. The interventions can be subtle by destabilizing homeostasis and altering the sequential behavioral patterns that perpetuate the original problems.

Reframing

Reframing involves presenting a new or alternative perspective on the presented complaint in a way that makes clients feel open to trying something different (Fisch et al., 1982). When reframing, MRI therapists consider clients' positions and adjust their approach to tailor the reframing to each client's preferred frame of reference. Reframing must be contextually relevant to clients' worldviews, so it makes sense to them and is readily accepted.

As MRI interventions are designed to alter clients' behavioral and communication sequences, therapists frame clients' presented problems behaviorally and interactionally, such as what happens, how clients handle it, and in what sequences. They reframe the underlying meanings of the attempted sequential behaviors to loosen and alter clients' rigid perspectives. In the Daniels family, the MRI therapist reframes their rigid interactional pattern of control, withdrawal, and resistance and states,

> As I hear your sharing of attempting to resolve Pam's eating issue, I notice everyone is doing their best to keep the family safe and protected. For Fran, when you keep commenting and monitoring Pam's eating, I see your worries and deep care for Pam's health, even though your constant monitoring may sound like nagging and leave no room for Pam to breathe. So, she gradually runs away from you. For Murray, you often take a step back when the relationship between Fran and Pam gets tense, so you can keep the peace in the family without further stirring the fire. However, the further you pull yourself away, the lonelier Fran feels and the harder she works to control Pam's eating, and the more intense her relationship with Pam becomes. For Pam, when Mom comments on your eating at meals or things get intense, you resist and gradually silence yourself, as this is one way you learn to preserve your space to feel like yourself. However, the more you resist or pull away, the more worried your mom is for your health and the more she nags at your eating. Everyone is making it hard to protect each other, but this cycle pushes each one further away.

Punctuation Shift

Based on cybernetic theory, MRI therapists perceive problematic behaviors as embedded in circular interactional sequences. Oftentimes, family members blame the identified client for causing the problematic situations. The **punctuation shift** refers to changing how family members or individuals interpret the start point of problematic interaction cycles (Watzlawick et al., 1967; Watzlawick & Weakland, 1977). Therefore, they can understand their role within interactional sequences, which influence and are influenced by others' actions and reactions, thereby maintaining problematic cycles. By shifting this punctuation, clients and family members change their linear blame on one individual and see the circular nature of their interactions with each other, which opens the possibility of alternative interactions.

Fran worries that if Pam does not eat, she will die, so she pushes harder to save Pam's life. Pam perceives Mom's constant monitoring as the problem and her push as controlling, and she restrains eating to preserve her autonomy. An MRI therapist might state,

> When mother worries and constantly reminds Pam's eating, Pam feels pressure and wants to be independent by pulling away more. When Pam keeps her distance and does not listen to the mother, the mother feels more anxious, tries harder, and wants to convince Pam more. You are both caught in interactions where each's action and reaction make sense, but also keep the cycle going without achieving any productive goals. There is nothing wrong with what you do, but it's more like a dance where both people move at the same time and get trapped in the movement.

Paradoxical Interventions

Paradoxical intervention is a counterintuitive strategy to direct a client "to continue an undesired symptomatic behavior and even increase it to show that the client has voluntary control over it" (American Psychological Association, 2018). The purpose of the intervention is to reduce or better control problematic behavior (Weakland et al., 1974). Grounded in Bateson's theories of double-bind communication and systemic feedback loops, MRI therapists perceive that double-bind communication creates confusing, inconsistent, and contradictory situations that make individuals feel stuck (Weakland, 2009b); it is a no-win situation. Paradoxical intervention strategically uses the same communication structure that the double-bind theory perceives as harmful to break the self-perpetuating interactional patterns and transform them into a win-win situation. In paradoxical situations, if clients agree to take the therapist's intervention, they comply with the suggested change. If clients disagree with the intervention, they become rebellious and do not participate in the problematic behaviors, therefore voluntarily gaining control over the problems. There are two main types of paradoxical interventions: **prescribing the symptoms** (paradox by doing the problem more) and **restraining change** (paradox by not changing too fast).

Prescribing the symptoms. This type of paradoxical intervention asks clients to intentionally worsen or amplify problematic behaviors, or to practice them more often or more intensely for specific periods (Weakland et al., 1974). For example, MRI therapists ask a client with insomnia to make efforts to stay awake tonight and not fall asleep. By taking this intervention, clients can experience their autonomy to produce the symptoms (insomnia, staying awake for the whole night) and realize they have control over the symptoms to make them happen or not. If they do fall asleep, the insomnia problem is resolved as well. To interrupt Fran's controlling and Pam's resistance, the MRI therapist suggests that Fran and Pam practice "overcontrol and resistance" on certain days and times. For example, Fran must comment on Pam's eating for 15 minutes a day for a week, including what to eat and how much. During that time, Pam is free to resist and argue to preserve her autonomy. After 15 minutes of practice, they must stop and converse about something else. The purpose of this intervention is to make this overcontrolling and resistance pattern visible to family members, so they will not perceive Pam's eating behavior as her only problem and realize this rigid pattern is not helpful for Pam's recovery from anorexia.

Positioning. This type of paradoxical intervention involves therapists agreeing with and intensifying clients' positions, symptoms, or worldviews to increase clients' cooperation (Fisch et al., 1982). Clients can recognize the absurdity of their logic and invite reflection that alters their perspectives. As Murray often withdraws from the relational tensions between Fran and Pam, and he also plays these complementary roles in relation to Fran's overcontrolling and functioning roles, the MRI therapist might state,

> Murray, I have noticed that you seem to be a peacemaker in the family while keeping quiet and distant from Fran and Pam's power struggle as you do not want to add the fuel to the fire. I wonder what would happen to your family if you kept this distance further.

Up to this point, the therapist joins and invites Murray to acknowledge the impact of his continuous withdrawal behavior on the family. Depending on Murray's response, he could reflect that his distance would make Fran feel even more alone, acting like a single parent solely responsible for Pam's issue, and his children would mimic his withdrawals, gradually distancing themselves from each other. The therapist can suggest that he speak up for at least one sentence before he steps away and see how the family responds to his presence.

If Murray cannot acknowledge the consequences of his withdrawal behaviors on the family, this shows that the family system requires Murray's distance to protect the status quo. The therapist would go with Murray's persistence in his distance and silencing (again, positing deeper with Murray) and would use "restraining changes" with Murray.

Restraining changes. In this type of paradoxical intervention, MRI therapists discourage or warn clients against changing too quickly, even though clients desire change and often want it to happen quickly. When giving an intervention, therapists are taking away clients' autonomy for changes (Fisch et al., 1982). Therefore, clients might resist being told what to do, even when it would be beneficial to resolve their problematic situations. In this case, restraining changes removes pressures for changes from clients, and they can experience spontaneous changes. This also gives MRI therapists and clients more maneuverability and does not immaturely commit to a position for change before contextually understanding the nature of the presented problem.

When Murray persists in his roles of a peacemaker and continues distancing himself from parenting, the MRI therapist might state, "Murray, that makes sense for you to keep the family's calmness through your constant distancing and even distracting the boys from family tensions by focusing on sports. If you step in, you might mess up Fran's discipline of Pam." The absurdity of Murray's distance and silence might provoke Fran's objection by stating, "That is also the problem! I have been doing this on my own. He has not supported me enough. I am the one who always plays as a bad cop, and he is the good one." Fran's complaints require Murray to take a different approach. Restraining change makes the rigid complementary pattern between Fran's overcontrolling and Murray's withdrawals more vivid to the couple and requires further systemic changes.

Go Slow. The "Go Slow" intervention is a softer version of restraining changes. When clients change too rapidly and quickly, the system's homeostasis feels threatened. MRI therapists suggest that clients slow down to match the system's homeostatic balance and prevent further backlash (Fisch et al., 1982; Weakland et al., 1974). The purpose of slowing down is to break the "basic thrust" (underlying principles) of working too much or being driven by anxiety for change. When slowing down, clients feel less pressured to change, which decreases further resistance and creates space for autonomous change.

As the MRI therapist notices the Daniels family working so hard to "fix" Pam's eating issue, which further reinforces Pam's restricted eating, the therapist suggests that the family slow down to interrupt the pressure to change, which leads to Pam's resistance. The therapist states that

> Pam's slowing to eat may be one way for her to regain her control and handle all those pressures for change. It might be better for the family to join her at this slow pace. For the next week, no one should push for any eating changes. For Fran, rather than commenting on Pam's eating, you would be attentive to your body and emotion while observing this slow move. If you cannot help but want to talk at the dining table, talk about something unrelated to food.

This Go Slow intervention invites the family to do something different that interrupts their attempts to solve the problem by working too hard and putting pressure only on Pam to change.

The dangers of improvement. The **dangers of improvement** are another extension of restraining changes. When a client's presenting problem improves, family members may resist change or react defensively to maintain or restore the previous balance. Oftentimes, clients may report relapses or another problem emerges, which may make clients wonder or question the suggested intervention. As MRI therapists warn of the potential negative consequences of making changes, it paradoxically reassures clients' ambivalence and anxiety about change and mobilizes change indirectly (Fisch et al., 1982; Weakland et al., 1974).

Assuming that Pam's eating habit improves and she starts gaining weight, the MRI therapist prepares the family to be aware of the potential consequences of this positive change and states,

> As Pam is getting better, her body might need time to adjust. This principle also applies to the family, taking time to adjust to this change. Fran, you might not know what to do, since it doesn't require you to get involved that much with Pam. Murray, you might feel weird, as there is no need for you to be the peacemaker anymore, since the relational tension between Fran and Pam is gone. If this does happen, it means the family needs time to adjust to the change and explore another way to connect.

Making a U-Turn

Making a U-turn means an intervention in which clients are encouraged to intentionally reverse their rigid pattern of attempted problem-solving by doing the opposite of what they have constantly tried (Fisch et al., 1982). This intervention is to break up more of the same first-order changes and to seek second-order changes by doing something different. For example, Fran and Murray will shift away from "concerning too much" or "making comments/control on Pam's eating" to "stop trying to solve the symptoms directly" or "withdraw their efforts/control." Pam can feel space to maintain her autonomy without having to fight back against her parents and learn how to take good care of herself.

Making a U-turn can also be used when MRI therapists shift from one position to another, such as moving from a directive stance to taking a one-down position (Weakland et al., 1974). This happens when the suggested intervention is not working, or the therapist may unwittingly argue with clients. To increase therapists' maneuverability and avoid doing more similar interventions that are not productive in therapy, MRI therapists acknowledge their mistakes and use them as opportunities to shift direction and do something different.

Evaluating Outcome

The general treatment goal of MRI therapy is to resolve the client's presenting problem and interrupt the underlying principles that drive problematic behaviors. As therapists and clients establish clear treatment goals, they use those goals to evaluate treatment outcomes and decide if they no longer need therapy. This happens when clients no longer have complaints or no longer perceive the problem as bothering them (Fisch et al., 1982). It involves a qualitative shift in perceiving the problem behavior or executing alternative attempted solutions. The clients may have alternative perspectives on the problem, or they may report that their attempted solutions have changed, and they do not need to return to the identified old interaction patterns in which they feel stuck. Fran and Murray may state,

> I realize that Pam is learning how to be independent now and needs more autonomy for trial and error. In fact, compared to other teenagers at this stage, her academic performance has improved significantly, from C to B and A-. Her eating habits have changed. I am grateful to have her as my daughter, and her health has stabilized for now. We decided to give her space and to support her whenever she needs it. It is not a big issue now.

Sometimes therapy termination occurs when the clients' complaints remain unresolved. In this case, therapists acknowledge the situation and check in with clients about what has been done and what has not been done to prevent further improvement. Therapists may present other alternatives, such as referrals. Therapists may also initiate termination when they assess that the risks of resolving the problem outweigh the benefits of continuing therapy. The resolution of the problematic situation might result in an unanticipated change for clients. For example, a couple sought help with communication and intimacy issues. After initial assessments, the therapist uncovered an interactional pattern of coercive control with ongoing emotional abuse and situational physical altercations by one partner. MRI therapists may terminate couples therapy and recommend individual sessions for each partner to ensure safety. In this case, continuing couples therapy may become part of the problem as it risks perpetuating harm or invalidating safety needs. Ending couples therapy symbolizes shifting from unsafe reciprocity (e.g., the perpetrator uses power to control and manipulate the therapeutic process) to protected individual work.

The Therapeutic Process

In the first session, the MRI therapist would understand the clients' complaints, their attempted solutions, and their desired goals. Through therapists' inquiries and clients' sharing, the therapist also assesses clients' positions for change, and who is motivated for change. If appropriate, the therapist may suggest an intervention that challenges the basic thrust (organizing principle) of the attempted solution, so the Daniels family can explore alternatives among themselves.

Case Transcript

Therapist: Hello, everyone. I am glad to meet you all today, and thanks for making the effort to come to the clinic. I briefly reviewed the intake and was informed that Murray (Father), Fran (Mother), and Pam (daughter) will attend family therapy, as Oliver and George are in school now. How's everyone doing?

Intervention: The therapist greets and welcomes the family to build therapeutic rapport.

Fran: Overall, we're doing good. We're here for Pam and really concerned about her. She recently didn't eat well and lost quite a bit of weight. I'm not sure if this is related to her school performances, as the grades are dropping.

Therapist: I see. Glad to know you are doing well, and thanks for briefly highlighting your concern. I will certainly get back to that topic later. How about Murray and Pam? How are you both doing?

Murray: I'm doing well. Like Fran, I also have a concern for Pam.

Therapist: Ok, glad to know you are doing well as well. It looks like you and Fran have a common concern about Pam. So, Pam, how are you doing today?

Intervention: The therapist continues checking in with each family member and acknowledges their perspective, which helps to explore their interactions about Pam's eating later.

Pam: I'm doing fine.

Therapist: Thanks for all your sharing. Mom and Dad touched a bit on why you're here for therapy. Tell me more about what exactly happened that brought you all here today?

Intervention: Identify the presented problem—The therapist inquires into what the problem is.

Fran: I'm really worried about Pam. She's not been eating well; in fact, she's eating less and losing weight. She's skinny compared to girls her age. We brought her to see a psychiatrist who gave the diagnosis of Anorexia Nervosa two years ago. She started seeing a therapist, but things have gotten worse. The therapist suggested putting Pam in an inpatient facility. So, I have to talk to her about this and ensure she's eaten something at the table. This is our last try to see you. If this doesn't work, we'll need to send her to the inpatient facility and get her weight loss controlled.

Therapist: It seems you've tried hard to help her feel better. I'm curious about what you talked to her about and how you ensured she ate something.

Intervention: Inquire more about attempted solutions—The therapist acknowledges Fran's efforts and begins to inquire further about Mom's attempted solutions, which reveal her interactional behaviors with Pam.

Fran: Well, I cook her favorite meals and sit with her to make sure she eats. We usually sit at the table together when eating breakfast and dinner. For breakfast, I remind her to have at least one egg and drink milk to get protein and energy. If she doesn't, I make sure to put the protein bar in her lunchbox. At dinner, I check how she's doing in school. I would make sure she eats some vegetables and meat, like stew chicken with potatoes. She really needs to gain some weight.

Therapist: How did Pam respond when you reminded her of what to eat?

Intervention: Assess the nature of circular causality between Fran and Pam—The therapist is curious about Pam's responses to Fran's attempted solution of monitoring and reminding Pam's eating, and wants to gather information about the interaction pattern between Fran and Pam. This helps the therapist to see the nature of feedback loops between Fran and Pam.

Fran: Well, she didn't respond to me. At first, she got some bits, but she told me she wasn't hungry. How can you feel not hungry? People eat to boost their energy, and the body needs nutrients. She finally put her earphones on when we were eating and pretended not to hear what I was saying.

Therapist: It sounds like you tried everything you could. However, the more you tried, the less response you got from Pam.

Intervention: Identify complementary feedback loops—Based on Fran's sharing, the therapist reflects on complementary feedback loops between Fran and Pam that maintain the problem.

Fran: Yeah, the more I tried, the worse it got. She continues losing weight.

Therapist: Pam, I want to check in with you. What's it like for you when Mom checks in on your eating and works so hard to ensure you eat at least something?

Intervention: Check the assessment of circular interactions between Fran and Pam from Pam's experiences—Inquire about Pam's response to Fran's intense monitoring, so the therapist can learn from Pam's perspectives as well.

Pam: I feel pressured. I don't like it. I know when I'm hungry and need to eat. Sometimes, I wish that everyone would stop talking about my eating and weight. Sometimes, I want to hide myself.

Therapist: You want some space and can decide on your own eating.

Intervention: Reframe—The therapist acknowledges Pam's perceptions and feelings. The therapist reframes her distance to preserve her autonomy to decide when and what to eat.

Pam: Yes, when Mom keeps talking and "monitoring" my eating, I feel annoyed and don't want to eat anything. It makes me want to run away.

Therapist: So, the more Mom works so hard to make you eat, the more you want to run away.

Intervention: Verify the assessment of complementary feedback loops between Fran and Pam from Pam's perspective. The therapist reflects Pam's responses to confirm that Fran's increased control and Pam's withdrawal.

Pam: Yes.

Therapist: How about you, Murray? How have you been handling this at home?

Intervention: Inquiring circular causality among three family members—The therapist also assesses Murray's participation in the ongoing cycle, such as how he responds when Fran and Pam argue, how he interacts with Fran's monitoring and Pam's resistance, and how these sequential interactions further contribute to the presented problem. The MRI therapist sees Pam's eating issues from an interactional perspective and is curious about how the presented problem serves a function in the interactional sequences among Fran, Pam, and Murray.

Murray: Well, I usually let Fran handle it. I don't want to bring more tension to the house, as I certainly see the arguments between Fran and Pam. I want to ease the tension out.

Therapist: You want to keep the peace at home. So, what exactly would you do when you see Fran and Pam get into an argument about Pam's eating?

Intervention: Inquiring more specific and behavioral information about Murray's responses to Fran and Pam's interactions—The therapist acknowledges Murray's perceptions of the argument and is curious about what actions Murray takes in responding to Fran and Pam's arguments. The MRI therapist continues to gather behavioral information to understand Murray's position in the sequential interactions that contribute to the problem maintenance.

Murray: I often step away. When the conversation heats up, I go to check with the boys and maybe take them out for sports, as I don't want them to hear the arguments. Or I go back to my office and work on my own stuff.

Therapist: So, when tension heats up, you tend to leave to avoid further conflicts and hope Fran and Pam can calm down.

Intervention: Reframe—The therapist reframes Murray's stepping back as a positive intention to avoid escalating the relational tensions between Fran and Pam and to maintain stability in the family.

Murray: That's right. It doesn't mean that I don't care about them. I just don't want to put more fuel on the fire.

Therapist: It seems that everyone is doing their best to assist Pam's eating. Fran works very hard to monitor and remind Pam to eat and protect her health. Pam tries to regain control of her own eating and autonomy by pulling herself away from mom's supervision. Murray has tried to keep things calm at home by staying out of the arguments between Fran and Pam. I see Fran and Murray's care and protection of Pam's health and family peace, but somehow, these attempted efforts do not work as you all expected. What do you think about my observations?

Intervention: Highlight attempted solutions and the problem-maintenance pattern—The therapist summarizes each family member's attempted solutions, points out the problem-maintaining cycle among the three family members, and invites the family to reflect on the interactional pattern.

(*All family members nod and agree with the therapist's observation.*)

Therapist: This gives us helpful information and tells us what is not working, so we can avoid repetitive solutions that lead us to the same unresolved deadlock. Have you tried any other solutions?

Intervention: Continuing to explore additional attempted solutions—The therapist acknowledges the family's agreement and continues to inquire if there are any additional attempted solutions the family has tried that may contribute to the problem-maintaining cycle.

Fran: We took Pam to see a psychiatrist and therapist, as I stated earlier. Pam has received individual therapy for a while, on and off. When she saw the therapist, things improved; when she stopped, her eating issues kicked back.

Therapist: I see. Pam, I am curious about your experiences in therapy. If you don't mind, please share it with me.

Intervention: Explore the 'basic thrust' (organizing principle) of the family's attempted solutions—The therapist gathers information about Pam's experiences in therapy and how the attempted therapeutic efforts fit into the Daniels family. The therapist hopes to understand how those therapeutic interventions may fit into their current interaction pattern, such as if the interventions interrupt the problem cycle among family members, how Pam responds to the suggested interventions, and how the family responds to Pam's changes or lack of changes.

Pam: I have nothing special to say. It's good to talk with the therapist, as I don't talk much at home. The therapist helped me to realize my thoughts about eating, and I honestly don't think my issues are that big. I don't understand why my parents send me there so often. If they feel bothered, they should seek therapy.

Therapist: So, on one hand, you feel that the therapist is helpful for you as you have an outlet to vent, but on the other hand, you feel that your parents seem much more worried than you are. Can you please clarify "if they feel bothered, they should seek therapy?" What did you notice that made you feel that way?

Intervention: Acknowledge Pam's change position and clarify the interactional pattern between Fran and Murray—The therapist validates Pam's experiences in the past therapy and acknowledges her position on change, as Pam does not perceive her eating as a big issue, but instead sees it as a relational issue among parents. The therapist further inquires about the relational patterns, as observed by Pam, that may contribute to the problem-maintaining cycle.

Pam: I know they care for me, but it's too much. My mom watches what I put on my plate and comments, "Take more, this is delicious," or "Are you sure this is enough?" This really makes me feel pressured, and eating is no longer enjoyable. My dad usually sits there and says nothing. He's closer to my brothers. Sometimes, I hear them talking about me, like my dad would say, "Let her eat whatever she wants," and my mother would argue, "You always put me through this and just go out with boys." I think their arguments are more dramatic than my eating.

Therapist: Fran and Murray, is this your experience being with each other as Pam described?

Intervention: Check in with the couple about their interactions. The therapist shifts the focus from Pam to the couple's relationship to verify Pam's observation, as the therapist wants to know how the couple's interactions may contribute to the problem cycle.

Fran: Well, I don't know how Pam sees us like this. We try not to have arguments in front of the kids. I guess we might not realize that our voices have grown louder and that they can hear our conversation. I feel that I sometimes act like a single parent, handling Pam's situations on my own, while Murray is the one who has fun with boys.

Therapist: It seems you both really care about Pam's eating and health, as shown by your hard work during those intense discussions. It also makes sense to feel that all parental responsibility is on you, and you can feel alone in handling Pam's eating. It seems that you wish he could be there with you when you need him. Murray, I want to hear your perspectives as well. When Fran stated that she carries things alone, you find a way to stay with the boys. What do you think about her comments?

Intervention: Reframe, Validate, and inquire about the couple's interaction pattern -- The therapist reframes the couple's arguments as expressions of care for Pam's eating. The therapist validates Fran's sense of caretaking alone, which aligns with Murray's disengagement. The therapist also checks Murray's experiences to clarify the couple's interaction pattern.

Murray: Well, I see her perspective. I guess we have different ways of handling Pam's eating. I appreciate Fran being on top of everything. However, I don't want to add more tension to the family, so I step back to maintain family peace. Or sometimes, when I want to step in, it's too late, as Fran already handled it. I care for Pam, but I feel like we can't force her to eat. She's got to start eating something she likes first and gradually gain weight. I know Fran can get anxious easily, but I don't want to fight with her in front of Pam. So, I let her handle it.

Therapist: It sounds like you take a different approach, such as stepping back to prevent further tension. Fran is good at getting involved right away. Both of you complement each other in caring for Pam and protecting the kids, as you both highlight avoiding a fight in front of them. To better understand what we might do from here, I would like to know, if the family tension around Pam's eating becomes less intense, what would look different at home?

Intervention: Identify the couple's complementary interaction pattern, acknowledge the couple's intentions, and clarify treatment goals—The therapist highlights the couple's complementary communication patterns in handling Pam's eating, such as Fran's pursuing and Murray's withdrawing. In addition, the therapist validates each approach while sharing a common intention: not fighting in front of children. The therapist further clarifies the therapy goals with family members to define the desired changes.

Fran: Pam will certainly eat more and start gaining weight. At that point, I would love to stop worrying about her so much. Our arguments might become fewer. I want her to eat normally and feel healthy again.

Therapist: Can you clarify what you mean by 'eating normally' and 'feeling healthy'? As you are not Pam, how do you know she would feel healthy?

Intervention: Positioning—The therapist uses Fran's language, such as eating normally and feeling healthy, to clarify the two vague terms and gently highlight that they are based on Fran's definition rather than Pam's. By gently reminding Fran that she is not Pam, the therapist positions Fran to separate her assumptions from Pam's and reveal how her attempted solutions, such as monitoring and defining Pam's eating, contribute to the problem-maintaining sequence. Then the therapist asks Fran to define the terms.

Fran: You're right. I'm not Pam. I mean, she eats at least three meals a day and starts gaining weight.

Therapist: How about you, Pam? What do you think about Mom's suggestion?

Pam: I would like Mom to stop checking everything I eat, as I can decide what and how much I want to eat.

Therapist: That makes sense. It seems you want to feel control over your eating, and this is a way for you to preserve your space to be yourself. Am I right?

Intervention: Reframe—The therapist reframes Pam's desire for autonomy as a way to preserve her sense of control, highlighting it as part of the interaction pattern rather than a problem perceived by the parents.

Pam: Yes, I'm not a kid anymore.

Therapist: Ok. So how do you decide what and how much to eat daily?

Intervention: Clarify concrete behavioral goals for Pam—The therapist asks Pam to clarify her daily eating behaviors, focusing on observable, behavioral actions she can commit to changing.

Pam: I eat when I'm hungry. I can certainly drink milk in the morning, as it's quick and easy. I ate a slice of pizza and some fresh fruit with friends at the school cafeteria. For dinner, I can eat some fruit and a veggie salad.

Therapist: That's good to hear that you did eat a little bit. That is more than I initially expected. Let's be careful not to progress too quickly, as your body might need time to adjust to increased food intake.

Intervention: Go Slow—The therapist acknowledges Pam's eating something and takes a "Go Slow" approach by framing gradual eating as necessary for her body to adjust. This reduces her pressure to change and supports her autonomy to change.

Therapist: How about you, Murray?

Murray: I would like to see less fighting at home, especially between Fran and Pam.

Therapist: That makes sense, but it's hard for us to control someone else. I'm more curious about what you think you could do to facilitate less fighting at home.

Intervention: Reframe responsibility—The therapist acknowledges Murray's expectation but redirects him from controlling others to reflecting on his role in the interaction pattern. This aligns with MRI's perspective of continuously assessing Murray's change in position and observing if he can acknowledge his role in altering the problem-maintaining cycles to solve the problem.

Murray: Let me think about it.

Fran: Well, I guess you can have more time hanging out with Pam as you take the boys out more often. This might make Pam feel like she can talk to you.

Therapist: What do you think about Fran's suggestion, Murray?

Intervention: Inquire Murray's perception of Fran's suggestion—The therapist assesses that Murray might not fully recognize his role in the problem-maintaining cycles and has a hard time doing something different at this point. The therapist observes Fran stepping in to answer Murray, which parallels the couple's complementary pattern (e.g., Fran's active pursuit and Murray's withdrawal). The MRI therapist holds a neutral stance and checks Murray's opinion, which disrupts the couple's relational pattern, even though Fran's suggestion aims to increase Murray's involvement with Pam and thereby interrupt the problem-maintaining cycles.

Murray: Of course, I'd love to do so.

Therapist: How about you, Pam? Will you be willing to hang out with Dad sometimes?

Intervention: Inquire about Pam's perception of Fran's suggestion—As Murray agrees with Fran's suggestion, the therapist also checks Pam's willingness to engage in this alternative pattern. Fran's suggestion will require the participation of both Murray and Pam to break the old problem-maintenance cycle. If both Murray and Pam agree to hang out more, it might create a different interactional sequence between them, weakening the problem-maintenance cycle.

Pam: Well, I don't have any preference.
Therapist: Ok, so you don't oppose that idea, am I right?
Pam: Yes. I'm fine to go out with Dad.
Therapist: Sounds good. Each of you came up with some specific ways you can contribute to that vision, such as Fran feeling less worried, Pam gaining control, and Murray seeing fewer fights in the family. Based on what you say, I'd like to suggest the following tasks for each of you to try this week. For Pam, as discussed earlier, I'd like you not to change your eating habits at all this week. Simply observe what you eat and how much you eat this week. You can write it down in a journal, so it's easy to track and share next time. Or you can take a picture or record a video, and we can review it later. To better assist you, we need to study it a little bit more. For Fran and Murray, I'd like to switch your parental positions. For Murray, per Fran's suggestion, I would like you to take Pam out once a week. Go for a walk, the mall, or whatever. For Fran, I know you worry a lot about Pam. As you already know, the more you argue and comment on Pam's eating, she feels pressured, and it doesn't create a "healthy and easy" eating environment that makes people want to eat more. So, during this week, at the table, please comment on Pam's eating only for the first 10 minutes. After 10 minutes, stop commenting and talk about something unrelated to food. During this 10-minute practice, Pam, you can argue back to Mom as much as you want. This is the only chance you can fight for your autonomy in eating. Murray, if you notice Fran commenting or nagging about Pam's eating for over 10 minutes, you need to stand up and stop her. Does this make sense to everyone?

Intervention: Restraining change for Pam's eating behavior, prescribing the symptom for the interaction pattern between Fran and Pam, and facilitating a U-turn for Murray and Pam—Throughout the conversation with the Daniels family, the therapist has observed and assessed the problem-maintaining cycles among three family members, such as Fran's controlling, Pam's resistance and withdrawal, and Murray's disengagement, and decides to change these rigid interactional patterns. The therapist assigns different tasks to each family member to disrupt repetitive attempts at solutions and create conditions for second-order changes. For Pam's eating issues, the therapist uses "Restraining change" for Pam not to change too quickly. This reduces the pressure she has felt from interacting with her parents and suggests that she observe her own eating behavior and record it. This also invites Pam to shift from reacting to Fran's monitoring to observing her own behaviors.

For Fran, Pam, and Murray, the therapist intervenes in the problematic-maintaining cycle with two behavioral modifications. One is to "Prescribe the symptom" by having Fran comment on Pam's eating, Pam's rebelling, and Murray's intervening within a set time limit. This paradoxical intervention allows Fran, Pam, and Murray to become aware of their rigid interaction pattern if they take the suggestion and practice it. If they fail to complete the assignment, they successfully break the cycle and try something different.

To increase Murray's presence with Pam and reduce Fran's control over Pam, Murray will spend time with Pam as Fran suggested. On the one hand, this suggestion parallels Fran's continued control in the family and can be considered a first-order change. On the other hand, if Murray and Pam take the suggestion and act on it, it creates a U-turn in the father-daughter dyad, leading to a decrease in Murray's disengagement and greater involvement with Pam. This shift might weaken the old problem-maintaining cycle and invite a second-order change.

The Therapeutic Story

At the end of therapy, the MRI therapist and the Daniels family clarify the presented problem, explore any attempted solutions, assess interaction patterns, and suggest several interventions that create a space for the family to explore alternative interactions and interrupt the rigid, repetitive problem-maintaining cycles.

1 The Daniels family's original problem, presented as Pam's anorexia, is changed to an interactional view that her symptoms are a response to the repetitive interactional pattern among family members, rather than her intrapsychic issues.
2 The MRI therapist identifies the family's attempted solutions as Fran's controlling, Murray's withdrawal, and Pam's resistance that maintain the problem. The therapist also reframes the intention behind the repetitive attempted solutions as a way each family member uses to protect family stability.
3 The therapist reframes Pam's resistance to preserving her autonomy as a pathology, as it was predicted responses within the feedback loops among family members. Therefore, the problem definition is shifted from blaming one individual to shared participation among family members.

4 Several strategic interventions are introduced to interrupt rigid repetitive problem-maintaining cycles so that the family can explore alternative interactions with each other.
5 As the family members alter their interactions with each other, the original organizing principles of the problem-maintaining cycles get weakened and create more space for second-order change to happen.

References

American Psychological Association. (2018). Paradoxical intention. In *APA dictionary of psychology*. Retrieved November 19, 2025, from https://dictionary.apa.org/paradoxical-intention

Anger-Díaz, B., Schlanger, K., Rincón, C., & Mendoza, A. (2004). Problem-solving across cultures: Our latino experience. *Journal of Systemic Therapies*, *23*, 11–27.

Bateson, G. (1972). *Steps to an ecology of mind*. Ballantine.

Bateson, G., Jackson, D. D., Haley, J., & Weakland, J. (1956). Toward a theory of schizophrenia. *Behavioral Science*, *1*(4), 251–254.

Fisch, R., Weakland, J. H., & Segal, L. (1982). *The tactics of change: Doing therapy briefly*. Jossey-Bass.

Keeney, B. P., & Ross, J. M. (1985). *Mind in therapy: Constructing systemic family therapies*. Basic Books.

Mental Research Institute. (n.d.). *Our past*. MRI. https://mri.org/about

Ray, W. A., & Schlanger, K. (2009). One thing leads to another: Reduc. In R. Fisch, W. A. Ray, & K. Schlanger (Eds.), *Focused problem resolution: Selected papers of the MRI Brief Therapy Center* (pp. xiv–xxv). Zeig, Tucker & Theisen, Incorporated.

Reiter, M. D., & Ray, W. A. (2014). Brief therapy: Mental Research Institute. In M. D. Reiter (Ed.), *Case conceptualization in family therapy* (pp. 105–125). Pearson.

Schlanger, K., Viorreta, R.T., Arnal, G.D., & Sánchez, A.P. (2020). 'My child is anxious because we might get deported': Brief therapy from MRI with an immigrant family in the United States. *Australian and New Zealand Journal of Family Therapy*, *41*, 355–366.

Soo-Hoo, T. (1999). Brief strategic family therapy with Chinese Americans. *American Journal of Family Therapy*, 27(2), 163–179.

Watzlawick, P., Beavin, J. H., & Jackson, D. D. (1967). *Pragmatics of human communication. A study of interactional patterns, pathologies, and paradoxes*. Norton.

Watzlawick, P., & Weakland, J. H. (1977). *The Interactional view: Studies at the Mental Research Institute, Palo Alto, 1965–1974*. Norton.

Watzlawick, P., Weakland, J. H., & Fisch, R. (1974). *Change: Principles of problem formation and problem resolution*. W. W. Norton.

Weakland, J. H. (2009a). Communication theory and clinical change. In R. Fisch, W. A. Ray, & K. Schlanger (Eds.), *Focused problem resolution: Selected papers of the MRI Brief Therapy Center* (pp. 65–82). Zeig, Tucker & Theisen, Incorporated.

Weakland, J. H. (2009b). The double-bind theory: Some current implications for child psychiatry. In R. Fisch, W. A. Ray, & K. Schlanger (Eds.), *Focused problem resolution: Selected papers of the MRI Brief Therapy Center* (pp. 141–152). Zeig, Tucker & Theisen, Incorporated.

Weakland, J. H., & Fisch, R. (1992). Brief therapy—MRI style. In S. H. Budman, M. F. Hoyt, & S. Friedman (Eds.), *First session in brief therapy* (pp. 306–323). The Guilford Press.

Weakland, J. H., Fisch, R., Watzlawick, P., & Bodin, A. M. (1974). Brief therapy: Focused problem resolution. *Family Process*, *13*(2), 141–168.

10 Milan Systemic Family Therapy

Carlos A. Ramos and Claire Loucka

Milan Systemic Family Therapy (MSFT) was founded in 1971 by a group of psychiatrists (Mara Selvini Palazzoli, Luigi Boscolo, Gianfranco Cecchin, and Giuliana Prata) from Milan, Italy, who were captivated by Gregory Bateson's systemic concepts and the work of the Mental Research Institute (MRI) in Palo Alto, California (Boscolo et al., 1987). In the 1960s, Selvini Palazzoli discovered that her efforts to work with young women with anorexia were ineffective (Amorin-Woods & Selvini, 2023). She noted that a long-lasting, individual approach (e.g., psychoanalysis) was limited in effectively treating her clients' symptoms. Selvini's frustrations led her to collaborate with her peers. The Milan group formed *the Centro per il Studio della Famiglia*—Center for the Study of the Family—where they embraced a systemic framework with families and couples. The Milan team soon noticed how quickly "anorexic girls abandoned their symptoms only after a few family sessions" (Amorin-Woods & Selvini, 2023, p. 112).

Like the MRI, the Milan group organized their approach to include therapists behind a one-way mirror for consultation and as part of the therapeutic process (Boscolo et al., 1987). The Milan group also expanded on the MRI's notion of the therapeutic double bind (Watzlawick et al., 1967) and phrased it as **counterparadox**, which became the foundation of their approach (Boscolo et al., 1987). The guiding hypothesis is that the family is a self-regulating system that governs itself based on the rules that are created over time through trial and error (Palazzoli et al., 1978a). The Milan group had three basic formulations: 1) Families are involved in unacknowledged family games; 2) Individual family members try to unilaterally control each other's behavior; and 3) The goal of the therapist is to discover and disrupt these games (Boscolo et al., 1987).

It is important to note that the original Milan team parted ways after about a decade of practice in 1980 (Amorin-Woods & Selvini, 2023; Barbetta & Telfener, 2021). Selvini Palazzoli split with Cecchin and Boscolo and then co-developed the Systemic Family Individual (SFI) approach (Codecá et al., 2024). Alongside her son, Matteo Selvini, and two of her students (Stefano Cirillo and Ana Maria Sorentino), Selvini created SFT with the intention of increasing flexibility by integrating multiple theoretical frameworks to help

DOI: 10.4324/9781003668510-10

better understand clients and families. Together they formed The New Center for the Study of the Family—*the Nuovo Centro per lo Studio della Famiglia* (Tomm, 1984). The group continued their research on anorexia-bulimia and associated four different personality types to this disorder: dependent, narcissistic, borderline, and obsessive-compulsive (Selvini Palazzoli et al., 1998), which they later conceptualized as post-traumatic personality (Selvini, 2018).

Cecchin and Boscolo dedicated their time to education and training as their approach shifted away from its early strategic interventions and techniques (Barbetta, 2019; Boscolo et al., 1987). Based on Bateson's critique of the work at the MRI, they gravitated toward nonauthoritarian practices (Cecchin et al., 2005) and referred to their practice as the Milan Approach (Barbetta, 2019). Cecchin and Boscolo distinguished their cybernetic understandings from the original family systems models, specifically Don Jackson's conceptualization of the family's homeostasis (Amorin-Woods & Selvini, 2023; Boscolo et al., 1987). Jackson suggested that the symptom served as a function that maintained the family's homeostasis. In other words, the family system creates and maintains the problem. This understanding reflects a first-order cybernetic epistemology that views the observer (e.g., therapist) as separate from the observed (e.g., client). The therapist can identify and diagnose the symptom or the problem (e.g., anorexia). This Milan group, however, embraced von Foerster's description of second-order cybernetics, which recognizes "that the observer enters into the description of that which is observed in such a way that objectivity is not at all possible" (Boscolo et al., 1987, p. 14). Cecchin and Boscolo argued that the notion of the therapist being separate from their client is misleading, so they viewed treatment as consisting of the therapist and the client "in one large bundle" (Boscolo et al., 1987, p. 14). Although the Milan approaches have evolved in different and separate ways, the Daniels' case study will be conceptualized mostly through the lens of the original model and founders (Cecchin, 1987; Palazzoli et al., 1978a).

The Therapeutic Story of Problem Formation

Milan systemic family therapists conceptualize problems, or symptoms of pathology, as transactional patterns that are unique to each family system (Palazzoli et al., 1978a). The family system is created through a series of transactions and corrective feedback loops. These recursive interactions create parameters (or family rules) that indicate what is acceptable and not acceptable in the family relationship. Through time, the family becomes a systemic unit that is held together "by rules peculiar to it alone" (Palazzoli et al., 1978a, p. 3). The rules are connected to the family's transactions or communicational dynamics. Thus, there is a recursive (or bidirectional) relationship between the family's behaviors and their rules—the family's interactions strengthen the rules of the game, and in turn, the rules of the game govern the family's transactions.

Palazzoli et al. (1978a) hypothesized that a member's symptoms of pathology are maintained by the family's interactions and "by the rules peculiar to the pathology" (p. 4). In other words, the family's problematic interactions are governed by their dysfunctional, oftentimes unnoticed, rules or games (Palazzoli et al., 1978b). The behavior, communications, and responses within the family have unique characteristics that maintain the rules and, thus, the pathological symptoms (Palazzoli et al., 1978a). It is epistemologically incorrect to consider the behavior of one family member as the cause of the behavior of others. Milan systemic family therapists "see the members of the family as elements in a circuit of interaction" (Palazzoli et al., 1978a, p. 5). Regardless of who is designated as the identified patient (IP), the first session includes all family members in the household with the intention of enhancing the therapist's knowledge of the family's relational dynamics (Palazzoli et al., 1980).

Palazzoli et al. (1978a) compared the family's paradoxical game to "a bizarre poker game" (p. 35), in which each player is committed to winning at all costs and is unaware of the motions and expressions of the others. The unspoken rules of the game perpetuate these symmetrical, competitive efforts, which in turn, further reinforce the game. Consequently, the game encourages each player not to quit, and it creates the idea that each player is winning if done in secret. The notion is that as long as "I keep playing, I have a chance of winning" (Palazzoli et al., 1978a, p. 35). Unfortunately, this limits the family from placing the cards on the table and ending or changing this everlasting game.

Palazzoli et al. (1978a) described symptoms of pathology within a family member as a manifestation of dysfunctional communication patterns within the family. During moments of crisis, dysfunctional families are susceptible to coalitions, subdivisions, or "factional battles" (Palazzoli et al., 1978a, p. 56) that are characterized by pathological labels (e.g., bad, weak, sick, etc.). The interactions within the Daniels family are understood as moves and countermoves that perpetuate impossible narratives for Pam. For instance, the family's message is that "it's not that you should do something different; you should be different" (Palazzoli et al., 1978a, p. 36).

This message creates an incongruency in communication that causes confusion and helplessness for Pam, who was diagnosed with Anorexia Nervosa. Pam finds that her responses "are always classified as 'wrong,' or better yet, as 'not exactly right'" (Palazzoli et al., 1978a, p. 37). In other words, if Pam says something, there is always another family member who will correct them, indicating that they did not communicate correctly. For instance, Fran is quick to educate and correct Pam's misuse of words or vocabulary during Pam's interactions with her siblings. If Pam tries to help someone, her efforts are inadequate. Conversely, if Pam does not attempt to help, her lack of effort is criticized. For example, Murray tends to criticize Pam's inability to set a good example for her younger siblings (e.g., grades, leadership, nutrition). Everyone within the system feels like Pam "has never done the right thing, without it ever being said explicitly what it is he should do to do the right thing" (Palazzoli et al., 1978a, p. 37). Pam is trapped in a "superparadox" with the implication that it's not just about her actions, but ultimately, it's about her identity, who she should be, which is also vague (Palazzoli et al., 1978a). Milan systemic family therapists would not pathologize the family's responses and reactions to Pam, meaning that they do not associate the family's interactions as the cause of the "symptom" (Pam's eating habits) (Palazzoli et al., 1978a).

With families with rigid boundaries, like those with someone with Anorexia Nervosa, every act of change is valued as a threat. All family members oppose any change that "presents a danger to their homeostatic ideal" (Palazzoli et al., 1978a, p. 59). This includes solicitations for change from outside of the family system (e.g., social, cultural, therapeutic) and pivotal experiences within the family (e.g., birth, loss, some form of crisis) (Palazzoli et al., 1978a). Barbetta (2005) suggested that anorexia was a common response to economic changes among middle and upper-class families in Western countries. The family encounters these experiences (or changes) with more rigidity, which in turn, further strengthens the rules of the game. With the Daniels family, Murray is the primary breadwinner, so his focus is on work and on sports with Oliver and George. Fran, as a stay-at-home mother, is responsible for the nurturing and development of the children. Fran's mother, Nancy, was also a stay-at-home mother with similar expectations. Fran's role, as the oldest of four siblings, was responsible for watching over the others, specifically the care of her youngest sister, Tamara, who was six years younger than Fran. Horace, Fran's father, was the primary breadwinner and was hardly involved with the parenting of the children. Thus, the Daniels' family rules or expectations are a reflection of their family's traditional views. The mother, Fran, is mostly responsible for caring for her "sick" child, Pam. Consequently, Pam's diagnosis and eating patterns have strengthened Fran's efforts with Pam, while Murray has further distanced himself from his interactions with Pam. Murray's responsibility is to financially provide for the family, and Fran is responsible for addressing any issues with the children.

Milan systemic family therapists must understand the family rules that organize the family's interactions and dysfunctional patterns of communication (Palazzoli et al., 1978a). Not understanding the rules or family patterns can result in patient-focused interventions or treatments that can maintain or exacerbate the problem. For instance, a therapist might primarily focus on Pam's anorexia and her eating patterns. However, if Pam improves, her family system will strive to reorganize the rules of the game according to Pam's improvement. In some instances, someone within Pam's family system (e.g., George) will develop similar pathological tendencies, ensuring the continuation of the game (Palazzoli et al., 1978a). Selvini (1977) argued that it was impossible to treat someone with anorexia with psychoanalysis in an individual setting; the approach must shift focus from the individual to the family system.

Families have rich and detailed descriptions of the problem(s) or of the person(s) they have labeled as the problem. They can provide a plethora of examples of the problem and how it has affected their lives. For instance, Fran and Murray could describe Pam's eating patterns and health habits and recount the number of meals she consumes (or refuses to consume) throughout the day or week. However, Milan systemic family therapists emphasize the importance of the family's interactions and reactions rather than their descriptions of the pathological symptoms (Palazzoli et al., 1980). In other words, it's a focus on the process rather than on the content. Rather than spending time on pathological descriptions (e.g., Pam's eating habits), the therapist asks questions that focus on how each family member reacts to the person with the problem or symptoms and how that individual reacts to their reaction (Palazzoli et al., 1980). Thus, it is a focus on responses and reactions—the recursive interactions of the family.

Palazzoli et al. (1978a) underscored the importance of questioning our linguistic conditioning, which is guided by a linear and causal epistemology. They highlighted that therapists' greatest obstacle to working with families is their conditioned conceptualization of "reality" through a linguistic model. Palazzoli et al. (1978a) emphasized that language is not reality; language is linear, descriptive, and static, while reality is living and circular. Cecchin (1987) suggested that we can accept our clients' linear descriptions if we do not believe these assumptions. These constructions of reality limit our curiosity and "have the effect of terminating dialogue and conversations" (Cecchin, 1987, p. 405). Once a therapist assumes they have an explanation for a problem, they stop searching for other alternatives or descriptions. Thinking they have "discovered" a "cause" stifles their systemic curiosity and hinders their neutrality toward the family.

Causal descriptions result in either/or thinking (true or false), which in turn assumes that some descriptions are more accurate than others (Cecchin, 1987). Consequently, this leads to the supposition that complex human interactions are trivial and can be explained by "a few simple, procedural postulates" (Cecchin, 1987, p. 405). For instance, if a therapist believes there is an accurate description of the family's situation, they might embrace the family's best description. The therapist might accept one family member's explanation or combine some or all of the family's descriptions to formulate the most accurate explanation. Alternatively, the therapist can present their explanation using certain facets of the family's descriptions of the problem. Cecchin (1987) referred to this as providing the family with a "scientific" or the "most logical" explanation.

Since we use language to communicate, we are forced to describe transactions through arbitrary dichotomizations. For example, we use language to punctuate the timing of an experience or exchange (before and after), and we also use language to define a "subject" or an "object," meaning one "who performs the action and [one] who receives the action" (Palazzoli et al., 1978a, p. 53). With the Daniels family, Pam's weight and eating habits are labeled by the family as pathological. Pam's reluctance to eat or finish her meals is considered the cause of the family's stress and frustration. On the other hand, the therapist might view Pam as the victim of her family's responses and thus, attribute Pam's anorexia to Fran's "overbearingness." Consequently, this linear, cause-and-effect thinking leads to moralism in therapy, meaning a person(s) (e.g., Pam) or a set of actions (family's responses) is deemed responsible for the pathology in the family.

Milan systemic family therapists challenge their linguistic and cultural understandings that limit their thinking to that of "things" and "objects" (e.g., viewing anorexia as a "thing" that can be identified and treated) and embrace an approach that emphasizes relationships (Palazzoli et al., 1980). Circularity in practice refers to the ability of the therapist to inquire about relational information about the family and to respond to their feedback in search of difference and change. As Palazzoli et al. (1980) underscored, "what we perceive easily is difference and change and difference is a relationship" (p. 173). Thus, Milan systemic therapists work under the assumption that information is difference and that difference is a relationship or a change in the relationship.

Diversity Conceptualization

Although MSFT was developed in Milan, Italy, therapists from all over the world have been captivated by the Milan group's complex ways of thinking about families (Barbetta & Telfener, 2021). They appreciated the Milan group's exploratory and non-judgmental stance with all families regardless of the circumstances. As Palazzoli et al. (1978a) suggested, every family is unique and different, so the family rules and games will vary across situations, cultures, and experiences. Currently, there are four Milan schools (*Scuola di Psicoterapia Mara Selvini Palazzoli*) across Italy and one location in Switzerland (Amorin-Woods & Selvini, 2023).

In 1980, Cecchin and Boscolo expanded their systemic framework to include different areas or professions beyond the therapy room (Barbetta & Telfener, 2021). These settings included schools, hospitals, violent settings, and foster care organizations. As Barbetta and Telfener (2021) suggested, a Milan approach (or systemic framework) allows practitioners to work with any complex systems or institutions. Boscolo and Cecchin inspired many international professionals who later formed the post-Milan teams (Telfener et al., 2025). These institutional and community efforts have continued through the work of Milan associates across the globe.

Telfener et al. (2025) explained why the Milan approach is conceptualized as an "approach," rather than as a "model." They suggested that a model is finite, so it does not evolve with the dimensions of time and context. On the other hand, an approach values therapists' diverse epistemological and socio-cultural frameworks; it is not simply a collection of theories or concepts. Thus, the Milan approach has experienced many changes since its inception (Amorin-Woods & Selvini, 2023). These changes have been guided by different settings and contexts, but, more importantly, through the work with a diverse range of individuals and families across the globe. For instance, in the United Kingdom (UK), the Milan approach has been modified to embrace solution-focused brief therapy (SFBT) and narrative therapy concepts (Campbell, 1999). Amorin-Woods and Selvini (2023) suggested that these changes have been mostly influenced by evolving societal, cultural, and political factors such as migration, substance addiction, divorce, suicide, and unemployment.

Lately, the Milan approach has placed more of an emphasis on "discrimination, poverty, social issues, and human rights" (Barbetta & Telfener, 2021, p. 14). The approach's curiosity has shifted to the social factors that create discrimination and pathology and to exploring the links between the violation of human rights and pathology. For instance, Barbetta and Telfener (2021) described marginalized discourses as *out of order*, rather than using the psychiatric discourse *disorder*. Unfortunately, therapists are confronted with institutional demands to provide efficient and cost-effective interventions that are valid, measurable, and verifiable, which are normally supported by some kind of assessment and diagnosis (Telfener et al., 2025). Milan therapists, however, embrace their clients' individual and cultural differences and engage in efforts to try "to empower them rather than 'change' them, believing that one can always choose in life" (Telfener et al., 2025, p. 10). It is important to consider that the personal history and experiences of the therapist become part of the therapeutic process, so there may be life events "that make us temporarily vulnerable and incapable of dealing with some difficult issues" (Barbetta & Telfener, 2021, p. 15).

The Therapeutic Story of Problem Resolution

Milan Systemic family therapists avoid true or false descriptions and generate descriptions within a frame of curiosity. They celebrate the complexities of human interactions and invite a polyphonic orientation to the explanation of family interactions (Cecchin, 1987). The goal is to invite the family members to share multiple descriptions and interpretations of the behaviors to develop a more systemic view.

Cecchin (1987) emphasized that a systemic framework embraces a shift toward esthetics and "the multiplicity of possible patterns" (p. 406). He highlighted that this approach provides therapists with the opportunity to explore a plurality of alternatives while maintaining a curious stance. It's a stance that enhances curiosity because it appreciates "a myriad of applicable 'stories' describing one interaction" (Cecchin 1987, p. 406). For example, the therapist might wonder about how all of the family's descriptions fit together; how do they reflect the therapist's assumptions about the problem; how are the descriptions similar and/or how are they different? Milan systemic family therapists also wonder about past descriptions of the problem and the family's potential future descriptions. For instance, a therapist working with the Daniels family might ask about the family's activities if Fran was no longer worried about Pam. Thus, they are not invested in the best (most accurate) description(s) but rather in searching for a pattern that connects the family's descriptions. Cecchin (1987) emphasized that "the more curious we are about the possible array of patterning, the more esthetically pleasing our analysis" (p. 406).

Guided by a systemic framework, Milan systemic family therapists assume that each family system has a logic or rationale to its interactions (Cecchin, 1987). They do not judge this logic, meaning that they do not interpret the family's engagement as either "good" or "bad" or "right" or "wrong." Therapists value and respect the integrity of the system. By valuing its integrity, therapists can approach the family members with enhanced curiosity about their experiences, behaviors, ideas, and their ways of communicating that have created and maintained the family's beliefs and interactions (Cecchin, 1987). The family's interactions are "simply operative," meaning "that the system is simply doing what it does and that this doing is the it that does it" (p. 406).

Hypothesizing

Palazzoli et al. (1980) suggested that therapy starts with the first phone call to schedule an appointment. Milan systemic family therapists use the information discussed over the phone and the information shared on any assessment or intake forms to develop an initial hypothesis. A hypothesis is the starting point for the therapist that guides their investigation and interview with the family (Palazzoli et al., 1980). The hypothesis should be a relational assumption of the family's patterns of communication or their family games. It organizes the therapist's engagement with the family (e.g., their relational questions, interruptions, control of the session). This approach helps to limit the therapist from being flooded with meaningless chatter from the family.

The first session starts with gathering information about the family (Palazzoli et al., 1980). The therapist then engages in a verification or falsification process to assess the validity of their hypothesis. If their hypothesis is proven false, then they must develop a second hypothesis dependent on the information gathered during the assessment of the first hypothesis. It is important to note that a hypothesis "is neither true nor false, but rather, more or less useful" (Palazzoli et al., 1980, p. 5). The purpose of the hypothesis is to guide the therapist's questions to elicit new information that can support, modify, or reject the therapist's hypothesis. Every hypothesis must be systemic, which includes all descriptions and components of the family.

Cecchin (1987) suggested that the metaphor of storytelling can be foundational in the development of a useful hypothesis. Cecchin described families as wonderful storytellers who present detailed scripts of their family's experiences. The family's scripts are oftentimes tightly or rigidly written. The issue is that their scripts do not help the family function in ways that are beneficial or useful. The intention of a hypothesis is to offer the family new scripts that encourage the members to modify their interactions (or current scripts), which consequently helps to adjust the therapist's script or hypothesis; this is an ongoing recursive process. When therapists are unable to develop a new hypothesis, this indicates that they have accepted the family's story or script and have lost their notion of curiosity (Cecchin, 1987).

Milan systemic family therapists use circular questions to create, refine, and abandon hypotheses about the family (Cecchin, 1987). This form of questioning helps to create a context where therapists can embrace their curiosity and neutrality with all family members. Cecchin emphasized that a troubling sign (or a red flag) for a therapist is when their hypothesis limits their use of circular questions and curiosity with a family. This is normally an indicator that the therapist has accepted or has "married" their own hypothesis. When therapists are unable to generate a new hypothesis, they "have no doubt lost [their] curiosity and become social controllers" (Cecchin, 1987, p. 411).

Circular Interviewing

Milan systemic family therapists embrace their relational framework by asking the family circular questions. The therapist takes the role of a scientist, researcher, or explorer with the intention to discover new information (Tomm, 1988). The purpose of **circular interviewing** is to create curiosity within the family and the therapeutic system (Palazzoli et al., 1980). It is a form of curiosity that inquires about the connection between the family's events and the problem, rather than the precise origins of the problem (Tomm, 1988). The therapist's engagement in circular interviewing creates a context that shifts from the family thinking in terms of objective "truths" and "reality" to thinking about relationships (Palazzoli et al., 1980). In other words, Milan systemic family therapists inquire about patterns and not facts. Normally, a family's belief system relies heavily on linear, cause-and-effect explanations for pathology. For instance, Fran might describe Murray as "dismissive" or Pam as "stubborn." The implication is that Pam or Murray is the IP and that they need to be different for therapy to be successful.

Tomm (1985) described the differences between circular questions and circular questioning. With **circular questioning**, the therapist is intending to understand the system and to generate change. There are two forms of circular questioning—descriptive circular questions and reflexive questions. A therapist uses **descriptive questions** to generate new information about the family or to modify their systemic understanding of the problem. They are genuinely curious about the unique family's descriptions and interactions. Milan systemic family therapists invite every member of the family to share how they see the relationship of two other family members (Palazzoli et al., 1980). The goal is to explore a dyadic relationship from the perspective of a third family member. For example, the therapist might ask Oliver to share how he sees his father's relationship with his younger brother, George. This technique or form of descriptive questioning helps to illuminate the various triadic relationships, secret coalitions, and alliances within the family. It also encourages the person (e.g., Oliver) to metacommunicate about the relationship of two other family members while present, which then facilitates a shift in their dysfunctional patterns of interactions (Palazzoli et al., 1980). The family's responses provide new information for the therapists to develop a hypothesis of the family's relational dynamics.

The purpose of **reflexive questions** is to initiate an immediate change within the family system. They are meant to challenge the family's polarizations by undermining their belief system by using the language of relationship (Palazzoli et al., 1980). Milan systemic family therapists identify "good" moments or opportunities during a session where they could use reflexive questions to offer therapeutic input (Tomm, 1985). Rather than being direct and telling the Daniels how they should behave, the therapist might ask Pam, "What would happen if your father expressed his concerns instead of your mother"? This form of intervention respects the autonomy of the system, which is different from the therapist presenting a directive or prescription.

Although circular questions and circular questioning overlap, circular questions are intended to explore *differences* between interpersonal relationships (and perceptions) and experiences across time and context (Tomm, 1985). For instance, a categorical or interpersonal circular question could explore, "Who gets more upset when Pam doesn't eat, Fran or Murray"? The therapist is searching for differences in reactions to Pam and in perceptions of each other's responses. **Categorical questions** are also useful in exploring differences among ideas and the family's belief systems. They can also inquire about the past and into the future (Tomm, 1985). The therapist could ask the Daniels family, "What would potentially be the most comforting approach to Pam at the dinner table"? This question would encourage the family to share their individual ideas while exploring potential possibilities in the future.

Temporal questions "focus on a difference between category differences at two points in time, in other words, on a change" (Tomm, 1985, p. 41). For example, the therapist could ask Murray, "Was there more arguing between Fran and Pam before or after Pam was diagnosed with Anorexia Nervosa"? The time marker of the diagnosis allows the therapist to explore Pam and Fran's relationship before and after a major family event. Another temporal question that can compare the past to the present could be, "Was Murray closer to Pam when she was younger or is he closer now"? This type of question can illuminate alliances or shifts in alliances, which then can be further explored. Temporal questions can also be future-oriented, connecting the present to the future or two points in the future (Tomm, 1985). One way of examining the differences between the present and the future could be by asking the Daniels family, "If Fran and Pam continue to argue over Pam's weight, what would their relationship be like in two years?" The therapist could connect two points in the future by asking Pam, "If your mother stopped worrying about your father, how would their relationship be different"? Palazzoli et al. (1980) suggested that once a question challenges the family's belief system, it provides the possibility for new stories to emerge.

Furthermore, Tomm (1988) suggested that circular interviewing has "the potential of having *liberating effects* on the family" (p. 7). As the therapist explores patterns and connections, the family makes their own connections. For instance, Murray, listening to Fran and Pam's interactions, might realize his lack of participation (or absence) in these interactions. With this increased awareness, Murray (and others) may shift from their linear perspective to one that provides new possibilities and options.

Neutrality

An additional concept that Milan systemic family therapists consider essential in therapy is neutrality. Palazzoli et al. (1980) conceptualized **neutrality** as the pragmatic effect of the therapist (their behavior or language) on the family's engagement in the session. There is an emphasis on behavioral interactions (circularity) rather than the therapist's "intrapsychic disposition" (p. 11). The initial description of neutrality was for the therapist to recognize their role in the therapeutic system and to embrace a neutral stance with each family member and presenting problem.

Palazzoli et al. (1978a) compared the role of the therapist to a player in a chess tournament who has little information on their opponents. The authors described this approach as playing "in as detached as a manner as possible" (p. 125). Therapists focus their attention on *how* the players (the family members) play the game rather than trying to familiarize themselves with the personalities and qualities of each family member.

Palazzoli et al. (1978a) suggested that therapists must free themselves from the motivations that inspired them to pursue this profession, such as the desire to give and help others. They argue that these aspirations make therapists vulnerable and sensitive to believe the interpretations of the family; families that are well trained in enticing others into their web of interactions. Palazzoli et al. (1978a) also stated that feelings of compassion or pity for families result in other emotions such as frustration due to little progress, boredom, or hostility toward certain individuals. A detached position prevents therapists from judging the responses, reactions, and behaviors of the family. Therapists view the interactions within the family with admiration, respect, and authenticity in the way a chess player would value the moves of his adversary.

Cecchin (1987), however, underscored that it is impossible for therapists to remain neutral because of how language is structured. Cecchin noted that all behavior (and language) is "politically laden" (p. 405). The language or behavior(s) that the therapist uses shapes, organizes, and constrains the patterns of communication in the session. This, in turn, influences the language and descriptions shared by the family in session. Thus, the therapist and family's behavior (or language) are always in relation to each other. As Cecchin (1987) accentuated, "we act in relation" (p. 405).

Cecchin (1987) argued that the concept of neutrality has been misunderstood. Therapists have assumed that neutrality means taking a position of "non-involvement" with the family. This approach often limits therapists from sharing their perspective or opinions, from not taking responsibility when needed, or from committing to certain ideas or perspectives. In other words, it's the position of "a cold and aloof," relativist therapist (Cecchin, 1987, p. 405).

To clarify these misunderstandings, Cecchin (1987) proposed a new definition for neutrality. Cecchin described "neutrality as the creation of a state of curiosity in the mind of a therapist" (p. 405). By embracing a curious stance, the therapist can explore the family's different perspectives or views. As a result, this enhances the therapist's curiosity in the family's alternative descriptions, which then increases curiosity in these descriptions (and so on, and so forth). This approach also leads to the invention of novel perspectives that were not present during the family's ways of understanding their situation. Therefore, there is a recursive, interlinked relationship between neutrality and curiosity, with the implication that the therapist commits to the exploration of different perspectives, but without an attachment (or marrying) to one description (Cecchin, 1987).

Cecchin (1987) stated that family members may have different opinions of the therapist's personality or personal qualities. Some of the family members may describe the therapist as being "warm" and "kind" while others may describe them as "naïve" or "ignorant." However, when the family is asked about who the therapist supported or sided with, they should respond with uncertainty. In other words, the family should have a difficult time suggesting who the therapist favored or disagreed with (or disliked) during the interview.

Cecchin (1987) emphasized that the intention of the therapist is to align with all family members during the interview process. These alliances may shift during the session. For instance, the therapist might ask Pam to describe her father's relationship with her mother. At that moment, the therapist appears to be allied with Pam. However, the alliance then shifts once the therapist asks Fran or Murray a similar circular question. The result of these building alliances "is that the therapist is allied with everyone and no one at the same time" (Cecchin, 1987, p. 405). To ultimately be effective, the therapist must maintain this "metalevel" from the family.

These three principles, hypothesizing, circularity, and neutrality, are recursively interconnected. Neutrality helps therapists create a context of curiosity that facilitates the construction of multiple hypotheses (Cecchin, 1987). The development of multiple hypotheses guides the therapist to explore circular patterns rather than thinking in terms of cause-and-effect relations, meaning that a person(s) or a group of actions are responsible for the family's problem. It is important to note that although the Milan approach has evolved over time, hypothesizing, circularity, and neutrality (curiosity) remain foundational to this approach (Barbetta & Telfener, 2021).

Positive Connotation

Boscolo et al. (1987) described **positive connotation** as "the most compelling invention of the Milan team" (p. 7). It is a concept that was initially influenced by the MRI's technique of paradox or prescribing the "symptom." For instance, a therapist could instruct a woman diagnosed with agoraphobia to stay home as if she was on house arrest (Boscolo et al., 1987). It is an effort to support and connect with the symptom, rather than engaging in efforts to eradicate it (Fisch et al., 1982). The Milan team, however, perceived that the therapist's actions of supporting the "symptom" negatively connoted the anti-symptomatic views of the family. Although the therapist was positively reframing the IP's behaviors, they were inadvertently pathologizing the family's perception of the circumstances. Consequently, the symptom would disappear but so would the family. This form of division, where an individual is exonerated and the family challenged, "made it impossible to envision the family as a systemic unity" (Boscolo et al., 1987).

Palazzoli et al. (1978a) described their frustrations with parents when they correlated their children's symptoms of anorexia to their behaviors. They described their arbitrary divisions as labeling some behaviors as "good" and others as "bad." For example, with the Daniels family, a therapist might positively reframe Pam's eating behaviors as a form of "protection" through "fasting." However, this discounts the family's concerns and perceptions of Pam's weight and nutritional habits. Thus, to embrace a systemic stance, a Milan systemic family therapist makes a positive connotation of both the IP's experiences and the behaviors of the family. With the Daniels family, the therapist could suggest that their behaviors and actions are intended to strengthen their family connection and cohesion. Through positive connotations, the therapist places the family on the same level and avoids the involvement of coalitions, alliances, or divisions, which tend to be the cause of the system's dysfunction (Palazzoli et al., 1978a).

Unlike strategic therapists (Haley, 1976), Milan systemic family therapists do not use persuasive rhetoric to communicate positive connotations (Boscolo et al., 1987). They are not used to "trick" the family out of their problem or to accepting change. They also do not provide prescriptions in a vacuum, meaning they do not target their interventions to a single individual. The intention is to consider the family's social context and to value their homeostatic tendencies. This approach respects the family's efforts to protect their equilibrium and, as a result, decreases the likelihood of the family's efforts to resist change. It is important to note that a positive connotation is not the only explanation for the family's experiences. As mentioned, Milan systemic family therapists are not searching for "truths" or "facts" (Palazzoli et al., 1980). A negative connotation of the family's experiences can be equally possible. However, Boscolo et al. (1987) suggested that from a multiview perspective, the therapist could explore which of the "truths" could be most useful to the family, "since none [are] less 'true' than the others" (p. 9).

Process-Oriented

As noted, Milan systemic family therapists emphasize **process-oriented questions** that focus on the family's interactions rather than inquiring about the descriptions of pathological symptoms (Palazzoli et al., 1980). One of the intentions is to prevent the family from meaningless chatter that often interferes with therapeutic intervention. Palazzoli et al. (1978a) suggested that certain families have the ability and tendency to disqualify the context (sessions) as therapeutic. The authors provide the example of "social" or "talkative" families who interact with the therapist as if they are at a social event or party. The family's ways of engagement consist of laughter, jokes, and "word games" in response to the therapist's attempt to be therapeutic.

The same logic applies to the withdrawn family that provides minimal information during the session. As Palazzoli et al. (1978a) described, "the family sits stiffly in a closely drawn-together group" (p. 68) staring at the therapist, wondering, "Well, we are here, what do we do now" (p. 68)? The family's silence or minimal communication implies that their participation depends on the efforts of the therapist. It appears as if it was the therapist's idea for the family to seek therapy. One way to encourage the family to therapeutically engage is to comment on the family's interactions or lack of participation. This effort, however, results in the therapist taking a moralistic stance or a particular interpretation of the family's dynamics that inevitably interferes with the therapist's neutrality or curiosity.

Instead, Milan systemic family therapists incorporate the use of "prescriptions" based on the family's responses and reactions during the session (Palazzoli et al., 1978a). A **prescription** is a specific task or homework assignment provided to the family, which is then discussed during the next session. The goal is to contextualize and structure therapy in a way that motivates and provokes all family members to focus on treatment. In other words, a prescription provides a format for the family to follow during the following sessions. It provides parameters that prevent families from going off on tangents or from deviating from the purpose of therapy. As Palazzoli et al. (1978a) suggested, with some "talkative families," the next session runs the risk of the family repeating what they shared during the previous session. With the use of a prescription, the family is restricted during the follow-up conversations to discuss the task(s) that the therapist recommended.

A therapist working with the Daniels family could present the following prescription: During dinner every other night for the next week, each family member will individually thank Pam for her eating habits and nutrition. They will each share one benefit connected to Pam's health habits. The family must make sure that everyone has an opportunity to share. These experiences are then discussed during the follow-up session.

Family Rituals

Milan systemic family therapists prescribe family rituals as an intervention to encourage all family members to engage in a specific task (Palazzoli et al., 1977). The authors defined a **family ritual** as "an action or a series of actions, sometimes accompanied by verbal formulas or expressions, that are to be carried out by all members of the family" (p. 452). Palazzoli et al. (1978b) stated that the therapist must quickly identify the family rules that are perpetuating the family dysfunction. Once identified, the therapist creates a prescription or ritual that targets the disruption of the family's dysfunctional games or rules. The therapist must present the family ritual, or sequences of actions, with complete instructions and specific details. This includes the location of the ritual, the date and time, the number of repetitions, and the family members who are going to communicate and in what order (Palazzoli et al., 1978a).

Palazzoli et al. (1978b) underscored the differences in the use of prescriptions, family rituals, and ritualized prescriptions. The primary difference is that ritualized prescriptions can be repeated in identical formats, specifically with couples who have children with pathological symptoms. These couples tend to disqualify one another in the discipline or nurturing of their children. The idea is that one parent "knows better" than the other. This disqualification undermines or sabotages each parent's initiatives with their children, which results in symptoms of pathology in the child (e.g., eating disorders). The ritualized prescription is intended to block the interference from the parents. However, the content of the ritualized prescription is cryptic. The therapist only provides the couple with the parameters for their engagement with their children.

Palazzoli et al. (1978b) described this intervention as **odd days and even days**, which the therapist assigns to each parent with the task of responding to their child on certain days. For example, the mother is responsible for responding to her child on even days of the week (Tuesdays, Thursdays, and Saturdays). Although the father is present, he must behave as if he is not there. It is fully up to the mother to decide how she is going to behave and interact with the child. This information is not provided by the therapists or any other family member. The same applies for the father on odd days (Mondays, Wednesdays, & Fridays); he is solely responsible for the discipline of the child. On Sundays, the family must figure out, or collaborate, how they are going to approach the child. The parents are also instructed to write down any instances or attempts by the other parent to intervene or interfere during their days off. The therapists could also instruct the child or other children to note any interferences if they are capable of completing the task.

The purpose of prescribing a family ritual is to shift the family's epistemology, or their family games, without having to explain or criticize their dysfunctional interactional patterns (Palazzoli et al., 1978a). In other words, the primary focus is to change the rules of the family games (Palazzoli et al., 1977). The intention is not to enhance the family's awareness or recognition of the interactions perpetuating the family games but rather "to introduce into the system a ritualized prescription of a play whose new norms silently take the place of old ones" (Palazzoli et al., 1978a, pp. 67–68). The therapist can generate recognition or insight with the family once the change has occurred. Palazzoli et al. (1978b) suggested that insight prior to shifting the family's rules or dynamics could result in the family becoming combative and resistant to participating in the prescribed ritual.

This form of intervention requires due diligence and great effort from the therapist (Palazzoli et al., 1978a). Milan systemic family therapists pay close attention to the details or the information shared by the family. Since every family is unique and different, Milan therapists embrace their ability to improvise and creatively come up with family rituals that are closely related to the family's dynamics. Family rituals that were effective with one family are more than likely not going to be useful with another family; the family games, myths, and rules vary across situations, cultures, and experiences (Palazzoli et al., 1978a)

Palazzoli et al. (1978a) described their approach as long-term brief therapy. They suggested that a change in the actions of one family member does not immediately influence the behavior of others. Although the intervention was helpful for one member, "it takes a certain span of time before a corrective maneuver in another member or members becomes exasperated to the point of being evident" (Palazzoli et al., 1978a, p. 15).

Five-Stage Format

The Milan group conceptualized their approach as an interview and divided the interview process into five phases: the pre-session, the session, the intersession, the intervention, and the post-session reflection (Palazzoli et al., 1978a). During the **pre-session**, the team creates an initial hypothesis of the family's problem based on the information shared by the clients before the first session. For instance, with the Daniels family, the team could use the information shared by Fran or Murray on the intake form or during their phone calls before the appointment. Next, the therapist(s) conduct(s) the **session**. If working with four team members, only two of the members would join the session with the family. The other two members would observe the session behind a one-way mirror, and their goal is to "validate, modify, or change the hypothesis" (Boscolo et al., 1987, p. 5). About halfway through the session is the **intersession** where the four team members would meet alone to discuss the hypothesis and to develop an intervention. The two therapists would then return to the family with an **intervention**, which consists of a positive connotation of the family's problem or a family ritual intended to introduce change (Boscolo et al., 1987). The **post-session** consists of the team discussing the family's reactions to the intervention and to plan for the following session.

Boscolo et al. (1987) underscored that this format can consist of fewer than four team members, and it could also be done alone. The therapist working alone can step outside of the therapy room for a brief reflection. They then return and share their ideas with the family. The therapist could also share that they consulted with a colleague or group of colleagues, and this is the message they wanted to share. Boscolo et al. (1987), however, suggested that these are normally imaginary colleagues.

Case Transcript

The following case demonstrates how a Milan systemic family therapist, Millie, approaches the Daniels family, listening closely for their unique family rules and ways of engagement. Millie develops her initial hypothesis using the information shared during a phone call with Fran and a brief pre-session discussion with the team members. The team suggested that Fran's concerns for Pam indicate Fran's ongoing efforts to help Pam. There was little to no mention of Murray's involvement, leaving the team curious about his role (and the other children) in the family's dynamics. Millie continues to develop her hypothesis during the first portion of the session. This is one iteration of how a Milan systemic family therapist would interview the Daniels family.

Participants: Therapist (Millie), Murray (father), Fran (mother), Pam (17), Oliver (15), George (13)

Team (behind one-way mirror): *Observing team members taking notes for discussion during the intersession (consultation break).*

Therapist: Good afternoon, everyone. I appreciate you all being here. I'd like to hear from each of you. Briefly, what do you all hope might happen because of coming here?

> **Intervention**: The therapist quickly starts with a question that sets the parameters for a therapeutic conversation to avoid meaningless chatter. She is interested in each family member's perception of the problem and their hopes for therapy. The therapist and the team are interested in communication patterns and behavioral transactions within the family. The therapist is closely observing who volunteers to share first (their order) and their responses/reactions to each other. Just as important, the initial open-ended question has a future-oriented implication. From the start, the therapist is creating a context that provides the possibility for new patterns and stories (family scripts) to emerge.

Fran: We're scared. Pam isn't eating much again, and I don't know what else to do. She has struggled with her weight for quite some time. We're hoping that maybe, if we can talk as a family, things might get better before she must go into treatment, which we really don't want.

Murray: Yeah, I just want Pam to be healthy. I don't know how this happened. We've always been a close family. I'm hoping this helps us figure out how to help Pam get back to normal.

Pam: I don't really know. I'm here because they want me here. I don't want to talk about eating all the time. That's all they think about.

Oliver: I just want everyone to stop arguing at dinner. It's intense.

George: Yeah, same. I kind of miss when things were just normal. Back when this wasn't all we spoke about.

Therapist: It sounds like "normal" feels pretty far away right now, and each of you misses it in your own way. I'd like to explore how each of you responds when something feels different or doesn't feel "normal." How does that sound?

(*All nod slightly.*)

Intervention: The therapist maintains neutrality, a non-judgmental stance, avoiding taking sides or aligning with any one family member. This is to prevent polarization, maintain trust with all members, and encourage the family to think systemically rather than defensively (or cause-and-effect thinking). The therapist is also listening for the family's response to change (challenging of homeostasis or family rules).

Hypothesizing Phase (the therapist is exploring patterns)

Therapist: Fran, when you first noticed that Pam wasn't eating much, what did you think was happening for her?

Intervention: The therapist is gathering information to develop a working hypothesis of the family interactions and functions of the symptom. Once the therapist creates a hypothesis, she will test it through questions and observations. The goal is to explore the function of Pam's anorexia within the family system, rather than viewing it as an isolated medical issue. This form of circular questioning (reflexive) was intended for Fran to reflect on Pam's experience (e.g., personal, emotional challenges).

Fran: I thought it was stress, perhaps issues at school, maybe body image stuff. This could be also related to her low self-esteem. I tried to encourage her to eat, but it turned into fights.

Therapist: So it seems like, Fran, that your encouragement to eat led to fights with Pam. And Murray, when you saw Fran and Pam fighting about food, what would you do?

Intervention: The therapist uses circular questioning (descriptive) to invite Murray to explore his response to Fran and Pam's interactions. The goal is to shift the focus to the family's interactions, rather than asking questions to discover (or reveal) "objective truths."

Murray: I'd usually stay quiet. Fran was handling it. I didn't want to make things worse.

Therapist: Pam, when your mom and dad were reacting that way, Mom was worrying, and Dad was staying quiet. What was that like for you?

Intervention: The therapist uses circular questioning (reflexive) to invite Pam to describe her experience in relation to her parents' interactions. This shifts the focus from Pam's individual symptoms to the relational pattern among the three of them. The therapist is also encouraging Pam to meta-communicate her perception of her parents' dynamics.

Pam: Like I was being watched. Like every bite was a test. And dad not saying anything just made it worse, like he agreed but didn't want to deal with it and get in mom's way.

Therapist: So your dad does not get involved during conversations at dinner?

Pam: Nope. Just sits back and watches. He might say something, but it's meaningless. Again, I don't think he wants to interfere with Mom.

Therapist: That's helpful, thank you. Oliver, what do you notice that happens between your mom and dad when Pam isn't eating?

Intervention: The therapist continues to engage in circular questioning (descriptive) to learn Oliver's perspective of the situation. This question also helps to provide Fran and Murray with a different perspective on their interactions and the responses to their interactions. It's a question intended to shift the family's linear thinking to a circular focus.

Oliver: Mom gets upset, and Dad says, "Just let Pam be." Then they kind of argue. Then Mom cries or gets really upset.

Therapist: Ok. And George, what happens after your mom cries?

Intervention: The therapist continues to value and collect perspectives from each family member. The therapist continues to embrace neutrality by remaining curious and non-judgmental of the family's interactions. The therapist is also exploring the family dynamics to continue to develop hypotheses.

George: Then Pam leaves the table, and everyone is upset. And Dad tells us to finish eating. He doesn't say much after. He just wants us to finish our meals. Dad sometimes tries to change the subject, but at that point, no one really wants to talk.

Therapist: So, when Pam eats less, Fran worries and pushes more, Murray steps back to calm things, which feels like withdrawal to Pam. This leads Pam to pull away even more. This appears like a dance none of you want to be in.

Intervention: The therapist continues to explore the family dynamics and ongoing patterns. Remaining neutral, the therapist suggests the circular nature of the existing pattern. It is important to note that the therapist is not punctuating or placing blame on any individual during these interactions. The therapist is searching for patterns and not "facts."

(*Family looks thoughtful.*)

Therapist: Pam, who here first notices when you're having a harder day?

Intervention: The therapist is exploring how Pam perceives her relationship with other members, rather than just inquiring about her own perspective on her experience. This helps to reveal reactions/responses, alliances, and feedback loops in the system. The goal is to shift the family's thinking from individual blame (Pam is sick) to relational dynamics (how we all influence one another). This is another example of a descriptive question.

Pam: Mom. Always my mom. She is always the first to say something. She always has something to say. It's so hard to even tell her I'm fine. Just drop it.

Therapist: So, your mom is quick to notice first. Fran, who notices next? After you notice?

Intervention: The therapist keeps her neutrality and avoids othering Pam's perspective or correcting her. She also avoids pathologizing or placing blame on Fran's reactions.

Fran: Normally, Murray. Or he pretends not to, but I can tell he knows. He'll pretend as if he doesn't notice, but I can tell he notices.

Therapist: Murray, when Fran worries, who do you feel more responsible for in that moment, Pam or Fran?

Intervention: The therapist continues to develop a hypothesis based on the family's responses through the use of reflexive questions, which are also intended to introduce the possibility of change.

Murray: Honestly, Fran. I want her to calm down and just let it go. I guess, I think if she relaxes, everything else might mellow out.

Therapist: So sometimes your way of helping Pam is to first take care of Fran's emotions?

(*Fran looks surprised, nods slowly.*)

Murray: Yeah.

Therapist: Pam, when you see your dad focus on helping your mom stay calm, how does that affect you?

Intervention: The therapist uses a reflexive question to gather Pam's perception of how Fran and Murray's interactions influence her. The therapist continues to search for patterns and not "facts." The therapist is also encouraging Pam to metacommunicate her perception of her parents' dynamics.

Pam: It makes me feel like I'm the problem. Like I'm the cause and reason my mom needs to relax and calm down.

Therapist: Your perception is that you're the problem. Oliver, if Pam feels like she's the cause of the problem, what happens to the rest of you?

Intervention: The therapist continues to explore how the rest of the family responds during these experiences (descriptive question). She continues to avoid placing blame on Pam or identifying her as the patient.

Oliver: We don't want to make things worse. We know that our parents are stressed, so we try to stay out of it. We don't get involved.

George Yeah. We just go play outside or something. We find something else to do. I agree with Oliver, we don't want any piece of what's going on.

Systemic Reflection (Therapist sharing hypothesis)

Therapist: I'm beginning to imagine that this family has learned some creative ways to maintain a sense of balance. When one part feels shaky, for example, when Pam's eating changes, the rest of you move in predictable ways to steady things. For example, Fran increases her care, Murray brings a sense of calmness, the boys find ways to not get involved and make things worse, and Pam takes on the role of holding everyone's emotions. It's almost like she's saying with her body what can't be said out loud.

(Pam looks down; Fran looks tearful.)

Intervention: The therapist shares a hypothesis that reflects a systemic understanding of the family's interactions. The hypothesis is also a reflection of a positive connotation. The descriptions of the family's experiences are conceptualized from a positive viewpoint that underscores the family's efforts to support each other. The therapist does not place blame on any individual, and she also presents it as one potential description of the family's circumstances. It is not an objective "truth." The therapist is also suggesting that Pam is limited in her ability to metacommunicate on her family's belief system.

Fran: I never thought of it that way. I thought she was hurting herself by avoiding meals. I didn't think she was holding our emotions.

Therapist: Perhaps, both could be true. I'd like to consult with the team to hear their thoughts. I'll be back in 10 minutes.

Consultation Break

(*Therapist steps out to speak with observation team behind the mirror.*)

Team Reflection

A hallmark of the Milan model is that a team observes the session and offers systemic reflections or alternative hypotheses from behind a one-way mirror. The purpose is to maintain therapist neutrality and curiosity, to generate multiple perspectives, and to demonstrate that no single narrative is "the truth." The team shared the following feedback: 1) Pam is trapped in a "superparadox;" 2) they underscore the strong mother-daughter imposition and father-son subsystem; and 3) they hypothesize that Pam's anorexia may serve as a bridge or protest (a form of communication) between the two family halves. Based on this information, the team recommends a family ritual that invites Fran and Murray to consciously swap roles for a week (Fran to step back, Murray to step closer to Pam). All family members will be invited to journal their experiences, including the children, after dinner is complete. This means that both George and Oliver will be invited to observe and journal the family interactions, rather than engaging in other activities. Pam will also take note of her interactions with her parents.

The Therapist Returns to the Family

Therapist: I'd like to share the team's thoughts and suggestions. The team noticed how much strength this family shows through connection, even when it looks like conflict. They wondered what might happen if, for one week, Murray took the lead in connecting with Pam, and if Fran allowed herself to rest from worrying, trusting that Murray would handle it. Murray will specifically, and only during these moments, take the lead during dinnertime each night of the week except on Sundays. On Sundays, you all can decide how to best approach it. Murray is responsible for all comments about food or eating with Pam. Fran, your role is to just observe how Murray interacts with Pam. You will try your best not to interject during their interactions. I want to encourage both Murray and Fran to journal these experiences. Please make sure to journal once dinner is complete and away from the dinner table. For Murray, what was it like to take the lead? For Fran, what was it like to observe Murray and Pam? As for Oliver and George, you all will also stay at the dinner table but will take note of the family interactions. This means that you both would use journals to reflect on how these interactions unfold once done with dinner. The same applies to you, Pam. Your goal is to journal your interactional experiences with your dad outside of the dinner table. Just as important, you're also going to keep a note of any instance where your mom interferes or discusses food with you at the dinner table. This will be an experiment for this week until our next session. We will discuss your experiences, including the information in your journals. How does that sound?

Intervention: The therapist prescribed a family ritual designed to disrupt dysfunctional patterns. It was intended to promote new interactions, rather than to create awareness. This creates a systemic change by temporarily shifting alliances, rules, or roles in the family. The purpose of the ritual is to shift the family games or scripts. The goal is to get all family members involved in the process, including George and Oliver. The information the family gathers during the week will set the stage and structure for the following session. The information will also contribute to the therapist's working hypotheses of the family's interactions.

Murray: I think I can try that. I don't want Fran to feel alone in this experience.

Fran: I'm not sure I can stop worrying. It will be hard for me to just sit back and observe. I can give it a shot.

Pam: That would be different. I'm not used to dad saying something about food at the dinner table. He normally just sits back. Let's see.

Therapist: Oliver and George, can I count on you all to find journals or notebooks to write some notes?

Oliver: I can try!

George: Yeah, me too!

Therapist: Great! Let's see what happens when you all shift your interactions a bit this week. Next time, we'll talk about what each of you noticed and what you all wrote down in your journals. See you next week.

Post-Session

Team Reflection

The team discusses the family's responses to the family ritual. They underscore how each family member was receptive to the prescription. They mention that the family's acceptance of the family ritual is an indicator that the task more than likely respects and values the family's belief system, which, ultimately, minimizes their resistance for change.

The Therapeutic Story

The Daniels' perception of their problem primarily focused on Pam's anorexia and her reluctance to engage in healthier eating habits. They had a cause-and-effect epistemology that identified Pam as the cause of the family's circumstances. In other words, Pam was to blame for all the disagreements and arguments within the family system. If only Pam improved, then the rest of the family would be in a better place. The therapist, however, conceptualized the family's experiences from a systemic epistemology. Embracing her curiosity, the therapist engaged in circular interviewing to gather information on the recursive and relational patterns within the family. The therapist was mostly interested in the family's responses and reactions during certain experiences, rather than trying to identify a diagnosis or the "cause" of the problem. Unlike the family's understanding of the problem, the therapist did not blame Pam or her anorexia for the family's circumstances.

By embracing neutrality and circular interviewing, the therapist was able to gather information that helped her (and her team) develop a working hypothesis on the family's relational dynamics. This information also provided the therapist with a better understanding of the family's rules and games. Most of the family's disagreements and arguments were at the dinner table, where there was an expectation that Fran was responsible for addressing Pam's disruptive behaviors. Once the therapist and the team developed a hypothesis, they were able to construct a family ritual.

The intention of the family ritual was to disrupt the family's dysfunctional interactions by encouraging each family member to do something different. For example, Murray was informed to take the lead at the dinner table with Pam, while Fran took more of a passive role. The boys were encouraged to stay at the dinner table, rather than engaging in other activities. Pam was to pay close attention to her parental interactions and journal these experiences, especially if there were instances where Fran interfered with Murray's parenting at the dinner table. The therapist placed the family in a paradoxical situation that allowed them to metacommunicate about their norms, rules, and interactions. Ultimately, the therapist's intention was to shift the family's conventional rules and games.

References

Amorin-Woods, D., & Selvini, M. (2023). The influence of the Milan approach: Five decades of intergenerational change. A conversation with Matteo Selvini. *Australian and New Zealand Journal of Family Therapy*, *44*(1), 108–121.

Barbetta, P. (2005). *Anoressia e isteria*. Rafaello Cortina editore.

Barbetta, P. (2019). Milan systemic family therapy. In J. L. Lebow, A. L. Chambers, & D. C. Breunlin (Eds.), *Encyclopedia of couple and family therapy*. Springer.

Barbetta, P., & Telfener, U. (2021). The Milan approach, history, and evolution. *Family Process*, *60*(1), 4–16.

Boscolo, L., Cecchin, G., Hoffman, L., & Penn, P. (1987). *Milan systemic family therapy: Conversations in theory and practice*. Basic Books.
Campbell, D. (1999). Family therapy and beyond: Where is the Milan systemic approach today? *Child & Adolescent Mental Health*, *4*(2), 76–84.
Cecchin, G. (1987). Hypothesizing, circularity, and neutrality revisited: An invitation to curiosity. *Family Process*, *26*, 405–413.
Cecchin, G., Barbetta, P., & Toffanetti, D. (2005). Who was von Foerster, anyway, *Kybernetes*, *34*(3–4), 330–342.
Codecá, L., Russon, J., & Selvini, M. (2024). The systemic-family-individual approach: The heritage and continuation of Mara Selvini Palazzoli's work in integrative psychotherapy. *Journal of Marital and Family Therapy*, *50*, 706–725.
Fisch, R., Weakland, J. H., & Segal, L. (1982). *The tactics of change: Doing therapy briefly*. Jossey-Bass.
Haley, J. (1976). *Problem-solving therapy*. Jossey Bass.
Palazzoli, M. S., Boscolo, L., Cecchin, G., & Prata, G. (1977). Family rituals: A powerful tool in family therapy, *Family Process*, *16*, 445–453.
Palazzoli, M. S., Boscolo, L., Cecchin, G., & Prata, G. (1978a). *Paradox and counterparadox: A new model in the therapy of the family in the schizophrenic transaction*. Jason Aronson.
Palazzoli, M. S., Boscolo, L., Cecchin, G., & Prata, G. (1978b). A ritualized prescription in family therapy: Odd days and even days, *Journal of Marriage and Family Counseling*, *4*, 3–9.
Palazzoli, M. S., Boscolo, L., Cecchin, G., & Prata, G. (1980). Hypothesizing-Circularity-Neutrality: Three Guidelines for the conductor of the session, *Family Process*, *19*, 3–12.
Selvini, M. (1977). *Self-starvation*. Jason Aronson.
Selvini, M. (2018). A challenge to borderline personality diagnosis: Investigating post-traumatic personality disorders. Connecting personality traits to development in family. In R. Pereira, & J. Linares (Eds.), *Clinical interventions in systemic couple and family therapy*. Springer.
Selvini Palazzoli, M., Cirillo, S., Selvini, M., & Sorrentino, A. M. (1998). *Ragazze anoressiche e bulimiche*. Raffaello Cortina.
Telfener, U., de Bustis, E., Cazzaniga, E., Ferrari, F., Floris, R., Ganda, G., Giordano, C., Giuliani, M., La Barbera, C., Marchiori, R., Mosconi, A., Mreule, S., Pasini, B., Pezzolo, M., Rosas, R., Sacchelli, D., Sannasardo, P., Sbattella, F., Tettamanzi, M., & Troielli, W. (2025). The Milan approach today. *Family Process*, *64*(1), 1–20.
Tomm, K. (1984). One perspective on the Milan systemic approach: Part I. Overview of development, theory, and practice. *Journal of Marital and Family Therapy*, *10*(2), 113–125.
Tomm, K. (1985). Circular interviewing: A multifaceted clinical tool. In D. Campbell & R. Draper (Eds.), *Applications of systemic therapy: The Milan approach*. Grune & Stratton.
Tomm, K. (1988). Interventive interviewing: Part III. Intending to ask lineal, circular, strategic, or reflexive questions? *Family Process. 27*(1), 1–15.
Watzlawick, P., Beavin, J., & Jackson, D. (1967). *Pragmatics of human communication: A study of interactional patterns, pathologies, and paradoxes*. Norton.

11 Strategic Family Therapy

Roxanne Bamond, Anastasia B. Hanson, and Rosemary A. Leone

Strategic therapy emphasizes the power of structure, planning, and directive interventions to bring about change in individuals, couples, and families (Haley, 1986). Unlike traditional talk therapies that seek insight through reflection, Strategic Therapy operates with the belief that problems are often maintained by repetitive patterns of interaction (Haley, 1969). By disrupting these patterns through purposefully designed strategies, therapists help clients resolve issues in a focused and efficient manner. Strategic Therapy is part of the broader school of brief therapy, often requiring only a few sessions to achieve meaningful change. This is based on the belief that insight is not always necessary for transformation—strategic actions can be more effective (Madanes, 1981).

A central figure in the development of Strategic Therapy is **Jay Haley** (1923–2007), a pioneering psychotherapist, author, and theoretician. Haley was instrumental in shaping modern family therapy and is best known for his innovative work at the Mental Research Institute (MRI) in Palo Alto and later at the Philadelphia Child Guidance Clinic. Influenced by thinkers like Milton Erickson and Gregory Bateson, Haley emphasized the use of paradox, metaphor, and direct interventions tailored to the unique dynamics of each case (Haley,1984; Keim & Lappin, 2002). His approach was pragmatic, often provocative, and centered on changing the present rather than analyzing the past.

Chloe Madanes was also a major figure in developing Strategic Therapy. She believed difficulties occur in families due to the imbalance in the family structure and problematic patterns among the family members (Madanes, 1981). She also posited that pretending to enact the symptom gave the client influence over the problem; shifting the involuntary into something within the control of the client would eliminate the need for the original symptom (Madanes 1981). Madanes' work will be especially helpful in addressing parent-child interactions later in this chapter. For a time, Haley and Madanes were married and jointly developed the Family Therapy Institute of Washington, D.C.

Strategic therapy is about *changing the doing, not just the thinking* (Haley, 1986). By leveraging strategic interventions, therapists aim to quickly interrupt dysfunctional cycles and empower clients to take new and more effective actions.

DOI: 10.4324/9781003668510-11

Haley's vision of therapy as a strategic, creative, and purposeful process continues to shape contemporary practice across many therapeutic disciplines.

The Therapeutic Story of Problem Formation

Strategic therapy posits that problems form in human systems when people rely on behaviors and interactions that create distress to retain the essential structures and functions of those social systems (Haley, 1987). These dysfunctional behaviors and interactions are, in fact, functional in that they create organization and predictability in relational systems. Like Structural Family Therapy, Strategic therapy orients the therapist to structures and hierarchies within families and sees emergent and chronic behavioral issues from children and young adults as reflective of issues of adaptability within the family (Haley, 1980). Problems reflect a family's struggle to adapt to new roles and responsibilities and serve to keep the family from having to fundamentally restructure their relationships with one another.

A Strategic family therapist might note the division of hierarchies, roles, and responsibilities between Murray and Fran in taking care of Pam, Oliver, and George. Early in the family's formation, Murray and Fran decided that Murray's role in the family would be to provide the family with money and to manage the boys' social and athletic lives, while Fran's role would be to care entirely for Pam and for the nutritional and functional needs of all the children. Pam is seen as needing to be fed by Fran, while Murray is busy running the family business and focusing his limited attention on Oliver and George. The family is mostly split by gender: Pam and her mother in one subsystem and Oliver, George, and their father in another. Strategic therapy would see the division of the Daniels family into two subsystems as an organizational structure, which the therapist must interface with to properly affect or resolve Pam's symptoms.

As we will see, this organization of relationships within the Daniels family is being challenged by the family's natural evolution from one stage to the next, where the relationships, communications, and interactions between family members all must change as the Daniels children enter adulthood. A strategic family therapist would need to conceptualize what would be happening in the family if they were functionally adapted to their new stage of family life, and to question the role of the family's concern for Pam in preventing their collective evolution.

Family Life Cycles

Strategic therapists understand that an individual's symptoms are a form of communication regarding the family system's rules, and are about how the larger family system is organized, rather than about one individual in that family system being sick or dysfunctional (Madanes, 1981). An individual's symptoms are the behavioral result of maladaptive family communication and interactions. The therapist does not attempt to diagnose an individual with a pathology but rather understands that problems serve as a distraction for the family and begin to emerge at certain points in the **family life cycle** (Haley & Richeport-Haley, 2003).

Haley (1971) established the need to evaluate a psychiatric patient's family system in understanding the patient's behavior. Without the context of the family system, the early family therapists found that extreme behaviors in individual patients would resolve in inpatient settings, only to later reemerge when the patient would transition to outpatient and resume interactions in their family systems (Haley, 1971). This led the founders of family and systemic therapy to seek to understand *why* this would happen. Haley (1971) definitively concluded that "[the] symptom is a signal that a family has difficulty in getting past a stage in the life cycle" of the family (p. 42).

Haley so emphasized the role of the family in producing erratic or extreme behaviors in an individual, writing that "the particular life stage of the family is more important than the symptom category of the young person" (Haley, 1980, p. 2). A strategic therapist is not too preoccupied with distinguishing one extreme behavior from another, whether it is arson, suicidality, or an eating disorder. More important is considering the stage of family life a child, adolescent, or young adult exists within.

Haley (1971) theorized six primary phases of a family life cycle: the courtship period; marriage; childbirth and beginning parenthood; middle parenthood and childhood; "weaning parents from children" during adolescence and young adulthood; and finally, retirement and growing old. Haley (1971) noted crises may emerge between and during each stage of the family life cycle.

Homeostasis

From a Strategic frame of reference, problems occur when people are blocked in certain developmental stages. The strategic therapist seeks to prompt the client(s) into the next stage of development (Haley, 1980, 1986; Haley & Richeport-Haley, 2003). At this point in the Daniels' family life cycle, Pam is approaching adulthood. While she appears regressed, and her parents doubt her ability to care for herself, she is actually keeping the family stable. If the family's attention is on caring for Pam, it is not on weaning from their adult child or what could happen when Pam leaves home.

While often unintentional, and almost always painful for the family, the problematic behavior of children may thus be seen by a strategic therapist as helping maintain a kind of **homeostatic**, or stable, organization of the family (Haley, 1971; Hoffman, 1976). Homeostasis is the combination of stability and change, and while families may want change, their dysfunctional sequences provide stability. The strategic therapist must consider why it may be advantageous for the family to remain organized in such a structure. Pam's refusal to eat may mask the lack of attention that Murray and Fran are paying to their own relationship since Murray's attention has been centered on the family business. While Pam is in crisis, Fran and Murray are forced to put aside any of their own individual or relational tensions and focus on Pam. If Pam were to be capable of launching into the next stage of development by perhaps attending college, it is quite possible that the parents would be forced to look at their own relationship and the difficulties presented if and when the children (Pam in this case) are not there as a focus of attention. Neither Fran nor Murray may be ready for the transition to empty nesting. Fran has spent her married life devoted to her children, mostly to Pam, and without another outlet of attention, Pam would surely be abandoning her mom if she did, indeed, launch. A strategic therapist might go so far as to understand that Pam's abstinence from feeding herself is doing her parents a favor—diverting their attention to her instead of their relationship and preventing Murray and Fran from beginning to transition into being empty nesters.

Repetitive Interactional Sequences

To maintain homeostasis and predictability within the family, all members of families and similar social organizations establish **repetitive interactional sequences**, which promote cohesion of the system along certain patterns of communication and behavior (Hoffman, 1976). These repetitive interactional sequences maintain the ingrained roles and hierarchies within the family's existing organization and reflect a family's operation within a certain stage in the family life cycle. However, in situations such as those observed in the Daniels family, these repetitive interactional sequences often contribute to the maintenance of problematic behavior, which limits the family's ability to adapt to new circumstances.

In situations such as a split in parental roles, family members may become stuck in repetitive interactional sequences that contribute to the maintenance of the problem (Haley, 1980). Some such patterns may grant a hidden benefit to a family, even though they would all agree that the current state of things is unbearable. Therefore, families sometimes engage in behaviors that unknowingly sustain a maladaptive organization, seeing change as something to be fearful of and avoided. Strategic therapy was developed primarily to target these dysfunctional sequences, using the hesitancy toward change as a catalyst for it. Dysfunctional sequences create behavioral issues in children, whom strategic practitioners saw as providing their parents with a primary objective by trying hopelessly to address the problematic behavior itself (Madanes, 1981).

In the Daniels family, the homeostatic organization has become maladaptive because the family is not accepting or preparing for change in the family life cycle. Murray and Fran are not facilitating the children's transitions into autonomy and adulthood, Pam's most especially. Similarly, the children are not effectively learning to become autonomous adults and remain dependent on their parents for direction.

We can see specific repetitive interactional sequences play out, which maintain this overarching structure in the presenting issues. To start, Murray and

Fran have decided on a family organization in which Murray's role in the family is to consistently provide the family with income, and then to interact with the children (specifically the boys) via recreation and sports. Fran's role, meanwhile, involves interactions with the children, wherein the children are dependent on her to eat, as she is responsible for feeding the family. In Pam's case, her attempts to gain control over her autonomy by way of refusing Fran's food are creating copious amounts of distress for her parents, such that they feel they must remain in control of her eating for her to survive. She continues to seek control by rejecting her parents' attempts for control and thus participates in a locked sequence of interactions that escalates the crisis without resolving the actual dilemma of the family. George and Oliver, who are close in age but still younger than Pam, watch these sequences play out between Pam and Fran, and participate by repeatedly becoming quiet and fading into the background at dinnertime, failing or refusing to acknowledge that they will soon need to negotiate their own autonomy and launching from their parents. In doing so, they maintain a family organization in which the children—who are now teenagers and will soon be adults—must be fed by their mother. This maintains a "stability" by ensuring no one family member goes to the next stage in life, therefore contributing to dysfunction.

For strategic therapists, the understanding is that children's symptomatic behaviors often function less as signs of individual dysfunction and more as protective mechanisms for parents (Madanes, 1981). The symptomatic child(ren) represent the unspoken struggles of the parents, thereby inverting traditional family hierarchies and assuming a position of power through symptom expression (Madanes, 1981). When parents are preoccupied with marital discord, professional stress, or unresolved conflicts with extended family, the child's disturbances serve to divert attention from these problems and mobilize parental unity around a shared concern (Haley, 1980). In this way, the child's difficulties paradoxically stabilize the family system, even while appearing to destabilize it.

In this model, symptoms are strategic solutions to relational problems. Problem behaviors frequently serve communicative or protective purposes within the family, offering indirect strategies for coping with conflict without directly confronting it (Haley, 1986). Pam, as the symptomatic child needing the full attention from her mother, diffuses any struggles that would arise between her parents, therefore stabilizing the marital system, and in so doing, the family system. So long as Pam's abstinence from eating necessitates Fran's direct oversight and intervention, the family repeats interactional cycles from a stage of family life which needs to be outgrown.

Diversity Conceptualization

The Strategic family therapy model, rooted in cybernetics and systems theory, reflects a foundational assumption that change can occur by targeting patterns of interaction rather than by evoking insight in clients (Weakland, 1976).

In contrast to insight-oriented approaches like psychodynamic therapy, which emphasize personal narratives, introspection, and deep psychology as central to therapeutic growth, Strategic Family Therapy sees change as arising from interventions that shift interactional sequences. As such, cultural or ethnic identities may be important to note for their influence in such behavioral interactional patterns but are not prioritized.

An attribution of the Strategic model is its deemphasis on ethnicity as a necessary lens through which to understand client problems or solutions. As Haley and colleagues stated, Strategic therapy "minimizes a focus on ethnicity as an essential factor for bringing about change in therapy" (Haley & Richeport-Haley, 2003, p. 18). Instead, it is understood that cross-cultural similarities in family systems—particularly in terms of power structures, communication patterns, and hierarchies—allow the therapist to work effectively even when they do not share the client's cultural background. What matters most is not the cultural narrative but the pattern of behaviors that perpetuate dysfunction.

From a Strategic perspective, ethnic identity may become salient if it provides leverage toward behavioral change or provides context for maladaptive interactions (Haley, 1996). Cultural values or expectations that align with hierarchical family structures—such as respect for parental authority and matriarchal family structures—can be used by the therapist to elicit cooperation or compliance with interventions. For example, when working with immigrant families, therapists may identify cultural beliefs that reinforce functional parental leadership, thereby helping to reestablish the family hierarchy in ways congruent with both the family's culture and therapeutic goals.

It would be incorrect to assume that the strategic therapist entirely ignores the family's unique ethnic identities. Rather, ethnicity is acknowledged primarily to the extent that it impacts the effectiveness of the therapeutic alliance. Respect and courtesy are important for the strategic therapist to exemplify when working with families whose cultural backgrounds differ from those of the therapist. As Haley and Richeport-Haley (2003) noted, "therapists must adapt to certain basic premises of a culture" to engage clients effectively in therapy (p. 19). This adaptation is not for the sake of deeper cultural insight or ideological exploration, but for the pragmatic purpose of client engagement and therapeutic influence. A strategic therapist can always add a feminist or multicultural lens in which to do their work, strengthening their ability to observe how experiences rooted in cultural identity are affecting the client system.

Moreover, historically, Strategic therapy shows a preference for action over cultural exploration when addressing issues arising from immigration or cultural displacement (McGoldrick et al., 2005). When culturally situated behaviors are maladaptive in a new sociocultural context—such as rigid disciplinary practices or disproportionate delegations of power to certain family members over others—strategic family therapists aim not to explore or interpret these behaviors but to intervene directly to adjust them. In such cases, "insights" are traded in favor of behaviorally-based directives (Haley & Richeport-Haley, 2003).

In effect, the goal becomes the functional assimilation of the family's interactions into the dominant cultural framework, rather than the analysis and reification of any sort of family identity.

This orientation may be criticized as too narrow, especially by those who value cultural humility in therapeutic practice. However, it reflects the strategic model's core premise: that therapy is not about dealing with abstract concepts or ideology, but about producing observable change. Diversity considerations are respected insofar as they play a role in the therapist's ability to interact respectfully with the family, but are not coveted as a source of deep meaning foundational to the family's collective identity. The therapist's role, then, is not to understand or validate cultural identity, but to intervene skillfully in the behavioral system to promote desired outcomes.

The Therapeutic Story of Problem Resolution

Strategic therapy is a structured, directive form of psychotherapy that focuses on identifying and altering the patterns of interaction that maintain a client's problem. While a clear conceptualization of problem formation is integral to a Strategic approach, Haley (1971) emphasizes that "[therapy] can be called strategic if the clinician initiates what happens during therapy and designs a particular approach for each problem" (p. 17). The action-oriented nature of the therapist is paramount, and it is the therapist's willingness to take responsibility for a family's problems that defines a Strategic approach.

Thus, Strategic therapy is a form of psychotherapy that identifies and alters the patterns of interaction that maintain a client's problem (Haley, 1986). Rather than exploring the origins of a problem in depth, Strategic therapy aims to interrupt and break maladaptive cycles and introduce practical, deliberate, and creative interventions (Madanes, 1981). The therapist identifies dysfunctional patterns that necessitate the family's reported problem, then develops targeted strategies to interrupt or reframe them by changing the meaning of the symptom. Through these deliberate interventions, clients are guided toward resolution in a focused and effective way (Haley, 1996).

While the strategic therapist plays an active, authoritative role in planning and guiding therapy by assessing how the system functions and then designing targeted interventions to create change, the therapist and client work collaboratively to establish specific, achievable goals (Haley, 1987). The therapy is brief and time-limited, aiming to produce measurable change in a short period. Rather than **first-order change**, wherein specific actions in a system are changed but the same problem-solving strategies are repeated (Weeks & L'Abate, 1982), strategic therapists attempt **second-order change**, which involves a radical alteration of the system's underlying structure, rules, or principles by disrupting the existing framework.

Once the core operating principles of the system are changed, a new pattern of behavior ensues, and the existing problem disappears (Weeks & L'Abate, 1982).

Second-order change can often "appear abrupt, illogical, and unexpected" (Weeks & L'Abate, p. 19). A second-order change intervention is seldom aimed at the symptomatic behavior, yet has a direct impact on the larger problem and therefore seems unexpected and illogical to the client. A strategic therapist will rarely be credited as the solution provider, as the directives they give may appear unrelated. Still, those directives are effective in getting the client out of the binds in which they find themselves (Watzlawick et al., 1974). What is happening in the Daniels family is that the more they try to encourage Pam to eat, thus avoiding hospitalization, the more her symptoms escalate and hospitalization becomes a reality. This reflects the family's attempts to create problem resolution, yet these attempts continue to perpetuate and worsen the problem behavior. In Strategic therapy, "the task is to have the person 'spontaneously' behave differently, not behave differently because he is told to" (Haley, 1984, p. 72). Thus, a successful strategic intervention based on second-order change will target the family's cohesion so that Pam's symptoms are eliminated.

Second-order change shifts the context and the focus that is sustaining the problem. In the Daniels family, second-order changes would mean that Pam starving herself would no longer organize the family, and that it would no longer make sense for Pam to enact this behavior. The symptom that brought the family to therapy, Pam's refusal to eat, would no longer keep the family stable, and another focus would take its place. If the therapeutic intervention is successful, and the family's rules change, a child no longer must sacrifice themselves for the stability of the family. An example of second-order change might be that Pam helps her mother *find a life*; or Pam is challenged to help out with the family business so Murray can spend more time with Fran and the kids. Anything that allows focus to shift away from Pam: ideally, something that communicates to Pam that she is a trusted member of the family and is seen as a responsible caregiver to herself.

This shift in context, from Pam being the child who needs monitoring and feeding to Pam being the young adult assisting in the care of the family business, and helping care for her siblings, solves multiple issues. This makes it possible for the family to spend more time together, encourages the timely and appropriate launching of all members, promotes meaningful change in the family system, and allows each member freedom to access individual pursuits while staying connected. A strategic therapist would have to assess over time whether the desired outcome (Pam eating and family cohesion) actually results from this intervention, prescribing an intervention at a more surface level if not (first-order change). The hope of second-order change in this case is that Pam shifts into young adulthood, allowing the family members to launch into their next developmental stages. There is also a recursive effect; the family spending more time together allows Pam to shift into adulthood. This would be a radical perspective shift in identity that would no longer support the belief that Pam needs care. She becomes integral to the family's success. Fran, released from the role of monitor, may be able to pursue the dreams or goals she had prior to having children.

Problem-Focused and Goal-Oriented

Strategic therapy begins with a clear definition of the presenting problem (Haley, 1971). The therapist and client work collaboratively to establish specific, achievable goals. The therapy is brief and time-limited, aiming to produce measurable change in a short time (Haley & Richeport-Haley, 2007). The strategic therapist wants to make sure that the therapeutic goal addresses the problematic behavior which is often serving the larger family system in some way, so it is wise for the therapist to make sense of what often can appear like crazy or sick behavior. This "making sense" can be in the form of a **reframe**, or a new way to frame a problem that is equally plausible but frames it in an addressable and less threatening way, while providing context which motivates the client or family toward change (Haley & Hoffman, 1997). Pam is no longer the helpless child but rather the person giving Fran 'a life' or someone on which Fran may focus her attention.

In the Daniels family, the problem bringing them to therapy appears to be Pam's refusal to eat and thereby risking her health and her life. The family wants to see if therapy could help Pam before considering inpatient treatment. At the beginning of therapy, the family believes that Pam, and her refusal to eat, is the problem. The strategic therapist must join in that same concern, that Pam's refusal to eat is problematic, while holding a different way of understanding the solution to the problem. At resolution of therapy, Pam would healthily feed herself, and the change in the structure of the family system is addressed so that the goal can be met.

Pattern Identification and Disruption

As previously discussed, rather than locating pathology within the individual, Strategic therapy looks at how repetitive interactional sequences contribute to the maintenance of the problem. Once these patterns are identified, the therapist devises strategies to disrupt or reframe them. The clients' symptoms have a function in maintaining the homeostasis, or the "repeating sequence of behaviors" (Haley, 1996, p. 81) of the family that allows the problem to continue. In Strategic therapy, the repetitive interactive patterns, not the symptomatic person, are the problem. So rather than attempting to change the symptomatic person, the strategic therapist attempts to change the pattern that maintains the problem. Strategic therapy avoids prolonged exploration of the past. While family history and dynamics may be considered, the main emphasis is on how problems are being sustained in the present and what can be done to change them now.

In the Daniels family, Fran had planned prior to having children to become a teacher, but after getting pregnant with Pam, she devoted herself to raising her children. Now that Pam is seemingly at the launching stage of development, and her brothers are close behind, Fran's "job" as caretaker of her children may be coming to an end. Two years ago, Murray took over the family business, spending less time with Fran and Pam, but he still finds time to coach Oliver and George's teams. Just before this time, when Pam entered high school, she became symptomatic, increasing her refusal to eat to a point of crisis and malnutrition. Due to Pam's diagnosis of Anorexia Nervosa, Fran finds herself doubling down on parenting Pam. Fran finds herself consumed with creating appealing meals, taking Pam to doctor appointments, consulting with Pam's educators, and monitoring Pam's weight and food intake. Murray steps back, allowing Fran to take the lead in Pam's care. His reaction is to put his energy into the family business, as well as raising the boys, making sure they get to games, coaching their teams, and trying to support Fran in her advocacy for their daughter. The family has become split, Fran consumed with caring for Pam, and Murray focused on the family business and on George and Oliver. According to Strategic therapy, if Pam's symptoms are to abate, the family's structure would have to reorganize such that the parental hierarchy was no longer split, and Fran would also be focused on her own goals. At that point, Pam would be free, or even encouraged to grow up.

Use of Directives and Ordeals

The strategic therapist plays an active, authoritative role in planning and guiding therapy (Haley, 1987). They assess how the system functions and then design targeted interventions to create change. This role requires keen observation, flexibility, and creativity.

Strategic therapists give clients specific tasks or instructions, which they call **directives**, to complete between sessions, and sometimes even in sessions. These directives are designed to alter stuck and problematic patterns of behavior, communication, or relationships. Tasks may appear paradoxical or counterintuitive. **Paradox** occurs when the family or client engages creatively with the very behavior they came to eliminate, which can challenge clients' beliefs and expectations and lead to change, sometimes without the client knowing how the change came about (Watzlawick et al., 1974). Haley and Richeport-Haley (2003) admit that to design a beneficial directive, the therapist must understand the wisdom in the problem first, and how the client benefits from it. In the case of the Daniels family, the problem appears to be Pam's eating disorder. This problem keeps the family stuck in an earlier stage of development, and the family members are unable to launch. This primary focus on Pam prevents the possibility that the family would collapse in some way. The therapist must understand the wisdom in this problem. Pam is, in a sense, sacrificing herself for the stability of the family. If all eyes are on her, then other problems will cease to exist. To get a client out of this protective bind, a strategic therapist respects the problem and uses a client's resistance to change as a catalyst for change. Common examples of strategic directives include prescribing the symptom, rewarding inaction, permitting avoidance, "going slow," etc.

Some directives can be a paradox that creates a "no-win" situation for the client. If they obey the directive and intentionally perform the symptom, they gain control over a behavior that previously felt involuntary. If they defy the directive and stop the behavior, they are also forced to give up the symptom in the process. A good directive works whether a client follows through or not (Watzlawick et al., 1974). A paradox is unlike a contradiction in that a "paradox gives a person no choice" (Weeks & L'Abate, 1982, p. 5). If they perform the paradoxical directive, the problem is under the client's control. If they do not perform the paradoxical directive, the problem is eliminated. It is imperative to get the clients' buy-in to change before using directives. Clients often feel that to change has the greater risk of being a "no-win," but a strategic therapist helps a client to see that *not* changing is also a "no-win," so they might as well trust the therapist's seemingly nonsensical directive.

Haley (1984) also noted that specific directives known as ordeals are given to clients to interrupt the repetitive interactional sequences, "is more than technique- it is actually a theory of change that encompasses many therapy techniques" (p. 19). An **ordeal** is a task that is more troublesome to perform than the symptom itself. The client is instructed to perform this arduous task whenever the unwanted behavior occurs, making the symptom less appealing. For example, an insomniac might be told that if they can't sleep, they must get out of bed and polish the silverware for an hour (Haley, 1984). Ordeals are a type of directive that may persuade the clients to relinquish the problem, rather than carry out the ordeal prescribed by the therapist.

Because Strategic therapy can be understood as provocative and intense, the therapist has unique ethical responsibilities. Haley and Richeport-Haley (2003) discussed the ethical issues of directives. First and foremost, the therapist must commit to helping and not harming the clients. While the interventions can seem radical, the therapist is not attempting to trick the clients. **Directive interventions** are not meant to damage relationships, hurt individuals, or take advantage of or exploit clients, but rather restructure the family so that the presenting problem is eliminated. Given that the presenting problem seems to be Pam's dangerous health behaviors, the therapist must be careful not to encourage Pam to exacerbate her symptoms. The therapist would understand the interactions in the family that prompt Pam's symptoms as what needs to change (the focus on Pam). The therapist strives to create a new homeostasis where it is no longer beneficial to defer launching. Pam's leaving home and the impending empty nest becomes something to look forward to rather than something to be feared or avoided.

Paradox

Drawing from Milton Erickson's influence (Haley,1986), strategic therapists often use paradoxical interventions. For example, instructing a client to *intentionally continue* a symptom or pretend to have a symptomatic behavior may reduce its power or alter the client's relationship to it. When one believes they are powerless to the problem, and then must enact the problem as prescribed, they often find that they have some agency.

We see the current family structure working when Fran "needs" to continue to care for the children, especially Pam. A strategic therapist might offer a paradoxical suggestion to Pam that her mom 'can't get a life' because her life is her children. Pam cannot become an autonomous or independent adult because she is unconsciously trying to sustain Fran's role of caring for the children. An example of a possible introduction of paradox into the system would be that Fran has to work harder to care for Pam, even accompanying her to school and dressing her. Murray would have to give up the family business or quit coaching the boys so that *more* attention could be given to Pam. George and Oliver would have to forfeit their extracurriculars so that the family could come together to care for Pam, sit with her at breakfast, lunch, dinner, and snacks, each making her favorite foods. Perhaps Fran has not paid enough attention to her sons, and they need to demand more attention from her. This might not be the way the strategic therapist chooses to intervene, but by giving the family a paradox (*you are not caring for Pam ENOUGH* or *Fran is neglecting her responsibilities*), the current interactional cycle could be relinquished since it would be near impossible to do. The family might respond with "We can't monitor or care THAT much," thus reckoning with the impossibility of the paradox.

Often, clients are already in a paradox of their own making (e.g., if Pam gets better, and she is no longer the focus of attention, the family could get worse), and implementing a paradox as an intervention can lead them out (Madanes, 1981). "What was heretofore perceived to be out of one's control is brought under conscious control by the [paradox]—a second-order change" (Weeks & L'Abate., 1982, p. 23).

If the family decides that the problem is the focus on Pam (as seen in the transcript below), then the paradox created by the family is that the more Fran tries to push Pam to health, she pushes her to sickness. And that sickness is doing the family "a favor" by allowing them to remain arrested in individual development. The only way Pam can maintain autonomy is by resisting care. The more Pam is entrusted to be autonomous, and in fact relied on to be autonomous and in charge, the less she needs to "not eat." Therefore, the target of a paradoxical intervention would be to redirect Fran's focus from Pam (and on to her husband, a personal project, the family business, etc.).

Prescribing the Symptom

Prescribing the symptom rests on the strategic therapist's understanding of paradox (Nardone & Watzlawick, 2005). Symptoms serve a purpose in the system, and by instructing the client(s) to do more of it, clients understand that they have agency in their behavior. If they can do more, then they can do less or none at all (Weeks & L'Abate, 1982). If we see the symptom as Pam not eating, it would be unethical to prescribe the symptom. This intervention, gone bad, could lead to Pam's death. But if we choose to see the symptom as Fran monitoring Pam's eating and well-being, which leads to Pam increasing her need to be monitored, and therefore giving her mom a primary task, then a strategic therapist could prescribe monitoring as a directive. Or if the strategic therapist understood that Murray relinquished all responsibility for Pam to his wife, the therapist could tell him to back off completely and give no support, maybe doubling down on the family business. In fact, it might be better if Murray and the boys moved out temporarily to allow Fran no distractions. It would be imperative for a strategic therapist to gradually and hesitatingly offer smaller steps to a directive to get the clients' buy-in along the way (Weeks & L'Abate, 1982). It is also possible that the clients would see this prescription as untenable and give up the symptom altogether.

Reframing is also common—offering a new interpretation of behavior or context that shifts the client's understanding and emotional response (Haley, 1984). Currently, the problem is framed as Pam is sick and needs Fran's (and the family's) care. A potential reframe could be that if Pam was not the center of Fran's life, she would be alone, nearly abandoned by her husband and sons. She would have "no life." By not eating, Pam is giving her mother a primary goal (Madanes, 1981). Pam's symptom is allowing her mother to have a focus, allowing her to have a life partner. Pam is sacrificing herself so that she does not abandon her mother. While the family remains split between genders, Pam would also be abandoning her mother if she were to launch. A reframe could be that Pam is actually taking care of her mother, not the other way around.

Metaphor

Informed by the work of Milton Erickson, strategic therapists use metaphor as an indirect directive (Godin & Oughourlian, 1994). Clients are not requested to do anything, nor are their opinions or behaviors criticized. Clients can hear the metaphor or story that relates to their situation and find ways to conquer the problem through those stories. The problem behavior is externalized, therefore making it possible for the therapist to refer to it without the client becoming defensive. The therapist offers the metaphor as a way of fascinating the clients, helping them to hear a new perspective or a way out of the binds in which they find themselves.

In the Daniels family, Pam is *starving* herself to avoid *abandoning* her mother and family. Fran is *sacrificing* her life to keep her daughter alive. Murray is *consumed with work* to provide for the family. The family is literally arrested in their development as long as Pam continues to lose weight or not eat (Haley, 1980). In a sense, these family members are sacrificing so that the pain or uncertainty of the next developmental stage is avoided. Metaphors like *starving for attention, consuming issues, eating away at, throwing up, sacrificial lamb, a lot on their plates*, or any number of eating/sacrificing metaphors can be used to indirectly get the therapist's message across without actually calling the family out on their literal behaviors (Haley, 1980). By using metaphors like "a lot on your plate" or telling stories of heroes conquering problems, the clients can find a way to relate. In so doing, they find a way out of their own binds.

Ultimately, the strategic therapist must help the family reorganize such that to *not* enact change will be equally painful, if not more-so, than adjusting to a new organization. Similarly, a strategic therapist works for an outcome wherein any benefits the family currently experiences could also be experienced when the family has readjusted to appropriate life stages and undivided family positioning. For example, a task for the Daniels family could include assigning meaningful and important roles to Fran in the family's new mode of functioning, such that Pam's leaving home will not leave Fran abandoned and adrift. An assignment for the strategic therapist would be to have the family choose the momentary confusion and discomfort of a loss of family homeostasis over the prolonged pain of a family in crisis.

Stages of Strategic therapy

In Strategic therapy, the primary goal is not to analyze or explain the dysfunction within a family system, but rather to change interactional sequences so that the presenting problem is resolved (Haley, 1987). Therapy is understood as a strategically guided process, with each session deliberately structured to produce specific, observable change.

***Conducting the First Session*:** Haley (1987) describes five distinct stages in the first family therapy interview:

The first is the **social stage**, in which the therapist greets each member of the family, and welcomes each family member individually into the therapy room, and into a relationship with the therapist. The therapist's initiative in welcoming or greeting each family member defines the therapy process to the family "as one in which everyone is involved and important" (Haley, 1987, p.15). It is anticipated that members of the family will be eager to shift quickly into discussing the problems which have brought them in; however, the therapist wants to invite each person into the process such that the family is aware that what each family member has to say will be important. During the social stage, the therapist additionally may observe important dynamics, such as the family's mood, the way the family organizes themselves relationally and spatially in the room, and how comfortable or defensive family members feel toward the therapist (Haley, 1987).

The transition from the social stage to the **problem stage** shifts the therapist and family toward the patterns and events that brought them to seek out family therapy. Here, the therapist speaks with each member of the family to understand their perspective regarding behaviors or interactions being labeled as problematic, either by one, some, or all members of the family. The therapist seeks from each family member a description of what that person sees as something that needs to change. In doing so, the therapist must consider how to ask the family about what problems are bringing them to therapy, and in what sequence the therapist elicits answers from family members. The therapist demonstrates respect, especially for the member of the family who has the most ability to bring the family back to therapy, and to avoid starting with eliciting a response from the identified client (Haley, 1987).

In listening to each family member's definition of the problem the family is experiencing, the therapist must be intentional in several ways. The strategic therapist focuses on clarifying what specific actions or events the family member defines as problematic, and abstains from shifting anyone's perspective, offering advice, or inquiring on the emotional or meaning-making levels of the family's experience (Haley, 1987). The strategic therapist does not share their observations, interpretations, or beliefs with the family as they are explaining their perspective on the problem but rather reflects and clarifies with each family member their understanding of what is happening that needs to change.

The therapist ensures they receive each family member's unique perspective on the family's problem before shifting into the **interaction stage** of the first session, in which the therapist takes a backseat from directing who responds to allow the family members to talk to each other about how they see the family's problem. Often, family members will disagree with what was said and then proceed to challenge or argue with one another regarding the definition of the family's problem. Here, if the family members continue to interact directly with the therapist, as they did in the problem stage, the therapist consistently redirects them to talk with the rest of the family instead of the therapist (Haley, 1987).

The family's organization around the problem they are experiencing emerges during this phase. The therapist will have the ability to observe the family's interactional process in addressing and attempting to resolve their problem. For this reason, if two family members become locked into a back-and-forth conflict, the therapist may ask another family member to enter the conversation, so that the therapist understands the third family member's way of maintaining or participating in the conflict. The strategic therapist wants the family to not only describe what they are conflicted about, but to begin demonstrating their interactional patterns, which the therapist will need to ultimately disrupt.

After adequate time is given for the therapist to understand each family member's role in the behavioral sequences that create an impasse from problem-solving, the therapist steps back into a more directive role during the **goal-setting stage**. The therapist moves to synthesize the formulations of the problem given by all family members into a central problem and goal definition that all members of the family can agree on. This involves ensuring the agreed-upon problem definition is action-oriented and sequential, as opposed to static, meaning-derived, or diagnostic. In the case of the Daniels family, the strategic therapist would not accept the definition of the problem as being that "Pam has anorexia" (even if Pam were to agree to that definition). Instead, they would seek a problem definition which "one can count, observe, measure, or in some way know one is influencing" (Haley, 1987, p. 39). This means in Pam's case that the therapist is thinking less about the diagnosis of Anorexia Nervosa and more about the specific activities and behaviors that the family considers to be Anorexia Nervosa. These factors contribute to the therapist's ability to identify ways to change or disrupt how the problem is acted out and to guide the therapist and family toward clear markers of improvement. For example, if Fran can spend the same amount of time she spends focused on Pam on spending time with Murray and the family business instead, it frees Pam to be autonomous in ways appropriate to her life stage.

The goal-setting stage will likely follow naturally into the **task-setting stage**, where the therapist assigns the family a task or directive to complete before they are seen again in family therapy. Once the family has been able to actionably define both their problem and their desired changes, the strategic therapist will conceptualize and assign a directive appropriate to the context. The task the therapist assigns the family at the end of the first session does not need to be thought of as one single cure-all intervention for the family, but rather as an intervention that begins to target and disrupt key interactional patterns among the family. The therapist tends to have the first task they assign the family be something relatively simple, so the family understands exactly what is expected of them between now and the next session. Clarifying any confusion is very important to the strategic therapist, as the family must explicitly understand what is being asked of them to feel confident enough to try to enact the directive.

Strategic therapists maintain a focus on resolving the presenting problem and planning targeted interventions aimed at eliminating the symptom rather than uncovering its roots. As Madanes (1980) explained, therapy begins by assuming that symptoms are both messages and attempts at solutions—they are metaphorical expressions of deeper relational dynamics. For example, a child's refusal to eat could indicate a child's unwillingness to grow. In the Daniels family, the presenting problem is not the eating disorder; it is the maladaptive family structure, which requires Fran's focus on Pam, and the eating disorder gives Fran good reason to focus on Pam.

The therapist then determines whom the child is protecting through the symptom and designs a strategy to restore a functional family hierarchy, in which parents resume a position of authority. Directives are central tools in this process, and may be straightforward or paradoxical, involving one or more family members. A strategic therapist may utilize a straightforward directive to require a client's follow-through, or they may present a paradoxical directive that they suspect the client will refuse to do. Either way, the directive is aimed at changing the communication patterns and restructuring familial organization, along with relational roles (Madanes, 1980).

Like Haley, Madanes (1980) outlines a structured sequence for intervention that begins with defining the problem and setting clear goals. The child's symptoms are reframed as protective behaviors within the family system, and directives are then designed for parents or other family members to give to the child. These directives often involve playful or symbolic tasks such as enacting the symptom, pretending to experience it, or pretending to offer help. The intervention is first practiced in session and later implemented at home, with progress reviewed in subsequent meetings. Positive changes are reinforced by crediting the parents, while unresolved issues are either addressed through new directives or therapy is ended. Madanes (1981) emphasized that these techniques rely heavily on child-appropriate communication strategies, particularly role-play and pretend scenarios. For example, feigning disinterest when a child is caught coming home late after sneaking out. In this case, the symptom (reckless behavior) is not resulting in the expected reaction (anger from parents). While highly effective in loving and stable families, these methods require caution in cases of violence or abuse, where playful interventions may be misinterpreted or even cause harm (Madanes, 1981).

Case Transcript

After introducing themselves, the therapist addresses each family member in the Social Stage. It is important that each member responds; their mood will be communicated to the therapist, and the therapist should match it. The therapist seeks to understand what the interaction is in the family by their verbal and non-verbal cues.

Therapist: Hi folks, I'm glad you all could come today. I know it can be difficult getting your schedules to align. I'm happy to have the chance to meet with you all. Can each of you tell me your name and who you are in the family?

> **Intervention**: By making a general request to the whole family for each family member to introduce themselves, the therapist notes the way responses and interactions are organized and standardized by the family. This is the Strategic therapist's first glimpse into the family rules.

Fran: Hi, I'm Fran. Let's see…well, I'm Murray's wife and the mom of Pam, George, and Oliver here.

Therapist: Great, nice to meet you, Fran. [*Fran looks to Murray*]

Murray: I'm Murray–Fran's husband and father of George, Oliver, and Pam.

Pam: Well, I'm Pam. I guess I'm the reason we're here today!

Therapist: Oh? [*looking at George and Oliver*] And would you two be Pam's brothers?

Intervention: The therapist is careful during the social stage to meet and establish individual rapport with each member of the family before transitioning into the problem stage.

George: Yes, I'm George. And Pam's right, we're here because of her.
Therapist: Hello, George. [*Looks expectantly at Oliver*]

Intervention: Here, the therapist makes sure to speak with Oliver before addressing George's problem definition.

Oliver: I'm Oliver, and in 8th grade. I play soccer and basketball for our city's traveling teams. Oh, and I'm going into high school after this summer.
Therapist: Hi, it's nice to meet you, Oliver. Is that why your family is here? Going to high school is a huge transition! *[Therapist has the idea that the family may be arrested in an early stage of development, so places the idea of "transitioning" as a way to frame the potential problem.]*
Oliver: [*laughs*] Yeah, it is, but I don't think that's why we're here…

[*Therapist may spend a bit more time getting to know the individuals in the family*]

Therapist: Well, on that note, I wanted to hear from each of you regarding what is going on in your family. Fran, I had a short opportunity to hear from you when you called to set the appointment, so could I start with you, Murray? What do you believe brought your family here today?

Intervention: The therapist now transitions to the Problem Stage. In this stage, the therapist hears how each member of the family defines the problem. Since Fran has thus far been the initiator in the family's interactions with the therapist (e.g., reaching out for the initial appointment, answering first for the family in the social stage), the therapist makes sure to speak first to "the adult who seems less involved with the problem" (Haley, 1987, p. 22). Here, that is Murray.

Murray: Well, Fran is really worried that Pam will have to go into inpatient treatment because she hasn't been eating. It's gotten to the point where Pam is really losing weight, and nothing we've tried with her has worked. Fran says Pam just refuses to eat anything she cooks for her. It scares her—and I guess I am worried about my little girl too.
Therapist: Wow, I can hear your concern for your wife and daughter.

Intervention: The therapist wants to join with Murray's concern for Pam. The therapist privately notes that Murray referred to Pam, who is nearly an adult, as his "little girl," which may inform how the therapist understands Pam's symptoms as communication within the family.

Fran: Yes, I called because I'm really scared for my daughter. She keeps losing weight, and her therapist thinks we should put her into a residential treatment center. I don't want her to go inpatient, but I'm at a loss and hoping that all of us coming to therapy could help us figure out what to do.

Therapist: So it sounds like you are both really confused and uncertain. When did you both notice that this problem had developed?

Fran: Pam used to be my little helper in the kitchen, especially for dinners, from the time she was young. She always liked to help me. Even when she was really little, she loved doing things like cracking eggs and rolling out dough. She would test out sauces and tell me if they were ready or if they needed more seasonings. She even would help with feeding her brother Oliver when he was learning to eat solids. As a teenager, she would help me prepare dinner and clean dishes. But as Pam's been growing up, and especially in the last year, she's completely lost interest in being around for meals and participating.

Therapist: Wow, it sounds very different! [*turns to Pam*] Pam, what do you think about you all coming here today?

Pam: Like I said, I guess I'm the problem. Everyone is just so up in my business, they need to get a life and worry about themselves.

Therapist: So I'm hearing that you see a different problem in the family. Am I hearing that correctly?

Pam: Yeah, I guess so.

Therapist: What do you think the problem here is?

Pam: I'm fine, if my mom could just leave me alone-she hovers all the time.

Fran: Leave you alone? Who's gonna take care of you?

Therapist: Pam, do you think there wouldn't be a problem if your mom would, as you say, leave you alone?

Pam: Yes!

Therapist: So, to you, the problem that's happening in your family is that your mom is very concerned about you not eating?

Pam: Yeah, I mean, she treats me like a child, and I'm almost 18.

Therapist: Huh. So, George and Oliver, what do you think?

Intervention: With each response from the family, the therapist gathers more information through which to understand the behavior of not eating as communication in the family dynamic. The therapist makes sure to obtain each family member's individual conceptualization of the family's problem.

George: I'm not really sure, but mom and Pam fighting during meals is really stressful.

Fran: Pam used to be really close with her brothers when they were little, and now the boys hang out more with each other, and with the other boys on their soccer team. That leaves Pam and me to deal with a lot going on in the house.

Therapist: Hmm. So Oliver, what are your thoughts about all of this?

Oliver: [*shrugs*] I don't really know. Pam just stopped eating during meals. It used to only happen sometimes, but lately, Pam and mom fight about it every meal.

Therapist: What do you mean "lately"?

Murray: A couple years ago, after my dad retired, I assumed full control of the business, things have really changed. I just roll in after dinner to take the boys to soccer. I know a lot of this falls on Fran, especially when she had plans to restart her career, but right now it really is just impossible to get home in time to help out. There are days I don't even eat until after their soccer practice is over. Sometimes I don't eat at all.

Therapist: So, Murray—a couple years ago, things changed in your family. Your dad retired, you took over the business, Fran put her career on hold to take care of the kids, and there's been a bit of a shift in how you all spend your time? Lots of reshuffling of the way you spend your time. Lots *on your plate, huh?*

Intervention: The therapist now transitions to the **Interaction Stage**. The therapist sits back and allows the family to talk to each other about the problem. If the clients turn toward the therapist, the therapist turns them back to talk to each other (Haley, 1987). This gives the therapist the opportunity to witness the interactional patterns that take place in the family around the problem. It's important to note that the family naturally began the interaction stage themselves during the problem stage, when Pam challenged Fran directly about her focus on her; the therapist encourages the family to continue interacting directly with one another.

Murray: Yeah, that's it pretty much.

Therapist: Pam, it sounds like things at home changed when your dad had to take on more responsibility at work. Can you talk to your parents about what changes you noticed around then?

Intervention: The therapist encourages Pam to address her parents directly. This begins to shift her from helpless to more powerful in the family hierarchy.

Pam: Well, you both used to spend more time during meals talking to each other about your days. Now, it's just mom making me eat. And dad, by the time you're home, you grab left-overs, get on your computer, and then go to bed. You haven't even been able to go to Parent's Night at school. Mom took me and cared more about how the classrooms were set up than me going to college out of state.

Fran: I don't think you're ready to go to college- especially out of state.

Murray: I thought we were going to do college tours later in the year? She can also go to Community College, like we did. We lived at home and went to school before we got married.

Pam: (*rolls her eyes and says under her breath*)—I am not going to 13th grade…

Fran (to Murray): Honey, if she can't feed herself, how is she supposed to go to college and live on her own?

Murray (to Fran): Well, how else is she supposed to learn to feed herself?

Pam (to therapist): I KNOW how to feed myself…

Therapist: Tell your parents that.

Intervention: Therapist continues to encourage Pam to engage with her parents in a more adult manner.

Pam (to Murray): Remember when we used to go out to Cracker Barrel, we'd always play with those games on the table? We never do that anymore since you started working late. Mom never takes us out, and you, George, and Oliver get to grab dinner before leaving for practice or eat after.

Murray (to therapist): Since taking over the family business, I really don't have time anymore to eat with the family. I really need more help at the business so I can free up some time to be home.

Therapist: Did you all know that about the business?

Intervention: Therapist doesn't engage with Murray directly but turns to the family to expand on what Murray said.

Oliver: Dad never really talks about what happens at work.

Fran (to Murray): Honey, you said everything was working out and you had it together.

Murray (to Fran): You have enough to worry about. I didn't want to give you another damn thing to worry about.

Fran (sarcastically to Murray): Maybe I can run the business, and you can take care of everything else!

Murray (to Fran): I didn't know you wanted to run the business?

Fran: Well, I want to do SOMETHING. I thought by now I'd either be back at school getting an advanced degree or working in my field.

Therapist: It really sounds like you have all sacrificed so much in the last couple years to keep everything and everyone above water. It's almost like you all are just treading water in a rough ocean. I get this image of your family *starving* for more time together, and also getting time to focus on your own things too. To be able to swim forward in smooth seas.

Intervention: In this interaction, we are starting to see that the problem in the family may not necessarily be Pam's weight loss. We begin to hear that since Murray's father's retirement, the time the family gets to spend together, especially Fran and Murray and Murray and Pam, has shifted. The parental roles have changed. Pam may seem arrested in her development, but it becomes clearer that she is giving Fran a focus that she would not otherwise have. The therapist adds a metaphor of sacrifice, drowning, and swimming, and reframes the problem from Pam's eating issues to clients being split—and not having the opportunity to launch into their next stage of development. In the Goal-Setting Stage, the therapist narrows in on a goal definition the whole family can agree on. The therapist needs to define what specific, measurable, operational changes the family wants to see.

Therapist: Wow, it sounds like everyone here is in the middle of a big transition. Murray, you've been so involved in transitioning the family business after your father's retirement and making sure that your sons are active. Fran, that leaves you to take care of "everything else" and Pam, there seems to be some thought of either going to college or staying home. And Oliver and George, you are a stone's throw away from following in your sister's footsteps—George, you're going to high school, and Oliver, you're in middle school. There's a lot of change in the family!

Intervention: The therapist reframes the family's problem from centering on Pam's eating, to focusing on the family's shift in the family life cycle and the various changes with which each member of the family is reckoning.

Murray: Since my dad's retirement and taking over the business, yeah, I think that we've all had to become focused on other things. I make sure that George and Oliver are active, that's the least I can do, I guess. Fran and Pam were always so close; I just thought everything would be fine.

Fran: I would have liked to help with transitioning the business, but given this is Pam's senior year, I have had to focus completely on her.

Pam: Wow mom, thanks for your vote of confidence. If you weren't so focused on me, you would be completely alone. What would you be focused on?

Fran: I'd love to figure that out!

Pam: Really??

Therapist: Yes, that is a great question, Pam. [*turning to Fran*] What would you get to do when you're not so needed by Pam?

Intervention: The therapist reframes Fran's focus on Pam to Pam needing her.

Fran: Hmm, I don't really know. I've always wanted to work with kids, but I don't think I want to be a teacher anymore. I'd be more interested in being a school counselor. But I guess I'd need to think more about it.

Therapist (to Pam): It sounds like you are taking lots of time that your mom could be figuring her life out! No good mom would let her kid starve to death even if that kid wanted her to get a life.

Intervention: Once again, the therapist reframes the family's interactional sequences, suggesting that Pam's extreme refusal to eat is functioning to prevent Fran from transitioning into a new role in the family.

Pam (to Therapist): She CAN get a life, I can take care of myself! I know how to cook!

Murray: You do???

Pam: Well, not like mom. I can make grilled cheese and chicken nuggets. I used to cook that for George that one summer when mom was taking her stained-glass classes. We used to eat grilled cheese out on the porch, and Oliver only wanted the chicken nuggets.

George: Yeah! I loved those mini pizzas too! Then we'd eat ice cream. That was fun.

Oliver: And then Pam could take us to practice. We could bike there since dad wouldn't be doing a photo-finish! "Boys, grab your shit quick, we gotta go NOW!"

Sorry dad but that is what you say! (*Murray looks embarrassed*)

Murray: Well, I guess that would help a bit.

Therapist (to Fran, but indirectly to Pam): So, Fran, I am not sure what Pam could do or say that would allow you to trust she could feed the boys and take them to practice a couple of days during the week?

Intervention: The therapist and family have developed several goals where Fran is able to focus on her own life goals, and Pam gets to prove she can take care of herself, which leads to her being able to launch, and Fran being able to let go of her need to monitor Pam's eating.

Pam: (*Under her breath*) With my eyes closed....

Therapist: Murray, you said that would relieve you a bit. You and Fran could leisurely get to the field, and Pam could choose to stay or bike home? ...then on Fridays and the weekends you can be in full force with the family?... George and Oliver, it sounds like there may be more chicken nuggets, pizza, and grilled cheese.

Oliver: Cool!

Intervention: In the Task Stage, the therapist elicits a common goal from the family, and "takes what has been learned about the family members in the session and uses what seems most evident and matter-of-fact as the basis for persuading them to do the task" (Haley, 1987, p. 62). Ideas in relation to launching are framed as the idea of the client's, not the therapist's, which is the therapist's ultimate aim (Watzlawick et al., 1974). However, the therapist is very intentional by the end of the first session to co-identify with the family the specific changes that will occur in the family's interactions, which are measurable and observable, by the next time the therapist meets with the family (Haley, 1987).

Therapist (to Parents): There are a lot of things going on in your family and many decisions to make. The big one that brought you in today is "What do we do with Pam?" And Murray, I get that the business is sustaining the family now, and it is quite possible that the business will be what affords medical care for Pam if she needs it, or college if she's ready, but this decision is too big for Fran to make alone. I wonder if, between now and our next appointment, you and Fran could figure out what would be financially feasible to allow these different options? I am not sure that is what would be needed, but I am sure that figuring out the finances, and if Fran would have to restart her career to make any of the options feasible. You both would need to decide what is the right course of action, you will have made a joint decision together.

Intervention: The therapist targets the repetitive interactional sequence of Murray disengaging from Fran and from parental decision-making and care. Murray's new interactions with the family destabilize old sequences of interaction between Pam and Fran, and also have Fran and Murray spend increased time together, beginning to address the gender split in the family structure.

Therapist: And Fran, I know that there is a *lot on your plate* right now with taking care of Pam and monitoring her eating, but I think it is crucial that you are involved in the decisions alongside Murray. Meanwhile, Murray, I wonder if you could take the lead on helping Pam figure out what her next steps might look like?

Murray: Yeah, I always wanted to help my little girl figure this part out. I always thought her next steps would be going to college. I've just been concerned that she'll get there and won't be able to stay, given the state of everything…

Therapist: Yes, I'm sure she would need some help in figuring out how she could *sustain herself* through such a big transition.

Intervention: The therapist uses the metaphor of food and feeding to engage the family in their dilemma.

Therapist: Regardless, would it be possible for both of you to connect and spend time this week to research your finances to figure out how you might afford medical care, if that is what it comes down to? This might take some time together and lots of discussion and planning… Of course, when or if you make any decisions, you can include Pam…maybe in our next meeting?

Murray: (*hesitating*)… I have to get Oliver and George to their respective games this week…. Not sure how I can…

Oliver: Maybe Pam can take us?

George: We can go to McDonalds first!!

Pam: I don't mind taking them to their games, but why can't mom and dad take me on campus tours! I'd rather be looking at colleges than having them try to figure out if they can lock me away in hospitals!

Therapist: I like that idea. But it seems like your parents are really concerned that you might not be able to go away to college this next year...

Fran (to Pam): We'll have to see if that is possible.

Pam (to Therapist): I'll be 18 soon, and I can make my own decisions- my grades are good enough to get into the State University.

Therapist: Hmmm... Maybe you can talk to your school counselor... bring some information home...Not sure how you will convince your parents that you can make such a big decision... But I guess if they trust you to feed yourself and your brothers and transport them to their games this week....

Pam: I can definitely do that myself!

Therapist: Listen, this is a big risk for all of you. Murray, Fran, this means sacrificing a lot of time and energy to come together and research the best possible outcome for Pam—it could be home, or as Pam says, "thirteenth grade", it could be researching different options for Pam's medical care, or it could be that Pam finds out that she can handle State U without your monitoring. She talks to her school counselor, gets information about State U. And Pam having to step in and covering for you, Fran, can allow you to consider your next move. For you, Pam, there is a lot put *on your plate right now. Can you handle it?* Cooking for yourself and your brothers, taking them to games... Talking to your school counselor. Seems like a LOT! *This responsibility thing is not child's play*, your mom can tell you that! And George and Oliver—you two will have to sacrifice some time with Dad... maybe eat some fast food for a bit or pizza and chicken nuggets.... It's a lot for all of you. I wouldn't doubt it when you come back, you all tell me that it was just too hard to do.... or that you found out a better resolution, or that things are fine just the way they are.... I look forward to hearing about how you all figure this out together....

Intervention: The therapist summarizes the family's respective directives moving forward, as well as using a simple paradox, prompting the family to rebel against the concept of the directive being unattainable.

The Therapeutic Story

In this case, the strategic therapist quickly recognizes that the problem lies not in Pam herself, nor even in the eating disorder, but in the family's organization. The eating disorder functions as a symptom of a larger systemic pattern.

Pam is "taking care" of her mother by allowing her to extend her identity as caretaker long after it is developmentally necessary. In other words, Pam's suffering sustains her mother's role.

From this perspective, the therapist explores the benefit of the family's focus on Pam. The therapist notes the timing of her symptoms: they surface just as each family member faces a new life stage—her father preparing to take over the business, her mother anticipating an empty nest, her brother entering high school, and her transition to college. Pam's disordered eating provides the family with a compelling reason to halt these developmental transitions. Her symptoms allow everyone to remain in familiar roles rather than moving forward.

The therapist carefully considers where and with whom to intervene strategically within the interaction sequence, guiding the family toward their shared and individual developmental goals, each member successfully launching into the next stage of life. Doing so requires careful placement of interventions and, at times, paradoxical reframing. For Fran, this means loosening her attachment to the caretaker role that has come to define her. The therapist first initiates this shift by inviting Fran to consider directing her energy toward her husband Murray and the family's finances. This redirection serves as a manageable first step, distributing focus across more family members while relieving Pam of the relentless scrutiny that fuels her symptoms. Yet the therapist must also consider whether this redirection is merely "more of the same" (Watzlawick et al., 1974). A true second-order change would require Fran to move beyond caretaking altogether, investing instead in her own passions and identity.

In parallel, the therapist works with Pam directly, supporting her autonomy and encouraging greater responsibility. As Fran gradually releases control, the therapist offers her ideas for how to fill the newly available space with pursuits of her own. There are many Strategic interventions to consider, the best being that which gets the family to their agreed-upon goal. Here, a Madanes-inspired intervention may prove powerful: reframing Fran's caretaking as a noble sacrifice. To go "above and beyond" as a caretaker, the therapist suggests, Fran must make an even greater "sacrifice"—turning her attention away from Pam and toward her own deferred dreams, regardless of external pressures (Madanes, 1981). By positioning self-investment as an ultimate act of sacrifice, the therapist leverages Fran's identity while simultaneously moving her closer to authentic growth and allowing Pam to relinquish her partnership with Fran so as to be able to launch into her next stage of development.

This process may occur over a series of sessions, wherein the family and the therapist meet and follow up on the successes and failures of the family to implement the previously discussed changes. For each follow-up session, the therapist must be deliberate to keep the family focused on assessing what happened when they attempted to meet the identified desired changes. If the family successfully implemented the changes identified in the previous session's goal-setting stage, the therapy is seen as working effectively, whereas if the family avoided, forgot about, or otherwise neglected to implement such changes, the therapy is seen as a failure (Haley, 1987). The strategic therapist continues to clarify with the family the specific actions the family will implement, with each session building off the successes or failures of the previous session. This helps the strategic therapist to keep family therapy brief and intensive.

As with any systems-oriented approach, a strategic therapist may want to follow up with the family a couple of months after therapy has concluded (Stanton & Welsh, 2012). This would be to assess for desired, sustained change. During a follow-up such as this, the therapist would assess to ensure that no unforeseen side effects of the therapeutic directives have resulted. In this case, the therapist would hope to see evidence that each member of the family was moving toward their unique dream or goal as it pertains to their stage in life. The therapist would ask questions to see if Fran and Murrey have been able to sustain connection, no longer finding themselves in a gendered split structure. If the therapist were to find that Pam's symptoms have resolved but Oliver, for example, has started to become symptomatic in a way that requires Fran's attention, the therapist would know that second-order change has yet to be completed, that the functional rules of interaction within the family have not effectively changed.

References

Godin, J., & Oughourlian, J. M. (1994). The transitional gap in metaphor and therapy: The essence of the story. In Jeffery K. Zeig (Ed.) *Ericksonian methods* (pp. 182–192). The Milton H. Erickson Foundation, Inc.

Haley, J. (1969). The art of being a failure as a therapist. *American Journal of Orthopsychiatry*, *39*(4), 691–695.

Haley, J. (1971). Family therapy: A radical change. In Jay Haley (Ed.) *Changing families: A family therapy reader* (pp. 272–285). Grune & Stratton, Inc.

Haley, J. (1980). *Leaving home: The therapy of disturbed young people*. McGraw-Hill.

Haley, J. (1984). *Ordeal therapy: Unusual ways to change behavior*. Jossy-Bass, Inc.

Haley, J. (1986). *Uncommon therapy: The psychiatric techniques of Milton H. Erickson, MD*. W. W. Norton & Company, Inc.

Haley, J. (1987). *Problem-solving therapy*. Jossey-Bass Inc.

Haley, J. (1996). *Learning & teaching therapy*. The Guilford Press.

Haley, J. & Hoffman, L. (1997). *Techniques of family therapy: Five leading therapists reveal their working styles, strategies, and approaches*. Basic Books, Inc.

Haley, J., & Richeport-Haley, M. (2003). *The art of strategic therapy*. Taylor & Francis.

Haley, J., & Richeport-Haley, M. (2007). *Directive family therapy*. Routledge.

Hoffman, L. (1976). Breaking the homeostatic cycle. In P.J. Guerin, Jr. (Ed.), *Family therapy: Theory and practice*. (pp. 501–519). Gardner Press.

Keim, J., & Lappin, J. (2002). Structural-strategic marital therapy. In A. S. Gurman & N. S. Jacobson (Eds.), *Clinical handbook of couple therapy* (3rd Ed.) (pp. 86–117). Guilford.

Madanes, C. (1980). Protection, paradox, and pretending. *Family Process*, *19*(1), 73–85.

Madanes, C. (1981). *Strategic family therapy*. Jossey-Bass Inc.

McGoldrick, M., Giordano, J., Gracia-Preto, N. (2005). Overview: Ethnicity and family therapy. In McGoldrick, M., Giordano, J., and Garcia-Preto, N. (Eds.), *Ethnicity and family therapy* (3rd ed). The Guilford Press.

Nardone, G., & Watzlawick, P. (2005). *Brief strategic therapy*. Jason Aronson

Stanton, M., & Welsh, R. (2012). Systemic thinking in couple and family psychology research and practice. *Couple and Family Psychology: Research and Practice*, *1*(1), 14–30.

Watzlawick, P., Weakland, J. H., & Fisch, R. (1974). *Change: Principles of problem formation and problem resolution*. W.W. Norton.

Weakland, J. (1976). Communication theory and clinical change. In P.J. Guerin, Jr. (Ed.), *Family therapy: Theory and practice* (pp. 111–128). Gardner Press.

Weeks, G. R., & L'Abate, L. (1982). *Paradoxical psychotherapy: Theory and practice with individuals, couples, and families*. Brunner/Mazel, Inc.

12 Structural Family Therapy

Michael D. Reiter

Structural family therapy (SFT) was originally formulated by Salvador Minuchin, a physician from Argentina who later trained as a child psychiatrist and emerged as a central figure in the development of contemporary family therapy. The theoretical and practical foundations of SFT were further refined through Minuchin's collaborative work with colleagues at key institutions, including the Wiltwyck School for Boys and the Philadelphia Child Guidance Clinic. These developments eventually influenced systemic therapy practices on a global scale. Minuchin became widely recognized for his confrontational yet transformative therapeutic style, which involved challenging both his clients and the broader institutional and systemic contexts in which families and clinicians function (Reiter, 2017a).

SFT is grounded in three core axioms, as articulated by Minuchin (1974/2012). First, individuals both shape and are shaped by their relational and environmental contexts. Second, modifications in a family's structural organization are accompanied by changes in individual behavior and intrapsychic processes. Third, the initiation of therapy constitutes the formation of a new system—the therapeutic system—in which mutual influence occurs between the therapist and the family.

The Therapeutic Story of Problem Formation

Structural family therapists conceptualize problem formation as arising from dysfunctional patterns within a family's organizational structure. Importantly, these structural arrangements are not inherently pathological; rather, they often represent previously functional adaptations to earlier developmental stages. For example, heightened parental vigilance may serve an important protective function when children are young, yet this same level of oversight can become maladaptive as children transition into adolescence. As Minuchin and Nichols (1993) noted, families experience difficulties "not because there is something inherently wrong with them but because they've gotten stuck—stuck with a structure whose time has passed, and stuck with a story that doesn't work" (p. 43).

DOI: 10.4324/9781003668510-12

Families construct narratives and myths that shape both individual and collective identities. These stories contribute to and reinforce the family's structural organization. Minuchin (1974/2012) described family structure as "the invisible set of functional demands that organizes the ways in which family members interact" (p. 39). When family members remain entrenched in rigid identity narratives, they often fail to recognize or realize their full relational potential (Colapinto, 1982).

The family system is best understood as an open, dynamic entity that is constantly evolving. Although the current structure may promote a temporary sense of equilibrium or homeostasis, external and internal inputs—especially those occurring at transitional points in the family life cycle—introduce the potential for structural reorganization and growth (Colapinto, 1982).

In the Daniels family's current homeostatic arrangement, Fran assumes primary caregiving responsibilities, particularly for their daughter, Pam. Murray, the father, functions chiefly as the financial provider and maintains involvement in the lives of their sons, Oliver and George, through extracurricular activities. However, he remains largely disengaged from Pam. The family has coalesced around a shared narrative in which Pam is viewed as a troubled adolescent suffering from mental illness—in this case, anorexia. Within this framework, Pam's anorexia is seen as an individual pathology, disconnected from the family's relational dynamics.

In contrast, the structural therapist interprets the symptom bearer—often referred to as the identified patient (IP)—not as the sole locus of dysfunction but as a representative of broader systemic issues. Anorexia, from this perspective, is not merely a psychosomatic condition of the individual but may be indicative of a "psychosomatic family" context (Minuchin et al., 1978). This reframe can be challenging for families, who are frequently heavily invested in maintaining the narrative of the IP rather than exploring the relational dynamics that sustain the symptom. Families typically enter therapy presenting an "official story"—a familiar, well-rehearsed account of family identity and roles, often centered on the IP (Minuchin et al., 2006).

Symptoms

Families typically enter therapy with an IP—a family member whose behaviors or symptoms are perceived as the primary source of distress. Within this framework, the prevailing assumption is that if the IP were to change or improve, the family as a whole would return to a state of well-being. This perspective reflects an individualistic understanding of problems, wherein the symptom is viewed as residing solely within the person, detached from the broader relational dynamics (Minuchin et al., 2021). In contrast, SFT adopts a systemic lens, emphasizing that symptoms emerge within and are maintained by patterns of familial interaction. Accordingly, therapy becomes a dialectical process: the family enters with an individualistic narrative, while the therapist introduces and promotes a systemic perspective.

Minuchin et al. (2021) argued that "all families that come to therapy are 'wrong' in their assumptions" (p. 4), not because their perceptions lack validity, but because those perceptions are constrained by an individualistic frame that overlooks the relational context of behavior. The task of the structural therapist, therefore, is to facilitate the co-construction of a *therapeutic story*—a redefined story in which individual symptoms are understood within the matrix of the family system. This therapeutic story links each member's behavior to the functioning of the family as a whole.

In the case of the Daniels family, Pam is identified as the symptomatic member due to her anorexia. Both the family and Pam herself likely conceptualize her illness as isolated from the rest of the family system. However, the therapist's role is to expand this narrative, reframing Pam's symptoms as meaningful within the context of family relationships and dynamics. This shift from an individual to a relational narrative is essential to therapeutic progress.

Minuchin emphasized that one of the primary impediments to change in therapy is the family's *certainty*—their firmly held belief in the fixed nature of roles, identities, and problems. As he noted, "One of the certainties that a family brings to therapy is the knowledge that the identity of their members is unique and unchangeable, and this certainty is maintained by years of daily transactions among its members" (Minuchin et al., 2021, p. 32). The structural therapist challenges this certainty by creating opportunities for new patterns of interaction that support more adaptive forms of connection and belonging.

Underlying this approach is the assumption that individual identity is shaped by two fundamental forces: autonomy and belonging (Minuchin, 1974/2012; Minuchin et al., 1978). In the Daniels family, Pam's current experience is one of marginalization. While she maintains a connection to her mother, Fran, this bond is characterized more by conflict than by emotional attunement. The family story appears to position Pam as an outsider—there seems to be a foursome of Fran, Murray, Oliver, and George. And then there is Pam, who needs to get help. The therapeutic task is to restructure this narrative and create new avenues of belonging, allowing Pam and the rest of the family to renegotiate their roles and relationships in more constructive and inclusive ways.

Subsystems

The family is conceptualized as a dynamic, interactive system composed of individual members whose functioning is interdependent and organized toward maintaining the integrity of the whole. Within this larger system, smaller units known as **subsystems** serve specific relational and developmental functions. The three primary subsystems typically observed in nuclear families are the *spousal*, *parental*, and *sibling* subsystems (Minuchin & Fischman, 1981; Minuchin et al., 1978). However, families frequently contain additional subsystems organized around variables such as age, gender, interests, or roles. An individual's participation in multiple subsystems contributes significantly to the formation and maintenance of their identity within the family system (Minuchin, 2017).

The **spousal subsystem** generally consists of two partners; however, in non-traditional relational structures, such as polyamorous arrangements, this unit may include more individuals. The primary developmental task of the spousal subsystem is to establish and maintain clear boundaries that distinguish it from other subsystems, including those involving extended family (e.g., in-laws) and children (Minuchin & Fischman, 1981). This subsystem functions as a template for intimate relationships, influencing the values, expectations, and relational models that children internalize.

When conflict or tension arises within the spousal subsystem, it often reverberates throughout the larger family system. In such cases, unresolved issues between partners may be redirected toward a child, forming what Minuchin (1974/2012) termed a **detouring triangle**. This occurs when both partners focus their attention on a symptomatic child—often the IP—rather than addressing their own relational distress. In the Daniels family, Fran and Murray constitute the spousal subsystem. A structural therapist might hypothesize that Pam has, at times, been triangulated into this subsystem, with Fran's preoccupation with Pam's anorexia functioning to diffuse potential conflict between Fran and Murray. This detouring process can give the appearance of spousal harmony while underlying tensions remain unaddressed.

The **parental subsystem** is primarily responsible for the care, guidance, and socialization of children. Often, the same individuals who form the spousal subsystem also serve in parental roles, although additional caregivers—such as grandparents or older siblings—may also be included depending on the family context. This subsystem is frequently characterized by challenges related to authority, control, and role differentiation (Minuchin & Fischman, 1981). In the Daniels family, Fran and Murray comprise the parental subsystem, though their participation is uneven. Fran is the primary caregiver, while Murray assumes a more peripheral parenting role, engaging mostly with the boys—Oliver and George—particularly through organized sports on evenings and weekends.

The **sibling subsystem** consists of the children in the family and serves as the child's first peer group. Within this subsystem, children develop essential interpersonal competencies such as conflict resolution, cooperation, emotional regulation, and the capacity to function as part of a group (Minuchin & Fischman, 1981). In the Daniels family, Oliver and George form the core of the sibling subsystem, characterized by a strong sense of mutual belonging. Pam, by contrast, appears isolated from this subsystem, interacting minimally with her brothers. Her exclusion from this peer group may contribute to her sense of disconnection and reinforce her identification as the family's symptomatic member.

Beyond the foundational subsystems, additional configurations may emerge based on gender, interests, or patterns of alignment. In the Daniels family, two prominent subsystems can be identified along gender lines. The *male subsystem*—comprising Murray, Oliver, and George—tends to coalesce around shared activities, particularly sports. Conversely, the *female subsystem*, consisting of Fran and Pam, appears to be organized around the central issue of Pam's anorexia. These gender-based groupings reflect patterns of alliance and differentiation that influence the family's overall structure and relational dynamics.

In SFT, **boundaries** are the defining features that distinguish one subsystem from another, both within the family and between the family and its external environment. Boundaries are informed by implicit and explicit rules that govern who participates in a given subsystem and the nature of their interactions (Minuchin et al., 1978). These boundaries determine relational proximity and hierarchy, and they shape patterns of communication, power, and role clarity within the system. Boundaries exist along a continuum and can be categorized into three primary types: *rigid*, *diffuse*, and *clear* (Minuchin & Fischman, 1981).

Rigid boundaries are characterized by excessive separation between family members or subsystems. Information and emotional expression are limited, and interactions tend to be formal, detached, or rule-bound. The family hierarchy in such systems is often inflexible, and members are discouraged—either implicitly or explicitly—from engaging outside of their prescribed roles. This can lead to **disengagement**, where family members function in parallel rather than in coordination (Minuchin et al., 1978).

Families with rigid boundaries typically prioritize stability and control over adaptability, which can impair their ability to respond to developmental transitions or external stressors. Emotional isolation, low empathy, and minimal support are common consequences. For instance, in rigid systems, parents may enforce strict rules with little room for negotiation, siblings may maintain distant or avoidant relationships, and spouses may build emotional walls that hinder vulnerability and intimacy.

In the Daniels family, several rigid boundaries appear to exist. One notable example is between Murray and Pam; Murray has largely deferred parenting responsibilities for Pam to Fran, resulting in emotional distance and minimal engagement. Pam, in turn, has learned to bypass her father entirely, reinforcing the disconnection. Another example is the boundary between Pam and her siblings, Oliver and George, who seem to form a distinct sibling dyad with little inclusion of Pam. These rigid boundaries isolate Pam both vertically (from parental support) and horizontally (from sibling connection), which may contribute to her symptomatic presentation.

In contrast, **diffuse boundaries** are overly permeable, leading to blurred roles, enmeshment, and a lack of individual differentiation. In these systems, family members are often overly involved in one another's emotional lives, and autonomy is compromised in favor of cohesion (Minuchin & Fischman, 1981). Although this can foster a sense of closeness, it frequently results in excessive dependence, poor role definition, and challenges with individuation—particularly in adolescence and early adulthood.

Enmeshment within diffuse systems can manifest in several ways. Parents may intrude upon their children's emotional or decision-making processes, siblings may lack a clear sense of individuality, and spouses may struggle with maintaining healthy separation. Diffuse boundaries can impair conflict resolution and contribute to being emotionally overwhelmed, as individuals find themselves entangled in the psychological experiences of others.

Within the Daniels family, the most prominent diffuse boundary exists between Fran and Pam. Their relationship appears enmeshed, with Fran exerting significant control over Pam's eating behaviors, routines, and possibly even her thought processes. For Pam, who is navigating the developmental task of identity formation and separation, this dynamic may feel constraining or even suffocating. From an SFT perspective, a key therapeutic goal would involve helping Fran and Pam renegotiate this boundary to foster greater individuality, autonomy, and mutual respect.

Clear boundaries are considered optimal in family functioning. These boundaries are flexible, allowing for emotional connection and support while maintaining individual autonomy. Clear boundaries support effective communication, mutual respect, and the capacity to adapt to developmental and environmental changes (Minuchin & Fischman, 1981).

In families with clear boundaries, parents provide appropriate structure and leadership while respecting their children's growing independence. Siblings are able to maintain emotional closeness without overreliance, and spouses can cultivate intimacy while sustaining personal identities and interests. Clear boundaries promote relational health by allowing for both connection and differentiation.

In the Daniels family, there appears to be a relatively clear boundary between Murray and his sons, as well as between the brothers, Oliver and George. These relationships are likely facilitated through shared interests, such as sports, and suggest a healthy balance of involvement and autonomy. While on the surface Fran and Murray may appear to have clear boundaries in their spousal relationship, further exploration may reveal whether underlying dynamics—such as detouring or avoidance—complicate that appearance.

Boundaries exist on a continuum, and families often exhibit a combination of boundary types across subsystems. Functioning at the extremes—either rigid or diffuse—can be problematic, particularly during periods requiring flexibility and adaptation, such as developmental transitions or crises (Minuchin et al., 1978). In anorectic families, diffuse boundaries are especially common. These families often place a premium on loyalty, group cohesion, and emotional fusion, which can impede the adolescent's capacity for individuation and increase symptomatic behavior as a form of resistance or expression of unmet developmental needs.

SFT seeks to help families move toward clear, functional boundaries. By restructuring interactional patterns and promoting healthier relational hierarchies, the therapist supports families in fostering both cohesion and autonomy—core components of adaptive family functioning.

Complementarity

A central concept in SFT is **complementarity**, which refers to the patterned ways in which family members interact to mutually reinforce, balance, or sustain each other's behaviors (Minuchin & Fischman, 1981). These reciprocal roles often operate outside of conscious awareness and contribute either to the adaptive functioning or dysfunction of the family system. For example, a dynamic may emerge in which one spouse adopts a highly assertive stance while the other becomes increasingly passive, or one parent may overfunction by being overprotective, while the other underfunctions through emotional or physical disengagement.

Such complementary interactions help maintain the family's homeostasis, even when the patterns are maladaptive. In SFT, the therapist works to identify these implicit interactional cycles and bring them into the family's awareness. Through this process, families can begin to understand how their roles co-create and reinforce one another, thus opening the door to relational flexibility and healthier functioning.

In the Daniels family, complementarity is evident in the distribution of parenting responsibilities. Fran assumes primary responsibility for caretaking and managing household affairs, while Murray maintains a peripheral role, particularly in relation to their daughter, Pam. This pattern doesn't imply individual blame but reflects the principle that relational roles are co-constructed. As Fran increases her involvement with Pam, Murray is allowed to disengage; conversely, the more Murray remains uninvolved, the more Fran intensifies her focus on Pam. Complementarity, therefore, illustrates how family members shape one another's behavior in a reciprocal, often unconscious, manner.

While functional families possess the capacity to engage in open disagreement and conflict resolution, families characterized as psychosomatic tend to avoid conflict altogether (Minuchin et al., 1978). In these families, overt disagreement is minimized or suppressed, and the expression of conflict is often redirected through the development of symptoms in a child, frequently the IP.

Minuchin et al. (1978) identified three primary patterns by which conflict is deflected in psychosomatic families: The first is **triangulation**—In this pattern, a child is drawn into parental conflict, often subtly encouraged to align with one parent against the other. Although the process may be unconscious, the child becomes a vehicle through which unresolved spousal tensions are expressed. The second pattern is **Parent-Child Coalition**—This occurs when a stable alliance forms between one parent and a child in opposition to the other parent. Unlike triangulation, which may shift depending on circumstances, a coalition is more fixed and enduring. The third pattern is **Detouring**—In detouring, the parents divert attention away from their own relational difficulties by focusing on a symptomatic child. The child's behavior becomes the locus of concern, thereby allowing the parental subsystem to avoid confronting its own conflict. This strategy often results in a facade of parental unity while the underlying issues remain unresolved.

In the case of the Daniels family, there is evidence of detouring. Fran's intense focus on Pam's anorexia may serve as a relational function—providing a distraction from unresolved issues between Fran and Murray. This dynamic may contribute to a superficially harmonious spousal relationship while masking deeper emotional or interpersonal disconnects.

Families with an anorectic child often exhibit distinct structural and interactional characteristics (Minuchin et al., 1978). These families are typically child-oriented, with parents displaying heightened levels of vigilance and concern over the child's behavior. Simultaneously, the anorectic individual tends to internalize this surveillance, becoming acutely self-monitoring and emotionally attuned to the expectations and responses of others (Minuchin et al., 1978). Despite potentially appearing emotionally distant or detached, these children are often highly sensitive to interpersonal dynamics—a phenomenon sometimes referred to as being a parent-watcher.

In such families, the anorectic child frequently occupies a central role in the family's emotional life. Their symptoms—such as food restriction, compulsive control, and perfectionism—are both expressions of individual distress and reflections of broader systemic dynamics. SFT seeks to understand these symptoms in relational context and to restructure the family system in ways that support both autonomy and connection.

Family Development

According to SFT, families evolve through a series of developmental stages, each marked by increasing structural complexity and the need to master new relational tasks (Minuchin & Fischman, 1981). Successful progression through these stages requires the family to adjust its organizational structure, role expectations, and boundaries in response to internal and external demands. Transitional periods between stages are particularly significant, as the family's established homeostasis may no longer suit the changing developmental context, prompting a need for structural reorganization.

Minuchin and Fischman (1981) delineated four primary stages in the family life cycle: **Couple Formation**—The establishment of a new spousal subsystem, with boundaries that separate the couple from their families of origin. **Families with Young Children**—The integration of a new parental subsystem and the negotiation of caregiving roles. **Families with Adolescents**—A shift toward increased autonomy for children and a restructuring of hierarchical boundaries. **Families with Grown Children**—The launching of adult children and a redefinition of parental roles, often accompanied by the reemergence of the spousal subsystem as central.

Each stage presents unique challenges and requires the development of new structural competencies. When families struggle to adapt, dysfunction often emerges, particularly when they rely on outdated interactional patterns or resist the necessary boundary shifts required for developmental progression.

Families often construct explanatory narratives around the presence of IP. This individual is typically presented as the source of the family's difficulties and is the person whom the family offers up to the therapist for treatment. From the family's perspective, change in the IP is assumed to be sufficient to resolve the presenting problem. However, SFT challenges this linear, individualistic view of pathology. Minuchin et al. (2021) argued that families are "wrong" in assuming that the problem resides solely in the IP. Rather, symptoms are understood as embedded within the family's broader relational patterns and structural dynamics. The more the family maintains a problem-saturated narrative focused on a single individual, the more constrained their capacity for systemic change becomes.

The therapist's task, therefore, is to **deconstruct the symptom**—to reveal its relational context and demonstrate how the problem is co-created and maintained across family members (Minuchin et al., 2007). Through restructuring interventions, the therapist helps the family shift from an individual-focused problem story to a systemic and relational understanding of dysfunction.

The Daniels family is currently navigating the transition from the families with adolescents stage to the families with grown children stage. Pam, at age 17, is nearing legal adulthood. In many cultural contexts, including the United States, this developmental period signals the beginning of the emerging adulthood phase, in which the individual prepares to assume greater autonomy and independence.

Developmentally, this transition requires a recalibration of the boundaries within the family system—particularly between the parental and sibling subsystems. Ideally, these boundaries should become clear: flexible enough to allow Pam increased independence while maintaining emotional connection and support. However, the Daniels family continues to operate as though Pam remains in early adolescence. Parental decision-making remains centralized, and Fran and Murray continue to exert considerable control over Pam's behavior, routines, and personal choices.

This incongruence between Pam's developmental needs and the family's structural patterns contributes to psychological distress and symptomatic behavior. From an SFT perspective, part of the therapeutic work will involve supporting the Daniels family in restructuring their roles and boundaries to support Pam's transition into adult functioning. This includes empowering her autonomy while redefining the parental role in a way that is developmentally appropriate and relationally supportive.

Diversity Conceptualization

SFT is grounded in the assumption that while all families share universal characteristics, each family also exhibits unique, context-specific patterns of functioning (Minuchin et al., 2006). From the structural perspective, every family possesses an organizational framework composed of subsystems (e.g., spousal, parental, sibling) demarcated by boundaries, and each family itself functions as a subsystem embedded within larger sociocultural systems. These universal elements offer a foundational blueprint for therapeutic assessment and intervention.

At the same time, SFT recognizes that families are inherently idiosyncratic in how they express and embody these universal principles. Family organization, relational roles, patterns of communication, and responses to stress or change are shaped by a confluence of factors, including but not limited to ethnicity, socioeconomic class, religion, immigration history, and cultural traditions. The structural therapist must, therefore, navigate both the universal and the idiosyncratic—using general structural principles as a guide while carefully attuning to the distinct characteristics and relational dynamics of the family system at hand.

As Simon (1995) emphasized, the outcomes of any therapeutic intervention depend not only on theoretical accuracy but also on the uniqueness of the family's structure and relational style. The therapist does not impose a one-size-fits-all solution, but rather facilitates change by collaborating with the family to explore how universal structural principles manifest in their specific context.

Minuchin et al. (2006) highlighted the necessity for therapists to understand how cultural variables such as ethnicity, class, and social norms influence both the structure and functioning of the family system. While all families perform critical developmental tasks—such as providing care, promoting autonomy, and fostering belonging—how these tasks are accomplished varies significantly across cultural groups. The therapist must remain culturally responsive, allowing the family's values, meanings, and lived experiences to shape the therapeutic process.

Fundamentally, the family serves as the primary site for identity formation. Across cultures, individuals develop their sense of self through the dynamic interplay between autonomy (the development of individuality) and belonging (the experience of connection and acceptance) (Minuchin, 1974/2012). While these dual needs are universal, their expression and negotiation are deeply informed by cultural worldviews and social positioning.

Though initially developed in the 1960s to address the needs of low-income, minority families in the northeastern United States, SFT has since been adapted and applied in diverse sociocultural contexts around the world. Its foundational principles—subsystems, boundaries, hierarchy, and systemic interaction—are sufficiently robust and flexible to accommodate culturally specific adaptations while preserving the integrity of the model.

International applications of SFT have included work with Chinese families (Ma et al., 2020) and Iranian families (Dehghani & Bernards, 2022), demonstrating the model's cross-cultural applicability. Within the United States, SFT has been effectively adapted for African American (Williams et al., 2016), Asian American (Kim, 2003), Latino (Zafra, 2016), Mexican American (Soto-Fulp & Del Campo, 1994), Italian American (Yaccarino, 1993), and Native American families (Napoliello & Sweet, 1992). Furthermore, it has been applied with family systems involving same-sex couples and LGBTQ+ identities, reflecting an evolving responsiveness to contemporary family forms and configurations (McAdams III et al., 2016).

Importantly, the structural model offers not only a diagnostic and intervention framework but also a flexible scaffolding for collaboration between therapist and family. Families and clinicians can use the structural lens to organize their understanding of family dynamics while simultaneously integrating their own values, meanings, and cultural processes (Minuchin et al., 2007). In this way, SFT remains both theoretically grounded and contextually adaptable, supporting therapists in working effectively across a broad spectrum of cultural and relational diversity.

The Therapeutic Story of Problem Resolution

In SFT, the resolution of psychological and relational issues is situated primarily within the context of the family unit. As Minuchin and Fischman (1981) assert, "The family is the natural context for both growth and healing, and it is the context that the family therapist will depend on for the actualization of therapeutic goals" (p. 11). Therapeutic change is facilitated when the therapist assists the family in reorganizing its internal structure and interactional dynamics (Minuchin et al., 1978). These authors explained, "The goal of therapy is to facilitate the growth of a system that encourages the freedom to individuate while preserving the connectedness of belonging" (p. 91), emphasizing a dual focus on individual autonomy and systemic cohesion.

Central to the structural approach is the concept of **restructuring**, a deliberate therapeutic intervention aimed at transforming the organization of the family system. This process extends beyond the mere delineation of boundaries; it encompasses the active modification of the family's hierarchical arrangements and relational subsystems. The therapist engages directly with the family to promote the development of a more functional organizational structure, thereby enhancing the system's capacity to manage conflict, support individual development, and achieve collective goals (Minuchin & Fischman, 1981).

Restructuring may involve a range of clinical techniques designed to shift power dynamics, reconfigure alliances, and clarify roles within the family. For instance, the therapist might empower a disempowered parent to restore parental authority or constrain a child whose influence has become disproportionate. Similarly, interventions may target maladaptive coalitions—such as an exclusive alliance between a parent and child that marginalizes the other parent—aiming to establish more balanced and inclusive family relationships.

Ultimately, restructuring seeks to alter the family's habitual modes of functioning at a structural level. By addressing these foundational patterns, the therapist facilitates the emergence of more adaptive interactional strategies. These changes typically result in improved communication, more effective problem-solving capacities, and enhanced emotional well-being across the family system.

Deconstructing the Symptom

Within many families presenting for therapy, a prevailing story often emerges in which the IP is viewed as the primary source of dysfunction. This individual is positioned as the bearer of symptoms that, if resolved, would ostensibly restore harmony to the family system. SFT challenges this reductive narrative by introducing a more complex, systemic conceptualization of the problem. Rather than locating the symptom within the individual, the therapist constructs a therapeutic story that situates the problem within the broader network of family relationships and interactions.

This re-narration involves a process of **symptom deconstruction**, through which the problem is externalized and reframed as a product of systemic dynamics. The aim is to shift the focus away from the individual and toward the family as a whole. As Minuchin et al. (2007) assert, "But the first, or perhaps most important, question a systemic therapist asks is: What are family members doing that helps maintain the identified patient's symptoms?" (p. 17). This question marks the beginning of a therapeutic shift from an individual pathology story to a transactional story, where behaviors are understood in the context of recursive interactional patterns.

For example, in the case of Pam's refusal to eat, the behavior is conceptualized not in isolation, but as emerging from a web of relational patterns: Fran's overinvolvement, Murray's emotional disengagement, and Pam's disconnection from her siblings, Oliver and George. SFT draws upon general systems theory, which holds that a change in one part of the system can initiate transformations throughout the system. Thus, symptoms are interpreted as signals of systemic imbalance rather than as intrinsic defects within the individual.

Minuchin et al. (2007) identify several strategies for deconstructing the symptom and redefining its meaning within the family context:

- focusing on areas of competence of the identified patient;
- giving a different meaning to the problem that the family has decided upon (reframing);
- exploring the ways in which the symptom presents itself and paying attention to details;
- looking at the problem from different perspectives until the symptom loses its toxicity;
- exploring the context in which the symptom appears;
- exploring other family members' difficulties, similar to or different from those of the identified patient;
- encouraging the identified patient to describe the symptom and the meaning he or she attributes to it, to describe other aspects of himself or herself, to describe the family, in other words, to give him or her respectful space while the other family members become the audience. (p. 9)

One of the initial interventions in this deconstruction process often involves **amplifying the voice of the IP**. In families where the IP is a child or adolescent, it is common for parents to attempt to begin sessions by listing grievances or concerns about the child's behavior. Rather than permitting an extended monologue that pathologizes the IP, the structural therapist intervenes by facilitating the direct involvement of the IP in the conversation. This not only disrupts the unilateral flow of blame but also begins to reposition the IP as an autonomous and competent participant in the family dialogue.

For instance, in work with the Daniels family, Fran may begin a session by expressing concern over Pam's weight. The therapist, instead of allowing Fran to dominate the narrative, might invite Pam to share her own perspective. This intervention initiates a subtle restructuring of the family dynamic, wherein Pam is not merely the subject of concern but an active contributor to the understanding of the problem. Such moments foster parental recognition of the child's agency and begin to alter the power dynamics within the family system.

Joining

In traditional therapeutic practice, *joining* is often conceptualized as a discrete, early-stage intervention—typically occurring during the first session—where the therapist establishes rapport by eliciting background information from the client, separate from the presenting problem. However, in SFT, **joining** is understood not as a procedural step but as a **therapeutic stance** or mindset that permeates the entire course of treatment, from the initial contact to termination (Minuchin et al., 2021). It is regarded as the foundational element upon which all effective structural interventions are built.

The process of joining enables the therapist to form a **therapeutic system** with the family. Within this system, the therapist typically assumes a leadership role, guiding the family through restructuring processes and systemic change (Minuchin et al., 1978). Importantly, interventions in SFT are not applied in a detached or mechanical manner. Rather, the Structural therapist exercises their "membership rights" within the therapeutic system, making interventions from a position of embedded participation (Colapinto, 2017).

Structural therapists engage with families along a **continuum of relational proximity**, moving fluidly between three primary joining positions—*close*, *median*, and *distant*—depending on the dynamics emerging in the session and the therapist's working hypotheses regarding the most therapeutically effective stance at a given moment.

In the **close position**, the therapist becomes deeply engaged with the family, mirroring their communication styles, affect, and behavioral patterns. This technique, referred to as *mimesis* (Minuchin, 1974/2012), involves adapting to the family's natural modes of interaction—whether through emotion, language, or even physical positioning. This approach facilitates trust-building and is particularly effective when working with disengaged families or when attempting to realign rigid or maladaptive alliances.

In the **median position**, the therapist remains involved and empathetic while maintaining a degree of professional distance. This balanced stance allows the therapist to observe family transactions objectively, while still providing relational support. The median position is often suitable for families where both connection and clinical neutrality are required.

In the **distant position**, the therapist deliberately steps back, minimizing emotional involvement to maintain a high level of observational clarity. This position is often assumed following an **enactment**, where the therapist encourages family members to interact directly. The distant stance is instrumental in working with enmeshed families, allowing the therapist to identify and challenge problematic structural patterns without being absorbed into the family's emotional field.

Minuchin is widely recognized as one of the most confrontational figures in the development of family therapy. His style involved direct challenges to clients' narratives and behaviors, grounded in a belief in their untapped potential. He explained, "Challenge is the capacity of the therapist to feel the dynamic of the group; to observe the invisible patterns that entrap each of them in their particular sense of identity" (Minuchin, 2017, p. 97). Yet, as Minuchin frequently emphasized, confrontation must emerge from a place of relational alignment: "Challenge comes from a place of connection" (Reiter, 2017b, p. 47).

To operationalize this balance between support and confrontation, Structural therapists often employ what Minuchin termed the **stroke and kick** technique (Minuchin et al., 2007; Minuchin et al., 2021). The "stroke" involves an affirming or complimentary statement directed at the family—e.g., "You are three very nice people" or "Each of you seems quite intelligent." This is immediately followed by the "kick," a pointed challenge to the family's maladaptive interactional patterns—e.g., "So how is it that you make your lives so nicely miserable?" or "Yet you continue doing something so wrong."

This technique reflects the dual role of the therapist as both ally and disruptor: by first affirming the family's strengths, the therapist builds rapport and increases receptivity to change. The subsequent challenge underscores the need for transformation and invites the family to confront their own contributions to dysfunctional dynamics.

The utility of the stroke and kick approach lies in its applicability across diverse family presentations. Every family brings both **competencies** and **constraints** into the therapeutic context. The therapist's task is to amplify the former while respectfully confronting the latter, thereby facilitating structural reorganization and long-term change.

Enactments

One of the most defining and frequently utilized techniques in SFT is the **enactment**. As Minuchin and Fischman (1981) famously described, "Enactment is the technique by which the therapist asks the family to dance in his presence"

(p. 79). This metaphor captures the essence of enactment: it is not a role-play or dramatized re-creation, but rather a spontaneous outgrowth of the therapeutic conversation in which the therapist invites family members to engage with one another directly. The therapist shifts the dialogue away from descriptions of problems and toward live interaction, thereby allowing the family's habitual **transactional patterns**, implicit rules, and interactional dynamics to emerge in real time.

Rather than relying on clients' self-reports—which are often shaped by personal bias, impression management, or limited awareness—the structural therapist privileges observable behavior. As Minuchin frequently noted, he was less interested in what people said than in how they acted (Reiter, 2017b). The enactment allows the therapist to bypass distorted narratives and instead assess how problems are maintained through ongoing relational sequences. In fact, enactments are considered so integral to SFT that Aponte (1992) stated: "The enactment is to Structural Family Therapy what transference is to psychoanalysis" (p. 271).

Once an enactment is initiated, the therapist typically adopts a **distant position**, stepping back physically and emotionally to become an observer. This detachment allows the therapist to maintain a systemic perspective, tracking patterns and alliances without becoming enmeshed in the family's process. Minuchin instructed his trainees to achieve this by finding a physical anchor—such as looking at their left foot—to remain disengaged from the content of the conversation (Minuchin et al., 2021). The key is to avoid being pulled into the family's interaction by leaning forward or appearing overly attentive, which might inadvertently reinforce triangulation or reactivity.

In addition to revealing structural patterns, enactments serve another important function: they slow down the tempo of interaction in the therapeutic space (Reiter, 2017b). As family members speak to one another under the therapist's observation, they become more self-aware and deliberate. This shift from reactive to reflective behavior fosters new insights and increases the possibility of behavior change. Clients begin to recognize their own contributions to dysfunctional cycles, opening the door to intentional reorganization of the system.

A compelling example of enactment in clinical practice is Minuchin's use of the **lunch session**, developed specifically for families in which a member was experiencing anorexia nervosa (Minuchin et al., 1978). This extended session—typically lasting two hours—was divided into two phases. In the first phase, the therapist focused on joining, forming therapeutic alliances with each family member, and emphasizing individual competencies. This stage creates a secure therapeutic system in which enactments can take place effectively.

In the second phase, the family shared a meal—either brought into the session or ordered ahead of time. This shared meal became the context for a powerful enactment, allowing the therapist to observe how the family organized itself around the issue of food. The objective, as Minuchin et al. (1978) articulated, "is to transform the issue of an anorectic patient into the drama of a dysfunctional family" (p. 120). In this setting, patterns such as overinvolvement, avoidance, or power struggles around food could be observed directly and then addressed therapeutically.

One specific intervention often used during enactments is **blocking**, in which the therapist restricts a particular family member from participating in an interaction that should occur between others. For instance, if Pam and her brother Oliver are attempting to communicate during a session and their mother, Fran, interjects, the therapist may intervene by saying, "Fran, hang on a moment. This is something to be handled by siblings. Let's see how they do it." This technique serves to reinforce appropriate subsystems, challenge triangulations, and promote more functional interactions aligned with the family's developmental and structural needs.

In sum, enactments provide a live and dynamic window into the family's organization. They are not only diagnostic but also transformative, allowing the therapist to both assess and restructure maladaptive family patterns in the here-and-now of the therapeutic encounter. As such, they are foundational to the practice of SFT and remain its most distinctive and powerful intervention.

Reframing

Reframing is a central therapeutic intervention within SFT, designed to alter a family's interpretive lens rather than the objective facts of their situation. The aim is to shift how family members perceive behaviors or relational patterns, thereby promoting more constructive interactional responses. Reframing facilitates the redefinition of meaning around problematic behaviors, encouraging family members to adopt more flexible, empathic, and solution-oriented perspectives.

Minuchin and Fischman (1981) emphasized the importance of this shift in perspective, noting,

> The family's framing is relevant for the continuity and maintenance of the organism more or less as it is; the therapeutic framing is related to the goal of moving the family toward a more differentiated and competent dealing with their dysfunctional reality.
>
> (p. 74)

In essence, while the family's current framing reinforces homeostasis, the therapist's reframing serves as a disruptive yet constructive force that opens new avenues for change.

For example, a therapist might reframe a child's oppositional behavior not as mere defiance, but as a bid for autonomy or connection. Similarly, a parent's intrusive involvement may be reinterpreted as a form of misdirected care rather than simple control. These reframes are not offered as empirical truths, but as alternative narratives that reduce blame, soften rigid attributions, and allow family members to re-engage with one another from a place of understanding rather than judgment.

With the Daniels family, the therapist is likely to encounter numerous opportunities for reframing entrenched perceptions. Fran's overinvolvement in Pam's eating behaviors, for example, might be reframed as a manifestation of maternal concern and a desire to protect. Pam's anorexia may be interpreted not solely as an individual symptom but as a systemic function—perhaps serving to unify her parents around a shared concern. Similarly, the emotional distance exhibited by her brothers, Oliver and George, could be reframed as a developmental attempt to support Pam's individuation and eventual transition toward autonomy.

Importantly, reframes do not require objective accuracy in the conventional sense. Their utility lies in their capacity to be accepted by the family and incorporated into their shared narrative. Once integrated, these new framings can help to destabilize maladaptive patterns and initiate new, more adaptive cycles of interaction.

Boundary Making

Family members are interconnected through various subsystems, with the sense of belonging serving as a central organizing principle within the family system. From an SFT perspective, therapists intervene by reshaping patterns of belonging through the technique of boundary making (Colapinto, 2017). Dysfunction often emerges when individuals operate at the extremes of subsystem boundaries—either overly diffuse or excessively rigid (Reiter, 2016). As such, the therapist's goal is to help reposition family members toward a functional middle ground by reconfiguring relational boundaries to become clearer.

Boundary making is the clinical process by which the therapist clarifies and redefines who is included in specific subsystems. Establishing developmentally appropriate and functional boundaries allows individuals to cultivate a stronger sense of self while simultaneously maintaining nurturing and supportive connections with others. This restructuring fosters greater systemic stability and resilience.

There are multiple methods for engaging in boundary making. For example, a therapist might address the parental subsystem explicitly by stating, "Fran and Murray, you two are the parents. So why don't you two talk about what you want to do in this situation," thereby affirming their roles within the family hierarchy. Similarly, the therapist might highlight a gender-based subsystem by asking, "What do the men in the family think about this?" Each of these interventions serves to demarcate and reinforce subsystem boundaries.

One of the most well-established techniques for boundary making involves manipulating the physical arrangement of seating during a session (Minuchin & Fischman, 1981). For instance, if a child is seated between both parents, it may signal an inappropriate involvement in the spousal subsystem. In such a case, the therapist may intervene by saying, "Pam, could you switch seats with your mother since she and your father have some important things as parents that they need to discuss right now." This spatial reconfiguration visually and symbolically clarifies the boundaries of the spousal and parental subsystems, reinforcing appropriate family structure and roles.

Unbalancing

While boundary making seeks to redefine the composition of subsystems within the family, the technique of *unbalancing* is aimed at altering hierarchical structures among family members (Minuchin & Fischman, 1981). Unbalancing occurs when the therapist deliberately aligns with one individual or subsystem—typically one occupying a lower position in the family hierarchy—in a way that temporarily disrupts the existing relational balance. This strategic alliance serves to shift power dynamics and foster systemic change.

Minuchin and Fischman (1981) identify three primary categories of unbalancing interventions. The first involves therapist affiliation with a particular family member to elevate their influence or visibility within the system. The second entails the therapist deliberately ignoring or minimizing the input of another member, often someone in a dominant or overfunctioning role. The third strategy involves the formation of a temporary coalition with one member against another, thereby challenging entrenched relational patterns and alliances.

Unbalancing is especially effective in cases where one family member exerts disproportionate control over others, suppressing alternative perspectives, or where pathological coalitions—such as an enmeshed parent-child dyad—marginalize other members of the system. For instance, in the Daniels family, Pam occupies the lowest position in the hierarchical structure. By aligning with her, the therapist can amplify her voice and facilitate her recognition as the eldest child, rather than as the youngest or least powerful. This shift destabilizes the family's existing equilibrium, encouraging reconsideration of roles, boundaries, and expectations.

The application of unbalancing requires the therapist to adopt a directive and, at times, confrontational stance, while simultaneously maintaining empathy and preserving therapeutic alliance. Importantly, the technique does not reflect a permanent alignment with one member over another; rather, it represents a strategic, time-limited intervention aimed at empowering marginalized individuals within the system (Minuchin & Fischman, 1981). Because unbalancing inherently involves an element of inequity, it must be employed with particular caution and clinical sensitivity (Minuchin et al., 2021). Furthermore, the technique places significant demands on the therapist, who must remain actively engaged and emotionally present in what are often conflict-laden and emotionally intense sessions.

Unwrapping Family Identities

As individuals participate in multiple family subsystems, they simultaneously construct and inhabit a range of identities. The family, in this sense, functions as the "*matrix of identity*," a foundational context wherein children and other members form a multiplicity of selves through their varied relational roles (Colapinto, 2017, p. 91). When identities within the family become rigid or narrowly defined, dysfunction often follows. In such cases, "one of the functions of the therapy is to convince family members that they are not who they think they are" (Minuchin et al., 2021, p. 32). The therapist's task, then, is to initiate a process of **unwrapping family identities**—inviting family members to recognize both themselves and others as more complex and multifaceted than previously assumed.

One core method for unwrapping identity involves altering the relational context in which a family member is viewed (Minuchin et al., 2021). This typically occurs through reconfiguration of subsystems. For example, a woman may carry different relational labels depending on whether she is positioned as a spouse, parent, daughter, or coworker. Likewise, an adolescent may be understood differently when interacting with parents, siblings, peers, or teachers. By shifting the relational context, new aspects of the individual's identity can be activated and made visible.

Throughout the therapeutic process, the Structural therapist brings attention to how individuals function differently across contexts. As these varied presentations emerge, the individual is perceived as more nuanced and multidimensional. This expanded perception not only enriches the individual's identity but also transforms how other family members relate to them. The therapist emphasizes *relational identities* over purely individual traits (Reiter, 2017b). Rather than focusing on descriptors such as "smart," "funny," or "mean," the therapist highlights identities such as "peacemaker," "sheriff," or "overworked mother." A peacemaker actively mediates between others, a sheriff monitors others' behavior against perceived norms, and an overworked mother assumes disproportionate responsibility in the family—often in the absence of adequate support from a partner.

Within the Daniels family, multiple identities have emerged, but the most salient and organizing one at present is Pam's identity as "an anorexic." This label has become central to the family's current organization, conferring upon Pam considerable influence within the system (Reiter, 2016). However, this identity is primarily individual and decontextualized—one that could exist independent of the family structure. The therapeutic task involves expanding Pam's identity to encompass a broader range of characteristics and roles (Minuchin et al., 2021). These may include individual traits such as "bright," "friendly," or "competent." More critically, however, the therapist aims to surface relational identities such as "mom's focus" or "the oldest sibling." By re-situating Pam within these relational frames, family members are encouraged to reinterpret their interactions, roles, and expectations. This reorganization may catalyze the development of new patterns of engagement and more adaptive systemic functioning.

Intensity

Structural Family Therapists employ *intensity* as a strategic intervention to facilitate the development of a therapeutic story within the family system. **Intensity** serves to enhance the salience of therapeutic messages, ensuring they are internalized and integrated as meaningful, novel information within the family's cognitive and emotional frameworks (Minuchin & Fischman, 1981). One of the primary mechanisms for generating intensity is *repetition* (Minuchin & Fischman, 1981; Minuchin et al., 2021). While a single therapeutic intervention may have an immediate impact, its effects are often transient. Through the deliberate repetition of key messages or techniques, the therapist underscores their significance and increases the likelihood that these messages become embedded within the family's evolving narrative.

Another technique for heightening intensity involves the *prolongation of conflictual transactions* (Minuchin et al., 1978). Whereas some therapeutic models may prioritize resolution within the session itself, SFT allows for the maintenance—and even amplification—of interpersonal conflict as a catalyst for change. By sustaining an enactment involving two or more family members engaged in a maladaptive interaction, the therapist creates space for the family to confront habitual patterns. If such an interaction is maintained through the end of the session, it may serve as a powerful prompt for continued reflection and behavioral experimentation outside the therapeutic context. In this way, exceeding the family's typical stopping point can destabilize entrenched routines and encourage the emergence of new, more adaptive responses (Minuchin & Fischman, 1981).

Proximity is another tool used to generate therapeutic intensity (Minuchin & Fischman, 1981). The therapist may actively manipulate physical space in the room to either reinforce or challenge relational dynamics. For example, when a family member, such as Pam, demonstrates behavior indicative of a shift in hierarchical positioning, the therapist may amplify this moment by physically approaching her, shaking her hand, and offering verbal reinforcement such as, "Congratulations." These layered behaviors—movement, gesture, and affirmation—collectively mark the action as significant and desirable. Conversely, the therapist may use physical distance to disrupt problematic closeness. In cases of enmeshment, such as a diffuse boundary between Fran and Pam, the therapist may work to decrease their proximity. If Fran interferes with an enactment between Pam and Murray, the therapist might physically reposition her chair to create space. Should Fran persist in her involvement, the therapist may escalate the intervention by positioning themselves between Fran and the others, thereby reinforcing boundary clarity.

Intensity can also be introduced by resisting induction into the family's homeostatic system (Minuchin & Fischman, 1981). The family's prevailing narrative often serves to preserve dysfunctional patterns. Therefore, the therapist must consciously reject this narrative and introduce an alternative therapeutic storyline. This process involves the intentional disruption of the system's equilibrium through the presentation of *novelty*. Novel interventions and perspectives function as catalysts for systemic transformation, inviting family members to reconsider their roles, relationships, and shared understandings.

Novelty

At its core, SFT is a model centered on change—specifically, change in the structure of the family system. One of the principal mechanisms for facilitating such transformation is the introduction of **novelty**. By offering alternative explanations for family members' behaviors, the therapist disrupts familiar narratives, enabling them to consider new ways of understanding themselves and one another. A particularly powerful shift occurs when the family's story is reframed from an individualistic to a relational perspective. As Minuchin and Nichols (1993) stated, "But when family members learn to look at problems in an interrelated way, they see anew. Novel and more sensitive ways of being emerge" (p. 113).

A primary technique for introducing novelty is the use of **metaphor** (Reiter, 2017b). As Minuchin et al. (2007) noted, "Metaphors make it possible to challenge family members without making them feel defensive" (p. 6). Some metaphors Minuchin has used with families include talking about how chickens have a pecking order and once they organize into lower power and higher power there is peace, that a son's "problematic behaviors" have created a jail for the family where he is the jailor, or that parents are treating a child as being of a much younger age than they actually are. These figurative representations offer alternative framings that can be internalized more readily than direct confrontation.

Change within the family typically occurs after the therapist has successfully joined with the family system, developed trust, and then introduced a crisis—a moment of uncertainty that forces the system out of its habitual patterns (Minuchin & Nichols, 1993). In this moment, the family is invited to experiment with new roles, behaviors, or emotional responses.

In the context of families dealing with anorexia, for instance, Minuchin (1984) emphasized that "a capacity for direct challenge in an area not related to food is a prerequisite for improvement" (p. 99). In the Daniels family, for example, the therapist might align with Pam in a challenge directed toward one or both parents. Importantly, this would occur in a non-food-related domain such as negotiating curfew, choosing a television program, or deciding on clothing—areas that are less emotionally charged and more manageable, yet still capable of fostering change in relational dynamics.

Strength and Competence

SFT is grounded in a fundamental belief in the inherent competence and resourcefulness of all families (Simon, 1995). As such, it can be described as a therapy of hope and strength (Minuchin et al., 2021). Families typically enter therapy presenting their most dysfunctional patterns, often unaware of the adaptive or functional aspects of their relational system.

If asked outright, "What are the family's strengths?" the family might want to keep focused on the presenting problem. To circumvent this, the therapist might be a bit more covert. "Statements of puzzled curiosity are ways in which the therapist punctuates his disbelief in the presentation of the family framing" (Minuchin & Fischman, 1981, p. 278). Because the structural family therapist believes in the family and the members of the family, they tend to utilize members as resources for one another. That is, family members are placed in positions to be healers of one another (Minuchin et al., 2021).

Richness

Minuchin was known for asserting that "people are richer than they think they are" (Reiter, 2017b). Families often enter therapy with a fixed understanding of their problems, identities, and relationships, viewing their circumstances through a narrow and often deficit-based lens. Structural therapists, by contrast, work from the assumption that clients possess far more resources than they are currently able to recognize or utilize. These resources open up a wide range of possibilities for how the family can reorganize and function (Reiter, 2016).

SFT expands the family's narrative reality, which is always partial and limited. As the complexity of the therapeutic story grows, so too does the number of potential pathways for interaction, identity, and problem resolution. Relational identities, behavioral patterns, and transactional processes can all be reimagined. As Simon (1995) observed, "The therapist must simply convince families to risk the uncertainty of searching for alternatives of which they are already in possession" (p. 20).

In the case of the Daniels family, the family system has become entrenched in rigid roles and repetitive interactional cycles. The presentation they bring to therapy reflects only a narrow slice of their potential. The Structural therapist enters treatment with a deep awareness that the family has many more unexplored alternatives available to them. The objective of therapy, then, is to help uncover and activate the richness within the system—expanding roles, shifting perspectives, and enabling the family to engage in new, more adaptive ways of being.

The Therapeutic Process

While many people view Structural therapists (and Minuchin in particular) as being experts and authoritarian, the therapist operates from an influential position that is speculative. That is, "what the therapist sees is a hypothesis, one that provides a map in which to contact the family, but a map drawn in pencil rather than in ink" (Reiter, 2017b, p. 52). In essence, the structural therapist is an uncertain expert. While the therapist may see where the family may go (e.g., move from diffuse to clear boundaries or connecting two adults into the parental subsystem), how to get there is not yet clear.

This section presents many of the ideas and tools that Structural therapists tend to utilize. However, they are just tools and techniques. Therapy is about craft; knowing when and how to use these tools. This comes through the self of the therapist. The most powerful tool that the Structural family therapist has in their tool pouch is themselves (Minuchin et al., 2021; Minuchin & Fischman, 1981) since the therapist plays such a central position in the therapeutic system (Aponte, 1992). They need to have as much richness of experience, understanding of self, and freedom from restrictions to be as connected and involved in the session as they can.

Case Transcript

Therapist: Hi everyone, I'm really glad you all could come today. Before we dive in, could you each introduce yourselves and tell me one thing you enjoy doing?

Intervention: Joining—The therapist begins by entering the family system respectfully and begins developing the therapeutic system.

Pam: I'm Pam… I guess I like painting.
Oliver: I'm Oliver, I play soccer.
George: I'm George, and I like video games.
Fran: I'm Fran. I like gardening.
Murray: I'm Murray, and I enjoy woodworking.
Therapist: Thanks, everyone. Pam, your painting sounds interesting. Do you still do it often?

Intervention: Deconstructing the symptom—From the intake information, the therapist knows that Pam is the IP. One of the first maneuvers in family therapy is deconstructing the symptom. One way to do so is to provide the IP with a voice in the therapy room, perhaps highlighting their competencies.

Pam(shrugs): Not really anymore.
Therapist (gently): That's okay. It's great to hear you used to enjoy it. Who would like to tell me about what brings you all in today?

Intervention: Deconstructing the symptom—The therapist provides a door opener to the family concerns, but leaves it ambiguous as to who should respond. This provides information on who will start and how. The therapist will then track these maneuvers. Further, the statement of "all" begins seeding the idea that this is a family rather than an individual problem.

Fran:	Pam's barely eating. We try to get her to sit down at meals, but it's a struggle every time.
Murray:	She says she's not hungry or already ate. But we know she's losing more weight. It's terrifying.
Therapist:	Ok. So, Fran and Murray, you both are concerned about Pam's weight. You are trying to get her to eat and are finding that it then becomes a conflict.

Intervention: Tracking—The therapist gathers information about the presenting problem while maintaining neutrality. Begins identifying interaction patterns.

Therapist:	Pam, how is it for you when they bring this up?

Intervention: Reframing—Begins shifting the problem from being "Pam's" to a family dynamic issue. The therapist recognizes how family involvement may maintain the problem, albeit unintentionally.

Pam:	They make such a big deal out of it. It's always about food or weight. I just want them to stop watching me all the time.
Therapist:	So it sounds like the focus on your eating feels overwhelming and maybe even controlling at times?
Pam:	*(nods)*
Therapist:	Can you talk to your parents about this?

Intervention: Enactment—Therapist invites family to demonstrate interactions in session, providing data about their patterns and structure. The therapist has issued a challenge to Pam to become more competent by initiating a conversation with them. They don't know whether Pam will be able to stand up to them. If not, the therapist can join her to engage in unbalancing some time later in the session.

Fran:	I made pasta. I told Pam to come to the table. She said she wasn't hungry.
Murray:	I said she had to eat. She yelled, then went to her room.
Fran:	Then we just ate with the boys. Quietly.
Therapist:	So, Oliver and George, what's it like for you when your parents and Pam get into this sort of argument?
Oliver (quietly):	It's kind of normal now.
George:	Yeah, it's weird if she actually eats with us.

Therapist: That's really helpful. It seems like dinner has become a tense time, not just for Pam, but for all of you. I'm wondering, how do the three of you—Oliver, George, and Pam—get along outside of meals?

Intervention: Tracking and Mapping Subsystems—The therapist gathers data about sibling dynamics, disengagement, or possible parentification. Also notes accommodation to dysfunction (siblings normalizing Pam's isolation). Exploring subsystems—the therapist assesses the dynamics within the sibling subsystem.

Pam: They treat me like a freak.
Oliver: That's not true.
George (mumbling): You're always mad.
Therapist: It sounds like Pam is feeling a little isolated, maybe even misunderstood. I'm hearing her say that she feels watched and judged. And I'm also hearing from the rest of you that it's hard to know what to do or say. Pam, how old are you?

Intervention: Unbalancing—Therapist momentarily aligns with Pam to shift the existing structure and give her more voice/power within the system.

Pam: 17.
Therapist: Ok. And how old do your parents think you are?
Pam: I'm not sure I know what you mean?
Therapist: Sometimes, in our heads, we treat people a different age than they are. How old do your parents treat you?

Intervention: Intensity, Unwrapping Identities—One means of bringing the family life cycle into the session is to highlight how the family is stuck at the previous stage. This is a family that is soon to launch a child yet they behave many times in ways of a family with early adolescents. The therapist begins creating a story about age. If the parents treat Pam as 12 or 13, they will be more on top of her. As she gets older, to her current age of 17, she will be treated in ways that help create more autonomy.

Pam: Maybe twelve or thirteen.
Therapist: Fran, what are your thoughts on that? That you've been a very good mother for a young adolescent but that there may be some difficulties in that same type of parenting for an older adolescent?

Intervention: Stroke and Kick—The therapist presents a stroke and kick to the mother. They are seeding the idea that mother's overinvolvement with her daughter was previously beneficial, but not at the current stage of the family.

Fran: I treat her as seventeen. I don't know what she's talking about.

Therapist: I'm just getting to know you, and Pam is saying she gets treated much younger than she is. Can you switch seats with Oliver [who was sitting between Pam and Fran] so that the two of you could discuss this?

Intervention: Unbalancing, Increasing Intensity, Boundary Making—One of the visual hallmarks of SFT is having people shift their seating position. This technique is done to increase the intensity in the room and to delineate boundaries. However, the therapist knows that because of the enmeshment between Pam and Fran, at some point in the session, they will need to decrease the mother and daughter's proximity to one another. This will come by connecting Pam to her brothers in the sibling subsystem, possibly also to her father, and connecting Fran to Murray in the spousal subsystem.

Fran: Pam, why are you saying that? I don't treat you as a baby.

Pam: Not as a baby. But not as an adult. I am just about eighteen.

Murray: Then maybe you should start acting like it.

Therapist: Murray, hold on a second. The women were having a perfectly good conversation. Pam, how often does this happen, that one parent begins telling you something and then you feel ganged up on?

Intervention: Blocking, Tracking Patterns—The therapist engages in blocking, trying to stop a pattern; in this case, of mother and father entering a coalition against the daughter. Their coalition will make it harder for the daughter to establish independence.

Therapist: Murray and Fran, do you two ever talk privately about how to handle these moments with Pam?

Murray: We try, but we usually just end up disagreeing.

Fran: He thinks I'm too soft, and I think he's too harsh.

Therapist: That's important—it sounds like your approaches are different, and that may make it harder to present a united front. One thing we can work on is strengthening your partnership as parents so that Pam doesn't get caught in the middle.

Intervention: Boundary Making—Therapist identifies blurred or conflicted boundaries in the parental subsystem and begins work to realign them.

Fran(softly): I don't want to upset her more.

Murray: But if we don't push her, she could die.

Therapist: That's a painful and critical dilemma. It shows how deeply you both care—even if your strategies differ. Part of our work will be helping you two come together in a way that supports Pam but also protects her. I also want us to think about how everyone in this family plays a role—not in a blaming way, but in the sense that each relationship affects the others. What happens to one member affects the whole system. What about with the boys? Any concerns about them?

Intervention: Reframing, Restructuring—Therapist reframes their differences as care-driven and begins the work of strengthening the parental hierarchy and alliance. Relational Reframe—SFT sees symptoms as embedded in dysfunctional structures, not individual pathology.

Murray: None at all. They get good grades. They're nice and respectful.
Therapist: Why? I'm surprised.

Intervention: Intensity—Therapist uses humor to challenge the notion that Pam is the only one who is or can be a problem in this family.

Murray: Because they listen when we tell them things.
Therapist: Oliver, I'm going to say something that your parents won't like, but your sister will appreciate. It might help her if you start to do a little mischief. That way, they can focus on you a bit and don't have to focus so much on your sister.
Oliver: I don't like getting into trouble.
Therapist: Don't you want to help your sister? Aren't you on her side?
Oliver: She should listen more to mom and dad. And she should be nicer to me and George.
Therapist: So you tend to take mom and dad's side? That doesn't seem right. Your mom has your dad. Shouldn't your sister have you to support her?

Intervention: Intensity, Joining, Boundary Making—From a close position, the therapist uses humor to try to help solidify the sibling and parental subsystems. Pam feels fairly alone in the family. The therapist attempts to increase her belonging by connecting her with her siblings. This will also begin to shift the diffuse boundary between Pam and Fran to clearer.

Oliver: I don't know.
Therapist: Pam, talk with your brother about how you two would like to have your relationship.

Intervention: Enactment, Boundary Making—The therapist gets the two oldest siblings to begin talking with one another. Whereas in the past they have mainly ignored one another, the therapist provides a space for them to have a different type of conversation.

Pam: Well, Oliver doesn't seem to want me around him. He prefers George.

Therapist: Tell that to Oliver. I'm listening. [*Therapist then looks at their left foot. Brother and sister talk about how they don't want to have conflict with one another.*] Okay. Now, can you include George in this conversation? [*The three siblings begin talking*]

Intervention: Intensity, Distant Position—The therapist heightens the intensity of the enactment by taking a distant position. This helps to establish the boundary between the sibling subsystem and outside systems (in this case the therapist). Further, brother and sister have likely learned to quickly disengage from one another. The intensity of the situation is increased by prolonging engagement between two people who do not interact much with one another. Given that there may have been a coalition of Oliver and George against Pam, the therapist starts smaller by having only one brother talk with Pam, the one who is closest to her in age and might perhaps have more in common. Then, after that conversation goes fairly well, the therapist brings the second brother into the enactment to expand the sibling subsystem.

Therapist: That was very nice. The three siblings were able to talk and not have the parents come into it. Pam, as you saw, there are things about being in your generation that your brothers understand. It is more difficult for people in your parents' generation to know about. They haven't learned. And especially the differences of your generation when you are a girl rather than a boy.

Intervention: Intensity, Richness, Novelty, Reframing, Competence, Deconstructing the Symptom—The therapist begins to increase intensity by pointing out beneficial process (that the sibling subsystem functioned well independently). They then introduce novelty in the reframe that there is a generation gap in this family and that Pam has special competence (knowing what it is like to be an adolescent female in today's day and age).

Therapist: Pam, your father needs your help. He knows very well how to be a father for boys. For young women, he may not quite understand how to be a father. How can you teach him to be a father for a 17-year-old woman instead of a 13-year-old girl?

Intervention: Repetition, Recruiting Family Members to Heal One Another, Deconstructing the Symptom, Novelty—Here, the therapist recruits Pam to help her father. He has become the IP rather than she. Instead of being an incompetent teen, she has competence and knowledge that will be useful for her father's growth. Further, this begins to shift the rigid boundary between father and daughter that has led to disengagement toward a clear boundary, allowing mother to not be on constant alert about Pam's behaviors and eating practices. The parents' control attempts are tempered so Pam can develop more autonomous functioning in her pre-adulthood life. There is also the introduction of novelty. Rather than the parents being the only ones who can teach to the other generation, the daughter is put in a position where she can teach the older generation.

Pam: I don't know.
Therapist: You don't have to right now. This will be a process. Pam, this is important since when you are seventeen, you will eat. How can you get them to treat you like a 17 almost 18-year-old young woman?

Intervention: Repetition, Deconstructing the Symptom—The therapist ends the session with a repetition of the idea of a change in relational dynamics, using the metaphor of age. They then deconstruct the symptom by talking about how the anorexia is related to relationships.

The Therapeutic Story

At the end of the session, there has been movement from the Daniels' initial problem story that all is fine in the family except for Pam being anorexic. The therapist, through a variety of techniques and joining positions, has introduced several new ideas into the family.

1 Perhaps most prominently, the notion of age and development, the therapeutic story now includes the notion that Pam is acting and being treated younger than her age. That she is functionally 13 years old rather than her chronological age of 17.
    a That the anorexic symptoms are related to the dynamics around age treatment; that at 13, she is not fully eating, but at 17, she will eat more.
2 The therapeutic story also includes areas surrounding gender; the males and females in the house have been separated from one another.
3 Subsystems were highlighted, where the siblings were attempted to be connected.
4 The problem has shifted from within Pam to the relationships in the family.
5 The designation of Fran as the sole overseer of Pam was shifted to include Murray.
6 Pam was moved from the position of IP to have more competence, even being able to teach her father about this generation of adolescent females.

References

Aponte, H. J. (1992). Training the person of the therapist in structural Family therapy. *Journal of Marital and Family Therapy*, *18*, 269–281.

Colapinto, J. (1982). Structural family therapy. In A. M. Horne & M. M. Ohlsen (Eds.). *Family counseling and therapy* (pp. 112–140). F. E. Peacock.

Colapinto, J. (2017). Belonging. *Journal of Systemic Therapies*, *36*(4), 91–94.

Dehghani, M., & Bernards, J. (2022). The effectiveness of structural family therapy in repairing behavioral problems and improving family functioning in single-parent families in Iran. *Journal of Marital and Family Therapy*, *48*(4), 1040–1058.

Kim, J. M. (2003). Structural family therapy and its implications for the Asian American family. *The Family Journal: Counseling and Therapy for Couples and Families*, *11*(4), 388–392.

Ma, J. L., Wong, C. W., & Xia, L. L. (2020). Helping a depressed Chinese adult with high functioning autism reconnect with his family through structural family therapy. *Journal of Family Therapy*, *42*(4), 518–535.

McAdams III, C. R., Avadhanam, R., Foster, V. A., Harris, P. N., Javaheri, A., Kim, S., Kooyman, B. A., Joe, J. R., Sheffield, R. L., & Williams, A. E. (2016). The viability of structural family therapy in the twenty-first century: An analysis of key indicators. *Contemporary Family Therapy*, *38*(3), 255–261.

Minuchin, S. (1974/2012). *Families and family therapy*. Routledge.

Minuchin, S. (1984). *Family kaleidoscope*. Harvard University Press.

Minuchin, S. (2017). Deconstructing Minuchin. *Journal of Systemic Therapies*, *36*(4), 95–97.

Minuchin, S., & Fischman, H. C. (1981). *Family therapy techniques*. Harvard University Press.

Minuchin, S., Lee, W-Y, & Simon, G. M. (2006). *Mastering family therapy: Journeys of growth and transformation* (2nd ed.). Wiley.

Minuchin, S., & Nichols, M. P. (1993). *Family healing: Tales of hope and renewal from family therapy*. The Free Press.

Minuchin, S. Nichols, M. P., & Lee, W-Y. (2007). *Assessing families and couples: From symptom to system*. Allyn & Bacon.

Minuchin, S., Reiter, M. D., Borda, C. (2021). *The craft of family therapy: Challenging certainties* (2nd ed.). Routledge.

Minuchin, S., Rosman, B. L., & Baker, L. (1978). *Psychosomatic families: Anorexia nervosa in context*. Harvard University Press.

Napoliello, A. L., & Sweet, E. S. (1992). Salvador Minuchin's structural family therapy and its application to Native Americans. *Family Therapy*, *19*(2), 155–165.

Reiter, M. D. (2016). A quick guide to case conceptualization in structural family therapy. *Journal of Systemic Therapies*, *35*(2), 25–37.

Reiter, M. D. (2017a). Salvador Minuchin, M.D.: Innovator and challenger. *Journal of Systemic Therapies*, *36*(4), 16–22.

Reiter, M. D. (2017b). Ten things I learned from Dr. Salvador Minuchin. *Journal of Systemic Therapies*, *36*(4), 46–56.

Simon, G. M. (1995). A revisionist rendering of structural family therapy. *Journal of Marital and Family Therapy*, *21*(1), 17–26.

Soto-Fulp, S., & Del Campo, R. L. (1994). Structural family therapy with Mexican-American family systems. *Contemporary Family Therapy: An International Journal*, *16*(5), 349–362.

Williams, N. D., Foye, A., & Lewis, F. (2016). Applying structural family therapy in the changing context of the modern African American single mother. *Journal of Feminist Family Therapy*, *28*(1).
Yaccarino, M. E. (1993). Using Minuchin's structural family therapy techniques with Italian-American-families. *Contemporary Family Therapy*, *15*(6), 459–466.
Zafra, J. (2016). The use of structural family therapy with a Latino family: A case study. *Journal of Systemic Therapies*, *35*(4), 11–21.

13 Cognitive-Behavioral Family Therapy

Woochul Park

Cognitive-behavioral family therapy (CBFT) arose from the integration of the behavioral tradition (B. F. Skinner) and the cognitive tradition (Aaron Beck). Building on this foundation, Norman Epstein, Frank Dattilio, and Donald Baucom extended cognitive-behavioral therapy to couples and families, systematizing interventions for behavior, cognition, and emotion (Baucom & Lester, 1986; Dattilio & Padesky, 1990; Epstein, 1982). Similarly, Patterson applied operant conditioning to parent training (Patterson & Forgatch, 1987). CBFT assumes that the cognitions, behaviors, and emotions of family members are not linear but instead interact in reciprocal, circular ways of influence. In practice, these three domains may be addressed separately or integrated within assessment and intervention with the family system.

The Therapeutic Story of Problem Formation

CBFT holds that family problems stem from maladaptive patterns across cognition, behavior, and emotion that reciprocally influence one another (Epstein & Baucom, 2002; Epstein & Dattilio, 2020). Behaviorally, stressed families often fail to share deeper thoughts and feelings—reducing intimacy—and struggle with decision-making, which impedes conflict resolution. In this climate, macro patterns such as mutual attack or demand–withdraw frequently emerge, compounding stress. Parent–child relationships often involve ineffective practices, including coercive discipline by parents and oppositional actions of children. Cognitively, distressed families display distorted information processing and rigid beliefs that block adaptation. Emotionally, members may avoid or suppress feelings or regulate them poorly (e.g., through outbursts). These processes interact within the family system, amplifying one another. Pam's family demonstrates these maladaptive patterns across multiple members; their patterned, entrenched exchanges sustain the difficulties and intensify Pam's symptoms.

DOI: 10.4324/9781003668510-13

Behaviors

Communication and Problem-Solving

There are two major forms of family communication (Epstein & Baucom, 2002). One is everyday conversation, in which members share daily experiences, thoughts, and feelings. In distressed families, however, even when such talk occurs, people often fail to express the deeper thoughts and emotions connected to positive and upsetting events. This lack of depth hinders mutual understanding, and the resulting misunderstandings weaken family intimacy. The erosion of intimacy, in turn, undermines relationship satisfaction within the family.

Beyond sharing accounts of their lives and inner experiences, members of families must also make effective decisions about issues that arise both inside and outside the home. When problem-solving abilities are weak, families not only cope poorly with the many stressors of the life cycle, but the communication process itself can also become a source of hurt. In addition, the family's sense of collective efficacy—as a team—deteriorates.

Ineffective communication skills may stem from patterns in the adults' families of origin or from those socially learned in the broader ecological environment. During development, family members may have had limited opportunities to share thoughts and emotions in depth or to observe effective ways of resolving problems and conflicts. As a result, they may lack the knowledge needed for effective everyday conversation and problem-solving. Alternatively, even if they possess such knowledge, insufficient practice may prevent it from becoming habitual. Moreover, despite having relevant behavioral communication skills, strong negative cognitive or emotional responses can still disrupt effective communication.

Pam's family communicates, but they neither adequately express nor listen to one another's thoughts and feelings. Consequently, they fail to achieve deeper levels of mutual understanding and intimacy. Pam began struggling with her eating habits at age 14, but kept them hidden for a year. Early warning signs of an eating disorder—such as appearance-related stress and/or peer-related stress—may already have been present, yet there is little evidence that she ever shared these concerns with her family. Even if she did, Fran may not have listened attentively, empathized, or offered support, leading Pam to remain silent thereafter. This pattern applies not only to her eating disorder but also to her academic performance. Although her parents express concern about her declining grades, there has been no genuine communication about the reasons behind them.

Excess of Negative Interactions and Absence of Positive Interactions

In addition to communication behaviors, families engage in various other forms of interaction. These include instrumental behaviors (e.g., conducting household chores) as well as expressive and emotional behaviors that influence others' feelings (e.g., giving gifts, expressing affection). Under stress, families tend to exhibit more negative behaviors and fewer positive ones. Although negative and positive exchanges are interrelated, they are also partly independent and can occur together. Therefore, effective intervention requires both increasing the frequency and intensity of positive family behaviors while reducing those of negative behaviors. In Pam's family, there appears to be a marked absence of positive behaviors, particularly those that convey affection and care.

Epstein and Dattilio (2020) emphasize the importance of addressing behavioral patterns at the macro level. Core family patterns often emerge in domains such as power and control, relational investment, intimacy-building, social support, and boundary maintenance. Negative cyclical patterns that undermine the fulfillment of family members' needs—such as mutual attack, demand–withdraw, and mutual avoidance—are therefore a central focus. According to Epstein and Baucom (2002), effectively addressing broader dimensions of family patterns (e.g., power) first requires reducing the influence of these negative cyclical patterns.

In Pam's family, behaviors that foster intimacy and support are largely absent, and the boundary between mother and daughter is diffuse—characterized by excessive involvement and influence between them—thereby weakening the parental hierarchy. As a result, emotions such as intimacy, social support, autonomy, and respect are not adequately cultivated. In response to these unmet needs, the mother–daughter dyad has fallen into a demand–withdraw cycle: the mother persistently presses for behavioral change, while the daughter responds with defensiveness and increasing emotional withdrawal from the relationship.

Ineffective Discipline

Parents in families under stress often adopt disciplinary strategies that focus on severe punishment for problematic behaviors rather than attending to children's prosocial behaviors and providing positive reinforcement. As a result, they fall into a vicious cycle in which problem behaviors and ineffective discipline escalate together (Forgatch & Patterson, 1987). For example, corporal punishment may produce immediate compliance but, in the long term, exacerbates children's problem behaviors (Gershoff, 2002). Harsh disciplinary practices such as yelling, humiliation, or psychological aggression similarly increase problem behaviors over time. Moreover, when such harsh or coercive strategies are used, children may become unresponsive to lower-intensity disciplinary approaches (Patterson & Forgatch, 1987). Conversely, permissive parenting that fails to establish clear limits also does not succeed in reducing problem behaviors.

CBFT identifies and modifies parental behaviors that influence children's problems. It primarily emphasizes the use of behavioral reinforcement systems, such as incentive charts and systematic rewards, to strengthen positive child behaviors rather than merely eliminate negative ones. Rewards may take many forms—social, tangible, or activity-based—and should be tailored to the child's needs. By focusing on positive reinforcement, families can foster a more supportive emotional climate and restore attachment bonds between parent and child. Once this foundation is established, strategies such as privilege removal or time-outs can be applied effectively to reduce problematic behaviors. At the same time, parents are educated and trained to provide clear and effective instructions and explanations.

Pam's family, however, relies more on punishment than on positive reinforcement to modify her behavior. Her mother pressures Pam to eat and demands that she work hard to maintain her grades; yet no reward system is in place to support her eating habits or studying.

Cognitions

Event-Related Cognitions

Members of distressed families often experience cognitive distortions in their appraisals of specific events. **Cognitive distortion** refers to information-processing errors that are not objective or realistic, which become sources of stress and conflict in relationships. Three common types of these distortions occur in selective attention, negative attributions, and negative expectancies (Baucom & Epstein, 1990; Epstein & Baucom, 2002). **Selective attention** refers to the tendency to notice only certain aspects of another person's behavior or a given situation. Distressed families, in particular, tend to focus more on the negative behaviors of other members than on their positive behaviors. **Attributions** refer to how family members infer the causes of one another's behaviors. Distressed members often attribute others' negative behaviors to dispositional flaws, negative intentions (e.g., selfish motives), or lack of love. In contrast, they are more likely to attribute other members' positive behaviors to external or situational factors such as chance. When negative behaviors are attributed to hostile intentions, strong emotional reactions such as anger are more likely to arise. **Expectancies**, like attributions, involve inferences—specifically, predicting how another person will respond in a particular situation. For example, distressed members may avoid authentic communication because of expectancies that honest interactions will lead to catastrophic outcomes from the recipients.

The Daniels family, as their negative emotions and cognitions accumulate, may selectively perceive only one another's negative behaviors while failing to recognize positive ones. Although Pam likely demonstrates many competencies beyond her eating behaviors and academic performance, the family's focus tends to remain confined to these two domains. Pam, in turn, is also likely to focus primarily on her mother's negative behaviors. During adolescence, Pam interprets her mother's repeated urging to eat not as expressions of concern for her health and social adjustment, but rather as attempts to control her that undermine her autonomy. Conversely, her mother tends to attribute Pam's resistance to eating not to fear or confusion, but to defiance and hostility toward her as a parent. Pam also interprets her father's closeness with her brothers as a sign of her own worthlessness and a lack of love from him. Furthermore, the family as a whole harbors the expectancy that openly sharing their inner experiences will lead to negative responses, which prevents them from engaging in genuine communication.

Relationship Beliefs

Difficulties in family relationships can be rooted in beliefs about relationships (Eidelson & Epstein, 1982). General relational beliefs include both assumptions and standards (Baucom & Epstein, 1990; Epstein & Baucom, 2002). **Standards** refer to beliefs about what family relationships should look like. Rigid or unrealistic standards can contribute to unhappiness among members of a family (Baucom et al., 1996). **Assumptions**, on the other hand, refer to beliefs about what family relationships are actually like. Distressed families tend to carry many negative assumptions, which in turn influence other cognitive processes—such as attributional style or selective attention—in a negative direction.

These standards and assumptions form core components of cognitive structures, or schemas. A **schema** refers to "the basic assumptions that an individual has internalized over time, relatively stable, about how the world operates and one's place in it" (Epstein et al., 1988, p. 13). Through accumulated interactions, family members may also develop shared beliefs about family relationships, culture, or society, which are referred to as **family schemas** (Dattilio, 2005, 2010). Particularly, schemas developed during one's experience in one's family of origin are often transmitted to the next generation; these are called **transgenerational schemas**. Couples bring into their marriage the family schemas formed in their families of origin, and these schemas are reflected not only in their marital interactions but also in child-rearing practices.

Thus, the Daniels family holds a standard that it is acceptable for family members to be deeply involved in one another's lives. Both Murray and Fran married through their parents' arrangement, and in Murray's case, he inherited the family business as the third-generation owner. Fran had previously served as caretaker for her younger sibling. Based on their shared family schema, both partners considered it natural for parents to be closely involved in their children's careers, romantic relationships, and social lives. Accordingly, Fran is heavily involved in her daughter's eating and academic performance.

Another family assumption is that "men and women occupy separate spheres, and this division of roles within family life is natural." Murray fulfills his role as a provider but remains largely absent from domestic and emotional caregiving, instead focusing on interactions with his sons. Fran, by contrast, assumes primary responsibility for managing her daughter.

Automatic Thoughts

Automatic thoughts refer to fleeting cognitions that pass through our minds and are difficult to detect unless we deliberately pay attention to them. Because these thoughts are not easily recognized, they often contain irrational or dysfunctional elements. Although these cognitive distortions are common, they tend to occur more frequently in distressed families. Several types of these errors have been commonly observed and categorized as follows (Dattilio & Epstein, 2016).

- Arbitrary Inference: Drawing conclusions without sufficient evidence.
- Mind Reading: Believing that one knows another person's feelings and thoughts without direct communication.
- Selective Abstraction: Focusing only on a particular detail when receiving information while ignoring other important information.
- Overgeneralization: Broadly applying a specific incident from one context to many other situations.
- Magnification: Judging an event as more important than it actually is.
- Minimization: Judging an event as less important than it actually is.
- Personalization: Concluding that external events are related to or caused by oneself without sufficient evidence.
- Dichotomous Thinking (Black-and-White Thinking): Classifying experiences into mutually exclusive, extreme categories.
- Labeling: Attaching a fixed label to oneself or others based on a specific past experience.
- Catastrophizing: Predicting extreme negative outcomes in the future without adequate evidence.
- Emotional Reasoning: Concluding based on vague feelings rather than objective evidence.

Cognitive distortions are evident in the Daniels family. For instance, Pam may engage in dichotomous thinking—such as seeing her father spend time with her siblings and concluding, "My dad doesn't love me at all." Fran, on the other hand, may hold a catastrophic belief that if Pam does not eat at a "normal level," she will die, which leads her to pressure and criticize Pam in an effort to make her eat.

Emotions

Deficits and Excesses in Experiencing and Expressing Emotions

Epstein and Baucom (2002) distinguish between individuals whose emotional experience and expression are minimized or intensified. Individuals who avoid emotional experience and suppress emotional expression tend not to monitor or analyze their emotions, inhibiting their expression; at times, however, they may suddenly and destructively display emotions. While such individuals may benefit in the short term by avoiding discomfort through suppression and avoidance of negative emotions, in the long run, they are likely to encounter relational difficulties by failing to address important issues within the family.

By contrast, some individuals experience negative emotions with very high frequency and intensity and struggle to regulate them. These individuals may express strong emotions in pursuit of their needs, but such expression can provoke aggressive responses from other family members or lead to withdrawal, thereby making it more difficult to have their needs met.

The Daniels family exhibits a high degree of chronic and entrenched negative emotions. The most commonly observed emotions are anxiety, depression, and anger. Pam and Fran experience emotions intensely and exaggeratedly express them. In contrast, Murray tends to avoid or suppress emotional experience and rarely reveals his feelings. The younger brothers, having primarily learned their roles by modeling their father, may likewise experience somewhat suppressed emotional expression.

Interaction of Behavioral, Cognitive, and Emotional Factors

CBFT has advanced beyond a linear interpersonal model—in which cognition precedes behavior and emotional responses—to a circular causal model, in which cognition, behavior, and emotion exert complex reciprocal influences (Dattilio & Epstein, 2021). For example, when individuals chronically experience negative emotions, they may primarily perceive the negative aspects of other family members while failing to notice or reciprocate to their positive aspects with positive behaviors. This demonstrates how emotion shapes both cognition and behavioral responses. As a result, distress-prone families may become trapped in a vicious cycle of negative behavior, cognition, and emotion.

Pam experiences anxiety, depression, and anger, and these negative emotions trigger **emotional reasoning errors**, leading her to interpret other family members' behaviors negatively and respond with negative behaviors herself. These behaviors, in turn, elicit negative reactions from other family members, strengthening Pam's negative inferences (e.g., "My mother just wants to control me") and further intensifying her anger, depression, and other negative emotions.

Diversity Conceptualization

Cultural sensitivity is essential in applying CBFT. Because CBFT was originally developed within Western cultural traditions, therapists must carefully consider cultural differences when applying it in other contexts (Epstein et al., 2012). For instance, in collectivist cultures such as Korea, the cultural norm of ishin-jeon-shim (literally, "communicating through the heart without words") emphasizes understanding one another without explicit verbal expression. As a result, a family schema may develop in which spouses are expected to accurately perceive and meet each other's needs and emotions without direct communication. Within this cultural context, CBFT's emphasis on open and direct communication may feel unfamiliar or uncomfortable to clients. Therapists should therefore explore the cultural beliefs of each family in advance.

When approached with sensitivity, CBFT's communication training can provide Korean clients with a safe and constructive way to express themselves. Such expression not only enables the sharing of thoughts and feelings but also fosters respect for others' perspectives, thereby strengthening relationships (Epstein & Park, 2021). Similarly, Chinese families who place a high value on face may feel uncomfortable engaging in cognitive restructuring in front of other family members, as they may perceive it as losing face (Epstein et al., 2012). In such cases, it may be helpful to emphasize the universality of cognitive distortions or to use individual sessions to allow clients to preserve face.

Beyond national culture, therapists must also recognize the diversity of subcultures within a given society, shaped by factors such as class, ethnicity, religion, region, education, gender identity, disability, and others (Falicov, 1995). Thus, attention should extend not only to the general cultural characteristics of a country but also to the specific subcultural contexts of individual families. Moreover, cultural variation may exist even among members of the same family. When parents come from different sociocultural backgrounds, it may be helpful for the therapist not only to remain mindful of these differences but also to gently support the parents in developing a deeper appreciation of each other's cultural perspectives. In some cases, this very process of fostering mutual understanding can itself become an important part of the therapeutic work.

In particular, when applying structured techniques in CBFT, using them too rigidly without regard to cultural differences may reduce their effectiveness. It is therefore important for therapists to stand alongside families within their cultural context, engage in thoughtful dialogue, and collaboratively adjust the direction of interventions so that families can gradually cultivate new relational patterns aligned with their cultural values.

The Therapeutic Story of Problem Resolution

CBFT therapists set goals in ways that strengthen the therapeutic alliance with their clients through a collaborative process (Epstein & Falconier, 2024). In the early stages of therapy, the therapist reframes clients' concerns and complaints as expressions of their desire for change. When establishing goals, priority is given to identifying macro-level goals that address core relational concerns. For instance, the therapist helps the Daniels family identify and articulate macro-level goals, such as enhancing family intimacy. Then, throughout therapy, the therapist reviews progress with the family, complimenting them when signs of improvement are observed. However, initial goals are rarely static. As therapy unfolds, the therapist may observe new and important family patterns, and family members themselves may generate additional goals as their self-understanding deepens. Members of the Daniels family may come to recognize that greater intimacy can be fostered when they learn to accept one another as they are, while maintaining clear interpersonal boundaries. Thus, therapists must maintain a collaborative stance and remain flexible in adapting treatment goals to fit the therapeutic context.

CBFT Education

CBFT emphasizes a collaborative relationship with clients, ensuring that they clearly understand the treatment model and intervention methods being applied (Dattilio & Epstein, 2016). To this end, therapists may provide psychoeducation during sessions or recommend relevant books and materials for clients to read. These educational approaches help clients strengthen their sense of responsibility for their own behaviors, cognitions, and emotions. Therapists also inform clients in advance that the therapy process will be structured around agreed-upon goals and explain the specific behavioral guidelines and rules that clients are expected to follow both during and outside of sessions, such as honoring each person's right to have adequate time to express personal values and beliefs.

Interventions Modifying Behaviors

Behavioral interventions address both expressive and instrumental behaviors. **Expressive behaviors** convey affection and care (e.g., verbal reassurance, attentive listening, physical warmth), whereas **instrumental behaviors** involve task-oriented actions that maintain family functioning (e.g., doing chores, managing schedules). Epstein and Baucom (2002) distinguished between **guided behavior change**, which does not involve technical components, and **skills-based interventions**, which rely on technical training.

Guided Behavior Change

In guided behavior change, families, in collaboration with the therapist, may devise their own directions for behavior change, while the therapist may also suggest specific behavioral modifications (Dattilio & Epstein, 2021). The degree of structure for these new behavioral tasks is determined according to the family's preferences. Guided behavior change is often introduced early in treatment to help shift the overall emotional tone of the relationship.

Families often seek therapy when negative behaviors outweigh positive ones. Thus, increasing positive behaviors and reducing negative ones is essential to altering the overall emotional tone. Epstein and Baucom (2002) distinguish between **primary distress**, which occurs when core needs (e.g., intimacy) are unmet, and **secondary distress**, which arises when family members attempt to cope with the primary distress by escalating negative behaviors and reducing positive ones. Secondary distress is often intensified by patterned dynamics, such as demand–withdraw cycles. Guided behavior change primarily targets reducing this secondary distress, thereby establishing a stable foundation for addressing the more challenging issues of primary distress.

Pam's weight has dropped significantly over the past six months. This weight loss may be linked to the escalation of mother–daughter conflict over the past year. In other words, as the demand–withdraw pattern intensified, secondary distress increased. The therapist's initial focus is to reduce family tension and shift the overall atmosphere in a positive direction by guiding the family to generate and increase positive behaviors. The therapist also encourages them to reflect on and decrease behaviors that exacerbate conflict. In this process, the therapist repeatedly emphasizes the demand–withdraw pattern—primarily evident in the mother–daughter relationship but also present in the marital relationship—so that the family becomes more aware of it. Once family members begin to recognize these cyclical causal patterns, the therapist supports them in discussing and implementing concrete behavioral changes to weaken the demand–withdraw pattern.

Once secondary distress subsides and the overall family atmosphere improves, therapy shifts its focus to addressing unmet needs in domains such as intimacy, social support, and boundaries that allow space for each person's autonomous functioning. At this stage, the goal is not only to encourage general "positive" efforts but also to help family members develop concrete strategies for meeting one another's needs (Epstein & Baucom, 2002). In the Daniels family, issues related to intimacy, social support, and boundaries are particularly salient—for example, clarifying boundaries between mother and daughter and fostering greater intimacy between father and daughter. Because intimacy and social support represent general weaknesses in this family, the therapist discusses specific behavioral changes to address these concerns and encourages their implementation.

Communication Training

A question used to assess family-discussion patterns is, "How well would you say you, as an individual, share your thoughts and feelings and listen while the other person talks?" (Epstein & Baucom, 2002, p. 327). This directs clients to increase attention to their own communication behavior. Therapists then provide guidelines for effective communication which is simple, so as not to overwhelm clients. When teaching the guidelines, therapists keep the process conversational and concise, preventing it from becoming a lengthy lecture or a didactic monologue.

There are several key guidelines to facilitate effective family discussions (Epstein et al., 2018):

a Emphasize subjectivity.
b Express emotions openly.
c Share not only descriptions of situations but also feelings toward other family members.
d When expressing negative emotions, also include positive feelings.

e Be concrete and specific about both emotions and thoughts.
f Keep statements as brief and concise as possible.
g Express thoughts and feelings at an appropriate time and in an appropriate manner.

Among these, the guidelines for emotional expression are particularly emphasized. Emotions often reveal the essence of a person's experience and play a central role in fostering intimacy among family members.

Listeners, in turn, are encouraged to demonstrate attentiveness nonverbally and, once the speaker has finished, provide a reflective summary of the speaker's feelings, needs, and thoughts. They should avoid inserting their own thoughts or rushing into problem-solving. Importantly, reflection should not be formulaic but practiced in a way that feels natural.

The Daniels family lacks conversations in which emotions and thoughts are expressed at a deeper level. Pam's symptoms began at age 14, but she kept them hidden. Her anorexia may have been related to increased appearance-related dissatisfaction and stress, which likely began even before the age of 14, but the family neither noticed nor discussed it.

The therapist begins by training the family to engage in conversations on positive topics, encouraging them to express emotions and offer reflections. Once they practice listening and speaking skills in the context of less severe issues, the therapist gradually guides them to address more central concerns in ways that are both effective and conducive to fostering intimacy. In this process, if difficulties that impede the development of communication skills (e.g., intense emotions, interfering beliefs) are identified, the therapist should also address them (Dattilio & Padesky, 1990).

The guidelines for decision-making conversations follow a sequence:

a Clearly and explicitly state the issue.
b Clarify why the issue is important and specify your needs.
c Discuss possible solutions that reflect the needs of all family members.
d Decide on a solution that is both realistic and mutually agreeable.
e Implement the solution for a trial period and make revisions as needed.

Compared to guided behavior change, decision-making or problem-solving conversations are often used for more complex issues. When it is determined that adolescent children should be included in decision-making, families are encouraged to involve them, and the therapist coaches the family through problem-solving meetings during sessions (Forgatch & Patterson, 1987).

In the Daniels family, key issues include intimacy, boundaries, social support, hierarchy, trust, and eating behaviors. The therapist may facilitate family decision-making meetings that involve the adolescent children on relevant topics. Over time, more sensitive concerns—such as Pam's eating behavior—may also be addressed. In such cases, the principle of **shaping** can be applied to guide gradual changes in eating behavior, beginning with very small steps (e.g., reinforcing Pam simply for sitting at the dining table for 10 minutes at mealtimes) and progressively reinforcing more substantial changes until higher-level goals are achieved (Patterson & Forgatch, 1987). Emphasizing these small, gradual changes by incorporating Pam's opinions into family decisions through regular family decision-making meetings may help her experience a stronger sense of self-control and self-efficacy.

When training families in these conversations, the therapist may focus either on the dialogue process itself or on its content (Epstein & Baucom, 2002). When the emphasis is on training, the therapist frequently pauses the family conversation to reinforce effective communication and to coach members when adjustments are needed. Once a sufficient level of skill has been reached, however, the therapist can shift more flexibly to the conversation's content. In this phase, the therapist interrupts less often, allowing the family's emotional flow to continue while important relational themes and issues are addressed. At this stage, the dialogue can naturally transition into cognitive interventions or guided behavior change as appropriate.

Parenting

For discipline to be consistent, contingency arrangements or contracts to guide parents' use of consequences for child actions commonly are devised (Alexander & Parsons, 1973). In particular, negative parent–child interactions are reorganized around the use of positive reinforcement (Patterson & Forgatch, 1987). Although allowances often serve as effective reinforcers for adolescents, many parents balk at using money as a reward; therefore, they are encouraged to define desired behaviors clearly and provide alternative non-monetary rewards—privileges such as smartphone use or time with friends.

When children engage in behaviors that parents want to reduce or eliminate, or fail to comply with instructions, parents may reduce privileges. At the same time, parents should be educated about ineffective strategies (e.g., lecturing) that may actually exacerbate children's problem behaviors. Effective coparenting also requires parents to align their practices by agreeing on target behaviors and strategies for intervention (Epstein & Falconier, 2024).

In the Daniels family, discipline has been characterized by coercion, with little attention to positive reinforcement. The family, therefore, needs to identify meaningful rewards (e.g., preferred activities) and use them to encourage positive behavior change. In addition, Fran's anxious directive—"Eat"—can be collaboratively reframed into calmer and more effective instructions.

When punishment is necessary, it should be applied consistently and without emotional reactivity on the parents' part (which also provides a model of emotion regulation for the child).

Finally, decisions about discipline should be allocated appropriately—some determined by the parental dyad, others addressed in whole-family decision-making meetings. From a coparenting perspective, the therapist helps the couple assess whether they are approaching disciplinary issues as a unified team, and explore any factors that may be interfering with their collaboration (e.g., competition to be the more competent parent).

Interventions for Modifying Cognitions

When conducting cognitive interventions with families, the therapist's stance is of primary importance (Epstein & Baucom, 2002). In conjoint sessions, family members may perceive feedback from the therapist regarding their cognitive distortions as criticism in front of others, and may respond defensively rather than being open to re-evaluating their thinking. Therefore, the therapist must first establish a safe atmosphere and demonstrate empathy for clients' cognitions and their developmental backgrounds.

The therapist should then emphasize that, regardless of whether a thought is negative or positive, the central task is examining whether it corresponds with reality. The therapist should also stress that human thinking is inherently subjective, vulnerable to distortion, and that such distortions are normative.

Finally, feedback from other family members, when it is offered constructively, can broaden an individual's perspective. The therapist should facilitate the constructive delivery of feedback by family members and encourage the individual's open and objective reception of it. If, despite these efforts, a particular family member remains highly defensive, the therapist may schedule individual sessions. In such cases, session allocation should be distributed evenly among family members to maintain therapeutic alliance and balance.

Psychoeducation

Therapists may provide psychoeducation on the role of cognition in relationships, the types of cognitions, the principles of cognitive restructuring, and the various forms of cognitive distortions (Epstein & Dattilio, 2020; Epstein & Falconier, 2024). Through this process, families gain a clearer understanding of the principles of cognitive therapy, which helps them recognize that examining one's thoughts is a constructive process rather than an indication of personal failure, and thereby alleviates defensive reactions. Importantly, this educational process should not take the form of a formal didactic lecture but be conducted in a conversational and interactive format with family members.

Cognitive Interventions

A principle of cognitive interventions is that cognitive change does not come solely from directly targeting thoughts; it can also emerge from changes in behavior and emotion (Epstein & Baucom, 2002). Accordingly, cognitive interventions encompass both techniques that directly modify thinking and behavioral–affective methods that promote cognitive change through shifts in behavior and emotion.

Within cognitive techniques, clients are first given a concise introduction to the concept of automatic thoughts and the different types of cognitive distortions, enabling them to identify such distortions in their own thinking.

This process is most effective when conducted in a light and engaging manner, encouraging family members to share personal examples of distortions they have experienced. The overarching goal is to help them recognize that such distortions are common and not inherently pathological (Dattilio, 2010).

In cases like the Daniels family, where Pam is the identified patient, the therapist needs to prevent the family from overfocusing on Pam's cognitive distortions and instead foster a balanced exploration of how other members' distorted thinking has negatively influenced their emotions and behavior.

To help clients recognize automatic thoughts and cognitive distortions and develop more adaptive thinking, therapists can employ structured tools (e.g., the Dysfunctional Thought Record), which are especially useful in the early stages of treatment (Dattilio, 2010). Therapists often assign thought records as homework and review them during sessions, guiding family members to gradually revise their beliefs. Alternatively, more naturalistic methods—such as Socratic questioning—can be used during sessions. **Socratic questioning** involves asking the client questions that prompt them to reflect on the logic underlying a particular cognition, thereby challenging the validity of family members' in-the-moment thinking and schemas (Epstein & Baucom, 2002; Epstein et al., 2018).

Frequently used Socratic questions include (Dattilio & Epstein, 2016):

- From your past experiences or the events occurring recently in your family, what evidence exists that supports this thought? How could you get some additional information to help you judge whether your thought is accurate?
- What might be an alternative explanation for your family member's behavior? What else might have led that person to behave that way?
- We have reviewed several types of cognitive distortions that can influence a person's views of other family members and can contribute to getting upset with them. Which cognitive distortions, if any, can you see in the automatic thoughts you had about…?

Fran experiences intense fear about Pam's anorexia. This fear leads to controlling and anxious responses to her daughter's eating behaviors, which in turn strengthen the demand–withdraw pattern between them. Therefore, it is crucial to guide Fran in examining the validity of her negative expectancies. For instance, when Fran thinks, "If Pam does not eat sufficiently right now, she will certainly die within a few months," therapy focuses on testing how reasonable that prediction is. Through a process of reviewing Pam's chronic restricted eating over the past couple of years and her gradual weight loss, Fran can recognize that the severity of her expectancy reflects catastrophizing, which exacerbates the pressure she puts on Pam, and she can begin to revise it into a more rational expectancy (clearly a problematic eating pattern by Pam but not a crisis at present). Given that Fran suddenly lost her father to a heart attack, she may also harbor heightened fears of sudden death, making it necessary to explore the formative background contributing to these fears.

It is important not only to evaluate whether thoughts and beliefs are valid, but also to assess their usefulness in family life (Dattilio & Epstein, 2021). Fran's expectancy that Pam might starve herself to death leads her to pressure Pam, which in turn backfires by heightening Pam's defensiveness; therefore, this way of thinking is not helpful. Such a "utility check" is particularly relevant when examining the usefulness of schemas.

In the Daniels family, a belief such as "As long as each family member fulfills their role, the family functions normally and intimacy is automatically achieved" may be at work. The therapist first explores the usefulness of this belief with the family and then collaborates to revise it into a more constructive form—for instance: "Intimacy develops through concrete, expressive behaviors, such as affection and social support, beyond merely performing material family roles."

Such schemas may surface naturally during therapy, but techniques such as the **downward arrow** can also be used to elicit them. This method involves asking questions when a family member expresses a worry, for instance: "If that worry comes true, what consequences do you think it would lead to?" This process helps uncover the core beliefs underlying the cognition.

It is also essential to explore the developmental origins of these schemas within the client's family of origin, as understanding their roots often increases openness to cognitive change. Building on this exploration, therapy then focuses on examining the usefulness of schemas that may have been appropriate in one's family of origin but are no longer adaptive in present relationships. Clients might be asked, "What are the advantages and disadvantages of maintaining this standard in your life now?" In many cases, clients come to recognize that, although the schema may have been adaptive in the past, it no longer serves them in their current relationships—allowing them to modify it more flexibly and rationally. At the same time, therapists should recognize that deeply ingrained schemas often require considerable time and effort to change (Dattilio, 2010). This is especially true for older adults, whose schemas, shaped across the lifespan, may resist complete restructuring. Therefore, therapists must remain realistic and mindful that expecting full modification of such schemas may be impractical.

In Fran's case, applying the downward arrow technique to explore the meaning of her daughter's illness surfaced the thought: "My daughter being sick means that I am a failed caretaker. Since caregiving has been central to my identity from early on, this also signifies my failure as a person." Underlying this belief was the schema, "I must always take good care of my family members." The therapist can guide Fran in examining both the validity and the utility of this thought. In Murray's case, he may have internalized from his family of origin the schema, "A father is fundamentally someone who provides for the family and guides his son, but not someone who engages in relationships or contributes to his daughter's socialization."

It is equally important to cultivate relational and systemic thinking in families. In therapy, family members often fall into the tendency of blaming one another, when the behaviors they criticize are actually products of repetitive and circular interactional patterns (Dattilio, 1998; Epstein & Baucom, 2002). The therapist helps family members recognize this by introducing the concept of circular causality and by asking questions that illuminate how these patterns are co-created. In Pam's family, the demand–withdraw pattern is especially evident in the mother–daughter relationship and, to a lesser extent, in the marital relationship. Therefore, it is essential to help the family recognize and address this pattern. An advantage in realizing the circular causal process is that both participants potentially have an opportunity to disrupt it by changing their part.

Behavioral and Affective Interventions

Some family members may respond critically to the therapist's repeated use of Socratic questioning. In such cases, the therapist can shift to guided discovery interventions, facilitating new experiences that broaden perspectives (Epstein & Baucom, 2002). **Guided discovery** often integrates emotional and behavioral methods; in other words, the therapist invites shifts in behavior and affect that can, in turn, stimulate cognitive change.

Through role plays, role reversals, communication exercises, behavioral experiments, and psychoeducation, families acquire new insights and revise existing beliefs. For example, communication training helps members move beyond adversarial positions and relate to one another with greater empathy, cooperation, and support. To consolidate these improvements, therapists may ask families to compare earlier negative communication patterns with their current, more constructive ways of interacting.

Behavioral experiments promote cognitive change by moving beyond routine family behaviors (Dattilio, 2010; Epstein & Baucom, 2002). In the Daniels family, such experiments might involve asking Murray—who believes it is embarrassing for fathers to openly express love to their daughters—to practice new behaviors, such as verbally expressing affection toward Pam, and then, upon seeing that Pam expresses happiness from his affection, reflect on whether that experience changed his belief to some extent. When family members are hesitant, the therapist may introduce an "acting-as-if" strategy—temporarily behaving as though the motivating belief and feeling were already established—to enable experiential learning through practice.

The therapist and the family also co-design specific behavioral changes that align with a revised belief. Family members then practice these behaviors between sessions, reflecting on how they felt and what impact the behaviors had on their relationships, thereby testing the usefulness of the new belief. After Murray had his initial experience of expressing affection to Pam and observing her positive response, Murray and Pam could agree to behave in additional ways toward each other that would be consistent with sharing a belief that expressing affection is a desirable way of relating, not embarrassing. In subsequent sessions, the family reviews what was learned and makes further adjustments to behavior or cognition as needed.

On the emotional side, helping members recognize both their own and others' emotions broadens members' perspectives. For instance, Pam may experience sadness in addition to anger, and the therapist can assist her parents in recognizing this.

When emotions are intense and dysregulated, interventions may initially focus on down-regulation. Reducing reactivity decreases the tendency to focus solely on another person's negative behaviors and to interpret them in the worst possible light. The following section outlines emotional interventions of this kind in greater detail.

Interventions for Modifying Emotions

Contrary to the misconception that cognitive-behavioral therapy focuses solely on cognition and behavior, it also emphasizes interventions that target emotion (Baucom et al., 1990; Epstein & Falconier, 2024). For individuals who have difficulty adequately recognizing and expressing their emotions, therapists encourage emotional experience and expression, helping them articulate their feelings. Techniques such as questioning, reflection, and interpretation are used to elicit primary emotions such as hurt or fear. To further heighten emotional experience, therapists may employ strategies like repeating specific phrases, using metaphors or imagery, encouraging family members to verbalize emotions, or blocking avoidance of emotional expression. Within the Daniels family, Murray exemplifies this type of individual who avoids and suppresses emotional expression: having spent four decades centering his life around family roles and tasks, he has become emotionally unexpressive and detached from affective experience.

For individuals who experience and express negative emotions excessively, therapists work to confine the experience and expression of these emotions to specific times and contexts, thereby preventing negative affect from dominating other aspects of family life. Additional strategies include encouraging alternative outlets for emotional expression (e.g., sharing with friends or extended family members) or redirecting negative affect through positive activities or self-soothing techniques. For those who manifest negative emotions through physical or psychological aggression, anger management skills are introduced (Epstein & Falconier, 2024). In the Daniels family, Fran and Pam exemplify this category, both requiring training to regulate their excessive emotional experiences and expressions.

For all family members, the most fundamental component of emotion regulation is cultivating emotional awareness and acceptance (Epstein & Falconier, 2024). Mindfulness meditation training can be particularly effective in strengthening this capacity.

The Therapeutic Process

CBFT is sometimes mistaken for a model that relies too heavily on structured approaches. In reality, CBFT calibrates the level of structure needed by each family and flexibly adapts its intervention style to each family's circumstances, characteristics, and preferences. Because the present case transcript captures a first session, it represents a phase in which CBFT emphasizes alliance building and assessment, with full-scale intervention not yet underway. Even so, the transcript reveals the seeds of core CBFT techniques. The therapist avoids artificially redirecting the family's emotional flow while establishing ground rules, such as refraining from interruptions when others are speaking. By eliciting and clarifying family members' behaviors, cognitions, and emotions, the therapist highlights their close interconnections and fosters members' mutual understanding. Attention is directed not only to micro-level behaviors but also to macro-level themes and interactional patterns within the family. Although this is an assessment phase, foundational interventions targeting behavior, cognition, and emotion are initiated to catalyze early change. Thus, while this first-session transcript does not represent a definitive prototype of CBFT, it offers valuable insight into the model's defining features.

Case Transcript

Therapist: Welcome, glad to see you all. Could you each introduce yourselves?

(*They go around and say their names.*)

Therapist: Great, nice to meet you all. I'd like to begin to get to know each of you. Pam, what do you like to do for fun?
Pam: I guess I just like being on my phone.
Therapist: Oh, I see. Any shows or content you watch a lot?

(*Pam, Oliver, and George share about their hobbies and favorite content.*)

Intervention: Families often come into the therapy room in a state of high tension. Many arrive with the expectation that something frightening or unexpected might happen during the session. For this reason, lowering family tension is crucial. One effective way for the therapist to reduce tension and shift family members' suspicion into trust is to engage with the children. Children usually respond with openness and friendliness when the therapist adopts a warm and approachable attitude, and parents may also shift their perception of the therapist as they witness this interaction. In particular, the therapist pays close attention to the types of media Pam is exposed to. CBFT places importance on ecological influences (Epstein & Baucom, 2002; Epstein & Falconier, 2024), and media are a critical factor in shaping young people's body image schemas, a key predictor of eating disorders. In subsequent sessions, to help reduce family tension, increase emotional and cognitive awareness, and lower chronic anxiety levels, the therapist often begins the session with a mindfulness meditation exercise.

Therapist: I hope that we can all work together as one team. There is one ground rule I'd like to set for our sessions. Many times, I will want each family member to speak to me when I ask about their experiences in the family, not directly to each other. Sometimes, as you listen to another person, you might feel misunderstood or disagree with what's being said, and you may feel the urge to jump in. I ask that you hold back and let that person finish describing their thoughts and emotions. I promise I'll give everyone a chance to respond, so please wait until it's your turn. This space is meant to be a safe place where we can share feelings and thoughts more deeply. To make that possible, we need an atmosphere of listening. So if someone interrupts, I may need to step in. Also, if one person speaks for a very long time, I may have to stop them so that others also get their chance to talk. And at other times, I will ask you to speak directly to one another to give me a picture of how you usually talk to each other, and eventually, for you to practice different ways of communicating with each other.

Intervention: CBFT emphasizes collaboration, fostering the sense that "we are all one team." The alliance with the therapist, as well as among family members, is crucial (Sprenkle et al., 2013). Because CBFT values the sharing and understanding of thoughts and emotions, it also emphasizes clear structure. When this is introduced early as a key rule, families usually remember and follow it.

Therapist: What expectations do you have coming into therapy, and how do you think I could be most helpful to you? Murray, would you please start, and we'll go around and hear from everyone.

Intervention: At the outset, the therapist avoids directing the first question to Pam in order to shift the family's perception that Pam is the sole problem. Instead, by addressing the father—who intuitively appears the least involved—the therapist highlights this perspective, which is often silent within the family, and begins building a collaborative alliance.

Murray: Yeah, like I mentioned when we signed up for therapy, Pam has anorexia, and I just want her to be able to eat.

Therapist: And how do you feel about that?

Murray: I guess… I'm concerned.

Therapist: I see, you're feeling concerned. What kinds of thoughts do you have about that concern?

Murray: I sometimes worry she could get sick, maybe even seriously. At her age, kids are usually growing stronger, and it troubles me that this isn't the case for her.

Therapist: So, you're saying you're worried Pam isn't eating enough during a time when she should be growing, and you're afraid this could hurt her health. It sounds like she means a lot to you, and watching her struggle is really hard. Did I get that right?

Murray: Yes.

Intervention: In CBFT, the therapist often asks about thoughts and feelings. This is useful not only for assessment but also for fostering self-awareness, as well as understanding and empathy among family members. In particular, when the therapist models reflective listening, this highlights and checks the underlying emotions behind Murray's concerns, even if he doesn't explicitly state them. The therapist may use downward arrow questions to explore Murray's underlying fears for Pam further.

Therapist: Pam, what are your thoughts about your family and about taking part in family therapy?

Pam: Honestly, I don't even know why I'm here. My family's just going to say I'm the problem again. Being 90 pounds isn't going to kill me. I know my own body. I'm just sick and tired of their constant interference.

Therapist: It sounds like you feel worn out and frustrated from not being trusted to take care of yourself and from all the constant input from your parents. Does that sound right?

Pam: Yes. I'm not a kid anymore. I'll be graduating high school next year. I just want them to let me go.

Therapist: So it looks to you like they are treating you like a child when you're almost an adult now. Thank you for being open about how it looks to you. What emotions do you feel when that happens between you and them? If you have different kinds of interactions with your dad and mom, please tell me about how they seem similar and how they seem different.

(*The therapist then continues listening and uses the downward arrow method to explore each family member's experience, identifying how each person describes the problems and what they hope for.*)

Intervention: Listening to each family member's full description of their problems and desires is important not only from an assessment standpoint but also because reflective listening to each individual fosters connection with the therapist. This process, in turn, encourages family members to disclose more of their inner experiences, thereby creating a positive cycle of openness and trust.

Therapist: This time, I'd like us to take another look at the conflict between Pam and Fran, since that's something the whole family has mentioned. Fran, could you start by telling me more specifically how the conflict usually unfolds?

Fran: Well, usually when I tell her to eat dinner, she'll just sit there playing with her spoon or fork and then say she's done. And then I say, "Done? You only took one bite!"

Therapist: How do you say that, exactly? Do you raise your voice? What are your facial expressions or nonverbal cues like when you say it?

Fran: I don't think I'm yelling… maybe my voice just gets a little louder?

Oliver: Oh, come on. Honestly, it's kinda loud. Even I jump sometimes when I'm eating.

George: [*chuckling*]

Therapist: And then what happens?

Pam: Then I just don't want to hear it anymore, so I get up and go to my room.

Therapist: And what happens when Pam gets up and heads for her room?

Fran: Well, I can't just sit there and let it go. Two or three times a week, I'll follow her upstairs, knock on her door, and say, "Come out and eat more. You're going to die like this!"

Therapist: And then?

Pam: I blast my music and crawl under the covers. Then Mom gives up and goes back downstairs.

Intervention: Identifying concrete behavior patterns within the family is important, as it reveals not only the primary sources of distress (e.g., conflict between Fran and Pam when Pam does not eat) but also the interactional patterns that generate secondary distress (Pam's withdrawing and Fran's pursuing her). Clinically, mapping conflicts in detail helps family members recognize their own behaviors more objectively and increases the likelihood of interrupting problematic patterns. In this case, Fran relies more on aversive pursuit of Pam than on positive reinforcement as a method of behavior modification, and a Fran-demand/Pam-withdraw pattern is observed.

Therapist: So, in that moment, what kinds of thoughts usually run through your mind, Pam?

Intervention: It is important to identify the emotions and cognitions embedded within the family's specific behavioral patterns. Doing so enhances the family's capacity for awareness and deepens their understanding of the circular interaction among behavior, cognition, and emotion.

Pam: It just feels so discouraging. It's like nobody understands me and how my life is.

Therapist: When did those thoughts and feelings begin in your life? Did you have similar ones when you were a child?

Pam: Yes, constantly. Earlier, it wasn't about eating, but just anything I did or didn't do. I don't think I've ever really done anything of my own free will. My mom has always been the main character of my life—Not me!

Therapist: I hear you saying that you value yourself and your life, and you want to be the main character in your life, making your own choices. But it feels like—even though you know your mom loves you—she's taken over that role of making choices for you, and that makes you upset. It feels discouraging, like you can't break out of this pattern. Is that right?

Pam: Yes, I just want to breathe.

Therapist: Fran, as Pam shared how she's been thinking and feeling for a long time, what went through your mind?

Fran: That's heartbreaking. Pam has mentioned things like that in passing a few times, but I didn't realize she'd been thinking about it so seriously—and for so long.

Therapist: It sounds like you're beginning to see a deeper meaning behind Pam's refusal to eat during conflicts. You didn't intend it that way, yet your message may have reached her in a way you didn't want.

Intervention: Asking Fran about her emotional and cognitive reactions to Pam's inner experience fosters the family's mutual understanding. Through empathic reflection, the therapist clarifies her new perspective on the situation.

Therapist: So, Fran, going back to that moment—when you and Pam were arguing—what was running through your mind?

Fran: A deep sense of worry.

Therapist: What thoughts made you feel so worried?

Fran: I kept thinking, "What if Pam might die?" It felt as if the whole world would collapse. I was in total panic.

Therapist: Do you think this fear about your daughter's death could be influenced not only by the immediate risk her eating pattern seems to have for her health, but also any earlier experiences in your life?

Intervention: It is important to assess whether the behaviors, cognitions, and emotions currently observed are simply reflections of present family relationships or whether they originate from the family of origin or developmental history. Overall, such an understanding of formative background promotes a more open attitude toward modifying these behaviors, cognitions, and emotions.

Fran: Probably. I think it became stronger after my father's sudden death. About ten years ago, when I was still in my twenties, my father suddenly passed away from a heart attack. At that time, I was devastated—grief, trauma, depression. After that, my mother also grew distant. And for me… well, I do have a husband, but honestly, Pam is as close to me as my own mother. So I'm terrified of losing her.

Therapist: Thank you both for sharing in such detail. It really helps me understand what happens between you. From what I hear, it seems like one of you makes a demand, and the other resists. Then the demand increases, and in turn, the resistance or withdrawal does too. And as that cycle intensifies, it's easy to start feeling like the other person is ignoring you, which feels bad. It can even make you start seeing each other as if you're adversaries. But in fact, it seems to me that the negative pattern that keeps getting set off between you is an important issue that needs to be addressed, because it makes both of you feel so unhappy and helpless. It's not that either of you intends to dismiss or attack the other—rather, these reactions may be tied to fears and vulnerabilities that have developed from the past. For Fran, I hear something like: "I'm afraid of losing someone precious again. That loss caused such a huge change in my life, and I still struggle to cope with it." And for Pam, I hear something like: "I really want to be myself. At the very least, I want to be in charge of something as simple as what I eat. I'm afraid of losing myself." Those important needs of each of you get lost in the process.

Intervention: These statements can be seen as a reflective summary of the family's behavioral, cognitive, and emotional patterns. They aim to shift attribution away from a pathologizing perspective—one that views the other as an enemy—toward recognizing that cyclical patterns (secondary stress) are the true source of family distress, because they fail to address relatively normal needs of the two family members—Fran's anxiety over the prospect of losing another loved one (especially one whose well-being she sees as part of her parental responsibility), and Pam's need to fulfill needs for independence, autonomy, and personal achievement while still a member of a family. In addition, they encourage a change in each person's attributions about the other by reframing the other's behavior not as stemming from blame or disregard, but as a reaction rooted in fear and inner vulnerability.

Therapist: We've heard about what each of you fears and longs for. I'm also curious what thoughts and feelings run through Oliver's, George's, and Murray's minds when Fran and Pam tend to clash in the evenings.

Oliver: Honestly, I'm so used to them fighting that I don't really think or feel much anymore. It's just like, "Here we go again."

George: Same here—I just think, "They're at it again."

Murray: I tried to calm my wife down before, but it didn't go well. Now I feel like just ignoring her like our sons do—eating quickly and leaving the table.

Therapist: Given that, when those conflicts arise, how does your body respond—for example, with digestion?

George: Well, I get home from baseball starving, so I eat, but honestly, sometimes I have trouble digesting, because the atmosphere at dinner is so tense.

Therapist Do you think it might be that you're getting stressed in those conflict situations—even without realizing it?

George: Maybe… I'm not really sure.

Therapist: It sounds like your stomach might be speaking for your feelings. That's a common response. We'll have a chance to talk more deeply about that experience later.

Intervention: In exploring how the two sons and the father are affected by mother–daughter conflict, the therapist sought to view the functioning of the family system as a whole and to facilitate mutual understanding. Within CBFT, emotion is conceptualized not only as verbally expressed affect but also as embodied responses. Given the possibility that this family—Pam's anorexia included—may communicate affect somatically, the therapist also probed bodily reactions. This, in turn, informed the clinical judgment that other family members may benefit from guidance in developing more adaptive modes of emotional expression.

Therapist: Okay. Fran and Pam, now that you know what the other is vulnerable to, how might you respond a little differently in the same situation—so that you trigger each other's fears less and begin to break out of this cycle of demanding, defending, and withdrawing?

Pam: I'm not sure… it feels hard.

Therapist: It can definitely feel tough. But even if it's just something small, if you were to respond a little differently—something that reflects your mom's needs—what might that look like?

Pam: I guess I'd have to work something out with Mom. Usually, I only eat about two bites, but I could maybe do one or two more. At least that way we'd both know the minimum we can settle on.

Therapist: Thank you for that good idea. Fran, what about you?

Fran: Maybe I could've said it a bit more calmly—like telling her I'd just like her to eat a little more. I know that's not easy for me. And instead of chasing her into her room, knocking on the door and working myself up, maybe I could just give her some space.

Therapist: Very good. Moving forward, it seems important that we continue therapy to build new ways of responding—ways that involve deeply understanding each other's thoughts and feelings, taking into account both needs and fears, and, above all, breaking the old cyclical pattern that has become our common enemy. As a family, do you agree with this?

(*The family agrees.*)

Intervention: After the extended perception that comes from understanding each other's needs and vulnerability, the therapist conducts guided behavior change by asking for new behavioral responses grounded in this revised cognition.

Therapist: This time, I'm curious how the two of you—as Pam's parents—communicate to address Pam's issues, as well as any issues involving Oliver or George. In particular, when the two of you disagree, how do you work to bridge those differences?

Fran: Honestly, we hardly talk about any family issues. Sometimes I feel lonely, but I haven't really said much about it. We don't really argue, either. It's just that everything inside the family pretty much falls on me, and everything outside falls on my husband. That's just how it's split between us.

Therapist: Fran, it sounds like you and Murray are both committed to carrying out your respective roles. But at the same time, when the desire comes up—like when you think, "sometimes I just want to share what's inside"—you end up feeling alone. And as your conflicts with Pam have grown, it seems you no longer feel emotionally connected to anyone. Am I getting that right?

Fran: Yes.

Intervention: To assess how the parents, as co-parents, can engage in effective dyadic coping with their child's difficulties, the therapist explores how they share thoughts and emotions and how they resolve disagreements. When previously unarticulated emotions (e.g., loneliness) emerge, the therapist reflects and highlights them to facilitate a revised perception of one another among family members.

Therapist: How about you, Murray?

Murray: We don't really have deep conversations. We don't get into things that might turn into a fight. It's basically like, "You do your thing, I'll do mine."

Therapist: So, you don't discuss or share much when it comes to Pam's situation?

Murray: Sometimes Fran talks about how tough it is, but I mostly just listen. Honestly, I really only notice how stressed she gets with Pam when they're in conflict. I try to calm her down, but she doesn't really settle. I don't know what to do. I worry about Pam, sure, but I honestly worry even more about Fran breaking down emotionally. She just seems to be struggling a lot.

Therapist: When Fran talks about how difficult things feel for her, what kinds of thoughts and emotions usually come up for you?

Murray: It's just hard for me. I've never been good at listening when someone talks about their struggles. It just stresses me out, and half the time I don't even know what to say. So mostly, I just sit there and listen.

Therapist: Thank you for sharing your thoughts and feelings; it helps me better understand your family dynamics. The model I use places a lot of importance on sharing thoughts and feelings at a deeper level. I'll give you guidelines for this over time and help your family gradually strengthen communication skills, step-by-step. But for now, let's start with a simple exercise with Fran and Pam. We'll have this kind of conversation between Fran and Murray as well to support effective co-parenting later. Fran, please sit next to Pam and look at her. Pam, try saying something like this: "Mom, I know you work hard to make food for me, and I appreciate it. But when it feels to me like you're pressuring me to eat, I end up feeling upset—like I'm a powerless child again." The key here is to state your hurt feelings clearly without loading them with very intense emotion. That helps your mom not feel threatened by strong emotions. And Fran, would you be willing to make a statement to yourself as you hear Pam expressing her feelings, such as, "I don't need to feel too threatened or tense right now. She's just telling me how she feels, and that's a good step toward us communicating." Then take a deep breath, and reflect back what you hear from Pam with something simple, like, "You felt upset when you saw me yelling at you to eat, because it made you feel controlled, like a little kid."

(*They actually carry out the exercise.*)

Therapist: How was that for you?

Fran: As I mentioned earlier, Pam has said things like this in passing, but we'd never talked calmly face to face. Hearing it this way, I feel I understand a bit more what she's really trying to say, and her genuine feelings came through.

Pam: It was just a simple thing to say, but it took courage to open my mouth. Still, I feel okay—like I actually put myself out there. My mom saying my feelings back to me sounded a bit awkward. It didn't feel bad, though, and she did seem to understand.

Intervention: Interventions targeting communication can take the form of structured approaches in which guidelines are explicitly taught and systematically practiced. At the same time, during sessions, the therapist may also create natural conversational situations, encouraging the family to try out new communication behaviors. Such experiences can facilitate changes not only in communication but also in cognitions and emotions toward one another, as members' understanding of each other increases. In subsequent sessions, more systematic communication training and experiential practice can then be implemented. The therapist also provides Fran with simple cognitive interventions (e.g., relaxation self-statements) and emotional interventions (e.g., practicing deep breathing) to help her stay less tense and listen more effectively.

Therapist: We're almost at the end of our session. Often, families come to therapy very focused on the problems they are experiencing, which can seem unchangeable. But every family also has many strengths. Therapy isn't about changing everything—it's about preserving the aspects of family life that are already strong and working on the specific aspects that could improve. And even when you work on those parts that have been problematic, it's important to draw on the strengths you already have. So I'd like to hear about your family's strengths. Oliver, why don't you start, since you haven't spoken much yet?

Intervention: Because of the vicious cycle of selective perception and sentiment override, families often come into therapy with a markedly narrowed perspective on problems and complaints. In such situations, it is crucial to highlight the family's strengths as a way to broaden their understanding and foster a more constructive and positive atmosphere.

Oliver: I think we're still a pretty good family. Mom and Pam have been fighting more over the past year or two, but aside from that, we've had a lot of good times. We've made some really nice memories together. And… I guess another strength is that I'm kind of a cheerful person. Just having me around feels like a strength in itself. (*everyone laughs*)

Therapist: You said your family has made some nice memories together. Could you give me an example?

Oliver: Oh, like last year we went hiking in West Virginia, and it was really great. Everyone in the family seemed relaxed.

Therapist: Sounds great. How about you, George?

George: From my point of view, we all get along pretty well. Mom and Pam fight sometimes, but they also have good moments. I'm not that close to Pam, but that's mostly just because we're into different things. I'm into sports, so I hang out more with Dad and my brother. Still, I think of everyone in a positive way. Sure, I get annoyed when Mom or Pam gets annoyed with me, but that happens in any family.

Therapist: You mentioned there are good moments between Mom and Pam. Could you give me an example?

George: I can't think of anything specific right now, but they laugh around together a lot. I even saw them like that this morning.

Therapist: It's great to hear that. Fran, what about you?

Fran: When I look at the big picture, I'd say we're a pretty happy family. Thanks to hard work by my husband and me, we don't really have major financial problems. And Pam and I share some good moments too.

Therapist: For example?

Fran: Sometimes we just talk, go for a walk, or watch TV together. In those moments, it feels like I have a friend—like my daughter has grown up and become more of a companion to me.

Therapist: After losing your father and with your mother having moved away, has Pam's presence been a source of strength for you?

Fran: Definitely. Since I feel some distance from my husband because he's often so busy, Pam has started to feel more like a friend. But as our conflicts have grown, I'm afraid of losing her too—not just physically, but emotionally. I worry she might pull away from me.

Therapist: Family relationships can be viewed in many ways. Closeness can sometimes lead to conflict, but it also provides strong support. If we hold onto that closeness and work through the rough spots, it can become a real strength. In particular, to help Fran and Pam's closeness serve as a resource rather than a source of conflict, it may help to reflect on what "friendship" means between you. In future sessions, let's discuss which view of friendship is more sustainable and ultimately deepens intimacy for the two of you: a friendship that requires doing many things the same way with little autonomy, or one that recognizes and supports each other's differences. Lastly, Murray, what do you see as the family's strengths?

Intervention: The therapist interprets the situation through a strengths-based lens to keep the family from being pulled into overly negative views of their relationships. The therapist also introduces beliefs about friendship, thereby addressing the balance between connection and autonomy—i.e., boundary issues—and, in this respect, integrating elements of structural family therapy. This friendship-related belief system will be explored further in subsequent sessions. In addition, the therapist will address the couple's diminished intimacy and companionship associated with the husband's busy schedule and the impact this has on the relationship between Fran and Pam.

Murray: Honestly, none of us are really difficult people. We all have good hearts. Sure, when Fran and Pam get a bit sensitive with each other, it stresses me out. But they both mean well. And it's that good-heartedness that makes me believe we can get through these challenges.

Therapist: A kind person met another kind person, and together you've raised kind, caring children. Finally, Pam, how about you?

Pam: Honestly, at first I thought this felt kind of fake—like we were just sugarcoating our family. But the more I listened, I realized it's not all fake. We actually do have some good moments. However, I don't want us to avoid talking about the tough times too.

Therapist: Thank you for sharing your family's strengths as well as challenges—it really reassures me that your family has a lot going for it. However, you all have noticed that there are some troubling issues that deserve your attention. What I'd like us to do is focus on making some changes in the parts that feel less smooth. For now, our immediate goal should be to ease the tension in the family and create a more positive atmosphere. I see this as the foundation that will allow us to move forward smoothly and engage in more constructive work. Does this goal feel right to all of you?

(*The family agrees.*)

Therapist: To work on this, I would like to begin by focusing on changing communication patterns to increase your understanding of each other's concerns, goals, etc. But I'd also like us to think about some general behavioral changes too. What kinds of positive behaviors could you do toward each other more often, and what negative behaviors could you cut back on or stop, so the tension in your family might ease a bit? The key is to identify small, simple things you can actually do. They may not take away all the tension, but if they help even a little, that's what really matters.

Intervention: The therapist is asking the family about behavioral changes they can take personal responsibility for enacting, as part of guided behavior change, in order to shift the overall family atmosphere.

(The family members share their ideas.)
Therapist: Sounds good.

Intervention: The therapist chose not to formalize the ideas that emerged from this guided behavior change into a behavioral contract. This decision was made to avoid imposing an artificial structure on insights that had arisen naturally during the first session.

Therapist: For homework, I'd like you to try out some of these behaviors. But remember—it's not about saying, "I'll only take a step if the other person does first." Instead, I'd like you to come from a place of goodwill that you already share, and from your own sense of agency and dignity—regardless of how the other person responds. In other words, don't focus on "Are they doing their part?" but rather, "Am I doing my part?"

Intervention: Emphasizing the voluntary nature of behaviors encourages family members to shift their focus from others to themselves. This is especially important for motivating those who hold the expectancy, "Even if I try, other family members won't respond positively, so it's better not to try." It also helps family members attribute other family members' actions to their own choices.

The Therapeutic Story

CBFT fosters deeper understanding and empathy among family members by encouraging them to explore and share their behaviors, cognitions, and emotions. It also helps them modify these processes to meet relational needs such as intimacy and autonomy, using both structured interventions and more natural, unstructured approaches.

a In the first session, the therapist explores the Daniels family's concerns, thoughts, and feelings, using reflective listening to ensure accurate understanding, convey empathy, and build a therapeutic alliance.
b Family members are invited to describe conflicts in detail, which clarifies interaction patterns and allows them to observe their behavior more objectively, broadening the focus from Pam's individual symptoms to the rigid interaction patterns embedded within the family system.
c The therapist helps family members identify the cognitions and emotions underlying conflict situations and reflect on their formative background. This process helps shift the attribution of Pam's eating behavior from individual pathology to relational conflict, facilitating the modification of existing patterns and consideration of alternative behaviors.

d Family members are guided to express their thoughts and emotions openly and to practice reflective listening, fostering changes in how they perceive one another.
e To counter emotional override and selective attention to negative family interactions, the therapist emphasizes family strengths as well.
f Finally, behavioral changes aimed at reducing family tension are discussed and assigned as homework, helping redirect accumulated negative emotions and interactions.

References

Alexander, J. F., & Parsons, B. V. (1973). Short-term behavioral intervention with delinquent families: impact on family process and recidivism. *Journal of Abnormal Psychology*, *81*(3), 219–225.

Baucom, D. H., & Epstein N. (1990). *Cognitive-behavioral marital therapy*. Brunner/Mazel.

Baucom, D. H., Epstein, N., Rankin, L. A., & Burnett, C. K. (1996). Assessing relationship standards: The inventory of specific relationship standards. *Journal of Family Psychology*, *10*(1), 72–88.

Baucom, D. H., & Lester, G. W. (1986). The usefulness of cognitive restructuring as an adjunct to behavioral marital therapy. *Behavior Therapy*, *17*(4), 385–403.

Baucom, D. H., Sayers, S. L., & Sher, T. G. (1990). Supplementing behavioral marital therapy with cognitive restructuring and emotional expressiveness training: An outcome investigation. *Journal of Consulting and Clinical Psychology*, *58*(5), 636–645.

Dattilio, F. M. (Ed.). (1998). *Case studies in couple and family therapy: Systemic and cognitive perspectives*. Guilford.

Dattilio, F. M. (2005). The restructuring of family schemas: a cognitive–behavior perspective. *Journal of Marital and Family Therapy*, *31*(1), 15–30.

Dattilio, F. M. (2010). *Cognitive-behavioral therapy with couples and families: A comprehensive guide for clinicians*. Guilford.

Dattilio, F. M., & Epstein, N. B. (2016). Cognitive-behavior couple and family therapy. In T. L. Sexton, & J. Lebow (Eds.), *Handbook of family therapy* (pp. 89–119). Routledge.

Dattilio, F.M., & Epstein, N.B. (2021). Cognitive-behavioral couple and family therapy. In A. Wenzel (Ed.) *Handbook of cognitive behavior therapy* (Vol. 2, pp. 513–548). American Psychological Association.

Dattilio, F. M., & Padesky, C. A. (1990). *Cognitive therapy with couples*. Professional Resource Exchange.

Eidelson, R. J., & Epstein, N. (1982) Cognition and relationship maladjustment: Development of a measure of dysfunctional relationship beliefs. *Journal of Consulting and Clinical Psychology*, *50*(5), 715–720.

Epstein, N. (1982). Cognitive therapy with couples. *American Journal of Family Therapy*, *10*(1), 5–16.

Epstein, N. B., & Baucom, D. H. (2002). *Enhanced cognitive-behavioral therapy for couples: A contextual approach*. American Psychological Association.

Epstein, N. B., Berger, A. T., Fang, J. J., Messina, L., Smith, J. R., Lloyd, T. D., Fang, X. Y., & Liu, Q. X. (2012). Applying Western-developed family therapy models in China. *Journal of Family Psychotherapy*, *23*(3), 217–237.

Epstein, N.B., & Dattilio, F.M. (2020). Behavioral and cognitive-behavioral approaches in systemic family therapy. In K.S. Wampler, R.B. Miller, L.M. McWey, A.J. Blow, M. Rastogi, & R. Singh (Eds.), *Handbook of systemic family therapy* (pp. 365–390). Wiley.

Epstein, N. B., & Falconier, M. K. (2024). *Treatment plans and interventions in couple therapy: A cognitive-behavioral approach*. Guilford Press.
Epstein, N. B., & Park, W. (2021, October). Dialogue between CBT and Bowen model: How can we become good friends? [Conference presentation]. *Annual Conference of the Asian Academy of Family Therapy*, Seoul, South Korea.
Epstein, N., Schlesinger, S., & Dryden, W. (1988). Concepts and methods of cognitive-behavior family treatment. In N. Epstein, S. Schlesinger, & W. Dryden (Eds.), *Cognitive-behavior therapy with families* (pp. 5–48). Brunner/Mazel.
Epstein, N.B., Schlesinger, S.E., & Kim, H. (2018). Cognitive-behavioral family therapy. In P.C. Kendall (Ed.), *Cognitive therapy with children and adolescents: A casebook for clinical practice* (pp. 301–328). Guilford.
Falicov, C. J. (1995). Training to think culturally: A multidimensional comparative framework. *Family process, 34*(4), 373–388.
Forgatch, M. S., & Patterson, G. R. (1987). *Parents and adolescents living together: Part 2: Family problem solving*. Castalia Publishing Company.
Gershoff, E. T. (2002). Corporal punishment by parents and associated child behaviors and experiences: a meta-analytic and theoretical review. *Psychological Bulletin, 128*(4), 539–579.
Patterson, G. R., & Forgatch, M. (1987). *Parents and adolescents living together: Part 1: The basics*. Castalia Publishing Company.
Sprenkle, D. H., Davis, S. D., & Lebow, J. L. (2013). *Common factors in couple and family therapy: The overlooked foundation for effective practice*. Guilford Publications.

14 Solution-Focused Brief Therapy

Carol Messmore and Arlene Brett Gordon

Solution-focused brief therapy (SFBT), developed by Steve de Shazer and Insoo Kim Berg, is an evidence-based practice that focuses on clients' inherent strengths and competencies (Żak & Pękala, 2025). SFBT helps clients discover solutions to their challenges instead of focusing on the problems they currently face. This future-focused, goal-directed approach is effective because clients experience their own ability to make positive changes efficiently (de Shazer et al., 1986).

SFBT differs from traditional problem-focused models of family therapy, which focus on the past. It is an action-oriented approach that focuses on the present and the future, speculating on when the existing problem will be solved. This brief, strength-based approach was developed by Steve de Shazer, Insoo Kim Berg, and their team in Milwaukee (de Shazer et al., 1986).

In 1978, after training at the Mental Research Institute (MRI), de Shazer and Berg rejoined their team at the Brief Therapy Center (BFTC) in Milwaukee and set out to establish the "MRI of the Midwest" (Cade, 2007, p. 39). The team noticed commonalities among clients and grew curious about the times when the problem wasn't a problem, what they called **exceptions**. By the early 1980s, they discovered that problems did not occur all the time and sometimes varied in severity (Berg, 1994). Applying this notion to the Daniels family, there are times when the family argued less, enjoyed doing things together, and Pam would eat without a fight.

As the BTFC team explored exceptions to the problems, they noted these often existed unnoticed. "Exceptions are those occasions in client's lives when the problem could have occurred but did not- or at least were less severe" (De Jong & Berg, 2008, p. 16). Shifting past exceptions into future behaviors became the most important focus for solution-building change, "basically, all the therapist and client have to know is: 'How will we know when the problem is solved?'" (de Shazer, 1982, p. 3). Focusing on exceptions is a way of building on Milton Erickson's notion of **utilization**—using what is already present for the client (de Shazer, 1988).

DOI: 10.4324/9781003668510-14

The Therapeutic Story of Problem Formation

Clients seek family therapy because they want to have something different in their lives. Clients often come with complaints about family members, lack of communication, difficulty resolving conflicts, and navigating relationships. The complaints clients bring to therapists are constructs involving certain behaviors, in certain contexts, and the meaning of the behaviors in those contexts (de Shazer, 1985). Talk in therapy about the complaint is known as **problem talk** (De Jong & Berg, 2008). Often, the family has been struggling with the problem and has attempted the same solutions over and over again. Nothing seems to get better and may seem even worse. The problem talk has grown into a "fact," and its weight feels heavier (Berg & de Shazer, 1993).

To break it down even more, SFBT therapists distinguished between **difficulties** and complaints. de Shazer et al. (1986) stated, "Difficulties are the one damn thing after another of everyday life, which clients frequently call 'problems'" (p. 210). Every person has difficulties. In themselves, they are not problematic. They become a **complaint** when the person experiences repetitive unsuccessful attempts to resolve the difficulty, or the perception that the difficulty is unsolvable. In essence, difficulties turn into complaints when "one damn thing after another becomes the same damn thing over and over" (de Shazer et al., 1986, p. 210).

For over two years, the Daniels have attempted to find a solution to a serious family problem. Pam's poor eating habits and diagnosis of anorexia affected the entire family system. Fran became hypervigilant, constantly focusing on what Pam was eating and how much she weighed. Fran and Murray decided that Fran would handle the concerns with Pam, and Murray would focus on his two sons and their activities. This left Pam and Fran, who used to enjoy their activities together, to argue, developing a strained relationship. The more Fran tried to force Pam, the more Pam resisted, and the more arguing continued in the home. At the point of SFBT therapy, the family relationships have grown very strained and uncomfortable. The tension was increasing and causing escalating problems within the family system, affecting all the family members. The initial difficulty, of Pam not eating as much as the parents would like, has shifted to a complaint where the repetitive attempts to solve the difficulty have not worked. Fran's overseeing of Pam's eating, Murray's distant support, and Pam's attempts to maintain her autonomy have led the family to do the same damn thing again and again.

The central philosophy of SFBT follows three basic rules (Berg, 1994)

1 If it ain't broke, don't fix it.
Clients can have many challenges apparent in their lives, so they may not be able to identify those things that are already working for them. A solution-focused therapist would note that Fran and Murray continue to seek solutions to address family challenges and collaborate to make decisions together to support their family.

2 If it works, do more of it.
Focusing on the times when the client is successful is more beneficial than focusing on the times the client has failed. From a solution-focused perspective, clinicians highlight client competencies, asking them to do more of what is already working. The family has had thousands of interactions with one another that have led to all five members feeling happy. This included past vacations as well as many dinners together, before the current difficulties surrounding how they are dealing with Pam's eating behaviors.
3 If it isn't working, do something different.
People tend to try to solve their challenges by applying the same ineffective strategies. From a solution-focused perspective, if something does not work, clients are asked to do something different. The family's initial problem focused on Pam's eating problems and weight loss. Six months of previous therapy was not helpful. The harder Fran tried to get her daughter to eat, the more Pam resisted. Because this was a health issue, there was a heightened sense to get Pam help. Pam saw herself as the problem. Everyone in the family was upset about the arguing. No matter how hard they tried, nothing seemed to change.

Clients seeking therapeutic change often have difficulty navigating these rules within their relationships. Clients tend not to recognize when exceptions occur (de Shazer et al., 2007). They remain aligned with the problem in their problem talk. As a result, clients are more focused on the third SFBT rule and continue to do what is not working (Reiter, 2018). "An odd reality of human nature is the tendency to continue to try to solve problems by repeating the same things that have not worked in the past" (de Shazer et al., 2007, p. 2). However, they are hopeful that change may eventually occur.

Another reason that people become stuck in their current problems is that they are using an either/or position rather than a both/and position (Reiter, 2025). An **either/or position** occurs when a person uses a binary when looking at things. Fran views Pam as either eating or not eating. Or that she is healthy or not healthy. Pam may view her parents as either overbearing or too permissive. Fran may view Murray as either totally engaged or totally disengaged. This position leads people to concretize another's actions, leaving little room for hope of change. A **both/and position**, which SFBT practitioners utilize, holds that people are multitudes, simultaneously. Pam eats and doesn't eat and is healthy and not healthy. Fran is overbearing and permissive. Murray is engaged and disengaged. We all function on a continuum. When we view people in limited, restricted roles, we then limit and restrict the ways we perceive the situation and the potential available behavioral responses we might use.

Clients are often prepared to share details of the problems that brought them into therapy. They may want the therapist to understand the problem they are facing. Acknowledging and exploring the client's "problem can lead to pathways to solutions" (Reiter, 2018, p. 206). From the SFBT perspective, the therapist does not need to focus on the problem since the solution isn't necessarily related to the problem (Nelson, 2011). However, SFBT therapists benefit by giving the client an opportunity to share the problem that brought them to therapy (Reiter & Chenail, 2016). By acknowledging a client's initial focus, the therapist joins with the client and then is able to explore the unfocused focus—those times when things were going more as the client wanted them to. However, rather than go into seeking details through problem talk, the SFBT therapist tends to ask less about the problems and their causes (De Jong, 2019).

Clients generally seek therapy after failed attempts to solve their problem. In the case of the Daniels family, for over two years, Murray and Fran have been very concerned about their daughter's deteriorating health. The parents sought therapeutic support, during which time Pam was diagnosed as anorexic and participated in therapy for six months. The therapy was determined to be unsuccessful, with the therapist suggesting inpatient care. This solution did not fit for this family. For the next year and a half, Fran, an extremely engaged mother, continued to actively focus on Pam's eating and weight, which created difficulty between mother and daughter. The father, Murray, was very engaged with his two sons and their sports activities, and he stepped aside to let Fran take responsibility for Pam's eating and weight loss. Fran's constant monitoring of her daughter became a larger problem affecting the entire family system. Everyone was upset and sad.

Diversity Conceptualization

One of the main highlights of SFBT is viewing the client as the expert in their own lives, collaborating with them to find their best solutions. Working with members of diverse cultures, challenges, and environments, the use of specific solution-focused language often brings hope and has a positive effect on both the clients and the practitioners (Solution Focused Brief Therapy Association Research Committee, 2025).

SFBT highlights the individual client's specific strengths and solution-building skills. "One notable strength of SFBT is its flexibility for cross-cultural application in a way that honors and acknowledges the diverse cultural and human experiences in its various forms" (Solution Focused Brief Therapy Association Research Committee, 2025, p. 40). Each session starts as an individual meeting based on what the client currently brings to that session. Clients bring their culture through their language, values, and attempted solutions.

SFBT applies effectively in a wide range of cultural contexts without the need for new development of "culturally adapted" SFBT interventions. Clients from diverse cultures report feeling more encouraged, more hopeful (Neipp & Beyeback, 2022). SFBT has been utilized with diverse populations, including Hispanic families, immigrant families, African American families, and the LGBT community (Kim, 2014).

Since 2000, SFBT has been applied in a wider variety of diverse contexts, including schools, the WOWW program (Berg & Shilts, 2005), residential treatment centers, social service programs, hospitals, nursing, childcare programs, as well as in organizational settings. This approach respects each system's values and practices. The practitioner listens closely for specific exceptions, the client's desired future, and together co-constructs steps to meet their specific goals.

The Therapeutic Story of Problem Resolution

Solution-focused therapists learn to listen to their clients differently (De Jong, 2019). They listen to incorporate the client's specific language to collaboratively explore possible solutions based on the client's desired future, framed as a time when the problem that brought them to therapy is no longer a problem. This enables the SFBT therapist to focus on the times when the problem is not a problem and on past successes, increasing the focus on existing personal strengths and resources (Źak & Pękala, 2025).

SFBT is a socially constructed model of intervention in which therapists engage the clients as collaborators of change. From this perspective, the therapist takes a non-judgmental view and understands that the family is a working system (de Shazer, 1994). The problems clients bring to therapy are defined by the family, and the intervention is based on the nature of the problem.

The goal of the SFBT interview is to help clients construct their problem differently, with very little talk of the perceived problem (de Shazer, 1994). During the first session, SFBT therapists focus on a collaborative stance, providing clients with an opportunity to envision their desired future when the problem is solved. Conversations about the problem are co-constructed, highlighting the client's existing strengths, capabilities, resources, and exceptions.

Change

de Shazer noted "that only a small change is necessary, and therefore only a small and reasonable goal is necessary" (de Shazer, 1985, p. 16). SFBT is based on systems thinking, that no matter how difficult the problem, making "a small change in one person's behavior can make profound and far-reaching differences in the behavior of all persons involved" (de Shazer, 1985, p. 16). This small change often leads to progress. The primary goals of solution-focused interventions focus on what is working, what has worked in the past, and what may be likely to work in the future.

Therapists find that change often occurs once the client schedules a meeting (Berg, 1994). Initiating a first session with a conversation about change highlights the client's competencies and their ability to be resourceful. Early in the initial meeting, an SFBT therapist inquires about any changes made since scheduling an appointment. "Between the time you made the appointment for this therapy and our first session today, what has gotten better even just a little bit?" (Bannink, 2014, p. 130). Based on the response, the therapist initiates a collaborative conversation about what has gotten better, remained the same, or why things are not worse. To open the session, the SFBT therapist may ask the client: "How can I be helpful to you today," or "What would need to happen today to make this a really useful session?" or "How would your best friend notice if/that this session was helpful to you?" or "What needs to be different in your life after this session for you to be able to say that it was a good idea you came in and talked with me?" (Bavelas et al., 2013, p. 12).

Client Engagement: Joining

Clients' motivation to change, how clients see themselves in relationship to the problem, and in relationship within the client-therapist relationship are important aspects of therapeutic change. Traditionally, the professional was considered responsible for increasing the client's compliance (the acceptance and carrying out of interventions) and decreasing resistance (lack of cooperation with interventions) on the part of the individual, couple, or family (de Shazer, 1985). This position left the client blamed for the lack of engagement (Berg, 1989).

de Shazer (1984) refers to the concept of resistance as the practitioner's perspective, and that the client's unwillingness to work was the client's responsibility. This was the dominant understanding of problem-focused interventions. Conversely, de Shazer proposed that each client's show of "resistance" may be that unique individual's way of cooperating (De Jong & Berg, 2008).

Berg (1994) stressed the importance of assessing the nature of the client-therapist relationship based on several considerations: how the client came to work with the therapist; how invested the client is; and how hopeful the client is. Berg (1989, 1994) found it useful to consider clients in three types of relationships with the therapeutic process: the visitor, complainant, or customer.

1 The **visitor** is not invested in change and is sent by someone else (e.g., parent, spouse, or court order). A solution-focused therapist would likely compliment their participation in the therapy session, even though the visitor may feel they do not have anything to work on.
2 The **complainant** is very aware of the problem but does not see themselves as part of it. This client provides details about the problem but does "not see themself as part of the solution" (Berg, 1989, p. 1). Often, the solution-focused therapist will compliment the complainant for their participation and perspective. To further engage the complainant, the therapist may ask them to observe changes over sessions.
3 The **customer** is most vested in change, wants to do something differently, and provides an abundance of details about the problem. After complimenting

> this client's investment, the therapist is likely to ask them what they are already doing and highlight what is going well.
>
> (De Jong & Berg, 2008)

The members of the Daniels family approached the family session with different levels of engagement based on their relationship to the presenting problem. Everyone wanted change. During this initial session, both parents presented as customers desperately seeking ways to create change. Over two years, Fran and Murray attempted several solutions, including six months of unsuccessful therapy for Pam, before deciding that Murray would focus on the boys and placing Fran in charge of Pam. Historically, Fran had been the parent to push Pam to improve, to do better in school.

Brothers George and Oliver, as complainants, were tired of the focus on Pam's eating habits. The brothers had no complaints about Pam but wanted to see their mother handle the situation differently. They complained about the tension in the home, and they wanted their mother to change. Pam, a complainant, did not want to be forced to change and wanted everyone to stop focusing on her. Pam wanted her mother to stop pushing her and to have more family time. At this point, Pam felt as if she were the problem. In therapy, the therapist will attempt to shift each family member to become a customer for change, collaborating on possible solutions.

Client-Focused Therapy

SFBT's original interviewing protocol explicitly limited talk about problems and complaints (de Shazer et al., 1986). The therapist recognizes each client's ability to be proactive in creating change and building solutions, as the client is the expert in their own lives. SFBT emphasizes collaboration. Together, client(s) and therapist negotiate goals by asking questions such as "What needs to happen first?" and "What needs to happen next?".

Families bring multiple perspectives of what the solution might look like, and members may disagree about which is best. Perhaps the parents have different parenting views and are dealing with the problem differently. In the Daniels family, Murray distances himself from his daughter and her problem, leaving Fran to focus on Pam's eating habits. Fran, in her desire to help her daughter, becomes hypervigilant and controlling. The brothers want Pam to start eating again so that Mom would relax and they would be able to do things together as a family again.

Rather than taking sides, an SFBT therapist may take a more collaborative stance by complimenting the clients' commitment to the process and recognizing each person's ideas as possible solutions. This leads to a more collaborative conversation in which each member feels as if their perspective is considered. The therapist could compliment the Daniels on their support and love for Pam, explaining that the family is "loving" and "concerned."

Well-Formed Goals

Developing well-formed goals is an unfolding process in collaboration between the client and therapist. Solutions lie in changing interactions to better fit the needs of each client. Solution-focused, well-formed goals use the client's frame of reference and are stated in the client's language (De Jong & Berg, 2008).

According to de Shazer (1988, 1994), both clinical experience and research indicate that workable goals tend to be: important to clients; small rather than large; described in specific, behavioral terms; described as the "start" of something not as the "end" of something; described as a presence of something rather than an absence; perceived by clients as involving their hard work; realistic; achievable; and in the context of the clients' lives.

Solution-Building, Not Problem-Solving

SFBT was specifically designed to limit the talk about the problems and current challenges the family brings to therapy (De Jong & Berg, 2008). The focus on the time when the problem is solved moves the therapeutic conversation from problem talk to solution talk. Solution talk focuses on what has worked for the clients and shifts the emphasis from what the client does not want to what the client would like to see as the solution to their problem (De Jong & Berg, 2008).

Solution-focused questions provide the therapist with opportunities to build cooperation with clients using open-ended questions such as who, what, where, when, and how.

- What is the first small step that you can take to tell everyone that you know how to make healthier decisions?
- Where do you see yourself/the family a year from now?
- When the family is having more fun together, what will be happening?
- How will you know when Mom and Pam are enjoying their time together?

(De Jong & Berg, 2008)

Leading from one step behind provides clients with opportunities to be the experts in their own life experiences. The therapist may take a not-knowing stance, becoming curious about the client's perception of the situation (Anderson & Goolishian, 1992). This posture opens an opportunity for clients to provide more information about their current situation. Together, the client and therapist navigate next steps (De Jong & Berg, 2008).

The second and follow-up sessions may begin with the question "What's better?". Therapists ask clients to recall times the problem did not occur to highlight positive change. Asking this question maintains the position that the client is the expert on the situation. "The most fundamental reason for beginning later sessions by asking this question is it once again reflects the conviction that solutions are primarily built from the perception of exceptions" (De Jong & Berg, 2008, pp. 140–141). Therapists then focus on exceptions that occurred since the last meeting.

Questions and Intervention Tools

SFBT questions are critically important and used to gather more context about the solution rather than the problem. The questions are also used as interventions to move the clients toward change and to track progress. The questions can be used for all clients and problems and are designed to expand the conversation about times when the problem is not a problem. The talk between the therapist and the clients is focused on what the clients would like to see happening differently, instead of the problem. The flexibility of the questions was a reason that de Shazer (1986) referred to the questions as skeleton keys—broad constructs which can be used across unique client systems.

The therapist uses the client's words to not insert assumptions or meanings that are not aligned with the client's perspective. Following the path of "listen, select, and build" (Solution Focused Brief Therapy Association Research Committee, 2025), the therapist co-creates with the client a path toward change. The "problem" does not need to be deconstructed; rather, it is the solution that needs to be deconstructed. Sitting with the client to understand the "why" of the problem is not as helpful as working with the client to determine what has to be different in the future so that the problem is not a problem. The model paradigm, social construction, presents that reality is socially created. Through that lens, the therapist and client can focus on the future without the problem, using the questions and interventions of the model, essentially changing their future to not be dependent upon the problem that brought them into therapy (De Jong & Berg, 2008). Interventions such as the miracle question, scaling questions, exception questions, and coping questions are key to the development of solutions with clients (Reiter, 2024).

The Miracle Question

The **miracle question** is perhaps the most recognized question of the model. The purpose is for the clients to put into words what life looks like when the problem is no longer a problem because a miracle has occurred (de Shazer et al., 2007). The question invites the client to envision and verbalize what is happening when the problem is no longer a problem. While the presentation of the question is very simple, the facilitation of the question is complex. It is not just the act of asking a question. The therapist must carefully listen to the response (Listen) and choose what information to gather (Select) and when to prompt for more detail (Build). This is the essence of the question. The contextual information gathered can then be used to create and clarify goals, discover exceptions, and, most importantly, create hope for change (Lipchik, 2002; Solution Focused Brief Therapy Association Research Committee, 2025).

Developed in the midst of a session, the miracle question was created when Berg asked a client about what needed to happen for therapy to be useful. The client responded that only a miracle could help her. Using the client's language, Berg posed the first version of the miracle question, which helped the client put her goals into words about what would be happening differently for the family and moved the client's focus from problems to solutions (De Jong & Berg, 2008). The question has been refined through usage and is best asked in a soft voice, phrased using future-focused wording and spoken slowly:

> Now, I want to ask you a strange question. Suppose that while you are sleeping tonight and the entire house is quiet, a miracle happens. The miracle is that the problem which brought you here is solved. However, because you are sleeping, you don't know that the miracle has happened. So when you wake up tomorrow morning, what will be different that will tell you that a miracle has happened and that the problem which brought you in here is solved?
>
> (De Jong & Berg, 2008, p. 84)

This phrasing pushes the client into the future without the problem, moving the client from problem talk to solution talk. The therapist then gathers the details and context of what life is like for the client when the miracle has happened. This allows the client to see their desired change and offers hope that it is possible and even already happening as a picture of the miracle. The therapist deconstructs the next morning, asking what else is happening, who notices, and how the interactional patterns will be different (e.g., when your mother does that, what do you do?). This conversation should take time and be thoughtful, exploring the multiple differences that are happening; this disconnects the problem from the solution (Berg, 1994). The pacing of the question and the following discussion allows for collaboration between the therapist and client co-creating the picture of the miracle (Shilts et al., 2003).

SFBT is a systemic and collaborative model; if the question is asked individually to system members, the therapist then integrates the solutions from each member into a shared system goal. As a result, the system works together toward the solutions. Alternatively, the question can be asked of the system, and the therapist then deconstructs the solution through gathering responses from across the system members, whether present in the room or not (de Shazer, et al., 2007).

The concept of a "miracle" can have cultural implications for some. The purpose of the question is to prompt clients to think about what their life looks like when the problem is no longer a problem; the way the question is phrased is flexible. Therapists use different terms other than the word "miracle" to support the client in accepting the question. Talking to clients about "a dream," "a vision," or "a wish" are all ways to suggest the same meaning for the question (Blakesee & Jordan, 2014).

The Scaling Question

There are multiple uses for **scaling questions** as they can be used to identify exceptions to the program, assess client motivation, and track progress toward client goals. Using a scale of 0–10 or 1–10 (the low-end number is not important; de Shazer tended to start at 0 and Berg tended to start at 1 for no particular reason), the client rates their understanding of where they are in relation to where they wish to be (de Shazer, et al., 2007). The flexibility of the question makes it indispensable in therapy as the clients can be asked to scale anything, such as hope for change, self-esteem, and progress in therapy (De Jong & Berg, 2008). The question is also effective when combined with the miracle question, where the defined morning after becomes the "10" and asking when the last time parts of the description of the morning after the miracle happened. This supports the clients realizing that their miracle is happening, just not as much as they hope. The scaling question can then create actionable steps toward the miracle (de Shazer et al., 2007).

The wording of the scaling question is critical, with the two endpoints clearly defined using the client's language and the time frame specified, for example, "today," or "over the past week." This helps to assess the current situation when assessing progress and setting up steps forward (Berg, 1994). There are multiple follow-up questions to the scaling question to elicit strengths and actionable steps forward. For example, in a first session, the therapist might decide to assess pre-session change and ask, "On a scale of 1–10, with 1 being the day you decided to come into therapy and 10 being the day you feel that you no longer need therapy, where are you today?" The therapist listens for the number for the client, then asks, "How come a 3 and not a 2?" (inserting the client's number first and going down 1 point for the second number). This elicits pre-session change from the client, offering hope to the client that change can happen because it already has on a small scale (Berg, 1994).

How this change happened is explored to further develop the client's hope for change. The therapist then asks the client, "What has to happen for you to move from a 3 to a 3.5 on the scale?" The use of half a point allows the clients to focus on small changes to ensure success. The therapist then carefully works with the client to ensure the steps suggested are indeed just half a point. Larger steps up the scale can set clients up for failure, attempting to make changes that are too major a change for the time (Berg & Dolan, 2001). The half-point move can be assigned as homework for the client: "Between now and the next time we meet, what if you think about making (insert the half step) happen?" The therapist might also bring in other system members through asking relational questions about the change, "Who would notice first that you are a 3.5 on the scale?", "What would they notice?", and "What else would they notice?" The actionable steps should be in the client's language and be the client's idea, as it is more likely to happen. Clients become invested in their own change when it aligns with their perspectives, not the therapist's perspective (Berg, 1994).

The Exception Question

Exception questions are built upon the SFBT basic tenet of "doing more of what works." Asking **exception questions** allows the clients to discuss times when the problem was not a problem, although it could have been (Berg, 1994). Often, clients come into therapy with an understanding that the problem is happening all the time and do not pay attention to times when the problem is not their focus (de Shazer, 1985). Berg (1994) noted that no problem happens all the time; thus, it is the therapist's job to uncover what is different when the problem is not happening. Exceptions are also the past successes in the client's life. Therapists can explore exceptions by asking, "When is the problem not a problem?" Some clients can quickly answer this, offering up exceptions easily. Other clients will let the therapist know that the problem is always happening. Once the therapist knows what change is that the clients are seeking, the therapist can ask, "When was the last time [change clients discussed] happened?" When the client responds, the therapist then asks, "What was different then?" and "How did that happen?" These questions pull out more context of the solution and allow the clients to acknowledge that the solution has indeed happened in the past.

The therapist listens for small exceptions when clients are talking and then uses those to build the focus on how the client made that exception happen. Emphasizing the exception also helps the clients to pause and actually notice that the difference they are looking for is happening, just not as often as they would like (Solution Focused Brief Therapy Association Research Committee, 2025). Repeated emphasis on the exceptions allows the clients to continually build their hope for change. The instillation of hope supports the positive focus of the therapeutic process and allows the clients to expect that change can and is happening (Reiter, 2010).

The Coping Question

There are times when clients come into therapy with such an overwhelming sense of the problem that there is no way they can engage in a conversation about differences, exceptions, or conceptualize a miracle. Coping questions support clients in processing the problem and acknowledge small steps they are taking to deal with it, even when they are not consciously aware that they are doing so. The therapist first acknowledges where the client is and the serious nature of the issues.

The next step is finding out how the client is coping with the situation by asking what they have found helpful in managing their stress so far, how they managed to come into therapy, how they are getting out of bed, and whatever small daily steps they take yet don't have to. What the therapist hears is the strength of the client to want to move forward; however, the step might be so small that the client does not see it (De Jong & Berg, 2008). The therapist working with the Daniels family might ask the parents how they had been coping with the worry about their daughter. Fran would reply, "We love our children and would do anything for them!" and "We want to be the family we used to be, for Pam to be like she used to be." The response reveals the client's desire to have change and identify strengths, such as the motivation to change.

Additional Solution-Focused Tools

Additional solution-focused tools can be implemented to focus the therapeutic conversation on solution-building rather than problem-solving.

Overcoming the Urge Suggestion. de Shazer and the team found it useful to wonder how clients might overcome the urge to engage in the problem behavior, as it supports the client to realize episodes of success (De Jong & Berg, 2008). Examples may include feeling frightened, anxious, hopeless, or behaviors such as misusing drugs or harming someone. The SFBT therapist asks the client to pay attention or notice times when they might start [identified problem behavior], yet they were able to overcome the urge and not engage in the problem behavior; further wondering what was different at that time. For the Daniels family, the therapist would be curious about how the family was able to have fun together while at Disney and in the past as a family. It seems that when there is less conflict in the family and less control and focus on Pam's eating, things are better; Pam can and will eat. When Pam eats, her parents are less stressed and able to focus on the activities at hand and the entire family.

Normalizing. When clients are overwhelmed by a situation or problem, they might not be able to see how their reaction makes sense. **Normalizing** is an intervention used by therapists to be curious with the client about whether their response might be within the typical range of behaviors for a particular situation. Normalizing the "problem behavior" can de-escalate the problem talk and create more understanding of how the behavior makes sense (De Jong & Berg, 2008). Fran and Murray are very concerned about Pam not eating and are considering placement in a residential facility if family therapy doesn't work. The therapist can normalize their concerns, expressing that any parent who loves their child as much as they do would be scared and worried. This diffuses the tension between the parents and Pam. It helps to validate their concerns while highlighting their love and concern for their daughter (who saw them as critical and not meeting their expectations).

Reframing. **Reframing** helps clients see a situation from a different perspective by suggesting alternative views that are less problematic. The therapist can help the family understand that a behavior identified as a "problem" can have a positive purpose (Berg, 1994). Pam identifies her parents as "overbearing and critical." The therapist can reframe that presentation into parents who are concerned and love their daughter very much. Reframing helps a family see behaviors in a different light.

Compliments. According to Berg (1994), **compliments** are an effective intervention used from the start of therapy. Clients are empowered by the recognition that they have done something well, even if it is not related to the presenting problem. Compliments "should be reality-based, in the sense that it is derived from what the client communicates to you through words or client process" (De Jong & Berg, 2008, p. 35). Exploring previous solutions and highlighting what the client is doing well engages the client to collaborate in exploring new possible solutions with a level of confidence and hope.

Highlighting what the client is doing well is purposeful throughout the therapeutic process. Compliments punctuate what the clients are already doing well. Berg and De Jong (2005) described the distinctions between three different types of compliments to consider during SFBT sessions with clients.

Direct compliments. **Direct compliments** come from the therapist based on something the client has done or is doing. "*Wow. You must be very committed parents to seek support for your family.*" In working with a new client, the conversation might begin with complimenting the ability to come to the session at the right time. For the Daniels family, the therapist might compliment the family for being able to all make it to the session because they are all concerned about the fighting over Pam.

Indirect compliments. **Indirect compliments** come from the vantage point of another person in the system. The therapist poses a question using a positive statement from a relational perspective. For example, the therapist might ask, "Pam, did you know how proud your parents are about your artistic and musical talents?" (De Jong & Berg, 2008). Another way to implement an indirect compliment is to form a question that elicits a compliment through the perspective of another person. The therapist could ask, "Fran, if I asked Murray how you manage to be such an attentive mother, what would he say?" (Berg & De Jong, 2005).

Self-compliments. **Self-compliments** are found in the client's self-disclosure of successes. The client might mention that, during the past week, she was able to not get upset with her daughter. The SFBT practitioner might ask: "How were you able to do that?" The client would then respond with ways she was able to stay calm when she might have escalated the interaction. Highlighting their success brings the client's attention to their ability to do something different, which results in positive or desired behavior (De Jong & Berg, 2008). The therapist might ask the Daniels family how they were all able to make time for the therapy appointment, or how they were able to work together to plan their day when they were at Disney.

Formula first session task (FFST). de Shazer and Molnar (1984) formulated an intervention designed to assist both clients and therapists in forming a clearer idea of the goals of therapy and in creating a positive context for change. They termed this intervention the formula first session task (FFST). de Shazer (1985) describes the FFST as follows:

> Between now and the next time we meet, we would like you to observe, so that you can describe to us next time, what happens in your (pick one: family, life, marriage, relationship) that you want to continue to have happen. (p. 137)

The response to this task often allows the clients to note positive events already happening, which might have gone unnoticed before. This task can start the process of creating solutions as reported by the clients (De Jong & Berg, 2008). If used with the Daniels, this task would focus the family members' attention on the times when they are working together as a family, the times when the problem is not a problem.

The Therapeutic Process

The solution-focused brief therapist works from the position where the client is the expert on their lives. The therapist leads from one step behind (De Jong & Berg, 2008), being curious about what the client is seeking. Using the questions and interventions, the therapist works to understand what the client is seeking, what life looks like without the problem. Often, that is already happening, just not enough for the clients to notice as they are fixed on the problem. The therapist does not ignore the problem but explores around it; wondering when there are times the problem is not a problem and what else is happening at that time. The focus of the therapy shifts from the problem to what the client wants to be different. Building on the exceptions to the problem, the therapist and client co-construct the future that the client has identified.

The family transcript that follows highlights the therapist working to move the family from focusing on a family member as the problem to being the type of family they want to be. Eating disorders are serious, and the family has involved their family physician in the daughter's health. The diagnosis was made two years ago, and she has made positive progress in the past. The first session is about joining with the clients so all family members will participate in therapy and help remove the focus on Pam as the family problem.

Case Transcript

Therapist: Welcome, everyone. It's great that you were all able to make the appointment. Let's start by introducing ourselves and letting me know what has to happen for this session today to be helpful.

Intervention: Joining—The therapist works to create a relationship in the system with all the family members and gets to know what is important to each person. The therapist also started the session with a question about what the clients are seeking to be different. The therapist asks how the session can be helpful.

Fran: Hello, I'm Fran. I'm so concerned about my daughter, Pam. She's not eating and not understanding that she must eat; she must go back to being who she was before and stop this behavior.
Therapist: Ok, you said you want Pam to stop a behavior. What would you like her to do instead?

Intervention: Goal formulation—The therapist is learning what the goals of the client system are; focusing on the desired behaviors rather than the undesired behaviors.

Fran: Eat. She was diagnosed with Anorexia two years ago—Pam's always been thin and a picky eater, but she would eat. Her doctor wanted her to gain 15–20 pounds "to be safe." I tried. I made her favorite foods and charted her eating. I made her step on a scale twice a day, things were OK, but in the past six months, she just kept losing weight. Her therapist wanted us to put her in an inpatient facility…I…we just cannot do that.
Pam: I won't go. I'm just not hungry. You're just overbearing and critical of everything I do!
Murray: Pam, you're not fine. This is why we're here.
Therapist: This is what the family is supporting each other about; this is a loving, concerned family.

Intervention: Reframing—the daughter sees the parents as "overbearing" and "critical." The therapist reframes that behavior as supporting each other. The therapist also begins shifting the therapeutic conversation away from problem talk to solution talk.

Murray: I'm Murray. I agree with my wife, for today to be helpful, we need to understand why Pam won't eat. This is our last option. I mean, a residential treatment facility—which we don't want to have happen, is very costly.
Therapist: You're very concerned parents; you love your daughter very much.

Intervention: Normalizing—the therapist normalizes the parents' behavior—thinking about a residential facility for the daughter by acknowledging how scary it must be to worry about their daughter.

Fran: Yes, our children are our world.
Murray: Of course.

Therapist: That must be scary for you to worry about Pam. How are you coping with this worry?

Intervention: Coping question—The therapist uses the coping question to help the family recognize the love that the parents have for the children, the strength and commitment of the family.

Fran: By coming here—we love our children and would do anything for them! Murray is so busy at the store but he's here—Pam is so important to us. We want to be the family we used to be, for Pam to be like she used to be.

Therapist: Yes, parents who love their children would be concerned like you are. Tell me more about the family you used to be—you said you wanted Pam to be like she used to be—what does that mean?

Intervention: Goal formulation—The therapist continues to clarify and deconstruct the client goals.

Fran: Oh, she was a star student, involved in all sorts of activities in the community. We did all kinds of fun things together. She never wants to talk to me now.

Therapist: Ahh, a star student, wow! (*looking at Pam*) You must be Pam? What are you thinking needs to happen today for the session to be helpful?

Pam: (*looking away from the therapist and her family*) I don't know, it's not such a big deal. I'm just not hungry at the times my family sits down to eat. I just want my parents off my back and to leave me alone! I don't need to go into a hospital; they need to stop talking about that!

Therapist: Pam, you must have a good reason not to eat with your family. What do you think?

Intervention: Exceptions—The family is overwhelmed by their problem and having a difficult time visualizing when the problem is not a problem. Learning when the problem was not a problem in the past can identify past successes.

Pam: (*starting to cry*) I don't know. They threaten me all the time that I will have to go to the hospital and be force-fed.

Fran: Honey, we love you and can't ignore you when you are acting like this. You are disappearing in front of our eyes! (*She reaches for Pam who shrugs her away*). We used to be so close.

Therapist: This must be overwhelming for you, Pam. Your parents are talking about a residential facility. You said you've been to a therapist before. What was helpful?

Intervention: Finding out what works—The family has disclosed that Pam went to a therapist before and things were better until about 6 months ago. The therapist seeks to find out what was helpful for Pam when she was working with the therapist. One of the basic tenets of SFBT is doing more of what works.

(Berg, 1994)

Pam: Nothing was helpful. She would see me and then tell my mother everything I said, so I stopped talking to her.

Therapist: Mmm, so you did talk to her at the beginning, though? What did you talk about?

Intervention: Listen–Select–Build—The therapist ignores what did not work and continues to be curious about what did work in the therapy session. Listening for the small clues for what was helpful, the therapist builds on those to learn more about what worked in the past.

Pam: Yeah, we did talk. She was interested in my music. I play the piano, and she asked a lot about that. We also talked about my friends and school, which is really stressful. Then everything changed, my mom got involved, and we had to talk about my food.

Fran: I had to get involved because we were paying for weekly sessions and nothing was happening.

Therapist: OK, so Pam, you're a pianist! Wow! Fran and Murray, you have a talented daughter! I remember you said she's a star student!

Intervention: Compliments—The therapist offers compliments as a way of joining with clients and to highlight success.

Fran: Well, yes, but her grades have dropped in high school. She used to be a solid A student now she is almost a C student.

Murray: The boys are top athletes, baseball is their game, and I'm one of the coaches. They're top of the class too—A students.

Therapist: Wow, all your kids are so talented and smart! You must be so proud of them! Who do they get that from?

Intervention: Compliments—the therapist continues to offer compliments directly to the parents in an effort to shift the talk from problem talk to success or solution talk.

Murray: We are for sure—our kids are great…they didn't get this from me for sure. It must be their mom. Fran went to college to be a teacher, but she decided to stay at home once we decided to start our family. I just work with my hands.

Fran: Oh Murray, you run your family business! You worked your way up from a clerk in your grandfather's appliance store and am now the owner—it's the store everyone in the community goes to. You have kept your family business viable. You went to college too.

Therapist: Wow, quite a family, everyone is so talented!

Pam: Not me, didn't you hear them? I'm too skinny and dumb. I keep telling them that high school is different from middle school, the classes are tough…so much pressure about college too. Even when I did get A's they wanted more—advanced classes, cheer team, not satisfied with the school orchestra, they wanted me to try out for the National Youth Orchestra, said it would help me get into college.

Therapist: Yes, that's so true, Pam, high school is different, isn't it and thinking about your future can be confusing. You want to be more independent in your decisions as a young adult. Did you know your parents are so concerned and love you as much as they do?

Intervention: Validation—the daughter is used to being the problem. The therapist validates her feelings, so her voice is heard. This helps with the joining process between the therapist and the daughter.

Pam: No, this is the first time I've heard that I do anything well from my parents. I'm not a child anymore; I'm in high school and will be leaving for college in a couple of years.

Therapist: So Mom and Dad want Pam to continue with her music and focus on schoolwork. Pam wants to be more independent. George and Oliver, what has to happen today for the time spent to be helpful?

Oliver: I just want my parents to calm down. Pam knows what's good for her. They're always yelling and everything is about "What did Pam eat this morning?" "What can we get Pam to eat for dinner?" Geez. Pam is a great big sister. I mean, she leaves us alone.

George: Yeah, what Oliver said.

Therapist: Ok, so it seems like for today to be helpful the family is focused on something other than being upset and worrying about Pam. What would you all be doing instead?

Interventions: Goal formulation—the therapist works on finding exceptions to the problem and clarifies the goals for the family.

Oliver: We'd be at the ballpark—watching the game today!

Therapist: Oh, is that something you do as a family? Go to ball games?

Murray: No, the boys and I usually go to the games by ourselves. Fran and Pam aren't much into sports.

Fran: That is not true, honey. When the boys are playing, I'm always there.

Therapist: Ok, so Fran, what would you be doing?

Fran: Well, maybe Pam and I would be in the crafting room or planning a new craft project and out shopping for supplies. We used to do those kinds of things together all the time, but we don't anymore.

Pam: We used to do a lot of things mom that we don't do anymore.

Therapist: Oh, like what?

Pam: We used to do family things—game night, family trips, pizza dinners after my brother's ball games. We don't do any of that anymore.

Fran: Those were fun times. We still do that, sometimes.

Pam: Mom, get real! Dad works all the time, Oliver and George are at practice every day and Dad is there with them at the ball field if he is not at the store. Mom just watches me and asks what I've eaten today, or she's on the phone with her mother.

Therapist: OK, so it sounds like this is one busy family—when was the last time you had a family thing?

Intervention: Exception to the problem—The therapist has identified "a family thing" as a time when everyone was getting along and having fun. Exception questions allow the family to remember times when the problem was not a problem.

Fran: I don't know, can't think of a time right now…

George: When grandma was in town! She took us to the movies and let us have whatever we wanted. Grandma is the best.

Pam: Yeah, Grandma taught me a new song to play on the piano. She's really good.

Therapist: Wow! That sounds really fun. When was that?

Fran: That was last year. My mother comes to town and stays with the kids so Murray and I can get away.

Therapist: That sounds nice—important for parents to have time together as a couple. Ok, I'm going to ask you what might seem to be a weird question, just go with me, please. Suppose that today is just a typical day after you leave here. Murray, you and the boys head to the ball field, Fran, you head home with Pam and do what you both usually do in the afternoon. Later, everyone gets home and you have dinner, the kids get their homework done, things are just as usual, and you head to bed. However, while you are sleeping tonight, a miracle happens—just over your house—not your neighbor or friends, just your house. The miracle is that the problem which brought you here today is solved, gone just like that (*snaps fingers*). Yet, because you're sleeping, you don't know that the miracle has happened. So, when you wake up tomorrow morning, what will be different that tells you that a miracle has happened? The problem which brought you in here is solved?

Intervention: Miracle question—the miracle question is to support the clients visualizing their life without the problem. The phrasing of the question causes the clients to look forward, shifting the client view to their preferred future, one without the problem.

George: I will win the MVP award this year instead of Oliver.

Therapist: Wow, that would be great for you—perhaps a smaller difference?

Oliver: There would not be angry faces in the house…

Pam: There would be "faces" in the house; Dad would be at home.

Therapist: OK, so Pam and Oliver, tell me more about the "faces," what would they be doing?

George: They would be talking about good things, laughing, having fun.

Therapist: OK, so everyone will be home then, laughing and having fun doing what?

Intervention: Bridging—the therapist deconstructs the clients' miracles so that they can be woven together. This provides a unified focus on what life looks like when the problem is no longer a problem. This process is called **bridging**.

(Hoyt & Berg, 1998)

Fran: Making breakfast, the kids used to love doing that on the weekends! Pam is a great cook—she could even get the boys in line.

Therapist: Oh? Is that true, Pam? You're a great cook, and you can corral your brothers? What would you make?

Pam: Well, I never heard Mom say that before. I guess so. I used to make a breakfast casserole. I don't know why I haven't done that for a while. We just don't eat breakfast together. I just don't eat breakfast.

Therapist: (*Jumping in before Fran could talk about her eating*) Ok, so Murray, what else would be going on?

Murray: Well, like Fran said, those breakfasts were fun. We used to go to community festivals, things the school puts on. Those were fun.

Therapist: So, let's see, everyone would be up, eating a great breakfast and planning something the family would do together. Wow! What else is happening?

Oliver: Mom and Dad are happy; they wouldn't be having those arguments under their breaths… the slow tight talking.

Therapist: OK, so Mom and Dad would be happy, smiling. What would you boys and Pam be doing?

Pam: We'd be having breakfast and talking, as a family—like we did at Disney.

Oliver: Yeah, we always had breakfast and planned which parks and rides we were going to do that day. It was really fun.

Therapist: How did you do that at Disney? Have fun and everyone together?

Intervention: Exception to the problem—The therapist helps the family identify an exception; that when they went on their Disney trip everyone got along and had fun.

Fran: Well, it was a major family vacation we had planned for, and everyone was excited. So many things to do—we even had special reservations at the Castle for dinner and with Chef Mickey! Even Pam ate there!

Therapist: Really?! Wow, Pam, how did you do that?

Pam: They have fountains of chocolate and everything you could imagine—I don't know, everyone was happy and no one was watching my plate, no one was arguing.

Therapist: So Pam, when the focus is not on your eating but on the family fun, you're OK to eat?

Intervention: Exception to the problem—The therapist helps Pam identify an exception; a time when everyone was happy, getting along, and having fun.

Pam: Well, yeah, when mom focuses on my plate, it's full of things I don't like to eat—at Disney I got to choose what I wanted to eat and how much I wanted to eat.

Therapist: Wow, you *all* ate breakfast together and planned the day together? That sounds like a great time. Let me ask you another question—on a scale of one to ten, with ten being the family has those happy faces, you're sharing a meal that sometimes Pam, the great cook, has made and the boys helped, Mom and Dad are smiling. And one is when the family is busy, in different places, not smiling. What number are you at today?

Intervention: Scaling question—the therapist uses the scaling question at this time to find out where they are in relation to how close they are to what their lives look like when the problem is no longer a problem. Once the clients offer a number the therapist will find out what tells them they are not lower. This helps the client to identify exceptions and successes. The therapist will then find out what has to be different for the client to move up a small step. This helps identify steps towards achieving the 10.

Pam: I'm a 1.
Therapist: OK, a 1, what tells you that you're a 1 and not a zero?

Intervention: Scaling sequence—The therapist gathers details of how the client defines their position on the scale. Asking why the client is not lower prompts the client to bring up successes and highlights that they are moving up the scale already.

Pam: I didn't know I could go to a zero; everyone is here because of me so I'm at the low end of the scale. I'm the problem, can't make good decisions, am a poor achiever, too skinny, too stupid… maybe I should be a negative 10.
Therapist: Ah, OK Pam, let's get back to you about your number. Murray, what number are you?
Murray: I'm a 5.
Therapist: A 5, OK, how come a 5 and not a 3?
Murray: Well, we're all here today, aren't we? And we're talking too.
Oliver: You forgot the fun part, Dad.
Therapist: Oliver, what number are you?
Oliver: Maybe a 3.
Therapist: So how come a 3 and not a 1?
Oliver: Well, like dad said, we're all here, and we do have times when we're having fun as a family, like that Disney trip.
George: I'm a 5, like dad. And I know your next question. I'm a 5 and not lower because we're all here, and I am pretty sure we're headed out for pizza after.
Therapist: OK, wow, pizza! So dad and George are a 5, Oliver is a 3 and Pam is a 1. What about you Fran?
Fran: I guess I'm a 2 because it wasn't too difficult to get everyone to get in the car today. We all do care about each other.
Therapist: Pam, now that you've heard from the others, how come you are a 1 and not lower on the scale?
Pam: Well, I guess because this isn't what I expected. I thought it would be just about me, not about the family.
Therapist: OK, so Fran, what would have to be different for you to move from a 2 to a 2½?

Intervention: Scaling sequence—the therapist has the client detail an actionable step they can take to keep progressing up the scale towards their goal. Small steps towards the goal help keep the change process from overwhelming the clients.

Fran: For Pam to eat.

Therapist: That might be a bigger step; we're just talking about half a point up the scale towards the family fun, the happy faces talking.

Intervention: Scaling sequence—The therapist continues to focus the client on what she can do to move towards the goal rather than another client. Small steps are more attainable and support client success.

Fran: OK, I guess a smaller step would be Pam making good choices.
Therapist: What could *you* do, Fran, that would move *yourself* half a step?
Fran: I guess I could stop making Pam step on the scale multiple times every day. She hates that.
Therapist: What would you do instead, Fran?
Fran: I guess I could do something more enjoyable, like crafting.
Therapist: What kind of crafts do you do?
Fran: A little of everything, but my favorite is knitting. I used to make blankets for the nursing home near our appliance store. The kids would come with me when I delivered them, we loved doing that—not sure why we stopped.
Therapist: Wow, that sounds like fun things you did as a family. What about you, Murray, what could you do to move up the scale half a point, just a small step?
Murray: I guess I could stop working the weekends—I really don't have to be there.
Therapist: Oh? What would you do with this free time?
Murray: Maybe do things with the family.
Pam: The whole family, dad, or just Oliver and George?
Fran: Pam! You didn't mean that.
Therapist: Murray, tell us more about what things you are thinking about…
Murray: Pam, of course I meant the whole family…it's just the boys play ball and they need me more plus taking over the store fulltime. I was thinking about things like the state fair we used to always go to or everyone, the whole family, going to a ball game.
Therapist: You used to do that all the time? Sounds fun, tell me more about those times.
Fran: Oh, every weekend we planned a family day, it was before Murray was responsible for the entire business, so he had more time. I would pack food, and we'd go watch the boys play and picnic after with the other families from the team. The kids would all play and run around. It was the best of times.
Murray: We used to do more than that—we had Saturday night movies in the backyard for the kids and their friends. Kids, do you remember that?

Pam: Yeah, that was fun—we had a popcorn machine, and I got to run it.
George: It was fun. Why did we stop?
Pam: Dad got busy with work; he only has time for baseball now.
Fran: Pam, that is not true, your father works hard so you can go to a good college, and the boys can play ball. Travel teams are expensive you know.
Pam: Maybe I don't want to go to college?
Therapist: Pam if you don't go to college what would you do instead?
Pam: Well thank you for asking. No one in this family ever asks me what I want; they just tell me. I would get a job, save some money and maybe travel. See another country. I don't know.
Murray: Pam, I'm sorry if you think we don't ask about what you want. I thought you wanted to go to college and be a teacher like your mom planned to be. I thought you might teach art or music. Taking some time to work and perhaps travel does sound interesting. You can tell us what you want to do; it is your life.
Therapist: OK, so Pam, it sounds like you have an idea for your future which you've been thinking about for some time, and it seems like your father is interested in hearing about it too. Does that surprise you?
Pam: Yes, it does, I didn't expect my Dad to support me—he's all about my brothers. I didn't think he cared. He loves having boys to play ball with.
Murray: Pam, I love you, honey—you're the oldest, and as a girl, your mom just knew better how to raise you.
Therapist: OK, OK. Oliver, what could you do to move from a 3 to a 3½?
Oliver: I don't know, clean my room?
Therapist: So that would move you closer to family fun?
Oliver: Yes, because when my room isn't clean, I don't get to do anything fun, and Mom gets mad.
Therapist: OK, sounds like you are ready for the family fun. What about you, George? What would have to be different for you to move from a 5 to a 5½?
George: I don't know…do my chores so mom doesn't get mad?
Therapist: So that gets you moving towards family fun?
George: Yeah, when mom gets mad at us for not doing chores, she yells and is angry. Then dad comes home, and he gets mad because mom is mad and then the whole night is not fun.
Therapist: OK so when Mom is happy things are more fun. What about you, Pam? What would have to be different for you to move up ½ a point?
Pam: My parents would get off my back.
Therapist: OK, what could you do to move towards family fun?
Pam: I guess I could talk more with my mom like we used to. She always wants to talk, and I just go to my room because I don't want her to get mad at me because I won't tell her what she wants to hear.

Therapist: What do you think your mom wants to hear?

Pam: That I got all A's on my tests, and I'm spending the weekend filling out college applications and that I'm hungry enough to eat like my brothers.

Fran: No, Pam, that is not what I want to hear. I want to know what you are doing in school, talk about what you're interested in, your ideas about travel, I never knew you wanted to do that—anything. I just want to be with you like we used to be. I want us to have the mother-daughter relationship I don't have with my mother.

Therapist: OK, so it sounds like you all know that you can move towards that 10 by intentionally spending time with each other, talking, and having fun …and it's something you've done before. So, I'm thinking about giving you homework - don't worry, George, Oliver, and Pam, it's easy compared with your schoolwork! I'm wondering, between now and the next time we meet, if you all could observe times you are together as family—having fun. Notice those times – might be 10 minutes here, 20 minutes there, but it's time spent having fun with each other as a family. Those are things we'll want to make sure are not changed in therapy and continue to happen.

Intervention: FFST—the therapist creates a task for the family to observe or notice exceptions to the problem over the time until the next session. This shifts the focus of the family from the problem to what they have identified as steps towards their life when the problem is no longer the problem.

Murray: Yes, we can do that, and we can start today.

Fran: Yes—we can do that, right kids? (*Pam, Oliver, and George all nod*).

Therapist: OK, good, just notice times when you're together and having fun. See you next week then.

The Therapeutic Story

The session started with the focus on Pam and the goal for Pam to eat and ended with the family focused on how to spend time with each other. The family talked about times they had enjoyed being with each other and having fun together, not focusing on Pam's eating which was the problem they came in with. The therapist, through using exception questions and the miracle question, found that the family did miss the times they used to spend together. Pam felt like a disappointment to her parents because she did not align with her mother's expectations of going to college after high school. She also felt like no one listened to what she wanted.

When using this model, the therapist must move from problems to solutions. This was done by asking the family for more details and specifics about exceptions and tracking their progress using clearly defined and reachable goals. When the mother kept responding with problem talk, the therapist flipped it by asking what the mom would be doing instead.

In subsequent sessions, the therapist will find out what is better, to further focus on the exceptions and successes of the family. The same scaling question from the first session can be used each time to assess progress toward their goal. It is important not to ignore the anorexia diagnosis; however, it is also important to not make it the only focus of the family. The therapist learned that when the family was talking and spending time together, having fun, then the daughter was stable. The therapist also knows that the family physician is working with the daughter. It might also be wise for the therapist to consider asking for a release to speak with the family physician for collaboration and consultation purposes.

References

Anderson, H., & Goolishian, H. (1992). The client is the expert: A not-knowing approach to therapy. In S. McNamee & K. J. Gergen (Eds.), *Therapy as social construction* (pp. 25–39). Sage Publications, Inc.

Bannink, F. (2014). *Post-traumatic success: Positive psychology & solution-focused strategies to help clients survive and thrive*. Norton.

Bavelas, J. D. J., Franklin, C., Froerer, A., Gingerich, W., Kim, J., Korman, H., Langer, S., Lee, M.Y., McCollum, E., Jordan, S.S., & Trepper, T. S. (2013). *Solution focused therapy treatment manual for working with individuals* (2nd Ed.). Solution Focused Brief Therapy Association.

Berg, I. K. (1989). Of visitors, complainants, and customers: Is there really such a thing as 'resistance?'. *Networker*, January/February.

Berg, I. K. (1994). *Family based services*. Norton.

Berg, I. K., & De Jong, P. (2005). Engagement through complimenting. *Journal of Family Psychotherapy*, *16*(1–2), 51–56.

Berg, I. K., & de Shazer, S. (1993). Making numbers talk: Language in therapy. In S. Friedman (Ed.). *The new language of change: Constructive collaboration in psychotherapy* (pp. 5–24). The Guilford Press.

Berg, I. K., & Dolan, Y. (2001). *Tales of solutions: A collection of hope-inspiring stories*. W. W. Norton & Company.

Berg, I. K. & Shilts, L. (2005). *Classroom solutions: WOWW approach*. Brief Family Therapy Center.

Blakesee, S. & Jordan, S.S. (2014). Solution-focused approach with American Indian clients. In J. Kim (Ed.) *Solution-focused brief therapy: A Multicultural approach* (pp. 106–120). Sage.

Cade, B. (2007). Springs, streams, and tributaries: A history of the brief, solution-focused approach. In T. Nelson, & F. Thomas. (Eds.), *Handbook of solution-focused brief therapy: Clinical applications* (pp. 25–63). Haworth Press.

De Jong, P. (2019). A brief, informal history of SFBT as told by Steve de Shazer and Insoo Kim Berg. *Journal of Solution Focused Practices*, *3*(1), 1–5.

De Jong, P., & Berg, I. K. (2008). *Interviewing for solutions* (3rd ed.). Brooks/Cole.

Hoyt, M. F., & Berg, I. K. (1998). Solution-focused couple therapy: Helping clients construct self-fulfilling realities. In F. M. Dattilio (Ed.), *Case studies in couple and family therapy* (pp. 203–232). Guilford.

Kim, J. S. (Ed.) (2014). *Solution-focused brief therapy: A multicultural approach*. Sage Publications.

Lipchik, E. (2002). *Beyond technique in solution-focused therapy: Working with emotions and the therapeutic relationship*. Guilford Press.
Neipp, M. & Beyeback, M. (2022). The global outcomes of solution-focused brief therapy: A revision. *The American Journal of Family Therapy*, *52*, 1–18.
Nelson, T. S. (2011). Solution-focused brief couple therapy. In D. K. Carson & M. Casado-Kehoe (Eds.), *Case studies in couples therapy: Theory-based approaches* (pp. 275–287). Routledge.
Reiter, M. (2010). Hope and expectancy in solution-focused brief therapy. *Journal of Family Psychotherapy*, *21*(2), 132–148.
Reiter, M. D. (2018). *Systems theories for psychotherapists*. Routledge.
Reiter, M. (2024). *Family therapy: An introduction to process, practice and therapy* (2nd ed.). Routledge.
Reiter, M. (2025). Solution focused couple therapy. In M. D. Reiter (Ed.). *Case conceptualization in couple therapy: Comparing and contrasting theories*. Routledge.
Reiter, M. D., & Chenail, R. J. (2016). Defining the focus in solution-focused brief therapy. *International Journal of Solution-Focused Practices*, *4(1)*, 1–9.
de Shazer, S. (1982). *Patterns of brief family therapy: An ecosystemic approach*. Guilford Press.
de Shazer, S. (1984). The death of resistance. *Family Process*, *23*, 79–93.
de Shazer, S. (1985). *Keys to solutions in brief therapy*. Norton.
de Shazer, S. (1988). *Clues: Investigating solutions in brief therapy*. Norton.
de Shazer, S. (1994). *Words were originally magic*. Norton.
de Shazer, S., Berg, I. E. L., Nunnally, E., Molnar, A., Gingerich, W., & Weiner-Davis, M. (1986). Brief therapy: Focused solution development. *Family Process* (25), 207–221.
de Shazer, S., Dolan, Y., Korman, H., Trepper, T., McCollum, E., & Berg, I. (2007). *More than miracles: The State of the art of solution-focused brief therapy*. Routledge.
de Shazer, S., & Molnar, A. (1984). Four useful interventions in brief family therapy. *Journal of Marital and Family Therapy*, *10* (3), 297–304.
Shilts, L., Rambo, A., Huntley, E. (2003). The collaborative miracle: When to slow down the pace of brief therapy. *Journal of Systemic Therapies 22*(2), 65–73.
Solution Focused Brief Therapy Association Research Committee. (2025). *Solution-Focused Therapy Treatment Manual for Working with Individuals*, (3rd ed.). Solution Focused Brief Therapy Association.
Żak, A. M., & Pękala, K. (2025). Effectiveness of solution-focused brief therapy: An umbrella review of systematic reviews and meta-analyses. *Psychotherapy Research*, *35*(7), 1043–1055.

15 Narrative Family Therapy

Weston Crafton and Ashley McErlean

Michael White from Australia together with David Epston from New Zealand created narrative therapy as a different approach to standard therapeutic methods which placed problems inside patients. White and Epston (1990) posited that problems develop when people accept culturally based stories that stem from social power systems and dominant social norms. Narrative therapy enables clients to transform their problems through intentional meaning interpretation (Freedman & Combs, 1996; Morgan, 2000).

Narrative therapy serves as a different approach to studying human problems because it operates outside the standard models, which concentrate on treating internal psychological flaws (Payne, 2006; White & Epston, 1990). Narrative therapy identifies problems as narrative constructs that people learn through their exposure to cultural standards, social connections, power dynamics, and dominant language systems (Freedman & Combs, 1996; Morgan, 2000). People develop these stories through interactions with their family members, community environment, and social environment. For instance, as pertaining to anorexia, it exists as a pattern of meaning which has established itself around a person rather than being an internal personal trait (White, 2007). This chapter examines a narrative therapist's views about problem emergence before applying their concepts to study the Daniels family, who seek assistance for their daughter Pam's anorexia nervosa.

The Therapeutic Story of Problem Formation

Narrative therapy's foundational premise is that people live their lives according to stories shaped by dominant discourses (White, 1991; White & Epston, 1990). **Dominant discourses** are socially sanctioned ways of understanding reality—shared cultural assumptions about gender, success, beauty, family roles, morality, etc. These discourses exert subtle but powerful influence, providing criteria by which people judge themselves and others. When individuals or families measure themselves against these discourses and perceive a discrepancy, problems can take shape (Freedman & Combs, 1996).

DOI: 10.4324/9781003668510-15

In contemporary Western culture, discourses around thinness and bodily self-control are pervasive. Young women may feel pressure to conform to ideals that equate slenderness with worth, discipline, and desirability. Additional discourses surrounding female relational responsibility, academic achievement, and family image also influence identity formation (Morgan, 2000; Payne, 2006). When these cultural narratives saturate a young person's meaning-making, they can set the stage for problems such as eating disorders to emerge.

In family contexts, dominant discourses may intersect with local family stories, shaping expectations about who each member "should" be (White, 2007). In the Daniels family, traditional gender roles organize relationships: Murray identifies closely with the boys through sports, while Fran assumes responsibility for nurturing and emotional care. These powerful gendered storylines create a framework through which Pam interprets her place in the family system.

Narrative therapy describes **internalization** as the process through which individuals absorb dominant cultural messages and integrate them into their self-stories (White & Epston, 1990). When a person internalizes problem-saturated narratives, they may come to see the discourse as a personal truth rather than a socially constructed expectation. For example, a cultural message such as "discipline is measured by food restriction" may be internalized as "I am only valuable if I can control my eating." Once internalized, such beliefs can structure identity, behavior, and emotional experience.

Internalization often leads to **self-policing**, a process Foucault (1977) described as individuals monitoring and correcting themselves according to external norms. In the context of eating disorders, self-policing may manifest as meticulous calorie tracking, shame around eating, secrecy, or rigid self-judgment. These behaviors reinforce the problem's presence and make it difficult for the person to imagine alternative stories. Internalization is not a sign of personal failure; it is evidence of the profound influence of cultural narratives on identity (White, 2007).

Narrative therapists view problems as surviving within **life-support systems**—the relational, emotional, discursive, and environmental conditions that allow the problem to continue exerting influence (White, 2007). A problem cannot survive in isolation; it requires a set of sustaining interactions, beliefs, and patterns. These supports may include unspoken family expectations, conflict cycles, secrecy, fear-based reactions, or broader cultural narratives. Identifying these supports allows families to weaken the problem's influence by modifying the conditions that allow it to thrive (Freedman & Combs, 1996).

The life-support system is not about blaming families; rather, it highlights how problems recruit people into roles without their awareness (White & Epston, 1990; Winslade & Monk, 2008). For instance, when family members respond to an eating disorder with pressure, surveillance, or argumentation, the problem may exploit these reactions to intensify its hold. Life-support systems often include cycles of silence or avoidance, unmet emotional needs, transgenerational messages, or chronic stressors. Examining these factors helps families reclaim agency from the problem.

The Daniels family presents with deep concern regarding their 17-year-old daughter Pam, who has been struggling with anorexia nervosa despite previous outpatient treatment. Narrative therapy provides a lens through which to understand how the problem was constructed and how it continues to influence family life (Monk et al., 1997; White, 2007). By examining dominant discourses, internalization processes, and the life-support system surrounding the problem, therapists can help the Daniels family develop alternative narratives that re-author Pam's identity and strengthen family resilience.

Several dominant discourses appear to influence the Daniels family's relational context. First, their adherence to traditional U.S. gender roles positions Murray as the athletic, achievement-oriented father closely bonded with his sons. In contrast, Fran is positioned as the emotional caretaker and mother-daughter relational anchor. Pam, whose interests lie in music and arts rather than sports, may feel marginalized within a family culture that values athleticism. This dynamic reinforces a discourse that belonging is tied to sports-related competency—an identity Pam does not naturally inhabit.

Second, discourses around academic achievement contribute pressure. Pam's high school grades declined after middle school, and Fran's attempts to motivate her were interpreted by Pam as criticism rather than support. Within a dominant narrative that "good daughters succeed academically" and "good mothers ensure their daughters achieve," both Pam and Fran may experience shame, frustration, or self-doubt (Morgan, 2000; Payne, 2006). These discourses shape their relational interactions, setting the stage for conflict and misunderstanding.

Finally, cultural discourses surrounding body image and thinness intersect with Pam's stage of development as an adolescent girl. These narratives may contribute to a belief that thinness equates to control or worthiness, making Pam more vulnerable to the influence of anorexia (White, 2007; Winslade & Monk, 2008).

Pam's year-long concealment of her eating habits suggests significant internalization of problem-related messages. By repeatedly telling her family she "was not hungry," Pam acted as both subject and enforcer of the discourse that values restriction. Her secrecy illustrates the degree to which anorexia had taken up residence in her self-story, encouraging her to hide behaviors that aligned with its demands.

As anorexia gained influence, Pam likely engaged in intense self-policing, monitoring her eating, body shape, and weight with vigilance. This self-regulatory process is consistent with culturally supported ideals of self-discipline and bodily control. Once internalized, these narratives can eclipse other parts of a young person's identity, narrowing their experience and reinforcing the problem (Freedman & Combs, 1996). Pam's isolation within the family may have further amplified the problem's voice, offering Anorexia a sense of purpose or identity during moments when she felt emotionally disconnected.

The Daniels family provides several contextual conditions that may unintentionally support the problem's survival. One major factor is emotional distance and unspoken hurt. Pam feels disconnected from her father and brothers, but has not shared these feelings openly. Another life-support factor is the escalating cycle of meal-time conflict between Pam and Fran. Fran's fear leads her to frequently comment on Pam's eating, and these exchanges often devolve into arguments. This pattern inadvertently strengthens the problem by increasing stress, secrecy, and defiance—conditions that Anorexia often exploits (Monk et al., 1997; White & Epston, 1990).

The gender-based division in the household also contributes to Pam's isolation. Murray invests heavily in his sons' sports lives, leaving Pam without a parallel avenue for connection. Anorexia may use this relational gap as justification for its presence, reinforcing Pam's belief that she is separate or unseen.

Finally, transgenerational narratives influence the family system. Fran's childhood experiences of caring for her younger sister may lead her to assume disproportionate responsibility for Pam's wellbeing, intensifying pressure on both. Murray's limited emotional expressiveness, shaped by his own family-of-origin stories, may restrict opportunities for father–daughter connection (White, 2007). Together, these elements create a life-support structure that allows anorexia to maintain a foothold within the family.

Diversity Conceptualization

Narrative therapy focuses on diversity by understanding how culture, identity, and power dynamics affect family negotiations (Freedman & Combs, 1996; Winslade & Monk, 2008). Postmodern theory, which narrative therapy is predicated on, rejects the existence of any relationship between cultural background and universal standards for human development and mental health assessment. Narrative therapy examines human problems by studying dominant discourses that establish social norms for what society considers normal, acceptable, and preferred (White, 1991, 2007). The values, power structures, and historical background of dominant social groups determine what these belief systems contain. The Daniels family has spent multiple generations in the United States while maintaining a conventional U.S. family structure, which divides work responsibilities by gender and assigns men to sports and work while women care for children. The expectations within these discourses stem from European American and Christian-based family values, which have traditionally defined American family life.

Narrative therapists view diversity as a central aspect of identity construction, exploring culture and language as part of understanding people in context, while acknowledging that diversity also exists within cultural groups, within family systems, and within individuals, and that "no system of universal categories could capture people's lives in all their complexity" (Combs & Freedman, 2012, p. 1035). Rather than searching for universal truths, narrative therapists engage in contextualized meaning-making that deconstructs the contributions of cultural context and dominant discourses to the client's story while valuing the exceptionality and uniqueness of each person. At the same time, narrative therapy centers social justice by scrutinizing the truth status of cultural stories (Fitzsimmons & Zucker, 2004). Those cultural stories that have been taken for granted as universal truths can be re-examined in collaboration with the client to determine whether they are oppressive or limiting, or even to accept them as true for that client.

This approach to exploring diversity makes narrative therapy especially suited for application with diverse situations and populations. Since its inception, narrative therapy has been effective with diverse populations, including couples, older adults, women, children, neurodiverse people, adolescents, and people living with chronic pain, and with clients from vastly different cultural backgrounds, such as Indian, Spanish, Chinese, Aboriginal, and South African (Dulwich Centre, 2025). In just the last five years, researchers have recorded positive outcomes through the use of narrative therapy with caregivers of people with schizophrenia in Hong Kong (Zhou et al., 2023); older adults living with chronic pain in Hong Kong (Chow & Fok, 2020); women in Iran experiencing low marital satisfaction (Ghavibazou et al., 2020); Protestant couples dealing with relational issues in Spain (Chimpén-López et al., 2022); and orphaned and abandoned children in Rwanda (Karibwende et al., 2022).

The dynamics of the Daniels family demonstrate how their relationship problems stem from cultural norms about gender roles, parenting responsibilities, and personal identity. Murray maintains his closest bond with his sons because they share masculine interests and gender identity, which matches his relationship with his father through work and traditional male activities. Fran developed her identity through her family history of caring for her younger sister and through her close bond with her mother and siblings who shared her gender. The family members use their inherited discourses to establish their expectations and maintain their relationships, which determines Pam's family position. The family system positions Pam differently because she lacks the gender-based pathways to intimacy that her brothers have, and she does not share their mother's caregiving experiences. The family system creates these patterns through dominant cultural narratives, which narrative therapy views as evidence of how relationships become possible (White, 2007; Winslade & Monk, 2008).

Narrative therapy requires therapists to analyze how their own cultural background influences their interpretation of client stories. The way people understand family health, gender equality, and emotional expression stems from cultural influences (Anderson, 1997; Freedman & Combs, 1996). A therapist who supports equal relationships in relationships might view Fran and Murray's conventional gender roles as restrictive, even though the family members do not share this perspective. Narrative therapy requires therapists to maintain a position of a curious, humble, and unknowing stance (White, 2005). Narrative therapists check their cultural biases while avoiding forced interpretations of client stories and help clients discover their personal values and preferences. The therapist's non-judgmental stance enables them to work with clients who maintain their cultural heritage while helping them create their preferred life stories (Monk et al., 1997; Winslade & Monk, 2008).

The Therapeutic Story of Problem Resolution

Narrative therapists begin treatment by inviting clients to tell their story. They listen to these problem-saturated stories with the understanding that while they represent an important aspect of the client's experience, they do not fully encapsulate the client's lived experience or reality, and may even be contradicted by other stories (**alternative narratives**) that the client is unable to access when centering the dominant narrative (White & Epston, 1990). This narrow focus on a dominant narrative is called a **thin description**, and it limits the client's ability to interpret their experiences outside of this problem-saturated story or to consider complex or contradicting information (Morgan, 2000). The therapist's goal is then to bring attention to the alternative, subjugated stories that can offer new meaning and increase the accessibility of nuanced interpretation, referred to as **thickening the narrative** (Freedman & Combs, 1996; White, 2007).

The key to being open to both the problem-saturated story and alternative stories simultaneously is maintaining a therapeutic stance that does not assume expertise. White (2005) described the ideal position of the therapist in narrative therapy as **decentered and influential**, in which the therapist prioritizes the stories and knowledge of the clients over their own expert knowledge, and influences the process of therapy by asking questions that build the scaffolding on which the client can create new meaning. This decentered position can be achieved through curiosity and a not-knowing attitude that gives clients "primary authorship" over their own stories (White, 2005, p. 9). The idea of being influential refers not to the therapist's efforts to achieve an agenda, but to their effectiveness in building the scaffold necessary for the clients to explore alternative stories. The combination of varying levels of centeredness and influentiality results in four different quadrants a therapist can fall into: decentered and influential (ideal), centered and influential, decentered and non-influential, or centered and non-influential (White, 2005). A highly centered therapist will emphasize diagnosis and intervention in service to a pre-determined "best" outcome, while a non-influential therapist takes on a more conversational approach that does not steer the dialogue in any direction and therefore does not intentionally create the conditions necessary to explore and create preferred outcomes. A decentered and influential therapist, however, will not pursue a pre-determined outcome, instead allowing the client to take the lead, but at the same time will use intentional questioning and interventions that guide the client in identifying and exploring their preferred story (Freedman & Combs, 1996; Payne, 2006).

Deconstruction

In narrative therapy, the process of examining and understanding how a client's problem-saturated story is constructed is known as **deconstruction** (Freedman & Combs, 1996; White, 1991). According to White (1991), deconstruction "has to do with procedures that subvert taken-for-granted realities and practices" (p. 27), often by highlighting the absurdity of these realities, or "exoticizing the domestic." This process begins with an intentional approach to listening, then progresses to questioning. Freedman and Combs (1996) describe **deconstructive listening** as listening "guided by the belief that those stories have many possible meanings" (p. 47). The therapist listens for differences between their interpretations and the interpretations of the client, asking questions to fill in these gaps. Although at this point, the purpose is to understand the client's story, the therapist's presence and curiosity alone begin to reshape the client's interpretation (Morgan, 2000; Payne, 2006).

During deconstructive questioning, the therapist takes a more active role in shaping meaning and inviting clients to re-examine their stories through alternative lenses (Freedman & Combs, 1996). By bringing awareness to how a client's story has been constructed, the therapist opens the door for the client to see their story as something that can be re-constructed, and for the client to adopt different realities and practices that better align with their lived experience. White (1991, 2007) also emphasized that the therapist's role is not only active, but political, in that it is the therapist's responsibility to draw awareness to marginalizing discourses, such as those rooted in race and gender, that the client may not realize are subjugating.

Deconstruction also requires listening for what is not there—the absent but implicit. The concept of **absent but implicit** refers to the unspoken needs, desires, values, and purposes present in a client's story (White, 2000). In the background of stories about the presenting problem, it is possible to identify the preferred experiences, or what people value. Through **double listening** (Guilfoyle, 2015) and targeted questions, these preferred experiences and values can be brought to the forefront and considered. An impasse over the division of responsibilities in the home, for example, may reflect an unspoken need for a more equal partnership, or more explicit appreciation from a partner.

Externalization

Narrative therapy discards the once-prevailing notion that problems in living reflect individual identities, character flaws, or personality traits, a worldview upheld by "cultural practices of objectification of people" (White, 2007, p. 9). Instead, the narrative model separates the person from the problem through a process called externalization. White and Epston (1990) described **externalization** as "an approach to therapy that encourages persons to objectify and, at times, to personify the problems that they experience as oppressive" (p. 38). Instead of understanding a problem as inherent or a permanent characteristic of an individual, the client can now view it as external and view themselves as in relationship with the problem. People in relationship with a problem have increased influence and agency over how the problem affects them regularly (Freedman & Combs, 1996; Morgan, 2000).

Externalizing conversations modify the language the client uses to describe the problem, thereby objectifying the problem and making "it possible for many people to experience themselves as choosing responsibility for the first time" (Freedman & Combs, 1996, p. 63). The identified problem bringing the Daniels family to therapy is anorexia nervosa exhibited by Pam, which the family currently sees as something wrong within Pam herself. During therapy, the therapist will begin the process of externalization through metaphors and relative influence questions (White, 2007).

Metaphors

The use of metaphors is crucial to the process of externalization. As a language-based model, the words a therapist uses to frame the client's problem shape how the client sees themselves in relationship with the problem (White, 2007). Often, metaphors are used to identify **unique outcomes**, or "aspects of lived experience that fall outside the dominant story" (White & Epston, 1990, p. 15). For example, the Daniels family may describe an evening when Pam had dinner with the family and did not restrict her eating, or a moment when Murray felt a closeness with his daughter that is normally reserved for his sons, or a day when Fran enjoyed spending time with her daughter without feeling the need to act as a caretaker. The therapist can then build on these unique outcomes with metaphors that characterize the clients' behaviors as choices made in relationship with the problem.

White (2007) described two different types of metaphors—competition ("killing off" the problem; "beating back" the problem) and reclamation ("taking my life back" from the problem; "walking away" from the problem)—that are commonly used by clients. He argued that while **competition metaphors** are sometimes necessary when the problem is a matter of survival (for example, suicidality), more often, **reclamation metaphors** are preferred for promoting personal agency and revised action. Therefore, when both types of metaphors have been introduced by the client, the therapist may choose to lean into reclamation to avoid **totalizing**, or framing the problem as entirely adversarial, as this can lead to what White (2007) called a "fortress mentality" to life, ultimately resulting in increased vulnerability and decreased agency.

Relative Influence Questions

Another vital technique in the externalization process is **relative influence questioning**, an interviewing process comprised of two sets of questions focused on mapping the influences of the problem as well as the client (White & Epston, 1990). The first set of questions explores how the problem influences the client's life, relationships, and internal experience, while the second set of questions explores (often through metaphor and identifying unique outcomes) how the client influences the problem. These questions solidify the idea that the person exists separate from and in relationship with the problem rather than the problem existing within the person (Freedman & Combs, 1996).

When working with a system, such as the Daniels family, these questions also demonstrate that every member of the system has a personal relationship with the problem, not just the member who experiences symptoms most directly. Fran's relationship with anorexia nervosa, for example, causes her to excessively worry and to focus her interactions with Pam on her weight and eating. Murray's relationship with anorexia nervosa is one of detachment as he creates distance between himself and Pam and relies on his wife to handle the situation.

Mapping the Influence of the Problem

The first set of relative influence questions maps the influence of the problem on the client, to "identify the problem's sphere of influence in the behavioral, emotional, physical, interactional, and attitudinal domains" (White & Epston, 1990, p. 42). The therapist might ask how the problem is impacting the client at work or at school, how it is interfering in the relationships between the client and important people in their life, how it persuades the client to behave in ways that conflict with who they believe themselves to be, or how it changes the way society perceives the client (Monk et al., 1997). With the Daniels family, the therapist could map the influence of the problem on Pam's personal values by asking, "It seemed to be important to you to make it known that you were an above-average student before Anorexia came into your life. How has Anorexia impacted your ability to demonstrate this key part of your identity?" The therapist could also explore the impact on the family system's interactions with the outside world: "It seems like worrying about Anorexia takes up so much time and space in your lives. How does that impact your involvement in the community or with people outside of the family?"

Mapping the Influence of Persons

The second set of relative influence questions maps the influence of persons on the problem. The purpose of these questions is to "assist persons in identifying their competence and resourcefulness in the face of adversity" (White & Epston, 1990, p. 45). These tend to be more difficult for clients to answer, embroiled as they are in the problem-saturated story, but the preceding work toward externalizing and objectification of the problem sets the stage for this step (Freedman & Combs, 1996; Winslade & Monk, 2008). Metaphor is very useful at this point, as clients are invited to identify moments when they did not allow the problem to have its usual influence, or when their behaviors or actions dampened or interfered with the life of the problem.

For the Daniels family, questions like, "Tell me about a time when Anorexia tried to prevent you from achieving a goal you had set for yourself, but you were able to shut the door on it and persevere," or, "Describe a moment when you were able to interact without Anorexia taking your attention away from each other," begin to highlight personal agency and provide a more balanced perspective on the relationships between the family members and the problem.

Statement of Position Map

White (2007) coined the term the **statement of position map** to describe how externalizing conversations tends to be structured. He identified four categories of inquiry that establish "a context in which people, including children, can be radically consulted about what is important to their lives" (White, 2007, p. 39).

The first category of inquiry involves collaborating with the client to negotiate an "experience-near" definition of the problem that brings them to therapy. An **experience-near definition** draws from the language of the clients and their experiences of the problem to characterize and personify it in a way that illustrates its influence on their lives. The second category of inquiry is mapping the effects of the problem, which is described in more detail above. Following this, the third category of inquiry digs deeper by evaluating the effects through questions about how the client feels about the problem's activities, the client's position on different outcomes of the problem's activities, and reflections on whether developments related to the problem's actions are positive or negative (White, 2005, 2007).

Finally, the fourth category of inquiry asks the client to justify their evaluations; why they feel the way they feel. Why do they take the positions they take on different developments? White (2005) describes this fourth category as the client's opportunity to "put to words valued conclusions about their lives and identities" (p. 5), such as preferred values and purposes. The successful application of this technique relies on the decentered but influential position described previously.

Re-Authoring Conversations

White and Epston (1990) described **re-authoring** as "relocating a person/family's experience in new narratives, such that the previously dominant story becomes obsolete" (p. 127). The steps of deconstruction and externalization, and the identification of unique outcomes, create opportunities for questions that open the door to these possible alternative stories (White, 2007). These questions invite clients to ascribe meaning to the unique outcomes they identified. For example, the therapist might ask Pam, "How were you able to tune out Anorexia on this particular day when you were able to complete your school project? What does that say about you?" Through reflection on this question, Pam might realize that when she chooses her outfit the night before and does not start her day by examining her body in the mirror, Anorexia does not speak to her as loudly throughout the day, and she is better able to concentrate. The meaning she then ascribes may be that she has the personal agency to make choices that delay or quiet Anorexia's influence on her day.

White (2007) describes two landscapes that comprise all stories—the landscape of action and the landscape of consciousness, which he eventually referred to as the landscape of identity. A re-authoring conversation explores unique outcomes through both landscapes to develop alternative stories that better align with the client's lived experience and preferred narrative (Freedman & Combs, 1996).

Landscape of Action

The **landscape of action** is the plot of the story. It is made up of a series of events and the underlying theme (White, 2007). The problem-saturated, or dominant, story is often presented by the client as a sequence of events that "always" happens, and the underlying theme is often oppressive or limiting, rendering the client or family powerless to change the outcome. Regardless of the specific incident being described, the sequence of events leads to the same outcome. The Daniels family, for example, shares stories where the sequence of events leads to Anorexia controlling their behaviors, relationships, and health. The theme could be considered powerlessness, lack of control, or helplessness in the face of this dominant plotline.

In the process of re-authoring, the therapist and client work together to call forth previously ignored plotlines that resulted in different outcomes that perhaps challenge or alter the underlying theme (White & Epston, 1990; Winslade & Monk, 2008). Freedman and Combs (1996) described the questions used to accomplish this as **story development questions**. "Our hope when we ask story development questions is that people will come to experience their lives and themselves in new ways as they focus on previously neglected and unstoried aspects of their experience" (Freedman & Combs, 1996, p. 131).

To illustrate, let's assume that Fran and Murray shared a story of a rare evening when they were able to enjoy each other's company without Anorexia stealing their attention away from each other. There are several types of story development questions the therapist might ask to build on this unique outcome:

1 **Process questions** ask the client to notice the elements of an event (the plot, if you will). These questions ask what happened and how this particular series of events was made possible.
2 **Detail questions** encourage the client to relive an event to call to mind forgotten elements of the experience (Freedman & Combs, 1996).

3 **Time questions** seek to connect the event to previous moments in the client's history and to hypothetical futures.
4 **Context questions** explore the places, situations, and cultural values that support the new landscape of action.
5 **People questions** are concerned with understanding the characters who play a role in the story (Freedman & Combs, 1996; Monk et al., 1997).
6 **Hypothetical event questions** ask about past events that did not happen or future events that could happen to explore how different experiences can shape a story.

Landscape of Consciousness or Identity

The **landscape of identity** (originally referred to as the landscape of consciousness) refers to the client or family's knowledge, perceptions, emotions, and reflections on events (White, 2007). In short, this is where meaning comes into the story. It is worth noting that the dominant narrative a client presents in therapy is not necessarily the sequence of events that happens most frequently; rather, it is the sequence of events to which the client ascribes the most significant meaning (Morgan, 2000). White (2007) explained that the decision to change the name from landscape of consciousness to landscape of identity was rooted in the fact that a person's identity is drawn from the meaning ascribed to their narratives. A theme of helplessness in the dominant narrative contributes to the development of the identity of "helpless person." Alternative narratives, or subordinate storylines, offer opportunities for "the reconstruction of the identity" (White, 2007, p. 80).

Questions used to explore the landscape of identity are most effective when the therapist takes a subjunctive stance, using words like *might*, *if*, *possibly*, *could*, and so forth to remove certainty and leave room for loose and flexible interpretations of meaning (White, 2007). Re-authoring allows for the construction of new aspects of identity that do not align with the restrictive dominant narrative; these new parts of the self take up space previously occupied by the parts derived from the dominant storyline, thereby diminishing their influence. Freedman and Combs (1996) describe the category of questions used to explore the landscape of identity as **meaning questions**, including questions about implications, qualities, motivations, values, and learning. These questions allow clients to reflect on spiritual and moral principles they want to live by, and on the knowledge they gain through alternative storylines.

Ultimately, the process of re-authoring, and of narrative therapy in general, centers around and is reliant upon the therapist's effective use of questions (White, 2007; Winslade & Monk, 2008). What the narrative therapist asks, and when, can create space for the client to entirely reshape their understanding of the problem, their actions, and their identity to better suit their lived experience and preferred storyline.

Re-Membering Conversations

One of the core tenets of narrative therapy is that stories and identity are shaped within the context of relationships, or an "association of life" (White, 2007, p. 129). These associations are made up of those people and figures most significant to the client's past, present, and future, and their voices tend to be amplified when it comes to identity formation. This is something of a rejection of Western individualist ideals in that it acknowledges that identity is not innate and drawn from within the person but instead is "multi-voiced" and relationally constructed (Anderson, 1997; White, 2005). Sometimes, those amplified voices contribute to the problem-saturated story and to the subjugation of alternative stories. The purpose of **re-membering conversations**, then, is to reconsider the influence of these significant figures and to grant authority to those voices that support the alternative, re-authored storyline, while disqualifying those that attempt to maintain the dominant, oppressive narrative (White, 2007). White (2005) noted that while often these figures are people known personally by the client, they can also include pets, beloved toys, authors, songwriters, and others who had some sort of influence on identity.

Re-membering conversations are made up of two sets of inquiry, the first of which elicits the stories of how the significant figure contributed to the client's life and reflections on how that figure may have influenced the client's identity (White, 2007). The second set of inquiry elicits the stories of how the client contributed to the life of the significant figure and invites the client to reflect on how they may have influenced the identity of the figure. By amplifying supportive voices and repositioning unhelpful voices to the margins, clients can reshape their sense of self in ways that support preferred narratives (Freedman & Combs, 1996; White, 2007).

Counter-Documents

Counter-documents occupy a central place within narrative therapy because they actively support therapy clients by presenting their expressed values, preferred meanings, and commitments (White & Epston, 1990). The therapeutic documents include certificates, therapeutic letters, commendations, and poems, for example, which validate clients' resistance actions and their developing personal narrative. The main goal of counter-document narrative therapy work involves strengthening preferred identity conclusions against weak problem-focused descriptions which commonly affect clients.

The therapeutic letter serves as a primary counter-document tool, transforming session dialogue into written material that clients can apply in their daily lives. Typically composed during or immediately after each session, these letters document significant moments in which clients demonstrate agency and resistance to the influence of presenting problems. In this way, therapeutic letters act as narrative reconstructions that reinforce client authorship by highlighting their capacity to challenge and manage difficulties.

Therapeutic letters maintain their long-term value because they function as lasting reminders of preferred identity statements that extend past the brief time of spoken communication. Clients can use these letters for multiple purposes, including reading them multiple times, showing them to their family and supportive networks, and using them for support during problem-related crises. The letter functions as a witness that follows the client throughout their day to validate their alternative narrative even when the therapist is absent. The letters enable patients to combat problem dominance through demonstrations of their outstanding skills and vital qualities which others tend to overlook. The permanent nature of therapeutic letters enables clients to maintain their progress toward preferred identities because these documents can be carried with them.

Anti-Anorexia/Anti-Bulimia Leagues

Stephen Madigan developed the **Anti-Anorexia/Anti-Bulimia Leagues** to advance narrative therapy principles through externalizing problems and building social resistance against them. Madigan (1996, 2010) demonstrated that anorexia functions as a social system which uses cultural power to force people, especially girls and women, into controlling their bodies through thinness-based moral worth and self-surveillance. The leagues function as community-based programs that replace dominant eating disorder narratives through collective storytelling and identity development based on solidarity instead of social isolation. The leagues enable people to understand their experiences through social and cultural frameworks, which helps them overcome self-blame while showing anorexia as a political issue that affects relationships and discourse (Madigan, 2011; White, 2007).

The leagues operate as strong counter-story sites that support all types of resistance while demonstrating to members various methods people use to combat anorexia. The process of witnessing plays a crucial role because it turns the identity stories that anorexia tries to eliminate into stories which society acknowledges. The league activities consist of creating counter-documents which members share while they develop shared terms to describe anorexia's recruitment methods, loyalty requirements, and they support each other through recovery of their lost values and relationships (Madigan, 1996, 2011). The practices enable clients and their families to develop mutual comprehension about their recovery process. People can escape their personal battles against problems to unite against cultural norms through this process. The approach focuses on collective work which matches the core principle of narrative therapy that people develop their identities through social relationships and cultural environments (White, 2007; White & Epston, 1990).

Case Transcript

The Daniels family—Murray (39), Fran (38), Pam (17), Oliver (15), and George (13)—arrive for their first family therapy session following Pam's ongoing struggle with anorexia. The therapist arranges the room so the family sits in a semi-circle, allowing everyone to see one another. The intention is to reduce the symbolic hierarchy of typical living room arrangements (parents on the couch, children scattered elsewhere) and encourage a sense of collaborative work. The therapist sits slightly off to the side—not centered as an authority figure—reflecting a narrative stance of decentered yet influential.

Therapist: I'm glad all of you were able to be here today. Before we begin, I want you to know that in our work together, I don't assume that any one person is "the problem," nor that anyone here is broken or failing. Instead, I'm interested in understanding how something called Anorexia has been affecting your family's life. We'll explore how it operates, what it hopes to accomplish, and how each of you has responded to it in your own ways. Pam, as you hear me talk about Anorexia as something separate from you, what do you notice happening inside—emotionally or physically—right in this moment?

Intervention: The therapist begins with externalizing language, setting the tone by separating Pam from the anorexia. This reduces shame and invites a collaborative stance. It also frames the problem as an entity with intentions—consistent with narrative therapy's anthropomorphizing of problems. A process question helps Pam reflect on her immediate internal experience in response to externalization, validating her lived response to the therapeutic shift.

Pam: I like it better than thinking it's just me being messed up. It feels… I don't know. Less scary, I guess.

Therapist: That's really helpful to know. And I want you to feel free at any point to tell me if you want to call it something different. Sometimes people give the problem a different name—one that matches how it shows up for them, or the tricks it tries to pull. When does Anorexia tend to speak to you the loudest in your day—mornings, afternoons, nights?

Intervention: Offering Pam the authority to rename the problem supports agency and encourages her to participate in authorship. Time questions help map when the problem exerts influence, further externalizing its operations.

Pam: Usually mornings. Breakfast is the hardest.

Therapist: And where does Anorexia seem most active—at home, at school, around friends, or when you're alone?

Intervention: Context questions reveal situational patterns of the problem's influence, emphasizing that its power is environmentally shaped, not inherent within Pam.

Pam: Mostly at home. At school, it's easier to blend in.

Therapist: Now that we're starting from this shared understanding—that Anorexia is something acting on this family—I'd like to hear from each of you. When did you first notice that Anorexia was becoming part of your family's life story?

Intervention: This question maps the influence of the problem and positions every family member as a witness to the problem's impact, not spectators blaming Pam.

Fran: I think I saw it first. Pam started saying she wasn't hungry at dinner. At first I didn't think much of it... kids go through phases. But then it became a routine—avoiding meals, pushing food around her plate, cutting things into tiny pieces.

Murray: I didn't notice as quickly. I think I chalked it up to stress with school or teenage stuff. I never imagined it could become so serious.

Oliver: I don't think I noticed it at all until Mom and Dad talked to us about it.

George: Me neither. I guess I wasn't looking.

Therapist: That makes complete sense. Problems like Anorexia can be quite stealthy. They don't enter a family loudly. They slip in quietly, showing different faces to different people. It's not unusual for each of you to have recognized it in your own time and way. Pam, I'm curious what you've noticed about how Anorexia affects your relationship with your mom. And who else in the family does Anorexia seem to pull into its orbit?

Intervention: This removes blame or guilt, normalizes difference, and strengthens the externalized frame that the problem—not the family—creates distortion. A people question identifies how the problem organizes relational roles across the family system.

Pam: It... makes it hard. She's always watching me. Asking what I ate. Or what I didn't. And then I feel like I'm making her upset all the time.

Therapist: It sounds like Anorexia pulls your mom into a role she didn't choose—the role of "constant monitor." And it pulls you into a role you didn't choose either. Does that description feel accurate?

Intervention: The therapist names problem-generated roles without pathologizing either person. This supports deconstruction: the family sees relational patterns as orchestrated by the problem.

Pam: Yeah. I don't want her to be like that. I know she's scared. But sometimes I just want her to stop.

Fran: I just… I don't know what else to do. I worry every day.

Therapist: That makes sense. You're both being recruited into roles neither of you want or enjoy. Anorexia is clever—it knows how to pit love against fear. Pam, when Anorexia pulls your mom into that monitoring role, what are the specific things it has her do—what details stand out to you most?

Intervention: Humanizing the family's intentions helps them resist the identity conclusions the problem tries to impose. Detail questions slow down the narrative and make invisible operations of the problem visible.

Pam: Mostly her asking what I ate, or watching me during meals.

Therapist: What about with your dad, Pam? How does Anorexia influence your relationship with him?

Pam: I don't know. It just makes me feel… far away. I don't really talk to him about stuff. He's always with Oliver and George doing baseball or whatever.

Murray: I didn't realize you felt that way. I guess I thought you preferred being alone.

Pam: I didn't. Not at first. Then I felt like you guys just had your own thing.

Therapist: It sounds like Anorexia used that silence between you as an opportunity to widen the distance.

Intervention: Linking the problem to the relational gap helps prevent Murray from feeling accused while still acknowledging Pam's pain.

Murray: I didn't know how to connect with you, Pam. I should've tried harder.

Therapist: It's understandable you didn't know. You inherited a story of fatherhood based on sports and hands-on work—a story that didn't include connection through conversation or shared emotional space. Fran, I'm curious—what stories about mothering did you inherit?

Intervention: This brings in dominant discourse analysis, showing how cultural family scripts shape available roles.

Fran: In my family, the girls took care of the kids. I took care of my little sister. My mom took care of everyone. My dad worked and then relaxed.

Therapist: And has that story shaped how you see yourself as a mother to Pam?

Fran: Definitely. I feel like I have to fix everything. Protect her. Make sure she's okay.

Therapist: Which is a beautiful intention—but also a heavy responsibility. It makes sense that this story would make you feel you must carry the whole weight of fighting Anorexia alone.

Intervention: Highlighting intentions while easing pressure creates possibilities for new relational practices and alternative stories.

Therapist: Oliver and George, I'd like to ask each of you—what changes have you noticed in your relationship with your sister since Anorexia began showing up?

Oliver: She's quieter. More distant. I kinda miss talking to her.

George: I'm always scared I'll say the wrong thing. So I say nothing.

Therapist: That's understandable. Anorexia often tells siblings there's only one "right" way to talk—and that the risk of saying the wrong thing is too high. It limits your freedom to connect. Pam, despite Anorexia's influence, have there been moments—no matter how small—when you've done something you wanted instead of something Anorexia insisted on?

Intervention: Normalizes sibling uncertainty and portrays the problem as the inhibitor of connection, reducing tension and shame. Landscape of action questions uncover unique outcomes—actions outside the problem story.

Pam: Last week I went out for pizza with my friend. I didn't finish it, but… I ate some. I just wanted to be normal with her.

Therapist: That sounds like a moment when your value of friendship and connection became louder than Anorexia's voice.

Intervention: Identifying unique outcomes—actions that contradict the problem story—is foundational to re-authoring.

Fran: I had no idea. I wish you'd told me. I would've been so proud.

Pam: I didn't want you to freak out or turn it into a big deal.

Therapist: Pam, what did eating that pizza—even part of it—say about what matters to you?

Pam: I guess… that I miss my life. My friends. Being able to go out without thinking about calories.

Therapist: So it tells a story about longing for normalcy, for connection, for freedom. How long have those values been part of your life?

Intervention: Connecting behaviors to values strengthens alternative identity conclusions. The therapist has moved the conversation to the landscape of identity.

Pam: Always. I used to love sleepovers and hanging out and ordering food.

Therapist: That tells me that connection—and joy—have been long-standing companions of yours. Maybe even older companions than Anorexia. I'd like to invite each of you to share what you hear in Pam's story about the pizza. What stands out to you?

Intervention: This demonstrates that the client's preferred identity has always been present, making it more believable and resilient.

Fran: I hear courage. And I hear that she wants connection. I want that with her too.

Murray: I hear she wants her life back. And… I want to find a way to be part of that life.

Oliver: I think it's cool she hung out with a friend. I miss that version of her.

George: Same. I liked when she used to joke around with us.

Pam: I didn't know you guys missed me that much.

Therapist: That's the beautiful thing about stories—we often don't know the ones others hold about us unless the space is created to hear them.

Intervention: Encourages shared witnessing, which solidifies alternative stories socially.

Therapist: I want to shift to imagining a future where Anorexia has far less influence in this family. If Anorexia weren't calling the shots, what kind of relationships would each of you want with Pam, and with one another?

Intervention: This closing sequence invites re-authoring, articulating preferred futures and giving the family a narrative to move toward.

Fran: I want to laugh with her again. To talk about things other than food and health.

Murray: I want to be someone she can come to. I want to learn new ways of connecting with her—even if it's not through sports.

Oliver: I want us to hang out again. Watch movies. Talk about stuff.

George: I want things to feel lighter. I don't want her to feel so much pressure.

Pam: I want all of that, too. I want our home to feel… safe again.

Therapist: That is a powerful collective vision. This vision can become the new story this family authors together—one where connection, curiosity, love, and mutual support are the main characters. Before we close, I want to acknowledge something important. Each of you has resisted Anorexia in your own way. Fran, you resisted it by loving fiercely. Murray, by wanting to understand instead of shutting down. Oliver and George, by wanting connection. And Pam, by choosing friendship and moments of joy over isolation. These acts of resistance are seeds of a new story—one in which Anorexia shrinks and your voices grow louder. I want to let you all know that there is a local group, called the Anti-Anorexia League, where people meet and support one another in their resistance against Anorexia. This league is for everyone. I will give you the information about it in case that is something you all think would be useful for you.

Intervention: This final reflection strengthens preferred identities, validates multi-layered resistance, and solidifies therapeutic alliance through recognition of strengths. The therapist provides information about the Anti-Anorexia league to help the family start to circulate a different story of their lives; one in which they have more agency over Anorexia rather than just victim to it.

The family leaves with softened expressions, standing a little closer together than when they arrived. Pam walks between her parents, each placing a hand gently on her back—tiny but meaningful counter-stories to Anorexia's attempts to isolate her. Several days after the session, the therapist sent the family the following therapeutic letter.

Dear Daniels Family,

Thank you for the courage, honesty, and care you brought into our recent session. As I reflected on our time together, I was struck by the many ways each of you resisted Anorexia's attempts to isolate, silence, or divide your family. Pam's choice to spend time with a friend, Fran's devotion beneath her worries, Murray's openness to re-examining old stories about fatherhood, and Oliver and George's heartfelt expressions of longing for connection all revealed a family refusing to be defined by distress. These moments highlighted your shared values—connection, honesty, safety, caring, understanding, and openness to learning—that continue to hold you together even when things feel heavy.

Throughout our conversation, I noticed how consistently you turned toward empathy rather than blame. You listened closely to one another's hopes and fears, creating a space where vulnerability was met with compassion instead of defensiveness. This helped expose Anorexia's tactics—its efforts to pull Pam into withdrawal, Fran into vigilance, Murray into distance, and the boys into uncertainty. By recognizing these patterns as the work of the problem rather than the nature of any family member, you took an important step toward loosening Anorexia's grip and reclaiming agency over your relationships.

Near the end of the session, each of you described the kind of connection you long for if Anorexia were no longer in charge. Fran spoke of wanting ease and laughter with Pam, Murray expressed a desire to learn new ways of showing up for his daughter, Oliver and George shared hopes for renewed closeness, and Pam voiced her longing for safety, normalcy, and reconnection. These hopes harmonized beautifully, forming the early chapters of a shared family narrative that is already present—you are not inventing something new, but nurturing what has been there all along.

As you move forward, I invite you to notice moments of resistance—meals shared, conversations initiated, time spent together—and reflect on the values guiding them. Consider how each of you can continue supporting Pam's preferred identity and what new practices might help strengthen the story you want to co-author as a family. Narrative change does not require perfection; it asks for presence, curiosity, and a willingness to challenge the problem's narrow version of your lives. I am honored to walk alongside you as you continue reclaiming your stories, and I look forward to witnessing the unfolding of the more connected, hopeful future you are already creating together.

Sincerely,
Your Therapist

The Therapeutic Story

The therapist applied narrative therapy techniques to assist the Daniels family in creating their desired relationships and personal stories from their present problematic interactions. The therapist started the session by creating a narrative position that used decentered influence together with collaborative work and humble curiosity instead of relying on expert-based diagnostic power. The therapist started by making the problem outside of the family which served as the initial crucial move. The therapist demonstrated how "Anorexia" first entered the family system to begin controlling their actions. The entire session foundation emerged from this change because externalization enables people to escape shame while helping them overcome their self-critical behaviors and stopping family members from blaming each other. The therapist involved Pam in the process of naming Anorexia while asking for her preferred term to demonstrate her active role in developing the therapeutic approach.

The therapist initiated an externalizing conversation to support the mapping of the problem's influence, exploring how the problem operates within family relationships, emotional experiences, roles, and systems of meaning. The therapist asked each family member to describe their first encounter with Anorexia. This approach confirmed that each person brought their personal life experiences yet it did not establish any ranking system between their stories. The therapist focused on the problem instead of Pam to decrease family conflict because the problem caused confusion and distress. The family learned to grasp their intricate situation through the narrative metaphor, which stopped them from using basic explanations or blame.

The therapist employed mapping to show how Anorexia changed the social positions of family members in their relationships. The therapist described Fran's ongoing surveillance as an Anorexia-imposed duty which replaced her natural behavior of being controlling or Pam being uncooperative. The new perspective enabled Fran to observe her actions while freeing Pam from believing she failed her mother through her eating behavior. This helps people distinguish their personal identity from their problematic actions so they can develop fresh personal identities.

The narrative therapy process invites clients to study dominant discourses which represent cultural and family-based and social narratives that determine human relationships. The therapist studied family origins to understand how cultural standards about gender roles, childcare responsibilities, and emotional expressions affected their present family situation. The therapist worked with Murray to identify the sports-based, work-oriented, and practical-based bonding approaches he acquired from his father. The traditional masculine scripts lacked emotional and verbal connection models, which made it difficult for Murray to develop a bond with his daughter, Pam. The therapist used systemic and historical elements to explain Murray's limitations, which allowed him to escape self-criticism while discovering alternative relationship possibilities.

The therapist explained to Fran that she functioned as the eldest child who took responsibility for her younger brother. The social norms of femininity forced women to become protective, selfless servants, which influenced Fran's parenting style. The cultural story about motherhood forced Fran to defend her children from danger while she bore the responsibility of their emotional pain. The therapist worked to understand Fran's good intentions while showing how the dominant discourse restricted her to excessive worry, and Anorexia exploited this situation. This enabled Fran to understand her parenting approach while she discovered new methods to become a less burdened parent.

The therapist reduced Anorexia's control while helping the family understand their decision-making power and core values, and to recognize cultural boundaries and to develop better self-knowledge and family relationships. The therapist used three methods to help the family develop into a hopeful unit: resistance identification, alternative story enhancement, and collective re-authoring. The therapist used deconstruction to help the family create new preferred stories by freeing them from their current cultural and family traditions.

The therapist asked Pam to recall times when she fought Anorexia by choosing her personal wants instead of following its commands. The act of eating pizza with a friend became a vital act of resistance. Pam showed her core values for friendship, normal teenage life, and social connections during the incident while fighting against Anorexia.

The therapist employed alternative story thickening to link particular results with personal values, preferred identity, and life intentions. Pam discovered her fundamental values, which included friendship, normal teenage life, and social connections. These core values enable her to develop an empowered identity story because she wants to build relationships instead of allowing her illness to dominate her existence. The therapist established that these values had existed in Pam's life for many years to build a solid base for her preferred identity, which stems from her established self instead of her new or unstable self-perceptions.

References

Anderson, H. (1997). *Conversation, language, and possibilities: A postmodern approach to therapy*. Basic Books.

Chimpén-López, C. A., Pacheco, M., Teresa Pretel-Luque, Bastón, R., Chimpén-López, C. A., Pretel-Luque, T., & Chimpén-Sagrado, D. (2022). The couple's tree of life: Promoting and protecting relational identity. *Family Process*, *61*(4), 1403–1416.

Chow, E. O. W., & Fok, D. Y. H. (2020). Recipe of life: A relational narrative approach in therapy with persons living with chronic pain. *Research on Social Work Practice*, *30*(3), 320–329.

Combs, G., & Freedman, J. (2012). Narrative, poststructuralism, and social justice. *The Counseling Psychologist*, *40*(7), 1033–1060.

Dulwich Center (2025). *Collection: Evidence for the effectiveness of narrative therapy*. Retrieved from https://dulwichcentre.com.au/collection-evidence-for-the-effectiveness-of-narrative-therapy/

Fitzsimmons, K. J., & Zucker, L. M. (2004). Narrative therapy and the practice of advocacy: Emphasis on affirming difference when working with diverse clients. In R. A. Dorfman-Zukerman, M. L. Morgan, & P. Meyer (Eds.), *Paradigms of clinical social work: Emphasis on diversity* (pp. 205–224). Routledge.

Foucault, M. (1977). *Discipline and punish: The birth of the prison* (A. Sheridan, Trans.). Pantheon.

Freedman, J., & Combs, G. (1996). *Narrative therapy: The social construction of preferred realities*. W. W. Norton.

Ghavibazou, E., Hosseinian, S., & Abdollahi, A. (2020). Effectiveness of narrative therapy on communication patterns for women experiencing low marital satisfaction. *Australian & New Zealand Journal of Family Therapy*, *41*(2), 195–207.

Guilfoyle, M. (2015). Listening in narrative therapy: Double listening and empathic positioning. *South African Journal of Psychology*, *45*(1), 36–49.

Karibwende, F., Niyonsenga, J., Nyirinkwaya, S., Hitayezu, I., Sebuhoro, C., Gitimbwa, S. S., Ntete, J. M., & Mutabaruka, J. (2022). A randomized controlled trial evaluating the effectiveness of narrative therapy on resilience of orphaned and abandoned children fostered in SOS Children's Village. *European Journal of Psychotraumatology*, *13*(2): 2152111.

Madigan, S. (1996). The politics of identity: Considering the anti-anorexia/anti-bulimia league. In C. Smith & D. Nylund (Eds.), *Narrative therapies with children and adolescents* (pp. 211–232). Guilford Press.

Madigan, S. (2010). *Narrative therapy*. American Psychological Association.

Madigan, S. (2011). Hopelessness is possible but meaningless: The anti-anorexia/anti-bulimia league and narrative therapy. *Journal of Systemic Therapies*, *30*(3), 1–10.

Monk, G., Winslade, J., Crocket, K., & Epston, D. (Eds.). (1997). *Narrative therapy in practice: The archaeology of hope*. Jossey-Bass.

Morgan, A. (2000). *What is narrative therapy? An easy-to-read introduction*. Dulwich Centre Publications.

Payne, M. (2006). *Narrative therapy: An introduction for counsellors* (2nd ed.). SAGE.

White, M. (1991). Deconstruction and therapy. In D. Epston & M. White (Eds.), *Experience, contradiction, narrative & imagination* (pp. 109–151). Dulwich Centre Publications.

White, M. (2000). *Reflections on narrative practice: Essays and interviews*. Dulwich Centre Publications.

White, M. (2005). *Narrative practice, narrative possibilities: Essays & interviews*. Dulwich Centre Publications.

White, M. (2007). *Maps of narrative practice*. W. W. Norton.

White, M., & Epston, D. (1990). *Narrative means to therapeutic ends*. W. W. Norton.

Winslade, J., & Monk, G. (2008). *Practicing narrative mediation: Loosening the grip of conflict*. Jossey-Bass.

Zhou, D.-H. R., Chiu, Y.-L. M., Lo, T.-L. W., Lo, W.-F. A., Wong, S.-S., Leung, C. H. T., Yu, C.-K., Chang, Y. S. G., & Luk, K.-L. (2023). An unexpected visitor and a sword play: a randomized controlled trial of collective narrative therapy groups for primary carers of people with schizophrenia. *Journal of Mental Health*, *32*(1), 351–362.

16 Internal Family Systems

Keran Flynn-Kroska

The internal family systems (IFS) model was developed over 40 years ago by Dr. Richard Schwartz, who was a practicing licensed marriage and family therapist (Schwartz, 2021). The development of the model began when Schwartz noticed patterns in the ways in which clients reacted to stressors and the internal dialogues with which they used to calm their body systems. He also noticed that clients would talk about internal intrapsychic dialogues and stressful reactions to some of these dialogues. The foundations of the model incorporated structural, strategic, Bowen, and Satir, as well as being strongly informed by Gestalt, solution-focused therapy, and narrative therapy (Brenner et al., 2023). As the model evolved over decades, other practitioners and researchers added meditation, visualization, spirituality, and somatic work (Schwartz, 2021; Schwartz & Sweezy, 2021). Schwartz found that these additions enhanced the model and made it more useful in working with clients who had experienced different levels of trauma in their lives, whether from a single incident or developmental reoccurring incidents in childhood (van der Kolk, 2014).

IFS is a very popular model and is currently considered to be one of the premier evidence-based models for use in trauma therapy. IFS is generally thought of as an individual model, but it is used successfully with couples and families (Schwartz & Sweezy, 2021). The IFS model that is used with couples is called Intimacy from the Inside Out (IFIO; Herbine-Blank et al., 2021) and incorporates the use of external systems in work with internal systems. The main goal of IFS is to assist clients in unblending from parts and unburdening exiled parts to become more Self-led (Schwartz & Sweezy, 2021).

IFS rests upon core principles that form the foundation of the model (Schwartz & Sweezy, 2021):

- **Multiplicity of the Mind**: The mind is comprised of multiple parts (Schwartz, 2021; Schwartz & Sweezy, 2021).
- Parts have positive intent: Every part has a positive intent and is not inherently bad, even if its behaviors are destructive (Schwartz & Sweezy, 2021).

DOI: 10.4324/9781003668510-16

- Protective vs. Exiled parts: These parts can become polarized or extreme in their roles to protect the Self from pain, often leading to internal conflict (Schwartz & Sweezy, 2021), and
- The core **Self**: Everyone possesses a core Self, characterized by qualities such as compassion, curiosity, and calmness, which is the innate source of inner healing (Schwartz & Sweezy, 2021; Sweezy, 2023).

Multiplicity of the mind is a unique concept in IFS and is a core principle that posits that every mind is made up of multiple, distinct sub-personalities, or **parts**, which have their own personalities, emotions, beliefs, and so forth (Schwartz & Sweezy, 2021). As each part has a belief, their own experiences, and ways of dealing with stressors, the IFS therapist works with these parts with the goal to heal injured or wounded parts by accessing the core Self to harmonize parts rather than trying to eliminate or remove them. This is the "internal system" in IFS: the core Self and the many parts of the client. Even though this system is internal, it is still a system, so working holistically with the client and their parts, the system can be stabilized in an adaptive way without pathologizing the client.

The goal of IFS therapy is harmony by assisting in the connection and understanding between parts and the Self, leading to an internal balance (Schwartz & Sweezy, 2021). Think of this as being like an external family system in which, if you are using structural therapy, you would work with the system to realign the subsystems and improve adaptive rules, roles, and boundaries. The same is the goal in IFS, where aligning parts to the Self creates Self-leadership and improves adaptive subsystems, rules, roles, and boundaries for internal parts (Schwartz, 2021). The goal in IFS with the Daniels family would be harmony in the system with connection and understanding between each member of the family system and the Self of the parents and the children, which would then lead to an external balance and adaptive stabilization of the system (Schwartz & Sweezy, 2021). Another important factor in IFS is the therapist being a **Hope Merchant**, with the promise of hope and that extreme feelings and distorted beliefs will decrease and can be unloaded (Schwartz & Sweezy, 2021). Hope merchants also help in the stabilization of effective and safe communication between family members.

Within the internal system, there are three main types of parts:

- **Managers** are proactive protectors who try to keep exiles contained and prevent them from emerging by controlling their environment and relationships (Schwartz & Sweezy, 2021). **Polarized protectors** are controlling and severe managers who may utilize physical symptoms to do something to or for the person, and can hurt, punish, control, or distract (Schwartz & Sweezy, 2021). These may look similar to firefighters, yet the difference between polarized protectors and firefighters is that firefighters blend with the Self and create danger to the person in the form of suicidality, drug abuse, and unsafe impulsive acts (Schwartz & Sweezy, 2021). This is different than the internal controls of polarized protectors.

- **Firefighters** are **reactive protectors** that emerge when managers fail to contain exiles (Schwartz & Sweezy, 2021). They act impulsively with extreme actions to suppress exiled feelings of pain and shame, sometimes through destructive behaviors such as substance abuse, eating disorders, and suicidality (Schwartz & Sweezy, 2021).
- **Exiles** are vulnerable and childlike parts that hold the burdens of past trauma, pain, and rejection (Schwartz & Sweezy, 2021). Exiles can be created when a child is told (in verbal or non-verbal ways) that their energy is too much: too much activity, too much emotionality, too much sensitivity, too much physicality, and so forth (Schwartz, 2021).

When parts are **blended**, the person can believe that they are acting, speaking, or thinking from their core Self, yet often a part is blended with the Self (Schwartz & Sweezy, 2021). Parts that most often blend with the Self are called **Self-like parts**. These Self-like parts have an agenda to control and manage other parts and will often refuse to step away, and this is a clue to the therapist that a Self-like part is in charge (Redfern, 2023). A lack of progress in therapy may be a sign that a Self-like part has not unblended (Schwartz & Sweezy, 2021). An example of blended parts that get in the way of therapeutic progress could be specific manager parts or a firefighter (most likely a Self-like part) redirecting treatment effectiveness by being a good narrator and therefore mainly undetectable (Redfern, 2023). Thinking about Self-like parts in relation to the Daniels family and Pam's experiences with treatment and regression is a good example of a manager with an agenda in charge and not Pam's Self. This part would sound reasonable, and it would look like Pam was following treatment protocols and doing the work, yet there would be little movement toward real change and symptoms would not resolve. This could be seen, and there would be reactions of closing down, argumentativeness, defensiveness, and so forth. As an example from the case transcript below, Pam crosses her arms and says, "I keep telling you, I'm fine." An example of a polarized protector and a firefighter from the case transcript is when Pam says,

> Like, when I get mad at myself for being too fat? I hear this mean voice telling me I'm gross and it's unbearable. It's a really mean voice, and all I want to do is stop eating and go on a long run.

Unblending happens when the Self takes on the role of regulator for parts (Schwartz & Sweezy, 2021). A part must be willing to unblend for any unblending techniques to work (Sweezy, 2023). Controlling manager parts often internally unblend regularly from other parts to allow routine tasks to occur, yet this is not related to the techniques of unblending in IFS. Unblending in IFS refers to working with controlling parts, with permission, to take a step back from a part (or the Self) with guidance (Sweezy, 2023). This is where permission from parts or **negotiation with protectors** is so important. Unblending means that the therapist aids the person in communicating with controlling parts to learn about the part so that the part is willing to unblend.

In IFS, parts are individuals that have their own thoughts, beliefs, feelings, sets of experiences, and even their own "bodies" (Schwartz, 1995; Schwartz, 2021). Without a reliable parental figure (the Self Leader) to guide and help parts manage their experiences, these parts can "become emotionally flooded, cognitively confused, and over-burdened with intolerable beliefs" as well as feel bodily pain and discomfort (Herbine-Blank et al., 2015, p. 11).

Trauma happens when someone experiences frightening and threatening events that directly impact them. This can be an accident, abuse, recurring events, or observing dangerous things happening to someone close to the person. When someone has experienced trauma, this traumatic experience "injects their parts with beliefs and emotions that hijack them out of their naturally valuable state" (van der Kolk, 2014, p. 283). Parts can become distant, polarized, aggressive, dependent, and sad, similarly to people in an external system, especially if the Self has abdicated or is not very present (Schwartz, 2021). Bowlby's internal working model is evident in how parts seek Self-leadership when the Self is disengaged or absent in similar ways that infants and young children will do when seeking connection with absent or neglectful caregivers (Sherman et al., 2015). Bowlby's internal working model is a mental and emotional representation of an infant's first attachment relationship and forms the basis of an individual's attachment style throughout their life. This means that internal parts of people who have experienced inconsistent, neglectful, or frightening parenting replicate similar internal patterns to their historical external family patterns.

Attachment to internal objects (Sandler, 2003) is a good way to look at parts that are seeking connection, polarizing, or avoiding the Self of the person. This can be seen as those critical parts that appear as the parent or other authoritarian person from the client's childhood. Critical manager parts are sometimes those objects that more fearful parts will flock to for guidance and stability (Sandler, 2003). The goal in IFS is to create that object attachment between parts and the Self of the person rather than to a manager or other protector parts.

The Daniels family offers a useful example of parts and their roles. The protectors and managers in the external family would be the parents, demonstrated by their ability to provide care and support for the children in the family (possible exiles). Fran demonstrates reactive management, and Murray demonstrates proactive management for Oliver and George and avoidant management of Pam (Schwartz & Sweezy, 2021). In Murray's family of origin, the sons are more typical of Murray's expectations of typical behaviors and interests (sports and after-school activities), and so the boys appear non-reactive internally and possibly have less fearful parts as their father is more of a proactive manager and does not push them into exile as they do things their father likes and approves of. Murray demonstrates an inability to engage with Pam from the Self, so he avoids and shifts the management to Fran. In IFS, this is called **abdicated leadership** (Schwartz & Sweezy, 2021). Pam demonstrates as an exiled part that is not allowed to express anything but agreed-upon ways of conforming to the expectations of the system: fear and worry from Fran and avoidance by Murray. Interactions with parental parts pressure Pam's firefighters to emerge to keep the exile in. The firefighter in Pam's case is anorexia. Anorexia shows up when Pam feels left out by Murray's avoidance and is pressured by Fran's manager. Pam believes that she is operating from her Self, and does not realize that she is blended with a firefighter.

Each member of the Daniels family demonstrates blended parts as they believe that they are interacting from the Self rather than their parts being in charge. The goal, then, would be to assist family members to unblend so their external interactions are more Self-led and less parts-led (Schwartz & Sweezy, 2021). This would create a more Self-led system in which each member of the family would interact more from the Self than from blended managers, protectors, or firefighters.

The language of rules, roles, and boundaries is familiar, as it is the language of structural family therapy (Brenner et al., 2023). As Schwartz utilized a structural lens in his work with clients, and in his development of IFS, he incorporated some of the language from that model into IFS. When using IFS in work with individuals, couples, and families, it is noticeable that parts have a hierarchy and fill roles as necessary at specific times in a person's life. This hierarchy is similar to that in an external system. Boundaries are noticeable when parts blend, they battle over primacy, or when they work to supplant the Self. Similarly, this looks like how families demonstrate subsystems and boundaries. Thinking about IFS in this way can give an understanding of the ways in which internal parts are mapped for individuals, couples, or families as observed in external family systems. Boundaries and rules manifest the same way for internal systems as for external systems. Boundaries can be clear, diffuse, or rigid depending upon why a part has taken on a specific role. Patterns between parts can be stable, enmeshed, anxious, or cut-off. Cut-off is demonstrated by polarization or hidden parts. Mapping the external system uncovers patterns related to the ways in which internal parts manage the thoughts, actions, and behaviors of the individuals in the external system. In the Daniels family, the pattern of Fran's hyper-focus on Pam's actions and behaviors could reflect the manager part within Fran that used to manage the care for her younger, ill sibling. As there is no longer a younger, ill sibling for Fran to care for, this manager has taken on the role of managing Pam's "illness." Internal parts are always reflected in the outer system (Schwartz & Sweezy, 2021).

Polarization and coalition are typical in internal systems and can give a lot of information related to the interactions and functioning of the external family system. Two parts may go into coalition against another part in attempts to take leadership from the Self. Thinking about this, related to the external family system, constraints, polarizations, and coalitions can severely impact the Self-leadership and structure of parents/caregivers (Schwartz & Sweezy, 2021). Within the Daniels family, there are coalitions between Murray and his sons and between Fran and Pam, and there is a polarization between Murray and Pam. In cases where polarization is extreme, parental figures can abdicate leadership, which can happen if the leaders of the family become too overburdened by demands from the larger systems (Schwartz & Sweezy, 2021). In the Daniels family, coalition, abdicating leadership, and polarization are clearly visible in the ways in which the family interacts.

Often, the result of these coalitions is the blending of parts into the Self. This is seen in parts work when the IFS therapist thinks they are working with the Self, when in actuality, they are working with a part masquerading as the Self and can only really be recognized in the ways in which they visually manifest to the client(s). The therapist needs to ask the client to identify if the Self is speaking, or if it is a part speaking. This is called **parts detecting** and becomes an important skill for IFS therapists.

IFS is a system-centered model in which parts are to be acknowledged and appreciated (Schwartz, 2021). The goal is to elicit the assistance of parts to change roles and become more self-led. This act of asking permission to interact with parts relaxes defenses and creates a more trusting environment between parts and the Self. This could be reflected in the ways in which the Daniels family interacts once each family member becomes more Self-led which would then be reflected in the ways in which the family interacts.

The Therapeutic Story of Problem Formation

IFS therapists view problem formation as impacts on the Self from parts that interfere with optimal functioning and Self-leadership. In a family presentation, an IFS therapist might view problem formation as individual internal parts reacting to the internal parts of the other family members, creating triangulation and polarization between these parts.

The Daniels family presents with two parents and a daughter aged 17 for treatment. The two younger children, Oliver and George, are not present, as it currently appears that they demonstrate acceptable behaviors and needs within the system. The parents have identified that there are no presenting issues with the boys. The immediate issue appears to be a need to resolve issues between Fran, Pam, and Murray to stabilize both internal and external systems. This change in the system would automatically include Oliver and George.

The presenting issue is related to returning symptoms of anorexia nervosa and some isolation, disconnect, and enmeshment in the family system. The family of origin story for both sides of this family shows patterns of disconnect between fathers and daughters and enmeshment between mothers and daughters. Fran's family history detailed that Fran was the primary caregiver for her younger sister, who was ill, and now Fran's main focus is on the symptoms rather than the personal needs of Pam. The language of structural therapy is often used when describing inner systems as the hierarchy in internal systems is often relegated to the dominant parts rather than to the Self. Enactments are also useful in observing the influence of parts in external interactions (Schwartz & Sweezy, 2021). In the Daniels family, this would be noticed as external manager parts trying to regulate or suppress external exiles. In IFS language, this might be observed as overly enmeshed or avoidant parenting (external manager protector) as an attempt to suppress any expression of emotionality from the child (the external exile).

Pam was close to her mother, distant from her father, and the oldest of three children. Pam, as the identified client, appears to be the scapegoat of the family system as she "needs to get help." An IFS therapist would first look at trailheads to see where the parts are mostly blended both internally and externally for this family. The next steps are to begin to identify the most active internal parts that engage with the external active parts of each family member. What was identified was that Pam had been disconnecting from her mother, symptoms of anorexia had returned, and she had been ignoring anything to do with her father and brothers. Each of these issues is a trailhead that could lead to specific parts in charge of managing or protecting.

Sadness, anger, sensitivity, and other unwelcome emotions are often banished by controlling protectors and firefighters to stabilize the system (Schwartz & Sweezy, 2021). The emotions and traits pushed away due to fear of punishment, rejection, or shame are those exiles that the Self courageously nurtures, attends to, supports, and unburdens (Schwartz & Sweezy, 2021).

Symptoms

Families often present for therapy with a clear idea that their problems arise from the behaviors and actions of a single person in the system, most often a child or a spouse/partner. A therapist using an IFS lens sees that internal parts of persons in the system are driving external actions and reactions to the actions and behaviors of the person identified as the problem (Schwartz & Sweezy, 2021). This is an external reflection of the dynamics between parts happening internally for all persons in the therapy room. In IFS, there are no bad parts, only parts with maladaptive jobs, so a goal is to talk the parts into changing their jobs to other more adaptive ways to manage or protect (Schwartz, 2021). In the Daniels family, there are most likely protective parts reaching out externally to suppress the actions of other family members in the same way they interact with their own internal neighboring parts (Schwartz & Sweezy, 2021). In this way, the IFS therapist can see the external map as a reflection of the internal maps. This can be seen in Murray's disengagement with Pam and his engagement with his sons. Manager and protector parts can also be seen in Fran's hyper-focus on Pam's eating and behaviors.

Diversity Conceptualization

Families develop in their own ways within their cultures and larger systems, and even within larger cultural contexts, family systems can be unique (Bronfenbrenner, 1999). Each person in the family carries strengths and burdens from their families of origin and those systems within which the family developed. These people then meet and unite with other individuals who carry their strengths and burdens from their families of origin. These individuals have their own internal systems with parts that may clash or harmonize with the parts of the other. When the family system grows with the inclusion of children, the children's parts may experience conflict or harmony with their caregiver's parts (Schwartz & Sweezy, 2021). IFS is the systems within the systems within the larger historical and current contexts, which could be thought of as a "nano system" within Bronfenbrenner's (1999) micro system in the family unit.

It is within the context of the family system that the Self of children develops. With the development of the Self are the parts that manage, protect, or become exiled. This is strongly related to attachment in early childhood (Spiegel, 2017). Family systems are different across different cultures, and IFS has been shown to be useful with not only Indigenous populations in the Americas, but across the world as it is a relational model in which respect and permission are in the forefront (McVickers, 2014). IFS therapy honors listening to a variety of voices, which is important to all Indigenous peoples and has a construct of parts and the Self that makes sense to people in collaborative cultures (McVickers, 2014).

The Therapeutic Story of Problem Resolution

Problem resolution in the context of IFS is when parts become unblended and unburdened, and Self-leadership occurs. The therapist assists each family member to unblend and unburden parts and become more Self-led. This is reflected in the external system as maladaptive interactions become more adaptive, homeostasis is achieved, and the family is more flexible. The rest of this section will describe those areas in which unblending, unburdening, and Self-leadership happen.

The IFS therapist helps each person become more Self-led with the strength of the roles of reactive parts changing, assisting exiles to unburden, and to increase the person's ability to unblend from these parts (Schwartz & Sweezy, 2021). When each person works on their internal systems, it will change the ways in which external parts are reflected, which impacts the family system. It often is most beneficial to work with individual family members one at a time, then bring them all together to externalize identified internal parts into the external system to increase the likelihood of interpersonal healing (Herbine-Blank et al., 2015).

Trailheads

Identifying what is important to the client, couple, or family can be done through the search for trailheads. Trailheads are the entrance to greater knowledge and self-healing (Spiegel, 2017). **Trailheads** are those markers that show up as bodily reactions, emotional reactions, thoughts and beliefs, conflict with others, and external triggers. Following the breadcrumbs can lead to where parts are located or hidden. Once these parts are located and seen by the client, mapping can begin. Trailheads show up as things that are forefront in the mind (Spiegel, 2017).

For the Daniels family, locating trailheads might begin with identifying the main themes of conflict and disconnect. Identification of external entry points can be a good roadmap for identifying internal trailheads (Schwartz & Sweezy, 2021). Identifying the rules, roles, and boundaries in the family can help identify what types of parts might be present that are creating the problems for the family. It might be best to identify trailheads with each member of the family separately, then map where the parts are observed in the family interactions (somewhat like an internal and external enactment).

Mapping trailheads with the Daniels family would take multiple steps. The first step would be to map the trailheads in the external family (Spiegel, 2017). This would be identified by what the family says and how they react to what is said. The Daniels' interactions could direct an IFS therapist to note those times when the problems are discussed and the visible reactions to these discussions. An example of an external trailhead is Murray's disconnection from Pam, because Fran manages Pam's "illness." Noting that issue could be a labeled trailhead, "Reluctance to engage" or "Abdicating." Fran's need to manage Pam's eating behaviors and her hyper-focus could be labeled as "Caregiving manager." Pam's reiteration of "I'm fine" could be labeled as "Protector- keep away," which may also identify a possible firefighter who wants to keep others at a distance. Of course, each family member would label their own trailheads as the therapist would discuss each trailhead and ask the family what each trailhead could be named. The second step would be to map the trailheads for each family member individually. This would be done during individual sessions so that the focus could be on identifying the internal trailheads for each person. Mapping would be similar to mapping the external trailheads, yet might be more involved as each person may feel more comfortable disclosing while away from other family members (Herbine-Blank et al., 2015). This can assist with mapping parts, which would be the next step.

Mapping Parts and Externalization

Parts mapping can be a helpful process for clients. Identifying where the parts are in the body, their color, weight, physical description, sounds, or any other details can be mapped. Parts mapping entails drawing the body (or other visualized place) and identifying specifics, such as in an outline of the body, with parts drawn in, as well as including shapes, colors, dimensionality, emotions that come up relative to these parts, and so forth (Schwartz & Sweezy, 2021). Clients might see their parts as a variety of images, such as shapes with color, size, and weight, or as flowers and plants in a garden rather than simply housed within their bodies. There are as many ways to do parts mapping as there are imaginative people (Schwartz & Sweezy, 2021).

Externalization is a concept from narrative therapy related to objectifying problems rather than objectifying people (Lundby, 2014), which can help clients visualize and relate more solidly with their parts by using art, movement, journaling, figurines, objects, or models (Spiegel, 2017). Externalization can be utilized if a client is especially imaginative or if it is easier to describe parts if they are pulled from the body like a physical object. Another technique related to externalization is storage of externalized parts. Storage of parts for safekeeping can be helpful to those externalized parts that choose not to be returned to the internal system. The storage container can be imaginal, or it can be a physical object, such as a lock box or small box. Clients can keep their physical representations of parts in these chosen containers if they choose and the Self and parts feel comfortable with that. Parts should never be put away without permission and choice (Spiegel, 2017).

An example of parts mapping with Fran might be to identify which parts show up when she thinks about her daughter's diagnosis. A visual mapping process may be used to represent the internal system of parts—for example, a body outline or diagram in which parts are identified, named, and described according to their qualities, roles, and relationships. Labels, symbols, or colors can be incorporated in ways that align with Fran's preferences to support clear and meaningful representation of her internal experience. Once Fran has mapped relevant parts, then parts work can occur (Spiegel, 2017).

Parts work is the process of finding trailheads, mapping, and the other processes listed below. The goal of parts work is to help people develop a harmonious internal system by understanding, accepting, and integrating these different parts (Schwartz & Sweezy, 2021).

The 6 Fs

When an IFS therapist is learning more about identified parts, it's important to determine how the client feels about a part, because this can have a positive or negative impact on the therapy. The 6 Fs in IFS are (Spiegel, 2017):

- Find the part
- Focus on the part
- Flesh it out
- How do you feel about it
- Befriend the part, and
- Find out its fears

Finding the part aligns with locating trailheads. To locate trailheads, the therapist can observe interactions or identify important issues brought up when the client explains why they are in session. There are a few ways to find a part. The typical way is for a client to calm and still their body and search within themselves for a discomfort or a reaction of some kind. This can be challenging as some people are visual, and some aren't. Some can use imagination and creativity, and some can't.

Those clients who are imaginative and can visualize can search within their body and describe any parts that show themselves. This is called focusing on the part. If a person experiences challenges in focusing on a part, they can begin focusing with help from the therapist, who can ask focusing questions to aid the person in focusing on the part. An example might be sharpening the image where the part is located by asking the client, "Is it sharply in focus or does it have a vague outline or a misty appearance?"

Fleshing the part out entails identifying more details about the composition, size, shape, weight, volume, texture, etc. of the part. They can describe, give a shape, color, weight, tone, age, or anything that comes to mind. This can give the part more substance and a feeling of realness for the person.

Clients can then begin discussing how they feel about this part and any impacts from this part. Does the client have any curiosity about the part? Do they want to know more? Do they hate this part? Are they angry? Are they dismissive?

Is the client able to befriend the part? Is there anything about the part that the client can like? If the client still has negative feelings about the part, it may be another part that is blended and pretending to be the part.

Can the person talk to the part to learn about its fears or worries? If the client can learn what the part fears, this would demonstrate that the client has befriended the part. If this is the case, then it can be easier to work with the part as it can feel more accepted by the Self of the person. The client can learn to unblend from this part and show it that its fears are valid and that there are other ways to achieve desired results.

An example from the Daniels family could be that Fran feels resentful at the manager part that pushes her to worry about Pam all the time (blending) and hates it for controlling her life when she was younger, during the time she took care of her little sister (negative feelings about the part). Unpacking how Fran feels about the part leads to softening and befriending the part, which then leads to finding the part's fears of what would happen if it weren't doing its job. This then would be the Self of the person who orients the part to the Self and demonstrates that they are in charge so the part can relax.

Blending

Blending refers to how a part blends with the Self or another part. This can be challenging as a person may feel that it is the Self that is managing rather than a part. The person may believe that they are "this way," rather than a part being "this way." Blended parts can challenge experienced IFS therapists because a check-in needs to be done if certain information from a part appears to be not quite right. Some parts piggyback or control other parts and are not at all the parts that the therapist assumes they are, and this can also be challenging for both the therapist and the client. This is where mapping the parts is so important, as questions can be asked to identify whether a piggybacking or controlling part is responding, rather than the part that is thought to be responding.

Direct Access

When parts are blended to the point where it is unknown if another part is piggybacking, controlling, or blocking the Self of the client for some reason, the therapist can use a technique called **direct access** (Spiegel, 2017). When using direct access, the therapist communicates to the part as if it weren't a part but is the person. This can be very helpful, especially if the client believes that this is not a part but is the Self. Often, the therapist can communicate directly to a reactive part, which can often be faster than gaining access to the part through the client. This is often related to an inaccessibility of the Self for some reason (Schwartz & Sweezy, 2021). This intervention is often used until the client's Self is more available and the client is experiencing Self-leadership.

Direct access could be used with Pam, as Firefighters often take control and need to be placated and calmed. An IFS therapist using direct access would speak directly to the part and gain its approval to work with it and possibly the parts it is protecting; often this is a childlike exile. This could be as simple as asking Pam's firefighter to engage. Firefighters can be volatile, so care is needed, and the therapist can back off to relax the part (Schwartz & Sweezy, 2021). A therapist backing away from a firefighter might let the part know that they are moving away, thanking the part for engaging, and reassuring the part that they will not engage without permission (Schwartz & Sweezy, 2021). If Pam's firefighter is engaged without soothing, it might result in increased eating, exercising, or other self-harming behaviors. This is why training in IFS is so important for those therapists using the model—especially with clients who have experienced trauma (Schwartz & Sweezy, 2021).

Burdens

There are two main burdens in IFS: personal burdens and legacy burdens. These burdens are the reason why parts take on a specific role in the internal system. **Burdens** are the painful beliefs, feelings, and physical sensations that parts take on and carry (Spiegel, 2017). Schwartz (2021) described burdens as being powerful organizers of the part's experiences and activity, similar to the way in which a virus organizes a computer's hard drive. Burdens come into being as the result of trauma experienced by the person, or a child internalizing criticism or neglect from a caregiver (Schwartz, 2021).

Burdens present in many different ways, and burdens in the Daniels family might be related to the roles of sons and daughters in the generational family system, which parent takes on the caregiving role and which parent takes on other tasks such as coaching in sports and mowing the lawn, the roles of grandparents, and messages from the larger systems in the culture (Schwartz & Sweezy, 2021).

Personal burdens are those burdens the person takes on themselves, such as perfectionism, self-criticism, and so forth. These are either self-created or reinforced by interaction. Powerful personal burdens are the result of internal maps created by expectations of caregivers and the world in general (Sherman et al., 2015). These experiences and expectations create internal working models for infants and children that they carry throughout their lives (Sherman et al., 2015).

Legacy burdens are those that are handed down generationally, socially, and by others. These burdens impact the functioning of family systems. Cultural legacy burdens are the result of racism, patriarchy, individualism, and materialism (Schwartz & Sweezy, 2021). While other types of legacy burdens can be the result of generational transference, epigenetic, and harmful interactions by parents, caregivers, or others, there may be legacy burdens in the Daniels family transmitted to Pam in the form of generational patterns of father-son bonding, cut-off/isolation, agendas, and patriarchal gender role assignments. Individualism and materialism often create challenges in families in which parental roles are challenged due to time constraints. This could be an aspect of Pam's father seeking more time with his sons and moving attention from Pam to Pam's mother. While the Daniels are a Caucasian family, they could still be impacted by the larger cultural and societal norms in the United States and be perpetuating gender norms, expectations of behaviors and actions, and imbalances in power in the family system.

Transitioning IFS Concepts and Interventions in Work with External Systems

Due to stressors to a family system (political, social, generational, gender roles, financial, work, etc.), family members often divide into the same roles of exile, manager, protector, and firefighter and become bound in these roles by similar constraints placed upon inner parts to maintain their roles (Schwartz & Sweezy, 2021). It could be beneficial to locate trailheads and map external patterns, then meet individually with each family member to identify their internal trailheads and map their internal systems.

External family systems mirror how internal systems work: in response to danger or a threat, families develop managers, protectors, firefighters, and exiles, and the family members who take on these roles can polarize and form alliances the same way an internal system does (Schwartz & Sweezy, 2021). The first approach when using IFS with a family is to approach the managers first, just as it is for approaching the internal system. Family managers define the family's problems in understated ways and use tactics to control the discussion and to shift topics away from exiled topics (Schwartz & Sweezy, 2021). As family managers may polarize over less threatening things, such as the brothers and father being away for sports or mother's worries about anorexia symptoms, we see that the Daniels family's managers are pulling the focus to avoid dealing with any issues related to exiled issues (e.g., the reasons why Pam is not eating).

Fostering Skillful Communication

Fostering skillful communication is related to a client being able to communicate from the Self with their parts (Schwartz & Sweezy, 2021). When skillful communication is utilized, family members can notice and listen to their parts, speak for rather than from their parts, explore the fears their parts have, and lead from their Selves in discussion with one another rather than communicating from blended parts (Schwartz & Sweezy, 2021).

To begin the process of helping family members foster skillful communication, IFS therapists first identify individual internal parts and then map when the external parts activate and react to another member's internal parts. This entails identifying the family managers and their roles (enmeshed, controlling, abdicating, avoiding, etc.) and observe how the parts polarize, seek out, avoid, fight back, and so forth in the external family system, then map the parts that activate during family interactions, then use the 6 Fs so that each family member learns more about their parts and can begin to soften to their parts.

An example from the Daniels family might be Fran's need to manage Pam's eating habits. Fran reported that she was worried because Pam had been diagnosed with anorexia and had completed treatment for this two years ago, yet Fran has been noting behaviors that remind her of Pam's actions before treatment. Pam is observed to weigh very little for her height. Identifying the managers in Fran's internal system, how they interact, who is in charge, how blended Fran's Self is with these parts, and the roles these parts have taken on could lead to Fran's ability to communicate with these parts and lead to Fran becoming more Self-led. This, in turn, would create the ability for Fran to utilize skillful communication, rather than acting from blended parts.

Reassuring Family Managers

Reassuring family managers is called **relaxing the system** (Schwartz & Sweezy, 2021). It would be impossible to have access to both the external family system and the IFS without first reassuring the family managers. For the external managers and protectors (Murray and Fran), joining with the family and getting buy-in from parents is key, as parents are the permission-grantors of the family system (Schwartz & Sweezy, 2021).

Contracting

Contracting is usually utilized in IFS work with couples, yet it is important when used in work with families as well (Redfern, 2023). There are specific needs related to contracting with family members. The first being that each agrees to listen to parts without reacting to those parts with one another. The second is that they will need to allow others to witness their parts without reacting (Schwartz & Sweezy, 2021).

Another integral factor when contracting with a family is to regularly revisit the goals of IFS therapy with each person in the system to stay on track, as working with so many people and parts can become chaotic without structure (Redfern, 2023). Another aspect of contracting is related to the therapist's parts: Is the therapist not following through in making sure goals are discussed? Is there a part that might be getting in the way? Would the therapist benefit from IFS consultation to work through one of their own parts that might be hindering treatment?

It would be beneficial to contract with the Daniels family, as there appear to be polarizations in both the external system and the internal systems of each member in treatment. Each person would need to contract to move forward in therapy to not lose sight of goals as they may change as therapy moves forward.

Individual Work

Individual parts work is important in IFS with families because the internal system is reflected externally in the system. This is one of the areas in which IFS is often believed to be only an individualistic model, yet many of the same presenting issues are observed in both, so to work toward lasting change, individual work also needs to be done by each member of the family who is presenting for treatment. Individual work would be in the form of the therapist working with each family member to do parts work, then that would be reflected in the larger system. As a metaphor, this might look like a conductor conducting the entire orchestra, yet working with the strings, the brass, and the woodwind sections as well to create a uniform whole. If Fran, Pam, or Murray refused to work individually with the IFS therapist, this might limit the strength of treatment in that the remaining family members would do the bulk of the internal work necessary for external system change (Schwartz & Sweezy, 2021). It's not impossible to resolve systemic issues without one of the identified family members working individually, but it would be easier to see change more quickly. Reassuring the individual's managers and protectors can help reluctant family members do the individual work (Schwartz & Sweezy, 2021).

Self-Leadership and Self-Energy

The role of the Self. IFS as a model utilizes the core **Self** to assist parts in relinquishing unhelpful roles and aligning parts to the Self for structure and leadership (Schwartz & Sweezy, 2021). There are three main pathways toward healing: **the 8Cs**, **Self-leadership**, and **Self-energy**, with the goal of healing and transformation (Schwartz & Sweezy, 2021).

The **8 Cs** relate to the Self characterized by core qualities of the Self that are the roadmap of healing the internal system and increasing external connection (Schwartz & Sweezy, 2021). The 8 Cs are:

- **C**ompassion,
- **C**uriosity,
- **C**alm,
- **C**larity,
- **C**onfidence,
- **C**ourage,
- **C**reativity, and
- **C**onnectedness.

Self-leadership happens when the Self has cultivated the 8Cs and begins to lead the internal system, mediating conflicts, understanding parts, and fostering healing (Schwartz & Sweezy, 2021). Healing and transformation happen when the Self-led system works with its parts, protective and reactive parts relax their roles, and exiled parts can release their burdens, leading to personal growth and a more harmonious internal life, which then becomes reflected in external relationships (Schwartz & Sweezy, 2021).

Often, when parts are blended or polarized, there is no compassion in the system, and some parts are exiled and hidden, protectors and managers take over, and the system has little trust in the Self (Schwartz & Sweezy, 2021). Increasing compassion within the system is a goal to encourage change in protectors' beliefs about exiled parts and increase their trust in the Self.

When the Self is blended with protective and polarized parts, people lose access to curiosity. Curiosity happens when the Self is unblended a bit from polarized parts, and the Self can access these parts (Schwartz & Sweezy, 2021). When the person can work with a part and have curiosity about that part, its role, its needs, and its history can foster healing in the system, leading to the part's trust in the Self.

When the Self becomes calm, curious, and has compassion for parts—for their experiences, their anger, protectiveness, and so forth—parts begin to trust the Self more implicitly. This is where mindfulness and body calming are so helpful as additions to IFS to increase the person's ability to be calm (Schwartz & Sweezy, 2021).

Clarity is the act of recognizing the roles of parts as not inherently bad, just burdened (Schwartz & Sweezy, 2021). Clarity is being able to recognize parts and their roles and is sometimes thought of as "in-sight" and can open avenues to create trusting relationships between parts and the Self (Schwartz & Sweezy, 2021). **In-sight** is a communication method in which the client communicates with their own internal parts to gain clarity. If this is stressful or hard for the client, the therapist can use "direct access" and speak to the part as if it were the client (Schwartz & Sweezy, 2021). Direct access is often utilized with clients who experience dissociation, fear of their parts, who are sleepy, self-critical, and otherwise unable to communicate directly with their own parts.

Confidence, clarity, and calm in Self-leadership can foster a partnership with parts in which the Self is in charge and the parts can believe that the Self is self-reliant and can be safely in charge. This alignment to the Self mirrors what is seen in an external family system in which a parent becomes more attuned to their children and can recognize cues and bids for nurturance, and the parts do not need to retreat, hide, over-protect, or over-manage, which creates a more secure attachment of parts to the Self (Dugan et al., 2025). For the Daniels family, this could look like Fran telling Pam that she believes in her (confidence), that she recognizes Pam's need for independence (courage), and that she is there to support Pam (connectedness).

When people become more Self-led and begin to unburden exiles, there is more creativity, calmness, curiosity, connection, and caring within the internal system as well as in the external system (Schwartz & Sweezy, 2021). This lack of creativity, calmness, curiosity, connection, and true caring can be noticeable in those families in which family members are polarized, enmeshed, cut-off, or otherwise destabilized, yet once the external system can unburden and recognize their own Self-leadership, the external system will begin to resemble the internal systems that are more Self-led. The Daniels family experiences a lack of connection and true caring in that the parents are polarized and reactive, leadership has been abdicated by Murray, Fran is worried and often blended with her micro-manager parts, Pam is blended with a firefighter a lot of the time, and her brothers are simply doing their own things and not noticing that anything is going on.

Connectedness in IFS relates to three ways in which the Self and parts are connected: the connectedness between parts and the Self (Self-to-part) when inner balance and harmony are the result of compassion; compassion and kindness between the Self of one person and the Self of another person (Self-to-Self); and connectedness between unburdened parts (unburdened part-to-unburdened part); Schwartz & Sweezy, 2021). These relationships create a calm and resonant connection between a person's parts and the Self as well as between persons in external systems.

Unblending

Unblending is a process in which permission is asked for from the part that is either blending with the Self or another part. A part is reassured that they will not be asked to leave, die, be removed, and their feelings, concerns, and experiences will not be denied (Sweezy, 2023). Unblending cannot happen in an environment of fear or distrust. Honoring the sacrifices of the part, their hard work, noticing them, and allowing their voice to be heard and understood is important, as the Self can only lead with their consent (Sweezy, 2023).

Shared Vision

Maladaptive patterns in families can be seen as a consequence of parents imposing their personal visions of who their children are and how their children should live their lives. These are often powerful dreams of the parents that are passed down from legacy burdens in their own families of origin (Schwartz & Sweezy, 2021). These expectations often leave little room for difference or growth. In contrast, a shared family vision promotes flexibility, growth, and adaptability, leading to a more balanced and harmonious family system.

Unburdening

Exiles are hidden emotions or unwanted attributes of the person that were pushed down deep and hidden because of traumatic experiences or extreme and pervasive expectations from parents or others (Schwartz & Sweezy, 2021). Most exiles are very young, so unburdening often is tied to a protector part relaxing and allowing the Self to be the caring adult the child needed when the trauma occurred or when the exile was created because of extreme family expectations. The process begins with finding the part, fleshing it out, making friends with it, and identifying the fears of the protector. The IFS therapist guides the client in identifying why the protective part is there (using the 8Cs). The protective part has given itself the job of protecting this exiled part due to circumstances out of the child's control (Schwartz & Sweezy, 2021). When the protector can relax, the therapist can guide the client in finding out from the exile what it needs to release its burdens, which then releases the burdens of the protector part. Once the client can care for the exile and give it what it needs, the client can unburden the parts to the earth, air, water, fire, or spirit (Schwartz & Sweezy, 2021). For the Daniels family, it may be that Fran needs to work with a protector part to unburden a childlike exile. The protector may have developed as an adaptive response to Fran's early family environment, taking on a managerial and caregiving role toward her younger sister, while more vulnerable feelings—such as resentment, anger, anxiety, fear, and the desire to please her mother—came to be held by an exile.

Self-Energy of the Therapist

Working with clients to identify, unblend, and unburden parts can take a toll on the therapist and the therapist's parts (Anderson, 2021). It can be exhausting at times to maintain the Self-energy required to process with clients, especially in those times where a client's parts might activate parts in the therapist. To resolve this issue, most IFS therapists seek consultation or their own IFS therapy.

Case Transcript

This is the first session with the Daniels family. Present are Murray (39), Fran (38), and Pam (17). Murray and Pam's other two children, Oliver (15) and George (13), are not present at this session as Murray and Fran have reported that the younger children are doing well and that they do not demonstrate behaviors that challenge the status quo. The immediate issue appears to be a need to resolve issues between Fran, Pam, and Murray to stabilize both internal and external systems. This change in the system would automatically include Oliver and George (Schwartz & Sweezy, 2021).

Therapist: Hello, I'm glad to meet you all. Please tell me a bit about yourselves and why you're here today.

Intervention: Joining—taking steps to become more familiar and safer to the family system.

Fran: I'm Fran. I'm Pam's mom, and I used to teach in elementary school, but I became a stay-at-home mother after Pam was born. I'm worried about my daughter and her lack of eating. Look at her! She's too thin.

Pam (crossing arms and rolling eyes): I'm Pam, and could you stop it, mom? There's nothing wrong with me. You need a hobby, or something. I'm fine.

Murray (sitting on the outside and leaning back): I'm Murray. I work full-time and coach my sons' teams. I try to stay out of this (*he waves his hands at Fran and Pam*). My boys are so easy.

Therapist: Thank you. I'm glad you're here. Let's see how I can help. Tell me a bit more about why you're here.

Intervention: Mapping the system—The communication and body language are an enactment of how the internal parts of each person react to external family interactions.

Pam: Well, George and Oliver aren't here, so.... They never have to do anything but play sports and be boys.

Murray (leans across Fran): Well, they have practice, which I'm missing right now.

Fran (leans toward Murray):	You can be here for your daughter. She's going through a lot right now. I'm really worried about her.
Therapist:	You're both concerned about your children.

Interventions: Mapping the system—watching the interactions, the placement of family members, body language, and proximity to one another allows the therapist to map interactions looking for trailheads. Fran and Pam are sitting together, and Murray is off to the side, facing slightly away. Reassuring family managers—validating that the parents care for their children assists in gaining confidence from parents and allows Pam to see and hear that her parents care for her. Pam's internal parts might take notice of this.

Fran (leans forward):	Yes! I'm so worried because Pam went to treatment a few years ago for an eating disorder, and all the signs are there that it's happening again.
Pam (looks away):	I keep telling you, I'm fine.
Fran (reaching toward Pam):	I'm so nervous that you are getting worse again.
Murray (leaning back):	I get that Fran is worried, but why can't she just meet with you so I can do the things I need to do?

Pam (*rolls her eyes and tightens her crossed arms and looks away*).

Fran (looking at Murray):	You're her father; you need to be involved. (*To therapist*): Don't you think Murray needs to be involved?
Therapist:	I'm so glad you're all here so that you can resolve this. Fran, so that you feel less stressed. Murray, so you can feel that you can be there for your daughter yet do the things you need to do. And, so that you, Pam, will have both of your parents actively in your life.

Interventions: Mapping the system—watching the interactions, the placement of family members, body language, and proximity to one another allows the therapist to map interactions looking for trailheads. Fran is demonstrating a blended reactive manager, and Murray is demonstrating an avoidant manager. Pam is demonstrating a manager that is locking down to avoid a firefighter. Enactment—the therapist is watching the natural engagement of this family.

Pam (staring at therapist): I just want my mom off my case. My dad can ignore me all he wants.

Therapist (stopping parents from engaging): That is an interesting way to say that. (*To Fran*): Pam wants you off her case. What does that mean to you?

Fran (wiping at eyes): It makes me sad. I'm only trying to help Pam feel better so she can go to college happy and not sad. I want her to be happy, normal, and a good, healthy weight. I was never very close to my mother, and I wanted to be close to Pam. I wanted us to have a good relationship.

Therapist: It makes you sad, and you want to help Pam feel better so she can enjoy life.

Interventions: Reframing—Flipping the context of the message to move away from the negative. Validating—Pointing out that feelings are valid. Reassuring family managers—validating that the parents care for their children assists in gaining confidence from parental parts.

Fran: Yes.

Therapist: You wanted to have a close relationship with Pam, and you feel that she's distancing herself from you.

Fran: Yes. I wanted to have what my mother and I never had. I thought we were close until Pam started refusing to eat and began distancing herself from me.

Therapist: You wanted to be close. This sounds like something important. (*to Murray*): Pam is giving you permission to ignore her all you want. What does that mean for you?

Murray: I don't know. I don't think I ignore her; I just think Fran can handle all this emotional stuff. That's a mom's job. I don't know how to do any of that.

Fran (touching Murray's hand): I didn't know you felt like that. That sounds hard.

Murray (squeezing Fran's hand): Yes, it's hard.

Therapist: It can be hard to do things if you feel that you don't know how or feel unable to do things.

Interventions: Mapping the system—watching the interactions, identifying managers, protectors, and exiles. Reassuring family managers—validating that the parents care for their children assists in gaining confidence from parental parts. Challenging—challenging assumptions and identifying firefighters. Pam's firefighter was visible in the session and showed when challenged. Fostering skillful communication—Family members communicating from the Self, rather than from their parts.

Murray: Yes.

Therapist: What is it about not knowing how to do any of that stuff that is the hardest for you?

Murray: I don't know. I never really had to know how to do that stuff. My mother took care of the emotional stuff, and my father supported my sports, my work, and things like that. My dad was a good provider but wasn't available to do more than that. I was able to spend time with him doing things he enjoyed, or he would participate in my after-school sports or be with me when I was working in the business.

Therapist: Did anything else come up for you when you were thinking about your dad? Did you feel anything in your chest, or neck, or anywhere else?

Interventions: Mapping the system—watching the interactions, identifying managers, protectors, and exiles. Identifying trailheads—Where are there noticeable activations in the body when specific things are discussed?

Murray: Well, yes, my heart felt heavy, and my neck hurt a little.

Therapist: Okay, so your heart felt heavy, and your neck hurt a little. Which was most noticeable when you were talking about your dad?

Murray: That's a weird thing to ask.

Therapist: Yes, it does sound weird, yet we all have parts of ourselves that react to different things, like thinking about family members, or work, or things that we need to deal with. So, when people say things like "A part of me feels this way, yet another part of me thinks this…" it's natural to think about different parts of us reacting to different events.

Interventions: Introduction to IFS, especially parts—this is an open discussion related to introducing basic parts language to create familiarity before more in-depth work is done. Relaxing the system—this allows parts to become familiar with the language so that when the person seeks permission during parts work, the parts already know that there is no threat. This decreases the likelihood that parts will polarize with the therapist and the client.

Murray: Yeah, I've heard of that. I say that sometimes myself, like, "A part of me wants to watch football, but another part wants to work on the car." Is that similar?

Therapist: Exactly! That's exactly right. We all have parts of us that help us with different things. Some help us stay on task, some help us focus, some want to just be on social media, some are those voices we hear that tell us if we want to succeed we'll study, or that we don't fit in, or any number of things.

Pam: Like, when I get mad at myself for being too fat? I hear this mean voice telling me I'm gross and it's unbearable. It's a really mean voice, and all I want to do is stop eating and go on a long run.

Therapist: Thank you, Pam. Yes, very much like that. That is a great example.

Fran: Wow! When I'm not productive enough at home, you know, cooking, doing laundry, or finishing other tasks, I have these horrible thoughts that I'm a lazy, useless slacker!

Therapist: That was another great example. Thank you, Fran. See, we all have these parts of ourselves that show up in reaction to things that happen. The trick then is to begin understanding them and identifying when they show up. I have a couple of handouts for you about this and the different roles these parts usually have. Some are managers, which means they help us be on time, stay organized, like paying bills on time or getting to work or school on time, and push us to be prepared for presentations, job interviews, and so forth. I see each of you nodding, so this sounds familiar? Some are protectors, and these are like the older siblings that protect younger siblings from getting hurt or they keep possibly harmful things away from us. Some are called exiles, and these are young, childlike parts of us that have been pushed down due to family expectations, trauma, pressures of society, and so forth. These handouts describe what parts are, their roles, and the goals of working with them so that you achieve your goals as a family.

Interventions: Introduction to IFS, especially parts—this is an open discussion related to introducing basic parts language to create familiarity before more in-depth work is done. Normalizing experiences—this helps clients see how their experiences with parts are typical and everyone has experience interacting with parts. Psychoeducation—using IFS handouts to inform on the model and the rules, roles, boundaries, and motivations of parts (managers, protectors, and exiles).

Fran (looking at a handout): These look interesting. I've never seen this before.

Therapist: Are there any questions about the handouts? I know the ideas can seem odd at first. We're nearing the end of the session. Thank you for sharing your feelings and thoughts today. Sometimes it can be hard to do that. Please think about what happened in session today between now and next time we meet. Note those thoughts, images, or feelings that come up for you when you think about what was said today. You can write about it, draw it, or talk to each other. Bring this in with you next time we meet, and we can discuss anything that comes up. Pam, I would like to meet with just you next time. Is that okay? (*Pam nods but sits back and crosses arms tighter*). Pam, I see you closing up. It's okay, I won't intrude. You can tell me when you feel uncomfortable, and we can talk about other things (*Pam relaxes back and says, "Okay."*). Is that okay for you, Fran and Murray? (*they both nod*). Then, I would like to meet with you next, Murray, is that okay? (*Murray nods but sighs*). You sighed, Murray. It's okay, I'll tell you the same thing I told Pam. Is that okay (*Murray relaxes back and says, "Sounds good."*)? Then, I would like to meet with you, Fran. Is that okay? (*Fran nods and sits forward*). I see that you leaned in, Fran. We can go over what is important to you in our session. Is that okay? (*Fran leans back and says, "That sounds great!*)? Then, I would like to meet with all three of you again. Does this sound like a plan? (*they all nod*). Think of one goal each that you would like to work toward, and we will discuss that as a group when we all meet again. Thank you all for meeting me today, and I will see you next week, Pam.

Interventions: Relaxing the system and reassuring family managers--calming the activated parts. Mapping the system—passively by journaling, writing down, drawing, or discussing parts (unconscious, homework). Who is involved in the therapy—With IFS, it can be challenging to map the external system without first mapping each person's internal system to see how the external system mirrors the internal one or how internal parts present on the outside.

The Therapeutic Story

By the end of the first session, there has been some change in the system from managers and protectors being in charge to some softening so that there can be identification of trailheads and movement toward parts work with each member of the family presenting to therapy. Each will journal, draw, or identify in their own way what comes up for them when they think about the issues that brought them into therapy.

1 Mapping the system: This is challenging in a first session, so observing natural enactments and noting the ways in which each member interacts can give clues to trailheads and to which types of parts are activated.
2 The therapeutic story also includes burdens (both general and legacy) from generational family of origin stories and the larger society. This includes gender role expectations related to activities, emotional expression, and caregiving.
3 Emotional expression was validated, so manager parts may be more amenable to exploring this next session.
4 The system is becoming more relaxed, and activated managers have been calmed.
5 A possible firefighter was identified when Pam kept reiterating that she was fine and nothing was wrong.
6 Pam is the identified client, yet her parents will also be required to be in therapy—both as individuals and as a family. Identifying who needs to be present in therapy can structure sessions and treatment goal development. Younger brothers Oscar and George will not be required to be present for sessions as they really don't have power in the system for change.

References

Anderson, F. G. (2021). *Transcending trauma: Healing complex PTSD with internal family systems*. PESI Publishing.

Brenner, E. G., Schwartz, R. C., & Becker, C. (2023). Development of the internal family systems model: Honoring contributions from family systems therapies. *Family Process, 62*(4), 1290–1306.

Bronfenbrenner U. (1999). Environments in developmental perspective: Theoretical and operational models. In S. L. Friedman, & T. D. Wachs (Eds.), *Measuring environment across the lifespan: Emerging methods and concepts* (pp. 3–28). American Psychological Association Press.

Dugan, K. A., Fraley, R. C., Jones, J. D., Stern, J. A., Shaver, P. R., Lejuez, C. W., & Cassidy, J. (2025). Coordination of parent and adolescent attachment across time. *Developmental Psychology, 61*(9), 1721–1738.

Herbine-Blank T, Kerpelman D, & Sweezy, M. (2015). *Intimacy from the inside out: Courage and compassion in couple therapy*. Routledge.

Herbine-Blank T, Kerpelman D, & Sweezy, M. (2021). *Intimacy from the inside out: Couple therapy skills manual: Healing relationships with intimacy from the inside out*. PESI.

van der Kolk, B. A. (2014). *The body keeps the score: Brain, mind, and body in the healing of trauma*. Viking.

Lundby, G. (2014). Creating different versions of life: Talking about problems with children and their parents. *Australian and New Zealand Journal of Family Therapy, 35*(1), 31–45.

McVicker, S. A. M. (2014) Internal family systems (IFS) in Indian country: Perspectives and practice on harmony and balance. *Journal of Indigenous Research, 3*(1), 6.

Redfern, E. E. (2023). *Internal family systems therapy: Supervision and consultation*. Routledge.

Sandler, J. (2003). On attachment to internal objects. *Psychoanalytic Inquiry, 23*(1), 12–26.

Schwartz, R.C. (1995). *Internal family systems therapy*. Guilford Press.
Schwartz, R.C. (2021). *No bad parts: Healing trauma and restoring wholeness with the internal family systems model*. Sounds True.
Schwartz, R.C. & Sweezy, M. (2021). *Internal family systems therapy* (2nd Ed.). Guilford Press.
Sherman, L. J., Rice, K., & Cassidy, J. (2015). Infant capacities related to building internal working models of attachment figures: A theoretical and empirical review. *Developmental Review*, *37*, 109–141.
Spiegel, L. (2017). *Internal family systems therapy with children*. Routledge.
Sweezy, M. (2023). *Internal family systems therapy for shame and guilt*. The Guilford Press.

17 Emotionally Focused Family Therapy

Matthew Pace and Todd C. Workman Jesness

The primary proponent of emotionally focused family therapy (EFFT) is Susan Johnson. Originally of British origin, Johnson practiced and taught as a psychologist and couple and family therapist primarily in Canada at the University of Ottawa, while also teaching and researching at Alliant University in San Diego (Furrow et al., 2022). The EFFT approach is grounded in the same core tenets of emotionally focused couple therapy (EFCT), a highly researched and empirically validated model, which utilizes attachment theory as its organizing premise for understanding human and relational functioning (Furrow et al., 2019). The model is brief, experiential, systemic, and humanistic, with assumptions about honoring emotion and dependency that find resonance in feminist theory (Johnson, 2020).

The ideas of EFCT originally began to take shape as Susan Johnson and Leslie Greenberg (1985) examined the role of emotion and attachment in their work with couples in the mid to late 1980s (Johnson, 2019). With such rigorous research and robust outcomes established through the development and practice of EFCT over the years, it was perhaps simply a matter of time before the model was adapted to working with families and individuals as well, which Johnson became a stronger proponent of until her passing in 2024.

Recognizing that attachments are shaped through relationships, EFFT, per its namesake, incorporates a resolute focus on the internal emotional experiences of clients as they relate to the presenting relational dynamics that bring families to therapy (Furrow et al., 2022). In tandem with the focus on emotion, EFFT is also keen on identifying the interactional cycles coinciding with the emotional experiences of clients, both of which factor into problem formation as well as problem resolution in the model (Furrow et al., 2019).

In order to tell the story of EFFT, it is necessary to articulate a bit more about its foundation, attachment theory. Attachment theory was developed by John Bowlby (1969/1982, 1988), a psychiatrist and developmental psychologist, who posited that humans are shaped by their earliest and ongoing experiences with caregivers, which impact their sense of security in those relationships. This sense of security, or attachment, whether it is more broadly regarded as secure or insecure, is effectively ingrained in a person from these lived

DOI: 10.4324/9781003668510-17

experiences and shapes how people then relate and connect to others in their lives. This sense of security affects not only one's relationships but also has ramifications for one's day-to-day functioning in the world. For example, those hailing from secure attachments are, in a nutshell, more resilient, adaptive, and well-adjusted than those more broadly described as having insecure attachments (Bowlby, 1988; Johnson, 2019; Mikulincer & Shaver, 2016). While an exploration of the nuances of attachment theory has been copiously expanded on in the volumes cited by Bowlby, for this exploration, Johnson (2019) will be relied on primarily to distill and articulate the tenets of attachment theory in the context of EFFT.

EFFT is fundamentally grounded in attachment theory, holding that: the need for attachment and bonding is inherent and essential to the human condition; attention to emotion and emotional regulation, particularly around fear, is critical to understanding and working with a person's level of attachment security; and that "the close connection with trusted others is the ecological niche in which the human brain, nervous system, and key behavioral patterns evolved and is the context in which we can evolve into our best selves" (Johnson, 2019, p. 6).

The attachment theory tenets laid out by Johnson (2019) are as follows:

1 The need for connection is effectively "hard-wired," and we are driven by our need for both physical and emotional proximity to attachment figures. The human longing for this sense of connection is primary in organizing the human experience, and we become most aware of this longing "at times of threat, risk, pain, or uncertainty" (Johnson, 2019, p. 6). Within these attachment relationships, "shared vulnerability builds bonds precisely because it brings these needs to the fore and encourages reaching for others" (p. 6). EFFT argues that shared vulnerability that is validated and received effectively is what builds secure attachment bonds.
2 When caregivers afford reliable emotional and physical availability to children, this works to calm the child's nervous system and creates a safe haven, a place/relationship that one knows they can return to during times of turmoil or distress. This helps establish a working schema for the world, wherein the nervous system is less attenuated to stress, which "creates expectations of a relatively safe and manageable world" (Johnson, 2019, p. 6).
3 The emotional balance afforded by the safe haven helps develop an integrated, confident sense of self, wherein the child feels able to congruently communicate their needs to attachment figures, furthering the attachment bond(s). These experiences and interactions then help foster working models for positive attachments with others.
4 The experience of having a safe haven helps establish a secure base, a place from which a person feels greater confidence to go out into the world to explore and take risks. This yields a greater sense of autonomy and confidence. Having a safe haven, affording reliable closeness, and a

secure base, which provides confidence in one's greater ability to encounter the world, results in effective dependency, which is a source of strength and resilience. In sum, "Being able to reach out to and depend on reliable others and internalize a 'felt sense' of secure connection with others is the ultimate resource that allows our species to survive and thrive in an uncertain world" (Johnson, 2019, p. 6).

5 Secure attachment bonds are defined by the *accessibility, responsiveness*, and *emotional engagement* (A.R.E.) of caregivers/attachment figures. Johnson (2019) articulates this acronym as a mnemonic shorthand when exploring with clients around their attachment needs, effectively, "Are you there for me?" (p. 6).

6 When our sense of security or closeness is lost or threatened, we experience separation distress. Emotional or physical isolation from attachment figures is inherently traumatic and results in feelings of vulnerability and helplessness. These threats to or losses of attachment to loved ones are often referred to as **attachment injuries** or ruptures.

7 Through repeated interactional cycles, we develop working mental models for attachment, both in how we interpret the actions of others and how we respond. Attachment security is not set in stone, however, as new experiences afford the opportunity to develop new working models of attachment. One might have an insecure attachment with an unreliable attachment figure and a secure attachment with another, more reliable attachment figure. Automatically relying on these working models, shaped by repeated patterns of interaction, can result in distorted perceptions of the actions of others and, hence, color one's actions in response. In effect, if the working model does not fit the unique dynamics at hand, personal and/or interpersonal problems will likely result.

8 Those who have benefited from secure attachments are more at ease with closeness to others, are more likely to recognize their own needs, and to make congruent appeals to attachment figures to have those needs met. When the attachment figure reliably responds in kind to that outreach, trust in the attachment figure is affirmed, which acts to calm the central nervous system of the child or person making the outreach. This "attachment security appears to buffer stress and potentiate positive coping throughout life" (Johnson, 2019, p. 7).

9 When attachment figures are unresponsive, unavailable, or hostile to the person making an attachment bid, secondary attachment strategies are utilized. These secondary attachment strategies can more broadly be categorized as anxious or avoidant, which also tend to align with fight or flight survival responses. Under the **anxious attachment** style, we might see vigilant or hyperactivated strategies for outreach or regulation of attachment emotions, "characterized by sensitivity to any negative messages coming from significant others and by 'fight' responses designed to protest distance and get an attachment figure to pay more attention and offer

more reassuring support" (Johnson, 2019, p. 7). With **avoidant attachment** styles, deactivated, dismissive, or flight strategies are seen with "responses designed to minimize frustration and distress through distancing oneself from loved ones who are seen as hostile, dangerous, or uncaring" (Johnson, 2019, p. 7). With such responses from a caregiver, minimization of attachment needs occurs, and the child will develop compulsive self-reliance. The lack of A.R.E. during these times of vulnerability effectively leads to avoidance of the vulnerable state as well as distancing from the attachment figure(s) in question. The use of these fight/flight strategies is not inherently dysfunctional, as there may be circumstances where pursuing or distancing is merited by the circumstances at hand. Issues arise, however, if these strategies are relied on habitually, "rigidifying into a style that ends up constraining a person's awareness and choices and limiting his or her ability to engage constructively with others" (Johnson, 2019, p. 7).

When trauma is experienced with an attachment figure, a third kind of secondary attachment strategy can manifest, which is characterized by disorganized or fearful avoidant attributes. In such circumstances, the child reaching for their attachment needs to be met is "in a paradoxical situation in which loved ones are both the source of and the solution to fear" (Johnson, 2019, p. 7). The results are similarly paradoxical, with a person longing for connection and also being fearful of what their efforts might yield when they do reach out, often "demanding connection and then distancing, and even attacking when connection is offered" (Johnson, 2019, p. 7). Those who inflexibly exercise these **insecure attachment** strategies will likely have a more tenuous relationship with the very resources that are best understood to help ameliorate their underlying attachment needs, safe and reliable connections with loved ones (Johnson, 2019).

10 While child/parent attachments are more reliant on immediate physical proximity to develop and maintain secure attachments, adults are less reliant on these factors, given their ability to mentally internalize attachment figures "to create symbolic proximity" (Johnson, 2019, p. 8). Attachment theory recognizes two other behavioral systems for adults which interact with attachment, sexuality, and caretaking. Within the domain of caretaking, **secure attachments** have been "associated with more attuned attention to another adult and more responsive caregiving" (Johnson, 2019, p. 8). In the realm of sexuality, attachment security is associated with more gratifying sexual experiences characterized by greater arousal, intimacy, and pleasure (Johnson, 2019).

The Therapeutic Story of Problem Formation

EFFT incorporates the noted emphasis on attachment and emotion, and the experience thereof, as well as an emphasis on the interactional cycles within which the various attachment strategies and consequent emotions manifest

(Furrow et al., 2019). The model borrows from other models of family therapy focused on cybernetics, such as Structural Therapy, that problems manifest in the context of interactional cycles and become maintained by those stuck (or homeostatic) interactional cycles, which ultimately work to reinforce the issues at hand (Furrow et al., 2022). In short, the cycle is the problem, not the family nor the identified client(s).

Along with its emphasis on identifying problematic interactional cycles, the model incorporates a complementary emphasis on the experiential processing of emotions as those cyclic interactions unfold (Johnson, 2019). EFFT therapists hold a primary emphasis on caregiver/child relationships as they relate to identifying problematic emotions, attachment strategies, and patterns of interaction. The model also accounts for how these factors play out in other subsystems, such as parents/partners, siblings, and other parent/child alignments in a case. EFFT views unmet attachment needs as the prime ingredient in understanding the development and maintenance of problematic interactional cycles within a family. Within those problematic interactional cycles, parents or caregivers are navigating their challenges and life transitions with attachment strategies and behaviors, assumed to be well-intended by the emotionally focused therapist, that are ultimately unfruitful in meeting the attachment needs of their children during experiences of individual or familial stress (Furrow et al., 2019).

Daniels Family Considerations

The attachment histories and strategies of Murray and Fran as the parents would be assessed. The most salient attachment figure in Murray's story appears to be his father, with whom he spent a great deal of time with in light of being an only child and running the family business together. Murray's tendency to affiliate with the boys might stem from this experience, a comfort zone that he is familiar with, albeit at the apparent expense of closeness to Pam, as she has struggled. Murray's attachment strategy might be considered avoidant as he seems content to let Fran deal almost exclusively with her in their family life. This hands-off approach appears to have been tenable before Pam's struggles, with each parent seemingly content in their attachment roles for their children, which were basically stratified by gender. As Pam's struggles began to manifest and worsen, Murray continued to utilize the avoidant, disengaged strategy, which likely leaves Pam feeling further isolated from her father.

Fran's experiences of being a primary caretaker for her sister likely honed anxious attachment strategies involving hyperactivity and vigilance. Being left to fend for herself and her sister's health has likely led to a degree of compulsive self-reliance for Fran, an attribute that likely complements Murray's preference to let Fran and Pam have their relationship while he serves as the primary attachment figure for Oliver and George. Since the onset of the eating disorder, Fran's efforts to help appear to be organized by anxious, overactive engagement, with constant prompts and reminders of Pam's weight and diet. Pam's responses to these efforts would be identified as avoidant. As Fran pursues, Pam withdraws, shuts down, and feels more isolated. As Pam avoids, Fran feels spurred to pursue and help as she knows how. The cycle is likely complemented and exacerbated by Murray's own tendency to avoid. Effectively, Fran's self-reliance means she won't ask for Murray's help, and Murray's avoidance means that he is not a reliable attachment figure for his partner, nor his daughter. Murray's absence as a reliable, secure attachment figure for Fran as partner and Pam as father appears to facilitate the cycle between mother and daughter in tandem with the anorexia worsening.

The attachment strategies of George and Oliver appear to mirror that of Murray, unsurprisingly given the amount of time they spend together. The separation of genders in the family also appears to be a critical factor, as it seems to have robbed Murray and the boys of opportunities to understand how to relate and connect more securely with Fran and Pam, particularly in a time of need. As Pam has struggled, her attachment with her mother, her primary attachment figure, has grown increasingly insecure, all while her brothers are witnessed to have rich, gratifying connections with each other and their father. Pam is on the outside looking in, now emotionally alone, without her usual companion to afford her comfort and closeness in the family's prior story of gender-bifurcated attachment.

While the origins of the eating disorder have yet to be fully understood, the attachment strategies at hand, seemingly innocuous before these challenges, perhaps helped set the stage for some of Pam's struggles. While the EFFT therapist would not necessarily see the attachment distress as causative of the eating disorder, they would hold that it is best treated in the context of accessible, responsive, and emotionally engaged relationships (Johnson et al., 1998).

Growing Pains

The EFFT therapist asserts that problems emerge when family members are unable to create or maintain secure connections during times of stress (Furrow et al., 2022). In their efforts to better understand the factors at play in a case, EFFT therapists are attentive to the transitions or stresses the family might be experiencing in coming to therapy (Furrow et al., 2019; Johnson, 2019). For example, the stresses associated with family life cycle transitions like childbearing/childrearing, adolescence, launching, marriage, eldercare, and death, to name a few (McGoldrick et al., 2016), afford ripe opportunities for attachment distress to manifest within and between family members (Furrow et al., 2022). The Daniels family appears to be in the life cycle of families with adolescent children, typically marked with changing developmental and relational needs of the children, which parents need to adapt to (McGoldrick et al., 2016). While the anorexia was diagnosed two years ago, an EFFT therapist would likely be attentive to the transitional stresses Pam is experiencing now as they relate to the apparent worsening of her symptoms. For example, being a senior in high school, facing mediocre grades, and the prospects of launching and/or college on the horizon.

Absorbing States

One factor that feeds into a family's story of problem formation is **absorbing states**, which can be understood as negative emotional states, such as worry, sadness, depression, anxiety, and so forth (Furrow et al., 2019). Family members get pulled into these negative affective states, which then feed into interactional cycles that perpetuate or worsen the insecurity and/or distance in the relationship(s) at hand.

These absorbing states are inherently connected with others in the family by way of the coinciding negative interactional cycles (Furrow et al., 2019). As a parent experiences an absorbing state, possibly encountered as the result of something observed or experienced with their child, the parent's behavior, spurred by that state toward their child, then inspires the emotional reaction of the child. If the result of that parental effort effectively triggers or amplifies another absorbing state in the child, then the family members will likely become stuck in an interactional cycle defined by those respective states. For example, as Fran gets pulled into an absorbing state of worry for Pam, she might anxiously take on the role of a caretaking pursuer, aiming to get her daughter to eat more. If Pam is already experiencing an absorbing state of anxiety, these caretaking efforts might miss the mark and intensify Pam's absorbing state, ultimately resulting in avoidant responses. Pam's reactions to her mother's efforts might then spur more worry in her mother, which then perpetuates the cycle as well as the distance in the affectional bond. Further, the broader problematic cycle in and of itself can also be considered an absorbing state (Furrow et al., 2022). The problematic cycle can absorb the family system into it in the same way that a negative affective state can absorb the individual.

Caregiving Blocks

Another common thread to problematic interactional cycles in families, specifically between caregivers and children, is **caregiving blocks** (Furrow et al., 2019). Caregiving blocks occur within the problematic interactional cycle. For example, the reactions of a child might trigger the caregiver's own issues and *block* the caregiver's ability to attend to the attachment needs of their child. In effect, the caregiver's attempts to intervene might be more about their own attachment disposition than they are about the needs of the child.

Benevolent intent does not inherently remediate a block (Furrow et al., 2019). A block could be hailing from a well-intended desire for a parent to help their child avoid the parent's past pains. Similarly, a caregiver can be acting in what they see as beneficial for their child based on their own experience, motivated by what they received in their own childhood that they want to provide their child. Regardless of good intentions, when blocks are at hand, caregivers will typically be grounding their efforts around their own attachment experiences rather than the unique attachment needs of their child/children. Fran is attempting to promote the health of her daughter while also aiming to alleviate some of her own attachment fears. These attachment anxieties might be understood as spurred by Fran's childhood experiences as a primary caregiver for her sickly sister, an experience likely fraught with fear of loss, and would be understood as a caregiving block in this case, limiting her ability to be accessible, responsive, and emotionally engaged around Pam's needs.

Parental Attachment Considerations

The EFFT therapist recognizes the unique contributions that the attachment styles and histories of caregivers bring to the table in understanding a family's story of problem formation (Johnson, 2019). While EFFT acknowledges the reciprocal influences of the actions of a child that can affect the parent as it relates to attachment needs, there is an onus of responsibility placed on parents as the active, primary attachment figures and caregivers for their children. The hierarchical nature of the relationship cannot be overlooked, with its implications for understanding the attachment considerations at hand in the family's problematic interactional cycles. In essence, the parent is best able to lead in the process of navigating emotions, attachment, and vulnerability.

The broader emphasis in EFFT relating to this might be understood as helping parents become more attuned to the attachment needs of their children and working to address their personal attachment inventories to get a better sense of the unique intersections between those issues and how they might manifest in both caregiving blocks as well as absorbing states. If parents are engaging their child without accounting for their own absorbing states and caregiving blocks, the problematic cycle and resultant distance in the attachment bond are likely to be maintained or worsened (Furrow et al., 2019).

Diversity Conceptualization

The EFFT model is grounded in attachment theory, which emphasizes the universal human need for secure emotional bonds (Bowlby, 1969/1982), yet it also acknowledges that how attachment needs are expressed and met are shaped by cultural context. EFFT therapists view families through a culturally responsive lens, recognizing that caregiving practices, emotional expression, and relational norms vary widely across communities. This involves attuning not only to individual experiences but also to how cultural identities—such as race, ethnicity, gender, religion, socioeconomic status, and migration history—inform interactional patterns and expectations of closeness, authority, and caregiving. EFFT therapists validate and integrate these cultural meanings into the therapeutic process, ensuring that interventions respect and align with family values rather than imposing dominant cultural norms. By attending to both universal attachment needs and culturally specific expressions of those needs, EFFT strives to create a therapeutic space that fosters safety, responsiveness, and belonging across diverse family systems (Guillory, 2021; Sandberg et al., 2016).

Studies on EFT show that the model can be effectively applied to clients dealing with a broad spectrum of presenting problems, from a variety of backgrounds and social locations (Sandberg et al., 2024; Young et al., 2023), when clinicians utilize a culturally informed lens and adapt the model to account for cultural diversity as well as dynamics of power and oppression (Allan et al., 2023). The EFFT therapist's posture of A.R.E. lays the foundation for recognizing and integrating the cultural dynamics that shape attachment and caregiving. Other qualities inherent to the EFFT process, including a collaborative and egalitarian stance, help create a space for openness and respect of cultural differences and contextual dynamics within families, as well as between families and therapists (Furrow et al., 2022). Cultural differences within a couple or family system are met with validation and overt acknowledgment by an EFFT therapist (Furrow et al., 2019).

Some attachment-related dynamics that are important to view through a cultural lens include child-rearing practices and children's reaction to separation from parents (Bowlby, 1969/1982). Strand et al. (2019) found that individualist and collectivist cultural beliefs are correlated with insecure-avoidant and insecure-anxious attachment styles, respectively. An EFFT therapist needs to consider various aspects of context by examining how a family's beliefs, past experiences, and culture contribute to the issue at hand, acknowledging the important role these factors play in how family members make sense of the presenting problem (Furrow et al., 2019).

Due to the centrality of emotions to the EFFT process, it is important to understand how culture informs them. Like attachment, emotion is part of the communicative language that all humans experience (Bowlby, 1969/1982). This is echoed by Tomkins (2008), who articulated a set of universal basic emotions: surprise-startle, distress-anguish, anger-rage, enjoyment-joy, interest-excitement, fear-terror, shame-humiliation, and disgust. Culture strongly shapes which emotions are considered acceptable to display, how they are regulated, the relational contexts in which they are expressed (Butler et al., 2007; Matsumoto et al., 2008), and how they are made sense of and symbolized (Greenberg, 2010). For example, some cultures may emphasize emotional restraint to preserve group harmony, whereas other cultures may encourage overt expression of feelings to affirm autonomy and authenticity. These cultural scripts can influence the ways family members communicate vulnerability, anger, or care, as well as how they respond to others' emotional bids. EFFT therapists are therefore called to remain attuned to the cultural meanings attached to emotion, validating expressions that may not align with dominant cultural expectations while also helping family members recognize and respond to the attachment needs beneath those expressions (Furrow et al., 2019; Sandberg et al., 2016). By situating emotions within their cultural framework, therapists create greater safety for family members to share authentically and deepen their engagement in the EFFT process.

Ultimately, attention to culture is often therapist-driven and situation-specific, rather than embedded as a core, structured component of the EFFT model. Diversity considerations in EFFT call therapists to stay curious, flexible, and attuned to the cultural frameworks shaping family life. In practice, this means slowing down to ask about the meaning of particular interactions, validating emotional expressions that may differ from dominant cultural norms, and adjusting interventions so they resonate with the family's lived experience. By holding space for both universal attachment needs and culturally shaped patterns of relating, therapists create an environment where family members feel understood, respected, and safe to engage more deeply in the EFFT process.

In working with the Daniels family, initial cultural considerations to explore may include gender roles, religious beliefs, emotional expression, and family identity. Murray and Fran have followed traditional U.S. cultural norms, with Murray as financial provider and Fran as primary caregiver. These roles influence not only how they interpret Pam's struggles but also how they divide emotional labor within the family—Fran carrying the burden of daily worry and confrontation, while Murray stays more aligned with the sons around sports. The division between male and female subsystems reflects cultural scripts that can leave Pam feeling isolated and unsupported, particularly since her interests and emotional needs differ from the family's dominant activities. Religious and spiritual beliefs may also play a role and can be important to unpack in therapy (Marterella & Brock, 2008; Williams-Reade et al., 2019). Given Murray's Protestant background and Fran's Catholic upbringing, these traditions often carry expectations about parental authority, caregiving, and family unity that may influence how they make meaning of Pam's symptoms and their role in addressing them. An EFFT therapist can attend to these dynamics by validating Fran's fears without framing them as overreactions, while also helping Murray recognize how cultural patterns of father–daughter distance may amplify Pam's sense of disconnection. By situating these interactional patterns within their cultural and spiritual context, the therapist can support the family in creating new ways of expressing care that foster inclusion and security for Pam.

The Therapeutic Story of Problem Resolution

In EFFT, problems are resolved through a reorganization of family relationships and patterns so that they are characterized by reliable, secure attachment and emotional availability. Change happens when "new patterns of emotional accessibility and responsiveness increase a family's ability to engage and encourage felt security in response to changing developmental needs" (Furrow et al., 2019, p. 64). The EFFT model provides a framework for change that is organized into stages, with various steps to accomplish within each stage. The role of the therapist is critical in creating an environment that feels safe and secure enough to explore the challenges the family is facing and to effectively navigate the intricate dance between therapist and family members in the EFFT process (Furrow et al., 2019).

Secure Base

A secure base is a predictable and reliable place from which a child explores their surrounding environment (Ainsworth, 1967; Ainsworth et al., 1978; Bowlby, 1988). Parents, or attachment figures, provide an emotional anchor that includes encouraging autonomy and exploration, while also being prepared and available to lend support in a child's time of need (Furrow et al., 2019). Imagine a situation where a curious child wanders off from a parent in a public place like a playground. The parent encourages the child to venture out while, at the same time, is ready and willing to provide a comforting hug if they fall and scrape their knee. As this interaction is repeated, children gain a sense of confidence that their attachment figures will be there when needed. This reinforces the expectation of caregiver availability and ultimately provides the confidence to continue "venturing out" to accomplish key developmental tasks (Stavrianopoulos et al., 2014). A secure base is needed for problem resolution in the context of EFFT and will help the family to successfully navigate future issues that arise.

Emotion Regulation

Emotions are categorized as primary or secondary. **Primary emotions** include those that emerge in direct response to interactions or events. Conversely, **secondary emotions** are viewed as coping mechanisms in response to primary emotions (Johnson, 2020). Anger, sadness, fear, disgust/shame, joy or surprise are considered foundational emotions that qualify as primary or secondary based on the situation (Brubacher, 2017). Emotions are also understood as adaptive and maladaptive, with primary emotions seen as adaptive catalysts for action, while secondary emotions are often markers of maladaptation that need to be distilled—carefully unpacked and clarified—so that the core emotional processes that fuel them can be revealed (Greenberg, 2010). In EFFT, the therapist helps family members access, clarify, and process emotions that fuel negative interactional cycles. According to Johnson (2019), "affect regulation is a process of moving with and through an emotion, rather than reactively intensifying or suppressing it, and then being able to use this emotion to give direction to one's life" (p. 11). As distressing emotions are processed in a secure therapeutic environment, they become reorganized into more coherent and manageable experiences. This reprocessing allows parents and children to respond with greater awareness, flexibility, and emotional accessibility, fostering more secure and responsive caregiving relationships (Stavrianopoulos et al., 2014).

Corrective Emotional Experience

Perhaps the most important signal of change at the heart of problem resolution in the EFFT treatment process, a **corrective emotional experience** is typified by the moment when a child experiences a parent in the loving, emotionally available way that they have been longing for. With careful guidance from the therapist, it is "when a child's attachment needs are expressed to an available caregiver and the caregiver responds effectively to those needs" (Furrow et al., 2019, p. 179). In moments like this, the therapist draws attention to the warmth and relief that surface, helping the family recognize how these new emotional exchanges can become the building blocks of a different pattern—one where attachment needs are met with responsiveness rather than conflict.

For the Daniels family, these three concepts highlight important pathways for healing. A corrective emotional experience could occur if Murray responds to Pam's bids for closeness with warmth and availability, giving her a new felt sense of being seen and supported by her father. Emotion regulation will be critical for both Pam and her parents, as Pam learns to tolerate and share the intense emotions tied to her eating disorder while Murray and Fran manage their own fear, shame, and defensiveness in ways that allow them to stay engaged. Establishing a secure base within the family can help Pam trust that her parents are reliable sources of comfort and encouragement, reducing her sense of isolation and enabling her to explore challenges with more confidence. Oliver and George will also experience greater predictability and emotional safety, clearer permission to voice needs without competing for attention, and reduced triangulation as the family's secure base strengthens. Together, these processes can begin to shift the family's patterns away from distance and conflict toward trust, responsiveness, and safety.

The EFFT Model: Stages, Steps, and Interventions

The EFFT model consists of three main stages with nine coinciding steps. Stage 1, which includes steps 1 through 4, begins with a focus on de-escalation of the negative patterns that are causing or contributing to family distress. Restructuring these patterns is the hallmark of steps 5 through 7 of stage 2. Finally, the aim of steps 8 and 9 of stage 3 is the consolidation of patterns that are based on a newly gained sense of attachment security (Stavrianopoulos, 2019). What follows is a more in-depth look at each stage and step. This section also outlines the key interventions in each step and highlights how their use shifts across the stages of the model. Although the model is presented as a structured framework that appears to be linear, in practice, it is inherently systemic and circular. Flexibility on the part of the therapist is paramount as each intervention builds on and loops back to earlier processes to deepen emotional engagement and spark relational change.

Stage 1: De-Escalation (Steps 1-4)

Step 1: Alliance Building

As treatment begins, the therapist attends to the therapeutic alliance, building a secure foundation from which the family can gain the stability needed to work toward de-escalation. The therapeutic relationship is central in EFFT from the outset and remains vital throughout the process, as the therapist provides a secure attachment base for family members. In step 1 and across all stages, this alliance is nurtured by emphasizing family strengths and ensuring that every member's perspective is valued. The EFFT process flows through the therapist, who models leadership by demonstrating empathy, emotional availability, and responsiveness. If the process is likened to a dance, the therapist clearly leads the way (Furrow et al., 2019).

Validation

Although validation is considered a foundational microskill that therapists utilize with any model, it has a pivotal role to play in the EFFT approach. Validation is harnessed on many levels and during each phase of the process. Initially, in step 1, therapists use validation to connect with clients, establish rapport, and assure that each client feels valued, seen, and heard. Genuine and well-timed validation in early sessions sets the stage for the more intimate work of uncovering and sharing vulnerable emotions. Validation is at the heart of creating the environment necessary to build securely connected relationships (Furrow et al., 2019; Johnson, 2020). For example, with Fran, the therapist would begin by acknowledging both her fear for Pam's health and her long-standing closeness with her daughter. By validating her worry and honoring the effort she has already made, the therapist conveys respect and empathy. At the same time, this kind of reflection helps Fran feel that her perspective is valued and that she is not being blamed, laying the groundwork for trust. From here, the therapist can gently shift into exploring how Fran's emotional availability can become a powerful resource in the family's healing process.

Empathic Attunement

Therapists strive throughout the therapeutic process to utilize empathy to connect on a deep level with clients. The therapist taps into the emotional frequency of the client with the goal of "making contact with the client's world" (Johnson,

2020, p. 34). Like other aspects of the role of the therapist, this too has the ultimate intention in EFFT of modeling for parents how to attune to the emotional needs of children (Furrow et al., 2019). In step 1, therapists use **empathic attunement** to connect with each family member by carefully observing and reflecting their emotional experiences (Johnson, 2020). This involves resonating with both verbal and nonverbal cues and compassionately conveying understanding. By attuning to and validating these emotions in real time, therapists build trust, reduce defensiveness, and create a safe foundation for exploring deeper, unacknowledged feelings in later steps.

A.R.E.

Three pillars of secure attachment include A.R.E. (Furrow et al., 2019; Johnson, 2019). In EFFT, therapists actively work toward helping family systems possess these qualities to create new attachment patterns and resolve the problems that brought them to therapy. A.R.E. is also a hallmark of the role of the therapist in EFFT, as the therapeutic relationship includes "engaging each family member with emotional attunement, relational responsiveness, and accessibility" (Furrow et al., 2019, p. 65). Therapists model these qualities while simultaneously helping clients develop them. When working with the Daniels family, the therapist can model A.R.E. by being consistently present and emotionally attuned to each member's experience. This might be illustrated by the therapist inviting Fran to share her fears about Pam while maintaining steady eye contact and a calm, validating tone so she feels supported rather than criticized. In modeling A.R.E. this way, the therapist shows the family what secure emotional presence looks like, while guiding them to practice it with one another, laying the foundation for new patterns of safety and closeness.

Assessment

The assessment process in Stage 1 of EFFT is not confined to a single moment of data gathering, but unfolds as part of the therapeutic engagement itself. Early sessions are shaped by the therapist's dual task of establishing a secure alliance with each family member while also beginning to map the relational patterns that give structure to the family's distress. Although a conjoint family session is the springboard for starting the treatment process and initial assessment, it is common for EFFT therapists to meet separately with parental and sibling subsystems as well (Johnson et al., 1998). Of particular importance is the evaluation of the **parental alliance**, or the extent to which parents can work collaboratively in their parenting roles. This alliance forms the foundation for the therapeutic process, as parental unity communicates safety and predictability to children. Closely tied to this is the **caregiving alliance**, which extends beyond decision-making to the ways parents support and validate one another in the enactment of caregiving tasks. When fractures emerge in either domain, children are often left vulnerable to confusion or insecurity, amplifying the cycles of disconnection that bring families into treatment (Johnson, 2019).

Assessing **parental attachment history** provides important insight into how past experiences of caregiving and vulnerability are carried forward into present interactions. Unresolved fears of loss, rejection, or inadequacy may reverberate in the parent–child relationship, often outside of awareness, shaping how parents respond when their child expresses distress. By situating the presenting problem within this broader systemic and intergenerational context, the therapist begins to gently shift the family's focus away from viewing the child as the "problem" and toward an understanding of the ways attachment needs and histories intertwine to sustain negative cycles (Furrow et al., 2019).

Step 2: Exploring Negative Attachment Patterns

In step 2, the presenting problem is framed in the context of negative patterns that have to this point been sustained by failed attempts to meet attachment needs. Any blame that has been directed at a particular family member is systemically reframed and normalized, facilitating the de-escalation process (Furrow et al., 2019).

Process Consultant

As a **process consultant**, an EFFT therapist carefully tracks clients' emotional experiences and relational patterns to restructure them in ways that foster secure attachment and responsive caregiving. As Furrow et al. (2019) put it, the "goal is to help the family articulate an understanding of the predictable sequences that drive distress and uncertainty in the family" (p. 106). Therapists also guide the family's attention to the here-and-now emotional and relational processes unfolding between them. This entails helping family members notice, slow down, and make sense of their interactions, highlighting how their responses are part of a repeating cycle shaped by attachment needs. By doing so, the therapist empowers the family to recognize and shift their own patterns, creating new ways of engaging that foster safety and connection (Johnson et al., 1998).

Evocative Questions and Statements

To help clients explore more deeply, especially when their inner experience feels unclear or difficult to articulate, **evocative questions and statements** are used to gain access to the feelings beneath the surface that fuel conflict. This slow process creates space for emotions linked to rigid, negative patterns of interaction to emerge and be expanded upon. Early on, the therapist introduces such questions tentatively, balancing curiosity with sensitivity as they build understanding of the family dynamics. By drawing attention to the underlying relational dynamics, these evocative interventions help shift the family's focus from surface-level exchanges to the emotional realities that sustain the conflict that brings them to therapy. This redirection not only fosters opportunities for members to feel seen and heard but also provides a pathway into the emotions that shape meaning and drive problematic cycles (Johnson, 2020).

Steps 3 and 4: Accessing Unacknowledged Underlying Emotions and Redefining the Problem

Rounding out the initial stage includes uncovering the secondary emotions that support the negative interaction patterns and **relational blocks** (step 3), leading to redefining the presenting problems (Step 4). As clinicians move to the next steps, all previous skills and interventions are at the therapist's disposal. Tracking interactions, validation, and evocative questions are utilized to further strengthen therapeutic rapport and advance treatment. Attention turns to skills that help to address relational blocks, a key focus of the latter steps of phase 1 (Furrow et al., 2019).

Empathic Conjecture

In EFFT, **empathic conjecture** involves moving beyond a client's immediate expression to gently infer a deeper, often attachment-related layer of experience. Serving as a kind of careful hypothesis from the therapist, they frequently highlight a parent's motivation to nurture and/or protect the unmet attachment needs of a child that may be difficult to articulate directly. The therapist engages in this process by imaginatively stepping into the perspective of each family member and offering an attachment-informed reflection of what might be occurring beneath the surface. Because these are hypotheses rather than certainties, they are framed tentatively, allowing clients to affirm, refine, or reject them.

Within Step 3 of the model, empathic conjecture plays a crucial role in drawing attention to the attachment longings and caregiving responses that organize family interactions. By drawing on knowledge of separation distress and secondary attachment strategies, the therapist helps illuminate the emotional significance of present experiences and makes hidden needs more accessible for exploration (Furrow et al., 2019). Conjecture is used as part of a strategy to raise intensity between family members to create opportunities for new meanings and patterns (Johnson, 2020). The more emotionally attuned the therapist is to the clients, the more accurate the inferences will be, which increases the likelihood of a transformative experience. With the Daniels family, empathic conjecture would involve the therapist carefully noticing and naming the deeper attachment needs and caregiving intentions that may not yet be expressed. For Pam, this could mean highlighting that her sense of isolation from her father and brothers may mask an underlying longing for connection and reassurance.

Heightening

As attention turns to broadening emotional experience, **heightening** is used to bring family members' underlying emotions into sharper focus. The therapist weaves together diverse interventions to encourage deeper engagement, allowing each emotional moment to resonate with greater clarity. By reflecting a client's words or drawing attention to evocative imagery, present emotions become more vivid and tangible. Subtle changes in tone and pacing further enrich the experience, amplifying the depth of emotions (Stavrianopoulos, 2019). Building on previous interventions of evocative questions and empathic conjecture, heightening raises the collective intensity in the therapeutic interaction to spark further opportunities for change (Johnson, 2020).

Reframing

In EFFT, **reframing** becomes a powerful tool that helps achieve the de-escalation that is needed in stage 1. "The use of reframing shifts the focus on to the family's relationship patterns and how they interfere and disrupt the family's ability to respond effectively to distress" (Furrow et al., 2019, p. 132). Reframing also opens space for family members to explore the vulnerable emotions beneath their defensive stances. These defenses, rooted in universal attachment needs, often drive the negative interactional patterns that keep the family stuck (Johnson et al., 1998). In working with the Daniels family, the problem begins to expand beyond Pam and her eating disorder. Together, Pam, her parents, and her siblings start to see that each of them carries important attachment needs, and that the conflicts they face are less about one individual and more about the entrenched family patterns they have all been caught in.

Stage 1 lays the essential groundwork for EFFT by building safety, reducing reactivity, and shifting the family's focus from individual blame to systemic patterns rooted in attachment needs. Interventions such as validation, empathic attunement, and A.R.E. provide a secure relational base, while tools like evocative questioning, empathic conjecture, heightening, and reframing gradually bring underlying emotions into clearer view. What begins as an effort to calm conflict and establish rapport evolves into a deeper recognition of the attachment longings and fears that drive negative cycles. By the close of this stage, families are better able to see their struggles as shared patterns rather than individual faults, opening the door for the restructuring work of Stage 2.

Stage 2: Restructuring (Steps 5–7)

Steps 5 and 6: Accessing and Deepening the Child's Attachment Needs and Fostering Acceptance of These Needs

If one imagines stage 1 as pulling weeds and tilling new soil, stage 2 would be fertilizing and planting seeds in that soil. Steps 5 and 6 usher in stage 2 and are characterized by an important shift to the child's attachment needs and unacknowledged emotions. Care-seeking is associated with attachment behaviors in children, and step 5 is all about a deeper exploration and understanding of previously unacknowledged needs. Particular attention is given to creating space for acceptance of new attachment experiences. In step 6, EFFT therapists work with parents to be more available and responsive as this takes place. The therapist recruits the parents as the key attachment figures whose acceptance is a critical prerequisite to generating new patterns based on secure attachment, countering the negative interactions that have sewn conflict for families like the Daniels. These two steps go hand in hand as clinicians help family members traverse a delicate process of encouraging increased vulnerability on the part of the child, while parents meet them there with increased availability and responsiveness. Of course, parents are human too, with their own attachment issues that can hamper their ability to show up for their children during times of need. Therapists provide support to the parents as they find their way through these blocks and work toward responding to their children's needs with consistency and reliability (Furrow et al., 2019).

Evocative Responses: Evocative Responding, Heightening, and Empathic Conjecture

Therapists draw upon the trust and safety established in earlier steps and extend this into Steps 5 and 6 by employing evocative responding, heightening, and empathic conjecture. These interventions derive their power from being applied in the immediacy of the therapeutic encounter, where emotions are most accessible and alive. When integrated fluidly and used in concert, they guide clients more deeply into their emotional experience, opening pathways to new awareness and connection (Furrow et al., 2019). Taking advantage of the here-and-now, evocative statements and questions draw out and emphasize the newfound emotional vulnerability that family members are discovering. With Pam, the therapist might say "As you describe feeling apart from your dad, I notice your eyes drop and your voice softens. Can you stay with that feeling for a moment and tell us what it's like inside as you talk about the distance?"

Heightening serves to amplify the emerging emotional expression of clients. Therapists' deliberate actions here help to turn up the intensity by slowing the process down, using a soft tone, and repeating or reflecting poignant client language and feelings (Furrow et al., 2019). Staying with Pam here, in a gentle tone, the therapist would continue,

> You say it's not a big deal, but I can see your shoulders pull in, and your words get quieter, almost as if you're holding something back. That pulling in seems important right now—can we slow down here and pay attention to that?

Making the connection between these felt emotions and attachment needs is done through empathic conjectures. In EFFT, therapists proceed with tentative language, offering a hypothesis about the inner emotional world and attachment needs that aren't fully formed or understood (Furrow et al., 2019). Striking a tone of curiosity and possibility, not certainty or statements of fact, is more effective in these moments to facilitate clients taking ownership of their experiences. A therapeutic interaction can essentially be wrapped in tentative language from beginning ("I wonder if…" or "I get the sense that…") to end ("Does that fit for you?"). Here is an example follow-up with Pam: "I wonder if part of you longs to feel as close to your dad as your brothers do, but it feels safer to keep that hidden rather than risk being hurt or overlooked. Does that fit for you, Pam?"

Processing Interventions: Validation, Reframing

Processing interventions aim to further slow things down in a way that fosters understanding and provides opportunities to make sense of how family interactions and emotions have deep ties to attachment needs. These interventions "promote new relationship encounters, which are at the heart of EFFT change events" (Furrow et al., 2019, p. 162).

Validation

Therapists continue to use validation, with a slight difference in focus. It is important to balance validating the experiences of both children and parents. First, attention is appropriately fixed on the child's needs as they are encouraged to explore underlying emotions, which "invites the child to take a new position in relationship to their parents" (Furrow et al., 2019, p. 150). At the same time, it may be difficult initially for parents to accept what the child is expressing from this new vulnerable place and give rise to their own defensive reactions in the moment. Fears that they can't attend to their child's needs effectively can emerge and even uncover feelings of shame. Validation of these struggles is crucial in helping parents stay grounded emotionally and to respond with the empathy that is needed to reinforce more positive caregiving. Validation can also be used effectively within the parental dyad. As partners support each other, it helps create an opportunity to access empathy and be more emotionally attuned with their child. All in all, validation serves to help all family members accept each other's experiences (Furrow et al., 2019). Consider, for example, Murray's lack of confidence in connecting with Pam. His wife, Fran, can provide support through validation of his struggle to find common ground and closeness with his daughter in ways that he otherwise does so easily with his sons.

Reframing

In stage 1, reframing helped with de-escalation and shifted the focus of the problem from the identified patient to a broader family pattern. In steps 5 and

6 of stage 2, reframing serves to create more space for compassion and understanding of what has been seen by the family up to this point as problem behaviors. Past and current behaviors that have led to conflict are described as noble efforts to have attachment needs met and seek closeness with family members. Reframing extends to multiple systems, including the parental level and child/sibling level. EFFT therapists make room for parents' own attachment-related emotions and behaviors. Often at this stage, they emerge as parental guilt and shame, deeply connected to a desire to protect and care for their children (Furrow et al., 2019). Fran may come to see Pam's eating disorder not just as an act of defiance disrupting the family, but as an attempt to sound the alarm about rigid family patterns in hopes of generating the closeness they all need.

Step 7: Restructuring Family Interactions

Enactments

Enactments are a critical element of change in stage 2 of the EFFT model. As a pivotal intervention in step 7, **enactments** call family members into active dialogue with one another, opening channels between their inner emotional lives and the outward dynamics of their relationships. In the protected space of therapy, clients can voice emerging feelings in new and constructive ways (Tilley & Palmer, 2013). One can think of enactments along the lines of choreography, whereby parent–child interactions are ushered toward security at the gentle direction of the therapist (Furrow et al., 2019). It can be seen as the child taking an emotional risk by reaching out to the parent with growing trust and anticipation that the parent will respond in a supportive and effective manner. Therapists invite clients to turn toward each other and communicate directly. Instead of therapeutic dialogue moving through the therapist to each client, they are communicating with each other, significantly raising the vulnerability and intensity in the therapeutic interaction. What results is a corrective emotional experience. For example, picture Pam, with the therapist's encouragement, slowly shifting her body to face her father. At the same time, Murray is invited to fully turn toward Pam, aligning his posture and attention with hers. With their bodies oriented toward each other, space is created for Pam to share her fears and longings and for Murray to respond with care—transforming what was once a therapeutic conversation into a lived moment of attachment in action.

Evocative Interventions and Reframing

Each of the previous evocative interventions, including validation, heightening, empathic conjecture, along with reframing, continues to be relied upon to facilitate the goals of processing emotion to create change in step 7.

Through the coordinated use of these techniques, the therapist facilitates clients' access to more profound levels of experience. As challenges may arise with family members being reluctant to take emotional risks at times in therapy, reframing offers an important perspective and reminds clients of how powerful old negative patterns can be. This is particularly useful in helping parents stay grounded and present as their child works their way through new emotional experiences and relational interactions (Furrow et al., 2019).

Stage 2 marks a significant shift in how core EFFT interventions are applied. Whereas in stage 1 techniques were used to de-escalate conflict and establish safety, in stage 2, they are harnessed to deepen emotional engagement and restructure family interactions. Validation now balances attention to both child and parent experiences, helping each remain emotionally grounded as vulnerability rises. Reframing evolves from reducing blame to cultivating compassion by viewing problem behaviors as efforts to secure connection. Evocative responses, heightening, and conjecture, once tentative and cautious, are now used more boldly to amplify emotional risks and connect them explicitly to attachment needs. Most critically, enactments move from gentle, therapist-guided exchanges to direct, lived moments of attachment in action that restructure bonds between parents and children. In these ways, the familiar interventions of EFFT take on new depth and potency in stage 2, guiding families from stability toward transformation (Furrow et al., 2019).

Stage 3: Consolidation (Steps 8 and 9)

Steps 8 and 9 Interventions: Exploring New Solutions to Past Problems and Consolidating New Patterns

The third stage of the model culminates with a focus on consolidating progress that has been made to this point. Now that a new pattern of relating has emerged based on emotional availability and responsiveness to attachment needs, therapists help clients apply this to other sources of conflict the family has been unable to effectively deal with in the past (step 8). Finally, consolidation takes place in step 9 through highlighting the evolution of the family in terms of their newfound ability to foster a sense of security in their relationships as they navigate the individual, relational, and developmental problems of living (Furrow et al., 2019).

Evocative and Processing Interventions

Although it seems contradictory, interventions in these final two steps of EFFT focus on what's new *and* what's old. As new relational patterns emerge, they are emphasized and deepened with the use of evocative responses like conjecture, heightening, and enactments. Conjecture shifts focus to deeper attachment needs with the goal of helping clients take ownership of them, so they become fully integrated into the newfound ways of interacting in the family. Heightening amplifies key emotions, reinforcing them as corrective experiences that become part of newly established and reliable patterns rather than fleeting exchanges. Positive emotions that result from these interactions, including hope, joy, pride, trust, and even relief, take center stage. Therapists also seize opportunities to use enactments as experiential means to consolidate changes that are now indicative of secure attachment (Furrow et al., 2019).

An enactment in this step would lead Pam to really trust that her father is truly capable of showing up for her when she needs him. Murray is not just saying he will be there for her, but she experiences him making eye contact, staying emotionally present, reflecting her attachment fears, and offering comfort—so she *feels* him there rather than merely *hearing* that he will be. Pain points from hurtful moments of the past are revisited and reprocessed. However, family members are now equipped to attend to them with an ability to respond with accountability and leave each other with a sense that they are understood and cared for (Furrow et al., 2019). For example, a more confident Murray can manage the intense emotions that Pam expresses when talking about a time when she needed his help and encouragement for a challenging piano recital last year, but he was unavailable because his attention was focused on baseball with his sons as usual. Instead of getting defensive, Murray not only manages his own emotions to stay in contact with Pam, he acknowledges her pain around it and even validates her all without any new guidance from the therapist. Here, the therapist uses processing interventions like reflection and validation to highlight this pivotal moment and praises the open, honest, and loving interaction between father and daughter.

Attachment Rituals

In these late steps of the model, the therapist helps families find ways to maintain the sense of loving connection they've been working hard to establish throughout the treatment process. According to Furrow et al. (2019), rituals "provide a rich resource in EFFT for symbolizing in practice the value found in attachment relationships" (p. 206). Rituals have the greatest impact when they reflect a family's unique culture, values, and ways of making meaning, while also providing continuity, predictability, and a sense of belonging (Fiese et al., 2002). Ultimately, rituals serve as powerful anchors for secure bonds, offering families a way to sustain and strengthen their connections not only during treatment but long after therapy has ended (Furrow et al., 2019).

The interventions used in steps 8 and 9 take on a different purpose than in earlier stages of EFFT. While techniques were initially employed to de-escalate conflict and access primary emotions, here they are used to consolidate and deepen new attachment patterns. Enactments now demonstrate reliability and responsiveness in action, while heightening reinforces positive emotions that anchor secure bonds. Processing interventions shift from uncovering distress to revisiting painful moments with accountability, empathy, and validation, transforming old injuries into opportunities for connection. Finally, attachment rituals serve as enduring symbols of these changes, embedding the family's growth into daily life and ensuring that new ways of relating extend beyond the therapy room.

To better understand how these interventions move in a fluid and recursive process across sessions, it is helpful to turn to the EFT Tango, which provides a framework for guiding moment-to-moment interactions in therapy.

The EFT Tango

The **EFT Tango** is a guiding framework that structures the flow of therapeutic interactions in EFFT from session to session. It is a dance within a dance! It provides a flexible, five-move process through which therapists help clients track their inner experience, share it in new ways, and reshape patterns of interaction in key family relationships. By repeatedly moving through these steps, the EFT Tango provides both structure and fluidity, supporting transformative change while remaining responsive to the unique dynamics of each relationship (Johnson, 2019). Each session throughout the treatment process will include moves of the Tango.

Mirroring the Present Process, the first move of the EFT Tango, heightens clients' awareness of their immediate emotional experiences and interaction patterns (Furrow et al., 2019). The therapist tracks and reflects on what is occurring in the moment—both internally and relationally—highlighting emotional cues, bodily signals, and relational responses. This reflection fosters validation, clarity, and insight, enabling clients to observe how their emotions influence interactions and setting the stage for deeper exploration and restructuring of relational cycles.

Affect Assembly and Deepening is the second move in the EFFT Tango, in which the therapist helps clients access, articulate, and integrate core emotional experiences (Furrow et al., 2019). Building on initial awareness, this stage guides individuals to identify primary emotions underlying their reactions and relational patterns. Through careful exploration and validation, the therapist supports clients in organizing these emotions into a coherent narrative, deepening their understanding of how feelings drive interaction. This process not only clarifies emotional experience but also amplifies the motivational power of emotions, creating opportunities for authentic expression, corrective relational engagement, and therapeutic change.

What follows in move three is **Choreographing Engaged Encounters** between clients. Here, therapists lead clients through a deliberate interaction in which vulnerable emotions that are typically ignored become a central focus and driving force for creating new relational Experiences (Furrow et al., 2019). Using empathy and validation, therapists reflect the vulnerable emotions revealed by one client and earnestly guide them toward a more direct engagement with their family member. Although the dialogue was initiated between client and therapist, it now shifts to direct communication from one client to the other.

To integrate the previous steps of the Tango with the client, the fourth move focuses on **Processing the Encounter**. Because these are often novel ways of interacting that clients are experiencing, exploring their impact and meaning with clients is critical to gaining a deeper understanding of their significance. Space is created for all family members involved, assuring that each role and position is valued. What's more, this processing helps to crystallize new ways of viewing the relationship as a part of establishing new patterns (Furrow et al., 2019).

Each of the previous steps culminates in the final move: **Integrating and Validating**. Here, the therapist helps clients make sense of and consolidate their newly expressed emotional experiences. At this stage, the therapist affirms the significance of what has been shared, highlights shifts in relational engagement, and connects these changes to the broader attachment framework guiding therapy. By validating vulnerability and linking it to new interactional patterns, the therapist fosters coherence and strengthens emerging cycles of responsiveness. This integrative process not only solidifies therapeutic gains but also enhances clients' confidence in continuing to engage with one another in secure and transformative ways (Furrow et al., 2019).

In practice, the EFT Tango serves as a roadmap that helps therapists guide families through new emotional and relational experiences. The same five moves are revisited throughout treatment, but how they are used shifts depending on the moment—sometimes slowing things down to help a child risk sharing a vulnerable feeling, other times highlighting a parent's ability to respond in new ways. Interventions such as validation, conjecture, and enactments take on greater depth with each pass through the Tango, gradually reshaping how family members reach for and respond to one another. To see how these moves unfold in real time, the following case transcript demonstrates how the Tango and its interventions are applied in a first session.

Case Transcript

Therapist: I want to begin by saying how much I appreciate you all coming here today. It tells me that each of you cares deeply about this family, even though things have been hard.

Intervention: Validation; joining with the whole family by affirming their courage and commitment to being present.

Therapist: Fran, I understand from what you've shared that Pam's health has been weighing heavily on you. Can you tell me a little about what that's been like for you?

Intervention: Empathic attunement; therapist tunes into Fran's role as primary caregiver, inviting her perspective with warmth and accessibility (A.R.E.).

Fran: It's been terrifying. I feel like I'm constantly watching her, afraid something will happen.

Therapist: That sounds exhausting, almost like you've been carrying a lot of fear on your own while still trying to hold the family together.

Intervention: Validation and empathic reflection; demonstrating responsiveness by naming Fran's emotional burden and making her feel seen.

Therapist: Murray, hearing Fran describe how much fear she's been carrying, what has it been like for you?

Intervention: Accessibility; therapist turns to Murray to balance the conversation and show engagement with both parents.

Murray: I've been scared too. But I don't always know what to say, so I step back. Fran knows Pam better than I do.

Therapist: So part of you steps back not because you don't care, but because you're uncertain how to help. That sounds painful, wanting to do more but not knowing how.

Intervention: Validation and empathic attunement; therapist reframes Murray's distance as blocked caregiving, showing responsiveness to his unspoken feelings.

Pam, as you've listened to both your parents these last few minutes, I'm wondering what it is like for you to hear them talk about how worried they are?

Intervention: Engagement (A.R.E.); therapist makes space for Pam's voice, showing accessibility to her perspective and responsiveness to her role in the family.

Pam: It's weird. I feel like they talk about me but not to me. I just don't want it to always be about food (*Looks down and shakes head*).

Therapist (Gently): That makes a lot of sense, Pam—it must be frustrating to feel like the focus is always on food instead of on you as a whole person. And I can sense that frustration as you look away, shaking your head.

Intervention: Validation and attunement; therapist uses empathetic tone, notices Pam's non-verbal cues, is responsive to her feelings of frustration and affirms her need to be understood beyond her symptoms.

Therapist: Oliver, George, I want to hear from you, too. What has this been like for you as Pam's brothers?

Intervention: Joining and accessibility; therapist engages the siblings directly to demonstrate that every family member's perspective matters.

Oliver: I feel bad sometimes. Dad and I do sports a lot, and I know Pam isn't part of that.

George: Yeah... we just don't hang out much. It's not on purpose. It's just... different.

Therapist: I really appreciate you both sharing that. It shows how much you notice Pam, even if you're not sure how to include her. To me, that says something about how much you care about her.

Intervention: Validation; therapist responds warmly to the brothers' perspective, engaging them as important voices while framing their awareness as care.

Therapist: So what I'm hearing from all of you is Fran is carrying a lot of fear, Murray is feeling uncertain but really wants to do more, Pam feels frustrated being seen only through her eating, and Oliver and George notice that she's left out. Each of you is hurting in different ways, but I also hear how much you all care about one another.

Intervention: Empathic attunement and integration; therapist reflects the family's voices back to them, modeling engagement (A.R.E.) and beginning to frame the problem systemically rather than individually.

EFFT Tango: In this opening dialogue, the therapist begins to enact the first move of the EFT Tango, mirroring the present process, by tracking and reflecting each family member's emotional expressions and interaction patterns. Through validation and empathic attunement, the therapist highlights Fran's fear, Murray's uncertainty, Pam's frustration, and the brothers' sense of distance, giving each perspective a sense of clarity and legitimacy. Elements of the second move, affect assembly and deepening, are also present in subtle form as the therapist gently links Murray's withdrawal to blocked caregiving and reframes Pam's frustration as a longing to be seen beyond her symptoms. Finally, the therapist demonstrates the spirit of engagement that underlies the Tango as a whole, ensuring accessibility and responsiveness (A.R.E.) to every family member and laying the groundwork for future steps where enactments and deeper emotional risk-taking can occur.

Therapist: As I listen to each of you, I notice a pattern beginning to emerge. Fran, you become more anxious and push harder with Pam when you see her withdrawing. Murray, you often step back, feeling unsure how to help. And Pam, when you feel that pressure, you pull away even more. Oliver and George, you notice this distance, but it leaves you not knowing how to join in. It's like the harder everyone tries, the more stuck you all feel.

Intervention: Tracking the cycle as a process consultant; reframing the problem from an individual (Pam) to a relational pattern sustained by the attachment needs of the family system.

Fran: That's exactly how it feels. I push, Pam resists, and then we just argue or go silent.

Pam: I just feel smothered. Like no matter what I do, it's not good enough (*tears well in her eyes*).

Therapist (softly): Pam, when you say you feel smothered, I hear frustration—yet I see there is more happening for you as you tear up. I wonder if underneath that, there's also a longing to be understood for more than your eating. Almost like you want your mom to see the hurt behind the wall you put up. Does that fit for you?

Intervention: Empathic conjecture; tentative hypothesis to connect Pam's secondary emotion (frustration) to her deeper attachment need (longing to be understood).

Pam (quietly): Yeah… I just want her to stop watching every bite I take and notice me.

Therapist: Fran, when Pam says that she wants to be noticed beyond her eating—what's that like for you to hear?

Intervention: Evocative intervention; therapist slows the moment, directing Fran's attention to Pam's vulnerable disclosure.

Fran(tears forming): It hurts. I realize I've been so scared of losing her that I can't see past the food. I want to notice her… I just panic.

Murray: And I think Fran sometimes panics because some of this reminds her of how she grew up having to take care of her little sister, Tamara, who was always sick. Fran did more parenting for Tamara than her own mother from the way she's described it to me over the years.

Therapist: That is really insightful, Murray. Is that right, Fran? You had to be a mother sometimes to your little sister when your own parents weren't able to show up for her. That sounds like it was a lot to take on. (*Softly*) I wonder if some of that same fear and responsibility comes alive for you now with Pam, almost like you must watch her as closely as you did your sister or you might lose her.

Intervention: Validating Murray to strengthen the alliance and build his sense of competence. Linking present process to parental attachment history, setting the stage for new relational experiences in later steps; empathic conjecture is used to deepen Fran's awareness of how earlier caregiving roles may heighten her fear and inform her present relationship dynamics with Pam. This also fosters empathy in the parent–child dyad, introducing a new frame for Pam that her mom's reactions are connected to attachment patterns from her upbringing.

Therapist: So when you're afraid of losing her, that fear pushes you to focus on what she eats. And Pam, when your mom panics, you feel unseen and smothered, so you pull back. This is the cycle that traps you both—fear on one side, withdrawal on the other—even though underneath it all is love and longing.

Intervention: Cycle reframing and heightening; therapist highlights secondary emotions (panic, withdrawal), names the underlying attachment needs, and makes the negative cycle the problem rather than either person.

Murray: That sounds right. I see it too, but I don't know how to step in without making things worse.

Therapist: Murray, that uncertainty tells me how much you want to protect both Fran and Pam, but also how stuck you feel in knowing how to do it. It sounds like when you back away, it's not because you don't care, but because you're afraid you'll get it wrong.

Intervention: Empathic conjecture; reframes Murray's withdrawal as blocked caregiving driven by fear of failure.

Murray (nodding): Yes, that's exactly it. I don't want to mess up.

Therapist: Murray, I wonder if you would be willing to try something right in this moment. I want to invite you to turn directly to your daughter now and tell her that you do care very much about her and that she is important to you.

Intervention: Enactment. Therapist sees an opportunity to initiate this tender moment and have Murray communicate directly with Pam, creating an experience of caregiving that she has needed. Murray is part of this enactment intentionally instead of Fran, to invite him into a caregiving role as a preliminary shift in the caregiving dynamics between parents. This interaction can be used to build on in future sessions to create new patterns of relating.

Murray: (*Turning to face Pam*): I do care…I care so much about you, Pam, and I will really try to figure out how to do a better job showing you that.

Therapist: So as a family, you're caught in this cycle that just seems to take over: Fran's fear makes her pursue, Pam's hurt makes her withdraw, and Murray's uncertainty keeps him on the sidelines. And Oliver and George, you notice all this happening, but you don't know how to step in. This cycle is powerful—it keeps you apart—but I also hear the love underneath it. That sounds like something we can continue exploring during our session next week.

Intervention: Systemic reframing and integration; therapist consolidates insights from all members, externalizing the negative cycle and pointing toward attachment needs as the shared focus.

EFFT Tango: This section of the Daniels family session illustrates how the EFT Tango provides both structure and flexibility in guiding therapeutic interactions. In Move 1, Mirroring the Present Process, the therapist tracked the family's negative cycle, reflecting how Fran's fear, Pam's withdrawal, and Murray's uncertainty kept them caught in disconnection, getting the perspective of Pam's brothers. In Move 2, Affect Assembly and Deepening, empathic conjecture and validation helped surface the primary emotions beneath those patterns—Fran's fear of losing Pam, Pam's longing to be seen beyond her eating, and Murray's fear of failing as a father. A tentative step toward Move 3, Choreographing Engaged Encounters, was first taken as Fran responded directly to Pam's disclosure, allowing a new, more vulnerable exchange to occur between them. Then, a more direct Choreographed Encounter through an enactment intervention took place between Murray and Pam. The therapist then engaged Move 4, Processing the Encounter, by slowing the moment, highlighting its impact, and reframing it as a shift from blame toward connection. While the session did not yet step fully into Move 5, Integrating and Validating, the groundwork was laid as the therapist named the love underlying the family's distress and emphasized the possibility of new relational patterns. In this way, the Tango organized the flow of the session, allowing the therapist to attend to the goal of stage 1: de-escalate conflict while fostering safety and preparing the family for deeper work ahead.

The Therapeutic Story

At the conclusion of this first session, there is a shift away from a problem story that is centered on Pam's symptoms at an individual level, toward a therapeutic story revealing there are complex systemic patterns at work driven by the attachment needs of the family. This was made possible in part by the therapist creating a safe therapeutic space, attuning to the clients, and modeling a secure base.

1 Early on, a new therapeutic story emerges that is characterized by family members being more open and vulnerable with regard to their emotions.
2 The apparent distance in the affectional bonds between Pam and her father and brothers has begun to be reframed as not reflecting indifference, but coming from a place of caring limited by insecurities around how to approach and support Pam.
3 The therapeutic story includes an understanding that the attempts by family members to seek closeness are related to universal attachment needs. Pam's desire to be closer to her father is normalized and validated, while her eating disorder is seen in the context of her attachment environment.
4 Murray accesses vulnerable emotions related to his fears and lack of confidence in his relationship with Pam while affirming his wish to be closer to her. Fran gains new insight about how past attachment patterns from her family of origin inform her current family, including her anxious attachment to Pam.
5 The therapeutic story has become less about Pam's individual experience of anorexia and more so about her needs for greater security, support, and closeness from family members during a challenging time. Complementarily, the family has gained a budding awareness of their own attachment needs within their relationships with Pam and each other.
6 Family members have begun to have a new experience with each other that is indicative of increased A.R.E.

References

Ainsworth, M. D. S. (1967). *Infancy in Uganda: Infant care and the growth of attachment*. Johns Hopkins University Press.

Ainsworth, M. D. S., Blehar, M. C., Waters, E., & Wall, S. (1978). *Patterns of attachment: A psychological study of the strange situation*. Lawrence Erlbaum Associates.

Allan, R., Edwards, C., & Lee, N. (2023). Cultural adaptations of emotionally focused therapy. *Journal of Couple & Relationship Therapy*, *22*(1), 43–63.

Bowlby, J. (1969/1982). *Attachment and Loss: Vol. 1. Attachment*. Basic Books.

Bowlby, J. (1988). *A secure base*. Basic Books.

Brubacher, L. (2017). Emotionally focused individual therapy: an attachment-based experientially/systemic perspective. *Person-Centered & Experiential Psychotherapies*, *16* (1), 50–67.

Butler, E. A., Lee, T. L., & Gross, J. J. (2007). Emotion regulation and culture: Are the social consequences of emotion suppression culture-specific? *Emotion*, *7*(1), 30–48.

Fiese, B. H., Tomcho, T. J., Douglas, M., Josephs, K., Poltrock, S., & Baker, T. (2002). A review of 50 years of research on naturally occurring family routines and rituals: Cause for celebration? *Journal of Family Psychology*, *16*(4), 381–390.

Furrow, J. L., Johnson, S. M., Bradley, B., Brubacher, L. L., Campbell, T. L., Kallos-Lilly, V., Palmer, G., Rheem, K., & Woolley, S. R. (2022). *Becoming an emotionally focused therapist: The workbook*. Routledge.

Furrow, J. L., Palmer, G., Johnson, S. M., Faller, G., & Palmer-Olsen, L. (2019). *Emotionally focused family therapy: Restoring connection and promoting resilience*. Routledge.

Greenberg, L. (2010). Emotion-focused therapy: A clinical synthesis. *Focus*, *8*(1), 32–42.
Guillory, R. M. (2021). The integration of cultural humility in emotionally focused therapy. *Journal of Marital and Family Therapy*, *47*(1), 94–108.
Johnson, S. M. (2019). *Attachment theory in practice: Emotionally Focused Therapy (EFT) with individuals, couples, and families*. The Guilford Press.
Johnson, S. M. (2020). *The practice of emotionally focused marital therapy: Creating connection* (3rd ed.). Brunner/Mazel.
Johnson, S. M., & Greenberg, L. S. (1985). The differential effects of experiential and problem solving interventions in resolving marital conflicts. *Journal of Consulting and Clinical Psychology*, *53*, 175–184.
Johnson, S., Maddeaux, C., & Blouin, J. (1998). Emotionally focused family therapy for bulimia: changing attachment patterns. *Psychotherapy: Theory, Research, Practice, Training*, *35*(2), 238–247.
Marterella, M. K., & Brock, L. J. (2008). Religion and spirituality as a resource in marital and family therapy. *Journal of Family Psychotherapy*, *19*(4), 291–309.
Matsumoto, D., Yoo, S. H., & Nakagawa, S. (2008). Culture, emotion regulation, and adjustment. *Journal of Personality and Social Psychology*, *94*(6), 925–937.
McGoldrick, M., Carter, B., & Garcia Preto, N. (2016). *The expanding family life cycle: Individual, family, and social perspectives* (5th ed.). Pearson.
Mikulincer, M., & Shaver, P. R. (2016). *Attachment in adulthood: Structure, dynamics, and change*. Guilford Publications.
Sandberg, J. G., Calatrava, M., Andrade Urbina, D., Lybbert, R., Mazo, S., & Rodríguez-González, M. (2024). Toward a culturally sensitive application of emotionally focused couples therapy: A qualitative study of therapists' experience using EFT in Spanish-speaking countries/cultures. *Family Process*, 63(2), 648–666.
Sandberg, J. G., Knestel, A., & Suh, H. (2016). The role of emotion in culturally responsive EFT. *Journal of Couple & Relationship Therapy*, *15*(2), 95–112.
Stavrianopoulos, K. (2019). Emotionally focused family therapy: Rebuilding family bonds. In F. Irtelli (Ed.). *Family therapy: New intervention programs and researches* (pp. 67–83). Intechopen.
Stavrianopoulos, K., Faller, G., & Furrow, J. (2014). Emotionally focused family therapy: facilitating change within a family system. *Journal of Couple & Relationship Therapy*, *13*(1), 25–43.
Strand, P. S., Vossen, J., Savage, E. (2019). Culture and child attachment patterns: A behavioral-systems synthesis. *Attachment & Human Development*, *21*(4), 317–336.
Tilley, D., & Palmer, G. (2013). Enactments in emotionally focused couple therapy: Shaping moments of contact and change. *Journal of Marital and Family Therapy*, *39*(3), 299–313.
Tomkins, S. S. (2008). *Affect imagery consciousness: The complete edition*. Springer.
Williams-Reade, J. M., Lobo, E., & Gutierrez, G. (2019). Integrating spirituality into MFT training: A reflexive curriculum and qualitative evaluation. *Journal of Marital and Family Therapy*, *45*(2), 219–232.
Young, J., Tadros, E., & Gregorash, A. (2023). Cultural considerations for using emotionally focused therapy with African American couples. *International Journal of Systemic Therapy*, *34*(2), 63–82.

18 Feminist Family Therapy

Coreen Haym and Anne M. Prouty

Feminist family therapists (FFTs) are shaped by their own identities, values, interests, experiences, and social contexts. Rather than serving as a standalone therapy model, FFT is a meta-perspective that informs therapists and the models they utilize. Although FFTs have critiqued and improved systemic therapy models (e.g., Dankoski & Deacon, 2000; Dermer et al., 1998; Kim et al., 2014; Knudson-Martin, 1994; Leupnitz, 1988; Maier, 2015; McDowell et al., 2023; Walsh & Schneikman, 1988), many branches of feminism have evolved over time and differ based on country, sociopolitical influences, and global era. Since this chapter cannot cover all of FFT, we will reflect upon three generations of FFTs' work that helped us conceptualize the shared family case.

The Therapeutic Story of Problem Formation

Conceptualizing problem formation from any FFT meta-perspective requires the therapist to understand social identity and power dynamics at individual, familial, and contextual levels. FFTs understand the formation of problems by considering three interconnected levels of the system: people's individual identities and experiences, the family's interpersonal dynamics and family-level identity, and the clients' interactions with their broader social contexts (Goodrich, 1991). Their work helped the field recognize how gendered, social power dynamics were both personal and institutionalized and should not be replicated in our therapy models if family therapy was going to be able to promote mental health for individuals, families, and communities. It is important to note that feminist scholars and therapists typically engage with multiple branches of feminism rather than adhering strictly to one. Let us examine how FFT has evolved over the decades as different feminist communities examined identity, interpersonal and familial process, and social context dynamics.

DOI: 10.4324/9781003668510-18

First Generation of FFTs

In the United States, second wave feminism of the 1960s and 1970s brought attention to improving women's power and choice in many family-related experiences including: sexuality and reproductive rights, legal status rights, the recognition of interpersonal violence in family systems' power dynamics, and the need to challenge medical misogyny in both physical and mental health care. Within this context, Hare-Mustin (1978) is regarded as the first FFT for her critique of systemic therapy and its presupposition of therapist and theoretical neutrality. Hare-Mustin and others examined their own work with couples and families, as they unlearned and challenged sexist conceptualizations of gender roles, intergenerational patterns, and responses to social expectations. Feminists' critiques prompted systemic and relational therapists to redesign family therapy models (Leupnitz, 1988), to refocus of therapy, to include women's perspectives, and to promote gender equity in relationships and responsibility for change (Goodrich et al., 1988; Walters et al., 1988). During the 1980s and 1990s, several branches of systemic feminists emerged to expand thinking and practice such as Radical Feminism, Liberal Feminism, Social and Marxist Feminism, Queer Feminism, and Cultural Feminism. This history and foundation provided building blocks for future generations of FFTs. For the purposes of this chapter and the Daniels family, we will be focusing on second- and third-generation applications, including fourth-wave feminism.

Second Generation of FFTs

Decolonialist ideas and personal activism began emerging globally in the 1990s, prioritizing new conceptualizations and values in order to respect and include the nuanced, local, heterogenous experiences of women. These decolonial ideas gained prominence in the United States alongside Crenshaw's articulation of intersectionality in 1989. By the mid-1990s, the concept of intersectionality was widely embraced by the second generation of FFTs, leading to examination of clients' intersectional identities as well as consideration of parallel systems among supervisors, therapists, and clients (Hernández, 2008; Long et al., 2006). FFTs' publications emphasized families' cultural strengths, benefits, and lessons to be learned from interplay among culture, community, and social factors on individual and family development (Almeida et al., 1998; Aponte, 1994; Comas-Diaz, 2003; Falicov, 1999; Kim et al., 2014; Tamasese, 2003). FFTs helped intercultural couples navigate hegemony and move toward embracing their diverse cultural identities and traditions, thereby developing flexible, informed, and resilient families based on negotiation, adoption, and adaptation (Karis & Killian, 2008; Long & Andrews, 2007; Thomas et al., 2003).

Although both parents in the Daniels family came from Christian upbringings, a second-generation feminist would have explored the differences within Murray's protestant family upbringing and Fran's Catholic background.

At first glance, this is a White family. Murray and Fran may have ignored and minimized ethnic and religious differences, aspects of whiteness that were more socially dominant may have had more influence on the couple, or they may have included and celebrated a variety of cultural and religious values, priorities, skills, traditions, and spiritual rituals that their different backgrounds provided. FFTs would want to attend to intersections and cultural differences in the family, how Murray and Fran brought aspects of culture to be experienced, how they chose which aspects to emphasize, and which have been conscious and unconscious. How have their families, community, parenting values, gender and sexual identities, social class, and other intersectional identities influenced their accommodation, negotiation, priorities, couplehood, and parenting? How have they experienced the evolving changes in the Protestant and Catholic communities?

By the early 2000s, most feminist training and therapy publications were informed by social constructionism and intersectionality, including branches such as queer and post-gender FFT (Knudson-Martin & Mahoney, 2009; McGeorge & Carlson, 2011) and intersectional and post-colonial FFT (Almeida et al., 2011; Hernández-Wolfe & McDowell, 2013). FFTs wrote about developing ways of collaboration founded from within local perspectives and values like Tamasese and her colleagues in New Zealand (Tamasese, 2003). American cultural feminists and womanists emphasized culturally informed approaches in therapy that prioritized equity, fairness, justice, family loyalty, and courage (Boyd-Franklin, 2006; Falicov, 2015). FFTs attended to clients' self-preservation, cautious boundaries, and needing time to trust therapists, while valuing extended family and chosen family. FFTs promoted culturally informed practices to foster mutual respect, particularly in couples, where the focus was often on identifying and disrupting patterns of dominance and replacing them with mutual influence, flexibility, and bilateral accommodation (Knudson-Martin & Mahoney, 2009).

Interpersonal Power in Families. For FFTs examining interpersonal power, relative status is an important aspect of interpersonal power in human systems. **Relative status** includes who has the right to define what is important, who gets to express their opinions and needs, who can expect to receive accommodation, and who can expect support (Knudson-Martin, 2012). FFTs are interested in familial, cultural, and contextual layers of status, power and the effects on each member of the family, and trauma-informed methods. FFTs monitor pace and safety and name injustices within family members' lives, enabling families to clarify values, recognize resources, reframe individual responses with compassion, and reorganize around solidarity (McDowell et al., 2023), valuing what each member brings and mitigating temporary relational inequities through genuine gratitude (Jonathan, 2009). FFTs examine how life experiences, work histories, skills training, education, and monetary assets, like inheritance, impacted power dynamics within and across generations and migration histories (Falicov, 2012). The

Daniels family migration histories are several generations back, so let's look at three generations to understand the power dynamics at play in the Daniels family.

Power dynamics in the family represent macro-level problems manifested through a micro-level family system where traditional white, patriarchal U.S. social expectations create and maintain systems that work in favor of the dominant culture, such as devaluation of domestic work and raising children. Pam's likelihood of queer identity is not only marginalized but ignored as a possibility and could also exacerbate tension or conflict within the family if disclosed. These dynamics create and maintain a system where Murray holds more power than any other member of the family, as he provides financial resources that U.S. families see as an imperative for survival.

Whether consciously or not, imitation of the socially acceptable and unchallenged roles inherited by the culture in both Murray's and Fran's families of origin serves to sink Pam deeper into her isolation, seeking for a way to control something in her life, since empowerment is unreachable given these circumstances. Lack of empowerment can manifest through eating disorders in females, as pressure to be attractive to men is also carried through generational training. FFTs would conceptualize through inquisitive, curious questions below.

In the Daniels family, an FFT would be curious about how the parents negotiate decisions, asking, does either parent or a child generally get to have their way or have their needs met more than anyone else? Sometimes someone assigned as head of the family, due to cultural or religious beliefs, will be accommodated; while sometimes someone who is ill or is a premier athlete will be accommodated. An FFT would also ask, what are the systemic effects of accommodation on the centralized person and the marginalized family members? Have the parents established compensatory attunement and attending practices, or could the presenting symptoms be signs of cumulative distress?

FFTs would be curious about how gender is described, discussed, and reflected in both Murray's and Fran's cultures and religious communities. For example, have all of the children been given opportunities to develop spiritual lives, be included in spiritual education and leadership, and to develop peer groups related to their interests? Were their developmental milestones celebrated within their faith communities, or does gender limit the opportunities in any way? Have any family members or their neighbors experienced social violence related to their religious practices and identities, and if so, how have the Daniels responded as parents and as members of Christian communities?

In the Daniels family, have both Murray and Fran had equal access to financial and social resources? Have both of their roles as parents and people with extra-familial careers been equally prioritized, or did they negotiate a different way to balance their growing family's needs as they have moved through the years? Has this process been an open one in which both felt valued and appreciated, or did gendered assumptions covertly dictate decisions, leaving anyone out of either family roles or career opportunities? When they did have an imbalance that caused one person to take more of the family or money-earning burden for a while, did they recognize the sacrifice and use relational care and gratitude practices? FFTs would consider all or any of these questions to conceptualize, while learning how to integrate these queries into therapy, attuning to the Daniels family.

Integrating Emotional Skills. Early feminists in mental health disciplines did much of the scholarship on promoting emotional ways of knowing as mature, adult, necessary, requiring practice, and being culturally informed. Feminists adjusted Bowenian family systems to respect emotional processing on equal par with cognitive processing (Knudson-Martin, 1994) and suggested fusion did not fit for all cultures (Kim et al., 2014). Several feminists validated women's anger, noted that anti-anger norms were used to dismiss and control women in relationships and social systems, and addressed such coercion in therapy (Flemke & Allen, 2008).

FFTs also wrote about how to build emotional competency and skills for all family members, regardless of gender, while respecting family's cultural styles and preferences. FFT goals included the development of parent-child relationships, increased emotional self-awareness, interpersonal attunement, and mutual support (Knudson-Martin & Mahoney, 2009; Prouty & Lyness, 2011). FFTs integrate emotional skills to heighten understanding and closeness that helps families manage problems as they arise. Both Murray and Fran come from families that did not promote emotional connection and affection, as it was likely seen as feminine expression, which is again devalued. We can see these patterns played out through generations in the Daniels family cultures through generations.

Balancing Work and Family. During this generation, FFTs wrote about balancing work and family and developing equal partnerships (Haddock et al., 2001) and developed methods that promoted conscious collaboration in family work and parenting. Feminist therapists promoted varied configurations of equity and partnerships and supported collaborative family dynamics. Tamasese (2003) encouraged therapists to help uncover the traditions of gender arrangements that were traditional in people's cultures and that facilitated equity, respect, reciprocity, accountability, and empathy. We can see how with the Daniels family layered historical gender roles and work/family balance have played a significant role in splitting the family down gender lines, having a detrimental effect on family cohesion and closeness.

Third Generation of FFTs

Transnational feminism began appearing in family therapy literature around 2010, continuing and building upon a wider arena of feminist research, advocacy, pop culture, and personal experiences from around the world. This generation may or may not use the word feminist, and the definition varies by country. Those whose work we can identify as FFT continue to transform knowledge about activism, global belonging, identities, borders, family, and relational responsibility. Discerning women and their communities as unique and worthy of respect, transnational feminist scholars do not treat women in regions of the world as a homogenous group but seek to promote self-identification, nuanced identities, and more distinctive samples in research protocols. Perhaps due to their digital world and global perspective, this newest generation of FFTs is much more eager and willing to discern women's lives as existing in both local communities and unique intersectional identities. This willingness to see people as unique translates into being therapists who are familiar with diverse, non-static, nonbinary, even noncategorical, rich and personalized experiences of gender, culture, religion, sexuality, abilities, relationships, and nation associations.

Murray and Fran grew up in families, religious communities, and social circles that may have purposefully emphasized gender as either male or female, even if their generation was accepting of more flexibility in gender expression, emotional expression, educational expectations, career possibilities, and parenting roles than their parents' generation. Both came from families and religions that acknowledged the existence of heterosexual, gay, bisexual, and lesbian persons but only supported heterosexual unions as sanctified unions by their churches and thereby may have sent an overt or covert preference of both limited gender and heterosexual identities to their children. A FFT would note that Pam is developmentally at an age in which she is aware of her gender identity and sexual attractions. No matter the extent of exposure and discussion within her own family, peer groups, and community, she has been exposed to more information and a global peer group, expressing themselves, their attractions, and their dreams of relationships in which they find love and acceptance.

Within the Daniels family make-up and adherence to familiar social norms, they have unwittingly ignored a wider lens that does not assume heterosexuality. Pam already feels unseen, and cisheterosexual assumptions only exacerbate her invisibility and subsequent withdrawal. Once joined with the family, an FFT would explore how flexible Murray and Fran are with their children's development into gendered and sexual beings, to determine whether family therapy, individual therapy with Pam, or some combination would provide the safest means by which to promote Pam's development and her continued connection with her family.

Transnational feminists represent fourth wave feminism within third generation feminist family therapy and are living in a world with the highest rates of migration in history, so it makes sense that feminist family-centered scholarship has a stronger and more complex focus on migration (Espín & Dottolo, 2019) and the diverse and dynamic nature of modern women's identities, experiences, and perspectives, as well as challenging patriarchal and western-centric definitions of culture, class, religion, gender, age, ability, relationship boundaries, and conceptualizations of mental health fields themselves (Kiliçer et al., 2021; Phillips, 2010).

Transnational feminists are not eliminating FFT branches developed in earlier decades. Instead, they are de-centralizing the existing scholarship to represent diverse experiences, enabling expansion of earlier branches of feminist family therapy by being embedded in multiple, global contexts within an ever-shifting political and gendered landscape. Liberal/legal and policy-focused feminists have a very fast-paced and ever-changing discourse as family-focused and gender-based laws and policies are quickly shifting and influencing therapists' practices. For example, marriage has been storied in past decades of FFT mostly as a means of individual pleasure, sexual and bonding fulfillment, individual choice, and presumed heterosexual orientation. International FFTs are moving beyond these assumptions and focusing on people's local experiences, nonheterosexual marriage, as well as the influences on clients of legally/religiously enforced presumed heterosexuality, colloquial social norms like sexual respectability, and what roles might heterosexual marriage have embedded within collectivism and kinship responsibilities and values (Abeyasekera, 2017).

This FFT conceptualization would prove useful for the therapist in creating an environment for the Daniels family that allows for both individual and familial reflection as well as the possibility for alternative ways of thinking and interacting. Do the parents have similar or different ideas about coupling, dating, sexual identity, sexual behaviors, and parenting about these topics? Does this family have ways that they discuss human sexuality related to their children's development as well as human diversity and global cultures? What have been family members' experiences within their family, with extended family, with peers, with media, and on the internet? Are their values and beliefs similar or different from prior generations and their communities?

Women around the world have expectations to provide children to their families and communities, to marry within their community to persons approved and sometimes chosen by their families. Hence, heterosexual marriage is a vehicle for family and community preservation, and mothers may give up careers to ensure their daughter's eligibility (Merecek, 2019). FFTs engage and examine how cross-border social policies and economics influence families, and sometimes the lives of women working in the homes of our clients as we attend to the complex layers of a family's systems (Espín & Dottolo, 2019; Méndez-Pounds, 2024).

An FFT would wonder, what were the cultural, generational, religious, and economic influences of their meeting and decision to marry? What were the social, religious, cultural, socioeconomic, and familial influences in which Murray and Fran were immersed as Murray pursued a career, and Fran pursued the role of homemaker, primary family organizer, and primary parent? Was Murray's generation, citizenship, cis-male, heterosexual, married, Christian, white, male status an influence on his access to steady work with a retirement plan? What did they each gain and miss as a result of these choices?

Do they believe that their children will have other opportunities and options? Are there legal, economic, social, and educational differences that limit and expand their children's experiences? Will laws permit their children to marry whom they wish and adopt children if they choose? Will policies enable them to take paid leave from work to care for children, siblings, and elders whether they are family of origin or partner's kin? Continuing to ask these kinds of questions informs how to transform conceptualization into workable interventions specific to the Daniels family.

Diversity Conceptualization

FFTs are open to how people conceptualize and talk about their identities along every aspect of human diversity. Since identity and contextual variables are salient to FFT and have been discussed thoroughly above, let us just review a few key ideas in the following aspects of human diversity often discussed across systemic and relational models of therapy.

Sex and Gender

Among languages and cultures that discern sex from gender, **sex** usually denotes a person's genotype and/or the best guess of the external gonads present on a newborn's body, whereas **gender** is a social construction and infused with meaning, behavior, expression, and identity informed by a person's other identities (McGeorge et al., 2020).

Sexual Orientation and Relational Orientation

Sexual orientation refers to whom people are sexually attracted and **relational orientation** to the number of persons with whom one intimately bonds and creates partnerships and family units (Blumer et al., 2014). FFTs work with people across the lifespan, as clients parent queer children who have their own experiences of sexual orientation and gender identity (Boe et al., 2018). Queer adults' life experiences of illness and medical care, ability to marry, ability to become parents, employment, and safety are influenced by local and national policies and sometimes require multiple migrations when nations' governments and laws change (Underwood, 2024). Feminists have talked about sexuality since their voices were first raised, but the prevalence and public nature of this topic vary greatly by country, culture, and context. In the northern and western parts of the globe, FFTs have focused on supporting people to self-define and embrace their own sexuality, sexual pleasure, sexuality-related identities, sexual relationships, and intimate relationship orientations (Blumer et al., 2014; Dalton et al., 2020; Hertlein et al., 2016; Kilçer et al., 2021; Negy & McKinney, 2006), but sexuality and sexual attraction are not always the priority of FFTs in other parts of the globe, or even a safe topic to discuss. Considering the power dynamics and defined expectations discussed earlier, there is little room for Pam's ability to self-define or explore in terms of her gender, sexuality, or potential future relationships as a result of reinforced gender norms and possibly religious underpinnings related to family lineage and culture.

Ethnic Identity

Ethnicity is a complex tapestry of historical, social, artistic, religious, communal, and familial meaning systems aimed at enabling belonging to a group or groups of people who share a past, a present, and a future. McGoldrick et al. (2005) described ethnicity as denoting a group's shared peoplehood. Ethnic identity can bring a sense of belonging to a community of people with a shared history from a collective group or geographical region, with shared customs and traditions, values, ways of communicating and living, that have usually developed over years, decades, or centuries. FFTs seek to attune to clients' identities, priorities, and experiences and follow the clients' preferences as to whether and how ethnicity plays a role in therapy, rather than avoid or wait for the client to assert its importance. Religion is often a primary aspect of identity and ethnicity, defining and giving meaning to people's lives, providing purpose and rhythm to their days, and informing how they interact with themselves and others. Whether culture, religion, spiritual orientation, or attunement to the natural world, FFTs' practice and scholarship have long included this important aspect of identity in their work and continue to do so (Walsh, 1999, 2012).

Religion and Spirituality

Religious and spiritual engagement can act as a protective factor in dealing with discrimination, provide resistance from self-harm, and a guide for healing (Comas-Diaz, 2003; Falicov, 1999). Religious traditions define gender, inform gender roles, prescribe sexuality and sexual identity, and organize both altruistic and dominant power structures in families and communities, including loyalty and a collective sense of belonging. Practices, beliefs, sacred stories, and sacred places provide an experience of divine presence within the family (Fishbane, 1999). Religions and spiritual traditions define individual and family life cycles, provide rituals for important life transitions, and help us to set aside time to celebrate as well as grieve (Helmeke and Sori, 2006). Denominations within religions share a core set of beliefs and history, but their decades and eons of fracture and differences may have created chasms that can be difficult for interfaith couples and families to navigate.

The Daniels family may have a specific intersection with religion, ethnicity, and sexuality assumptions that need to be explored in session, while providing a strong respect for the role of religion in their relational dynamics, noting that Murray and Fran have different religious upbringings, suggesting unique yet associated Christian values.

Socioeconomics and Social Class

This category informs a complex set of experiences, knowledge, and resources that includes money, education, knowing how to navigate social systems, having a monetary safety net, having access to transportation, medical insurance, employment, safe housing, safe neighborhood, and food. Religion and government policies can also denote, constrain, and maintain social class and social immobility. Socioeconomics and social class are influenced by culture, geography, migration experiences, political climate, laws, policies, and regional conflict. One's ability to remain stable within a social class depends on many variables including networks, family ties, and many identity variables. Even in a "middle-class" family such as the Daniels, class values often manifest as concern for how the family is perceived in social settings, which is another area that must be addressed to empower the family to examine the influences that silently inhibit authentic living.

Age and Generation

FFTs seek to be sensitive to the influences of age and generational experiences, cultural traditions about human development and aging, and how age intersects with all other aspects of a person's experiences. Women are often care providers, sometimes of both the younger and older generations of their families (Kriseman & Claes, 1997; Long, 1997). Feminists have sought to understand how women age well, women's relational experiences as they age, how they thrive (Rossano & Cotter, 2024), and how they understand and cope with vulnerabilities and demonstrate resiliency (Rabig, 2024). Feminists have also asked difficult questions about dignified elder care and international policies (Wisensale, 2005).

Health and Ability

Finally, health and ability experiences intersect with every other facet of a person's identity, social context, and access to resources. FFTs have examined health disparities (Kissill & Davey, 2012) and many different chronic illnesses which challenge physical abilities both invisibly and visibly (Wetchler, 2006). Knudson-Martin (2003) designed a gender-informed framework for understanding biology and health in clinical practice. FFTs have provided women-based examinations and discussions of women's bodies, sexuality, fertility, health, and aging (Duarte-Silva et al., 2012). Although many areas of health and ability can be explored in the Daniels family, we will specifically focus on eating disorders in FFT, as Pam is presenting with a diagnosis of Anorexia that has brought the family to therapy as a last resort before residential treatment, which could serve to isolate her further.

Eating Disorders in FFT

FFTs have contributed to many discussions of women's bodies, including sexuality, fertility, infertility, breastfeeding, athleticism, pornography, trafficking, health, illness, gender diversity and affirmation, and eating disorders. Anorexia was constructed as a psychological diagnosis in the mid to late 1800s (Dell'Osso et al., 2016) and was included in the first version of the *Diagnostic and Statistical Manual of Mental Disorders* (1952) as a neurotic reaction—placing the blame and the diagnosis on the person, often a woman, with the symptoms. Feminists asked: A neurotic reaction to what? Rather than focusing on the diagnosis, FFTs investigated what social stimuli might be heinous enough to result in starving oneself through various painful and increasingly lethal means.

Anorexia, bulimia, and overeating (Stice, 1998) are important to examine as distinct experiences and cannot be minimized as methods to fulfill an increasingly thin-bodied idealization of beauty. So, what additional powerful social influences and ways of being in our bodies (Squire, 2003) could comprise etiologies that should be addressed in therapy? Could some behaviors be women's rebellion against patriarchal control of and demands on female bodies and identities (Maier, 2015; Peterson et al., 2008)? Responses to racist sexual objectification (Yokoyama, 2007)? Could disordered eating and related behaviors be a reaction to social and institutional attempts to dismiss women's minds, capabilities, choices, sexualities, and diverse identities (Pharr, 1997; Wacker, 2018), and responses to acts of violence in women's lives and relationships (Bretaña et al., 2025)? FFTs have contributed to efforts to treat these etiologies and the manifested symptoms of anorexia, bulimia, and binge-eating disorders.

FFTs, like Wacker (2018), have advocated for increasing social supports and significant positive relationships to subvert body dissatisfaction and disconnection. FFTs work to empower clients to find a style of expressing genuine thoughts, discontents, expectations, and needs to promote a healthy, culturally congruent voice with both themselves and others. An example of promoting close relationships in therapy came from Chan and MaMa (2006), who advocated for helping families organize through mutual love and care, rather than member control. Control of Pam's eating and behavioral modification would be of primary concern if residential treatment was chosen. As such, FFTs also empower clients to engage in their life goals, pathways, priorities, options, and the social systems in which they live and whether these systems produce access or barriers to dignity, power, and opportunities (McDowell et al., 2023).

FFTs examine underlying processes that support eating disorders in order to bring internal and external stressors to awareness where they can be challenged. For example, FFT might help clients to identify thoughts, emotional reactions, and behaviors that reflect embodiment of rage, disgust, or desire (Squire, 2003). For Pam, it is possible that she is harboring these feelings that contribute to her need for visibility. FFTs use methods to establish congruence and empowerment to not only identify experiences of racism, misogyny, ageism, and body shaming, but to promote active strategies of resistance (Maier, 2015). Feminist therapists like Yokoyama (2007) recognize that racial teasing, shame, and obligation are strategies used to dominate, control, and denote belonging or rejection to social groups. We can see how Pam's isolation has grown over time due to the aforementioned strategies that maintain a heteropatriarchal model of family and social acceptance. Further, diagnostic categories based on racial experiences of white, dominant groups may obscure the racialized-body experiences, interpersonal and internalized struggles, and resistance to the devaluation of physical features of women of color (Mintz & Kashubek, 1999) in which subsequent self-criticism may or may not manifest only in dieting behaviors.

Subsequently, FFTs focus on complex identity conceptualization where clients' bodies, social systems, and layers of social context are all considered. Feminist perspectives facilitate examination and reworking of family of origin (Carolan et al., 2010), couple (Maier, 2015), and societal messages where clients can raise awareness, develop a style of conceptualization and language, and utilize cognitive and emotional ways of knowing so that the body is not the primary method of expression. For the Daniels family, Pam has internalized the idea that the body serves as the primary mode of expression. Consequently, her invisibility and subsequent devaluation embedded in the inherited social and family culture have manifested as an eating disorder. This conceptualization applies directly to the Daniels' family goal to help heal Pam as a family unit rather than send her to a treatment facility that focuses primarily on behavioral eating changes.

The Therapeutic Story of Problem Resolution

It is common to think of FFT as focusing only on gender equality as a primary driver for all presentations in therapy. In actuality, as explored in the past section, FFT therapists focus on interrupting inequity and unspoken, socialized power dynamics with a family system, while remaining flexible, authentic, and transparent in their work (Bridges et al., 2023; Prouty & Bermudez, 2000). FFTs compassionately confront beliefs from dominant discourses regarding the role of gender and culture in the family. In the simplest terms, FFTs motivate change by utilizing feminist philosophies to create relevant systemic interventions through self-reflection woven into self-of-the-therapist (SOT) processes (Prouty & Twist, 2016). This requires that the therapist self-monitor for both implicit and explicit personalization and internalization of colonized norms that can decenter the presenting problems of the couple or family. SOT approaches and cultural humility are paramount to this process. FFTs approach clients with the curiosity needed to allow marginalized voices to be heard.

FFTs do not limit the use of interventions from other systemic approaches but continuously consider static hierarchy, power dynamics, and unacknowledged gender and cultural norms, while using theory to conceptualize and intervene. Influences from multiple systemic levels are addressed, from the microsystems of family, friends, and local culture to the ecosystems of government and media, to macrosystems of social norms, political systems, and culture (Bronfenbrenner, 2005). Systemic influences are deeply embedded, which silences marginalized family members, leading to patterns that may be detrimental to the family as well as family members.

The FFT focus on self-reflection and cultural positionality guides insight that explores the social norms that create problems for the family. As we can see in the Daniels family, gender roles are simply accepted as *what is*, rather than seeing a potential for change that can influence how the family members interact with one another. We can help the Daniels family recognize that oppressive gender, heterosexual, and religious norms maintained in the family contribute to, if not cause, Pam's isolation, lack of eating, and family gender division.

Role of the Therapist

The FFT is not the expert of the family (Cheon & Murphy, 2007; Penfold, 1989). A primary intervention in FFT is the use of self to understand each person's perspective, while refraining from judgment, empowering clients to recognize that they can create a family culture and system that is unique, rather than what social systems prescribe. Feminism informs the therapeutic approaches that resonate with the style and genuine personality of the therapist, while simultaneously considering the presenting problem and family culture. Feminist therapists consider the social location of family members without assumptions of heterosexuality, White-European descent, and other dominant culture identities, regardless of physical presentation (Kirk & Okazawa-Rey, 2003; McDowell & Hernandez, 2010). Feminist therapists have a responsibility to collaborate with supervisors, colleagues, and relevant literature and art to make the implicit "isms" explicit. SOT awareness and "a-ha" moments can create meaningful change, as the therapist and what they bring into the process is the primary tool of FFT (Larner, 1995; Prouty & Twist, 2016).

The Daniels family appears to present as occupying mostly dominant areas of social location. Although age/generation and SES/class may be confirmed through original case information, many may read the case study and assume the family members to be white, heterosexual, able-bodied, and cisgender. These immediate defaults highlight the common misnomer that anything outside of dominant culture is othered, minimally valued, and often ignored. This is only one example of the critical consciousness that feminist therapists employ to examine power dynamics at play between each unique family and therapist. Without this iterative and ongoing SOT reflection, the therapist cannot create space for minoritized people to develop trust in the process or the therapist.

Integrating Feminist Concepts into Therapy

Assessing integration of feminist thought into models of systemic family therapy can be challenging, and several tools can be helpful to this end. The *Power and Equity Guide*, authored by Haddock et al. (2000), supports ideas common to many of these measures. With this guide, therapists gain information about their integration and reflect on several goals: (a) eliminating or reducing power differentials between partners or family members; (b) empowering clients to embrace all aspects of themselves, particularly the parts that are not supported in dominant culture; and (c) attending to the therapist-client power differential. It is critical to engage in ongoing self-reflexivity and to seek out colleague and supervisory feedback.

Empowerment. The goal for clients is not necessarily to increase *power over* anyone but to increase *power with* (Goodrich et al., 1988). This is the difference between harmful, unchecked power and personal or collective empowerment. When the therapist recognizes these aspects of themselves, it becomes easier to see them in clients and assist the family in recognizing their own self-expertise regarding decision-making and choices (Blumer et al., 2010; Cheon & Murphy, 2007). The therapist automatically holds a certain amount of power, but it is interwoven with the identity characteristics of the therapist as well as the client(s), meaning that clients may hold power dependent upon their social locations and identities. Acknowledgment of these dynamics can bring voices to the surface as opposed to creating blocks in therapy, leading to unnecessary client withdrawal.

The power that occurs from therapist to client is encapsulated in the understanding that the therapist brings certain knowledge and skills, while clients enter into a situation where personal sharing is significantly unbalanced, as clients are experiencing distress and encouraged to share details of their pain with the therapist. In short, the intersection of personal and social characteristics will inform other power dynamics where the therapist will not have the power position, such as gender, ethnicity, etc. all framed within an intersectional context. Examining client-therapist-supervisor-context ***intersectionalities*** is a helpful exercise to understand the many dynamics at play within systemic layers (McDowell et al., in press). Empowerment within the Daniels family can ease the burdens of all family members. Heteropatriarchy has resulted in marginalizing Pam, pressuring Fran to act in a way that she feels a "good mom" should operate, all while distancing Murray and the boys from engaging in a family experience that values the uniqueness of each family member.

Collaboration. Collaboration between families and therapists, as well as between family members, provides space for reflection and managing inequitable power dynamics. This openness to alternative ways of existing and being in the world, outside of prescribed expectations and norms, can be a catalyst for self-motivated systemic change. Collaboration also acts as a safeguard for the therapist to remain cognizant of avoiding expert status, whether this is consciously recognized or not.

Post-colonial and Transnational feminist therapy approaches remind us to respect the client lens, while also bringing to awareness the possibility of different ways of interacting. In this way, we do not unknowingly exert power but instead spark untapped creative potential from our clients. In the Daniels family, there is currently little to no space for personal differences and alternatives to rise, as the family is steeped in a multitude of the aforementioned social norms influenced by many systemic levels, including their own families of origin.

Family rituals were promoted to help families include everyone while attending to emotional family transitions, improving cohesion, and removing the mother from carrying the burden alone (Imber-Black & Roberts, 2003). Helmeke and Sori (2006) edited two volumes of interventions to attend to spirituality in family therapy. Creating family rituals for the Daniels family could be an exceptional exploration of belief systems. Further, the attention on emotional closeness and parent-child family relations could help raise awareness to the fact that even though the Daniels see themselves as a close family, there is emotional integration that would benefit the family members and the family as a whole.

Modeling. As FFTs strive to call attention to inequities and interrupt societal and familial assumptions that inform functioning and self-awareness, they challenge these deep-seated beliefs with respect, compassion, and curiosity. Family systems must be considered with an understanding of unjust global realities. This means that therapist's patience, authenticity, and even well-timed humor can model that varying approaches to life are as valid as currently held beliefs regarding how to act, feel, and be. If the therapist can be genuine in their work, while sincerely displaying understanding of other worldviews, they can demonstrate that there are infinite ways to inhabit relationships and walk through the world.

Cultural training has traditionally been from parents to children, but in a globalized internet world, it is now more commonly flowing from children to parents (Akyil, et al., 2015). While parents continue to attempt to define reality for their children, generational clashes arise and look different from those in pre-internet eras. In the Daniels family, Pam likely has heightened awareness, and her developmental stage is one of self-discovery in identity and value formation. Through this understanding, an FTT can help the client, couple, or family gain "permission" to explore alternative realities for themselves. Succinctly, if a therapist can model flexibility, confidence in who they are, and how they inhabit the world, so can others. The therapist who works alongside the Daniels family can model empowerment and unique ways of looking at the world through modeling. For example, this can be magnified by presentation, such as office set-up and decor, intentional and purposeful self-disclosure, and an authentic presence.

Third-Order Change

Many systemic family therapy models utilize reframing in their therapeutic approaches. For example, EFT, Narrative, and SFBT all utilize the interruption of homeostasis to create new meaning and open pathways for understanding challenges in new ways to create hope, foster insight, and effect change (Kerr, 2001; Lee, 1997; Seponski, 2016). In FFT, the focus is on third-order change (McDowell et al., 2023) which focuses on social injustice and conformity, rather than simply focusing on the positive. This serves to validate clients, rather than support narratives that suggest internal or personal deficits. Since cultural and gender inequities are validated through years of research in various disciplines, these truths can encourage externalization of problems that were once internalized as character flaws.

It is a powerful realization when people understand that their reactions are "normal" given experienced oppression. These shifts in worldview can help to create new meanings that contextualize thoughts, feelings, and behaviors as believable. Conversely, invalidation of social inequities and lived experience will likely eliminate therapeutic trust. Nadal (2018) describes this as the **double bind of response** where people are silenced or face repercussions that heighten mental health struggles creating **minority stress** (Meyer, 2003) and further struggles. It is assumed within the Daniels family that Pam is heterosexual and cisgender. Pam's assumed cisheteronormativity can cause further isolation and loneliness when the focus is primarily on her eating behaviors, rather than the forces that have shaped this result. Pam likely feels as though what is important to her is not considered. When clients are seen, understood, and believed, we are able to create relationships that benefit therapeutic alliance.

Models of Application

We will focus on two applications that can help guide therapists in the incorporation of FFT into therapeutic approaches: The *Transtheoretical Socioculturally Attuned Guidelines* (McDowell et al., 2023) and *The Feminist Intersectional Couple, Relationship, and Family Therapy Model* (Walker et al., 2025), focusing on fourth wave feminism, transnational application. Infusing intersectionality and culture into FFT began to take shape in the third wave (Walker et al., 2025). Considering the complex, overlapping influences of identities and historical context, therapists need to recognize and challenge structural oppression. With this lens, FFTs can honor the multifaceted experiences of marginalization, rather than relying on narrow or dominant narratives. As such, you will see overlapping ideas in these models as well as specific variations within the two.

Transtheoretical Socioculturally Attuned Guidelines. As we have discussed, FFT is a meta-theory and a philosophical approach, not a set of interventions. It has been applied under the umbrella of multiple theories, such as Structural, Narrative, SFBT, and many others (Kerr, 2001; Knudson-Martin et al., 2019). It can be challenging to apply these concepts without some structure, and McDowell, et al. (2023) developed an organized approach to applying FFT concepts into family therapy models called ***ANVIET***, which are the guidelines that follow.

Attune to context and power. **Sociocultural attunement** is the dynamic process by which FFT can intentionally recognize, validate, and integrate clients' cultural, social, and historical identities into the therapeutic relationship. It requires sustained awareness of how systemic forces (e.g., race, ethnicity, class, gender, sexuality, religion, ability, and oppression) influence lived experience, while also continuously engaging in SOT reflections regarding one's own cultural positionality, assumptions, and power. Unlike the idea of static cultural competence, sociocultural attunement is a relational stance and ongoing practice that fosters trust and connection in the therapeutic space (McDowell et al., 2023), which is an MFT common factor and prerequisite to effective work (D'Aniello et al., 2020).

Name injustices. In feminist family therapy, explicitly naming injustices is essential because it situates clients' struggles within broader systems of power rather than reducing them to individual or relational deficits. A non-judgmental stance is not to be confused with neutrality, as FFTs purport that neutrality is not only impossible to achieve but unhelpful, often silencing marginalized groups and related cultures (Capozzi, 2022; Seponski, 2016). Silence around systemic oppression risks reinforcing dominant discourses that blame individuals for problems rooted in inequity (Goldner, 1985; McDowell & Hernandez, 2010). By acknowledging and naming injustices, therapists validate clients' lived experiences and challenge the invisibility of systemic oppression, fostering an environment grounded in recognition and empowerment.

This process allows families to externalize problems and recognize that many conflicts are shaped by societal hierarchies, not simply personal failings. In turn, naming injustice supports the feminist commitment to linking therapeutic practice with social transformation, a principle foundational to feminist-informed systemic practice (Almeida et al., 2019). Injustices within the Daniels family have been created and maintained by what members of the family, likely Murray and Fran, see as societal imperatives, such as Fran giving up her teaching career to raise a family and the boys receiving more attention to their activities, for example. This is not as simple as Murray working outside the home, Fran working domestically, and the boys being involved in sports. An empowered family can certainly be shaped this way, but only if these choices are made consensually within a lens of critical consciousness, knowing that many other choices are available, valued, and supported.

Value what is minimized. FFT emphasizes recognizing and addressing the needs that dominant cultural systems minimize, such as equitable access to resources and rich cultural narratives silenced through colonization and internalization of dominant values. Intersectionality reminds us that these erasures are compounded for families and individuals who manage multiple oppressions (Collins, 2000; Crenshaw, 1991). What may appear as individual or relational struggles, like gender-based domestic roles, financial stress, frustration, or silenced voices, are often symptoms of broader systemic inequities (Enns, 2019; Knudson-Martin & Mahoney, 2009).

In the Daniels family, we see minimization of Pam's ideas and voice, her potential gender and sexual orientation, the value of artistic expression as not as important as athletics, and the importance of the work of child-rearing throughout the years. By recognizing these stories, therapists validate lived experiences and invite clients to show up as themselves, while contextualizing unexamined external societal norms, rather than in the case of the Daniels where the sole focus is on Pam's eating behaviors.

Intervene in power dynamics. Sociocultural attunement is necessary to intervene, as internalized dominant, gendered client discourse is contributing to family struggles. The Daniels family has a multitude of examples of these patterns in their description alone. This is where we can take a "one-down" position using empathy, active listening, and expressive curiosity (Knudson-Martin et al., 2019). The concept of **listening otherwise** (Lipari, 2009) insists on listening without objectification or appropriation. The value of listening to others in all their complex diversity is key to addressing oppressive silencing. By intervening in destructive and unhelpful power dynamics within the family, such as the Daniels gendered construction that values economic and traditionally masculine roles, therapists can externalize blame as expected reactions to internalized social injustices, while simultaneously empowering clients to create new and alternative ways of operating both in the systems they inhabit.

To effectively address problematic power dynamics in the Daniels family, we must not only intervene but do so with understanding, effective pacing, and compassion, rather than with judgment or elitist exchange. Power differentials can be necessary, such as parents and children, but the FFT aims to minimize the therapists' power as the expert of the family, while also acknowledging that training and education can be of assistance.

Envision just alternatives. Helping create space for the family to create equitable, not necessarily "equal," alternatives is a result of engaging in the above practices. FFTs will assist the family to envision different ways of operating, thinking, and relational engaging that do not reinforce patriarchal, heterosexual dominated patterns, which is particularly relevant for the Daniels family, given their middle-class, white, Christian, heteropatriarchal structure. Merely offering alternatives can spark various ideas from family members, and as the family becomes more aware of possibilities, new visions can arise, further empowering the family and its members. Additionally, this can create hope, which leads us to the last component of the model.

Transform to make the imagined a reality. Imagining alternatives may not always immediately morph into a believable reality for families who have operated within similar confines for years. Here is where the therapist can help the clients initiate small changes in the system that ease unspoken tensions and interrupt what was originally thought of as an impossible situation, such as Pam's minimal eating. Once the family can see movement in a desired direction, they develop hope that new norms that may have once seemed unrelated to the presenting problem can be beneficial for the family.

The Feminist Intersectional Couple, Relationship, and Family Therapy Model. This model is explored through "tasks" that need to be applied in clinical FFT settings. The authors of this model (Walker et al., 2025) stress that we must also move beyond the dyadic assumption, as clients may present in many diverse relational structures with multiple partners in diverse relationships, such as polyamory and countless other versions of consensual/ethical nonmonogamy (Blumer et al., 2014). Below are five tasks that provide an outline for this model.

Therapist introspection. Similar to the self-reflexive process in the attunement section in the ANVIET model, introspection is core to this model. Walker et al. (2025) stress that "…perhaps of most importance is the consistency of the feminist therapist's ongoing process of self-awareness and willingness to address one's biases and distortions" (pp. 113–114). Additionally, through this task, the therapist attends to core therapeutic ethical principles of autonomy and empowerment, as full respect must be given to the client's decision-making and choices, a vital part of FFT and our profession (AAMFT Ethics, 2015, Standard 1.8).

Transparent egalitarian, therapeutic alliance. The idea of "joining" is a common therapist-client(s) concept that includes developing an alliance with clients. As FFTs, we strive to transparently navigate power dynamics to develop an equitable and balanced relationship in therapy. This provides a space for empowerment needed to make autonomous choices that fit for the client or family, while continuing to respect key cultural intersections and the family context.

Exploration of patriarchal influences. In this model, Walker et al. (2025) highlight intersectional power analysis, strength exploration, and the use of a feminist intersectional genogram, which can give a visual understanding of the influences of marginalization and its effects on both individuals and the families they inhabit. Historical power analysis will ideally strengthen understanding of societal and cultural influences that maintain and support marginalizing narratives, and strengths exploration should be employed with the individuals first and then within the system of the family as a whole. A feminist intersectional genogram, primarily focused on intersectional diversity and multi-generational patterns, is an ideal intervention for the Daniels family to consider how generational influences have impacted their situation.

Higher consciousness and choices. To enable clients to externalize valid reactions to system oppression and disenfranchisement, they need to recognize the strong and subtle ways that societal "rules" from the dominant narrative are implicitly and deeply internalized, rather than the story that their thoughts, feelings, and behaviors are solely attributed to personal shortcomings. The focus is on raising collective consciousness to empower both family members and the family, which can lead to choices that grow from critical consciousness, rather than prescribed norms at many systemic levels.

Equitable power may seem ideal in FFT but can sometimes ignore culture and is not always socioculturally attuned. As with transnational feminisms, operating within an immovable binary is limiting and unrepresentative of how people exist (Mason, 2019). FFTs strive to recognize this and attain flexibility regarding cultural and sometimes necessary uneven power dynamics. Walker et al. (2025) explain:

> Although the goals of FFT are for empowerment, there will be situations where uneven power differentials are unavoidable. For example, children will not have the same power as their parents in the family system. Navigating power within a family would allow a child to realize process power (i.e., being understood) and have a voice, even when overruled.
>
> (p.119)

FFTs would navigate power dynamics within the Daniels family through inquisitive challenges to the current family homeostasis that maintain problems. Further, FFTs will infuse with humility and questioning that allows for consciousness raising and collaborative exploration of new options that also respect the family culture.

Advocacy and ongoing empowerment. FFT includes advocacy as a significant factor for both the therapist and the family. Advocacy can occur on multiple levels. Although most counseling and MFT professions include the need for therapist advocacy within their code of ethics, an FFT framework explores client advocacy options without any pressure from the therapist. These can vary significantly and offer many choices for both individuals and families. It can be as simple as asserting a nondominant belief within the family system or externally, such as writing a letter to a local politician (Walker et al., 2025). For any of the family members in the Daniels family, the discovery that choices that may not have been made consciously but rather defaulted to internalized societal norms can be incredibly powerful.

The Therapeutic Process

By attending to these guidelines and FFT applications, we can engage in the process with our clients from a position of ultimate curiosity, while allowing the genuine therapist self to emerge through systemic therapeutic approaches. This is the art and science of family therapy. The example provided is just that—an example. Each therapist will approach this case within the context of their own authentic style.

Case Transcript

Therapist: I want to thank each of you for being here today. I know you're all here out of care and concern for Pam, and that's not easy for any family. I'd really love to hear from all of you. I'm curious how all of this has felt for each of you and hear a bit about how we can navigate all of this. It's important for everyone to have a voice to speak here. Since you all know your own family better than I do, would it be alright if we started with how things have felt for each of you lately? Pam, I'd like to check in with you first. What has it been like knowing the family is worried?

Intervention: The therapist positions the family as expert, while also collaborating with them in the therapeutic process. The transparency of process and invitation to raise Pam's voice can give rise to the beginning of an egalitarian therapeutic alliance with the entire family.

Pam: I guess I feel... sort of put under a microscope. It's like all of a sudden everything is about what I eat, or don't eat. It's overwhelming.

Therapist: That sounds like a lot to hold. When things get so focused on your eating, what do you wish people could see or understand about you, that maybe they're missing?

Intervention: Using a lens of valuing what is minimized, we can explore Pam's underlying reasons for her lack of eating. This is an intentional intervening in power dynamics within the family that values a heteropatriarchal way of looking at dangerous starvation.

Pam: I just wish people could notice me for more than that, like, who I am, not just if I finished dinner. Like, no one invites me to do the fun stuff. You treat me like I'm fragile or something.

Therapist: I get that. That feeling of wanting to be seen for your whole self is so important. Sometimes when families fall into routines, it's easy to miss parts of each other. Fran, what's it like to hear Pam say that?

Intervention: The therapist names injustices outright, while attuning to context and power and intervening in power dynamics with sensitivity by normalizing the effects of how families can fall into routines that are created and maintained through social norms and pressures.

Fran: I'm sad. I didn't realize that's how she felt. I thought being on top of her eating meant I was caring for her. Now I wonder if I messed up.

Therapist: It's so hard, isn't it? So many mothers get messages that their main job is to always keep their daughters perfectly safe and healthy. It can be an impossible standard.

Intervention: With the awareness that Pam asserted, Fran felt frustrated and possibly guilty regarding her own mothering. With the validation, understanding, and naming of unjust societal standards that create pressure to be the perfect mother, she can explore patriarchal influences and relieve blame, helping create a transparent, egalitarian alliance.

Murray: I had no idea Pam felt left out. I just thought the boys and I had common interests, and Fran and Pam were close in their own way.

Therapist: That makes sense. Families often drift into roles shaped by what's expected in society. But those traditional roles can sometimes leave people out, unintentionally. Pam, is there anyone in the family you do feel connected to right now?

Intervention: The therapist invites exploration of patriarchal influences that impede Murray's connection with his daughter and wife, while reducing the idea of personal failing with understanding higher consciousness and choice.

Pam: (*shrugs*) Not really, lately. I used to feel close to Mom, but now our talks are more like check-ups than real conversations. I just feel different and on the outside. Like, all the time.

Therapist: That sounds like a heavy weight to carry.

Pam: I hate it.

Therapist: Oliver, George, what are you hearing? Has it seemed to you like Pam is on the outside lately?

Intervention: This is both collaboration with the family and modeling inclusion, while valuing what is minimized, meaning children's voices, all while simultaneously continuing to form a transparent, egalitarian therapeutic alliance with all family members and the maintenance of the current family systemic habits.

Oliver: I didn't really think about it. We do stuff with Dad a lot, like going to baseball or playing games. Pam never seemed interested. She started spending less time around us. I just thought she wanted to do her own thing, you know? I guess I didn't realize how much she was feeling left out until now. It's weird, because we all used to do a lot together when we were younger, but now, it's more like Dad takes us out and Pam stays home with Mom.

George: I guess I just thought that was how things were with girls. But it would be cool if we all did things together sometimes, not just sports. Like, I don't know, maybe we should try not to always have things about sports, or boys versus girls. I want to spend time with Pam too, like we used to.

Therapist: Thank you both for saying that. Sometimes it's easy for brothers and sisters to end up in separate worlds, especially with family traditions about "what the boys do" and "what the girls do." It can really limit all of us. Pam, does that sound true for you?

Intervention: The therapist intervenes in power dynamics while having the boys explore patriarchal influences in an age-appropriate way. This almost always leads the way to higher consciousness and unique choices.

Pam: Yeah, totally. Honestly, it always felt like there was a big wall between me and the rest of the family. I used to try to join in, but mostly it felt like I didn't belong. Not just because I don't care about sports, but other stuff, too.

Therapist: That sounds really lonely. Sometimes, when families are divided along gender lines, it can feel like certain feelings or parts of ourselves have to stay hidden. It makes me wonder…are there things you wish you could share here but haven't?

Intervention: The therapist gives value to what is minimized—the reasons behind Pam's feelings of loneliness—and at the same time, intervenes in the power dynamics of the entire system's silencing of Pam's perspectives.

Pam: (*quiet, tears up, takes a deep breath*) Maybe…

Therapist: It's okay if you don't want to talk about them now, and you can let me know if and when you might like to share more. I sincerely want you to know that all parts of you are welcome here.

Intervention: This is an example of the therapist advocating for Pam's possible hidden identity and creating a place for her to feel supported and empowered. Additionally, this gives her room for choices and the ability to inhabit multiple identities while engaging in pre-adult awareness development in adolescence of identities, emotions, and attractions.

Pam: (*nods, looks away*)

Therapist (softly): Thank you, Pam. I know you're carrying a lot. (*to family*) Sometimes, when families get divided up by gender roles—like "Dad with the boys, Mom with the girl," it can leave people feeling boxed in. And for Pam, who is facing enormous outside pressures about what girls should be, look like, or care about, feeling disconnected inside the family may make it even harder. Fran and Murray, what do each of you think?

Intervention: The therapist models Pam's inclusion and creates a higher consciousness by including each family member in the process, by compassionately naming injustices, which helps to intervene in power dynamics. This, in turn, leads to envisioning just alternatives that empower the family as a whole.

Fran: I want Pam to feel like herself, not just an idea of what I think she should be. I want to be a good mom, but I was raised to think this is what I need to do. So many of my friends think this.

Therapist: Fran, I think it's beautiful that you both want that for Pam, and I understand how these outside influences from folks, and even media, etc. can feel like just "how it is." You do have choices though…even if it doesn't always feel that way.

Intervention: By transparently naming these influences and injustices, we create motivation for advocacy and ongoing empowerment and help to create alternatives.

Murray: I want that too. I truly didn't realize the ways we were repeating those old patterns from our own upbringings. I'm just trying to be a good husband and father.

Therapist: Of course you are. I can see that clearly. That's the hard part. These patterns are bigger than just your family. They come from the world outside: rules about what a girl is supposed to be, what moms "should" do, what dads pay attention to. We often think the problem is just in one person, Pam, in this case, but it's lived out in the whole system. Often, these issues are shaped by societal rules about what a family should be, so it's hard to realize that you can shape it differently and open up a whole world of choices.

Intervention: The therapist demonstrates intentional sociocultural attunement to context and power. They value what is minimized by examining gender roles and the pressure that Pam and Fran may experience in a different way than Murray and the boys do, further explaining that the outside pressures to conform can lead to unhelpful family patterns. Additionally, we see advocacy and empowerment by initiating higher consciousness and making new choices possible. Also, exploration of patriarchal influences magnified by the hyper-connected world is lifted to the surface.

Oliver: Is there stuff we could do together as a family? Not just sports?

George: I'd like that.

Pam: I think that would help. (*Slightly smiles*)

Therapist: It means so much when brothers and sisters are open to changing how things have always been. Maybe we can come up with ideas for things you'd all enjoy where Pam can feel just as much a part of the group.

Intervention: Hearing the openings, the therapist helps the family collaborate to envision just alternatives, continuing to promote an egalitarian therapeutic alliance.

Murray: Honestly, that sounds like a pretty good start.

Therapist: Great. (*addressing everyone)* If it's alright, we can keep thinking about what makes each of you feel seen and connected, how to break down those old walls, together, at your own rhythm. There are so many influences that we assume we have to do things a certain way. I'd love to map out something called a genogram in one of our future sessions. It's an activity we can do together and look at some patterns through generations. How does that sound?

Intervention: Collaborating with the family by asking permission to engage in a conscious-raising activity, such as a feminist, intersectional genogram, the entire group can work together to envision alternatives and transform to make the imagined a reality.

Fran: That sounds so interesting. (*Others nod*)

Therapist: It really is! I loved it when I did it when I was training to be a therapist.

Intervention: While attuned to context and power, the therapist uses authentic, intentional self-disclosure while modeling a genuine way of being that may fall outside what is socially expected by a therapist.

Therapist (Gentler, to Pam): And Pam, you don't have to carry anything alone here. When or if you're ready to talk about the other things that matter to you, we'll be here. Thank you all so much for all your work and sharing today.

Intervention: At this point, the therapist has helped raise critical consciousness, which allows the family to envision alternatives and transform to make what was once an unimagined possibility into a likely and creative potential.

The Therapeutic Story

The first session is just the beginning of the conscious-raising and collaborative process that integrates FFT. Through this meta-theory, the focus is removed from Pam's anorexia in a vacuum as an individual problem and instead engages the entire family system. From a feminist, intersectional lens and application, it becomes possible for the Daniels family to establish innovative ways to forge relationships and interactions where everyone is seen and heard.

1 Through therapeutic modeling and warm, authentic engagement, the creation of a socioculturally attuned egalitarian space is established.
2 The family is divided by gender lines and secrecy, and Pam's struggle with anorexia is reframed as an issue that is maintained by all members of the family due to multiple levels of societal influences.
3 The family members can recognize how these influences have created dynamics of gendered division as well as Pam's withdrawal and minimal eating patterns.
4 Personal blame is removed from family members and understood as a reflection of static default to societal expectations. Pam's assumed heterosexuality is gently brought to the surface to examine the possibility of an underlying reason for her presentation. Her feelings of being an outsider and fear of disclosure are layered and much more than a random choice to stop eating.
5 Through attunement to context and power, valuing what is minimized, and exploring patriarchal influences, all members of the family are beginning to recognize and envision new ways of connecting and making empowered choices that will help not only Pam but the entire family system.

References

Abeyasekera, A. L. (2017). "Living for others": Narrating agency in the context of failed marriages and singleness in urban Sri Lanka. *Feminism & Psychology*, *27*, 427–446.

Akyil, Y., Prouty, A., Blanchard, A., & Lyness, K. (2015). Experiences of families transmitting values in a rapidly changing society: Implications for family therapists. *Family Process*, *55*(2), 368–381.

Almeida, R., Woods, R., Messineo, T., & Font, R. (1998). The cultural context model: An overview. In M. McGoldrick (Ed.), *Re-visioning family therapy: Race, culture, and gender in clinical practice* (pp. 414–431). Guilford.

Almeida, R., Hernandez-Wolfe, P., & Tubbs, C. (2011). Cultural equity: Bridging the complexity of social identities with therapeutic practices. *International Journal of Narrative Therapy & Community Work*, *3*, 43–56.

Almeida, R. V., Werkmeister Rozas, L. M., Cross-Denny, B., Lee, K. K., & Yamada, A. (2019). Coloniality and intersectionality in social work education and practice. *Journal of Progressive Human Services*, *30*(2), 148–164.

American Association for Marriage and Family Therapy. (2015). *Code of ethics*. American Association for Marriage and Family Therapy.

American Psychiatric Association. (1952). *Diagnostic and statistical manual of mental disorders* (1st ed.). American Psychiatric Association.

Aponte, H. J. (1994). *Bread and spirit: Therapy with the new poor*. W. W. Norton.

Blumer, M. L. C., Green, M. S., Compton, D., & Barrera, A. M. (2010). Reflections on becoming feminist therapists: Honoring our feminist mentors. *Journal of Feminist Family Therapy*, *22*(1), 57–87.

Blumer, M. L. C., Haym, C., Zimmerman, K., & Prouty, A. (2014). What's one got to do with it? Considering monogamous privilege. *Family Therapy Magazine*, *13*(2), 28–33.

Boe, J. L., Maxey, V. A., & Bermúdez, J. M. (2018). Is the closet a closet? Decolonizing the coming out process with Latin@ adolescents and families. *Journal of Feminist Family Therapy*, *30*(2), 90–108.

Boyd-Franklin, N. (2006). *Black families in therapy: Understanding the African American experience*. Guilford.

Bretaña, I., Mendia, J., Díaz-Gorriti, V., & Rotaetxe, O. (2025). Intimate partner violence and eating disorders: A systemic review. *Current Psychology*, *44*, 1696–1716.

Bridges, D., Lewis, C., Wulff, E., Litchfield, C., & Bamberry, L. (2023). *Gender, feminist and queer studies. Power, privilege and inequality in a time of neoliberal conservatism*. Routledge.

Bronfenbrenner, Y. E. (Ed.). (2005). *Making human beings human: Bioecological perspectives on human development*. Sage

Capozzi, F. (2022). A multi-level guide to work with male clients in couple and family therapy from a gender-critical perspective. *Journal of Feminist Family Therapy*, *34*(1–2), 178–195.

Carolan, M., Burns-Jager, K., Bozek, K., & Escobar Chew, A. R. (2010). Women who have their parental rights removed by the state: The interplay of trauma and oppression. *Journal of Feminist Family Therapy*, *22*, 171–186.

Chan, Z. C. Y., & MaMa, J. L. C. (2006). A feminist family therapy research study: Giving voice to a girl suffering from anorexia nervosa. *Journal of Feminist Family Therapy*, *17*(2), 41–64.

Cheon, H. S., & Murphy, M. J. (2007). The self-of-the-therapist awakened: Postmodern approaches to the use of self in marriage and family therapy. *Journal of Feminist Family Therapy*, *19*(1), 1–16.

Collins, P. H. (2000). *Black feminist thought: Knowledge, consciousness, and the politics of empowerment* (2nd ed.). Routledge.

Comas-Diaz, L. (2003). The Black Madonna: The psychospiritual feminism of Guadeloupe, Kali, and Monserrat. In L. B. Silverstein & T. J. Goodrich (Eds.), *Feminist family therapy: Empowerment in social context* (pp. 147–160). American Psychological Association.

Crenshaw, K. (1991). Mapping the margins: Intersectionality, identity politics, and violence against women of color. *Stanford Law Review*, *43*(6), 1241–1299.

Dalton, M. R., Jones, A., & Stoy, J. (2020). Reducing barriers: Integrated collaboration for transgender clients. *Journal of Feminist Family Therapy*, *32*(3–4), 176–191.

D'Aniello, C., & Fife, S. T. (2020). A 20-year review of common factors research in marriage and family therapy: A mixed methods content analysis. *Journal of Marital and Family Therapy*, *46*(4), 701–718.

Dankoski, M. E., & Deacon, S. A. (2000). Using a feminist lens in contextual therapy. *Family Process*, *39*, 51–66.

Dell'Osso, L., Abelli, M., Carpita, B., Pini, S., Castellini, G., Carmassi, C., & Ricca, V. (2016). Historical evolution of the concept of anorexia nervosa and relationships with orthorexia nervosa, autism, and obsessive-compulsive spectrum. *Neuropsychiatric Disease and Treatment*, *12*, 1651–1660.

Dermer, S. B., Hemesath, C. W., Russell, C. S. (1998). A feminist critique of solution-focused therapy. *The American Journal of Family Therapy*, *25*(3), 239–250.

Duarte-Silva, M., Henriques-Calado, J., & Camotim, V. (2012). Growing older in Portugal: Gender issues in physical health and well-being. *Women & Therapy*, *35*(3–4), 221–232.

Enns, C. Z. (2019). *Feminist theories and feminist psychotherapies: Origins, themes, and diversity* (3rd ed.). Routledge.

Espín, O. M., & Dottolo, A. L. (2019). A transnational feminist perspective on the psychology of migration. In L. H. Collins, S. Machizawa, and J. K. Rice (Eds.), *Transnational psychology of women: Expanding international and intersectional approaches* (pp. 121–139). American Psychological Association.

Falicov, C. J. (1999). Religion and spiritual folk traditions in immigrant families. In F. Walsh (Ed.), *Spirituality and family therapy* (pp. 104–120). Guilford.

Falicov, D. J. (2012). Immigrant family processes: A multidimensional framework. In F. Walsh (Ed.), *Normal family processes* (4th ed., pp. 297–323). Guilford.
Falicov, D. J. (2015). *Latino families in therapy*. Guilford.
Fishbane, M. D. (1999). "Honor thy father and thy mother." Intergenerational Spirituality and Jewish tradition. In F. Walsh (Ed.), *Spirituality and family therapy* (pp. 136–156). Guilford.
Flemke, K., & Allen, K. R. (2008). Women's experience of rage: A critical feminist analysis. *Journal of Marital and Family Therapy*, *34*(1), 58–74.
Goldner, V. (1985). Feminism and family therapy. *Family Process*, *24*(1), 31–47.
Goodrich, T. J. (1991). *Women and power*. W.W. Norton.
Goodrich, T. J., Rampage, C., Ellman, B., & Halstead, K. (1988). *Feminist family therapy: A casebook*. W. W. Norton.
Haddock, S. A., Zimmerman, T. S., & McPhee, D. (2000). The power equity guide: Attending to gender in family therapy. *Journal of Marital and Family Therapy*, *26*, 153–170.
Haddock, S. A., Zimmerman, T. S., Ziemba, S. J., & Current, L. R. (2001). Ten adaptive strategies for family and work balance: Advice from successful families. *Journal of Feminist Family Therapy*, *27*(4), 445–458.
Hare-Mustin, R. (1978). A feminist approach to family therapy. *Family Process*, *17*(2), 181–194.
Helmeke, K., & Sori, K. (Eds.). (2006). *The therapist's notebook for integrating spirituality in counseling I & II*. The Haworth Press.
Hernández, P. (2008). The cultural context model in clinical supervision. *Training and Education in Professional Psychology*, *2*(1), 10–17.
Hernández-Wolfe, P., & McDowell, T. (2013). Social privilege and accountability: Lessons from family therapy educators. *Journal of Feminist Family Therapy*, *25*(1), 1–16.
Hertlein, K. M., Hartwell, E. E., & Munns, M. E. (2016). Attitudes towards bisexuality according to sexual orientation and gender. *Journal of Bisexuality*, *16*(3), 1–22.
Imber-Black, E., & Roberts, J. (2003). *Rituals in families and family therapy*. W. W. Norton.
Jonathan, N. (2009). Carrying equal weight: Relational responsibility and attunement among same-sex couples. In C. Knudson-Martin & A. R. Mahoney (Eds.), *Couples, gender, and power. Creating change in intimate relationships* (pp. 79–103). Springer.
Karis, T. A., & Killian, K. (Ed.). (2008). *Intercultural couples: Exploring diversity in intimate relationships*. Routledge.
Kerr, L. (2001). An assessment of adaptability to feminist principles of solution-focused brief therapy as practiced by Insoo Kim Berg. *Journal of Systemic Therapies*, *20*(3), 77–90.
Kilicer, B., Gurcag, S. N., Civan, A., Akyil, Y., & Prouty, A. (2021). Feminist family therapy in Turkey: Experiences of couple and family therapists. *Journal of Feminist Family Therapy*, *33*(2), 105–130.
Kim, H., Prouty, A. M., Smith, D. B., Ko, M., Wetchler, J. L., & Oh, J. (2014). Differentiation of self and its relationship with family functioning in South Koreans. *The American Journal of Family Therapy*, *42*, 257–265.
Kirk, G., & Okazawa-Rey, M. (2003). Identities and social locations: Who am I? Who are my people? In *Women's lives: Multicultural perspectives* (3rd ed., pp. 59–110). McGraw-Hill.
Kissill, K., & Davey, M. (2012). Health disparities in procreation: Unequal access to assisted reproductive technologies. *Journal of Feminist Family Therapy*, *24*(3), 197–212.
Knudson-Martin, C. (1994). The female voice: Applications to Bowen family system's theory. *Journal of Marital and Family Therapy*, *20*, 35–46.

Knudson-Martin, C. (2003). Gender and biology: A recursive framework for clinical practice. *Journal of Feminist Family Therapy*, *15*(2–3), 1–21.

Knudson-Martin, C. (2012). Changing gender norms in families and society: Toward equality and complexities. In F. Walsh (Ed.), *Normal family processes* (4th ed., pp. 324–467). Guilford.

Knudson-Martin, C., & Mahoney, A. R. (2009). *Couples, gender, and power. Creating change in intimate relationships*. Springer.

Knudson-Martin, C., McDowell, T., & Bermudez, J. M. (2019). From knowing to doing: Guidelines for socioculturally attuned family therapy. *Journal of Marital and Family Therapy*, 45(1), 47–60.

Kriseman, N. L., & Claes, J. A. (1997). Gender issues and elder care. In T. D. Hargrave & S. M. Hanna (Eds.), *The aging family: New visions in theory, practice, and reality* (pp. 199–208). Brunner/Mazel.

Larner, G. (1995). The real as illusion: Deconstructing power in family therapy. *Journal of Family Therapy*, *17*(2), 191–217.

Lee, J. (1997). Women re-authoring their lives through feminist narrative therapy. *Women & Therapy*, *20*(3), 1–22.

Leupnitz, D. A. (1988). *The family interpreted: Feminist theory in clinical practice*. Basic Books.

Lipari, L. (2009). Listening otherwise: The voice of ethics. *The International Journal of Listening*, *23*(1), 44–59.

Long, J. (1997). Alzheimer's disease and the family: Working with new realities. In T. D. Hargrave & S. M. Hanna (Eds.), *The aging family: New visions in theory, practice, and reality* (209–234). Brunner/Mazel.

Long, J., & Andrews, B. V. (2007). Fostering strength and resiliency in same-sex couples. *Journal of Couple & Relationship Therapy*, *6*(1), 153–165.

Long, J. K., Bonomo, J., Andrews, B. V., & Brown, J. M. (2006). Systemic therapeutic approaches with sexual minorities and their families. *Journal of GLBT Family Studies*, *2*(3–4), 7–37.

Maier, C. (2015). Feminist-informed emotionally focused couples therapy for eating disorders. *The American Journal of Family Therapy*, *43*(2), 151–162.

Mason, C. L. (2019). Buzzwords and fuzzwords: Flattening intersectionality in Canadian aid. *Canadian Foreign Policy Journal*, *25*(2), 203–219.

McDowell, T., & Hernandez, P. (2010). Decolonizing academia: Intersectionality, participation, and accountability in family therapy and counseling. *Journal of Feminist Family Therapy*, *22*, 93–111.

McDowell, T., Knudson-Martin, C., & Bermúdez, J. M. (2023, in press). *Socioculturally attuned family therapy. Guidelines for equitable theory and practice* (2nd and 3rded.). Routledge.

McGeorge, C., & Carlson, T. S. (2011). Deconstruction heterosexism: Becoming an LBG affirmative heterosexual couple & family therapist. *Journal of Marital & Family Therapy*, *37*(1), 14–26.

McGeorge, C. R., Walsdorf, A. A., Edwards, L. L., Benson, K. E., & Coburn, K. O. (2020). Sexual orientation and gender identity. Considerations for systemic therapists. In K. Wampler, R. B. Miller & R. B. Seedall (Eds.), *The handbook of systemic family therapy* (pp. 251–271). John Wiley & Sons.

McGoldrick, M., Giordano, J., & Garcia-Preto, N. (Eds.). (2005). *Ethnicity & family therapy* (3rd ed.). Guilford.

Méndez-Pounds, J. (2024). DREAMers' perceptions of relational impacts after DACA. *Journal of Feminist Family Therapy*, *36*(3–4), 88–112.

Merecek, J. (2019). Toward a transnational feminist psychology of women's reproductive experiences. In L. H. Collins, S. Machizawa & J. K. Rice (Eds.), *Transnational psychology of women: Expanding international and intersectional approaches* (pp. 185–209). American Psychological Association.

Meyer, I. H. (2003). Minority stress and mental health in gay men. In L. D. Garnets & D. C. Kimmel (Eds.), *Psychological perspectives on lesbian, gay, and bisexual experiences* (2nd ed., pp. 699–731). Columbia University Press.

Mintz, L. B., & Kashubek, S. (1999). Body image and disordered eating among Asian American and Caucasian college students. *Psychology of Women Quarterly*, *23*(4), 781–796.

Nadal, K. L. (2018). *Microaggressions and traumatic stress: Theory, research, and clinical treatment*. American Psychological Association.

Negy, C., & McKinney, C. (2006). Application of feminist therapy: promoting resiliency among lesbian and gay families. *Journal of Feminist Family Therapy*, *18*(1–2), 67–83.

Penfold, P. S. (1989). Family therapy: Critique from a feminist perspective. *The Canadian Journal of Psychiatry*, *34*(4), 311–315.

Peterson, R. D., Grippo, K. P., & Tantleff-Dunn, S. (2008). Empowerment and powerlessness: A closer look at the relationship between feminism, body image and eating disturbance. *Sex Roles*, *58*, 639–648.

Pharr, S. (1997). *Homophobia: A weapon of sexism*. Chardon Press.

Phillips, A. (2010). *Gender and culture*. Cambridge University Press.

Prouty, A. M., & Bermudez, J. M. (2000). Experiencing multiconsciousness. A feminist model for therapy. *Journal of Feminist Family Therapy*, *11*(3), 19–39.

Prouty, A. M., & Lyness, K. P. (2011). Feminist couple therapy. In J. L. Wetchler (Ed.), *Handbook of clinical issues in couple therapy* (pp. 271–289). Routledge.

Prouty, A. M., & Twist, M. L. C. (2016). Training feminist family therapists. In K. Jordan (Ed.), *Couple, marriage, and family therapy supervision* (pp. 347–367). Springer.

Rabig, J. (2024). Anticipatory grief: Vulnerability and resiliency in encore women. *Women & Therapy*, *47*(4), 439–453.

Rossano, J. M., & Cotter, K. N. (2024). Thriving through the arts: Pathways to social well-being for older women. *Women & Therapy*, *47*(4), 485–502.

Seponski, D. M. (2016). A feminist-informed integration of emotionally focused and solution-focused therapies. *Journal of Family Psychotherapy*, *27*(4), 221–242.

Squire, S. (2003). Anorexia and bulimia: Purity and danger. *Australian Feminist Studies*, *18*(40), 17–26.

Stice, E. (1998). Modeling of eating pathology and social reinforcement of the thin-ideal predict onset of bulimic symptoms. *Behavior Research and Therapy*, *36*, 931–944.

Tamasese, K. (2003). Gender and culture: Together. In C. Waldegrave, K. Tamasese, F. Tuhaka & W. Campbell (Eds.), *Just therapy-A journey: A collection of papers from the Just Therapy Team* (pp. 203–206). Dulwich Centre.

Thomas, V., Karis, T. A., & Wetchler, J. L. (Eds.). (2003). *Clinical issues with interracial couples: Theories and research*. Routledge.

Underwood, S. W. (2024). Gay dads to be: Reflections on gender, sexuality, family, and race in adoption and surrogacy. *LGBTQ+ Family: An International Journal*, *20*(5), 339–354.

Wacker, E. C. (2018). Application of the feminist relational model for the treatment of subclinical eating disorders. *Journal of Feminist Family Therapy*, *30*(2), 71–89.

Walker, J. N., Park, C. N., Brown, K. S., Hawkins, T. (2025). Feminist intersectional couple, relationship, and family therapy. In J. Jodry & K. McCleskey (Eds.), *Feminist intersectional therapy: Fourth wave clinical applications*. Bloomsbury Publishing USA.

Walsh, F. (Ed.). (1999). *Spiritual resources in family therapy*. Guilford.
Walsh, F. (Ed.). (2012). *Normal family processes: Growing diversity and complexity* (4th ed.). Guilford.
Walsh, F., & Schneikman, M. (1988). (Fe)male: The hidden gender dimension in models of family therapy. In M. McGoldrick, C. M. Anderson & F. Walsh (Eds.), *Women in families: A framework for family therapy* (pp. 16–41). W. W. Norton.
Walters, M., Carter, B., Papp, P., & Silverstein, O. (1988). *The invisible web: Gender patterns in family relationships*. Guilford Press.
Wetchler, J. L. (2006). Reflections from a single father of a teenage daughter with mental retardation. *Journal of Feminist Family Therapy*, *17*(2), 65–78.
Wisensale, S. K. (2005). Aging societies and intergenerational equity issues. *Journal of Feminist Family Therapy*, *17*(3–4), 79–103.
Yokoyama, K. (2007). The double binds of our bodies: Multiculturally-informed feminist therapy considerations for body image and eating disorders among Asian American women. *Women in Therapy*, *30*(3–4), 177–192.

Index

Pages in *italics* refer to figures.

For Product Safety Concerns and Information please contact our EU
representative GPSR@taylorandfrancis.com
Taylor & Francis Verlag GmbH, Kaufingerstraße 24, 80331 München, Germany

www.ingramcontent.com/pod-product-compliance
Ingram Content Group UK Ltd.
Pitfield, Milton Keynes, MK11 3LW, UK
UKHW022346190926
475702UK00015B/2132
* 9 7 8 1 0 4 1 1 3 1 8 4 7 *